RENAISSANCE
AND
REFORMATION

RENAISSANCE
AND
REFORMATION

EDITOR

JAMES A. PATRICK
Chancellor, College of Saint Thomas More

ADVISERS

CHRISTOPHER FLETCHER
Queen Mary, University of London
Department of History

NATALIA NOWAKOWSKA
Oxford University
History Faculty

NORMAN TANNER, SJ
Pontificia Università Gregoriana
Faculty of Theology

RENAISSANCE
— AND —
REFORMATION

Editor
James A. Patrick

Chancellor, College of Saint Thomas More

6

Index

Marshall Cavendish
Reference
New York

Marshall Cavendish
99 White Plains Road
Tarrytown, New York 10591-9001

www.marshallcavendish.us

MARSHALL CAVENDISH
EDITOR: Thomas McCarthy
EDITORIAL DIRECTOR: Paul Bernabeo
PRODUCTION MANAGER: Michael Esposito

WHITE-THOMSON PUBLISHING
EDITOR: Steven Maddocks
DESIGN: Derek Lee and Ross George
CARTOGRAPHER: Peter Bull Design
PICTURE RESEARCH: Amy Sparks
INDEXER: Cynthia Crippen, AEIOU, Inc.

Library of Congress Cataloging-in-Publication Data
Renaissance and Reformation / editor, James A. Patrick.
    p. cm.
    Includes bibliographical references.
    Contents: 1. Agincourt, Battle of-Dams and drainage -- 2. Descartes, René-
Households -- 3. Humanism and learning-Medicis, the -- 4. Michelangelo-
Portugal -- 5. Preaching-Wren, Christopher -- 6. Index.
    ISBN-13: 978-0-7614-7650-4 (set: alk. paper)
    ISBN-10: 0-7614-7650-4 (set: alk. paper)
    1. Renaissance--Encyclopedias. 2. Reformation--Encyclopedias. I. Patrick,
James, 1933-

CB359.R455 2007
940.2'1--dc22

                  2006042600

ISBN-13: 978-0-7614-7650-4   (set)
ISBN-10: 0-7614-7650-4   (set)
ISBN-13: 978-0-7614-7656-6   (vol. 6)
ISBN-10: 0-7614-7656-3   (vol. 6)

Printed in Malaysia

10 09 08 07 06 5 4 3 2 1

ILLUSTRATION CREDITS

COVER: Queen Elizabeth I of England at prayer, anonymous frontispiece to
Christian Prayers, 1569 (Art Archive).
TITLE PAGE: Giotto, *Meeting at the Golden Gate,* detail of Saints Joachim and Anne
embracing, fresco, c. 1305 (Bridgeman Art Library/Scrovegni [Arena] Chapel,
Padua).

Contents

Time Line

	Architecture, Painting, and Sculpture	Literature and Music	The Church, the Reformation, and the Counter-Reformation
1300	**c. 1305–c. 1308/9** Giotto decorates the interior of the Arena Chapel in Padua.	**1321** Dante completes the *Divine Comedy*. **1327** Petrarch meets Laura, the inspiration of his *Canzoniere*.	**1302** Boniface VIII asserts the temporal and spiritual supremacy of the papacy. **1309** The papal seat moves from Rome to Avignon.
1350		**1353** Giovanni Boccaccio's *Decameron* is published.	
1360		**1360s** Guillaume de Machaut's *Messe de Nostre Dame* is composed for performance at the Cathedral of Reims.	
1370			**1378** With the election of rival popes in Rome and Avignon, the Western Schism begins.
1380	**1386** Construction of Milan's cathedral begins.		
1390			
1400	**1401** Lorenzo Ghiberti wins the competition to design the baptistery doors of Florence's cathedral.	**1400** Geoffrey Chaucer dies.	
1410	**1415** Poggio Bracciolini finds a manuscript of Vitruvius's *De architectura*. **1419** Filippo Brunelleschi builds the facade of the Ospedale degli Innocenti in Florence.		**1415** The Czech reformer Jan Hus is convicted of heresy and burned at the stake. **1417** The Council of Constance ends the Western Schism.
1420			
1430	**1432** Donatello completes his *David;* Jan van Eyck's Ghent altarpiece is dedicated. **1436** Brunelleschi completes work on the main part of the dome of Florence's cathedral.		**1438** The Pragmatic Sanction of Bourges challenges papal authority over the French church. **1439** The Council of Florence fixes the number of sacraments at seven.
1440			

Philosophy and Scholarship	Politics, Economics, and Society	Science, Technology, and Exploration	
1330 Petrarch finishes compiling Livy's *History of Rome* from several manuscripts. **1349** William of Ockham dies.	**1337** The Hundred Years War, between France and England, begins. **1348** The Black Death strikes Europe.	**1335** The mechanical clock is invented in Milan. **1347** Portugal establishes the Colonial and Naval Institute.	**1300**
	1356 The Holy Roman Empire's constitution is set; the English capture King John II of France. **1358** The Jacquerie, a peasant rebellion, breaks out in France.		**1350**
	1360 The Treaty of Brétigny grants England control of much of France.	**1363** The French physician Guy de Chauliac publishes *Chirurgia magna* ("great surgery").	**1360**
			1370
	1381 Wat Tyler leads the Peasants' Revolt in England. **1386** Poland and Lithuania are united.	**1382** The French scientist Nicole d'Oresme dies.	**1380**
	1397 The Medici bank is formally established in Florence.		**1390**
1400 The University of Ferrara rises to a preeminent position among Italian universities.			**1400**
1416 Poggio Bracciolini discovers a complete manuscript of Quintilian's *Training in Oratory* in a Swiss monastery.	**1415** The Battle of Agincourt restores England's position in France. **1419** Jan Hus's followers, the Hussites, revolt in Bohemia.		**1410**
	1429 Joan of Arc engineers the coronation of France's disinherited dauphin as Charles VII.		**1420**
	1431 Joan of Arc is burned at the stake. **1435** France and Burgundy are reconciled. **1436** The Hussite rebellion formally ends.		**1430**
1440 The Donation of Constantine is exposed as a forgery.			**1440**

	Architecture, Painting, and Sculpture	Literature and Music	The Church, the Reformation, and the Counter-Reformation
1450			
	1452 Leon Battista Alberti publishes *Ten Books on Architecture*.		
1460			
1470			
	1475 Sandro Botticelli completes *Man Holding a Medallion of Cosimo de' Medici*. 1475–1480 Hieronymous Bosch paints *The Cure of Folly* and *The Conjurer*. 1478 Brunelleschi's Pazzi Chapel is completed.	1474 The French composer Guillaume Dufay dies.	1478 The Spanish Inquisition is set up.
1480			
	1485 Botticelli paints *The Birth of Venus*. 1486 Vitruvius's *De architectura* is published for the first time; Rafaelle Riario begins work on the Cancellaria in Rome.		1484 Pope Innocent VIII condemns witchcraft.
1490			
	c. 1490 Bosch paints *Death and the Miser*. 1497 Leonardo da Vinci paints *The Last Supper*.		1492 Rodrigo Borgia is invested as Pope Alexander VI.
1500			
	1502 Donato Bramante builds the Tempietto. 1506 Rebuilding of Saint Peter's Basilica begins in Rome; Leonardo paints the *Mona Lisa*. 1508 Michelangelo begins work on the Sistine Chapel ceiling; Raphael begins the *School of Athens* and *La Disputa*.		
1510			
	1514 Albrecht Dürer completes *The Knight, Death, and the Lady*; *Saint Jerome in His Study*; and *Melancholia I*. 1518 Titian completes *The Assumption of the Virgin*.	1511 Erasmus publishes *The Praise of Folly*. 1513 Niccolò Machiavelli writes *The Prince*. 1516 Thomas More's *Utopia* is published; Ludovico Ariosto writes *Orlando Furioso*.	1513 Giovanni de' Medici is invested as Pope Leo X. 1517 Martin Luther posts his Ninety-five Theses in Wittenberg.
1520			
	1520 Raphael dies; the age of mannerism as the dominant mode in European painting begins.	1521 The French composer Josquin des Prez dies.	1521 Luther is excommunicated from the church and declared a political outlaw. 1522 Luther completes his German translation of the New Testament. 1523 Giulio de' Medici becomes Pope Clement VII.
1530			
	1534 Parmigianino completes *Madonna with the Long Neck*.	1534 François Rabelais completes *La Vie de Gargantua et de Pantagruel*. 1536 Luis Milán's *El maestro* begins the era of instrumental music publication.	1531 Huldrych Zwingli is killed in battle. 1533 The English church separates from Rome. 1535 Münster, an Anabaptist stronghold, is seized by a Protestant and Catholic army. 1536 John Calvin founds the Academy of Geneva.
1540			
	1546 Michelangelo takes charge of the rebuilding of Saint Peter's Basilica.		1540 The Jesuits receive papal approval. 1542 The Roman Inquisition is established. 1545 The Council of Trent begins. 1546 Germany's Protestant nobles take up arms.
1550			
	1550 Giorgio Vasari publishes his seminal *Lives of the Most Eminent Painters, Sculptors, and Architects*; Andrea Palladio begins the Villa Rotonda.	1557 With the publication of Richard Tottel's *Miscellany*, new styles of English poetry become available to a wide audience.	1555 The Peace of Augsburg establishes the principle that in a territory of the Holy Roman Empire, the ruler's religion, whether Protestantism or Catholicism, shall be the official religion.

Philosophy and Scholarship	Politics, Economics, and Society	Science, Technology, and Exploration	
1453 Byzantine scholars fleeing the Ottomans bring Greek manuscripts from Constantinople to Italy. **1456** Johannes Argyropoulos is appointed professor of Greek at Florence.	**1452** A Hapsburg is elected Holy Roman emperor for the first time. **1453** Constantinople falls to the Ottomans; the Hundred Years War ends. **1455** The Wars of the Roses begin in England.	**1453** Johannes Gutenberg produces the first printed Bible.	**1450**
1460 The Vatican Library is founded.			**1460**
1471 Thomas á Kempis dies; Argyropoulos begins giving lectures on Greek philosophy and literature in Rome.	**1478** Lorenzo "the Magnificent" de' Medici becomes sole ruler of Florence. **1479** Spain becomes a united kingdom under Ferdinand of Aragon and Isabella of Castile.		**1470**
1484 Marsilio Ficino completes his translation of Plato's works. **1486** Giovanni Pico della Mirandola publishes *Oration on the Dignity of Man*.	**1481** Spanish Christian forces invade Muslim-held Granada. **1485** Henry VIII becomes king of England.	**1480** Martin Behaim develops the nautical astrolabe.	**1480**
	1492 Spain offers Jews and Muslims the choice of conversion or expulsion. **1494** France invades Naples; Florence expels the Medicis. **1499** France seizes Milan.	**1492** Christopher Columbus reaches the Americas. **1494** The Treaty of Tordesillas divides the New World between Spain and Portugal. **1498** Vasco da Gama reaches India.	**1490**
	1503 Giuliano della Rovere becomes Pope Julius II; Spain takes control of Naples. **1509** The Battle of Agnadello breaks Venice's power in Italy.		**1500**
1518 Philipp Melanchthon is appointed professor of Greek at Wittenberg University.	**1519** King Charles I of Spain becomes Holy Roman Emperor Charles V.	**1519** Hernán Cortés reaches Mexico.	**1510**
1527 Melanchthon establishes a Protestant university in Marburg.	**1520** Süleyman I becomes the Ottoman sultan. **1526** The Hapsburgs lay claim to Bohemia and Hungary. **1527** Rome is sacked by imperial troops. **1529** Vienna is besieged by Ottoman forces.	**1522** Juan Sebastián de Elcano completes the first circumnavigation of the globe, a voyage originally commanded by Ferdinand Magellan.	**1520**
1530 Professorships in Greek and Hebrew are established at the University of Paris.	**1530** Charles V is crowned in Bologna; Florence falls under Medici control once more. **1536** France invades Piedmont.		**1530**
	1547 Ivan IV "the Terrible" is crowned czar of Russia; central Hungary comes under Ottoman rule.	**1543** Nicolaus Copernicus publishes *On the Revolutions of the Heavenly Spheres*; Andreas Vesalius publishes *On the Structure of the Human Body*.	**1540**
	1552 Russia conquers Kazan. **1556** Charles V ends his reign. **1558** Elizabeth I becomes queen of England. **1559** The Treaty of Cateau-Cambrésis ends the French-Hapsburg wars in Italy.		**1550**

	Architecture, Painting, and Sculpture	Literature and Music	The Church, the Reformation, and the Counter-Reformation
1560	**1563** Building of the Escorial in Spain begins. **1567** Pieter Bruegel the Elder paints *Peasant Dance.*		**1563** The Council of Trent comes to a close. **1564** Pope Pius IV promulgates the first Index of Forbidden Books.
1570	**1570** Palladio publishes *Four Books of Architecture.* **1572** The first edition of Georg Braun and Franz Hogenberg's *Civitates orbis terrarum* is published.	**1578** Pierre de Ronsard writes *Sonnets pour Hélène.* **1579** Edmund Spenser's *Shepheardes Calender* is published.	**1572** During the Saint Bartholomew's Day Massacre, most of Paris's Huguenots (Calvinists) are killed.
1580	**1584** The Escorial is completed.	**1589** Christopher Marlowe's *Doctor Faustus* is first performed.	
1590		**1590** The first three books of Spenser's *Faerie Queene* are published. **1592** Marlowe's *Edward II* is first performed. **1595** Philip Sidney's *Defence of Poesie* is published. **c. 1598** Jacopo Peri completes *Dafne,* the first opera.	**1598** With the Edict of Nantes, King Henry IV of France gives Huguenots a measure of legal status and protection.
1600	**1600** Caravaggio produces his *Conversion of Saint Paul* for the Cerasi chapel in Rome's Church of Santa Maria del Popolo.	**c. 1600** William Shakespeare writes *Hamlet.* **1609** Lope de Vega writes his manifesto, *Arte nuevo de hacer comedias.*	
1610	**1619** Inigo Jones completes the Queen's House at Greenwich, south of London.	**1610** Claudio Monteverdi's *Vespers* is published. **1611** The King James Bible (also known as the Authorized Version) is published. **1615** Miguel Cervantes completes *Don Quixote.*	
1620	**1622** Jones completes the Banqueting House in Whitehall, in central London. **1629** Gian Lorenzo Bernini succeeds Carlo Maderna as chief architect of Saint Peter's.	**1629** Book 1 of Heinrich Schütz's *Symphoniae sacrae* is published.	**1629** The Edict of Restitution reclaims German lands taken from the Catholic Church; the Peace of Alais ends special protection for French Protestants.
1630	**1631** Jones renovates Saint Paul's Cathedral in London. **1633** Jacques Callot publishes *Miseries of War.* **1635** Peter Paul Rubens paints *Rape of the Sabines.*	**1635** Pedro Calderón de la Barca writes *La vida es sueño.* **1637** Pierre Corneille writes *Le Cid;* John Milton writes *Lycidas.*	
1640	**1642** Rembrandt paints *Night Watch.*	**1642** Monteverdi's *L'incoronazione di Poppea* is first staged.	
1650	**1665** Saint Peter's Basilica (Rome) is completed. **1675** Christopher Wren begins the new Saint Paul's Cathedral in London; Jan Vermeer dies. **1680** Gian Lorenzo Bernini dies.	**1665** Milton completes *Paradise Lost.* **1667** Molière writes *Tartuffe;* Jean Racine writes *Phèdre.* **1670** Blaise Pascal's *Pensées* is published.	**1685** King Louis XIV revokes the Edict of Nantes.
1700	**1711** Work finishes on Saint Paul's Cathedral.		

Philosophy and Scholarship	Politics, Economics, and Society	Science, Technology, and Exploration	
	1566 Süleyman I dies; the revolt of the Dutch United Provinces against Spain begins.	1569 The first Mercator projection map of the world is published.	**1560**
1575 The University of Leiden is founded.	1571 The Battle of Lepanto wrecks Ottoman naval ambitions; Tatars burn Moscow. 1572 The Saint Bartholomew Day's Massacre reignites civil war in France.	1578 Francis Drake rounds South America's southern tip.	**1570**
	1581 The United Provinces declare independence. 1582 The Gregorian calendar is established. 1584 Ivan the Terrible dies. 1588 An attack on the English by the Spanish armada ends in disaster for Spain.	1589 Richard Hakluyt's *Principall Navigations, Voiages, and Discoveries of the English Nation* is published.	**1580**
	1593 Henry IV of France converts to Catholicism. 1598 Russia sinks into a chaotic period known as the Time of Troubles.		**1590**
1600 Giordano Bruno is condemned for heresy by the Roman Inquisition and burned at the stake.	1603 After the death of Elizabeth I, James VI of Scotland becomes James I of England. 1608 The Fifteen Years War, between the Ottoman and Holy Roman empires, ends.	1609 Johannes Kepler's *Astronomia nova* is published; Galileo Galilei makes improvements to Hans Lippershey's telescope and points it upward to observe the night sky	**1600**
	1613 Michael Romanov is elected czar of Russia; his dynasty will rule until 1917. 1618 The Thirty Years War begins when Bohemian Protestant nobles rebel against the Holy Roman Empire.	1610 Galileo writes up his first observations of the night sky in *The Starry Messenger*.	**1610**
1625 Hugo Grotius's *Law of War and Peace* appears.	1629 Charles I of England dismisses Parliament.	1620 Francis Bacon's *Novum organum* is published. 1628 William Harvey's *Anatomical Exercises on the Movement of the Heart and Blood* is published.	**1620**
	1630 King Gustavus II Adolphus of Sweden invades Germany. 1635 French forces enter the Thirty Years War.	1633 Galileo is called before the Roman Inquisition. 1637 Russian explorers reach Siberia's Pacific coast; René Descartes sets out his new philosophy in *Discourse on the Method*.	**1630**
	1642 Parliament asserts the right to make laws. 1643 Louis XIV becomes king of France. 1648 The Peace of Westphalia ends the Thirty Years War. 1649 Charles I is executed.	1641 Descartes publishes *Meditations on First Philosophy*.	**1640**
1651 Thomas Hobbes's *Leviathan* appears. 1670 Baruch Spinoza's *Tractatus theologico-politicus* is published. 1690 John Locke publishes *An Essay concerning Human Understanding*.	1660 England's monarchy is restored. 1666 London is devastated by fire. 1682 Peter I "the Great" becomes czar of Russia. 1688 England's Glorious Revolution deposes James II.	1660 The Royal Society of London is founded. 1662 Descartes's *Treatise on Man* appears. 1687 Isaac Newton completes the *Principia mathematica*.	**1650**
	1713 The Peace of Utrecht ends Hapsburg claims to Spain. 1715 Louis XIV dies. 1725 Peter the Great dies.	1735 Carolus Linnaeus's *Systema naturae* is published.	**1700**

Glossary

absolution Part of the Catholic sacrament of penance; the remission of sins pronounced by a priest acting as instrument of both God and the church.

absolutism In politics, the principle that a monarch has absolute authority over the people he or she rules. During the Renaissance several European monarchs based absolutist claims on the divine right of kings—the theory that a monarch is answerable solely to God.

allegory A narrative form in which abstractions or generalizations are represented as characters or events.

alliterative revival A late-fourteenth-century flowering in England's northern Midlands of poetry that, like Anglo-Saxon verse, relied on alliteration, the repetition of initial consonants.

alliterative verse A style of verse, particularly associated with poets writing in Anglo-Saxon and other early Germanic languages, in which alliteration is the main structural principle.

altarpiece A painting or carving that adorns the space above and behind an altar.

Anglo-Norman A version of the Norman-French spoken in England from the twelfth century through the fourteenth, especially in aristocratic and official circles.

Apocrypha Those Old Testament books and additions that form part of the Septuagint (the Greek translation of the Old Testament made between the third and first centuries BCE) and the Vulgate (the Latin translation made by Jerome in the fifth century CE) but that are considered noncanonical by Protestants and Jews.

apology A form of autobiographical literature in which the writer, usually a Christian, makes clear the grounds for a particular belief or course of action.

apostolic succession The doctrine common to Roman Catholicism, Eastern Orthodoxy, and certain Protestant churches that traces an unbroken line of spiritual succession from the apostles to present-day bishops, who are thus endowed with the apostolic authority to ordain priests, consecrate bishops, and govern a diocese. The specifically Catholic doctrine of the apostolic succession of the popes is not shared by other Christians, however.

apprentice A young man or woman who serves a master for a given period in return for training in a trade or craft as well as food and lodging. Apprenticeship was a crucial component of the guild system.

apse A projecting part of a church that is usually semicircular and vaulted.

architrave In classical architecture, the lowest part of an entablature, the part that rests immediately on the column capital.

archivolt An ornamental molding around an arched opening; the part that corresponds to an architrave in a rectangular opening.

Arminian One who, following the teachings of Arminius (Jacob Harmensen; 1560–1609), rejects the Calvinist doctrine of absolute predestination and holds instead that salvation is in the reach of all.

Augustinian A member of any of several religious orders in the Roman Catholic Church that live a communal life in accordance with the Rule of Saint Augustine, which dates from the fifth century. The Reformer Martin Luther was a clerical friar of the order of the Hermits of Saint Augustine, whose present form of organization dates from 1256.

ballad A story told in rhythmic verse, often sung and sometimes accompanied by dancing. A popular component of European folk traditions from the Middle Ages through the Renaissance, ballads were passed orally from generation to generation for centuries.

baptistery A part of a church (in many Renaissance churches, a separate building) that is used for baptism.

baroque In painting and sculpture, the style that predominated in Europe from the late 1500s until the early 1700s. In general, baroque artists aimed to appeal to the senses and not just to the intellect. Hallmarks of the style are drama, dynamism, grandiosity, complexity, and a highly developed naturalism both in the depiction of human figures and in the illusion of great spatial depth.

barrel vault A semicylindrical vault, one having the form of a very deep arch or tunnel.

basilica In ancient Rome, a public building, originally used as a courtroom or assembly hall, that had a central nave with an apse at one or both ends and two side aisles formed by rows of columns. The conversion of Roman basilicas into churches and cathedrals began in the fourth century. A version of the basilica design modified to include a transept provided the blueprint for church building in western Europe through the Middle Ages and the Renaissance.

benefice An office of the Catholic Church (such as the see of a bishop or the parish of a priest) to which some form of income, usually revenue from an endowment of land, is attached.

bloodletting In ancient, medieval, and Renaissance medicine, the surgical practice of drawing blood from the body in order to treat physical ailments thought to have been brought on by a super-abundance of blood in the system.

bourgeois A burgher—that is, a member of the town-dwelling social middle class.

brace and bit A hand-operated machine used to drill holes, usually in wood. The U-shaped brace is a form of crankshaft that converts the reciprocal (back-and-forth) motion of the operator's arm into the circular motion of the rotating bit, the sharp piece that cuts the hole in the wood.

broadside The long side of a ship above the waterline; also, the simultaneous firing of all the guns or cannon mounted on that part of a warship.

buon' fresco Literally, "true fresco"; the art of decorating freshly spread, wet plaster with water-based paints, whereby the pigment bonds to the lime in the plaster as it dries. *Fresco secco* ("dry fresco") is the art of painting on plaster that has already dried.

buttress A projecting structure built against a wall, especially one supporting a vault, to stabilize and strengthen it.

capital The uppermost member of a column or pilaster, the part that supports the entablature.

Caravaggesque Having the stylistic hallmarks of the work of Caravaggio, whose naturalistic figures, captured at moments of high drama, are illuminated by strong light and set against dark backgrounds.

caravan A convoy of merchants or pilgrims, especially one traveling across the deserts of Asia and northern Africa.

catechism A summary of Christian doctrine written in the form of questions and answers and used for religious instruction.

chancel The part of a church, often at the eastern end, that contains the altar and seating for the clergy and choir.

chanson de geste Literally, "song of deeds"; a French epic poem of the kind written by trouvères from the eleventh century through the thirteenth.

charisma Strictly speaking, a talent exhibited by a person who claims, by the grace of God, to be possessed of the power of the Holy Spirit. During the early Christian centuries, itinerant charismatic preachers might have inspired their audiences by speaking in tongues or healing the sick.

charter A royal grant that confers on a guild or company the right to exercise a monopoly in a given region; in some cases, the monopoly covered all trade, in others, only trade in certain commodities.

chiaroscuro Literally, "light-dark"; the use of stark contrasts between light and shade for dramatic effect. The Italian painter Masaccio (1401–1428) is credited with developing the technique.

chorus In ancient Greek drama, a company of actors that comments on and sometimes participates in the main action of the play.

clientage A political situation in which one territory (a client state) is economically, politically, or militarily dependent on another.

Composite A modification of the Corinthian order of classical architecture that combines the acanthus-carved Corinthian capitals with angular Ionic volutes.

conclave A special meeting of Roman Catholic cardinals who remain in continuous seclusion for the purpose of choosing a new pope.

condominium An arrangement whereby two or more rulers share sovereignty over a territory. Condominium was practiced to varying degrees by those members of the Hapsburg dynasty who vested imperial authority equally in several individuals rather than in a single sovereign.

condottiere In Italy, the leader of a band of mercenary soldiers, especially from the mid-fourteenth century through the sixteenth. The term derives from the *condotta*, the contract by which the condottieri put themselves in the service of the employer offering the best remuneration.

confession Part of the Catholic sacrament of penance; the act of disclosing one's sins to a priest (the confessor).

Congregationalist A member of a body of Protestant churches that affirm the local congregations' right and responsibility to make decisions without recourse to any higher authority.

contrition Part of the Catholic sacrament of penance; the feeling and expression of remorse for a sin committed.

corbel A weight-bearing architectural member that projects from within a wall, especially one that is stepped upward and outward.

Corinthian The most ornate order of the five classical orders of architecture, characterized by large bell-shaped capitals decorated with rows of carved acanthus leaves.

cornice The uppermost part of an entablature; the molded and projecting member that crowns a composition in classical architecture.

council In the Roman Catholic Church, a gathering of bishops to discuss matters of doctrine, liturgy, or practice.

Counter-Reformation The organized response of the Roman Catholic Church to the Reformation; the term is applied especially to the decrees of the Council of Trent (1545–1563). Although the church staunchly upheld those areas of Catholic doctrine the Protestants repudiated, it addressed the moral decay the Reformers complained of and made major changes in the conduct of its affairs, notably in improving the education and spiritual discipline of the clergy, regularizing the liturgy (including the celebration of Mass), and clarifying the elements of orthodox belief with the issuance of a definitive catechism.

cruciform In the shape of a cross; the term is usually used to describe a church with transepts.

Crusade One of several Christian military expeditions, especially in the eleventh, twelfth, and thirteenth centuries, whose purpose was to regain the Holy Land from the Muslims. In an extended sense, *crusade* is used to describe many other Christian campaigns against non-Christians and heretical Christians through the late Middle Ages and even until the end of the seventeenth century.

cyclops In Greek mythology, one of a race of giants with a single eye in the middle of the forehead.

deesis A representation, associated particularly with Byzantine art, of Christ enthroned and flanked by the Virgin Mary and John the Baptist.

dialectic In philosophy, a formal method of intellectual investigation; the Socratic dialectical technique, for example, is to put forward a proposition and then to test its truthfulness with thorough questioning.

diet A formal assembly, akin to a parliament, of estates of the realm. Princes of the Holy Roman Empire gathered at diets to discuss matters of concern to the whole empire.

dike Either an artificial watercourse or an embankment built along the shore of a sea or lake or beside a river to hold back the water and so prevent flooding.

dit amoureux A short verse narrative on the subject of love. The genre flourished in fourteenth-century France.

doge The chief magistrate in the government of the republics of Venice and Genoa.

Dominican A member of an order of friars founded by Saint Dominic in 1215 and dedicated especially to preaching and theological study.

Doric The oldest and simplest order of the five classical orders of architecture, characterized by a deep and decorated architrave.

dream vision A medieval poetic genre in which the narrator describes himself falling asleep and experiencing a vision wherein allegorical or symbolic figures, adventures, or spectacles shed light on some unresolved issue of his waking life.

ecclesiastical Having to do with a church or church-related matters.

ecumenical Representing or promoting unity or cooperation among all Christian churches.

elect According to the doctrine of predestination, those for whom God has foreordained salvation and eternal life.

Enlightenment An intellectual movement of eighteenth-century Europe that rejected traditional social, political, and religious arrangements and ideas in favor of new ones more closely based on logic, reasoning, and scientific observation.

entablature A horizontal construction in classical architecture that rests on the columns and consists of an architrave, a frieze, and a cornice.

equinox A twice-yearly event, usually occurring around March 22 and September 22, when the sun crosses the celestial equator and day and night are of equal length everywhere.

esquire A member of the English gentry (the class of landed proprietors) ranking below a knight.

Eucharist A rite common to all Christian churches in which, in imitation of Jesus at the Last Supper with his disciples, consecrated bread and wine are consumed, according to various interpretations, as a memorial of Christ's death, as a symbol of the realization of a spiritual union between Christ and the communicant, or as the body and blood of Christ.

exarch In Eastern Orthodoxy, a bishop who, as the head of an independent church, ranks below a patriarch and above a metropolitan.

excommunication A formal censure that deprives a person of membership in a church.

fabliau A short, ribaldly humorous story in verse, often involving deception and cunning, produced in northern France in the twelfth and thirteenth centuries.

Fall In Christian thought, the lapse from innocence and goodness that followed upon Adam and Eve's disobedience to God in the Garden of Eden and their subsequent expulsion from that earthly paradise. Christianity ascribes humankind's knowledge of sin, misery, and death to the indelible stain of this original sin—which may be removed only by the grace of God.

farce A kind of comedy in which the plot and character contain elements of absurdity and the tone is usually broad and often satirical.

feudalism A pattern of social and political organization that prevailed in Europe in the later Middle Ages. The word derives from the fief, which usually took the form of a grant of land from a lord to a vassal. The lord undertook to protect the vassal, and the vassal repaid the lord with an oath of homage, allegiance, and military service.

flying buttress An arching masonry structure that carries the weight of a roof or vault to a fully grounded supporting element.

foot A metrical unit that in English verse may consist of any of several combinations of one stressed and one or more unstressed syllables and in classical verse, of some combination of long and short syllables.

form In Platonic philosophy, the underlying essence of a thing; forms are also called ideas. The idea of a tree, for example, underlies all the actual trees in the world. The unchanging forms reside in a divine and perfect realm out of reach of all except the philosopher, who alone may grasp the higher reality beyond this transitory world.

Franciscan A member of the Order of Friars Minor, founded by Saint Francis of Assisi in 1209, or one of its offshoots. A Franciscan's life is dedicated especially to preaching, missionary endeavor, and charitable work.

friar A member of any of the mendicant religious orders—those whose members abjure ownership of personal property and thus are dependent on others' charity to survive.

frieze The section of an entablature between the architrave and the cornice, often a broad band filled with sculpture.

full To cleanse, shrink, and thicken woolen cloth. The process involves pounding the cloth in a vat or a mechanical mill with a variety of naturally occurring clay known as fuller's earth in combination with hot water (or sometimes ammonia-rich urine).

galleon A large, square-rigged, multidecked, often heavily armed wooden ship of war or commerce; because of their size and mobility, galleons were widely used by the European powers from 1500 till the mid-1700s.

Ghibelline In medieval and early-Renaissance Italy, a member of an aristocratic political party that opposed the papacy and supported the efforts of the Holy Roman emperors to extend their authority into northern Italy. Rivalry with the Guelfs contributed to considerable strife in Italian city-states during the thirteenth and fourteenth centuries.

Golden Fleece In classical mythology, the item whose recovery inspired the quest of Jason and the Argonauts. In 1430 Duke Philip the Good of Burgundy founded the chivalric Order of the Golden Fleece in order to honor the finest members of his court. Grand mastership of the order, whose guiding principles were to defend Roman Catholicism and uphold the chivalric moral code, later fell to the Hapsburgs.

gonfaloniere A high ceremonial officer in Florence; several members of the Medici family occupied the position during and after the Renaissance.

grisaille Decorative painting using tones of a single color, especially gray; the method produces the strong illusion of three dimensions.

groom of the chamber An attendant at the English court whose duties varied but were generally concerned with public ceremony and display.

Guelf In medieval and early-Renaissance Italy, a member of a popular political party (in rivalry with the aristocratic Ghibellines) that supported the pope and opposed the efforts of the Holy Roman emperors to extend their authority into northern Italy.

guild An association of craft workers or traders working in the same locality that provided its members with a protected market, a source of investment capital, and economic assistance in times of hardship. Guilds played a crucial role in the economic and religious life of medieval European towns.

habit The distinctive outer garb of a member of a religious order. The nicknames of the Franciscans and the Dominicans, for example—Gray Friars and Black Friars, respectively—derive from the color of the habit their monks wore.

harrow An iron agricultural tool set with spikes, teeth, or disks that is used to break up the surface of the soil and remove weeds.

heretic One who holds religious opinions that are at variance with the accepted doctrines of his or her faith.

humanism A belief in the overriding worth of human beings and their interests and values. Humanists typically consider secular matters more important than religious or supernatural ones.

iamb A two-syllable metrical foot consisting of one unstressed syllable followed by one stressed syllable.

impasto The thick application of paint to a canvas or panel, often with a palette knife rather than a brush. The technique, which adds depth and texture to the painted surface, is particularly associated with Rembrandt.

indulgence A partial or full remission of the purgatorial punishment due a penitent sinner; in Roman Catholic doctrine, the power to grant indulgences is the pope's alone. The abuse of indulgences—whether through outright sale, illicit extension to the remission of unconfessed sins, or both—more than once occasioned widespread scandal and protest among pious Christians and was a prime factor leading to the Reformation

insignia The ceremonial trappings, badges, or distinguishing marks of a person's office or status.

intercalary Inserted in the calendar, as a day or a month might be in order to harmonize the calendar with the cycle of the sun or moon.

Ionic Of the five classical orders of architecture, the one characterized by base-mounted fluted columns and scroll-shaped volutes in the capitals.

Jesuit A member of the Society of Jesus, a Roman Catholic order of priests founded by Saint Ignatius of Loyola in 1534. The Jesuits, who are known particularly for their educational and missionary work, played a key role in the Counter-Reformation.

jubilee For Roman Catholics, a period (usually a year) proclaimed by the pope as a time of particular solemnity and celebration. During a jubilee year the pope typically grants all Christian pilgrims visiting Rome a plenary indulgence (a full remission of the punishment due for sin).

justification In Christian (particularly, Reformed) theology, the act by which God considers a person righteous, free from sin, and worthy of salvation.

Kirk The established national church of Scotland, which officially accepted Presbyterianism in 1689.

laity The body of nonclerical adherents of a religious faith; lay people.

langue d'oc A Romance language, also called Occitan, formerly spoken in southeastern France. It is named for its word for "yes," *oc.*

langue d'oïl A Romance language, the ancestor of modern French, formerly spoken in northern France. It is named for its word for "yes," *oïl.*

lantern In architecture, a small glazed or open-sided tower or cupola that sits atop a dome or roof and admits light or air into the building below.

lathe A machine on which a piece of wood (or another carvable material) is spun horizontally; the material is then shaped either by a handheld tool or by a tool fixed to the machine.

liturgy A body of rites and formulas constituting the public worship of a particular religion.

loggia A roofed gallery open to the elements on at least one side, where the opening (usually arched) is divided by columns. Loggias were a common feature of Italian palaces and villas, especially those built in the seventeenth century.

mannerism The dominant artistic style in Europe from the death of Raphael in 1520 until the end of the sixteenth century. Mannerist art, sometimes described as self-consciously refined and artificially elegant, is characterized by complex spatial relationships and arrangements of figures, which are often deliberately elongated or presented in contorted poses.

manorialism An agricultural and economic arrangement prevalent in Europe in the later Middle Ages. Each manor was a unit of territory that might comprise one or more villages, in which peasant tenants lived, and a large manor house that belonged to the lord, who enjoyed numerous rights over the land, its fruits, and his (frequently bonded) tenants.

mechanism The philosophical doctrine that views all natural phenomena and processes as mechanically determined and fully explicable according to the laws of physical and chemical science.

Middle English The form of English spoken in England from roughly 1100 to 1500.

missionary One who works, usually in a foreign country, to spread a religious faith (especially Christianity) and to give humanitarian assistance.

moldboard On a plow, the curved iron board into which the plowshare (the blade that cuts into the soil) is fixed. It is by means of the moldboard that the soil is lifted and turned over.

motet A polyphonic choral composition on a sacred text. A motet is usually performed without instrumental accompaniment.

motif A distinctive theme, repeated feature, or dominant idea in a musical, literary, or artistic work.

mullion A slender vertical member that divides panes of glass in a window, adjacent windows from one another, or sections of a door.

nave The central portion of a church, usually running from the main entrance to the chancel and separated from the side aisles by pillars.

niello The process of decorating metal, often silver, with incised designs usually filled with a black sulfur alloy made with silver, lead, and copper.

nominalism A late-medieval philosophy that rejected the existence in reality of Platonic forms—universal essences such as beauty and "treeness"—and instead posited that such forms are mere categories produced by the human mind.

notary A public officer who attests to or certifies deeds, wills, contracts, and other documents in order to give them legal force.

nymph In classical mythology, a semi-divine and beautiful maiden inhabiting and closely identifed with a feature of the natural world such as a stream, a wood, or a mountain.

order In architecture, a unit of style composed of a column and entablature.

ottava rima Literally, "eighth rhyme"; an originally Italian eight-line-stanza form that rhymes *abababcc*. In English poetry, each line has ten syllables; in Italian poetry, each has eleven.

page A boy or young man in service to a knight as a form of training for knighthood.

Papal States A territory of varying size in central Italy over which the pope had political sovereignty from 756 to 1870.

parchment Sheep- or goatskin prepared as a material for writing; also, a manuscript written on parchment.

Passion The suffering of Christ between the night of the Last Supper and his death on the cross; also, the Gospel narrative of this event or a musical setting or dramatic retelling of the Gospel account.

patronymic A personal name that derives from that of its bearer's father or paternal ancestor.

pediment A triangular part that crowns the front of a classical building with a low-pitched roof and that is usually filled with relief carvings.

penance In the doctrine of Roman Catholicism, Eastern Orthodoxy, and certain Anglican churches, the sacrament wherein a penitent gains forgiveness for sins and is reconciled with God and the church. Penance encompasses contrition, confession, absolution, and satisfaction.

pendentive A concave triangle that is formed in the space between arches supporting a dome over a square space. Pendentives taper at the bottom to concentrate the weight of the dome on the columns beneath and spread at the top to form the continuous circular base needed for the dome.

pentameter A line of verse that consists of five metrical feet.

perspective The artistic technique of creating the illusion of depth on a plane surface, such as a canvas or panel, to represent the spatial relation of objects or people as they appear to the eye.

picaresque Describing a genre of fiction dealing with the adventures of a rough, often dishonest, but likable protagonist.

pilaster A rectangular column that is embedded in a wall and projects a third of its width or less from the wall.

polder An area of low land reclaimed from the sea, usually for agriculture.

Poor Clare A nun of a Franciscan order founded by Saint Clare in the early thirteenth century.

portico A covered walkway with a roof supported by columns at regular intervals, usually attached as a porch at the entrance of a building.

predestination The belief or doctrine that God, in consequence of his foreknowledge of all events, has eternally chosen those (the elect) for whom salvation and eternal life are reserved.

Presbyterian A member of a Protestant denomination, Calvinist in its doctrine, that is governed by a system of presbyteries that exercise legislative and judicial authority.

presbytery In a Presbyterian church, a governing body consisting of ministers and elected elders from local congregations.

purgatory In Roman Catholic doctrine, an intermediate realm of the afterlife where the souls of penitent sinners who have died in God's grace are required to undergo a finite period of punishment in restitution for their sins to make them fit for admission to the eternal joys of heaven.

Puritan A member of a Calvinist Protestant group that arose in sixteenth-century England. Considering the Tudor reform of the church insufficient and incomplete, they advocated the abolition of numerous Anglican ceremonies and practices retained or adapted from pre-Reformation times.

putto A representation of an infant boy, often a cherub; putti are common features of Renaissance painting and sculpture.

recant To formally retract or disavow a previously held statement or belief.

recusant One who refuses to submit to authority; specifically, from around 1570 to 1791, an English Roman Catholic who, by refusing to attend services of the Church of England, committed a crime.

Reformation The early-sixteenth-century religious movement, originating with Martin Luther, that broke away from the Roman Catholic Church on moral and doctrinal grounds. Its religious result was Protestantism.

Renaissance A cultural movement, beginning in Italy in the fourteenth century and lasting into the seventeenth, that was marked by a flowering of artistic and literary achievement and a resurgence of interest in the values of ancient Greece and Rome.

repoussoir French for "a pushing back"; in a painting, a figure or object, generally in the foreground, that separates the pictorial space from the real space of the viewer and also serves to push back the figures in the composition in order to suggest greater depth within the illusory space.

retinue A company of followers, called retainers, in attendance upon an important individual, such as a knight.

rhetoric The art of using language effectively; especially, the skill of persuasive speaking. With grammar, logic, geometry, arithmetic, music, and astronomy, rhetoric was one of the seven liberal arts that formed the basis of the classical education championed by humanists during the late Middle Ages and the Renaissance.

rhyme royal A stanza of seven iambic pentameter lines rhyming *ababbcc*.

romance A genre of medieval literature originally associated with French and other Romance languages. Romances concern chivalric love and adventure and often involve elements of legend and the supernatural.

rood screen A structure, usually masonry, in many late-medieval and Renaissance churches that separates the nave, where the congregation gathers, from the chancel, or sanctuary, where the altar sits. Atop the screen there is often a crucifix, or rood—whence comes the structure's name.

rosary A Roman Catholic devotion dedicated to the Virgin Mary; also, the string of beads used to count the prayers involved in the rosary.

sacrament In Christian doctrine, a religious ceremony or act regarded as an outward sign of inward grace and believed to have been ordained by Christ. The term is applied in Roman Catholic and Orthodox doctrine to each of seven rites: baptism, confirmation, the Eucharist, penance, matrimony, ordination, and extreme unction; most Protestant churches regard only baptism and the Eucharist as sacraments.

sacristy The room in a church, adjacent to the altar, in which the sacred vestments and vessels are kept.

satire A brand of literary humor in which human follies or vices are held up to contempt, often through an exaggerated characterization of the very flaws that are being ridiculed.

satisfaction In the sacrament of penance, the reparation due for a sin.

serf In feudal societies, a peasant who, in exchange for the right to live on and work a given tract of land, paid the landowner dues (in labor, service, or a portion of the harvest, for example) and was entirely subject in legal matters to the authority of the landowner. In many places serfs were bound to the land—anyone acquiring a piece of land also acquired its serfs.

sfumato Literally, "smoked out"; the subtle blending of one tone into another in an effect that softens the edges of figures and objects and lends a smoky, atmospheric quality to an oil painting. The technique was perfected by Leonardo da Vinci.

signoria In the medieval and Renaissance Italian city-states, a government run by a signore (a lord) that replaced republican institutions either by force or by agreement.

silverpoint An artistic technique in which a design is drawn on specially prepared parchment with a small, sharpened rod of silver.

simony The buying or selling of ecclesiastical preferment or a church office.

sluice An artificial channel for water—a millstream, for example—that incorporates a floodgate or valve for stopping or regulating the flow of the water.

sonnet A verse form, Italian in origin, consisting of fourteen lines, usually in iambic pentameter, that follow a prescribed rhyme scheme. Petrarch and Shakespeare are among the form's most celebrated practitioners.

tempera A type of artist's paint in which egg yolk or white is used to bind powdered dyes. Tempera was the most commonly used paint in Europe and elsewhere until oil paint superseded it in the sixteenth century.

tenebrism Championed by Caravaggio, a development of the chiaroscuro technique in which heavily contrasting areas of light and shadow are used to heighten the dramatic impact of a painting.

terza rima Italian for "third rhyme"; a verse form consisting of tercets (three-line stanzas) linked by an interlacing rhyme scheme, such as *aba, bcb, cdc,* and so on. Dante composed the *Divine Comedy* in terza rima.

toponym A personal name that derives from the place its bearer was born in or is closely associated with.

transept The shorter part of a cruciform church that crosses the longer part at right angles; also, either of the arms that thus project from the main part of the church to the north or the south.

transubstantiation In Roman Catholic doctrine, the miraculous transformation at the Consecration of the Mass of the substance of the eucharistic bread and wine into the body and blood of Christ while the appearance of the sacramental elements remains unchanged.

triptych A three-paneled painting; the panels are often hinged so that the two side panels may be folded over the center panel.

trompe l'oeil Literally, "deceives the eye"; any form of optical illusion in painting, sculpture, or architecture.

troubadour One of a class of lyric poet-musicians who flourished in southern France and northern Italy from the eleventh through the thirteenth century. They included noblemen, crusading knights, and even kings; their verses, whose most common themes were courtly love and war, were sung in Provençal, a version of the langue d'oc.

trouvère From the eleventh through the fourteenth century, one of a school of poets in northern France who, in imitation of the southern troubadours, produced mostly narrative poems in the langue d'oïl.

truss In architecture, a supporting structure or framework consisting of several members (most commonly, beams) laid out in a single plane.

Tuscan One of the five classical orders of architecture; Roman in origin, the Tuscan order is characterized by a plain frieze.

vernacular The language of a particular people, country, or region rather than a literary or classical language, such as Latin or Greek.

volute A spiral or scroll-shaped architectural ornament, especially of the kind found in classical capitals.

weather gauge One ship's position relative to another and to the wind. In naval combat, the vessel said to be holding the weather gauge is the one whose relative position gives it the advantage.

woodcut A wooden block, carved with a design in relief, that is then inked to stamp printed images onto paper (the word also refers to the images produced by this method). Woodcuts could be inserted into a mechanical press and were used mainly for pictures, although the pictures often contained small amounts of text.

yeoman An attendant in a noble or royal household during the Middle Ages.

Resources for Further Study

BIBLIOGRAPHY

All Internet addresses were functional and accurate as of August 2006.

Editor's Recommendations

Thousands of books have been written about the art, politics, philosophy, and religion of the Renaissance. The few works mentioned in these paragraphs are either seminal—that is, they offer good broad descriptions of fundamental Renaissance themes—or else they are of interest with regard to a particular aspect of Renaissance life and thought. In addition, the reader should bear in mind that bibliographies form a more or less endless chain. The Further Reading section that concludes every entry in this encyclopedia offers a good starting point for a bibliographical search. Each title listed there will have its own bibliography, and each book in that bibliography will lead the reader to many further books, and so on.

Study of the Renaissance as a discrete period defined by certain ideas and represented by a particular culture began in earnest in the nineteenth century with Jacob Burckhardt's *Civilization of the Renaissance in Italy* (Basel, 1860). Burckhardt was the first historian to use the word *Renaissance* to describe the period that began with the rebirth of classicism in mid-fourteenth-century Italy. His seminal work (written in German) has been translated often since, most recently by S. G. C. Middlemore (New York, 2002). Although a specialist study, John Sandys's *History of Classical Scholarship,* first published in three volumes (Cambridge, UK, 1903–1908; reprint, 1999), should be dipped into by the adventurous reader who wants to know more about developments in the study of the language and literature of classical Greece and Rome, for it was these developments that underpinned much of the culture of the Renaissance.

Several important works take up the broad intellectual themes of the Renaissance. Among them are John H. Plumb's *The Italian Renaissance: A Concise Survey of Its History and Culture* (New York, 1965) and *The Italian Renaissance in Its Historical Background,* by Denys Hay (Cambridge, UK, 1961). Henry Osborn Taylor's *Thought and Expression in the Sixteenth Century* (New York, 1920) is typical of a certain kind of early-twentieth-century Renaissance scholarship that is written from a particularly English point of view.

The study of Renaissance art always begins with the work of Giorgio Vasari (1511–1574), the original art historian, who in 1570 published his famous biographies of the preeminent painters, sculptors, and architects of his day. A good modern edition is the one translated as *The Lives of the Artists* by Julia Conaway Bondanella and Peter Bondanella (Oxford, 1998). Two studies of important Renaissance artists by their near contemporaries are Filippo Baldinucci's *Life of Bernini*—the

translation by Catherine Enggass (University Park, PA, 1966) is recommended—and Antonio Manetti's *Life of Brunelleschi,* also translated by Enggass (University Park, PA, 1970). Howard Hibbard's *Bernini* (Baltimore, 1966) and his *Michelangelo: Painter, Sculptor, Architect* (New York, 1978) are readable modern studies. Rudolf Wittkower's *Architectural Principles in the Age of Humanism* (London, 1949) is a good introduction to the architecture of the Renaissance.

The principal source of Renaissance ideas was classical antiquity. The rebirth and recasting of classicism is explored in R. R. Bolgar's *The Classical Heritage and Its Beneficiaries* (Cambridge, UK, 1954). For the Renaissance interest in pre-Christian religion, see Edgar Wind's *Pagan Mysteries in the Renaissance* (New Haven, CT, 1958) and the later study by Joscelyn Godwin, *The Pagan Dream of the Renaissance* (Grand Rapids, MI, 2002).

More pervasive than just a philosophy, humanism was an all-encompassing attitude that placed humankind at the center of creation. For an exploration of the humanistic basis of all Renaissance philosophy, see Sem Dresden, *Humanism in the Renaissance,* translated from the Dutch by Margaret King (London, 1968). For biographical studies of the philosophers, see Paul Oskar Kristeller, *Eight Philosophers of the Italian Renaissance* (Stanford, CA, 1964), and also the same author's *Philosophy of Marsilio Ficino,* translated by Virginia Conant (New York, 1943).

There are several good studies of those leading Renaissance families whose wealth paid for many of the finest buildings and works of art and whose dynastic ambitiousness shaped the politics of Europe, especially Italy. One standard account of a leading family of the Renaissance is Christopher Hibbert's *The House of Medici: Its Rise and Fall* (New York, 1975). A more recent work about a great Florentine family is *Spinelli of Florence: The Fortunes of a Renaissance Merchant Family,* by Philip Jacks and William Caferro (University Park, PA, 2001). Giovanna R. Solari's *The House of Farnese,* translated by Simona Morini and Frederic Tuten (Garden City, NY, 1968), treats one of Rome's most prominent families.

For accounts of the blooming of great Italian cities in the fifteen and sixteenth centuries, see Francesco Guicciardini, *The History of Florence,* translated by Mario Domandi (New York, 1970); Charles L Stinger, *The Renaissance in Rome* (Bloomington, IN, 1985; reprint, 1998); and David Chambers, ed., *Venice: A Documentary History, 1450–1630* (Oxford, 1992).

Although the center and source of Renaissance art and thought was Italy, the Renaissance was a Europe-wide happening that had echoes even in the colonial dependencies of France, Spain, and England. Marina Belozerskaya's *Rethinking the Renaissance: Burgundian Arts across Europe* (New York, 2002) makes the case that if Giorgio Vasari had been a Burgundian rather than a Roman, modern scholars might have a very different view of the Renaissance.

Two standard works on the Reformation are Roland H. Bainton, *The Age of Reformation* (Malabar, FL, 1956; reprint, 1984), and Henri Daniel-Rops, *The Catholic Reformation*, translated by John Warrington (New York, 1962), which tell the story from the Protestant and Catholic points of view, respectively. Hartmann Grisar's *Luther,* translated by E. M. Lamond (London, 1913–1917; one-volume edition, New York, 1971), portrays the first great Reformer as the destroyer of the medieval church and the unity of Europe. An alternative view of Luther as a complex thinker who represented much of the best in modernity is presented in Richard Marius's *Luther* (Philadelphia, 1974). On the other crucial founder of the Reformed tradition, see Bernard Cottret, *Calvin: A Biography,* translated by M. Wallace McDonald (Grand Rapids, MI, 2000). The Anabaptists and other marginal groups are discussed in George H. Williams, *The Radical Reformation* (3rd edition, Kirksville, MO, 1992). For contrasting views of the English Reformation, see Leonard Elliott-Binns, *The Reformation in England* (London, 1937; reprint, Hamden, CT, 1966) and Philip Hughes's *Reformation in England* (London, 1950–1954; 5th edition, New York, 1963).

JAMES A. PATRICK

The books and journals below were written for mature readers. Works suitable for younger readers can be found on pages 1478 to 1480.

General
Books

Cameron, Euan, ed. *Early Modern Europe.* New York: Oxford University Press, 1999.

Campbell, Gordon. *The Oxford Dictionary of the Renaissance.* New York: Oxford University Press, 2003.

Grendler, Paul F., et al., eds. *Encyclopedia of the Renaissance.* 6 vols. New York: Scribner, 1999.

Hale, J. R. *The Civilization of Europe in the Renaissance.* New York: Atheneum, 1994.

Johnson, Paul. *The Renaissance: A Short History.* New York: Modern Library, 2000.

New, John F. H. *The Renaissance and Reformation: A Short History.* 2nd ed. New York: Wiley, 1977.

Teeple, John B. *Timelines of World History.* New York: Dorling Kindersley, 2006.

Journals

Renaissance Quarterly
Twelve to sixteen articles a year and around one hundred reviews per issue cover all areas of Renaissance studies. Published by the Renaissance Society of America.
www.rsa.org/rq.htm

Renaissance Studies
Articles and documents cover the history, art, architecture, religion, literature, and languages of Renaissance Europe. Published by the Society for Renaissance Studies.
http://srs.sas.ac.uk

Architecture, Painting, and Sculpture
Books

Benevolo, Leonardo. *The Architecture of the Renaissance.* New York: Routledge, 2002.

Bissell, R. Ward. *Artemisia Gentileschi and the Authority of Art.* University Park: Pennsylvania State University Press, 1999.

Boucher, Bruce. *Andrea Palladio: The Architect in His Time.* New York: Abbeville Press, 1994.

Brown, Jonathan, and Carmen Garrido. *Velázquez: The Technique of Genius.* New Haven, CT: Yale University Press, 1998.

Christiansen, Keith, ed. *The Age of Caravaggio.* New York: Metropolitan Museum of Art / Electa / Rizzoli, 1985.

Claessens, Bob, and Jeanne Rousseau. *Our Bruegel.* English version by Haakon Chevalier. Antwerp: Mercatorfonds, 1969.

Costantino, Maria. *Leonardo.* New York: Smithmark, 1995.

Derbes, Anne, and Mark Sandona, eds. *The Cambridge Companion to Giotto.* New York: Cambridge University Press, 2003.

Feghelm, Dagmar, and Markus Kersting. *Rubens and His Women.* New York: Prestel, 2005.

Foister, Susan, Susan Jones, and Delphine Cool, eds. *Investigating Jan van Eyck.* Turnhout, Belgium: Brepols, 2000.

Gibson, Walter S. *Hieronymus Bosch.* New York: Praeger, 1973.

Harris, Ann Sutherland. *Seventeenth-Century Art and Architecture.* Upper Saddle River, NJ: Prentice Hall, 2005.

Hartt, Frederick. *History of Italian Renaissance Art: Painting, Sculpture, Architecture.* 5th ed. New York: Abrams, 2002.

Hutchison, Jane Campbell. *Albrecht Dürer: A Biography.* Princeton, NJ: Princeton University Press, 1990.

Jardine, Lisa. *On a Grander Scale: The Outstanding Life of Sir Christopher Wren.* New York: HarperCollins, 2002.

King, Ross. *Brunelleschi's Dome: How a Renaissance Genius Reinvented Architecture.* New York: Penguin, 2001.

———. *Michelangelo and the Pope's Ceiling.* New York: Walker, 2003.

Leapman, Michael. *The Troubled Life of Inigo Jones, Architect of the English Renaissance.* London: Review, 2003.

Lightbown, Ronald. *Sandro Botticelli: Life and Work.* 2nd ed. New York, 1989.

Murray, Peter. *The Architecture of the Italian Renaissance.* New York: Schocken, 1986.

Palladio, Andrea. *Four Books on Architecture.* Translated by Robert Tavernor and Richard Schofield. Cambridge, MA: MIT Press, 1997.

Panofsky, Erwin. *The Life and Art of Albrecht Dürer.* Princeton, NJ: Princeton University Press, 2005.

Puglisi, Catherine R. *Caravaggio.* London: Phaidon, 1998.

Schwartz, Gary. *Rembrandt: His Life, His Paintings.* New York: Penguin, 1991.

Snyder, James. *Northern Renaissance Art: Painting, Sculpture, the Graphic Arts from 1350 to 1575.* 2nd ed. Upper Saddle River, NJ: Prentice Hall, 2005.

Stratton-Pruitt, Suzanne I.., ed. *The Cambridge Companion to Velázquez.* New York: Cambridge University Press, 2002.

Journals

Art History
Five annual issues include essays and reviews concerning all aspects and periods of the history of art from a variety of perspectives. Published by the Association of Art Historians.
http://aah.org.uk/publications/arthistory.php

DVDs

Leonardo and *The Divine Michelangelo*
These two lively documentaries chart the lives and analyze the talents of two of the most celebrated figures of the Renaissance. Made by and available from the BBC.
http://www.bbcshop.com/invt/bbcdvd1558

Daily Life
Books

Burke, Peter. *Popular Culture in Early Modern Europe.* Brookfield, VT: Gower, 1988.

Cameron, David Kerr. *The English Fair.* London: Sutton, 1998.

Harris, Tim, ed. *Popular Culture in England, c. 1500–1850.* New York: Saint Martin's Press, 1995.

Hutton, Ronald. *Stations of the Sun: A History of the Ritual Year in Britain.* New York: Oxford University Press, 1996.

Keen, Maurice Hugh. *Chivalry.* New Haven, CT: Yale University Press, 2005.

King, Margaret L. *Women of the Renaissance.* Chicago: University of Chicago Press, 1991.

Mendelson, Sara, and Patricia Crawford. *Women in Early Modern England, 1550–1720.* New York: Clarendon Press, 1998.

Muchembled, Robert. *Popular Culture and Elite Culture in France, 1400–1750.* Translated by Lydia Cochrane. Baton Rouge: Louisiana State University Press, 1985.

Muir, Edward. *Ritual in Early Modern Europe.* 2nd ed. New York: Cambridge University Press, 2005.

Panizza, Letizia, ed. *Women in Italian Renaissance Culture and Society.* Oakville, CT: David Brown, 2000.

Reay, Barry. *Popular Cultures in England, 1550–1750.* New York: Addison Wesley Longman, 1998.

Reynolds, Susan. *Kingdoms and Communities in Western Europe.* New York: Oxford University Press, 1997.

Rummel, Erika, ed. *Erasmus on Women.* Buffalo, NY: University of Toronto Press, 1996.

Scribner, Robert W. *Popular Culture and Popular Movements in Reformation Germany.* Ronceverte, WV: Hambledon Press, 1987.

Sharpe, James. *Instruments of Darkness: Witchcraft in Early Modern England.* Philadelphia: University of Pennsylvania Press, 1996.

Tester, S. J. *A History of Western Astrology.* New York: Ballantine, 1989.

Vale, M. G. A. *War and Chivalry: Warfare and Aristocratic Culture in England, France, and Burgundy at the End of the Middle Ages.* Athens: University of Georgia Press, 1981.

Woolley, Benjamin. *The Queen's Conjurer: The Science and Magic of Dr. John Dee, Adviser to Queen Elizabeth I.* New York: Henry Holt, 2001.

Literature and Music
Books

Atlas, Allan W. *Renaissance Music: Music in Western Europe, 1400–1600.* New York: Norton, 1998.

Bergin, Thomas G. *Boccaccio.* New York: Viking, 1981.

Blume, Friedrich. *Protestant Church Music: A History.* New York: Norton, 1974.

Boccaccio, Giovanni. *The Decameron.* Translated by G. H. McWilliam. New York: Penguin, 1995.

Boitani, Piero, and Jill Mann. *The Cambridge Companion to Chaucer.* New York: Cambridge University Press, 2003.

Brand, Peter, and Lino Pertile, eds. *The Cambridge History of Italian Literature.* New York: Cambridge University Press, 1999.

Braunmuller, A. R., and Michael Hattaway, eds. *The Cambridge Companion to English Renaissance Drama.* New York: Cambridge University Press, 2003.

Brown, Howard Mayer, and Louise K. Stein. *Music in the Renaissance.* Rev. ed. Upper Saddle River, NJ: Prentice Hall, 1999.

Byron, William. *Cervantes: A Biography.* New York: Paragon House, 1988.

Carter, Tim. *Monteverdi's Musical Theater.* New Haven, CT: Yale University Press, 2002.

Chaucer, Geoffrey. *The Riverside Chaucer* General editor, Larry D. Benson. Boston: Houghton Mifflin, 1987.

Cheney, Patrick, ed. *The Cambridge Companion to Christopher Marlowe.* New York: Cambridge University Press, 2004.

Fallows, David. *Dufay.* New York: Vintage, 1988.

Farrow, John. *The Story of Thomas More.* New York: Sheed and Ward, 1954.

Frame, Donald M. *François Rabelais: A Study.* New York: Harcourt Brace Jovanovich, 1977.

Fraser, Russell. *Shakespeare: The Later Years.* New York: Columbia University Press, 1992.

Hainsworth, Peter, and David Robey, eds. *The Oxford Companion to Italian Literature.* New York: Oxford University Press, 2002.

Hopkins, Lisa. *Christopher Marlowe: A Literary Life.* New York: Palgrave, 2000.

Howard, Donald Roy. *Chaucer: His Life, His Works, His World.* New York: Dutton, 1987.

Kinney, Arthur F., ed. *The Cambridge Companion to English Literature, 1500–1600.* New York: Cambridge University Press, 2000.

Krailsheimer, A. J., ed. *The Continental Renaissance, 1500–1600.* Atlantic Highlands, NJ: Humanities Press, 1978.

Lewalski, Barbara Kiefer. *The Life of John Milton: A Critical Biography.* Malden, MA: Blackwell, 2000.

Mann, Nicholas. *Petrarch.* New York: Oxford University Press, 1984.

Marius, Richard. *Thomas More.* New York: Knopf, 1984.

Marlowe, Stephen. *The Death and Life of Miguel de Cervantes.* New York: Arcade, 1996.

Milton, John. *The Major Works.* Edited by Stephen Orgel and Jonathan Goldberg. New York: Oxford University Press, 2003.

Mohl, Ruth. *Edmund Spenser: His Life and Works.* New York: Peter Lang, 1988.

Molière. *The Misanthrope and Other Plays.* Translated by Donald M. Frame. New York: Signet Classics, 2005.

———. *Tartuffe, and Other Plays.* Translated by Donald M. Frame. New York: New American Library, 1967.

More, Thomas. *Utopia.* Translated by Clarence Miller. New Haven, CT: Yale University Press, 2001.

Nicholl, Charles. *The Reckoning: The Murder of Christopher Marlowe.* University of Chicago Press, 1995.

O'Connor, Garry *William Shakespeare: A Popular Life.* New York: Applause, 2000.

Parker, William Riley. *Milton: A Biography.* New York: Oxford University Press, 1996.

Pearsall, Derek Albert. *The Life of Geoffrey Chaucer: A Critical Biography.* Cambridge, MA: Blackwell, 1992.

Petrarca, Francesco. *My Secret Book.* Translated by J. G. Nichols. London: Hesperus Press, 2002.

———. *The Portable Petrarch.* Translated and edited by Mark Musa. New York: Penguin, 2004.

Rabelais, François. *The Histories of Gargantua and Pantagruel.* Translated by Michael Screech. London: Penguin, 2006.

Reese, Gustave, ed. *The New Grove High Renaissance Masters: Josquin, Palestrina, Lassus, Byrd, Victoria.* New York: Norton, 1984.

Riggs, David. *The World of Christopher Marlowe.* New York: Henry Holt, 2005.

Sanders, Andrew. *The Short Oxford History of English Literature.* New York: Oxford University Press, 2004.

Schütz, Heinrich. *Letters and Documents of Heinrich Schütz, 1656–1672: An Annotated Translation.* Edited and translated by Gina Spagnoli. University of Rochester Press, 1992.

Smallman, Basil. *Schütz.* New York: Oxford University Press, 2000.

Sobran, Joseph. *Alias Shakespeare.* New York: Free Press, 1997.

Speaight, Robert. *Shakespeare: The Man and His Achievement.* New York: Cooper Square Press, 2000.

Sylvester, R. S., and G. P. Marc'hadour, eds. *Essential Articles for the Study of Thomas More.* Hamden, CT: Archon, 1977.

Thomson, Peter. *Shakespeare's Professional Career.* New York: Cambridge University Press, 1992.

Trinkaus, Charles. *The Poet as a Philosopher: Petrarch and the Formation of Renaissance Consciousness.* New Haven, CT: Yale University Press, 1979.

Walker, Hallam. *Molière.* Boston: Twayne, 1990.

Waller, Gary. *Edmund Spenser: A Literary Life.* New York: Saint Martin's Press, 1994.

Wells, Stanley. *Shakespeare: A Life in Drama.* New York: Norton, 1995.

Whinnom, Keith. *Medieval and Renaissance Spanish Literature.* Exeter, UK: University of Exeter Press, 1994.

Wraight, A. D. *In Search of Christopher Marlowe.* New York: Vanguard, 1965.

Journals

English Literary Renaissance

Offers current scholarship on English literature written between 1485 and 1665, including the works of Shakespeare, Spenser, and Milton. Features rare texts and newly discovered manuscripts, current annotated bibliographies of work in the field, and contemporary woodcuts and engravings. Published at the Massachusetts Center for Renaissance Studies.
www.umass.edu/english/ELR/elr2.html

Early Modern Literary Studies

Articles and reviews examine English literature, literary culture, and language during the sixteenth and seventeenth centuries and evaluate recent work of interest. As an online journal, *EMLS* is committed to gathering and maintaining links to the most useful internet resources for Renaissance scholars, including archives, e-texts, and discussion groups.
www.shu.ac.uk/emls

Philosophy, Religion, and Scholarship
Books

Allen, Michael J. B., Valery Rees, and Martin Davies, eds. *Marsilio Ficino: His Theology, His Philosophy, His Legacy.* Boston: Brill, 2002.

Armstrong, Karen. *Islam: A Brief History.* New York: Modern Library, 2002.

Bacon, Francis. *The Major Works.* Edited by Brian Vickers. New York: Oxford University Press, 2002.

Bainton, Ronald H. *Here I Stand: A Life of Martin Luther.* Nashville, TN: Abingdon, 1990.

Barnes, Jonathan. *Aristotle.* New York: Oxford University Press, 1982.

Baron, Hans. *In Search of Florentine Civic Humanism: Essays on the Transition from Medieval to Modern Thought.* 2 vols. Princeton, NJ: Princeton University Press, 1988.

Bedini, Silvio A. *The Pope's Elephant.* Nashville, TN: Sanders, 1998.

Berkey, Jonathan P. *The Formation of Islam: Religion and Society in the Near East, 600–1800.* New York: Cambridge University Press, 2003.

Boyd, William, and Edmund J. King. *The History of Western Education.* 12th ed. Lanham, MD: Rowman & Littlefield, 1994.

Bracciolini, Poggio. *Two Renaissance Book Hunters: The Letters of Poggius Bracciolini to Nicolaus de Niccolis.* Translated and annotated by Phyllis Walter Goodhart Gordan. New York: Columbia University Press, 1991.

Bruce, F. F. *The English Bible: A History of Translations from the Earliest English Versions to the New English Bible.* Rev. ed. New York: Oxford University Press, 1970.

Cassirer, Ernst, Paul Oskar Kristeller, and John Herman Randall Jr. *The Renaissance Philosophy of Man.* Chicago: University of Chicago Press, 1967.

Celenza, Christopher S. *The Lost Italian Renaissance: Humanists, Historians, and Latin's Legacy.* Baltimore: Johns Hopkins University Press, 2004.

Coleman, Janet. *A History of Political Thought: From the Middle Ages to the Renaissance.* Malden, MA: Blackwell, 2000.

Copenhaver, Brian P., and Charles B. Schmitt. *Renaissance Philosophy.* New York: Oxford University Press, 1992.

Coppa, Frank J., ed. *The Great Popes through History: An Encyclopedia.* 2 vols. Westport, CT: Greenwood Press, 2002.

Coquillette, Daniel R. *Francis Bacon*. Palo Alto, CA: Stanford University Press, 1992.

Cottingham, John, ed. *The Cambridge Companion to Descartes*. New York: Cambridge University Press, 1992.

D'Amico, John F. *Renaissance Humanism in Papal Rome*: Baltimore: Johns Hopkins University Press, 1983.

Daniell, David. *The Bible in English*. New Haven, CT: Yale University Press, 2003.

Dixon, C. Scott. *The Reformation in Germany*. Malden, MA: Blackwell, 2002.

Duffy, Eamon. *Saints and Sinners: A History of the Popes*. New Haven, CT: Yale University Press, 1997.

Eby, Frederick. *Early Protestant Educators: The Educational Writings of Martin Luther, John Calvin, and Other Leaders of Protestant Thought*. New York: AMS Press, 1971.

Edwards, John. *The Jews in Christian Europe, 1400–1700*. New York: Routledge, 1988.

Eire, Carlos M. N. *War against the Idols: The Reformation of Worship from Erasmus to Calvin*. New York: Cambridge University Press, 1986.

Elton, G. R. *Reformation Europe, 1517–1559*. 2nd ed. Malden, MA: Blackwell, 1999

Erasmus, Desiderius. *Christian Humanism and the Reformation: Selected Writings*. Edited by John C. Olin. New York: Fordham University Press, 1987.

———. *The Praise of Folly*. Translated by Clarence H. Miller. New Haven, CT: Yale University Press, 1979.

Evans, Gillian Rosemary. *A Brief History of Heresy*. Malden, MA: Blackwell, 2002.

Fine, Lawrence, ed. *Judaism in Practice: From the Middle Ages through the Early Modern Period*. Princeton, NJ: Princeton University Press, 2001.

Gill, Joseph. *The Council of Florence*. New York: AMS Press, 1982.

Goodman, Anthony, and Angus MacKay, eds. *The Impact of Humanism on Western Europe*. New York: Longman, 1990.

Gouwens, Kenneth, and Sheryl E. Reiss, eds. *The Pontificate of Clement VII*. Burlington, VT: Ashgate, 2005.

Grafton, Anthony, ed. *Rome Reborn: The Vatican Library and Renaissance Culture*. New Haven, CT: Yale University Press, 1993.

Grendler, Paul F. *Schooling in Renaissance Italy*. Baltimore: Johns Hopkins University Press, 1989.

Grisar, Hartmann. *Martin Luther: His Life and Work*. New York: AMS Press, 1971.

Guicciardini, Francesco. *The History of Italy*. Translated and edited by Sidney Alexander. Princeton, NJ: Princeton University Press, 1984.

Hall, Marcia B., ed. *Rome*. New York: Cambridge University Press, 2005.

Haugaard, William P. *Elizabeth and the English Reformation: The Struggle for a Stable Settlement of Religion*. London: Cambridge University Press, 1968.

Hay, Denys. *The Church in Italy in the Fifteenth Century*. New York: Cambridge University Press, 1977.

Hillerbrand, Hans J. *The World of the Reformation*. New York: Scribner, 1973.

Huppert, George. *Public Schools in Renaissance France*. Urbana: University of Illinois Press, 1984.

Imber, Colin. *The Ottoman Empire, 1300–1650: The Structure of Power*. New York: Palgrave Macmillan, 2002.

Jones, Tod E., ed. *The Cambridge Platonists: A Brief Introduction with Eight Letters of Dr. Antony Tuckney and Dr. Benjamin Whichcote*. Lanham, MD: University Press of America, 2005.

Kelly, J. N. D., ed. *The Oxford Dictionary of Popes*. New York: Oxford University Press, 1986.

Kempe, Margery. *The Book of Margery Kempe*. Translated and edited by Lynn Staley. New York: Norton, 2001.

Kenny, Anthony, ed. *Wyclif in His Times*. New York: Oxford University Press, 1986.

Koerner, Joseph Leo. *The Reformation of the Image*. Chicago: University of Chicago Press, 2004.

Kraye, Jill, ed. *The Cambridge Companion to Renaissance Humanism*. New York: Cambridge University Press, 1996.

Kristeller, Paul O. *Renaissance Thought and Its Sources*. New York: Columbia University Press, 1979.

Lambert, Malcolm. *Medieval Heresy: Popular Movements from the Gregorian Reform to the Reformation*. Malden, MA: Blackwell, 2002.

Levack, Brian P. *The Witch-Hunt in Early Modern Europe*. New York: Longman/Pearson, 2006.

Levillain, Philippe, ed. *The Papacy: An Encyclopedia*. 3 vols. New York: Routledge, 2002.

McCrum, Robert, William Cran, and Robert MacNeil. *The Story of English*. 3rd ed. New York: Penguin, 2003.

McKim, Donald K., ed. *Major Themes in the Reformed Tradition*. Grand Rapids, MI: Eerdmans, 1992.

McNeil, John Thomas. *The History and Character of Calvinism*. New York: Oxford University Press, 1954.

Moynahan, Brian. *God's Bestseller: William Tyndale, Thomas More, and the Writing of the English Bible—A Story of Martyrdom and Betrayal*. New York: Saint Martin's Press, 2003.

Mullett, Michael. *The Catholic Reformation*. New York: Routledge, 1999.

Nadler, Steven. *Spinoza: A Life*. New York: Cambridge University Press, 1999.

Nauert, Charles G., Jr. *Humanism and the Culture of Renaissance Europe*. New York: Cambridge University Press, 1995.

Nicolson, Adam. *God's Secretaries: The Making of the King James Bible*. New York: HarperCollins, 2003.

Partner, Peter. *The Pope's Men: The Papal Civil Service in the Renaissance*. New York: Oxford University Press, 1990.

Pastor, Ludwig. *The History of the Popes from the Close of the Middle Ages*. Vols. 1–30. Translated by F. I. Antrobus et al. Saint Louis: B. Herder, 1923–1956.

Pico della Mirandola, Giovanni. *On the Dignity of Man*. Translated by Charles Glenn Wallis. Indianapolis: Hackett, 1998.

Raffini, Christine. *Marsilio Ficino, Pietro Bembo, Baldassare Castiglione: Philosophical, Aesthetic, and Political Approaches in Renaissance Platonism*. New York: Lang, 1998.

Rex, Richard. *Henry VIII and the English Reformation*. Rev. ed. New York: Palgrave Macmillan, 2006.

Scarisbrick, J. J. *The Reformation and the English People*. Oxford: Blackwell, 1984.

Schmitt, Charles B. *Aristotle and the Renaissance*. Cambridge, MA: Harvard University Press, 1983.

Scruton, Roger. *Spinoza: A Very Short Introduction*. New York: Oxford University Press, 2002.

Siraisi, Nancy G. *Medicine and the Italian Universities, 1250–1600*. Boston: Brill, 2001.

Skinner, Quentin. *Machiavelli: A Very Short Introduction*. New York: Oxford University Press, 2000.

Sorrell, Tom., ed. *Descartes*. Brookfield, VT: Ashgate, 1999.

Strauss, Gerald. *Luther's House of Learning*. Baltimore: Johns Hopkins University Press, 1978.

Tanner, Norman P. *The Councils of the Church: A Short History*. New York: Crossroad, 2001.

———, ed. *Decrees of the Ecumenical Councils*. Washington, DC: Georgetown University Press, 1990.

Tomas, Natalie. *The Medici Women: Gender and Power in Renaissance Florence*. Burlington, VT: Ashgate, 2003.

Tuck, Richard. *Hobbes: A Very Short Introduction*. New York: Oxford University Press, 2002.

Von Loewenich, Walther. *Martin Luther: The Man and His Work*. Translated by Lawrence W. Denef. Minneapolis, MN: Augsburg, 1986.

Wandel, Lee Palmer. *Voracious Idols and Violent Hands: Iconoclasm in Reformation Zurich, Strasbourg, and Basel*. New York: Cambridge University Press, 1995.

Webb, Diana. *Medieval European Pilgrimage, c. 700–c. 1500*. New York: Palgrave, 2002.

Wilcox, Donald J. *In Search of God and Self: Renaissance and Reformation Thought*. Boston: Houghton Mifflin, 1975.

Williams, George H. *The Radical Reformation*. 3rd ed. Kirksville, MO: Truman State University Press, 1992.

Wilson, N. G. *From Byzantium to Italy: Greek Studies in the Italian Renaissance*. Baltimore: Johns Hopkins University Press, 1992.

Woodward, William Harrison. *Studies in Education during the Age of the Renaissance, 1400–1600*. New York: Teachers College Press, 1967.

Wootton, David. *Paolo Sarpi: Between Renaissance and Enlightenment*. New York: Cambridge University Press, 1983.

Yiannias, John J., ed. *The Byzantine Tradition after the Fall of Constantinople*. Charlottesville: University of Virginia Press, 1991.

Journals

Church History: Studies in Christianity and Culture
The quarterly journal of the American Society of Church History, which was founded in 1888, continues to develop along ecumenical and interfaith lines. The society encourages research into narrowly conceived areas of all aspects of church history as well as broader topics related to the entire history of Christianity and the relationship of Christianity to its surrounding culture.
www.churchhistory.org/churchhistory.html

Places
Books

Baumgartner, Frederic J. *France in the Sixteenth Century.* New York: Saint Martin's Press, 1995.

Boxer, C. R. *The Portuguese Seaborne Empire, 1415–1825.* New York: Knopf, 1969.

Brady, Thomas A. *Turning Swiss: Cities and Empire, 1450–1550.* New York: Cambridge University Press, 1985.

Brown, Patricia Fortini. *Private Lives in Renaissance Venice.* New Haven, CT: Yale University Press, 2004.

Brucker, Gene A. *Renaissance Florence.* Berkeley: University of California Press, 1983.

Chambers, David, and Brian Pullan, eds. *Venice: A Documentary History, 1450–1630.* Cambridge, MA: Blackwell, 1992.

Clough, Cecil H. *The Duchy of Urbino in the Renaissance.* London: Variorum Reprints, 1981.

Collins, James B. *From Tribes to Nation: The Making of France, 500–1799.* Fort Worth, TX: Thomson Learning, 2002.

Commynes, Philippe de. *Memoirs.* Edited by Samuel Kinser and translated by Isabelle Cazeaux. Columbia: University of South Carolina Press, 1969–1973.

Crummey, Robert O. *The Formation of Muscovy, 1304–1613.* New York: Longman, 1987.

Derry, T. K. *A History of Scandinavia: Norway, Sweden, Denmark, Finland, and Iceland.* Minneapolis: University of Minnesota Press, 1979.

Dunning, Chester S. L. *Russia's First Civil War: The Time of Troubles and the Founding of the Romanov Dynasty.* University Park: Pennsylvania State University Press, 2001.

Fudge, Thomas A. *The Magnificent Ride: The First Reformation in Hussite Bohemia.* Brookfield, VT: Ashgate, 1998.

Garrisson, Janine. *A History of Sixteenth-Century France, 1483–1598: Renaissance, Reformation, and Rebellion.* Translated by Richard Rex. New York: Saint Martin's Press, 1995.

Hughes, Michael. *Early Modern Germany, 1477–1806.* Philadelphia: University of Pennsylvania Press, 1992.

Jacobs, David. *Constantinople: City on the Golden Horn.* New York: American Heritage, 1969.

Jones, P. J. *The Italian City-State: From Commune to Signoria.* New York: Clarendon Press, 1997.

Kamen, Henry. *Spain, 1469–1714: A Society of Conflict.* New York: Pearson/Longman, 2005.

Kirby, D. G. *Northern Europe in the Early Modern Period: The Baltic World, 1492–1772.* New York: Longman, 1990.

Knecht, R. J. *The Rise and Fall of Renaissance France.* 2nd ed. Malden, MA: Blackwell, 2001.

Lavery, Jason. *Germany's Northern Challenge: The Holy Roman Empire and the Scandinavian Struggle for the Baltic, 1563–1576.* Boston: Brill Academic, 2002.

Lukowski, Jerzy, and Hubert Zawadzki. *A Concise History of Poland.* New York: Cambridge University Press, 2001.

MacQueen, John, ed. *Humanism in Renaissance Scotland.* Edinburgh: Edinburgh University Press, 1990.

Magnuson, Torgil. *Rome in the Age of Bernini.* 2 vols. Translated by Nancy Adler. Atlantic Highlands, NJ: Humanities Press, 1982–1986.

Manley, Lawrence. *London in the Age of Shakespeare.* University Park: Pennsylvania State University Press, 1986.

Osborne, June. *Urbino: The Story of a Renaissance City.* Chicago: University of Chicago Press, 2003.

Picard, Liza. *Elizabeth's London: Everyday Life in Elizabethan London.* New York: Saint Martin's Press, 2004.

Russell-Wood, A. J. R. *The Portuguese Empire, 1415–1808: A World on the Move.* Baltimore: Johns Hopkins University Press, 1998.

Simon, Kate. *A Renaissance Tapestry: The Gonzaga of Mantua.* New York: Harper and Row, 1988.

Stinger, Charles L. *The Renaissance in Rome.* Bloomington: Indiana University Press, 1998.

Stow, John. *A Survey of London: Written in the Year 1598.* Dover, NH: Sutton, 1994.

Thomson, David. *Renaissance Paris: Architecture and Growth, 1475–1600.* Berkeley: University of California Press, 1984.

Todd, Margo. *The Culture of Protestantism in Early Modern Scotland.* New Haven, CT: Yale University Press, 2002.

Vaughan, Richard. *Valois Burgundy.* Hamden, CT: Archon, 1975.

Waley, Daniel. *The Italian City Republics.* New York: Longman, 1988.

Welch, Evelyn S. *Art and Authority in Renaissance Milan.* New Haven, CT: Yale University Press, 1995.

Wheatcroft, Andrew. *The Habsburgs: Embodying Empire.* New York: Viking, 1995.

Politics and Economics
Books

Asch, Ronald G., and Adolf M. Birke, eds. *Princes, Patronage, and the Nobility: The Court at the Beginning of the Modern Age, c. 1450–1650.* New York: Oxford University Press, 1991.

Bertelli, Sergio. *The King's Body: The Sacred Rituals of Power in Medieval and Early Modern Europe.* Translated by R. Burr Litchfield. University Park: Pennsylvania State University Press, 2001.

Burns, J. H. *Lordship, Kingship, and Empire: The Idea of Monarchy, 1400–1525.* New York: Oxford University Press, 1992.

Cohn, Henry, ed. *Government in Reformation Europe, 1520–1560.* London: Macmillan, 1971.

Day, John. *The Medieval Market Economy.* New York: Oxford University Press, 1987.

Fleisher, Martin, ed. *Machiavelli and the Nature of Political Thought.* New York: Atheneum, 1972.

Goldsmith, Raymond W. *Premodern Financial Systems: A Historical Comparative Study.* New York: Cambridge University Press, 1987.

Goldthwaite, Richard A. *The Building of Renaissance Florence: An Economic and Social History.* Baltimore: Johns Hopkins University Press, 1980.

Guenée, Bernard. *States and Rulers in Later Medieval Europe.* Translated by Juliet Vale. New York: Blackwell, 1985.

Hadden, Richard W. *On the Shoulders of Merchants: Exchange and the Mathematical Concept of Nature in Early Modern Europe.* Albany: State University of New York Press, 1994.

Hunt, Edwin, and James M. Murray. *A History of Business in Medieval Europe, 1200–1550.* New York: Cambridge University Press, 1999.

Huppert, George. *After the Black Death: A Social History of Early Modern Europe.* 2nd ed. Bloomington: Indiana University Press, 1998.

Jansen, Sharon L. *The Monstrous Regiment of Women: Female Rulers in Early Modern Europe.* New York: Palgrave Macmillan, 2002.

Kindleberger, Charles P. *A Financial History of Western Europe.* 2nd ed. New York: Oxford University Press, 1993.

Lane, Frederic C., and Reinhold C. Mueller. *Money and Banking in Medieval and Renaissance Venice.* Vol. 1. Baltimore: Johns Hopkins University Press, 1985.

Levathes, Louise. *When China Ruled the Seas: The Treasure Fleet of the Dragon Throne, 1405–1433.* New York: Oxford University Press, 1996.

Marcu, Eva Dorothea. *Sixteenth-Century Nationalism.* New York: Abaris, 1976.

Miller, John, ed. *Absolutism in Seventeenth-Century Europe.* New York: Saint Martin's Press, 1990.

Miskimmin, Harry. *The Economy of Early Renaissance Europe, 1300–1460.* Englewood Cliffs, NJ: Prentice Hall, 1969.

Mokyr, Joel. *The Oxford Encyclopedia of Economic History.* New York: Oxford University Press, 2003.

Monod, Paul Kléber. *The Power of Kings: Monarchy and Religion in Europe, 1589–1715.* New Haven, CT: Yale University Press, 1999.

Mueller, Reinhold C. *Money and Banking in Medieval and Renaissance Venice.* Vol. 2. Baltimore: Johns Hopkins University Press, 1997.

Nenner, Howard. *The Right to Be King: The Succession to the Crown of England, 1603–1714.* Chapel Hill: University of North Carolina Press, 1995.

Rediker, Marcus Buford. *Between the Devil and the Deep Blue Sea: Merchant Seamen, Pirates, and the Anglo-American Maritime World, 1700–1750.* New York: Cambridge University Press, 1987.

Shatzmiller, Joseph. *Shylock Reconsidered: Jews, Moneylending, and Medieval Society.* Berkeley: University of California Press, 1990.

Sullivan, Vickie B. *Machiavelli's Three Romes: Religion, Human Liberty, and Politics Reformed.* De Kalb: Northern Illinois University Press, 1996.

Rulers and Ruling Families
Books

Bellonci, Maria. *The Life and Times of Lucrezia Borgia.* Translated by Bernard and Barbara Wall. London: Phoenix Press, 2000.

Brandi, Karl. *The Emperor Charles V: The Growth and Destiny of a Man and a World-Empire.* Translated by C. V. Wedgwood. London: Jonathan Cape, 1980.

Brinton, Selwyn. *The Golden Age of the Medici (Cosimo, Piero, Lorenzo de' Medici), 1434–1494.* London: Methuen, 1925.

Buckley, Veronica. *Christina, Queen of Sweden: The Restless Life of a European Eccentric.* New York: Fourth Estate, 2004.

Croft, Pauline. *King James.* New York: Palgrave Macmillan, 2003.

Doran, Susan. *Monarchy and Matrimony: The Courtships of Elizabeth I.* New York: Routledge, 1996.

Frieda, Leonie. *Catherine de Medici.* London: Weidenfeld and Nicholson, 2003.

Guy, J. A. *My Heart Is My Own: The Life of Mary, Queen of Scots.* New York: Fourth Estate, 2004.

————, ed. *The Reign of Elizabeth I: Court and Culture in the Last Decade.* New York: Cambridge University Press, 1995.

Kamen, Henry. *Philip of Spain.* New Haven, CT: Yale University Press, 1997.

Kent, D. V. *The Rise of the Medici: Faction in Florence, 1426–1434.* New York: Oxford University Press, 1978.

Knecht, R. J. *Catherine de' Medici.* New York: Longman, 1998.

————. *French Renaissance Monarchy: Francis I and Henry II.* New York: Longman, 1996.

————. *Renaissance Warrior and Patron: The Reign of Francis I.* New York: Cambridge University Press, 1994.

Liss, Peggy K. *Isabel the Queen: Life and Times.* Philadelphia: University of Pennsylvania Press, 2004.

MacCulloch, Diarmaid, ed. *The Reign of Henry VIII: Politics, Policy, and Piety.* New York: Saint Martin's Press, 1995.

Mallett, Michael. *The Borgias: The Rise and Fall of a Renaissance Dynasty.* London: Bodley Head, 1969.

Parker, Geoffrey. *Philip II.* 3rd ed. Chicago: Open Court, 1995.

Richardson, Glenn. *Renaissance Monarchy: The Reigns of Henry VIII, Francis I, and Charles V.* New York: Oxford University Press, 2002.

Scarisbrick, J. J. *Henry VIII.* Berkeley: University of California Press, 1997.

Sharpe, Kevin. *The Personal Rule of Charles I.* New Haven, CT: Yale University Press, 1992.

Starkey, David. *The Reign of Henry VIII: Personalities and Politics.* London: G. Philip, 1985.

————. *Elizabeth: The Struggle for the Throne.* New York, HarperCollins, 2001.

Troyat, Henri. *Ivan the Terrible.* Translated by Joan Pinkham. New York: Dutton, 1984.

Vaughan, Richard. *Charles the Bold: The Last Valois Duke of Burgundy.* Rev. ed. Rochester, NY: Boydell Press, 2002.

————. *John the Fearless: The Growth of Burgundian Power.* Rev. ed. Rochester, NY: Boydell Press, 2002.

————. *Philip the Good: The Apogee of Burgundy.* Rev. ed. Rochester, NY: Boydell Press, 2002.

Whitelaw, Nancy. *Catherine de' Medici and the Protestant Reformation.* Greensboro, NC: Morgan Reynolds, 2005.

Woodward, Geoffrey. *Philip II.* Chicago: Open Court, 1995.

Wormald, Jenny. *Mary, Queen of Scots: Politics, Passion, and a Kingdom Lost.* Rev. ed. New York: Saint Martin's Press, 2001.

Science, Technology, and Exploration
Books

Appelbaum, Wilbur, ed. *Encyclopedia of the Scientific Revolution: From Copernicus to Newton.* New York: Garland, 2000.

Bedini, Silvio A., ed. *Christopher Columbus and the Age of Exploration: An Encyclopedia.* New York: Da Capo, 1998.

Bergreen, Laurence. *Over the Edge of the World: Magellan's Terrifying Circumnavigation of the Globe.* New York: Morrow, 2003.

Boyer, Carl B. *A History of Mathematics.* Revised by Uta C. Merzbach. New York: Wiley, 1989.

Buisseret, David. *The Mapmakers' Quest: Depicting New Worlds in Renaissance Europe.* New York: Oxford University Press, 2003.

Cantor, Norman F. *In the Wake of the Plague: The Black Death and the World It Made.* New York: Free Press, 2001.

Caso, Adolph. *To America and around the World: The Logs of Christopher Columbus and of Ferdinand Magellan.* Boston: Branden, 1990.

Columbus, Christopher. *Four Voyages to the New World: Letters and Selected Documents.* Bilingual ed. Translated and edited by R. H. Major. Secaucus, NJ: Carol, 1992.

Crosby, Alfred W. *The Columbian Exchange: Biological and Cultural Consequences of 1492.* Westport, CT: Praeger, 2003.

Daumas, Maurice, ed. *A History of Technology and Invention: Progress through the Ages.* Vols. 2 and 3. Translated by Eileen B. Hennessy. New York: Crown, 1970.

Duncan, David Ewing. *Calendar: Humanity's Epic Struggle to Determine a True and Accurate Year.* New York: Bard, 1998.

Eisenstein, Elizabeth L. *The Printing Revolution in Early Modern Europe.* New York: Cambridge University Press, 2005.

Fuller, Mary C. *Voyages in Print: English Travel to America, 1576–1624.* New York: Cambridge University Press, 1995.

Gille, Bertrand. *Engineers of the Renaissance.* Cambridge, MA: MIT Press, 1966.

Grafton, Anthony. *Cardano's Cosmos: The Worlds and Works of a Renaissance Astrologer.* Cambridge, MA: Harvard University Press, 1999.

Hall, A. R. *The Scientific Revolution, 1500–1800: The Formation of the Modern Scientific Attitude.* London: Longmans, 1962.

Hoskin, Michael, ed. *The Cambridge Concise History of Astronomy.* New York: Cambridge University Press, 1999.

Inwood, Stephen. *The Man Who Knew Too Much: The Strange and Inventive Life of Robert Hooke, 1635–1703.* London: Macmillan, 2002.

Kaufmann, Thomas DaCosta. *The Mastery of Nature: Aspects of Art, Science, and Humanism in the Renaissance.* Princeton, NJ: Princeton University Press, 1993.

Krebs, Robert E. *Groundbreaking Scientific Experiments, Inventions, and Discoveries of the Middle Ages and the Renaissance.* Westport, CT: Greenwood Press, 2004.

Kuhn, Thomas S. *The Copernican Revolution.* New York: MJF, 1997.

Ley, Charles D., ed. *Portuguese Voyages, 1496–1633.* London: Phoenix Press, 2000.

Machamer, Peter, ed. *The Cambridge Companion to Galileo.* New York: Cambridge University Press, 1998.

Margolis, Howard. *It Started with Copernicus: How Turning the World Inside Out Led to the Scientific Revolution.* New York: McGraw-Hill, 2002.

Marland, Hilary, ed. *The Art of Midwifery: Early Modern Midwives in Europe.* New York: Routledge, 1993.

McGovern, James R., ed. *World of Columbus.* Macon, GA: Mercer University Press, 1992.

McNeill, William H. *Plagues and Peoples.* New York: Anchor, 1989.

Mokyr, Joel. *Twenty-five Centuries of Technological Change.* New York: Harwood Academic, 1990.

Morison, Samuel Eliot. *Admiral of the Ocean Sea: A Life of Christopher Columbus.* Boston: Little, Brown, 1942.

———. *The European Discovery of America.* 2 vols. New York: Oxford University Press, 1974.

O'Malley, Charles D. *Andreas Vesalius of Brussels, 1514–1564.* Berkeley: University of California Press, 1964.

Park, Katharine. *Doctors and Medicine in Early Renaissance Florence.* Princeton, NJ: Princeton University Press, 1985.

Parsons, William Barclay. *Engineers and Engineering in the Renaissance.* Cambridge, MA: MIT Press, 1968.

Reston, James, Jr. *Galileo: A Life.* New York: HarperCollins, 1994.

Richards, E. G. *Mapping Time: The Calendar and Its History.* New York: Oxford University Press, 1998.

Sale, Kirkpatrick. *The Conquest of Paradise: Christopher Columbus and the Columbian Legacy.* New York: Plume, 1991.

Schmidt, Benjamin. *Innocence Abroad: The Dutch Imagination and the New World, 1570–1670.* New York: Cambridge University Press, 2001.

Schnitter, Nicholas J. *A History of Dams: The Useful Pyramids.* Rotterdam: A. A. Balkema, 1994.

Sharratt, Michael. *Galileo: Decisive Innovator.* New York: Cambridge University Press, 1996.

Shea, William R., and Mariano Artigas. *Galileo in Rome.* New York: Oxford University Press, 2003.

Siraisi, Nancy G. *Medieval and Early Renaissance Medicine: An Introduction to Knowledge and Practice.* Chicago: University of Chicago Press, 1990.

Solbrig, Otto T., and Dorothy J. Solbrig. *So Shall You Reap: Farming and Crops in Human Affairs.* Washington, DC: Island Press, 1994.

Usher, Abbott Payson. *A History of Mechanical Inventions.* Rev. ed. New York: Dover, 1988.

Walker, Christopher, ed. *Astronomy before the Telescope.* New York: Saint Martin's Press, 1996.

Waters, David W. *The Art of Navigation in England in Elizabethan and Early Stuart Times.* New Haven, CT: Yale University Press, 1958.

Watt, Tessa. *Cheap Print and Popular Piety, 1550–1640.* New York: Cambridge University Press, 1991.

Wear, A., R. K. French, and I. M. Lonie, eds. *The Medical Renaissance of the Sixteenth Century.* New York: Cambridge University Press, 1985.

Wright, Louis B. *Gold, Glory, and the Gospel: The Adventurous Lives and Times of the Renaissance Explorers.* New York: Atheneum, 1970.

Ziegler, Philip. *The Black Death.* New York: John Day, 1969.

Journals

The Mariner's Mirror
Published quarterly by the Society for Nautical Research, this journal covers naval and maritime history, nautical archaeology, and all aspects of seafaring and lore of the sea worldwide and in all ages.
www.snr.org/%20Mirror.html

CD-ROMs

The Catholic Encyclopedia
The electronic version of the 1914 New Advent edition of this major reference work is hyperlinked and searchable. More than 11,600 articles cover the achievements of Catholics not only in the context of church history and Catholic doctrine but across all intellectual and artistic fields.
http://store.newadventcd.com/caencd.html

Wars and Battles
Books

Allmand, C. T. *The Hundred Years War: England and France at War, c. 1300–c. 1450.* New York: Cambridge University Press, 1988.

Arnold, Thomas F. *The Renaissance at War.* New York: Smithsonian, 2006.

Asch, Ronald G. *The Thirty Years War: The Holy Roman Empire and Europe, 1618–48.* New York: Saint Martin's Press, 1997.

Baumgartner, Frederic J. *From Spear to Flintlock: A History of War in Europe and the Middle East to the French Revolution.* New York: Praeger, 1991.

Black, Jeremy. *A Military Revolution?: Military Change and European Society, 1500–1800.* Atlantic Highlands, NJ: Humanities Press, 1991.

Bonney, Richard. *The Thirty Years' War, 1618–1648.* Oxford: Osprey, 2002.

Curry, Anne. *The Hundred Years War.* 2nd ed. New York: Palgrave Macmillan, 2003.

Cust, Richard, and Ann Hughes, eds. *The English Civil War.* New York: Arnold, 1997.

Dunn, Alastair. *The Great Rising of 1381: The Peasant's Revolt and England's Failed Revolution.* Charleston, SC: Tempus, 2002.

Eltis, David. *The Military Revolution in Sixteenth-Century Europe.* New York: Tauris, 1995.

Fowler, Kenneth Alan. *The Age of Plantagenet and Valois.* New York: Exeter, 1980.

Froissart, Jean. *Chronicles.* Edited and translated by Geoffrey Brereton. Baltimore: Penguin, 1968.

Green, David. *The Black Prince.* New York: Longman, 2006.

Guilmartin, John Francis. *Gunpowder and Galleys: Changing Technology and Mediterranean Warfare at Sea in the Sixteenth Century.* Rev. ed. Annapolis, MD: Naval Institute Press, 2003.

Hale, J. R. *War and Society in Renaissance Europe, 1450–1620.* Baltimore: Johns Hopkins University Press, 1986.

Hall, Bert S. *Weapons and Warfare in Renaissance Europe: Gunpowder, Technology, and Tactics.* Baltimore: Johns Hopkins University Press, 1997.

Hanson, Neil. *The Confident Hope of a Miracle: The True History of the Spanish Armada.* New York: Knopf, 2005.

Heller, Henry. *Iron and Blood: Civil Wars in Sixteenth-Century France.* Buffalo, NY: McGill-Queen's University Press, 1991.

Holt, Mack P. *The French Wars of Religion, 1562–1629.* New York: Cambridge University Press, 1995.

Kaeuper, Richard W. *War, Justice, and Public Order: England and France in the Later Middle Ages.* New York: Oxford University Press, 1988.

Knecht, R. J. *The French Wars of Religion, 1559–1598.* New York: Longman, 1996.

Konstam, Angus. *Lepanto, 1571: The Greatest Naval Battle of the Renaissance.* Westport, CT: Praeger, 2005.

———. *Pavia, 1525: The Climax of the Italian Wars.* Westport, CT: Praeger, 2005.

Lucie-Smith, Edward. *Joan of Arc.* New York: Norton, 1977.

Mattingly, Garrett. *The Defeat of the Spanish Armada.* Boston: Houghton Mifflin, 1984.

Mitchell, John. *Life of Wallenstein, Duke of Friedland.* New York: Greenwood Press, 1968.

Pepper, Simon, and Nicholas Adams. *Firearms and Fortifications: Military Architecture and Siege Warfare in Sixteenth-Century Siena.* University of Chicago Press, 1986.

Perroy, Édouard. *The Hundred Years War.* New York: Oxford University Press, 1951.

Rodger, N. A. M. *The Safeguard of the Sea: A Naval History of Britain, 660–1649.* New York: Norton, 1998.

Salmon, J. H. *Society in Crisis: France in the Sixteenth Century.* New York: Saint Martin's Press, 1975.

Seward, Desmond. *Henry V: The Scourge of God.* New York: Viking, 1988.

Shaw, Christine. *Julius II: The Warrior Pope.* Cambridge, MA: Blackwell, 1993.

Smith, D. L. *A History of the Modern British Isles, 1603–1707: The Double Crown.* Malden, MA: Blackwell, 1998.

Sullivan, Karen. *The Interrogation of Joan of Arc.* Minneapolis: University of Minnesota Press, 1999.

PLACES TO GO

ASIA
India
National Museum
Janpath, New Delhi
(+91) 11 2301 9272
Among the treasures on display are weapons, armor, textiles, and miniature paintings from the Mughal period.
www.nationalmuseumindia.gov.in

NORTH AMERICA
United States
CALIFORNIA
Huntington Library
1151 Oxford Road
San Marino, CA
626-405-2100
This library's holdings include a Bible printed by Johannes Gutenberg and a manuscript of *The Canterbury Tales.*
www.huntington.org

J. Paul Getty Museum
1200 Getty Center Drive
Los Angeles, CA
310-440-7300
Peter Paul Rubens and Raphael are among the Renaissance masters whose works are represented here.
www.getty.edu/museum

Los Angeles County Museum of Art
5905 Wilshire Boulevard
Los Angeles, CA
323-857-6000
Highlights at this museum include works by Rembrandt.
www.lacma.org

COLORADO
Denver Art Museum
100 West 14th Avenue Parkway
Denver, CO
720-865-5000
Renaissance artwork figures heavily in this museum's collection of over three thousand paintings and statues.
www.denverartmuseum.org

DISTRICT OF COLUMBIA
Folger Shakespeare Library
201 East Capitol Street, SE
Washington, DC
202-544–4600
This world-class research facility stages exhibitions from its holdings as well as period concerts and plays.
www.folger.edu

National Gallery of Art
National Mall, Washington, DC
202-737-4215
Italian, Dutch, and Flemish paintings of the Renaissance are well represented in this gallery's collection.
www.nga.gov

ILLINOIS
Art Institute of Chicago
111 South Michigan Avenue
Chicago, IL
312-443-3600
This museum boasts impressive examples of French, Spanish, and German art from the fifteenth century.
www.artic.edu

Newberry Library
60 W. Walton Street
Chicago, IL
312-943-9090
Renaissance art and the exploration of the Americas are among this research center's areas of specialization.
www.newberry.org

INDIANA
Indiana University Art Museum
1133 East 7th Street
Bloomington, IN
812-855-5445
Among the many works of art held at this university museum are several important paintings by Italian Renaissance artists.
www.iub.edu/~iuam

MARYLAND
Walters Art Museum
600 North Charles Street
Baltimore, MD
410-547-9000
The Renaissance and baroque section here features works by numerous artists, among them Raphael and El Greco.
www.thewalters.org

MASSACHUSETTS
Isabella Stewart Gardner Museum
280 The Fenway
Boston, MA
617-566-1401
Renaissance works held here include two by Raphael: *Pietà* (c. 1505) and *Count Tommaso Inghirami* (c. 1513).
www.gardnermuseum.org

Museum of Fine Arts
465 Huntington Avenue
Boston, MA
617-267-9300
The almost 24,000 pieces of European art here include works by Donatello, Titian, Botticelli, and Tintoretto.
www.mfa.org

MISSOURI
Saint Louis Art Museum
Fine Arts Drive
Saint Louis, MO
314-721-0072
Works on view at this museum include Titian's *Christ Shown to the People (Ecce Homo;* c. 1576) and Bartolomeo Manfredi's *Apollo and Marsyas* (c. 1520).
www.slam.org

NEW JERSEY
Princeton University Art Museum
Princeton, NJ
609-258-3788
Albrecht Dürer's *Melancholia I* (c. 1514) and Bonifacio Veronese's *Rest on the Flight into Egypt* (c. 1540) are two of this museum's highlights.
www.princetonartmuseum.org

NEW YORK

Brooklyn Museum
200 Eastern Parkway
Brooklyn, NY
718-638-5000
This museum has a striking assortment of early-Renaissance paintings, especially from Florence and Siena.
www.brooklynmuseum.org

The Cloisters
Fort Tryon Park
New York, NY
212-923-3700
This reconstructed monastic cloister houses approximately five thousand works of art from late-medieval Europe, including manuscripts, tapestries, panels, and stained glass.
www.metmuseum.org/Works_of_Art/
 department.asp?dep=7

Frick Collection
10 East 71st Street
New York, NY
212-288-0700
Giovanni Bellini's *Saint Francis in the Desert* (c. 1480) and eight portraits by Anthony Van Dyck are among this museum's treasures.
www.frick.org

Metropolitan Museum of Art
1000 Fifth Avenue
New York, NY
212-535-7710
The more than two million pieces of art held at this globally renowned museum include signature works of the Renaissance and Reformation.
www.metmuseum.org

Morgan Library
225 Madison Avenue
New York, NY
212-685-0008
This collection boasts period manuscripts, drawings by Rembrandt and Rubens, and three Gutenberg bibles.
www.morganlibrary.org

OHIO

Cleveland Museum of Art
11150 East Boulevard
Cleveland, OH
216-421-7350
This museum has more than a thousand works of European art, including extensive Renaissance and baroque holdings.
www.clevelandart.org

Toledo Museum of Art
2445 Monroe Street
Toledo, OH
800-644-6862
This wide-ranging collection of over 30,000 items features many Renaissance and baroque works.
www.toledomuseum.org

PENNSYLVANIA

Philadelphia Museum of Art
26th Street and Benjamin Franklin
 Parkway
Philadelphia, PA
215-763-8100
This museum, one of the largest in the United States, has paintings, sculpture, furniture, and decorative objects from throughout Renaissance Europe.
www.philamuseum.org

TEXAS

Museum of Fine Arts, Houston
1001 Bissonet Street
Houston, TX
713-639-7300
This museum holds works by a dozen Italian and Flemish masters of the Renaissance and baroque eras.
www.mfah.org

Canada

Montreal Museum of Fine Arts
1380 Sherbrooke Street West
Montreal, PQ
1-800-899-MUSE
Mantegna, Pieter Brueghel the Younger, and Rembrandt are among the masters found in this museum's collection.
www.mbam.qc.ca/en

EUROPE

Austria

Kunsthistorisches Museum
Maria Theresien-Platz
1010 Vienna
(+43) 1 525 24 403
The personal collections of deceased Hapsburg potentates form the heart of this world-famed art treasure-house.
www.khm.at

Belgium

Musée d'Art Ancien
Rue du Musée 9
Brussels
(+32) 02 508 32 11
Flemish art from the fifteenth century through the seventeenth is especially well represented at this museum.
www.fine-arts-museum.be

Denmark

Rosenborg Castle
Øster Voldgade 4A
1350 Copenhagen K
(+45) 3315 3286
This castle, built in the Dutch Renaissance style as a royal residence in the seventeenth century, now houses a museum.
www.rosenborgslot.dk

France

Musée du Louvre
75058 Paris Cedex 01
(+33) 0140 205317
Possibly the world's most famous museum, not least because it contains Leonardo da Vinci's *Mona Lisa* (c. 1507).
www.louvre.fr

Musée National du Moyen Age (Musée de Cluny)
6 Place Paul Painlevé
Paris
(+33) 0 1 53 73 78 16
This museum presents a wide array of paintings, sculptures, and other artworks from the dawn of the modern world.
www.musee-moyenage.fr

Germany

Bayerisches Nationalmuseum (Bavarian National Museum)
Prinzregentenstrasse 3
D-80538 München
(+49) 89 211 24 01
Treasures amassed by the former royal family of Bavaria provide the museum's Renaissance and baroque holdings.
www.bayerisches-nationalmuseum.de

Gruenes Gewoelbe (Green Vault)
Taschenberg 2, 01067 Dresden
(+49) 0 3 51 / 49 14 2000
A sumptuous treasure chamber at the Royal Dresden Palace; contains artworks that belonged to the Wettin electors.
www.skd-dresden.de/en/museen/
    gruenes_gewoelbe.html

Kunstgewerbemuseum (Museum of Decorative Arts)
Herbert-von-Karajan-Strasse 10
10785 Berlin-Tiergarten
(+49) 0 30 266 2902
This museum houses works by some of the greatest names of Renaissance and baroque painting.
www.smb.spk-berlin.de/smb/
    sammlungen/details.php?
    objID=7&lang=en

Hungary

Iparmuveszeti Muzeum (Museum of Applied Arts)
IX. Üllői út 33–37
1450 Budapest, Pf.3
(+36) 1 456 5100
The metalwork, ceramics, and other examples of applied art on display here include many works of the Renaissance.
www.imm.hu/angol/index.html

Italy

Castel Sant'Angelo
Lungotevere Castello 50, Rome
(+39) 06 399 677 00
This former papal prison and fortress is now a museum.
www.roma2000.it/zmusange.html

Galleria dell'Accademia
Via Ricasoli 58–60, Florence
(+39) 055 2388612
Michelangelo's *David* (1504) is just one of the works found in this superb assemblage of Renaissance art.
www.mega.it/eng/egui/monu/galacc.htm

Gallerie dell'Accademia
Campo della Carità, Venice
(+39) 41 522 2247
Tintoretto, Titian, Giovanni Bellini, and other Venetian masters feature heavily in the collection held here.
www.gallerieaccademia.org

Museo Poldi Pezzoli
Via Manzoni 12, Milan
(+39) 02 79 63 34 / 79 48 89
This museum's collection includes Renaissance sculpture, painting, enamelwork, and jewelry.
www.museopoldipezzoli.it

The Netherlands

Rembrandt House Museum
Jodenbreestraat 4, Amsterdam
(+31) 0 20 5200 400
The house where Rembrandt lived for almost two decades is now a museum devoted to his life and work.
www.rembrandthuis.nl

Russia

Hermitage Museum
2 Dvortsovaya Square
190000, St. Petersburg
(+7) 812 710 96 25
This museum's more than three million works of art include numerous Renaissance masterpieces.
www.hermitagemuseum.org

Spain

Monasterio de El Escorial
Calle Juan de Borbón y Battemberg
28200 San Lorenzo de Escorial, Madrid
(+34) 91 890 59 02
This vast complex, built on the orders of Philip II in the sixteenth century, houses an array of Renaissance artworks.
www.patrimonionacional.es/escorial/es
    corial.htm (in Spanish)

Museo Nacional del Prado
Paseo del Prado
28014 Madrid
(+34) 91 330 28 00
Works by El Greco and Velázquez highlight one of the world's greatest collections of European art.
http://museoprado.mcu.es/ihome.html

Museo Thyssen-Bornemisza
Paseo del Prado, 8
28014 Madrid
(+34) 91 369 01
All phases of the Renaissance are represented in this museum's collection of almost a thousand works of art.
www.museothyssen.org

Palacio Real de Madrid
Calle Bailén
28071 Madrid
(+34) 91 454 88 00
This vast palace showcases many acclaimed artworks of the Renaissance and baroque periods.
www.patrimonionacional.es/preal/
    preal.htm (in Spanish)

Turkey

Hagia Sophia
Sultanahmet, Istanbul
(+90) 0212 522 17 50
This magnificent Byzantine church, built during the sixth century under the emperor Justinian, was converted into a mosque during the fifteenth century.
http://english.istanbul.gov.tr/
    Default.aspx?pid=343

Topkapi Sarayi
Sultanahmet, Eminonu
Istanbul
(+90) 0212 512 04 80
This complex of buildings where the Ottoman sultans lived and governed offers a glimpse of a lost empire.
www.ee.bilkent.edu.tr/~history/
topkapi.html

United Kingdom
Banqueting House
Whitehall, London
(+44) 0 870 751 5178
Designed by Inigo Jones and built between 1619 and 1622, the Banqueting House witnessed the execution of Charles I.
http://www.hrp.org.uk/webcode/
banquet_home.asp

British Library
96 Euston Road, London
(+44) 020 7412 7332
This institution houses one of the world's greatest collections of books, maps, and manuscripts and stages regular exhibitions of its prized holdings.
www.bl.uk

Burrell Collection
Pollok Country Park
2060 Pollokshaws Road, Glasgow
(+44) 0141 287 2550
Fine arts and crafts from early modern England and Scotland can be found in this collection.
www.glasgowmuseums.com/venue/
index.cfm?venueid=1

The Commandery
Worcester
(+44) 01905 361821
Here visitors can see the command post where Charles II lost the Battle of Worcester, the last battle of the English civil wars.
www.worcestercitymuseums.org.uk/
comm/commind.htm

Hoghton Tower
Hoghton, Lancashire
(+44) 01254 852 986
This Lancashire manor house, a beautiful example of Tudor design, was visited by James I.
www.hoghtontower.co.uk

National Gallery
Trafalgar Square, London
(+44) 020 7747 2885
Leonardo Da Vinci's *Virgin of the Rocks* (c. 1508) is one of the countless treasures found in the collection held at this celebrated gallery.
www.nationalgallery.org.uk

National Gallery of Scotland
The Mound, Edinburgh
(+44) 0131 624 6200
This gallery holds works by numerous Renaissance masters, including Velázquez, Sandro Botticelli, and Gian Lorenzo Bernini.
www.nationalgalleries.org

National Portrait Gallery
Saint Martin's Place, London
(+44) 020 7312 2463
This collection includes a wealth of portraits of English notables from the sixteenth and seventeeth centuries.
www.npg.org.uk

Royal Shakespeare Company
Waterside, Stratford-upon-Avon
(+44) 01789 403444
The town of Shakespeare's birth is home to one of the world's leading theater companies, which stages the plays of Shakespeare and his contemporaries.
www.rsc.org.uk

Shakespeare's Globe Theatre
New Globe Walk, Bankside, London
(+44) 020 7902 1400
In this faithful reconstruction, audiences may experience Shakespeare's works in the space for which they were written.
www.shakespeares-globe.org

Victoria and Albert Museum
Cromwell Road, London
(+44) 020 7942 2000
Raphael's sketches for a set of papal tapestries are among the riches found in more than a dozen rooms devoted to the Renaissance.
www.vam.ac.uk

Wallace Collection
Manchester Square, London
(+ 44) 0 20 7563 9500
This collection includes medieval and Renaissance works of art and European and Oriental arms and armor.
www.wallacecollection.org

Vatican City
Saint Peter's Basilica
Piazza San Pietro
(+39) 06 698 834 62
This breathtaking church, itself one of the greatest achievements of Renaissance architecture, is filled with many masterpieces of Renaissance and baroque art.
www.stpetersbasilica.org

Vatican Museums
Viale Vaticano
(+39) 06 698 849 47
The Sistine Chapel and its decorations by Michelangelo crown a glorious assemblage of Renaissance and baroque treasures.
http://mv.vatican.va

AUSTRALIA
National Gallery of Australia
Parkes Place, Parkes ACT 2600
(+61) 2 6240 6502
Renaissance and baroque items in this gallery's collection include a 1623 self-portrait by Peter Paul Rubens.
www.nga.gov.au

Architecture Online
Photographs, architectural drawings, and 3-D models help students explore great buildings from throughout history.
www.greatbuildings.com

British Civil Wars, 1638–1660
This site includes short but detailed portraits of the wars' key protagonists and examines the crucial battles.
www.british-civil-wars.co.uk

The British Library: Turning the Pages
Visitors to this site can use their mouse to turn the pages of the first atlas of Europe, one of Leonardo da Vinci's notebooks, and other manuscripts.
www.bl.uk/onlinegallery/ttp/
   ttpbooks.html

Calvinism Resources Database
This site gives access to hundreds of articles, essays, and lectures dealing with John Calvin himself and Calvinism in general.
www.calvin.edu/library/database/card

Development of the Papacy in Christian History
The papacy's roots and its development through the Middle Ages are examined in capsule form on this site.
www.religionfacts.com/christianity/
   history/papacy.htm

Digital Scriptorium
Renaissance and medieval manuscripts held at libraries across the United States can be examined page by page here.
http://sunsite.berkeley.edu/Scriptorium

Discover the Ottomans
War, art, and the ruling dynasty are examined in this well-illustrated site devoted to the Ottoman Empire.
www.theottomans.org

Discoverers Web
Short biographical essays on a wide range of explorers are accompanied by links to other sites and primary sources.
www.win.tue.nl/cs/fm/engels/discovery

Discovery and Reformation
A combined analysis of these two important issues in early modern European history.
www.wsu.edu:8080/~dee/REFORM

Early Modern Resources
This site offers links to numerous resources of relevance to students of early modern history.
www.earlymodernweb.org.uk

The End of Europe's Middle Ages: Fourteenth and Fifteenth Centuries
This online tutorial is for those engaged in Renaissance, Reformation, and early modern studies who lack a background in medieval European history.
www.ucalgary.ca/applied_history/
   tutor/endmiddle

Francesco Petrarch—Father of Humanism
Background information, audio clips, and original and translated excerpts illuminate Petrarch's life and work.
http://petrarch.petersadlon.com/
   petrarch.html

The Galileo Project
Short essays examine Galileo's life and achievements in the context of his world and the work of his contemporaries.
http://galileo.rice.edu/index.html

The Gutenberg Bible at the Ransom Center
Every page of a Gutenberg Bible can be magnified and inspected at this site.
www.hrc.utexas.edu/exhibitions/
   permanent/gutenberg

Henry IV of France
Text and occasional illustrations trace the life and reign of Henry of Navarre.
www.henri-iv.com/

The History Guide: Lectures on Early Modern European History
Topic headings include "Renaissance Portraits" and "The Impact of Luther and the Radical Reformation."
www.historyguide.org/earlymod/
   earlymod.html

The History Guide: Lectures on Modern European Intellectual History
Among the essays presented here is one titled "The Medieval Synthesis and the Renaissance Discovery of Man."
www.historyguide.org/intellect/
   intellect.html

History of Spain: Primary Documents
English translations of documents relating to the early history of the Spanish nation are available here.
http://eudocs.lib.byu.edu/index.php/
   History_of_Spain:_Primary_Documents

History of the Papacy
This segment of the HistoryWorld site follows the papacy from its origins through the Renaissance and the Reformation.
www.historyworld.net/wrldhis/
   PlainTextHistories.asp?historyid=ac65

History of Western Philosophy
Includes biographical studies of Hobbes and Machiavelli and an essay titled "Humanism and Science."
www.philosophypages.com/hy/
   index.htm

The Imperial House of Hapsburg
The past glories of Europe's foremost dynasty are commemorated on this site.
www.hapsburg.com

The Internet Modern History Sourcebook
Primary documents relating to the economic and social upheavals of Renaissance Europe are collected here.
www.fordham.edu/halsall/mod/
    modsbook.html

The Italian Renaissance
This thorough and lively analysis traces the birth of modern Europe.
www.wsu.edu:8080/~dee/REN/
    REN.HTM

Libro: the Library of Iberian Resources Online
The texts of around eighty academic works on the medieval and Renaissance Spanish kingdoms can be read here.
http://libro.uca.edu/title.htm

Luminarium
The site contains writings by English authors from the Middle Ages through the seventeenth century.
www.luminarium.org

Martin Luther
Links to English translations of a variety of writings by Martin Luther make up the bulk of this site's offerings.
www.educ.msu.edu/homepages/
    laurence/reformation/Luther/
    Luther.htm

The Medici Archive Project
The archives of the Medici grand dukes, established in 1569 by Cosimo I de' Medici, are now available online.
www.medici.org

The Medici: Godfathers of the Renaissance
This site, which accompanies a PBS television production, features profiles and a virtual tour of Florence.
www.pbs.org/empires/medici

Medieval and Early Modern Russia and Ukraine
This site links to such primary sources as Ivan IV's 1497 law code and a sixteenth-century travel journal.
http://faculty.washington.edu/dwaugh/
    rus/ruspg1.html

Medieval Writing: Vernacular Languages
The production of manuscripts and the role of vernacular languages in late-medieval culture are discussed in detail.
http://medievalwriting.50megs.com/
    writing.htm

Michelangelo Buonarroti
This illustrated site follows the artist's career from one masterpiece to another.
www.michelangelo.com/buon/
    bio-index2.html

Monarchs of Britain
Profiles assess the lives and legacies of English and British monarchs and of Oliver Cromwell and his son Richard.
www.britannia.com/history/h6f.html

Papal Encyclicals Online
Translations of encyclicals and other official documents of the Catholic Church can be accessed here.
www.papalencyclicals.net

Perseus: English Renaissance Texts
All the plays of Christopher Marlowe are available here, some of them in as many as twenty different versions.
www.perseus.tufts.edu/Texts/
    Marlowe.html

Philipp Melanchthon 500th Anniversary Exhibit
The life and work of Martin Luther's close intellectual ally are discussed on this site.
http://chi.lcms.org/melanchthon

The Protestant Reformation: Religious Change and the People of Sixteenth-Century Europe
Detailed chronologies of key events accompany a thorough analysis of the Reformation's roots and course.
www.st-andrews.ac.uk/jfec/cal/
    reformat/contents.htm

Rome Reborn: The Vatican Library and Renaissance Culture
The site presents some of the library's most precious manuscripts, books, and maps, including key humanist texts.
www.ibiblio.org/expo/vatican.exhibit/
    Vatican.exhibit.html

Splendors of Christendom
Links at this site offer tours of the world's most important churches, cathedrals, and monasteries.
www.christusrex.org/www1/splendors/
    splendors.html

Theatre History
Includes analyses of theater in Elizabethan England and of Italian and Spanish drama from 1600 to 1650.
www.theatrehistory.com

Thirty Years War
The site traces the many phases of the three-decade pan-European conflict that changed the face of the continent.
www.pipeline.com/~cwa/
    TYWHome.htm

The Web Gallery of Art
Visitors to this site will find more than 15,400 works of art from the Gothic, Renaissance, and baroque periods, each accompanied by a short essay analyzing the painting's significance, as well as numerous biographical studies and a comprehensive glossary.
www.wga.hu

RESOURCES FOR YOUNGER READERS

Books

Nathan Aaseng
You Are the Explorer
Minneapolis: Oliver Press, 2000

Aliki
William Shakespeare and the Globe
New York: HarperCollins, 1999

Catherine M. Andronik
Copernicus: Founder of Modern Astronomy
Berkeley Heights, NJ: Enslow, 2002

Steve Arman, Simon Bird, and Malcolm Wilkinson
Reformation and Rebellion, 1485–1790
Oxford: Heinemann, 2002

Marc Aronson
John Winthrop, Oliver Cromwell, and the Land of Promise
New York: Clarion Books, 2004

Marc Aronson
Sir Walter Raleigh and the Quest for El Dorado
New York: Clarion Books, 2000

Ceciel de Bie and Martijn Leene
Rembrandt
Los Angeles: J. Paul Getty Museum, 2001

Luther Blissett (translated by Shaun Whiteside)
Q
Orlando, FL: Harcourt, 2004

William J. Boerst
Galileo Galilei and the Science of Motion
Greensboro, NC: Morgan Reynolds, 2004

William J. Boerst
Johannes Kepler: Discovering the Laws of Celestial Motion
Greensboro, NC: Morgan Reynolds, 2003

William J. Boerst
Tycho Brahe: Mapping the Heavens
Greensboro, NC: Morgan Reynolds, 2003

Peter Chrisp
Welcome to the Globe: The Story of Shakespeare's Theater
New York: Dorling Kindersley, 2000

Alison Cole
Perspective
New York: Dorling Kindersley, 2000

Alison Cole
Renaissance
New York: Dorling Kindersley, 2000

Sean Connolly
The Life and Work of Leonardo da Vinci
Des Plaines, IL: Heinemann, 2000

Bruce Coville
William Shakespeare's A Midsummer Night's Dream
New York: Dial Books, 1996

Nancy Day
Your Travel Guide to Renaissance Europe
Minneapolis: Runestone Press, 2001

Leonard Everett Fisher
Galileo
New York: Macmillan, 1992

Jean Fritz
The World in 1492
New York: Henry Holt, 1992

Marzieh Gail
Life in the Renaissance
New York: Random House, 1968

Jim Gallagher
Vasco da Gama and the Portuguese Explorers
Philadelphia: Chelsea House, 1999

Todd Goble
Nicholas Copernicus and the Founding of Modern Astronomy
Greensboro, NC: Morgan Reynolds, 2004

Mary Gow
Johannes Kepler: Discovering the Laws of Planetary Motion
Berkeley Heights, NJ: Enslow, 2003

Neil Grant
The Atlas of the Renaissance World
Columbus, OH: Peter Bedrick Books, 2003

Miriam Greenblatt
Suleyman the Magnificent and the Ottoman Empire
New York: Benchmark Books, 2003

Kathryn Hind
Life in the Renaissance (4 vols.: *Church, City, Countryside, Court*)
New York: Benchmark Books, 2004

Brendan January
Science in the Renaissance
New York: Franklin Watts, 1999

David Scott Kastan and Marina Kastan, eds.
William Shakespeare
New York: Sterling, 2000

Bruce Koscielniak
Johann Gutenberg and the Amazing Printing Press
Boston: Houghton Mifflin, 2003

Andrew Langley
Renaissance
New York: Knopf, 1999

Tanya Larkin
Vasco da Gama
New York: PowerKids Press, 2001

Vicki Leon
Outrageous Women of the Renaissance
New York: Wiley, 1999

Fiona MacDonald
The Reformation
Austin, TX: Raintree Steck-Vaughn, 2003

James MacLachlan
Galileo Galilei: First Physicist
New York: Oxford University Press, 1997

Antony Mason
In the Time of Michelangelo
Brookfield, CT: Copper Beech Books, 2001

Rupert Matthews
The Renaissance
New York: Peter Bedrick Books, 2000

Milton Meltzer
Ferdinand Magellan: First to Sail around the World
New York: Benchmark Books, 2002

Milton Meltzer
The Printing Press
New York: Benchmark Books, 2003

David Nicolle and Viacheslav Shpakovsky
Armies of Ivan the Terrible: Russian Armies 1505–1700
New York: Osprey, 2006

Barbara O'Connor
Leonardo da Vinci: Renaissance Genius
Minneapolis: Carolrhoda Books, 2003

Tina Packer
Tales from Shakespeare
New York: Scholastic, 2004

Michael Pollard
Johann Gutenberg: Master of Modern Printing
Woodbridge, CT: Blackbirch Press, 2001

Josephine Poole
Joan of Arc
New York: Knopf, 1998

Deborah Mazzotta Prum
Rats, Bulls, and Flying Machines: A History of the Renaissance and Reformation
Charlottesville, VA: Core Knowledge Foundation, 1999

Francesca Romei
Leonardo da Vinci: Artist, Inventor, and Scientist of the Renaissance
New York: Peter Bedrick Books, 2000

Michael Rosen
Shakespeare: His Work and His World
Cambridge, MA: Candlewick Press, 2001

Philip Sauvain
Changing World
Cheltenham, UK: Thornes, 1992

Peter Sis
Starry Messenger: A Book Depicting the Life of a Famous Scientist, Mathematician, Astronomer, Philosopher, Physicist, Galileo Galilei
New York: Farrar Straus Giroux, 1996

Diane Stanley
Joan of Arc
New York: Morrow Junior Books, 1998

Diane Stanley
Leonardo Da Vinci
New York: Morrow Junior Books, 1996

Diane Stanley and Peter Vennema
Good Queen Bess: The Story of Elizabeth I of England
New York: HarperCollins, 2001

Sally Stepanek
John Calvin
New York: Chelsea House, 1987

Sally Stepanek
Martin Luther
New York: Chelsea House, 1986

Sally Stepanek
Mary, Queen of Scots
New York: Chelsea House, 1987

Richard Tames
Michelangelo Buonarroti
Chicago: Heinemann, 2001

Jane Resh Thomas
Behind the Mask: The Life of Queen Elizabeth I
New York: Clarion Books, 1998

Mike Venezia
Da Vinci
Chicago: Children's Press, 1989

Mike Venezia
Giotto
New York: Children's Press, 2000

Mike Venezia
Raphael
New York: Children's Press, 2001

Diane Yancey
Life in the Elizabethan Theater
San Diego: Lucent Books, 1997

Web Sites

Age of Exploration
Learn how to make navigational instruments on this site, which also features time lines and biographies.
www.mariner.org/educationalad/ageofex/intro.php

Arms and Armor in the Age of the Musketeer
Images and descriptions of seventeenth-century weapons are available here.
http://users.wpi.edu/~jforgeng/17cIQP/index.htm

British History: Tudors
"Henry VIII: Majesty with Menace" and "An Overview of the Reformation" are among this site's essays.
http://www.bbc.co.uk/history/british/tudors

Channel 4 History
Includes "A Time Traveller's Guide to Stuart England," "Galileo's Daughter," and "The Medici: A Chronology."
www.channel4.com/history

The Costumer's Manifesto
This site includes a Puritan sermon on clothing and pictures of baroque ball gowns and other period items.
www.costumes.org/History/100pages/17thlinks.htm#1600-1630

The English Civil War
The origins and course of the wars are traced in time line form; the early conflicts receive the most attention.
www.theteacher99.btinternet.co.uk/ecivil/index.htm

Essentials of Music
This site allows students to acquire a basic understanding of Renaissance and baroque music.
www.essentialsofmusic.com

Eyewitness to the Middle Ages and Renaissance
Firsthand accounts are combined with informative discussions of events in the life of key figures of the period, including Ferdinand Magellan.
www.eyewitnesstohistory.com/mefrm.htm

Francis Drake
Period illustrations at this site ornament an account of the voyages of the great English seaman.
http://sirfrancisdrakehistory.net

Galileo Galilei
Read about the astronomer's life and achievements; includes a bibliography.
http://scienceworld.wolfram.com/biography/Galileo.html

Gutenberg Bible
The British Library's two copies of the Gutenberg Bible can be viewed here.
www.bl.uk/treasures/gutenberg/homepage.html

Heretics History Tour
Time lines, arranged by country and even by city, trace the stories of the Reformation's dissident sects.
www.geocities.com/Athens/Forum/5578

History Learning Site
The focus here is England, with essays on Tudor manor houses, the 1666 great fire of London, and more.
www.historylearningsite.co.uk

Leonardo da Vinci: Scientist, Inventor, Artist
The text of this handsome site sums up Leonardo's career, and visual features explore key topics.
www.mos.org/leonardo

Privateering History
The Barbary corsairs and their fellow maritime marauders from England and other European nations are all described at this site.
http://privateer.omena.org/privateerhistory.htm

Queen Elizabeth I
Essays at this site include "The Queen's Wardrobe," "Power and Government," and "The Spanish Armada."
www.elizabethi.org

Renaissance
Exploration, printing, life and politics in Florence, and breakthroughs in art techniques are all explored here.
www.learner.org/exhibits/renaissance/

A Renaissance Childhood
This essay describes the nature of the family in the Renaissance and the era's general attitude toward children.
www.suite101.com/article.cfm/history_for_children/23417

William Shakespeare
This site provides a lively overview of the life, times, and works of the greatest playwright of all time.
www.william-shakespeare.info

The Witching Hours
Witches and their spells and witch hunters and their techniques are topics at this site about Europe's great frenzy.
www.shanmonster.com/witch

Women in History
Catherine de Médicis, Isabella I, Joan of Arc, and Mary, Queen of Scots, are among the figures profiled here.
www.womeninworldhistory.com

Directory of Articles and Contributors

Volume 1

Agincourt, Battle of
DONALD CARLSON

Agriculture
BRIAN BLACK

Architecture
JAMES A. PATRICK

Aristotle
CHARLES FREEMAN

Armada, Spanish
JOHN HAYWOOD

Astrology
HANS PETER BROEDEL

Augsburg, Peace of
ANDREW SPICER

Bacon, Francis
JESSICA L. MALAY

Banking
TOM LANSFORD

Bearbaiting and Blood Sports
HANS PETER BROEDEL

Bernini, Gian Lorenzo
JAMES A. PATRICK

Bibles
JAMES A. PATRICK

Boccaccio, Giovanni
DANIEL HORACE FERNALD
ZACHARY C. PARMLEY

Bohemia
PHYLLIS G. JESTICE

Borgia, Lucrezia
JESSICA L. MALAY

Bosch, Hieronymus
PHYLLIS G. JESTICE

Botticelli, Sandro
ERIC NELSON

Bramante, Donato
CHARLES FREEMAN

Bruegel, Pieter
CAROLINE S. HULL

Brunelleschi, Filippo
CHARLES FREEMAN

Burgundy
JOHN HAYWOOD

Byzantium
BRIAN A. CARRIERE

Calendars
ELIZABETH D. SCHAFER
JOHN HAYWOOD

Calvinism
JAMES A. PATRICK

Caravaggio
RICHARD COCKE
Norwich, UK

Catherine de Médicis
JESSICA L. MALAY

Cervantes, Miguel de
JESSICA L. MALAY

Charles V
CHRISTINE SHAW

Chaucer, Geoffrey
KEVIN MARTI

Chivalry
CHRISTINE SHAW

Christina
JOHN HAYWOOD

Church of England
JAMES A. PATRICK

Clement VII
KENNETH GOUWENS

Columbus, Christopher
DOUGLAS J. WEATHERFORD

Constantinople
JAMES A. PATRICK

Copernicus, Nicolaus
CHARLES FREEMAN

Dams and Drainage
ELIZABETH D. SCHAFER

Volume 2

Descartes, René
DANIEL HORACE FERNALD

Disease
BRIAN BLACK

Dürer, Albrecht
CAROLINE S. HULL

Education
TOM LANSFORD

Elizabeth I
ALEXANDRA GAJDA

England
LEIF DIXON

English Civil Wars
ANNA BAYMAN

Erasmus, Desiderius
DANIEL HORACE FERNALD

Established Churches
JAMES A. PATRICK

Exploration
ELIZABETH D. SCHAFER

Eyck, Jan van
SUSAN FRANCES JONES

Ferdinand and Isabella
GRETCHEN STARR-LEBEAU

Feudalism
CHRISTINE SHAW

Florence
ROBERT J. PAULY JR.

Florence, Council of
NORMAN TANNER

Volume 2 *(cont.)*

France
ERIC NELSON

Francis I
ERIC NELSON

French Civil Wars
MAX VON HABSBURG

Galilei, Galileo
CHARLES FREEMAN

Gentileschi, Artemisia
JO HALL

German Towns
ROBERT J. PAULY JR.

Giotto
CAROLINE S. HULL

Guilds and Companies
DANIEL HORACE FERNALD

Hanseatic League
BRIAN A. CARRIERE

Hapsburg Empire
DANIEL HORACE FERNALD

Henry IV
ERIC NELSON

Henry VIII
ALEXANDRA GAJDA

Heresy
ERIC NELSON

Hobbes, Thomas
TOM LANSFORD

Holy Roman Empire
MAX VON HABSBURG

Households
DANIEL HORACE FERNALD
ZACHARY C. PARMLEY

Volume 3

Humanism and Learning
DYLAN REID

Hundred Years War
RACHEL C. GIBBONS

Iconoclasm
JAMES A. PATRICK

Islam
PHYLLIS G. JESTICE

Italian City-States
ERIC NELSON

Italian Wars
CHRISTINE SHAW

Ivan IV Vasilyevich
JOHN SWIFT

Joan of Arc
ERIC NELSON

Jones, Inigo
JAMES A. PATRICK

Judaism
PHYLLIS G. JESTICE

Languages, Classical
CHARLES FREEMAN

Languages, Vernacular
GORDON C. THOMASSON

Leo X
PIERRE DE CRAON

Leonardo da Vinci
BRIAN A. CARRIERE

Lepanto, Battle of
JOHN HAYWOOD

Literature
JESSICA L. MALAY

Lombardy
CHRISTINE SHAW

London
JESSICA L. MALAY

Lutheranism
JAMES A. PATRICK

Machiavelli, Niccolò
TOM LANSFORD

Machines
BRIAN BLACK

Magellan, Ferdinand
JOHN HAYWOOD

Magic
HANS PETER BROEDEL

Manufacturing
BRIAN BLACK

Markets and Fairs
BRIAN BLACK

Marlowe, Christopher
JESSICA L. MALAY

Mathematics
SHEILA J. RABIN

Maximilian I
BRIAN A. CARRIERE

Medicine
PAUL F. GRENDLER

Medicis, The
ROBERT J. PAULY JR.

Volume 4

Michelangelo
RICHARD COCKE

Milton, John
JESSICA L. MALAY

Missionaries
JAMES A. PATRICK

Molière
DONALD CARLSON

Monarchy
TOM LANSFORD

Monteverdi, Claudio
PHYLLIS G. JESTICE

Volume 4 *(cont.)*

More, Thomas
  Tom Lansford

Muscovy
  John Swift

Music
  Phyllis G. Jestice

Nationalism
  Christine Shaw

Nobility and Rank
  Christine Shaw

Painting and Sculpture
  Caroline S. Hull

Palladio, Andrea
  James A. Patrick

Papacy
  Paul F. Grendler

Paris
  Eric Nelson

Paul V
  Christine Shaw

Peasants' Revolts
  Rachel C. Gibbons

Petrarch
  Daniel Horace Fernald

Philip II
  Andrew Spicer

Philosophy
  James A. Patrick

Pico della Mirandola,
  Giovanni
  Donald Carlson

Pilgrimage
  Gretchen Starr-LeBeau

Pius II
  Christine Shaw

Platonism
  Daniel Horace Fernald

Poland
  John Haywood

Popular Culture
  Hans Peter Broedel

Population
  Eric Nelson

Portugal
  John Haywood

Volume 5

Preaching
  Hans Peter Broedel

Printing
  Anna Bayman

Rabelais, François
  Max von Habsburg

Raphael
  Brian A. Carriere

Reformation
  Brian A. Carriere

Religious Orders
  Norman Tanner

Rembrandt
  Caroline S. Hull

Renaissance
  Paul F. Grendler

Rome
  Kenneth Gouwens

Rubens, Peter Paul
  Caroline S. Hull

Schütz, Heinrich
  Phyllis G. Jestice

Science and Technology
  Brian Black

Scotland
  Anna Bayman

Shakespeare, William
  Tom Lansford

Spain
  Jessica L. Malay

Spenser, Edmund
  Jessica L. Malay

Spinoza, Baruch
  Lisa R. Holliday

Stuarts, The
  Alexandra Gajda

Sweden
  John Haywood

Switzerland
  John Haywood

Theater
  Joseph Sterrett

Thirty Years War
  James A. Patrick

Trade
  Brian Black
  John Haywood

Trent, Council of
  Norman Tanner

Universities
  Daniel Horace Fernald

Urbino
  Christine Shaw

Velázquez, Diego Rodríguez de Silva
  Caroline S. Hull

Venice
  Christine Shaw

Viscontis, The
  Robert J. Pauly Jr.

Warfare
  Tom Lansford

Women
  Jessica L. Malay

Wren, Christopher
  Brian Black

List of Maps

A **boldface** number preceding a colon indicates the volume.

Agincourt, Battle of **1**:18

Armada, Spanish **1**:65

Bohemia **1**:116

Burgundy **1**:160

Columbus, Christopher **1**:252

Constantinople **1**:257

Disease **2**:305

English Civil Wars **2**:349

Exploration **2**:381

Ferdinand and Isabella **2**:393

France **2**:437

German Towns **2**:475

Hapsburg Empire **2**:508

Hundred Years War **3**:596

Islamic World, c. 1300 . . . . **3**:610

Islamic World, c. 1600 . . . . **3**:628

Italian City-States **3**:631

Lepanto, Battle of. **3**:718

Lombardy **3**:741

Magellan **3**:789

Muscovy **4**:937

Poland **4**:1106

Scotland **5**:1260

Spain **5**:1278

Sweden **5**:1309

Switzerland **5**:1314

Thirty Years War **5**:1330

Venice **5**:1393

Index of Maps

This index includes place-names appearing in the maps. For place-names mentioned in the articles and captions, see the Index of Places.

A **boldface** number preceding a colon indicates the volume.

A

Aargau **5:**1314
Aberdeen **5:**1260
Adrianople Gate **1:**257
Adriatic Sea **3:**631, 741, **5:**1393
Adwalton Moor **2:**349
Aegean Sea **3:**718
Africa **1:**252, **2:**381, **3:**610, 628, 789
Agincourt **1:**18, **2:**437, **3:**596
Alcalá **2:**393
Alexandria **3:**610, 628
Algiers **3:**628, **5:**1278
Alps **1:**116, **2:**475, **3:**631
Alsace **5:**1330
Amiens **2:**205
Anatolia **3:**628
Andalusia **2:**393
Angoulême, county of **2:**437
Anjou, county of **2:**437, **3:**596
Apennine Mountains **3:**631
Appenzell **5:**1314
Arabia **2:**381, **3:**628, 789
Aragon **2:**393, **5:**1278
Aral Sea **4:**937
Arctic Ocean **4:**937
Armagnac, county of **2:**437
Artois **2:**437, **3:**596
Asti **3:**631
Astrakhan, khanate of **4:**937
Athens **3:**718
Atlantic Ocean **1:**65, 252, **2:**305, 381, 508, **3:**610, 628, 789, **5:**1260
Augsburg **2:**475
Australia **2:**381, **3:**789
Austria **1:**116, **2:**475, 508, **5:**1314, 1330
Avignon **1:**116, **2:**305
Azores **1:**252

B

Baghdad **3:**610, 628
Bahamas **1:**252
Balearic Islands **2:**508, **5:**1278
Baltic Sea **2:**305, 475, **4:**937, **5:**1309, 1330
Baltiysk **5:**1330
Bar, duchy of **1:**160
Barcelona **2:**305, 393
Bari **3:**741
Barletta **3:**741
Basel **5:**1314
Basel, bishopric of **5:**1314
Bavaria, duchy of **2:**475, **5:**1330
Bayonne **3:**596
Béarn **2:**393
Belgrade **1:**116
Berg, county of **1:**160
Bergamo **3:**631, **5:**1393
Berlin **5:**1309
Bern **5:**1314
Berwick **5:**1260
Beury, duchy of **1:**160
Biscay, Bay of **2:**437, **3:**596
Biserta **5:**1278
Black Forest **2:**475
Black Sea **2:**305, **4:**937
Blekinge **5:**1309
Böblingen **2:**475
Bohemia **1:**116, **2:**475, 508, **5:**1330
Bohemian Territory **4:**937
Bologna **3:**741, **5:**1393
Bordeaux **3:**596
Bosporus **1:**257
Boulogne, county of **1:**160
Bourbon, duchy of **1:**160, **2:**437
Brabant, duchy of **1:**160
Brandenburg **5:**1330
Brazil **2:**381, **3:**789
Breisach **5:**1330
Breitenfeld **5:**1309, 1330
Bremen **2:**205
Brescia **3:**741, **5:**1393
Breslau **1:**116
Brittany, duchy of **2:**437, **3:**596
Bruges **1:**160

Brunswick **2:**475
Brussels **1:**160
Buda **1:**116
Budapest **2:**205
Bugia **5:**1278
Bukhara **3:**610
Burgundy, duchy of **1:**116, **1:**160, **2:**437, **2:**475, 508, **3:**596, **5:**1314

C

Cádiz **1:**65, 252, **2:**305
Caesarias, Harbor of **1:**257
Calais **1:**18, 65, 160, **2:**437, 475, **3:**596
Cambridge **2:**349
Canary Islands **1:**252
Cancer, Tropic of **3:**789
Cape Verde Islands **1:**252, **3:**789
Cape Virgenes **3:**789
Capricorn, Tropic of **3:**789
Caribbean Sea **1:**252
Carinthia **1:**116, **2:**475, 508
Carniola **1:**116, **2:**475, 508
Carpathian Mountains **1:**116
Caspian Sea **4:**937
Castile **2:**393, **5:**1278
Catalonia **2:**393, **5:**1278
Cebu **3:**789
Ceuta **2:**393
Chablais **5:**1314
Chalcedon **1:**257
Chiavenna **5:**1314
China **2:**381, **3:**628, 789
Chrysopolis **1:**257
Circus Gate **1:**257
Cleves, duchy of **1:**160, **5:**1330
Cologne **2:**508
Constance **5:**1314
Constantine, Wall of **1:**257
Constantinople **1:**257, **3:**628
Córdoba **5:**1278
Corinth, Gulf of **3:**718
Corsica **2:**305, 508, **3:**741, **5:**1278

Crécy **2:**437, **3:**596
Crema **3:**631
Cremona **3:**631, 741
Crete **2:**305
Cuba **1:**252
Cyprus **2:**305

D

Danube River **1:**116, **2:**305, 475, 508, **5:**1330
Danzig **2:**205, **4:**937, **5:**1309
Delhi **3:**610, 628
Delhi, Sultanate of **3:**610
Denmark **1:**116, **2:**475, **5:**1330
Denmark-Norway **5:**1309
Dijon **1:**160
Dnieper River **4:**937
Dordogne River **3:**596
Dorpat **5:**1309
Dresden **1:**116
Dublin **2:**205

E

Eastern Pomerania **5:**1330
East Indies **2:**381
Edgehill **2:**349
Edinburgh **2:**205, 349, **5:**1260
Elbe River **1:**116, **2:**475, **5:**1330
Elbing **5:**1309
Emilia **3:**631
England **1:**65, 116, 160, **2:**381, **3:**596, 789, **5:**1260, 1330
English Channel **1:**65, 160, **2:**349
Equator **3:**789
Estonia **5:**1309
Europe **1:**252

F

Falkland **5:**1260
Fatehpur Sikri **3:**628
Ferrara **3:**631, **5:**1393
Fiji **2:**381
Finland **5:**1309
Flanders, county of **1:**160

Flodden **5**:1260
Florence **1**:116, **2**:305, 508, **3**:631, 741, **5**:1393
Florence, republic of **2**:508, **3**:631, **5**:1393
Foix, county of **2**:437
Forchheim **2**:475
France **1**:65, 116, 160, **2**:349, 381, 393, 437, 475, 508, **3**:596, 610, 628, 631, 789, **5**:1278, 1314, 1330
Franche-Comté **1**:116, 160
Franconia **2**:475
Frankenhausen **2**:475
Frankfurt **2**:205
Frankfurt an der Oder **5**:1330
Freiburg im Breisgau **2**:475
Fribourg **5**:1314

G

Galata **1**:257
Galicia **2**:393
Garonne River **3**:596
Geneva **2**:305, 437, **5**:1314
Genoa **1**:116, 252, **2**:305, 475, **3**:741, **5**:1393
Genoa, Republic of **1**:116, **5**:1393
German towns **2**:475
Glarus **5**:1314
Glasgow **5**:1260
Golden Gate **1**:257
Golden Horde, khanate of the **4**:937
Golden Horn **1**:257
Good Hope, Cape of **2**:381, **3**:789
Gorizia **2**:508
Göteborg **5**:1309
Gotland **5**:1309
Granada **2**:393, **3**:610, **5**:1278
Granson **5**:1314
Graubünden **5**:1314
Gravelines **1**:65
Greenland **2**:381, **3**:789
Guadalquivir River **2**:393
Guam **3**:789
Guelders, duchy of **1**:160
Guyenne **2**:437, **3**:596

H

Hagia Sophia **1**:257
Hainault, county of **1**:160
Halberstadt **5**:1330
Hamburg **2**:205, 475, **5**:1309
Hapsburg Empire **2**:508
Harfleur **3**:596
Härjedalen **5**:1309
Hebrides **1**:65, **5**:1260
Hippodrome **1**:257
Hispaniola **1**:252
Höchst **5**:1330
Holland, county of **1**:160
Holstein **2**:475
Holy Apostles, Church of **1**:257
Holy Roman Empire **1**:116, 160, **2**:508, **3**:631, 741, **5**:1309, 1330
Hull **2**:349
Hungary **1**:116, **2**:475, 508, **4**:937, **5**:1330
Huntingdon **2**:349

I

Ibiza **2**:393
Il-Khan Empire **3**:610
India **2**:381, **3**:789
Indian Ocean **2**:381, **3**:610, 628, 789
Ingria **5**:1309
Ionian Sea **3**:718
Ireland **1**:65, **2**:349, **5**:1260
Irish Sea **2**:349
Isfahan **3**:628
Islamic world, c. 1300 **3**:610
Islamic world, c. 1600 **3**:628
Istanbul **3**:628
Italian city-states **3**:631

J

Jamaica **1**:252
Jämtland **5**:1309
Jankov **5**:1330
Japan **2**:381, **3**:789
Jülich, duchy of **1**:160, **5**:1330
Jutland **5**:1330

K

Kaffa **2**:305
Kaliningrad *see* Königsberg

Kappel **5**:1314
Karelia **5**:1309
Kariye Cami **1**:257
Kasimov **4**:937
Kazan, khanate of **4**:937
Kiev **4**:937
Klaipeda **5**:1330
Königsberg (Kaliningrad) **4**:937, **5**:1309
Königshofen **2**:475
Kontoskalion, Harbor of **1**:257
Kraków **2**:205, **4**:937
Kulikovo Field **4**:937

L

La Coruña **1**:65
Languedoc **2**:437
Lapland **5**:1309
La Rochelle **2**:437
Lausanne **5**:1314
Leipheim **2**:475
Leipzig **1**:116
León **2**:393, **5**:1278
Lepanto **3**:628, 718
Leventina **5**:1314
Liège **2**:205
Liguria **3**:631
Ligurian Sea **3**:631, **5**:1393
Linlithgow **5**:1260
Lisbon **1**:65, M252, **2**:305
Lithuania **1**:116, **2**:475, **4**:937, **5**:1309
Livonia **4**:937, 1105, **5**:1309
Loire River **2**:437, **3**:596
Lombardy **3**:631, 741
London **2**:205, 349
Lorraine, duchy of **1**:160
Los Toros de Guisando **2**:393
Lot River **3**:596
Lower Palatinate **5**:1330
Lübeck **1**:116, **2**:475, **5**:1309
Lublin **4**:1106
Lucca **3**:741
Lucerne **5**:1314
Lusatia **5**:1330
Lutter am Barenberg **5**:1330
Lützen **5**:1309, 1330
Luxembourg, duchy of **1**:160
Lvov **4**:937
Lyons **2**:305

M

Mâcon, county of **1**:160
Mactan Island **3**:789
Madeira **1**:252
Madrid **2**:305, **5**:1278
Magdeburg **2**:475
Magdeburg-Halberstadt **5**:1330
Magellan, Straits of **3**:789
Magnaura Palace **1**:257
Maine, county of **2**:437, **3**:596
Mainz (Mayence) **2**:508, **5**:1309
Maisoncelles **1**:18
Mallorca **2**:393
Mamluk Empire **3**:610
Mantua **3**:631, 741, **5**:1393
Mariana Islands **3**:789
Marienberg **4**:937
Mark **5**:1330
Marmara, Sea of **1**:257
Marston Moor **2**:349
Mauritius **2**:381, **3**:789
Mayence *see* Mainz
Meaux **3**:596
Mecca **3**:610, 628
Mecklenburg **5**:1330
Medina **3**:610, 628
Mediterranean Sea **1**:252, **2**:305, 393, 508, **5**:1278
Melilla **5**:1278
Messina **2**:305
Milan **1**:116, **2**:305, 508, **3**:631, 741, **5**:1393
Milan, duchy of **2**:508, **3**:631, **5**:1314, 1330, 1393
Minsk **4**:937
Modena **3**:631, 741, **5**:1393
Moers, county of **1**:160
Mogul Empire **3**:628
Moldavia **4**:937
Molucca Islands **3**:789
Morat **5**:1314
Moravia **1**:116, **2**:475, **5**:1330
Moscow **4**:937
Moscow, principality of **4**:937
Mülhausen **2**:475
Munich **2**:475, **5**:1309
Murcia **2**:393
Muscovy **4**:937

N

Namur, county of **1:**160
Nancy **1:**160
Nantes **2:**437, **3:**596
Naples **2:**508, **3:**741
Naples, kingdom of **1:**116,
    2:305, 508, **3:**741, **5:**1278
Narva **5:**1309
Naseby **2:**349
Navarre, kingdom of **2:**393,
    437, **5:**1278
Navidad **1:**252
Netherlands **1:**116, **2:**381,
    475, 508
Netherlands, Spanish **5:**1330
Neuchâtel **5:**1314
Nevers, county of **1:**160
Newark **2:**349
Newbury **2:**349
New Zealand **2:**381, **3:**789
Nizhniy Novgorod **4:**937
Nördlingen **5:**1309, 1330
Normandy **2:**437, **3:**596
North America **1:**252, **2:**381,
    3:789
North Sea **1:**65, **2:**305, 349,
    5:1260, 1309
Norway **2:**205, **5:**1309
Nottingham **2:**349
Novgorod **5:**1309
Nuremberg **2:**205, 475

O

Oder River **1:**116
Oesel **5:**1309
Okhotsk, Sea of **4:**937
Oran **5:**1278
Orbe **5:**1314
Orkney Islands **1:**65, **5:**1260
Orléans **3:**596
Orléans, duchy of **2:**437
Orsha **4:**937
Ottoman Empire **1:**116,
    2:508, **5:**1330
Oxford **2:**205, 349

P

Pacific Ocean **2:**381, **3:**789
Padua **3:**741, **5:**1393
Palermo **2:**305, **3:**741
Palos **1:**252

Papal States **1:**116, **2:**508,
    3:631, 741, **5:**1393
Paris **1:**160, **2:**305, 437,
    3:596, **5:**1330
Parma **3:**631, 741
Patras **3:**718
Patras, Gulf of **3:**718
Pavia **3:**631, 741
Peloponnese **3:**718
Pfeddersheim **2:**475
Philippine Islands **3:**789
Piacenza **3:**631, 741
Picardy **2:**437
Piedmont **3:**741
Pisa **2:**305, **3:**631, 741
Plate River **3:**789
Plymouth **1:**65, **2:**349
Poitiers **2:**437, **3:**596
Poitou **2:**437, **3:**596
Poland **4:**937, **5:**1309, 1330
Poland-Lithuania **1:**116,
    2:475, **4:**937 *see also*
    Lithuania
Portugal **1:**65, 252, **2:**381,
    393, 508, **3:**789, **5:**1278
Poznań **1:**116
Prague **1:**116, **2:**205, 475,
    5:1330
Preston **2:**349
Pripes River **4:**937
Provence, county of **2:**437
Prussia **1:**116, **2:**475, **5:**1309,
    1330
Pskov **4:**937
Puerto San Julián **3:**789

R

Rain **5:**1309, 1330
Ravenna **3:**741, **5:**1393
Reims **2:**205, **3:**596
Rethel, county of **1:**160
Reval **5:**1309
Rheinfelden **5:**1330
Rhine River **1:**116, **2:**205,
    475, 508
Rhône River **2:**437,
    3:596
Riga **2:**205, **5:**1309
Romagna **3:**631
Rome **1:**116, **2:**305, 508,
    3:741

Rostock **5:**1330
Rothenberg **2:**475
Rouen **3:**596
Roundaway **2:**349
Roussillon **5:**1278
Russia **2:**381, **3:**789, **5:**1309
Ryazan **4:**937

S

Safavid Empire **3:**628
Saint Andrews **5:**1260
Saint Irene, Church of **1:**257
Saint Mary Pammakaristos,
    Church of **1:**257
Saint Petersburg **4:**937
Saint Romanus, Gate of **1:**257
Salzburg **2:**475
Samar **3:**789
Samoa **3:**789
Sankt Jakob an der Birs **5:**1314
San Salvador **1:**252
Santa Maria de Belén **1:**252
Santander **1:**65
Santiago de Compostela **2:**393
Santo Domingo **1:**252
Sarai **4:**937
Sardinia **2:**305, 508, **3:**741,
    5:1278
Sätulsund **3:**1509
Sauchieburn **5:**1260
Savoy, duchy of **1:**160, **2:**508,
    3:631, **5:**1314
Saxony **2:**508, **5:**1330
Schaffhausen **5:**1314
Schladming **2:**475
Schleswig-Holstein **5:**1330
Schwyz **5:**1314
Scotland **1:**65, **2:**349, **5:**1260
Seine River **1:**160, **2:**437,
    3:596
Seljuk Turk region **3:**610
Senta **2:**508
Sibir (Siberia) **4:**937
Sicily, kingdom of **2:**305, 508,
    3:741, **5:**1278
Siena **2:**305, **3:**631, 741,
    5:1393
Siena, republic of **3:**631,
    5:1393
Silesia **1:**116, **2:**475, 508,
    5:1330

Skåne **5:**1309
Sluys **3:**596
Smolensk **4:**937
Solothurn **5:**1314
Solway Moss **5:**1260
Sophia, harbor of **1:**257
South America **1:**252, **2:**381,
    3:789
Spain **1:**65, 252, **2:**381, 508,
    3:610, 628, 789, **5:**1278
Spanish Netherlands *see*
    Netherlands, Spanish
Stettin **5:**1309
Stirling **5:**1260
Stockholm **2:**205, **5:**1309
Strasbourg **2:**475
Styria **1:**116, **2:**475, 508
Swabia **2:**475
Sweden **1:**116, **4:**937, **5:**1309,
    1330
Swiss Confederation **1:**116,
    160, **2:**475, 508, **3:**631,
    5:1314, **5:**1330

T

Tannenberg **4:**937
Teutonic Order, territory of
    the **1:**116, **4:**1106
Theodosius, Harbor of
    1:257
Theodosius II, Wall of **1:**257
Thurgau **5:**1314
Ticino **5:**1314
Toggenburg **5:**1314
Toledo **2:**393, **5:**1278
Tordesillas **5:**1278
Toro **5:**1278
Tours **3:**596
Tramecourt **1:**18
Transylvania **5:**1330
Treves **2:**508
Trevino **5:**1393
Tripoli **5:**1278
Trondheim **5:**1309
Troyes **3:**596
Tsaritsyn **4:**937
Tunis **2:**508, **3:**628, **5:**1278
Turin **1:**116
Tver **4:**937
Tyrol **1:**116, **2:**475, 508
Tyrrhenian Sea **3:**741

U

Udine **5**:1393
Ulm **2**:475
United Provinces **5**:1330
Unterwalden **5**:1314
Upper Palatinate **5**:1330
Urbino **3**:631
Uri **5**:1314
Utrecht **1**:160

V

Valais **5**:1314
Valencia **2**:393, **5**:1278
Valladolid **1**:252, **2**:393,
    5:1278
Vaud **5**:1314
Veltlin **5**:1314
Venice **1**:116, **2**:305, 475,
    508, **3**:628, 631, 741,
    5:1393
Venice, republic of **1**:116,
    2:508, **3**:631, **5**:1314,
    1330, 1393
Verona **3**:741, **5**:1393
Vicenza **5**:1393
Vienna **2**:205, **5**:1330
Vilna **4**:937
Vistula River **4**:937
Vladimir **4**:937
Volga River **4**:937
Voralberg **2**:508

W

Wales **1**:65, **2**:349
Wall of Constantine *see*
    Constantine, Wall of
Wall of Theodosius II *see*
    Theodosius II, Wall
    of
Warsaw **4**:937
Weser River **5**:1330
Western Pomerania **5**:1330
Westphalia **5**:1330
White Mountain **5**:1330
White Sea **4**:937
Wight, Isle of **2**:349
Wismar **5**:1309, 1330
Wittenberg **2**:475
Wittstock **5**:1309
Wurzach **2**:475
Würzburg **2**:475

Y

York **2**:349

Z

Zabern **2**:475
Zeeland, county of **1**:160
Zug **5**:1314
Zurich **2**:305, **5**:1314
Zutphen, county of **1**:160
Zweibrücken, principality of
    5:1330

Biographical Index

A **boldface** number preceding a colon indicates the volume. Numbers in *italics* refer to captions. Numbers entirely in **boldface** refer to a full article.

A

Albert III, archduke of Austria **2**:507, 508

Abbas I, shah of Persia **3**:612, 622

Abbas II, shah of Persia **1**:*280*

Abraham (prophet) **3**:610, **4**:1084, 1085

Abulafia, Abraham **3**:680

Acquaviva y Aragon, Giulio **1**:202

Adams, John **4**:887

Adolf II of Schauenburg **2**:503

Adorno, Antoniotto **3**:650

Adorno, Giuliano **5**:1420

Adramyttenus, Emanuel **4**:1073

Adrian VI, Pope **1**:210, 241, 242, **4**:1023, **5**:1380

Aeken, Anthonis van **1**:127, 128

Aeken, Goossen van **1**:128

Aeschylus **3**:685

Afonso V, king of Portugal **4**:1144, **5**:1277

Agricola **1**:*279*

Agrippa, Marsilio **3**:799

Ahnlund, Nils **5**:1339

Akbar, Mogul emperor **1**:*71*, **3**:615

Alba, duke of **1**:*190*, **2**:454, 556, **4**:1057, 1060, **5**:1233

Albergati, Niccolò **4**:1086

Alberquerque, Afonso de **4**:1143

Albert III, archduke of Austria **2**:507, 508

Albert IV, archduke of Austria **2**:508

Albert V, archduke of Austria **2**:508

Albert I, king of Germany **2**:509

Albert II, king of Germany **2**:509

Albert, archduke of Spain **5**:1241

Alberti, Leon Battista **1**:139, 154, **2**: 418, **3**:745, 847, **4**:984–985, 987, 989, 1001

architecture **1**:30–31, 32, 34, 35–36, 37

mathematics **3**:827

Rome **5**:1229

Albert of Brandenburg **3**:704, **4**:1107, **5**:1190

Albertoni, Ludovica **1**:100

Albertus Magnus **1**:52, 56, **3**:797

Albizzi, Rinaldo **2**:417, 420

Albizzis, the **2**:417, **3**:850

Albornoz, Gil Álvarez Carillo de **5**:1378

Albret, Charles d' **1**:17, 18

Alcalá, duke of **2**:471

Alciati, Andrea **1**:179

Alcionio, Pietro **5**:1233

Aldus Manutius *see* Manutius, Aldus

Alemán, Mateo **3**:738, 739

Alembert, Jean d' **2**:466, 516

Alençon, duke of **2**:456, 457, 517

Alexander III, Pope **4**:1137

Alexander IV, Pope **3**:693

Alexander VI, Pope **4**:948, 1011, 1016, **5**:1231, 1279

Borgia, Lucrezia **1**:123–124, 126

exploration **2**:381

heresy **2**:533

Leo X **3**:700

missionaries **4**:888–889

Pico della Mirandola **4**:1074, 1077

Urbino **5**:1379

Alexander VII, Pope **1**:100, 229–230, 231

Alexander VIII, Pope **2**:372

Alexander II (the Great), king of Macedonia **1**:*59*, 167, 224, **3**:*595*

Alexander Nevsky **4**:933

Alexander of Aphrodisias **1**:56

Alexis I, emperor of Russia **4**:940, *941*, 1113

Alfonso V (the Magnanimous), king of Aragon **2**:412, **3**:619, **4**:1091, **5**:1279

Alfonso VI, king of Castile and León **4**:1137

Alfonso X (the Wise), king of Castile **3**:693

Alfonso III, duke of Mantua **5**:*1206*

Alfonso I, king of Naples *see* Alfonso V, king of Aragon

Alfonso II, king of Naples **3**:644

Alfonso V, king of Portugal *see* Afonso V

Alfonso of Aragon **1**:124

Alfonso of Cartagena **1**:54

Alfonso of Castile **2**:393

Ali ibn Abi Talib **3**:620, 621

Allde, John **5**:1324

Allegretti, Allegretto **1**:281

Alleyne, Edward **3**:824, **5**:1268

Almeida, Francisco de **3**:787, **4**:1142

Álvarez, duke of Toledo **5**:1164

Alviano, Bartolomeo Liviano d' **3**:651

Amati, Andrea **4**:943, 958

Ambrose, Saint **3**:745

Amman, Jost **5**:*1344*

Ancona, Ciriaco d' **3**:587

Andrea del Castagno **1**:*111*

Andrew, Saint **5**:1230

Andrewes, Lancelot **2**:346

Andrew of Wyntoun **5**:1260

Andronicus IV, Byzantine emperor **1**:*262*

Angelico, Fra **2**:428, **5**:1229

Angelos, Christopher **1**:262

Anger, Jane **5**:1420

Angevins, the **2**:412, **3**:596, 655, **4**:965, 1090

Angus, earl of **5**:1261, 1262

Anjou, duke of. *see* Henry III, king of France

Anna, princess of Saxony **5**:1236

Anne, Saint **5**:*1220*

Anne, countess of Arundel **5**:1424

Anne of Bohemia **1**:217

Anne of Brittany **3**:*644*

Anne of Cleves, queen consort of England **2**:522, 527

Anne of Denmark, queen consort of England **3**:663, 665

Anne of Hungary **2**:510

Anne of Montmorency **2**:452

Annibaldis **1**:39

Annius of Viterbo **3**:594

Anthony, Saint **5**:1201

António of Crato **4**:1140, 1145

Apuleius **1**:41

Archias **3**:682

Archimedes **2**:297, 461, 462, **3**:831

Arcimboldo, Giuseppe **2**:559

Areopagus **5**:1287

Aretino, Pietro **3**:733

Argonauts **2**:515

Arguin **5**:1345

Argyropoulos, Johannes **1**:55, 169

Ariosto, Ludovico **1**:125, 223, **3**:721, 733, **5**:1289

Aristarchus of Samos **1**:265

Aristotle **1**:**50–61**, 81, 181, **2**:357, 359, **3**:*595, 703*, **4**:1049, 1054–1055, *1055*, *1061*, 1075

astrology **1**:69

classical languages **3**:684, 686

Constantinople **1**:169, 170, 258, 261

cosmology **1**:265, 267, **5**:1253

dramatic unities **3**:727, 729, **5**:1321

English translation **2**:336

exploration **2**:384

Galileo **2**:460, 461, 463

Hobbes vs. **2**:543

humanism **3**:582, 583, *586*

Latin translation of **1**:261, **3**:685, 693

Luther vs. **3**:761, 763, 767

on monarchy **4**:903

Aristotle *(cont.)*
  philosophy **4:**1061–1062, 1063, 1064, 1065, 1066, 1072, 1099, 1102
  Pico della Mirandola **4:**1073, 1074, 1076
  Platonism **1:**261, **4:**1095
  printed editions **3:**688
  Reformation **1:**181, **2:**320
  science **5:**1248
  Thomas Aquinas **1:**52, 56, 59, **3:**604
  on tragedy **4:**920
  universities **5:**1365, 1367, 1369
Arminius, Jacobus **1:**190, **2:**346
Arnolfini, Giovanni **2:***389, 390*
Arran, earl of *see* Hamilton, James
Arsenius, Saint **1:***168*
Arthur, prince of Wales **1:**232, **2:**521, 522, 523
Artusi, Giovanni Maria **4:**918
Arundel, earl of **1:**83
Ascham, Roger **2:**327
Aske, Robert **1:**235, **2:**340, 526
Asper, Hans **5:***1315*
Atticus **3:***584, 589, 682, 683, 684*
Aubrey, John **2:**547
Augustine, Saint **3:**606, 696, **5:**1229, 1248, *1284*
  Aristotle vs. **1:**53, **2:**357
  bibles **1:**104, **2:**467
  Erasmus **2:**357
  ideas **1:**182
  Lutheranism **3:**758–759, 765, 767
  Petrarch **4:**1052, 1055
  philosophy **4:**1069
  Platonism **4:**1098, 1100
  preaching **5:**1158, *1159*
  Vives commentary **5:**1282
Augustine of Hippo *see* Augustine, Saint
Aurispa, Giovanni **3:**685
Averroës *see* Ibn Rushd
Aviz dynasty **4:**1137–1140

Azaro, Ambrosio Mariano **1:**280
Azzolino, Decio **1:**230, 231

B

Babington, Anthony **2:**330, 331, **5:**1298, 1299
Babur (Muhammad Zahir ud-Din), king of India **3:**612, 615
Baburen, Dirck van **4:**997
Bach, Johann Sebastian **4:**960
Bacon, Anthony **5:**1419
Bacon, Francis **1:**79–83, **2:**542, **3:**775, **4:**929, **5:**1419
  Aristotle **1:**60, 61
  philosophy **4:**1065, 1067–1068, 1069, 1072
  Platonism **4:**1103
  science **5:**1251, 1256
  Shakespeare **5:**1276
Bacon, Nicholas **1:**79, **5:**1419
Bacon, Roger **1:**174
Baglione, Giovanni **1:**192, 194
Baglioni, Grifoneto **5:**1185
Balboa *see* Núñez de Balboa, Vasco
Baldinucci, Filippo **1:**34, 101, 230
Baldung, Hans Grien **4:***1080*
Ball, John **4:**1044, 1045, 1047, 1048
Baltellina **5:**1334
Balten, Pieter **4:***1122*
Baltimore, Lord *see* Calvert, George
Bandello, Matteo **3:**711, 736
Banér, Johan **5:**1338
Banister, John **5:***1254*
Barbara, Saint **5:***1221*
Barbaro, Daniele **1:**33, **4:**1001
Barbaro, Ermolao **1:**56, **4:**1075
Barbaro, Marc'Antonio **4:**1001
Barberini, Francesco **4:**882
Barberini, Maffeo *see* Urban VIII
Barbosa, Duarte **3:**793
Barcilon, Pinin Brambilla **3:**713

Bardi, Donato di Niccolò di Betto *see* Donatello
Bardi, Giovanni **2:**567, **4:**920
Bardis, the **2:**567
Barents, Willem **2:**374, 384
Barezzi, Stefano **3:**713
Barocci, Federico **5:***1380, 1381*
Baron, Hans **3:**585
Baronio, Cesare **5:**1205
Barozzi, Giacomo *see* Vignola, Giacomo da
Barrow, Isaac **3:**833
Bartolomeo, Fra **4:***1077, **5:**1184*
Bartolomeo da Venezio **1:***123*
Bascio, Matteo da **5:**1206
Basil, Saint **1:**257, **3:**684, 685, **5:**1419
Basil, Simon **3:**665
Basil of Caesarea *see* Basil, Saint
Basil the Great *see* Basil, Saint
Bastard of Vaurus **4:**1115
Bastwick, John **2:**346
Báthory, Stephen *see* Stephen Báthory
Battista della Porta, Giovanni **4:***1073*
Bauer, Georg *see* Agricola
Bautista de Toledo, Juan **1:***46, 47, **4:**1060*
Bavaria, duke of **1:**78
Bayart, Pierre de **1:**221
Bayezid I, Ottoman sultan **3:**616, 617
Bayezid II, Ottoman sultan **3:**619
Bazán, Álvaro de **5:***1401*
Beatrice del Sera **1:**112–113
Beaufort, Henry **1:**17
Beaufort, Thomas **1:**17
Beaumont, Francis **3:**733, **5:**1325
Becerra, Francisco **1:**279
Becket, Thomas **1:**218, **4:**1083
Bedford, duke of **3:**601, 602
Bedford, earl of *see* Russell, Francis
Beeckman, Isaac **2:**294, 295
Behain, Martin **3:**775

Béjar, duke of **1:**205
Béjart, Armande **4:**900
Béjart, Madeleine **4:**898, 899, 900, 901
Béjarts, the **4:**897, 898
Belisarius **1:***166*
Belknap, Robert **4:**1043
Bellarmine, Robert **2:**465, **5:**1253
Bellay, Jean du **5:**1176, 1177–1178
Bellay, Joachim du **3:**729, **5:**1286
Bellini, Gentile **1:***263*, **3:**618, *635*, **4:***1099*, **5:***1396, 1399*
Bellini, Giovanni **2:**312, **4:**988, 989
Bellori, Giovanni Pietro **1:**196
Belskys, the **3:**652
Bembo, Pietro **1:**125, 241, **2:**310, **3:**703, 721, **5:**1383
Benavente **5:**1323
Bendido, Lucrezia **3:**721
Benedict, Saint **5:**1201
Benedict XIII (antipope) **3:**672
Bening, Simon **4:***1134*
Benozzo di Lesse Gozzoli, Francesco **1:***52*
Bentheim, Luder von **1:***49*
Bentivoglios, the **3:**701
Benvenuto di Giovanni **1:***86*
Bérenger, Jean **2:**557
Berkman, Hendrik **5:***1252*
Bernáldez, Andrés **3:**678
Bernard, count of Armagnac **1:**159
Bernardino of Siena **5:**1160, 1162, 1163
Bernat, Martin **5:***1279*
Bernhard of Saxe-Weimar **3:**839, **5:**1337–1338
Bernini, Gian Lorenzo **1:97–101**, 195, **2:***458*, **3:**668, **4:**1000, **5:**1225
  architecture **1:**32, 33, 34, 38, 40, 44–45, 48, 49
  Caravaggio as influence **1:**195

Christina **1:**230
painting and sculpture
4:993, 994
Rome **5:***1234,* 1235
Saint Peter's colonnade
4:*1008,* 1026
Urban VIII **5:**1333
Bernini, Luigi di Pietro **1:**44
Bernini, Pietro **1:**44, 97, 98
Beroaldo, Filippo (the
Younger) **1:**41
Berruguete, Pedro **2:***397*
Bertendona, Martín de **1:**64
Berthelot, René **4:**897
Berthold of Henneberg **2:**550
Bérulle, Pierre de **2:**296,
5:1205, 1208
Bessarion **1:**260, 261, **3:**688,
690, 728, 829
humanist learning **2:**430,
431, **4:**1023
Platonism **4:**1063,
1099–1100
Bethlen, Gábor von **5:**1335
Bettes, John (the Elder)
5:*1272*
Bèze, Théodore de **1:**107, 108,
2:369, 566–567
Bigordi, Domenico di
Tommaso *see* Ghirlandaio,
Domenico
Bilhères-Lagrulas, Jean de
4:871
Bill, John **1:***82*
Binchois, Gilles **4:**944
Biondo, Flavio **3:**587
Bisticci, Vespasiano da **5:**1229
Black Prince *see* Edward, the
Black Prince
Blaeu, Jan **1:***275*
Blanche of Lancaster **1:**215,
4:1047
Blomberg, Barbara **3:**716
Boabdil **2:**397–398
Bobadilla, Francisco de **1:**254
Boccaccio, Giovanni
1:111–115, **3:**735, 736,
4:963, 1051
Chaucer **1:**216, 217,
218–219
Florence **2:**423

religious orders **5:**1202
vernacular **1:**217, **3:**694
Bodenehr, Gabriel **4:**1114
Boethius, Anicius Manlius
Severinus **1:**213, 217
Bogomils **3:**605
Boiardo, Matteo Maria **1:**223
Boleyn, Anne **3:**735, **4:**931,
1014, 1015, 1123, **5:**1297
Elizabeth I **1:**236, **2:**326
Henry VIII **1:**233, 234, 235,
240, **2:**338, 522, 523,
524, 525, 527
Boleyn, Thomas **1:**234
Bolingbroke, Henry *see* Henry
IV, king of England
Bolton, Herbert Eugene **2:**383
Bolton, Robert **3:**663
Bona of Savoy **3:**742
Bonaventure **3:**760, **4:**1062
Boniface VIII, Pope **2:**366,
491, **4:**903, *1079,* 1080,
5:1227, 1235
Bonvesin de la Riva **3:**631
Booker, John **1:**70
Bora, Katharina von **3:**762,
5:1201
Borghese, Camillo *see* Paul V
Borghese, Marcantonio **4:**1037
Borghese, Scipione **1:**97,
4:1037
Borgia, Cesare **1:**123, 124,
126, **3:**707, 769, **4:**1011,
5:1379, 1428
Borgia, Juan **1:**123
Borgia, Lucrezia **1:123–126,**
5:1427, 1428
Borgia, Rodrigo *see* Alexander
VI
Borgias, the **4:**1011, **5:**1231
Boris Godunov *see* Godunov,
Boris
Borja, Alfonso de *see* Calixtus
III
Borluut, Elizabeth **2:**387
Borromeo, Carlo **1:**32, **3:**747,
4:1036, **5:**1197
Borromini, Francesco **1:**33, 38,
40, 44–45, 49, **5:**1235
Boscán Almogáver, Juan **3:**726,
5:1284

Bosch, Hieronymus
1:127–132
as Bruegel influence **1:***144,*
145, 146, 148
Bosse, Abraham **5:***1423*
Bossuet, Jacques-Bénigne
2:372
Bothwell, earl of *see* Hepburn,
James
Botticelli, Sandro **1:***114,*
133–138, **2:***424,* **3:**706,
852, 856, **4:**985, **5:***1219,*
1220, 1230
Florence **2:**424–425
Boucicaut *see* Meingre
Boucicaut, Jean II le
Bourbon, Antoine de **1:**199,
2:516
Bourbon, Antoinette de **1:**198
Bourbon, Armand de, prince
of Conti **4:**898
Bourbon, François de **1:**198
Bourbons, the **2:**437, 443
Henry IV **2:**516–520
Thirty Years War **5:**1330,
1333
Bourbon-Vendôme, Louis de
1:199
Bourchier, John **1:**224
Bourdon, Sébastien **1:***227,*
2:*300,* **5:***1293*
Bourgeois, Louis **4:**954
Bourguignon, Le (Jacques
Courtois) **5:***1337*
Bouscal, Guérin de **1:***204*
Bouts, Dirck **4:**982
Bower, Walter **5:**1260
Boyle, Elizabeth **5:**1289
Boyle, Richard, earl of Cork
5:1289
Boyle, Robert **5:**1256
Bracciolini, Poggio **1:**33,
2:359, **3:**583, 683, **5:**1229
English translation **2:**336
Bradley, Humphrey **1:**276
Bradley, William **3:**824
Bragança family **4:**1145
Brahe, Per **1:**229
Brahe, Tycho **1:**121, *268,* 271,
272, **2:**559, **3:***831,* 832,
5:1251

Bramante, Donato **1:**31, 32,
36, 37–38, 39, **139–143,**
3:710, **4:**873, 878, **5:**1186
Palladio **4:**1002, 1004
Saint Peter's Basilica **1:**140,
142, 143, **4:**1026, **5:**1231
Bramhall, John **2:**543, 546
Branagh, Kenneth **3:**603
Brandenburg, elector of **1:**76
Brant, Isabella **5:**1238–1239,
1241–1242
Brask, Hans, bishop of
Linköping **5:**1305
Braun, Georg **1:***78, 281,*
5:1316, *1350*
Bregno, Andrea **1:**40, **5:***1230*
Breton, Gilles le **1:**45
Bridgewater, earl of *see*
Egerton, John
Bronckhorst, Arnold van
5:1265
Bronckhorst, Jan Gerritsz von
5:*1338*
Bronzino, Il **4:**990
Broquière, Bertrandon de la
1:*264*
Bruegel, Pieter (the Elder)
1:131, **144–148,** **4:***1119,*
1125
Brueghel, Pieter, III **2:***405*
Brueghel, Jan **1:**144, **4:***1124*
Brueghel, Pieter (the Younger)
1:144, **4:***1128,* **5:***1319*
Bruhl, Nikolaus **5:***1191*
Brunelleschi, Filippo **1:**139,
149–156, **3:**668, 856,
4:876, 878
architecture **1:**32, 34–35, 37,
47
classicism **4:**983
Florence **2:**424
perspective **2:**312, **4:**984
Brunfels, Otto **3:**840, **5:**1250
Bruni, Leonardo **1:**125, *155,*
3:640, 855
Aristotle **1:**54, 55
Chrysoloras **1:**264
classical languages **3:**684,
685
English translation **2:**336
Florence **2:**422, 423

Bruni, Leonardo (*cont.*)
humanism **2:**357, **3:**584,
585, 586, 588
tomb of **1:***155*
Bruno, Saint **4:**926
Bruno, Giordano **1:**57, 272,
4:*1019,* 1065, 1071
Brus, Anton **1:**121
Bruschi, Arnaldo **1:**143
Bry, Theodore de **1:***251,*
5:*1346*
Bucer, Elizabeth **5:**1423
Bucer, Martin **5:**1423
Buchanan, George **5:**1263,
1264, 1299
Buckingham, duke of *see*
Villiers, George
Budé, Guillaume **1:**179,
3:590, **5:**1176
Bueil, Jean de **5:***1410*
Buil, Bernado **4:**895
Bullinger, Henry **2:**369
Buonacorsi, Filippo de
(Callimachus) **4:**1109
Buonarroti, Michelangelo *see*
Michelangelo
Buonarroti, Michelangelo (the
Younger) **2:**469
Buoninsegna *see* Duccio di
Buoninsegna
Buontalenti, Bernado Timante
1:276
Burbage, James **5:**1270,
1326
Burbage, Richard **5:**1270,
1271
Burckhardt, Jacob **5:**1220
Bure, Idelette de **1:**179
Burghley, Lord *see* Cecil,
William
Burke, Thomas **5:***1290*
Burley, Simon **4:**1043
Burlington, Lord **3:**668,
4:1007
Burton, Henry **2:**346
Busenello, Giovanni **4:**923
Busnois, Antoine **4:**946
Busti, Agostino **3:***645*
Butler, James, earl of Ormond
2:353
Buxtehude, Dietrich **4:**960

Byrd, William **4:**943, 952
Byron, Lord **1:**126, **5:**1290

C
Cabot, John **4:**888, 914, 915,
5:*1350*
Cabot, Sebastian **2:**383
Cabral, Pedro Álvares **2:**374,
381
Caccini, Giulio **4:**920
Cade, Jack **4:**1042
Caesar, Julius **1:**174, **4:**1024,
5:1232
Caffarelli, Scipione *see*
Borghese, Scipione
Cailleau, Hubert **5:***1317*
Calderón de la Barca, Pedro
3:726, 727, 728, **5:**1284,
1323
Caliari, Benedetto **1:***58*
Caliari, Paolo **5:**1399
Calixtus III, Pope **3:**619,
4:1011, 1086
Callimachus (Filippo de
Buonacorsi) **4:**1109
Calvert, George (Lord
Baltimore) **4:**894
Calvin, Gerard **1:**179
Calvin, John **1:**178, 181, 183,
184, 185, 186–187, 188,
189, **2:**369, 483, **3:**761,
762, **4:**906, 1032
bibles **1:**107, 108
catechism **5:**1174
Church of Scotland **2:**369
divorce grounds **2:**566–567
education **2:**321, 324–325
France **2:**439–440, **5:**1191
Geneva **5:**1315–1316, 1423
humanism **1:**190,
2:324–325, **3:**593
hunting critique **1:**96
iconoclasm **3:**607, 608
interest-bearing loans **1:**85,
5:1316
on Islam **3:**618
music ban **4:**952
nationalism **2:**364
overview of **1:**179
philosophy **4:**1062–1063,
1064, 1065

preaching **5:***1164,* 1165
Puritanism **2:**342
Rabelais **5:**1179
Reformation **5:**1194–1196
religious wars **1:**183
sacraments **5:**1358
Switzerland **5:**1312
witch hunts **2:**535
Camden, William **5:**1290
Camerarius, Joachim **5:***1372*
Camões, Luíz Vaz de **2:**385,
4:1144
Campanella, Tommaso **1:**31,
4:1103
Campbell, Colin **4:**1007
Campion, Edmund **4:**896,
5:1206, 1323, 1324
Campofregoso, Ottaviano
3:650
Canaletto **4:***1039,* **5:***1433*
Canigiani, Sandra di Matteo di
Giovanni **5:**1185
Canossa, Lodivico da **5:**1383
Capponis, the **2:**417, **3:**850
Capranica, Domenico **4:**1086,
1088
Carafa, Gian Pietro *see* Paul IV
Carafa, Olivero **1:***140*
Caravaggio **1:**191–196, **4:**878,
993, 994, 997, **5:**1235,
1386
Gentileschi **2:**469, 470, 471,
472, 474
as Rembrandt influence
5:1211
Rubens **5:**1237–1238
Carda, Bernardino della
5:1379
Cardano, Girolamo **1:**70, 71,
72, *73,* **3:**828, 829, 830
overview of **1:**70, **3:**830
Carew, Thomas **2:**402
Carlos, Don, prince of Spain
4:1059
Caro, Joseph **3:**680
Caron, Antoine **4:***1102*
Carpaccio, Vittore **1:***87, 91,*
5:1399
Carpio, marquess del **5:**1389
Carr, Robert **5:**1300
Carracci, Agostino **1:**195

Carracci, Annibale **1:**41, 193,
195, **4:**993, **5:**1235,
1237–1238
Carrara, princes of **2:**318
Casaubon, Isaac **1:**58
Casimir, John *see* John II, king
of Poland
Casimir III (the Great), king
of Poland **3:**675, **4:**1104
Cassotti, Marsilio and
Faustina **5:***1420*
Castagno, Andrea del **1:***216,*
5:*1229*
Castelli, Benedetto **1:**277
Castiglione, Baldassare **1:**48,
3:685, 736, **5:**1221, 1383
Castillo, Juan del **5:**1386
Castro y Bellvís, Guillén de
3:728, 730, 731
Castro y Velasco, Antonio
Palomino de **5:**1384–1391
Catalina Micaela, princess of
Spain **1:**203, **5:**1281
Catherine, Saint **1:***125,* **3:**657
Catherine de Médicis
1:197–201, **3:**722, 827,
5:1426
astrological prediction **1:**73
Clement VII **1:**242, 245
France **2:**440–441
French civil wars **2:**452, 454
Paris **4:**1031
Thirty Years War **5:**1333,
1334
Catherine of Aragon **4:**930,
1014–1015, 1123, **5:**1297,
1417
Ferdinand and Isabella
5:1280
Henry VIII **1:**232–233, 234,
235, 240, 242, 244,
2:338, 340, 521,
522–523, 524
Mary Tudor **1:**236, 240
Reformation **5:**1196, 1197
Catherine of France **3:**601
Catherine of Siena **5:**1424
Catherine of Valois **1:**17
Cattanei, Vannozza **1:**123
Cauchon, Peter **3:**661–662
Caulery, Louis de **4:***1021*

Cavalieri, Bonaventura **3**:833

Cavalieri, Tommaso de' **4**:877

Cavalli, Marino **2**:447

Cavallini, Pietro **2**:491

Cavallino, Bernardo **2**:474

Cavazza, Bartolomeo **4**:1000

Cavenaghi, Luigi **3**:713

Cavendish family **2**:542

Caxes, Eugenio **5**:*1322*

Caxton, William **1**:223

Cecil, Robert **2**:333, **3**:665

Cecil, William (Lord
    Burghley) **1**:81, **5**:1287,
    1289, 1419

  Elizabeth I **2**:327, 328, 331

Cellini, Benvenuto **1**:243,
    2:450, **3**:767, **4**:989

Celtis, Conradus **2**:550, *551,*
    552, **3**:590

Cenami, Giovanna **2**:*389*

Cennini, Cennino **2**:490

Cerasi, Tiberio **1**:193, 194

Cervantes, Catalina de **1**:203

Cervantes, Miguel de
    1:202–206, **3**:728, 736,
    739, **5**:1221, 1284, 1323

  chivalry **1**:223–224

Cervantes, Rodrigo de **1**:202

Cestius, Caius **1**:37

Chacón, Pedro **1**:175

Chaerephon **4**:1093

Chancellor, Richard **3**:654,
    4:933

Chandoux, Monsieur
    (alchemist) **2**:296

Chapman, George **3**:825,
    5:1327

Chappell, William **4**:880

Charlemagne, king of the
    Franks **1**:180, **2**:493,
    3:721

  chivalric literature **1**:222,
    223

  Constantinople **1**:257,
    258–259, 264

  missions **4**:888

Charles I, king of Bohemia *see*
    Charles IV, Holy Roman
    emperor

Charles I, king of England
    1:*96*, **5**:1257

architecture **1**:47, **3**:663,
    665, 666–667, 668

banking **1**:90

Church of England **1**:239,
    2:372

divine right **1**:239

English civil wars **2**:346,
    347–355, 544, **3**:668,
    4:883

execution of **1**:239, **2**:344,
    346, 351, 354–355, *543,*
    4:884, 906, **5**:1303, 1325

iconoclasm **3**:609

Jones **3**:663, 665, 666–667,
    668

monarchy **2**:344–346

painting **1**:97, **2**:475, **3**:745,
    4:883, 884, 894, **5**:1242,
    1243

Roman Catholicism **2**:343,
    346

Scotland **5**:1262, 1267

Stuarts **5**:1301, 1302–1303

theater **3**:733, **5**:1325, 1328,
    1329

Thirty Years War **5**:1302,
    1336

Charles II, king of England
    1:262, **3**:666

architecture **1**:33, 48

astrological prediction **1**:72

Church of England **1**:239

divine right **1**:239

Hobbes **2**:543, 546

Restoration **1**:240, **4**:886,
    5:1322, 1329

Royal Society charter **5**:1256

Stuarts **5**:1302, 1303

Wren **5**:1429, 1430, 1431,
    1432

Charles IV, king of France
    2:433

Charles V, king of France
    2:406, *432,* 434, **4**:910,
    1029–1030, 1031

Charles VI, king of France
    2:434, 435, **3**:660,
    5:1416

  Agincourt **1**:16

  Burgundy **1**:158, 159, 160

  Byzantine Empire **1**:261

Hundred Years War **3**:599,
    600–601

  Paris **4**:1030

Charles VII, king of France
    1:*260,* **2**:435, **4**:946, 965,
    968, 1030, **5**:1371, 1427

  Burgundy **1**:159, 160,
    162–163

  Hundred Years War **3**:601,
    602

  Joan of Arc **3**:657–662

Charles VIII, king of France
    2:445, 550, **3**:619, 853,
    4:870, 965, 986, 1077,
    1088

  Burgundy **1**:164

  Florence **2**:419, 420, 421

  Italian wars **2**:310, 412, 421,
    3:642, 644, 648

Charles IX, king of France
    2:440–441, 442, 452, 454,
    455, 456, 517, **3**:722, 857,
    4:958, 1033

  Catherine de Médicis **1**:197,
    198–200

Charles IV, Holy Roman
    emperor **2**:478, 549, **4**:910,
    1052

  Bohemia **1**:117–118

Charles V, Holy Roman
    emperor **1**:**207–211,** 222,
    2:476, 557, **3**:677, 845,
    5:1335, 1400

  Americas **5**:1285

  architecture **1**:46

  Augsburg, Peace of **1**:75

  Bohemia **1**:120–121

  Burgundy **1**:157

  Clement VII **1**:241,
    242–243, 244

  Erasmus **2**:357

  family of **5**:1280, 1281,
    1283, 1426

  Ferdinand and Isabella **2**:400

  Florence **2**:419, 421, **4**:871

  Francis I **2**:445–446, 448

  German towns **2**:477–478,
    482, 483

  Hapsburg Empire **1**:207,
    209, **2**:445–446, 476,
    510, 511, 512, 515, 556

Henry VIII **1**:234, **2**:522,
    523

humanism **5**:1280, 1282,
    1283

Isabella of Portugal **4**:1056,
    1139

Italian wars **2**:413, 421,
    3:643, 644, 646, 647,
    648, 649, 650, 702

lands inherited **4**:966

Leo X **3**:702, 705

Lombardy **3**:743, 744, 745,
    853

Lutheranism **2**:553, 554,
    556, **3**:762, 765, *766,*
    767

Magellan **3**:788, 789

Ommegang procession
    5:1317

Ottoman expansion **3**:176,
    624, 715

papacy **1**:210, **4**:1013,
    1014–1015, 1017, 1023

Philip II **1**:211, **4**:1056,
    1058, 1060

Renaissance painting
    5:1222

Roman Catholicism **2**:364,
    513–514, **5**:1191, 1200

sacking of Rome **1**:38,
    5:1232–1233

ship musicians **2**:*379*

Trent, Council of **5**:1352,
    1353, 1357, 1359

Charles, duke of Nevers
    5:1336

Charles I, king of Spain *see*
    Charles V, Holy Roman
    emperor

Charles II, king of Spain
    2:512

Charles VIII, king of Sweden
    5:1304

Charles IX, king of Sweden
    5:1307, 1308

Charles X Gustav, king of
    Sweden **1**:228, 229,
    4:1114, **5**:1311

Charles of Blois **3**:597

Charles of Bourbon **1**:243,
    2:518

Charles of Luxembourg *see* Charles V, Holy Roman emperor

Charles the Bold, duke of Burgundy **2:**509, **4:**944, **5:***1313,* 1314, 1425

Charles the Great *see* Charlemagne

Charles the Rash, duke of Burgundy **1:**162, 163, 164

Charlier, Jean *see* Gerson, Jean de

Charron, Pierre **4:**1071

Chastillon, Odet de **5:**1178

Chaucer, Geoffrey **1:212–220, 3:**801, **4:**931, *1081, 1083,* **5:**1289, 1290

  Boccaccio **1:**112, 113

  religious orders **5:**1202

  vernacular language **3:**694

Chaucer, Philippa **1:**213, 214

Chávez Alvarado, Diego de **1:**280

Cheng Ho **2:**373, **5:**1342, *1343*

Cherbury, Lord *see* Herbert, Edward

Cherubin de Centelles, Juan **1:**123

Chieracati, Girolamo **4:**1004

Chigi, Agostino **1:**39, 40, 41, **5:**1186

Childe, Maccabaeus **5:**1287

Chrétien de Troyes **1:**222, **4:***1101*

Christian I, prince of Anhalt-Bernburg **3:**838

Christian I, king of Denmark and Norway **5:**1304

Christian II, king of Denmark, Norway, and Sweden **5:**1305

Christian IV, king of Denmark and Norway **3:**665, **5:**1246, 1251, 1308, 1335, 1338

Christian of Brunswick (Mad Christian) **5:**1335

Christina, queen of Sweden **1:227–231, 4:**1068

  abdication of **1:**229–230, **5:**1311

Descartes **1:**228, **2:**301

Oxenstierna regency **5:**1307, 1310

Christine de Pisan **5:**1418

Christopher III, king of Denmark, Norway, and Sweden **2:**506, **5:**1304

Christopher, duke of Württemberg **1:**75

Christus, Petrus **4:**982

Chrysoloras, Manuel **1:**261, **3:**584, 684–685, **5:**1220

  overview of **1:**264

Chu Ti, emperor of China **5:**1342

Cicero **4:**1102

  classical languages **3:**682, 683, 684, *685,* 686, 687

  humanism **2:**336, **3:**583, 584, 588, 589, **5:**1219

  Petrarch **4:**1053, 1054

Cid, El **3:**695, 728

Cignani, Carlo **5:***1209*

Cimabue **2:**484, *485,* 488

Cino dei Sighibuldi (Cino da Pistoia) **1:**111, **5:***1366*

Ciompi, the **2:**415, **3:**849, 853

Civedati, Marco **5:***1403*

Clare of Assisi **5:**1201

Claude, duchess of Lorraine **1:**198

Claudian **1:**112

Clavius, Christoph **1:**175

Clement V, Pope **4:**905, 1052, 1109, **5:**1227

Clement VI, Pope **1:**174, **3:**757, **5:**1367

Clement VII (antipope) **4:**1010, **5:**1427

Clement VII, Pope **1:241–246, 2:**426, **4:**930, 1014–1015, 1023, **5:**1196

  Catherine de Médici **1:**197

  Charles V **1:***208,* 209, 210, 241, 242, 243, 244

  Hapsburgs **2:**513

  Henry VIII **1:**234, 242, 244, **2:**523

  Italian wars **3:**647, 648, 649

  Judaism **3:**677

  Machiavelli **3:**773

Medicis **2:**418, 420, 421, 426, **3:**850, 851, *854,* 855

Michelangelo **2:**426

Paul V **4:**1037

Rome **5:**1232, 1233

Urbino **5:**1380

Venice **5:**1400

Clement VIII, Pope **2:**370, 517, 519

Clement IX, Pope **1:**330

Clement XI, Pope **5:**1209

Clement XIV, Pope **5:**1209

Clement of Alexandria **4:**1098

Cleves, duke of **4:**1088

Clifford, Anne, countess of Dorset **5:**1290, 1427

Clinton family **2:**542

Clouet, François **1:***198,* **5:***1262*

Clouet, Jean **3:***590,* **4:**990, **5:***1298*

Clough, Richard **5:**1164

Cock, Hieronymus **1:**145, 146

Cocq, Frans Banning **5:**1213

Coeck van Aelst, Mayken **1:**144, 146

Coeck van Aelst, Pieter **1:**144, 145, 146

Coke, Edward **1:**79

Colantonio, Niccolò **2:**391

Coles, Isaac **4:**1007

Colet, John **2:**337, **4:**879, 1103, **5:**1373

Coligny, Gaspard II de **1:**199, 200, **2:**452–453, 454, 455

Colombo, Domenico **1:**247

Colonna, Ascanio **5:**1238

Colonna, Caterina **5:**1379

Colonna, Giovanni **4:**1051, 1052, 1053, **5:**1228

Colonna, Oddo *see* Martin V

Colonna, Prospero **3:**651

Colonna, Sciarra **5:**1227

Colonna, Vittoria **4:**877

Columbus, Bartolomé **1:**255

Columbus, Christopher **1:**46, **247–255, 3:**693, 782, 788, 829, **4:**1138, 1142, **5:**1345

  armed trade **3:**775

  disease **2:**306, 308

exploration **1:**247–251, **2:**373, 374, 381–382, **4:**914, 915, **5:**1220

  Ferdinand and Isabella **2:**393, 394, 399

  missions **4:**888, 889, 891, 895

  writings of **1:**253

Columbus, Diego **1:**248

Columbus, Ferdinand **1:**248

Columella, Lucius **1:**277

Commynes, Philippe de **1:**162, 163, 164

Comyn, John **4:**905

Condé, prince of *see* Louis, prince of Condé

Condulmaro, Gabriele *see* Eugenius IV, Pope

Conrad of Mazowsze **4:**1107

Constance of Castile **1:**214

Constantine I (the Great), emperor of Rome **1:**38, 99, **2:**366, 512, **3:**594, 686, **4:**1026, **5:**1201

  Byzantium **1:**165, 166, 172

  Constantinople **1:**256, 257

Constantine IX, Byzantine emperor **1:**258

Constantine X, Byzantine emperor **1:**258

Constantine XI, Byzantine emperor **1:**263

Constantius, emperor of Rome **1:**172

Contarini, Gasparo **5:**1400

Cook, James **2:**384, **5:**1258–1259

Cooke, Anne **1:**79

Cooke, Anthony **1:**79, **5:**1419, 1427

Cooke sisters **5:**1418, 1419, 1422, 1427

Cooper, Samuel **2:***351,* **3:***663*

Cop, Nicholas **4:**1032

Copernicus, Nicolaus **1:***57, 60,* **265–272, 2:**539, **3:**699, 783, 827, 829, 831, 832, **4:**1036, 1069, **5:**1221, 1251

  circular planetary path **1:**31, 60, 265, 270

Descartes **2:**296
Galileo **2:**463, 465, 466, 467, **5:**1226
Polish Renaissance **4:**1109
universe model **1:**265, **2:**296, **4:**1109, **5:**1226, 1250, 1252–1253
Cordier, Mathurin **1:**179
Cordovero, Moses **3:**680
Corelli, Arcangelo **1:**230
Cork, earl of *see* Boyle, Richard
Corkine, William **3:**825
Cornaro, Luigi Alvise **4:**1001
Corneille, Pierre **3:**729, 730, 731, **4:**898
Cornyshe, William **4:**948
Coronado, Francisco Vásquez de **2:**382
Correa, Juan **5:***1199*
Cortés, Hernán **4:**890, **5:**1285, 1345
disease **2:**307
exploration **2:**374, 382
Cortona, Pietro da **1:***32*
Corvus, Hans **5:***1373*
Cossa, Baldassare *see* John XXIII
Courbet, Gustave **5:**1391
Courtois, Jacques (Le Bourguignon) **5:***1337*
Coverdale, Miles **1:***106,* 107
Covilhã, Pero da **2:**381
Cranach, Lucas (the Elder) **1:***95,* **2:***324,* **3:***704, 705, 760, 762,* **4:**1064, *1066, 1115,* **5:***1163,* 1171, *1188*
Cranmer, Thomas
bibles **1:**106–107
Book of Common Prayer **5:**1267
Church of England **1:**235, 236, 237, 238, 240
English vernacular **3:***699*
established church **2:**338
Henry VIII **2:**524, 526, 527, 528, **3:**608, **5:**1197
overview of **1:**237
Craponne, Adam de **1:**280
Credi, Lorenzo di **3:**706, 708, **5:***1428*

Cremonini, Cesare **1:**57
Crescas, Hasdai **3:**679
Crivelli, Taddeo **3:***686*
Crocyn, William **5:**1373
Cromwell, Oliver **2:**544, **4:***884,* 887, **5:***1303,* 1427
English civil wars **1:**239, **2:**351–352, *353,* 354
Cromwell, Richard **2:**351
Cromwell, Thomas
biblical translation **1:**106, **2:**339
Henry VIII **1:**235, **2:**338, 522, 524, 525, 526, 527
Crosby, Alfred **1:**255, **2:**306
Cudworth, Ralph **4:**1070
Culverwell, Nathaniel **4:**1070
Cuylenborch, Abraham van **4:***1037*
Cydones, Demitrius **1:**261

D
Dakin, Margaret (later Hoby) **3:**749, **5:**1416, 1422
Daniel, grand prince of Muscovy **4:**933
Dante Alighieri **1:**53, **2:**484, **4:***963,* 1050, **5:**1249
Boccaccio **1:**111, 112, 113, 114, 115
as Chaucer influence **1:**216, 217–218, 219
overview of **1:**217
vernacular language **1:**217, **3:**694
Danti, Ignatio **1:***175*
Darby, Abraham **3:**811
Darnley, Henry (Lord Darnley) **2:**330, **5:**1298
Darwin, Charles **1:**110
Dati, Carlo **4:**883
Dati, Gregorio **5:**1420
Daumier, Honoré **1:***206*
David II, king of Scotland **3:**597
David, Jacques-Louis **4:***1093*
Davis, Natalie **2:**459
Dee, John **2:**384, **4:**1065
astrology **1:**72, **3:**800, 801
calendar **1:**176, 177
overview of **3:**800

Defoe, Daniel **4:**1108
Dekker, Thomas **1:**93, **3:**733, 748, **5:**1326, 1327, 1329
Delaroche, Hippolyte **4:***1074*
Delhi Sultanate **3:**613, 615, 629
Del Lama, Guaspare di Zenobio **1:**138
Della Robbia, Andrea **1:***151*
Della Robbia, Luca **1:***154,* **3:***682*
Della Rovere, Federico Ubaldo **5:**1381
Della Rovere, Felice **5:**1420
Della Rovere, Francesco Maria I **3:**701, **5:**1379, 1380–1381, 1382, 1383
Della Rovere, Francesco Maria II **5:**1381, 1383
Della Rovere, Giovanni **5:**1379, 1380
Della Rovere, Giuliano *see* Julius II, Pope
Della Rovere, Guidobaldo II **5:**1380, 1381, 1382–1383
Della Rovere, Livia **5:**1381
Della Rovere, Vittoria **5:**1380, 1381
Della Roveres, the **5:**1380–1381, 1420
Della Torres, the **3:**741, **5:**1403
Deloney, Thomas **3:**738
Delumeau, Jean **5:**1160
Dering, Edward **5:**1419, 1424
Descartes, René **1:**60, **2:294–301,** 544, **3:**783, **5:**1206, 1251
Christina **1:**228, 229
dualism **2:**300
mathematics **2:**294, 295, 296, 301, **3:**828, 830, 833
philosophy **4:**1069–1070, 1071, 1072
Spinoza **5:**1291–1292, 1293, 1294
Deschamps, Eustache **1:**215
de Vere, Edward *see* Vere, Edward de
Devereaux, Walter **5:**1416

Devereux, Robert, earl of Essex **1:**79, 93, **2:**332–333, **5:**1290, 1416
Dias, Bartolomeu **2:**374, 381, **4:**1138, 1142, **5:**1341
Diderot, Denis **2:**466
Diefendorf, Barbara **2:**459
Diego, Juan **4:**890
Diodati, Charles **4:**879, 880, 882, 883
Diodati, Giovanni **4:**882
Dionysius the Areopagite **4:**1102, 1103
Diotima **4:**1092, 1095
Dmitry, prince of Russia **4:**937, 938–939
Dmitry Donskoi **4:**934
Dolet, Étienne **5:**1177
Dominic, Saint **2:***398,* **5:**1201
Dominique, Jean **3:**659
Donatello **1:**35, 36, *152,* **2:***424,* 428, **3:**856, **4:***871, 874,* 984, 985, **5:***1395*
Donatus **3:***682*
Don John *see* John of Austria
Donne, John **3:**726, **5:**1166
Doré, Gustave **1:***205*
Doria, Andrea **3:**650
Dorigatti, Niccolò **1:***186,* **4:***1016*
Dowland, John **4:***957,* 959
Drake, Francis
armada, Spanish **1:**62, 63, 64
Elizabeth I **2:**331
exploration **2:**374, 382, 383, 385, **3:**791
London **3:**751
privateering **5:**1347
Drayton, Michael **3:**755, 824, **5:**1329
Drost, Willem **5:**1217
Drury, William **5:**1287
Dryden, John **4:**887
Dubois, François **1:***200, 201,* **4:***1033*
Duccio di Buoninsegna **2:**489, 492
Dudley, Robert, earl of Leicester **2:**329, 331, **5:**1287

Dufay, Guillaume **4:**943, 944–946

Dumas, Alexandre **1:**126

Dumonstier, Pierre **2:***469,* 471

Dunn, Alastair **4:**1047

Duns Scotus, John **4:**1075

Dunstable, John **4:**944

Duran, Diego **5:***1285*

Dürer, Albrecht **2:311–316,** 550, *551,* **3:**828, **4:**983, 993, **5:***1220,* 1221

   printing **5:**1171

Dyck, Anthony van *see* Van Dyck, Anthony

Dyer, Edward **3:**725, **5:**1287

E

Eanes, Gil **2:**380, **4:**1140

Edward I, king of England **4:**905, **5:***1301*

Edward II, king of England **3:**825, **4:**903

Edward III, king of England **1:**16, 89, **2:**433, 497, 567, **4:**1047, **5:***1412*

   Chaucer **1:**213, 214, 216

   chivalry **1:**161, 223, 224

   feudalism **2:**406, 410

   Florentine debt default **2:**416

   Hundred Years War **3:**595, 596, 597, 598, 603

   nationalism **4:**965, 968

Edward IV, king of England **1:**162–163, **2:**408

Edward VI, king of England **1:**71, 79, **2:**340, 514, **4:**954

   bibles **1:**107

   Calvinism **1:**188, 189

   Church of England **1:**236, 237, 240, **2:**326, 368

   Elizabeth I **2:**326, 327

   Henry VIII **2:**522, 527, 528

   humanism **5:**1419

   iconoclasm **3:**608

   mercenaries **5:**1411

   papacy **4:**1015

   printing **5:**1175

   Reformation **5:**1197, 1267, 1325

   Scotland **5:**1262

Edward, the Black Prince (England) **3:**597, 598

Edward, duke of York **1:**18

Edward of Woodstock *see* Edward, the Black Prince

Eertvelt, Andries van **5:***1351*

Egerton, John, earl of Bridgewater **4:**880–881

Egerton, Thomas **3:**749

Elcano, Juan Sebastián de **2:**374, **3:**793–794

Eleanor (daughter of Joan I) **1:**208, **5:**1281

Eleanor of Aquitaine **3:**596

El Greco *see* Greco, El

Eliot, John **4:**892

Elizabeth, queen consort of Bohemia **1:**117

Elizabeth I, queen of England **1:***189,* **2:326–333,** **4:**894, 906, 909, **5:**1419

   armada, Spanish **1:**62, **2:**331

   astrological prediction **1:**71–72, **3:**800

   Bacon **1:**79–80

   bearbaiting **1:**93

   bibles **1:**105, 107

   calendar **1:**176

   Catherine de Médicis **1:**198, 201

   Christina compared with **1:**227, 229

   Church of England **1:**235, 236–239, 240, **2:**326, 328–329, 331, 341, 343, 368–369, **4:**1015, **5:**1198

   companies **2:**499, 501

   courtiers **5:**1427

   established church **2:**368–369, 370, 371, 372

   excommunication of **1:**238, **2:**330

   exploration **2:**382

   Henry VIII **2:**524, 527, 528

   humanist education **5:**1418

   iconoclasm **3:**608–609

   literature **2:**335, **3:**724, 725, 732, 733, 735, 737

   London **3:**748, 750

   Marlowe **3:**823

nationalism **4:**963, 966

   Philip II **4:**1059, 1060

   printing **5:**1175

   Puritans **1:**188

   Reformation **1:**176, 187, 188, *189,* 237, **2:**340–341, 342, 343, 345, 365, **5:**1198, 1325, 1424, 1426

   religious music **4:**953

   Renaissance **5:**1221, 1225

   Scotland **5:**1262, 1263

   Shakespeare **5:**1269, 1271, 1272

   Spain **5:**1283

   Spenser **5:**1285, 1287, 1289, 1290

   Stuarts **5:**1297, 1298, 1300, 1301, 1426

   theater **2:**335, **5:**1322, 1324–1325, 1328

   tournaments **1:**225

   universities **5:**1371

Elizabeth, princess of England (wife of Frederick V of the Palatinate) **5:**1336

Elizabeth, queen consort of Spain *see* Elizabeth of Valois

Elizabeth of Spain **2:**454, 466

Elizabeth of Valois **1:**198, 199, 202, 203, **4:**1059

Elizabeth of York **2:**521

Elsheimer, Adam **5:**1211

Elyot, Thomas **4:**1122

Empoli, Jacopo Chimenti **1:***197*

Encina, Juan del **4:**956

Enden, Franciscus van den **5:**1291

Enders, Ernst Ludwig **5:***1192*

Engelbrekt (Swedish rebel) **5:**1304

Enrique IV *see* Henry IV, king of Castile

Enriquez, Joan **5:**1278

Enriquez de Arana, Beatriz **1:**248

Erasmus, Desiderius **2:356–363,** 482, **3:**762

   Aristotle **1:**58, 59

   biblical interpretation **2:**538

   biblical translation **1:**58, 104, 109, 181, **2:**358, **3:**585, 591, 684, 688–689, 697, **5:**1357

   Colet curriculum **4:**879

   Dürer **2:**316

   on foolery **5:**1221, 1319

   French Protestant Reformation **2:**439

   humanism **2:**337, 339, 356, 423, **3:**585, 589, 590, 591, 592, 593, **5:**1282, 1283, 1370, 1371, 1373

   iconoclasm **3:**606

   Latin language **3:**684

   Leo X **3:**703

   Luther vs. **2:**339, 552, **3:**767

   on Margaret of Navarre **3:**735

   on marriage **2:**565

   More **4:**925

   northern Renaissance **2:**552

   papacy **4:**1023

   pilgrimage **4:**1079

   printed works **3:**688

   as Rabelais influence **5:**1176

   Roman Catholic Church **1:**180, **5:**1189

   Rome **5:**1232

   women's education **2:**322

Erastus, Thomas **2:**367

Erik VII, king of Denmark **5:**1304

Erik XIV, king of Sweden **5:***1306,* 1307, 1308

Erik of Pomerania **2:**506, **4:**911

Erpingham, Thomas **1:**18

Erri, Bartolomeo degli **3:***676*

Espinel, Vicente **1:**205

Essex, earl of *see* Devereux, Robert

Este, Alfonso d' **1:**124–125, 126

Este, Ercole d' 124, **1:**125

Este, Isabella d' **1:**125, **3:**745, **5:***1383*

Este, Lucrezia d' **5:**1381

Estes, the **2:**413

Estienne, Henri **3:**585

Estienne, Henri II **3:**592

Estoile, Pierre de l' **1:**179
Euclid **1:***143,* **3:***827,* **5:**1294
Eudocia, Saint **3:***605*
Eudocia, Byzantine empress
   1:257
Eugene of Savoy **2:**512–513
Eugenius IV, Pope **3:**672,
   4:946, 1086, *1087,* **5:**1229,
   1379
   Florence, Council of **1:**260,
     2:427, 428, 429, 430
Euripides **3:**688, 729
Eustachi, Bartolomeo **3:**840,
   846
Evelyn, John **3:**667
Eyck, Bartélemy d' **2:**391
Eyck, Hubert van **2:**386,
   4:983
Eyck, Jan van **1:**129, 163,
   2:316, **386–392, 4:**981,
   982, 983
Eyck, Lambert van **2:**386, 391
Eyck, Margaret van (Jan's wife)
   2:391
Eyck, Marguerite van (Jan's
   sister) **2:**386
Ezpelcta, Gaspar de **1:**205

F

Fairfax, Thomas **2:**352
Falconetto, Giovanni Maria
   4:1001
Faleiro, Rui **3:**788, 789
Falloppio, Gabriele **3:**840, 846
False Dmitrys **4:**938–939
Farel, Guillaume **1:**179,
   5:1315
Farnese, Alessandro *see* Paul III
Farnese, Ottavio **1:**210, **3:**644,
   648, **5:***1362*
Farnese, Pierluigi **3:**644, 648
Farnese, Ranuccio II **1:**195,
   2:470
Farneses, the **1:**40, *41,* **3:***648,*
   744, **5:**1353
Fawkes, Guy **1:***238,* **2:**342,
   343, **5:**1301
Fazio, Bartolommeo **2:**389
Fedele, Cassandra **5:**1417
Federigo II, duke of Mantua
   4:991

Federigo II, king of Naples *see*
   Ferdinand II (Ferrandino),
   king of Naples
Federigo II, duke of Urbino
   5:1181
Felix V (antipope) **2:**429,
   4:1086
Felton, John **2:**343
Felton, Nicholas **4:**880
Feltre, Vittorino da **3:**584,
   5:1220, 1379, 1417
Fenelon, François **2:**372
Fenizi, Ascania **1:**277
Ferdinand II (the Catholic),
   king of Aragon *see*
   Ferdinand and Isabella
Ferdinand, archduke of Austria
   1:209, 211, **3:**624
Ferdinand I, Holy Roman
   emperor **2:***365,* **5:**1281
   Bohemia **1:**120, 121,
     2:510–511
   Hapsburg Empire **2:**555,
     556, 557
   Maximilian I **3:**837, 838,
     839
Ferdinand II, Holy Roman
   emperor **2:**371
   Bohemia **1:**120, 121, 122,
     3:837
   Counter-Reformation **2:**514
   German towns **2:**477–478,
     560
   Thirty Years War **5:**1330,
     1332, 1333, 1336, 1337,
     1339, 1415
Ferdinand III, Holy Roman
   emperor **2:**371, 514,
   5:1330, 1338
Ferdinand I, king of Naples
   1:123, 124, **4:**1088,
   1089–1090
Ferdinand II (Ferrandino),
   king of Naples **3:**643, 644
Ferdinand I, king of Portugal
   4:1137
Ferdinand and Isabella, king
   and queen of Spain
   2:393–400, *411,* 510,
   5:1394, 1425
   Bramante commission **1:**141

Catherine of Aragon **1:***233*
Charles V **1:**207, 209
Christian conversions **3:**613
Columbus's voyages **1:**247,
   248, 250, 253, 254
exploration **4:**914
heirs **1:**207, **5:**1280–1283
heresy **2:**532, 533
holdings **4:**965–966
humanism **5:**1280, 1417
Inquisition **5:**1278
Italian wars **3:**643, 645
Jewish expulsion **3:***670,*
   678–679
knight in livery **2:***411*
missions **4:**889
monarchy **4:**907
Renaissance **5:**1220, 1225
Rome **5:**1231
Spain **5:**1277–1279, 1285
theater **5:**1322
Fermat, Pierre de **3:**833–834
Fernández de Avellaneda,
   Alonso **1:**206
Fernel, Jean **1:**197
Ferrandino *see* Ferdinand II
   (Ferrandino), king of
   Naples
Ferrari, Benedetto **4:**917
Ferrari, Defendente **1:**182
Ferrari, Ettore **4:***1019*
Ficino, Marsilio **2:**538, **3:**799,
   4:*1075*
   Florence **2:**422, 423, 424
   humanism **3:**584, 586, *587,*
     588
   Medicis **3:**852, 855, 856
   philosophy **4:**1063, 1065,
     1068
   Pico della Mirandola **4:**1073,
     1074, 1075, 1076, 1103
   Platonism **1:**57,
     4:1100–1103
Fieschi, Catherine **5:**1420
Figueroa, Francisco de **1:**204
Figueroa, Lope de **1:**203
Filipepi, Alessandro di
   Moriano *see* Botticelli,
   Sandro
Filmer, Robert **3:**803
Fisher, John **1:**235, **2:**340, 525

Fitzjames, bishop of London
   1:232
Fitzroy, Henry, duke of
   Richmond **3:**723
Fletcher, John **3:**733, **5:**1325
Flicke, Gerlach **3:**699
Flores, Isabel de *see* Rose of
   Lima
Foix, Gaston de **3:**645
Fontana, Domenico **1:**38, 44,
   47
Fontana, Lavinia **4:***1024*
Fontanarossa, Susanna **1:**247
Foppa, Vincenzo **3:**685
Ford, John **5:**1327
Forster, George **4:**947
Foscari, Francesco **5:***1396*
Foscarini, Paolo Antonio
   5:1253
Four Evangelists **1:***152, 154,*
   2:316
Fourment, Helena **5:**1242
Foxe, John **1:***187, 232,*
   5:1325
Foxe, Richard **5:**1373
Fracastoro, Girolamo **2:**310,
   3:840
Franca de Rojas, Ana **1:**204
Francavilla, duchess of **3:**714
Francesca, Piero della *see* Piero
   della Francesca
Francis, duke of Anjou **1:**198,
   2:327, 329
Francis II, duke of Brittany
   2:406
Francis I, king of France
   2:437, **445–450,** 522, 555,
   3:590, 735, 742, **4:**990,
   1031, 1064, **5:**1264
   Calvin **1:**188
   Catherine de Médicis **1:**197,
     198
   Charles V **1:**208, 209, 210,
     211, 222, 242, 243
   chivalry **1:**221
   Islam **3:**618
   Italian wars **3:**643, 645,
     646–647, 650
   Leonardo da Vinci **3:**707,
     714
   Rabelais **5:**1176, 1178

Francis II, king of France 2:440, 452, **3:**857, **5:**1262, 1266
Catherine de Médicis 1:197–198
Stuarts 1:198, **5:**1297, 1298
Francis of Assisi **5:**1162, 1201, 1206
Francis of Lorraine 1:198
Francis of Sales 1:188
Francis Xavier *see* Xavier, Francis
François, Jean-Charles **4:***1067,* **5:**1295
François, Simon **5:***1208*
Frangipanes, the 1:39
Franklin, Benjamin **4:**887
Fray, Agnes 2:312
Frederick I (Barbarossa), Holy Roman emperor 2:505, 509, **3:**740
Frederick II, Holy Roman emperor **3:**743
Frederick III, Holy Roman emperor 2:508, 509, **3:**673, **4:**1086, 1088
Burgundy 1:161, 162
Frederick III, elector of the Palatinate 1:76, 77, 2:453
Frederick IV, elector of the Palatinate 2:508, **3:**836, 837, 838
Frederick V, elector of the Palatinate **5:**1301, 1302, 1334, 1335, 1336
Bohemia 1:122, **3:**837, 838
Frederick II (the Great), king of Prussia **3:**773
Frederick III (the Wise), elector of Saxony 2:370, 553, **3:**705, **4:**1013, **5:**1190, 1191
Frederick, duke of Württemberg **3:**753
Frederick William (the Great), elector of Brandenburg **5:**1332
Frescobaldi, Girolamo **4:**960
Frick, Henry Clay **5:**1217
Frizer, Ingram **3:**822, 825
Frobisher, Martin 1:63

Froger, François **5:***1349*
Froissart, Jean 1:*16,* 215, 216, 224, **4:***1045,* **5:***1405*
Fuchs, Leonhard 1:*29*
Fugger, Anton 2:477
Fugger, Hans 2:477
Fugger, Jacob (the Rich) 2:477
Fugger, Jacob II 2:*478*
Fugger, Raimond 2:477
Fuggers, the 2:476, 477, 478, **5:**1344
Fust, Johann **3:**781, **5:**1169
Fyodor I, emperor of Russia **3:**656, **4:**937, 938

G

Gabriel, archangel **3:**611, 657
Gabrieli, Andrea **4:**952
Gabrieli, Giovanni **4:**952, **5:**1244
Gadio, Bartolomeo **5:***1403*
Gailde, Jean **5:***1160*
Gainsborough, Thomas **5:**1243
Galen **3:**840, 844–845, 846, **5:**1177
Galilei, Galileo 1:262, **2:460–468,** 539, 543, **3:**828, **4:**882, 917, 961
Aristotelianism 1:57, 60, 61
Copernicus 1:*272,* **4:**1109
Descartes 2:296, 297
disease 2:309
heresy trial 2:296, 297, **3:**783, 784, **5:**1226, 1234–1235, 1251, 1254, 1256, 1258
Inquisition **4:**1036
inventions 1:271, 2:309, **3:**775, 783, **5:**1252
mathematics **3:**831, 833
philosophy **4:**1068–1069
rehabilitation chronology 2:466
vernaculars 2:465, **3:**690, **5:**1254
water dynamics 1:277
Galilei, Vincenzo (father of Galileo) 2:460, 462, **4:**961
Galilei, Vincenzo (son of Galileo) **4:**882
Galluzzi, Tarquinio 1:59

Gama, Vasco da 2:374, 381, **3:**782, **4:**1139, 1142, 1144, **5:**1342, *1345*
Gamba, Marina 2:462–463, 468
Garcia Infanzon, Juan **5:***1323*
Gardiner, Stephen 1:236, **3:**608
Gargiulo, Domenico 2:*370,* 474
Garnier, Robert **3:**730
Garovo, Leone 1:44
Gascoigne, George **3:**738
Gaston, duke of Orléans **4:**899
Gattinara, Mercurino da 1:209, 2:555
Gaulli, Giovanni 1:100
Gavari, Domenico **5:**1182
Gaveston, Piers **3:**825
Geiler von Kayserberg, Johann **5:**1159
Gemistus Plethon, George 1:261, **4:**1063, 1099, 1100
Genghis Khan **3:**617, *692*
Gennadius II Scholarios 1:170, 261
Gent, Justus van 2:*431*
Gentileschi, Artemisia **2:469–474**
Gentileschi, Orazio 2:469, 474
Geoffroy d'Estissac **5:**1177
George, Saint 1:224
George Dósza **4:**1042
George of Podebrady 1:120, 121
George of Trebizond 1:261
George William, prince of Brandenburg **5:**1337
Gerardino, Antonio and Alessandro **5:**1281
Gerard of Cremona **3:**728
Gerónimo *see* John of Austria
Gerson, Jean de (Jean Charlier) 2:367
Gessler (Austrian baliff) **5:**1312
Gesualdo, Carlo **4:**955
Ghiberti, Lorenzo 1:34, 2:428, **3:**641, **4:**981, 983
Brunelleschi 1:149, 150, 151

Ghirlandaio, Domenico 1:169, *247,* **4:**870, 871, 985, **5:**1230
Ghirlandaio, Ridolfo del **5:**1185
Giacomo da Vignola *see* Vignola, Giacomo da
Giacondo, Fra 1:33
Gianuzzi, Giulio *see* Romano, Giulio
Gibbs, James 1:140
Gilbert, Humphrey 2:383
Giocando, Francesco del **3:**714
Giocondo, Fra 1:38
Giorgio, Francesco di 1:34, **5:***1379*
Giorgione **4:**988, 989, **5:**1389, 1399
Giotto di Bondone 1:145, *156,* **2:484–492,** **4:**980, 981
Giovanni, Agostino di **5:***1366*
Giovanni, Benvenuto di **5:***1411*
Giovanni, Bertoldo di **4:**870
Giovanni di Bicci 2:417
Giovio, Paolo **4:**875
Giraba, Jerónimo 1:280
Girard, Albert **3:**830
Giunta, Tommaso 1:58
Giustiniani, Vincenzo 1:194
Glamorgan, earl of 2:352
Glendower, Owen 1:17
Glinskaya, Yelena **3:**652, 653, **4:**933
Gloucester, duke of *see* Humphrey, duke of Gloucester
Godunov, Boris **4:**937, 938–939
Goes, Hugo van der **4:**982
Gogh, Vincent van **4:**996
Gombert, Nicholas **4:**921, 949
Gonçalves, Nuño **4:***1138,* 1144
Gonzaga, Cecilia **5:***1416,* 1417
Gonzaga, Elisabetta **5:**1383
Gonzaga, Federico **3:**744, 745

Gonzaga, Gianfrancesco
3:745, **5:***1416*
Gonzaga, Ludovico **3:**745
Gonzaga, Ludovico II **3:**745
Gonzaga, Vincenzo I **3:**745,
4:917, 919, 921, **5:**1238
Gonzaga, Vincenzo II **3:**745
Gonzaga de Nevers, Carlo
3:745
Gonzagas, the **1:***224,* **3:**642,
744, 745
Goodman, Christopher
5:1267
Googe, Barnaby **5:**1288
Gossaert, Jan (Mabuse) **1:**145
Gosson, Stephen **3:**725
Goudimel, Claude **4:**954
Gowrie, earl of **5:**1262
Goya, Francisco de **4:***1123,*
5:*1391*
Gozzolo, Benozzo **1:***262*
Gracián, Juan **1:**204
Gramani, Dominico **2:**357
Granacci, Francesco **2:***419*
Grandi, Alessandro **5:**1246
Granen, Blasco de **3:***695*
Greco, El **1:**131, **4:**957, *1058,*
1060, **5:**1284
Greene, Robert **3:**732, 755,
823, 824, **5:**1325
Greenhill, John **5:***1273*
Gregory I (the Great), Pope
1:258
Gregory VII, Pope **2:**366, 529
Gregory IX, Pope **2:***532*
Gregory X, Pope **3:**673,
4:1010
Gregory XI, Pope **5:**1227
Gregory XII, Pope **1:**264,
2:318
Gregory XIII, Pope
1:175–176, **4:**1024
Gregory XV, Pope **1:**33,
5:1205
Gregory, James **3:**828, 833
Gregory of Nyssa **4:**1024
Gregory of Valencia **4:**906
Gresham, Thomas **3:**750, 762
Grevenbroek, Jan van **1:***89*
Greville, Fulke **3:**725
Grevin, Jacques **3:**729, 730

Grey, Arthur (Lord Grey of
Wilton) **5:**1287
Grey, Lady Jane **1:**236, **2:**326
Grey, William, bishop of Ely
2:336
Grimald, Nicholas **3:**723
Grindal, Edmund **2:**341
Grindal, William **2:**327
Grosseteste, Robert **2:**529
Grünewald, Matthias **2:**316
Guacanagari (Taino chief)
1:250–251
Guangzhou **4:**1142
Guarini, Guarino **5:**1229
Guarino da Verona *see*
Veronese
Guercino, Il **4:***993*
Guericke, Otto von **3:**775
Guerrero, Francisco **4:**949
Guevara, Antonio de **1:**204
Guicciardini, Francesco **1:**242,
244, 245, **3:**856
Guienne, duke of **5:**1277
Guillaume de Lorris **1:**214,
5:1202
Guise, Charles de **1:**198
Guise, Claude de **1:**198
Guise, Henry de **1:**201, **2:**517
Guise, Marie de *see* Mary of
Guise
Guise family **2:**440, 442
    Catherine de Médicis **1:**198,
        199, 201
    French civil wars **2:**452, 453,
        454, 455
    Stuarts **5:**1264, 1265, 1266,
        1297, 1298, 1426
Guntram the Rich **2:**507
Gustav I Vasa, king of Sweden
4:1112, **5:***1304,*
1305–1306, 1307,
1308–1309
Gustavus II Adolphus, king of
Sweden **2:**371, **3:**839,
5:1307, 1308–1309, 1339
    Christina **1:**227, 228
    military tactics **5:**1309
    Thirty Years War **5:**1332,
        1333, 1336–1337, 1415
Gutenberg, Johannes **1:**102,
103, **3:***688,* 697, 775,

780–781, 783, 805,
5:1168, 1169, 1193, 1218,
1220
Guzmán, Gaspar de
5:1384–1385
Gyllenstierna, Christina
5:1305

H
Haddon, Walter **5:**1419
Hagar **4:**1085
Hagenberg, Franz **1:***183, 184*
Hakluyt, Richard **2:**375, 384,
385
Hales, Robert **4:**1046
Hall, Joseph **3:**609
Hals, Franz **4:**996, 997, 998
Hameel, Alart du **1:**131
Hamilton, James, earl of Arran
5:1426
Handel, George Frideric
5:1247
Hannibal **4:**1052
Hardouin-Mansart, Jules
4:1007
Hardwick, Elizabeth **3:**753,
5:1420
Hardwick, Henry **5:**1420
Hardwick, Mary **5:**1420
Harmensen, Jacob **1:**190,
2:346
Haro, Luis Méndez de **5:**1284
Harriot, Thomas **3:**825, 830,
831
Harris, Henry **5:***1273*
Harrison, Stephen **3:**665
Hart, James D. **2:**383
Hartmann, Adam Samuel
1:122
Hartog, Dirk **2:**385
Harvey, Anne **5:**1329
Harvey, Gabriel **5:**1286–1287
Harvey, Thomas **5:**1329
Harvey, William **3:**840,
5:1251, 1255
Hasan **3:**620
Hathaway, Anne **5:**1268, 1269
Hatzfeldt, Melchior von
5:1338
Hawkins, John **1:***63,* **2:**378
Hawksmoor, Nicholas **1:**140

Haywood, Thomas **5:**1325
Hegel, Georg Wilhelm
Friedrich **4:**1072
Heinz (the Younger), Joseph
1:*273*
Helena, Saint **5:***1279*
Heller, Henry **2:**459
Helliot, Nicholas **3:**825
Hendrick, Frederick **5:**1213
Henrietta Maria, queen
consort of England **2:**474,
4:894, **5:**1257, 1328
    Jones's architecture
        3:666–667
    Stuarts **5:**1302
Henry, duke of Anjou **2:**327,
329, **4:**1112
Henry X (the Proud), duke of
Bavaria **2:**505
Henry, duke of Burgundy
4:1137
Henry IV, king of Castile
2:393, 394, 395, 396,
5:1277
Henry I, king of England
3:815
Henry II, king of England
1:*218,* **2:**505, **3:**596
Henry IV, king of England
1:17, 261, **5:**1418
    Byzantine Empire **1:**261
    Chaucer **1:**218
    chivalry **1:**221–222
Henry V, king of England
1:*232,* **2:**434–435, **4:**968
    Agincourt **1:**16–20
    Burgundy **1:**159, 160,
        4:1030
    Hundred Years War
        3:599–601, 603, 660
Henry VI, king of England
2:*404,* 408, **3:**601, 602,
4:949
Henry VII, king of England
1:72, **2:**521, 522, **4:**1042
    Cabot voyages **4:**914, 915
    chapel of **1:**30
    More **4:**926–927, 929
    Scotland **4:**916, **5:**1261,
        1297
    Yorkist challenges **1:**233

Henry VIII, king of England **1**:187, **2**:334, 337, 521–528, **3**:655
bibles **1**:106–107
Church of England **1**:178, 232, 235–236, 237
Clement VII **1**:234, 242, 244
court entertainments **4**:948
divorce **1**:232–235, 240, **2**:338, 340
Elizabeth I **2**:326, 327
established church **1**:257, **2**:338, 339, 367, 368, 371, 372, **4**:913, 930–931, **5**:1374
French claim **4**:968
iconoclasm **3**:608
interest-bearing loans **1**:85
literature **3**:723
London **3**:748
monarchy **4**:906, 909
monastery dissolution **5**:1202, 1203
More **4**:927, 929–932, **5**:1371
music **4**:958
nationalism **2**:364
naval power **5**:1412
papacy **1**:240, **4**:1014–1015
printing **5**:1175
Reformation **1**:62, **2**:338–340, 342, 346, 364, 365, **3**:748, **5**:1191, 1196–1198, 1325, 1350
Renaissance **5**:1220
Scotland **5**:1261, 1262, 1265, 1297
succession **5**:1411
tournaments **1**:225
wives **1**:233–234, 240, 242, 244, **4**:1014–1015, 1123, **5**:1197, 1280, 1297, 1417
Henry II, king of France **1**:245, **2**:*438*, 440, 449, 452, **3**:857, **4**:1059
Catherine de Médicis **1**:197, 198, 201, 242, 245
Charles V **1**:208, 209, 211
Florence **2**:*420*
Paris **4**:1031, 1032

Scotland **5**:1262, 1264, 1265
tournaments **1**:225
Henry III, king of France **2**:442, 452, 456, 457, 458, 516, 517, 519, **3**:857, **4**:1033, 1034
Catherine de Médicis **1**:197, 198, 200, 201
Venice **1**:277
Henry IV, king of France **2**:437, 441, 442–443, **516–520**, **3**:666, **4**:903, **5**:1240
Catherine de Médicis **1**:200, 201
dams and drainage **1**:276
Descartes **2**:296
French civil wars **2**:452, 455, 456, 457, 458, 516–520, 540, **4**:1060
papacy **4**:1039
Paris **4**:1033–1034
Thirty Years War **5**:1333, 1334
Henry IV, Holy Roman emperor **2**:366
Henry VII, Holy Roman emperor **5**:1227
Henry II, king of Navarre **3**:735
Henry III, king of Navarre *see* Henry IV, king of France
Henry, duke of Orléans *see* Henry II, king of France
Henry, king of Portugal **4**:1140
Henry (the Navigator), prince of Portugal **2**:373, 379, 380, **3**:693, 775, **4**:914, 1137–1138, 1139, 1140, 1144, **5**:1345
Henry (the Lion), duke of Saxony **2**:503, 505
Henry, prince of Scotland **5**:1299
Henry I of Lorraine, duke of Guise *see* Guise, Henry de
Henry of Montmorency **2**:455
Henry III of Nassau **1**:131
Henry of Orléans *see* Henry II, king of France

Henry the Lion *see* Henry (the Lion), duke of Saxony
Henslowe, Philip **5**:1323
Hentzner, Paul **3**:749
Hepburn, James, earl of Bothwell **2**:330, **5**:1298
Heraclitus **4**:1097
Herbert, Edward (Lord Cherbury) **4**:1071
Hermes **4**:1065
Hermes Trismegistus **3**:799
Herodotus **3**:688
Herrera, Francisco de (the Elder) **5**:1384
Herrera, Juan de **1**:*46*, 47, **4**:1060
Hertford, earl of *see* Seymour, Edward
Hertz, Solange Strong **5**:1253
Heyden, Jakob van der **5**:*1377*
Heywood, Thomas **3**:733
Hideyoshi Toyotomi **4**:896
Hilliard, Nicholas **5**:*1269*
Hippocrates **3**:840, 844, **5**:1177
Hitler, Adolf **5**:1312
Hobart, John **4**:886
Hobbes, Thomas **1**:51, 59, **2:542–547**, **4**:1066–1067, 1071, 1072
Hoby, Margaret Dakin **3**:749, **5**:1416, 1422
Hoby, Thomas **5**:1419, 1422
Hogarth, William **4**:*1116*
Hogenberg, Franz **1**:*64, 78, 211, 281*, **2**:*371*, **5**:*1165, 1301, 1316, 1350*
Hohenstaufen dynasty **2**:505
Holbein, Ambrosius **2**:*318*
Holbein, Hans (the Younger) **1**:*181, 235*, **2**:*337*, **5**:*1198, 1223, 1371*
Hollar, Wenzel **3**:*749*
Homer **1**:59, 258, 264, **2**:373, **5**:1289
Honthorst, Gerrit van **4**:997
Hood, Thomas **1**:*67*
Hooke, Robert **5**:1258, 1433
Hooker, Richard **2**:367, 369
Hopkins, Matthew **3**:802, **5**:*1425*

Horace **1**:59
Howard, Catherine **2**:522, 527
Howard, Charles (2nd Baron Howard of Effingham) **1**:*62, 63, 66*
Howard, Henry, earl of Surrey **3**:723, 724, 823
Howard, Thomas, duke of Norfolk **2**:330, 331, 527
Howard, Thomas, earl of Arundel **3**:665
Hoyos, López de **1**:202
Hudson, Henry **2**:374, 383, **5**:1342
Hugo, Victor **1**:126
Huizinga, Johann **5**:1160
Hume, David **4**:1068, 1070
Humphrey, duke of Gloucester **2**:336, **3**:601
Huntingdon, earl of **5**:1416
Hurtado de Mendoza, Diego **3**:649
Hus, Jan
Bohemia **1**:118–119
heresy **2**:537
Holy Roman Empire **2**:549, 550, 557
Lutheranism **3**:764, 766
nationalism **4**:969
Reformation **5**:1192
Thirty Years War **5**:1334
universities **5**:1367
Husayn **3**:620
Hutten, Ulrich von **2**:552
Huygens, Christiaan (son) **3**:775
Huygens, Constantijn (father) **5**:1211

I

Ibn Battutah **3**:611, **4**:1084
Ibn Rushd (Averroës) **1**:51, 52–53, 58, **4**:1054, 1064, *1098*, **5**:1367
Ibn Sina **5**:1367
Ibrahim (prophet) *see* Abraham
Ignatius, patriarch of Constantinople **1**:259
Ignatius of Loyola **1**:59, **4**:894, 955, **5**:1205–1206

Jesuits **4**:1015, *1017*
Spiritual Exercises **1**:99,
  5:1199, 1206
Incas **2**:374, 382, **3**:776, 788,
  4:892
Ingegneri, Marc'Antonio
  4:917
Inglis, Esther **5**:1427
Ingram, Lady **2**:342
Innocent III, Pope **1**:260,
  2:531, **5**:1158
Innocent VII, Pope **2**:318
Innocent VIII, Pope **3**:700,
  4:1074, 1075, 1076
Innocent X, Pope **5**:1388,
  1389
Innocent XI, Pope **2**:372
Institoris, Henricus **3**:802
Irene, empress of Byzantium
  3:605
Ireton, Henry **2**:352
Isaac, Heinrich **4**:946, 950,
  951, 957
Isabella I, queen of Castile *see*
  Ferdinand and Isabella
Isabella, Holy Roman empress
  and regent of Spain **1**:209,
  4:1056, 1139, **5**:1281
Isabella, princess of Spain
  5:1237, 1241, 1280, 1426
Isabella of Portugal (wife of
  Charles V) *see* Isabella,
  Holy Roman empress and
  regent of Spain
Isabella of Portugal (wife of
  John II of Castile and
  León) **2**:387, **5**:1277
Isabelle of France (daughter of
  Charles VI) **3**:599
Isabelle of France (daughter of
  Philip IV) **3**:595
Ismail **3**:612, 621, 622
Ivan I, grand prince of
  Moscow **4**:933
Ivan III (the Great), emperor
  of Russia **4**:934, 936, 1109
Ivan IV Vasilyevich (the
  Terrible), emperor of Russia
  3:652–656
  Muscovy **4**:934, 936, 937,
  940

Poland **4**:1109, 1112
Sweden **5**:1306–1307
Ivan Ivanovich **3**:653, 656

J

Jackman, Charles **2**:384
Jacques le Grant **1**:85
Jadwiga, queen of Poland
  4:1104–1105
Jagiello, grand duke of
  Lithuania *see* Wladyslaw II
Jagiellonian dynasty **1**:120,
  4:911, 1105, 1109, 1111,
  1112
Jagiellonka, Anna **4**:1112
James, Saint **4**:1060, *1078,
  1080,* 1082, **5**:1356
James I, king of England
  architecture **1**:47, **3**:663,
  664–665, 666
  astrological prediction **1**:72
  Bacon **1**:80
  bibles **1**:104, 108, 109, **3**:698
  Calvinism **1**:189, **2**:328, 343,
  345, 349
  Church of England **1**:239,
  5:1166, 1329
  cockfighting **1**:96
  divine right **1**:239
  Elizabeth I **2**:330, 332, 333
  Gunpowder Plot **4**:880, 1039
  iconoclasm **3**:609
  as James VI of Scotland
  1:189, **5**:1299–1301
  Marlowe **3**:825
  monarchy **2**:335, 342–343,
  344, 345, 346, 347, **4**:907
  Paul V **4**:1039
  Reformation **2**:342–343
  Scotland **5**:1260, 1262,
  1263, 1264, *1265*
  Shakespeare **3**:732, 737,
  5:1269, 1272
  Spenser **5**:1289
  Stuarts **5**:1296, 1298,
  1299–1301
  theater **3**:755, **5**:1324
  Thirty Years War **5**:1336
  women **5**:1425, 1427
James II, king of England
  5:1302

Church of England nonjurors
  1:262
divine right **1**:239
Glorious Revolution **1**:24,
  2:346, **4**:906
James I, king of Scotland
  5:1296
James III, king of Scotland
  5:1261, 1264, 1296
James IV, king of Scotland
  4:927, **5**:1296–1297
James V, king of Scotland
  1:198, **2**:527, **3**:722,
  5:1262, 1263–1264, 1265,
  1296, 1297, 1299, 1426
James VI, king of Scotland *see*
  James I, king of England
Janequin, Clément **4**:948
Jan Kazimierz *see* John II
  Casimir Vasa
János Zázpolya **2**:511
Janssen, Zacharias **3**:775
Jean de Gerson *see* Gerson,
  Jean de
Jean de Meun **1**:214, **5**:1202
Jean de Venette **4**:1029
Jeanne of France **3**:595
Jean of Luxembourg **1**:215
Jefferson, Thomas **2**:545,
  4:887
Jem (Ottoman) **3**:619
Jeremias II, patriarch of
  Constantinople **1**:262
Jeremias III, patriarch of
  Constantinople **1**:262
Jerome, Saint **1**:104, **3**:*682,*
  688, 689, 696, **4**:1024,
  5:1357
Jerome of Prague **2**:549
Jewel, John **1**:238
Jimenez, Miguel **5**:*1279*
Jiménez de Cisneros, Francisco
  5:1282
Joan I (the Mad), queen of
  Castile **2**:510, 515, **5**:1277,
  1280
  Charles V **1**:207
  overview of **5**:1281
Joan of Arc **1**:160, **2**:435,
  3:602, **657–662**, **4**:968,
  5:1427

Joan of Kent **4**:1046
João II *see* John II (the
  Perfect), king of Portugal
Jodelle, Étienne **3**:720, 729
Jogues, Isaac **4**:893
Johannes (artist) **5**:*1341*
John, Saint **2**:316, 485, 487
John XXII, Pope **4**:905
John XXIII (antipope) **1**:87
John II, king of Aragon **2**:393,
  394, 395, **5**:1278–1279
  peasants' revolt **4**:1042
John, duke of Bedford **3**:601,
  602
John, king of Bohemia *see*
  John of Luxembourg
John, duke of Brittany **2**:406
John VII Palacologus,
  Byzantine emperor **1**:*262*
John VIII Palaeologus,
  Byzantine emperor **1**:169,
  260, 261, **2**:429
John I, king of Castile and
  León **4**:1137, 1145
John II, king of Castile and
  León **2**:393, **5**:1277, 1279
John I, king of Denmark and
  Norway *see* John II, king of
  Sweden
John, king of England **4**:905
John II (the Good), king of
  France **1**:157, **2**:433,
  3:597, **4**:1029, 1042
John II Casimir Vasa, king of
  Poland **1**:230, **2**:453,
  4:1114
John III Sobieski, king of
  Poland **4**:1114
John I, king of Portugal **2**:380
John II (the Perfect), king of
  Portugal **1**:247, **2**:380,
  403, **4**:1138–1139, 1140
John III, king of Portugal
  4:1139, 1140, 1144
John IV, king of Portugal
  4:1145
John, elector of Saxony **2**:370
John II, king of Sweden
  5:1304, 1305
John III, king of Sweden
  5:1307, 1308

John Climacus, Saint **1**:168

John Frederick (the Magnanimous), elector of Saxony **5**:*1188*

John George I, elector of Saxony **5**:1245, 1246, 1247, 1332, 1337

John George II, elector of Saxony **5**:1247

John of Austria (Don John) **3**:626, 716, 717, 718
    Cervantes **1**:202

John of Aviz **4**:1137

John of Bavaria **2**:388

John of Burgundy (doctor) **4**:1125

John of Capistrano **5**:1160, 1163

John of Damascus **1**:168, **3**:604, 761

John of Fordun **5**:1260

John of Gaunt, duke of Lancaster **1**:214, 215, 216, **2**:410, **4**:963, 1043, 1046, 1047

John of Holywood *see* Sacrobosco, Johannes de

John of Luxembourg **1**:117, 118, **3**:598, **4**:943

John of the Cross **5**:1207

John Paul II, Pope **2**:466, **4**:1023, **5**:1226

Johnson, Paul **5**:1179

John the Baptist **2**:485, **5**:1184, 1185

John the Evangelist *see* John, Saint

John the Fearless, duke of Burgundy **1**:158, 159, 160, 162, **3**:600, 601, **4**:1030

Jones, Inigo **1**:47–48, 49, **3**:**663–668**, **4**:1007, **5**:*1431*

Jonghelinck, Nicolaes **1**:146

Jonson, Ben **2**:335, **3**:663, 732, 733, 739, 755, **5**:1325, 1326

Joseph II, emperor of Austria **2**:372

Joseph, patriarch of Constantinople **1**:260

Joseph II, patriarch of Constantinople **2**:429

Josquin des Prez **4**:946–948, 949, 951, 952

Juana the Mad *see* Joan I

Juan de Flandes **5**:*1281*

Juan of Austria *see* John of Austria

Julius II, Pope **1**:*50*, 245, **3**:756, 757, **5**:*1420*
    architecture **1**:36, 38, 141–142
    Florence **2**:420
    Henry VIII **1**:232
    Italian wars **3**:643, 645, 648, 649, 702
    Leo X **3**:700–701, 702
    Medicis **2**:420
    Michelangelo **4**:871, 873–875, 876
    papacy **4**:1012, 1025, 1026
    Raphael **5**:1186, 1187
    Rome **5**:1230, 1231–1232
    Urbino **5**:1380
    Venice **5**:1394

Julius III, Pope **3**:672, **4**:*954*, 955
    Italian wars **3**:648
    Trent, Council of **5**:1353, 1357, 1359

Justinian I, emperor of Rome **1**:*166*, 171, 172, *256*, **4**:1095

Justin Martyr **3**:765

Justus of Ghent **4**:*1055*, **5**:1181

K

Kalff, Willem **4**:*996*, 997

Kalm, Pehr **5**:1259

Kant, Immanuel **4**:1070

Karl Gustav *see* Charles X Gustav, king of Sweden

Karlstadt, Andreas **3**:606, 758, 761, **5**:1193

Keats, John **5**:1290

Kelley, Edward **3**:800, 801

Kempe, Margery **4**:1081, **5**:1427

Kempis, Thomas *see* Thomas à Kempis

Ken, Thomas **1**:262–263

Kepler, Johannes **1**:121, **2**:463, 559, **3**:783, 828, **4**:1109
    astronomy **3**:1250, 1251–1252
    Copernicus **1**:271, 272
    mathematics **3**:828, 831, 832

Kerseboom, Johann **5**:*1256*

Ketelhodt, Christian **5**:1164

Khmelnytsky, Bohdan **4**:1113

Kiefuss, Johann **3**:782

Kieser, Eberhard **3**:*836*

Killigrew, Henry **5**:1419

Killingworth, John **1**:*174*

Klinkicht, Moritz **5**:*1372*

Kneller, Godfrey **5**:1303, *1429*

Knight, Gowin **3**:779

Knox, John **1**:189, **5**:1265–1266, 1423, 1424, 1426
    overview of **5**:1267

Knutsson, Karl *see* Charles VIII, king of Sweden

Koburger, Anthony **5**:*1171*

Kochanowski, Jan **4**:1109

Kölderer, Jörg **5**:*1413*

König, Gustav **5**:*1376*

Koster, Laurens Janszoon **5**:*1168*

Kottannerin, Helene **5**:1418

Kraus, Martin **1**:262

Kurbsky, Andrey Mikhailovich **3**:654

Kyd, Thomas **3**:732, 822, 824, **5**:1286, 1325

L

Ladislaus Postumus **2**:508, 509

Ladislav, king of Bohemia *see* László V, king of Hungary

Lajos, king of Hungary **3**:623

Lalaing, Yolanda de **1**:164

Lampsonius, Dominic **5**:1236

Lancaster, James **2**:379

Lancasters, the **1**:17, **2**:408, **4**:903, 912, **5**:1273
    John of Gaunt **1**:214, 215, 216, **2**:410, **4**:963, 1043, 1046, 1047

Landi family **3**:744

Landriano, Lucrezia **5**:1428

Langland, William **1**:220

Langley, Francis **5**:*1326*

Lanier, Emilia **3**:726, **5**:1423

Lannoy, Charles de **1**:243

Lanzani, Bernardino **5**:*1402*

La Ramée, Pierre de *see* Ramus, Petrus

Larkin, William **4**:*1068*

Lascaris, John **1**:261

Las Casas, Bartolomé de **1**:*253*, **2**:400, **4**:891

Lasso, Orlando di **4**:971

Lastman, Pieter **5**:1210–1211, 1212

László V, king of Hungary **1**:120

La Taille, Jean de **3**:730

Latimer, Hugh **1**:*187*

La Tour, Georges de **4**:995, 997, *1120*

Laud, William **2**:372, **3**:*608*, 609, **4**:881, **5**:1267, 1302
    anti-Calvinism **2**:345, 346, 348, 349
    Church of England **1**:239
    execution of **2**:351
    theater **5**:1325, 1329

Laura (Petrarch's muse) **4**:1050, 1051

Laurana, Luciano da **5**:1181, *1378*, 1382

Lawes, Henry **4**:880

Leeghwater, Jan Adriaanszoon **1**:275

Leeuwenhoek, Antoni van **5**:1258

Lefèvre d'Étaples, Jacques **1**:108

Le Gallois de Grimarest, Jean **4**:897

Leibniz, Gottfried Wilhelm **3**:828, 834, **5**:1295

Leicester, earl of *see* Dudley, Robert

Lely, Peter **5**:1243

Lemercier, Jacques **1**:48

Le Nain, Louis **4**:995

Leo III, Pope **1**:257, 258–259

Leo IV, Pope **5**:1187

Leo IX, Pope **4**:1073

Leo X, Pope **1**:152, 277,
  2:*426*, **3**:*700–705, 763,*
  765, **4**:929, **5**:1194
 architecture **1**:38, 40
 Charles V **2**:513–514
 Clement VII **1**:241, 242,
   245, 246
 Counter-Reformation
   5:1197
 elephant gift **4**:1012, 1037
 Erasmus **2**:357
 France **2**:442, *446*, 447,
   3:701
 Henry VIII **1**:240, **5**:1191,
   1196
 hunting **1**:95
 indulgences **2**:421, **3**:704,
   855
 Italian wars **3**:646, 648, 649
 Luther **1**:242, **3**:701, 703,
   704–705, 757, *763*, 765,
   4:1013, **5**:1192, 1232
 Medicis **2**:418, *420*, 421,
   426, **3**:850, 851, 853,
   855, 857
 Michelangelo **4**:876
 music **4**:946, 949
 Pontine Marshes drainage
   1:277
 Raphael **5**:1186, 1187
 Rome **5**:1232
 Urbino **5**:1380, 1382, 1383
Leo XIII, Pope **4**:932, 1022
Leo III (the Isaurian),
   Byzantium emperor **3**:605
León, Isaac de **3**:679
Leonardo da Vinci **1**:133,
   2:437, 450, 560,
   3:*706–714*, **4**:873
 as Bramante influence **1**:139
 contributions of **5**:1249
 Florence **2**:424, 425
 hydraulic engineering **1**:277,
   278, 279
 machines **3**:775, 782, 783
 Medicis **3**:852, 856
 painting **4**:986, 987, 988,
   999
 as Raphael influence **5**:1183,
   1184, 1185, 1187
 Renaissance **5**:1220, 1224

Leoniceno, Niccolò **3**:840,
   844
Leopold I, Holy Roman
   emperor **2**:513
Leopold III, margrave of
   Styria, Tyrol, and Carinthia
   2:507
Leo the Philosopher,
   archbishop of Thessalonica
   1:258
Lerma, duke of **5**:1284
Lescot, Pierre **1**:45
Lese Gozzali, Benozzo di **1**:*52*
Lesser, Aleksandr **4**:*1104*
Le Vau, Louis **4**:1007
Leyden, Jan van **5**:1195
Lezcenco, Juan Gabrielle de
   4:892
Liceti, Fortunio **2**:461
Lichfield, Richard **3**:*738*
Lievens, Jan **5**:1211, 1212
Lilio, Antonio **1**:175
Lilio, Luigi **1**:175
Lilly, William **1**:70, *72*, 73
Linacre, Thomas **4**:924,
   5:1373
Linnaeus, Carolus (Carl von
   Linné) **5**:1258, *1259*
Linschoten, Jan Huyghen van
   5:*1343*
Lionel of Ulster **1**:213
Lippershey, Hans **2**:464,
   5:1252
Lippi, Filippo **1**:133, 135
Littleton, Elizabeth **5**:1422
Livy **3**:584, 682, 684, 686,
   770, 772
Lobkowitz, Wenzel Eusebius
   von **2**:559
Locke, Anne Vaughan
   5:1423–1424
Locke, John **2**:545, **5**:1295,
   1348–1349
Lockley, Rowland **1**:*62*
Lodge, Thomas **3**:755, **5**:1286
Lodowick Bryskett **5**:1287
Lombards **1**:89
Lomi, Prudentia **2**:471
Longhi, Martino (the Elder)
   1:40
Lope de Vega *see* Vega, Lope de

Loqman **1**:*69*, **4**:*1084*, **5**:*1409*
Lorenzetti, Ambrogio **2**:492,
   4:980
Lorenzetti, Pietro **2**:488, 492,
   4:980
Lorenzo the Magnificent *see*
   Medici, Lorenzo de'
Lorrain, Claude **4**:994–995
Lotto, Lorenzo **5**:*1420*
Louis, duke of Bavaria **1**:112
Louis, prince of Condé **2**:451,
   452, 453, 454
Louis II de Male, count of
   Flanders **1**:157
Louis IX, king of France
   2:517, 531, **3**:601
Louis X, king of France **3**:595
Louis XI, king of France
   2:406, **3**:735, **4**:965
 Burgundy **1**:162, 163–164,
   2:413
 Spain **5**:1277
Louis XII, king of France
   1:124, **2**:429, 445, 555,
   3:742, 853, **4**:965, **5**:1394
 Florence **2**:419
 Italian wars **3**:643, 644, 645,
   646
Louis XIII, king of France
   2:371, 443, 458, 519,
   4:882, 897, 908,
   1034–1035, **5**:1240
Louis XIV, king of France
   1:48, **2**:367, 444, 450, 519,
   541, **5**:1256, 1390, *1419*
 absolutism **2**:367, **4**:907
 Aristotle **1**:59
 Bernini portrait bust **1**:97, 98
 established church **1**:257,
   2:372
 gardens **1**:26
 Molière **4**:899, 900, 901,
   902, 911
Louis I, king of Hungary
   4:1104
Louis II, king of Hungary
   2:510
Louis II, cardinal of Lorraine
   2:456, 517
Louis, duke of Orléans **1**:159,
   4:1030

Louis of Nassau **2**:453
Louise of Savoy **2**:446
Loukaris, Kyrillis *see* Lucaris,
   Cyril
Loves, Matteo **5**:*1206*
Loyola, Ignatius *see* Ignatius of
   Loyola
Lubomirska, Katarzyna
   4:*1108*
Lucan **3**:590, 649
Lucaris, Cyril, patriarch of
   Constantinople **1**:109, 263
Lucas, Margaret **5**:1257
Lucena, Vasco Fernández de
   4:1143–1144
Lucian **4**:925
Lucretius **1**:136
Ludolphus of Saxonia **1**:125
Luke, Saint **1**:*145*, **2**:380
Lull, Ramon **1**:224
Lully, Jean-Baptiste **4**:900
Lupicinia, Antonio **1**:276
Lupton, Donald **3**:748
Luria, Isaac **3**:680
Lusatia **1**:116
Luther, Martin **1**:99, 246,
   262, **2**:339, 370, 438, 439,
   448, **3**:756–768, **4**:906,
   929, **5**:*1188*
 alchemy **3**:801
 Aristotle **1**:58, **4**:1065
 biblical authority
   1:104–105, 106–107,
   5:1352, 1354, 1356,
   1371, 1372
 biblical translation **1**:102,
   103, *180*, **2**:316, **3**:698,
   4:931, 970, **5**:1193,
   1222, 1357
 calendar reform **1**:175
 Calvinism **1**:181, 183, 185
 Charles V vs. **1**:211, 242,
   2:514
 on divorce **2**:566
 doctrine **5**:1192, 1194,
   1195, 1197, 1198
 Dürer **2**:315–316
 Eastern church **1**:262
 education **2**:321–322, 324
 English Reformation **1**:232,
   240

Luther, Martin (cont.)
Erasmus **2**:339, 356, 357, 358, 359–362, 552, **5**:1283
excommunication of **1**:242
German towns **2**:479, 481, 482
Henry VIII **1**:232, **2**:338
heresy **4**:1032
Holy Roman Empire **2**:553
humanism **2**:423, **3**:585, 593
Hus as forerunner **1**:118
Hussites **2**:537
iconoclasm **3**:606
indulgences critique **2**:423, **3**:757, 763, **4**:929, 1012–1013, **5**:1360
Islam **3**:618
Judaism **3**:675
Leo X **1**:242, **3**:701, 703, 704–705, 757, *763*, 765, **4**:1013, **5**:1192, 1232
on marriage **2**:569
music **4**:947, 952, 957
nationalism **2**:364
Ninety-five Theses **3**:758, **5**:1190–1191, 1221
overview of **3**:762, **5**:1189
papacy **1**:246, **4**:1012–1013, **5**:1400
peasant revolts **2**:555
philosophy **4**:1063, 1064, 1065–1066
preaching **5**:1163–1165
Reformation inception **1**:178
religious orders **5**:1201, 1203, 1362
religious wars **1**:183
Rome **5**:1232
sacraments **5**:1358
Shorter Catechism **5**:1174
Swiss Reformation **5**:1305, 1315, 1316
universities **5**:1368, 1371, *1376*
usury condemnation **1**:85
witch hunting **2**:535
women's education **2**:322
Luttrell, Geoffrey **1**:*165*
Luxembourg family **1**:117, **2**:549

Lyell, Charles **1**:110
Lyly, John **3**:732

M

Mabuse (Jan Gossaert) **1**:145
Machaut, Guillaume de **1**:*214*, 215, **4**:943
Machiavelli, Niccolò **1**:164, 245, **2**:337, 395, 419, **3**:655, 769–773, 853
Borgias **4**:1011
on Ferdinand of Spain **2**:395
Florence **2**:419
literature **3**:376, 770, 772
Medicis **2**:419
monarchy **2**:337, 419, **3**:771
political philosophy **4**:1066–1067
Renaissance **5**:1221, 1224
theater **3**:733
Madariaga, Salvador de **1**:211
Madeleine de Valois **3**:722, **5**:1264
Maderna, Carlo **1**:38, 40, 44, 99, 100, **4**:1026
Magellan, Ferdinand **2**:373, 374, 382, **3**:787–794, **4**:888, **5**:1250
Mahdi **3**:620–621, 622
Maiano, Giuliano di **1**:*153*
Maimonides **3**:*678, 679*
Maintenon, Madame de **5**:*1419*
Major, John **1**:182
Malatesta, Sigismondo **4**:1090, 1091
Malatestas, the **5**:1379
Malatesti, Antonio **4**:882
Malory, Thomas **1**:223, 224
Maltby, William **2**:551
Malthus, Thomas Robert **4**:1127, 1128, 1129
Mami, Arnaute **1**:202
Mander, Carel van **1**:144, 146, 148, **5**:*1308*
Manelli, Francesco **4**:917
Manet, Édouard **4**:996
Manetti, Antonio di Tuccio **1**:34, 155
Manfredi, Bartolomeo **4**:997
Manners family **3**:665

Mansart, François **1**:45, 48
Mansfeld, Peter Ernst von **5**:1335
Mantegna, Andrea **1**:139, **2**:312, 314, **3**:642, 745
Manuel II Palaeologus, Byzantine emperor **1**:*260*, 261, *262*
Manuel I, king of Portugal **4**:1012, 1139, 1141, 1144, 1145
Manutius, Aldus **1**:56, 59, **2**:357, **3**:584, 688, **5**:1399
Manuzio, Paolo **4**:1024
Maratti, Carlo **5**:*1204*
Marcello, Magdalucia **5**:1420
Marcellus II, Pope **5**:1353, 1355, 1359, 1360
Marenzio, Luca **4**:918
Margaret, Saint **3**:657
Margaret I, queen of Denmark and Norway **4**:911
Margaret of Angoulême **3**:735–736, **5**:1176, 1177, 1178, *1179*
Margaret of Anjou **3**:*601*
Margaret of Austria **1**:131, 210, **3**:648, **4**:912, 1057, **5**:1281, *1362, 1417*, 1426
Margaret of Flanders **1**:157, 207, *242*
Margaret of Navarre see Margaret of Angoulême; Margaret of Valois
Margaret of Parma see Margaret of Austria
Margaret of Savoy **2**:446
Margaret of Valois **1**:198, 200, **2**:*455*, 517
Margaret Tudor, queen consort of Scotland 1298, **5**:1261, 1297, 1298
Margarita, princess of Spain **5**:1391
Margolin, Jean-Claude **5**:1179
Marguerite of Valois see Margaret of Valois
Maria Anna of Austria **3**:836
Maria d'Aquino **1**:111
Maria Eleonora of Brandenburg **1**:227

Maria Maddalena of Austria **2**:471
Mariana, queen consort of Spain **5**:1390, 1391
Maria of Hungary **5**:1281, 1426
Maria of Portugal **4**:1058, 1059, **5**:1280
María Teresa, queen consort of France **5**:1390
Marie Céleste (Galileo's daughter) **2**:468
Marieschi, Michele **5**:*1392*
Marillac, Louise de **5**:1208
Mark, Saint **2**:316
winged lion of **5**:*1400*
Mark of Ephesus **1**:260, **2**:429
Marlowe, Christopher **2**:335–336, **3**:671, 726, 728, 732, **822–826**, **5**:1269, 1270, 1325
Marot, Clément **2**:450, **5**:1176, 1177
Marprelate, Martin (pamphleteer) **5**:1175
Marsilius of Padua **1**:53, 257, **2**:367
Marston, John **3**:733
Martellus, Henricus **1**:*249*
Martin V, Pope **2**:428, **4**:1011, 1052, **5**:1162, 1227, 1379
Martin, Gregory **1**:108
Martinelli, Caterina de Cattaneis **4**:918
Martini, Francesco di Giorgio **1**:280, **5**:1181
Martini, Simone **2**:488, 491, 492
Martin of Arles **3**:798
Marvell, Andrew **4**:886
Mary I (Mary Tudor), queen of England **1**:62, 107, **5**:1225, 1325, 1374, 1424, *1427*
Elizabeth I **1**:237, **2**:326–327, 328
Henry VIII **1**:233, **2**:522, 524, 527, 528
humanist education of **5**:1417, 1418

iconoclasm **3**:608, 609
Philip II **1**:209, 236, **2**:327,
    328, **4**:1056, *1057*, 1059
printing **5**:1170, 1175
Protestant martyrs **1**:*232*
Roman Catholicism **1**:187,
    188, 189, 236, 237, 238,
    239, 240, **2**:340, 342,
    5:1198, 1265, 1267, 1426
Mary II, queen of England *see*
    William and Mary
Mary, Queen of Scots **1**:62,
    79, **2**:527–528, **3**:722,
    5:1289, 1426
 Calvinism **1**:189
 Elizabeth I **1**:238, **2**:327,
    330–331, 332
 Francis II **1**:198, **2**:452
 James I **2**:332
 Reformation **5**:1266
 Scotland **5**:1262, 1264
 Stuarts **5**:1297–1298
Mary of Burgundy
    1:163–164, **2**:509, 511,
    515, 550, **4**:966, **5**:1426
Mary of Guise **1**:198, **5**:1264,
    1265, 1266, 1297, 1298,
    1426
Masaccio (Tommaso Guidi)
    1:35, **2**:492, **3**:*589*, **4**:984,
    5:1185
Masi, Antonia **5**:1420
Massimi, Piero **1**:40
Massys, Quentin **1**:*84*
Master John (artist) **5**:*1427*
Mästlin, Michael **3**:832
Matejko, Jan **4**:*1107*
Mathewes, Augustine **5**:*1325*
Matilda, queen consort of
    England **2**:505
Matthew, Saint **1**:193
Matthiae, Johanne **1**:227
Matthias, Holy Roman
    emperor **1**:121, **2**:559, 560,
    3:836
Maurice, Saint **1**:224
Maurice of Nassau **2**:294
Maurice of Saxony **1**:75
Maximian, Archbishop **1**:*166*
Maximilian I, duke of Bavaria
    2:558, **5**:1332

Maximilian I, Holy Roman
    emperor **2**:445, 553,
    3:835–839, **4**:946
 Burgundy **1**:164
 Charles V **1**:207
 Dürer **2**:315
 German towns **2**:477, 478
 Hapsburg Empire
    2:509–510, 511, 515, 556
 Italian wars **3**:643
 Judaism **3**:674
 nationalism **4**:964, *965, 966*
 reforms **2**:550
 Venice **5**:1394
Maximilian II, Holy Roman
    emperor **1**:121, **2**:510, 556,
    557
Mayenne, duke of **2**:457, 458
Mazarin, Cardinal **1**:230,
    2:*459*
Mazzola, Girolamo *see*
    Parmigianino
Medici, Alessandro de'
    1:244–245, **2**:420, **3**:649,
    850, 856
Medici, Claudia de' **5**:1381
Medici, Cosimo de' (the Elder)
    1:87, 113, 169, **3**:649, 742,
    850, 851, 852, 853, 855,
    856, 857
 Byzantine scholars **1**:169
 Florence **2**:413, 417, 418,
    419, 420, 422
 Florentine Academy **1**:261,
    4:1063, 1090
 humanism **2**:422
 Platonism **1**:261
Medici, Cosimo I de' **2**:418,
    3:850, 851, 857
Medici, Cosimo II de' **2**:464,
    469, 471, 474, **3**:857
Medici, Cosimo III de' **3**:*849*
Medici, Ferdinand II de'
    3:*849*, 857, **5**:1380
Medici, Francesco de' **3**:857,
    5:1240
Medici, Giovanni Angelo de'
    see Pius IV
Medici, Giovanni de' *see* Leo X
Medici, Giovanni de' (Sforza's
    son) **5**:1428

Medici, Giovanni di Averado
    de' **1**:152
Medici, Giovanni di Bicci de'
    1:87, **3**:850, 851, 852, 857
Medici, Giuliano de' **1**:277,
    4:876–877, **5**:1383
 son Clement VII **1**:241
 tomb of **1**:42
Medici, Giulio de' *see* Clement
    VII
Medici, Ippolito de' **1**:244
Medici, Lorenzo de' (son of
    Piero) **3**:701
Medici, Lorenzo de' (the
    Magnificent) **1**:57, 87, 197,
    246, **3**:*587*, 687, 708, 771,
    850, 851, 854, 855, 856,
    857, **4**:946, 951, **5**:1353,
    1428
 Clement VII **1**:241
 daughter Lucrezia **1**:246
 Florence **2**:418, 420, 422,
    423, 424, 426
 Florentine Academy **4**:1063,
    1076
 humanism **1**:261, **2**:422,
    423, 424
 Leo X **3**:700
 Michelangelo **4**:870, 871,
    876–877
 Urbino **5**:1380
Medici, Pierfrancesco de'
    5:1428
Medici, Piero de' **1**:34, **3**:648,
    702, 707, 850, 852, 853,
    856, **4**:945
 exile from Florence **2**:419,
    420
Medici, Salvestro de' **3**:849,
    850, 853
Medicis, the **1**:277, **2**:413,
    477, **3**:747, **849–857,**
    4:986, **5**:1428
 architecture **1**:35, 42
 banking **1**:87–88,
    2:415–416, 417, **5**:1342
 Botticelli **1**:135, *136*, 137,
    138
 Brunelleschi **1**:*152*
 Catherine de Médicis
    1:197–202

Charles V **1**:208, 242
Ciompi revolt **2**:415, **3**:849,
    853
Clement VII **1**:241–246
coat of arms **1**:*152*
della Roveres **5**:1380, 1381
exiles **2**:420
Florence **1**:152, 208, 242,
    243, 244, 261, **2**:415,
    416, 417–420, 421, 423,
    424, 425, 426, **3**:637,
    638, 641, 642, 648–649,
    702, 703, 705, **4**:1077,
    5:1224
Hapsburgs **2**:421
humanism **3**:*587*, 588, 687,
    703, **4**:1073
Leo X **3**:700–705
Machiavelli **3**:769, 770, 771,
    772, 773, 853
Michelangelo **2**:424,
    425–426, **3**:852, 856,
    4:870, 871, 872,
    876–877
music **4**:945, 946, 951
opera **4**:920
papacy **4**:1029
prominent women **1**:246,
    2:459, **5**:1240, 1241
tomb sculptures **3**:707
Viscontis **5**:1404, 1405
Medina Sidonia, duke of **1**:53,
    65, 66
Mehmed I, Ottoman sultan
    3:617, 680
Mehmed II (the Conqueror),
    Ottoman sultan **4**:1089,
    5:1408
 Byzantium **1**:170, 171, 172,
    269
 Constantinople **1**:263
 Islam **3**:617, 618–619, 625
 overview of **1**:169
Meingre Boucicaut, Jean II le
    1:224
Melanchthon, Philipp **2**:483,
    566, **3**:585, 593, 767–768
 educational reform **2**:320,
    324
 universities **5**:1371, 1372,
    1373, 1377

Meli da Crema, Antonio
1:126

Melozzo da Forlì 4:*1023*

Memel (Klaipeda) 5:1334

Memling, Hans 4:982, *985*

Menabuoi, Giusto 4:*1062*

Mendes, Francisco 3:681

Mendoza, Iñigo López de
5:1279

Mendoza, Pedro de 4:892

Mendoza, Pedro González de
5:1279–1280

Mercator, Gerardus 2:384,
385, 5:1248, 1250

Mercoeur, duke of 2:458

Merian, Matthäus (the Elder)
1:*75,* 5:*1293, 1310*

Merisi, Michelangelo *see*
Caravaggio

Mersenne, Marin 2:294, *295,*
544

Mervenne, Aleyt van der
1:128

Meteren, Emanuel van 5:1286

Meulen, Steven van der
5:*1306*

Michael, archangel 1:224

Michael III, Byzantine
emperor 1:258, 259

Michael V, Byzantine emperor
1:258

Michael VII, Byzantine
emperor 1:258

Michael VIII Palaeologus,
Byzantine emperor 1:258,
260

Michael I, emperor of Russia
4:940, 5:1309

Michael Constantine Psellus
1:168, 258

Michelangelo 1:97, 2:466,
469, 492, 3:668, 703,
4:870–878, 946, 948,
5:*1226,* 1232, *1354,* 1387
architecture 1:36, 42, 44, 47,
2:424–425, 4:871, 876,
877, 5:*1226*
Bramante 1:143
Clement VII 1:241, 242,
244
mannerism 1:32–33

Medicis 2:424, 425–426,
3:852, 856, 4:870, 871,
872, 876–877
melancholia of 2:*315*
painting and sculpture 4:986,
988, 990, 992, 999
Palazzo Farnese 1:40
Palladio 4:1000, 1003, 1004
papal patron 4:1025
as Raphael influence 5:1183,
1184–1185, 1187
Renaissance 5:1220, 1221,
1225
Saint Peter's Basilica 1:32, 38,
98, 4:871, 873, 878,
1026, 5:1353
Sistine Chapel 1:135, 244,
4:870, 871, 873,
874–875, 877, 878, 1025,
5:1220, 1231

Michelazzo 3:*702*

Michel de Marillac 2:459

Michieli, Giovanni 1:200

Middleton, Thomas 3:733,
5:1323, 1325, 1326, 1329

Mikulas of Kadan 3:779

Mila, Adriana de 1:123

Milán, Luis 4:959

Mildmay, Walter 5:*1374*

Milton, Christopher 4:879,
887

Milton, Elizabeth Minshull
4:886, 887

Milton, John 3:609, 726, 823,
4:879–887

Milton, Mary Powell 4:879,
883, 884, 885, 887

Minin, Kuzma 4:939

Minshull, Elizabeth 4:886,
887

Mirk, John 5:1159

Mocenigo, doge of Venice
4:*1058*

Molcho, Solomon 3:677

Molesworth, Robert 5:1311

Molière 3:730, 731,
4:897–902, 5:1322, 1323

Molina, Luis de 1:205

Molina, Tirso de 1:205

Monaldeschi, Gian Rinaldo
1:230

Monstrelet, Enguerrand de
1:*159*

Montagu, Richard 2:346

Montaigne, Michel de 1:*80,*
95, 96

Monte, Francesco Maria del
1:191, 192

Monte, Giovanni Battista da
3:847

Montecavallo, Antonio da 1:40

Montefeltro, Antonio da
5:1378

Montefeltro, Federigo da
1:139, 5:1379, 1382

Montefeltro, Giovanna da
5:1379

Montefeltro, Guidantonio da
5:1378–1379

Montefeltro, Guidobaldo da
5:1379, 1380, 1383

Montefeltro, Oddantonio da
5:1379, 1382

Montefeltros, the
5:1378–1379

Monteverdi, Claudio 3:745,
4:916–923, 943, 961,
5:1244

Monteverdi, Julio Cesare 4:918

Montezuma, Aztec ruler
2:307, 4:890

Montmors, the 1:179

Montrose, earl of 2:351

Morales, Cristóbal de 4:956,
957

Morandi, Orazio 1:*74*

Moray, earl of 1:189

More, Anne 5:1166

More, Henry 4:1070–1071

More, Margaret 5:1418

More, Thomas 1:235, 3:698,
4:924–932, 1074, 5:1319,
1418
bibles 1:106
Erasmus 2:357, 362, 363
Henry VIII 1:235, 2:525
humanism 2:335, 339–340,
3:585, 590, 593, 5:1370,
1371, 1373
Platonism 4:1063, 1103
printing 5:1173
Reformation 2:339–340

Moritz, landgrave of Hessen-
Kassel 5:1244, 1245

Moro, Antonio 2:*327,* 5:*1422*

Morone, Giovanni 5:1355

Moroni, Andrea 5:*1370*

Morris, William 4:1048

Mortimer, Edmund 1:17

Morton, John 4:924

Mosca, Giovanni il 4:112

Motteux, Peter 1:205

Mountjoy, Lord 2:333

Mouton, Jean 4:949

Muezzinade Ali Pasha 3:715,
717, 718

Muhammad 3:610, 611, 614,
620, 626, 4:1084

Mulcaster, Richard 5:1286

Mulder, Joseph 1:*60*

Müller, Johann *see*
Regiomontanus

Mumford, Lewis 3:775,
779–780

Munday, Anthony 5:1324,
1329

Munk, Jens 2:383

Munster, Sébastien 1:179

Münzer, Thomas 1:178,
5:1193

Murad I, Ottoman sultan
3:616

Murad II, Ottoman sultan
3:618, 627

Murillo, Bartolomé Esteban
5:1242, 1386

Murray, Margaret 3:803

Mus, Decius 5:1237

Mussato, Albertino 3:584

N

Nanni, Giovanni *see* Annius of
Viterbo

Napier, John 3:831

Napoléon I, emperor of the
French 2:512, 3:773

Nash, Thomas 3:738, 823

Nasi, Gracia 3:681

Nasi, Lorenzo 5:1185

Nasiruddin Mahmud
Chiragh-i Dihli 3:615

Nebrija, Elio Antonio de
2:399, 3:694, 699, 5:1280

Neckham, Alexander
3:778–779
Neile, Richard 2:346
Neri, Philip 4:956, 5:1204
Nettesheim, Cornelius
Agrippa von 5:1417
Neville, Richard, earl of
Warwick 2:408
Nevsky, Alexander see
Alexander Nevsky
Newcomen, Thomas 3:785
Newton, Isaac 1:262, 2:467,
3:783, 801, 4:1072
calculus 3:827, 828, 833,
834
Cambridge University
5:1375
science 5:1251, 1256–1257,
1258, 1259
Wren 5:1430
Niccolò de' Niccoli 3:583,
584, 585, 587
Nicholas, Saint 2:378
Nicholas I, Pope 1:259
Nicholas IV, Pope 1:44
Nicholas V, Pope 1:34, 39,
142, 4:1022–1023
Bessarion 1:261
humanism 3:584, 586
Rome 5:1228–1229, 1230
Nicholas of Cusa 3:618,
4:1098 1099, 1101
Nicolls, Allen 3:825
Nikon, patriarch of
Constantinople 4:936
Nobili, Roberto de 5:1206
Noort, Adam van 5:1236
Noot, Jan van der 5:1286
Norden, John 3:751
Norfolk, duke of 2:330, 331,
527
Norris, Thomas 5:1290
Northumberland, earl of see
Percy, Henry
Norton, Thomas 3:823
Nostredame, Michel de
(Nostradamus) 1:70, 71, 73
Noves, Laura de 4:1051
Nowell, Robert 5:1286
Núñez de Balboa, Vasco
2:374, 382

O

Obrecht, Jacobo 4:949
Ochino, Bernardino 5:1209
Ockham, William of 2:366,
367, 3:759, 763
nominalism 1:181, 4:1062,
1063
Okeghem, Jean d' 4:946
Olier, Jean-Jacques 5:1361
Olivétan, Pierre-Robert 1:108,
181
Oman, Charles 4:1044–1045
Ond, earl of see Butler, James
O'Neill, Hugh 5:1290
Origen 1:109, 4:1098
Orkhan, emir of Anatolia
3:616
Orléans family 2:434, 437
Orley, Bernard van 1:145, 207,
242, 5:1417
Orsini, Alfronsina 1:194
Orsini, Clarice 3:700, 857
Orsinis, the 5:1227
Orsis, the 5:1428
Orte, Juan de la 1:208
Osiander, Andreas 1:269
Osman I, emir of Anatolia
3:616
Ostrogski, Janusz 4:1108
Otrepev, Gregory 4:938
Otto IV, Holy Roman emperor
2:505
Oudin, César 1:203
Oughtred, William 3:830, 831
Ovid 1:112, 136, 2:336,
3:823, 4:1053, 5:1321
Oxenstierna, Axel 1:227, 228,
5:1307, 1309, 1310, 1337
Oxenstierna family 5:1304
Oxford, earl of see Vere,
Edward de

P

Pacheco, Francisco 5:1384,
1385
Pacheco, Juana 5:1384, 1385
Pachomius 5:1201
Pacino, Al 3:671
Pacioli, Luca 3:828
Padovano, Annibale 4:960
Paiva, Alfonso de 2:381

Pajou, Augustin 4:1070
Palaeologus dynasty 1:166,
169, 172, 3:744
Palestrina, Giovanni Pierluigi
da 4:954, 955–956, 957
Palladio, Andrea 1:32, 33, 34,
42–43, 140, 141, 3:664,
665, 666, 667, 668,
4:1000–1007
Venice 3:664, 668, 4:1000,
1006–1007, 5:1399
Palladio, Leonida 4:1000
Palladio, Marc'Antonio 4:1000
Pallavicino, Benedetto 4:918
Palmieri, Matteo 5:1218, 1219
Pampaloni, Luigi 1:149
Panfili, Pio 5:1356
Pannini, Giovanni Paolo 1:39
Paolo de Perugia 1:111, 114
Papin, Denis 3:785
Paracelsus 3:843
Paré, Ámbroise 3:840
Pareja, Juan de 5:1389, 1390
Parker, Matthew 1:237, 3:822
Parmenides 4:1097
Parmigianino 1:209, 242
Parr, Catherine 2:522, 527,
3:735
Paruta, Paolo 3:719
Pascal, Blaise 3:775
Pastor, Ludwig von 1:243
Patrick, patron saint of Ireland
5:1317
Paul, Saint 3:605, 689,
4:1102, 5:1230
bibles 1:105, 110
Calvin commentary 1:179
conversion of 1:193
Dürer image 2:316
humanist learning 2:337
letters of 2:337, 5:1356
missionizing 4:894
preaching 5:1158, 1160,
1163
Paul III, Pope 2:361, 3:648,
836, 4:1009, 1025
astrology 1:72
Charles V 1:210
Counter-Reformation
4:1016, 1017, 1019
Inquisition 5:1197, 1234

Jesuits 4:1015, 1017,
5:1191, 1197, 1199,
1205, 1353
Michelangelo 4:871, 877
overview of 4:1016
Rome 5:1232, 1234
Saint Peter's Basilica 4:1026
Trent, Council of 5:1352,
1353, 1357
Urbino 5:1381
Venice 5:1400
Paul IV, Pope 4:992, 1058,
5:1353, 1360, 1363
Inquisition 5:1197
Italian wars 3:644
religious orders 5:1204
Rome 5:1233, 1234
Paul V, Pope 1:97, 2:465,
4:921, 1020, 1021, 1026,
1036–1040
Venice 5:1400
Paul VI, Pope 5:1363, 1364
Paulet, Amias 1:79
Paul of Thebes 5:1201
Pazzi, Andrea di Guglielmo
1:153
Pazzis, the 3:852
Peake, Robert 4:1071
Pearl Poet 1:220
Pedemuro, Giovanni da
4:1000
Pedro (the Cruel), king of
Castile 3:598
Peele, George 3:732, 824
Pellicioli, Mauro 3:713
Pembroke, countess of see
Sidney, Mary
Percy, Henry (Hotspur) 1:17
Percy, Henry, earl of
Northumberland 3:825
Pereira, Nuno Álvares 4:1137
Perestrello e Moniz, Felipa
1:247, 248
Perez, Martin 4:890
Peri, Jacopo 4:920, 943,
5:1246, 1321
Périers, Bonaventure des
3:736
Peringer, Dietrich 2:479
Perrissin, Jean 1:185
Persons, Robert 4:906

Perugino, Pietro **3**:706, **5**:1181, 1182, 1185, 1230

Peruzzi, Baldassare **1**:32, 38, 40, 41, 281, **4**:1003

Pesaro **5**:1380, 1382

Pet, Arthur **2**:384

Peter, Saint **1**:37, 99, 100, 105, 141, 193, **3**:798, **4**:1026

  Dürer image **2**:316

  papacy **1**:257

  preaching on **5**:1160

  Rome **5**:1230, 1231, 1234

Peter I (the Great), emperor of Russia **1**:49, **4**:941, **5**:1311

Peters, Edward **2**:398

Peterzano, Simone **1**:191

Petrarch **3**:720, 721, 722, 724, 725, 726, **4**:963, **1049–1055**, 1072, 1143

  Boccaccio **1**:111, 112, 114, 115

  Borgia, Lucrezia **1**:125

  Chaucer **1**:216

  Greek studies **2**:320

  humanism **2**:357, **3**:583–584, 585, 589, 682–683, 684, 686, **4**:1049, 1053–1055, 1075, **5**:1218

  papacy **4**:1009, 1052

  Rome **5**:1227, 1228

  Spenser translations **2**:335, **5**:1286

  vernacular **3**:694

  Viscontis **5**:1405–1406

Petrarch, Giovanni (son) **4**:1051

Petrucci, Alfonso **3**:701

Petrucci, Ottaviano **5**:1399

Peurbach, Georg **3**:828, 829

Pfefferkorn, Johann **3**:674

Philaret, patriarch of Constantinople **4**:940

Philip, archduke of Austria *see* Philip I, king of Spain

Philip (the Bold), duke of Burgundy **1**:157–158, 159, **4**:944, 981

Philip (the Good), duke of Burgundy **1**:160–162, 163,

223, 226, **2**:388, 515, **3**:602, 661, **4**:944

Philip (the Handsome), duke of Burgundy **1**:207, **2**:399, 400, **5**:1280, 1281

Philip I, king of Castile *see* Philip (the Handsome). duke of Burgundy

Philip II, king of Macedonia **1**:167

Philip III, king of France **2**:433

Philip IV (the Fair), king of France **2**:366, **3**:595, **4**:911, 913, **5**:1227

Philip V, king of France **3**:595

Philip, landgrave of Hesse **3**:768

Philip I, king of Portugal *see* Philip II, king of Spain

Philip I, king of Spain **1**:131, **2**:510, 515

Philip II, king of Spain **1**:46, 88, 203, **2**:442, 453, 511, 515, 556, **4**:892, 956, **1056–1060**

  Bosch collection **1**:131

  Charles V **1**:208, 209, 211, **2**:413

  Elizabeth I **2**:328, 331, 332

  Elizabeth of Valois **1**:198, 199, 203

  England **1**:238

  established church **2**:370

  Florence **2**:*420*

  Italian wars **3**:647, 648, 649, 650

  Mary Tudor **1**:209, 236, **2**:327, 328, **4**:1056, *1057,* 1059

  military tactics **5**:1414

  Netherlands revolt **2**:331

  Ottoman expansion **3**:715, 718

  papacy **4**:1036, 1037, **5**:1234

  Portugal **4**:1140, 1145

  Spanish armada **1**:62, 66, 238, **2**:331

  Spanish Empire **5**:1283–1284

  theater **5**:1322, 1323

  waterworks **1**:280

Philip III, king of Spain **5**:1238, 1284

Philip IV, king of Spain **2**:471, **3**:837, **4**:994, **5**:1284

  Rubens **5**:1237, 1242

  Thirty Years War **5**:1333

  Velázquez **5**:1385, 1387, 1388, 1390, 1391

Philip Julius, duke of Stettin-Pomerania **3**:751

Philip of Évereux **2**:433

Philip of Hesse **2**:569

Philippa of Hainaut, queen consort of England **1**:214, 224, **3**:598

Philippa of Lancaster, queen consort of Portugal **2**:380, **4**:1137

Phocas, Byzantine emperor **1**:258

Photius, patriarch of Constantinople **1**:259

Pia, Emilia **5**:1383

Piasts, the **4**:1104, 1108, 1112

Picart, Bernard **5**:*1232*

Piccolomini, Andrea **4**:1091

Piccolomini, Antonio **4**:1091

Piccolomini, Enea Silvio *see* Pius II, Pope

Piccolomini, Francesco *see* Pius III, Pope

Piccolomini, Jacopo **4**:1091

Piccolomini, Octavio **5**:1338

Piccolomini, Silvius **4**:1009

Pico, Giovanni Francesco (nephew) **4**:1074

Pico della Mirandola, Giovanni **4**:**1073–1077**

  Florence **2**:422–423, 424

  humanism **2**:482, **3**:*588,* 589

  magic **4**:1065

  Medicis **3**:852, 855, 856

  More **4**:924

  optimism **2**:537, 538, **4**:1064, 1066

  Platonism **4**:1100, 1103

  Renaissance **5**:1220

Pierce, Mark **1**:*28*

Piero della Francesca **1**:139, **3**:*630,* 827–828, **4**:985, *987,* 1090, **5**:*1181,* 1379

Pierre, Jean-Baptiste **4**:*1067*

Pierre de Beauveau **1**:*112*

Pietro de Crescenzi **1**:*25, 26*

Pigafetta, Antonio **3**:789, 791, *792, 793*

Pilate, Pontius **5**:1232

Pindar **4**:1092

Pine, John **1**:*66*

Pinturicchio (Betto di Biago) **1**:*125,* **2**:*428,* **4**:*1086, 1087, 1088,* 1091, **5**:1183

Pinzón, Martín Alonso **1**:248, 250, 251, 252

Pinzón, Vicente Yañez **1**:248

Piombo, Sebastiano del **1**:41, *241,* **3**:*650*

Pippi de' Gianuzzi, Giulio *see* Romano, Giulio

Pirkheimer, Willibald **2**:339

Pisanello, Antonio **1**:*224,* **2**:*428,* **5**:*1416*

Pittoni, Girolamo **4**:1000

Pius II, Pope **2**:*428,* **3**:619, **4**:**1086–1091,** **5**:1230

Pius III, Pope **4**:1091

Pius IV, Pope **2**:453, **3**:747, **4**:1020, 1024, **5**:1226, 1353, 1360

Pius V, Pope **3**:715, *717,* **4**:*967, 975, 1058,* 1059

  excommunication of Elizabeth I **1**:238, **2**:330

Pius XI, Pope **4**:932

Pizarro, Francisco **2**:374, **4**:892

Platiensis, Michael **1**:261, **2**:304

Platina *see* Sacchi, Bartolomeo

Plato **3**:*703,* **4**:*1054, 1061,* 1092, 1096, 1097, 1098

  Academy **4**:1063, 1090, 1095, **5**:1365

  English translation **2**:336

  Latin translation **1**:264, **2**:422, **3**:685, 687

Platter, Thomas **3**:753

Plautus, Titus Maccius **3**:683, 729, 732, 733

  Italian stage revival **5**:1320

Plessis, Armand-Jean du *see* Richelieu, Cardinal

Plethon *see* Gemistus Plethon, George
Pliny the Elder **1:**58, **3:**583, *687*
Pliny the Younger **3:**583
Plotinus **2:**422, 538, **4:**1061, 1063, 1070, 1096–1097, 1098, 1099, 1100, 1101
Plutarch **1:***59,* **3:**684, 685, 729
 English translation **2:**336
Poitiers, Diane de **1:**198
Pole, Reginald **1:**234, 236, **5:**1355
Poliziano, Angelo **1:**54, **3:**585, 587, *588, 687,* **4:**1074
Pollaiuolo, Antonio **2:**425, **4:**98
Pollaiuolo, Piero del **1:**133, 134
Polo, Marco **2:**373, **3:**804, **5:***1341*
Pombal, Marqués de **4:**1141
Pomponazzi, Pietro **1:**56, 261, **4:**1064, 1069
Ponce de León, Juan **2:**374, 382, **4:**888–889, 891
Ponet, John **5:**1419
Ponsonby, William **5:**1288, *1289*
Pontormo, Jacopo **4:**989, 998
Pope, Alexander **5:**1257
Poquelin, Jean-Baptiste *see* Molière
Porcari, Stefano **5:**1229
Porphyry **4:**1098
Porta, Giacomo della **1:**38, 40, 47
Pourbus, Frans **1:***234*
Poussin, Nicolas **4:**994, 995, **5:**1243, 1388
Powell, Mary (later Mary Milton) **4:**879, 883, 884, 885, 887
Powell, Richard **4:**880, 883, 887
Pozhansky, Prince Dmitry **4:**939
Praetorius, Michael **4:**950, 955, 958
Predis, Ambrogio da **3:**709

Přemyslid dynasty **1:**116–117
Prester John **2:**380, **4:**1140
Prete, El **1:**125
Pride, Thomas **2:**354
Primaticcio, Francesco **4:**990
Procida, Gasparo de **1:**123
Proclus **1:***271,* **2:**422
Protagoras **5:**1368
Prowse, Anne Locke **3:**724
Prynne, William **2:**346
Psellus, Michael Constantine *see* Michael Constantine Psellus
Pseudo-Dionysius *see* Dionysius the Areopagite
Ptolemy, Claudius **1:***60*
 astrology **1:**69, **3:**830
 Columbus's worldview **1:**249
 Copernicus vs. **1:**265, 268–269, 270, 271, **2:**463, **3:**825.272
 exploration **2:**373, 374, 384
 Galileo **2:**466, **3:**699
 mathematics **3:**829, 830
 universe model **1:**266–269, **2:**296, **5:**1249–1250
Pucci, Antonio **2:**484
Purchas, Samuel **2:**375, 377, 379
Puttenham, George **3:**723
Pym, John **2:**350, 351
Pythagoras **2:**334

Q

Quevedo y Villegas, Francisco de **3:**738–739
Quintilian **3:**583, 584, 588, 590, 683, 686, **5:**1373

R

Rabelais, François **3:**735, 736, **5:1176–1179**
Racine, Jean **3:**730, 731
Radboto, Count **2:**507
Raleigh, Walter **3:**726, 751, 825, **5:**1288
Ramus, Petrus **4:**1064
Raphael **1:**39, 40, 41, *50, 97,* 242, **3:***700,* **4:**957, 981,

1012, 1061, **5:1180–1187,** 1221, 1224, *1383,* 1387
Bramante **1:**37, 38, 142, *143,* **4:**1002, 1004
Clement VII **1:**242
Dürer **2:**316
High Renaissance **4:**986, 988, 990
Julius II **1:**36, **4:**1025
Leo X **3:**703
Palladio **4:**1002, 1003, 1004
 as Rembrandt influence **5:**1213, 1214
Saint Peter's Basilica **1:**48, **4:**1026
Sistine Chapel **1:**135, **5:***1158*
Ravaillac, François **2:***457,* 520
Recamati, Franco **1:**279
Recorde, Robert **3:**829
Regiomontanus **1:**174–175, 265, 269, **3:**828, 829, 831
Reinhard, Anna **5:**1315
Rej, Mikolaj **4:**1109
Rembrandt **1:***59,* **4:**996, 997, 998, **5:1210–1217,** 1243, 1387
 Caravaggio as influence **1:**196
Rembrandt, Titus **5:**1212, 1214, 1217
Renata, Elisabeth **3:**836
René of Anjou **4:**1088, 1089
Reni, Guido **4:**1040
Repin, Ilya Efimovich **3:***656*
Reubeni, David **3:**677
Reuchlin, Johann **3:**592, 593, 674, 689
Reynolds, Joshua **5:**1242
Reynolds, Susan **2:**405
Reza, Imam **3:***621*
Rhaw, Georg **4:**957
Rhenanus, Beatus **3:**590
Rheticus, Georg Joachim **1:**266, 269
Riario, Girolamo **5:**1427, 1428
Riario, Pietero **5:**1230
Riario, Rafaello **1:**40, **4:**870
Ribera, José de **4:**994
Ricci, Matteo **4:**894–895, 1015, **5:**1206

Ricci, Otilio **2:**460
Richard II, king of England **1:**17, **2:***378,* 499
 Chaucer **1:**216, 217, 218
 Hundred Years War **3:**599
 Peasants' Revolt **4:**1043, 1046–1047, 1048
Richard III, king of England **1:**233
Richard, 3rd duke of York **2:**408, **3:***601*
Richard of Wallingford **3:**780
Richelieu, Cardinal (Armand-Jean du Plessis) **4:**882, 908, 1034–1035, **5:**1240
 French civil wars **2:**458–459
 Thirty Years War **5:**1333, 1336, 1337
Richental, Ulrich von **1:***119, 158,* **4:***1010*
Richmond, duke of *see* Fitzroy, Henry
Ridley, Nicholas **1:***187*
Ridolfi, Roberto **2:**331
Rienzo, Cola di **4:**1052, **5:**1227
Riley, John **5:***1255*
Rinuccini, Ottavio **4:**920, **5:**1321
Ripa, Cesare **2:**472
Rizzio, David **5:**1298
Robbia *see* Della Robbia
Robert, king of Naples **1:**111, 112, **2:**487
Robert I (the Bruce), king of Scotland **4:**904, 905
Robert II, king of Scotland **5:**1296
Robert de Sorbon **5:***1369*
Robertello, Francesco **1:**59
Robert of Anjou *see* Robert, king of Naples
Robert of Artois **3:**595
Robles, Francisco de **1:**205
Robsart, Amy **2:**329
Roche, Lord **5:**1288, 1289
Rodriguez Juarez, Juan **5:***1205*
Roet, Gilles de **1:**213–214
Roet, Philippa de (later Chaucer) **1:**213–214

Rogers, Daniel **5:**1287
Rogers, John **1:**107
Roland **1:**222, 223
Rolin, Nicholas **2:***388*
Romana, Francesca **4:**1036
Romana, Giulio **5:**1187
Romano, Giulio **1:***38,* 39, 97, 242, **4:**991, 1003, 1004, 1012
Romanov, Michael *see* Michael I, emperor of Russia
Romanov dynasty **1:**166, **4:**940–941, **5:**1309
Romanus II, Byzantine emperor **1:**257
Romier, Lucien **2:**459
Ronsard, Pierre de **3:**721, 722, 723, 725, 735
Rosenblatt, Wibrandis **5:**1423
Rose of Lima **5:**1209
Rosselli, Cosimo **3:***588*
Rossellino, Antonio **5:***1218*
Rossellino, Bernardo **1:***155,* **3:***585,* **4:***1089,* 1090
Rossi, Luigi di **2:***426*
Rossi family **3:**744
Rossini, Gioacchino **5:**1312
Rosso, Franco dei **3:***686*
Rosso, Giovanni Battista *see* Rosso Fiorentino, Il
Rosso Fiorentino, Il **1:**242, **4:**990
Roubillac, Louis-François **1:***79*
Rovere *see* Della Rovere
Rowlett, Ralph **5:**1419
Roydon, Matthew **3:**824
Rubens, Jan **5:**1236
Rubens, Peter Paul **3:**666, **4:**917, 993, 994, 995, *1117,* **5:***1200,* **1236–1243** *1359*
  Caravaggio **1:**194
  Rembrandt **5:**1210, 1212
  Velázquez **5:**1386–1387, 1388
Rucellai, Giovanni **1:**36
Rudolf I, king of Bohemia **1:**117
Rudolf II, king of Bohemia **3:**801

Rudolf IV, king of Bohemia **2:**507
Rudolf I, king of Germany **2:**509
Rudolf II, Holy Roman Emperor **1:**121, **2:**556, 558, 559, 560, **4:**990, **5:**1334, 1415
Rue, Pierre de la **4:**951
Rueda, Lope de **3:**727, **5:**1323
Ruggieri, Michele **4:**895
Runciman, Steven **1:**171
Russell, Elizabeth **5:**1419, 1427
Russell, Francis, earl of Bedford **3:**820
Russell, John **5:**1419, 1427
Rustici, Cristofano **5:***1421*
Ryabushkin, Andreii Petrovich **3:***655*

S

Saavedra, Isabel de **1:**204, 205
Sacchi, Bartolomeo (Platina) **4:**1022, *1023*
Sachs, Hans **4:**960
Sackville, Thomas **3:**823
Sacrobosco, Johannes de **1:**174
Sadoleto, Jacopo **1:**179, **3:**703
Safavid dynasty **3:**612, 620–621, 622–623, 626, 628–629
Safi al-Din **3:**612, 620
Sahagun, Bernardino **2:**308
Salazar y Palacios, Catalina de **1:**204
Salmon, Pierre **4:***1050*
Salutati, Coluccio **3:**584, 589, 684, 685
Salviati, Francesco **4:***1009*
Salviati, Giovanni **1:**246
Salviati, Jacopo **1:**246
Salviati, Lucrezia de' Medici **1:**246
Salvini, Antonio **5:***1403*
Sambucus, Johannes **1:***54*
Sánchez Coello, Alonso **1:***121*
Sandoval y Rojas, Francisco de **5:***1238*
Sangallo, Antonio da (the Elder) **1:**38, 39, 44

Sangallo, Antonio da (the Younger) **1:**32, *33,* 38, 40, 44, 47, **4:**1026
Sangallo, Giuliano da **1:**44
Sanmicheli, Michele **4:**1002, 1004
Sansovino, Jacopo **1:**43, **3:**664, *690,* **4:**1001, 1002, 1004, 1005, 1006, **5:**1399
Santángel, Luis de **1:**251, 253
Santi, Giovanni **5:**1180, 1181, 1185
Sanzio, Raffaello *see* Raphael
Saraceni, Carlo **1:**194
Sarpi, Paolo **4:**1038
Savery, Thomas **3:**775
Savonarola, Girolamo **1:**137, 138, **3:**707, 769, 855
  Florence **2:**422, 423
  Pico della Mirandola **4:**1076–1077
  preaching **5:**1160
Savoy, duke of *see* Felix V
Scaliger, Joseph **3:**585, 592, 594
Scamozzi, Vincenzo **1:**34, **3:**664, 665, 668
Scarlatti, Alessandro **1:**230
Sceve, Maurice **4:**1051
Schertlin, Sebastian **1:**243
Schiller, Friedrich von **5:**1312
Schilling, Diebold **5:***1313*
Schöffer, Peter **5:**1169
Scholastic (hermit) **1:**168
Scholastica, Saint **5:**1201
Schongauer, Martin **2:**311, 314
Schooten, Joris van **5:**1211
Schütz, Heinrich **4:**952, **5:1244–1247**
Scipio **4:**1052
Scot, John **5:**1425
Scrovegni, Enrico **2:**486, 487
Scrovegni, Reginaldo **2:***486*
Scudéry, Madeleine de **4:**898
Seager, Jane **5:**1427
Sebastian, king of Portugal **4:**1140
Segni, Bernardo **1:**59
Selim I, Ottoman sultan **2:**555, **3:**622–623

Seneca **3:**590, 729, 732, 734
  Calvin's commentary **1:**181
  Italian stage revivals **5:**1320
Senfl, Ludwig **4:**950, 951
Senftenberg, Veit Wolff von **5:***1415*
Seripando, Girolamo *see* Marcellus II, Pope
Serlio, Sebastiano **1:**31, 34, 43, 45, 140, **3:**665, **4:**1001, 1002, 1004
Sermoneta **1:***124*
Serrur, Calixte-Joseph **5:***1262, 1426*
Servetus, Michael **1:**187, **2:**539
Seymour, Edward **2:**528, **3:**608, **5:**1411
  Calvinism **1:**188, 236
Seymour, Jane **1:**236, **2:**522, 524, 527, 528
Sforza, Ascanio **1:**123
Sforza, Bianca **2:**509, **4:**1087
Sforza, Bona **4:**1109
Sforza, Caterina **5:**1427, 1428
Sforza, Francesco **2:**417, **3:**709, 742, **4:**1087, 1088, 1090, **5:**1403, 1404
Sforza, Francesco II **1:**208, **3:**646, 647, 743
Sforza, Galeazzo Maria **3:**742, **5:**1428
Sforza, Giangaleazzo Maria **3:**742
Sforza, Giovanni **1:**123, 124
Sforza, Ludovico **1:**36, 139, 278, **3:**645, 710, 742
Sforza, Massimiliano **3:**645, 646, 742–743
Sforzas, the **1:**31, 42, 141, **3:**638, 641, 645, 646, **5:**1382, 1427, 1428
  Charles V **1:**208
  Lombardy **3:**742–743, 744, 745
  Venice **5:**1394
  Viscontis **5:**1403, 1406
Shakespeare, Hamnet **5:**1269
Shakespeare, Judith **5:**1269, 1275

Shakespeare, Susanna **5:**1269, 1275

Shakespeare, William **2:**335, **3:**600, *603, 664,* 671, 724–726, 727, 731, 732, 733, 737, **4:**880, 916, 928, **5:1268–1276,** 1322
- Aristotelian unities **5:**1321
- blank verse **3:**823
- English language **1:**108
- English theater **5:**1324–1325, 1326, 1328, 1329
- fool depiction **5:**1319
- history plays **1:**17, 19
- Jesuit plays **5:**1323
- London **3:**751
- Marlowe **3:**826
- Middleton collaboration **5:**1329
- nationalism **4:**963
- religion **5:**1326–1327
- Renaissance **5:**1223, 1225
- sonnet **4:**1052, **5:**1270
- Sonnet 18 **3:***726*
- Sonnet 130 **3:***725*

Shatir, Ibn al- **1:***271*

Shaw, George Bernard **3:**692

Shelley, Percy Bysshe **1:**113, **5:**1290

Shelton, Thomas **1:**205

Shrewsbury, earl of *see* Talbot

Shuisky, Andrew **3:**652, 653

Shuisky family **3:**652

Shute, John **1:**34

Shuysky, Vasily *see* Vasily Shuysky

Sidney, Mary **3:**725, 726, 738

Sidney, Philip **3:**724, 725, 737, 738, 823, **4:**1052, **5:**1287, 1416

Sidney, Robert **3:**824, **5:**1422

Sidney, Thomas **5:**1416

Sigismund, Holy Roman emperor **1:**119, **2:**318, 508, 509, 549, **3:**745, **4:**1073

Sigismund, king of Hungary **1:**158, **3:**616

Sigismund I, king of Poland **4:**1109, 1110, **5:**1307, 1308, 1310

Sigismund II, king of Poland **1:**200, **3:**654, **4:**1109, 1110, 1112

Sigismund III Vasa, king of Poland **4:**939, 1112–1113

Simeon, grand prince of Moscow and Vladimir **4:**933

Simmons, Samuel **4:**879

Simonetta, Cicco **3:**742

Simon of Trent (blood libel) **3:**673

Simons, Menno **5:**1195

Sinan Bey **3:***618*

Sindel, Jan **3:**779

Sitoni, Giovanni Francesco **1:**280

Sixtus II, Saint **5:***1221*

Sixtus IV, Pope **1:**133, 277, **3:**673, 852, **4:**907, 975, 1022, *1023,* **5:**1230–1231, 1278, 1379, 1428
- calendar reform **1:**175

Sixtus V, Pope **1:**40, 44, 45, 277, **2:**442, **4:**1022

Skála, Jan **1:**280

Slavs **1:**170

Sluter, Claus **4:**981

Smith, Adam **5:**1348–1349

Smith, Cyril Stanley **2:**383

Smith, J. C. **5:***1429*

Smythe, John **5:**1350

Snellick, Jan **5:***1414*

Snyders, Frans **5:**1241

Socrates **4:**1092–1093, 1094, 1095

Soderini, Pietro **4:**872

Solander, Daniel **5:**1258

Solothurn **5:**1314

Somerset, duke of *see* Seymour, Edward

Sonni Ali **3:**612

Sophocles **3:**685, 688, 729

Soto, Hernando de **2:**382, **4:**888

Southwell, Robert **4:**896, **5:**1424

Spadas, the **1:**40, 41

Sparrman, Anders **5:**1258–1259

Speed, John **5:***1297*

Spenser, Edmund **2:**335, **3:**721, 725, 726, 737, 754, **5:1286–1290**

Speusippus **4:**1095

Spinoza, Baruch **4:**1071–1072, **5:1291–1295**

Spranger, Bartholomeus **2:**559, **4:**990

Sprenger, Jacob **3:**802

Stafford, Edward **2:**375

Stalin, Joseph **3:**656

Stefaneschi, Cardinal **2:**487, 491

Sten Sture (the Elder), regent of Sweden **5:**1304

Sten Sture (the Younger), regent of Sweden **5:**1304–1305

Stephen, Saint **5:***1284*

Stephen Báthory, king of Poland **4:**1112

Stevin, Simon **1:**275, **3:**831, **5:**1250

Stewart, Walter **5:**1296

Stiatessi, Pierre Antonio **2:**469, 471

Stiatessi, Prudentia **2:**471, 474

Stimmer, Tobias **2:***367,* **4:***1075*

Stoffels, Hendrickje **5:**1212, 1215, 1217

Stoss, Veit **4:**1112

Stow, J. **5:***1161*

Strafford, earl of *see* Wentworth, Thomas

Strigel, Bernhard **2:**550

Striggio, Alessandro **4:**919

Stroganovs, the **4:**936

Strozzi, Clarissa **1:**197

Strozzi, Filippo **2:**420

Strozzi, Tito and Ercole **1:**125

Stuart, Mary *see* Mary, Queen of Scots

Stuarts, the **1:**189, 240 **5:1296–1303,** 1426
- architecture **1:**40, 47, 48
- Church of England **1:**239–240
- England **5:**1262

English civil wars **1:**109, **2:**347–355, **4:**906, **5:**1303, 1325
- iconoclasm **3:**609
- Jones's architecture **3:**663, 664–665, 666–667, 668
- monarchy **2:**342–346
- Puritans **1:**188
- Scotland **5:**1260–1267
- theater **5:**1322
- Thirty Years War **5:**1336

Stubbes, Philip **4:**1118

Sture *see* Sten Sture; Svante Sture

Styrian Hapsburgs **2:**508, 509

Sudbury, Simon **4:**1043, 1046

Sufi, Al- **1:***271*

Süleyman I (the Magnificent), Ottoman sultan **1:**210, **2:**512, 555, **3:**623, 625, 681

Sumerians **1:**173

Surgant, Johann Ulrich **3:**698

Surrey, earl of *see* Howard, Henry

Susato, Tielman **4:**950

Svante Sture **5:**1304

Swammerdam, Jan **5:**1258

Swanenburg, Jacob Isaaczoon van **5:**1210

Sweelinck, Jan Pieterszoon **4:**954, 960

Swinburne, Algernon Charles **3:**823

Swynford, Catherine **1:**214

Sylvester I, Pope **3:**594, 686

T

Taccola, Mariano **1:**280, **5:***1407*

Tacitus **3:**588, 590, **4:**923

Taikosama *see* Hideyoshi Toyotomi

Talbot, Elizabeth **5:***1264*

Talbot, George, earl of Shrewsbury **5:**1420

Talbot, Grace **5:**1420

Talbot, John, earl of Shrewsbury **2:***404*

Talbot Shrewsbury Book of Romances **3:***601*

Tallis, Thomas **4:**953

Tamerlane *see* Timur Lenk

Tapia, Gonzalo de **4:**890

Tartaglia, Niccolò **3:**829

Tasman, Abel **2:**385

Tassi, Agostino **2:**469–474

Tassman, Abel **2:**385

Tasso, Torquato **1:**223, **3:**721, **4:**922

Tauler, Johannes **1:**185, **3:**760, **4:**1065

Taverner, John **1:**280

Tebaldeo, Antonio **1:**125

Tell, William **5:**1312

Terbrugghen, Hendrik **4:**997

Terence **3:**683, 687, 729, 732, 733

Italian stage revival **5:**1320

Teresa of Ávila **1:**100, **5:**1207, 1427

Tetzel, Johann **3:***757,* **5:**1189, 1190, 1191

Tezio, Paulo **1:**98

Themistius **1:**56

Theodora, Byzantine empress **1:**258

Theodosius I (the Great), emperor of Rome **1:***168,* **2:**531, **3:**696

Theodosius II, Byzantine emperor **1:**256, 257

Theotokópoulos, Doménikos *see* Greco, El

Thevet, André **5:**1169

Thomas, Lord Camoys **1:**18

Thomas à Kempis **1:**99, 185, **3:**606, 760, **4:**1079

Thomas Aquinas **2:***398,* 461, **3:**696, 760, **4:**1075, **5:**1249

Aristotelianism **1:**52, 56, 59, **3:**604

astrology **1:**73

blood-sports critique **1:**96

divine right **4:**906

Erasmus vs. **2:**357, 358–359

Greek translation **1:**261

iconoclasm **3:**604, 606

idealism **1:**182

magic **3:**797

philosophy **4:**1062, 1064

Thomas Palaeologus **1:**169

Thomas Posthumous Hoby **5:**1422

Thomas the Apostle **2:**380

Thorne, Robert **2:**383

Thou, Jacques-Auguste de **4:**1033

Thucydides **2:**542, **3:**588

Thunberg, Carl Peter **5:**1259

Tilly, count of *see* Tserclaes, Johann

Timofeevich, Yermak **3:**656

Timur Lenk **1:***71,* **3:**617, 621

Tinctoris, Johannes **4:**944

Tintoretto **1:***259,* **5:**1236, 1387, 1388, 1399

Titian **2:***364,* **3:***701,* **4:**981, 986, 988, 989, 994, *1012, 1056,* **5:***1197,* 1222, 1236, 1237, *1352, 1353, 1360,* 1386, 1387, 1388, 1389, 1399

as Rembrandt influence **5:**1213, 1214

Tokugawa shogunate **4:**1142, *1143*

Toledo, Antonio de **1:**204

Tomasso da Messina **4:**1055

Tomassoni, Ranuccio **1:**191

Tomeo, Niccolò Leonico **1:**56

Torquemada, Tomás de **2:**533, **5:**1278

Torricelli, Evangelista **3:**775

Torriti, Jacopo **2:**488

Tottel, Richard **3:**723

Tovey, Nathaniel **4:**880

Toynbee, Arnold **1:**166

Trajan, emperor of Rome **4:**1040

Triana, Rodrigo de **1:**248

Trissino, Gian Giorgio **1:**43, 125, **4:**1000, 1001, 1002

Trivulzio, Giangiacomo **3:**651, 743

Tschudi, Aegidius **5:**1312

Tserclaes, Johann, count of Tilly **3:**835, 836, 837, 838, 839, **5:**1333, 1334, 1335, 1337, 1415

Tudor, Elizabeth *see* Elizabeth I, queen of England

Tudor, Margaret *see* Margaret Tudor, queen consort of Scotland

Tudor, Mary *see* Mary I

Tudors, the **1:**233, 236, **2:**410, 521, **4:**912

Elizabeth I **2:**326–333

Henry VIII **2:**521–528

male heir **1:**233

printing **5:**1175

Reformation **5:**1325

Scotland **5:**1261, 1297, 1298

Shakespeare **5:**1271

Tull, Jethro **1:**27

Tunstall, Cuthbert **1:**106

Turriano, Juanelo **1:**280

Tusi, Nasir ad-Din al- **1:**271

Tyler, Wat **4:**1044, 1046, 1048

Tyndale, William **1:**232, 234, *240,* **2:**524, **3:***697,* 698, **4:**931

bibles **1:**103, 105, 106, 107, 110

U

Uccello, Paolo **4:**985

Ulászló II, king of Hungary **1:**120, **2:**510

Ulster, countess of **1:**212–213

Uluch Ali **3:**718

Umberto I, king of Italy **2:**466

Urban V, Pope **1:**112, 115, **4:**1052

Urban VI, Pope **4:**1010, **5:**1424

Urban VIII, Pope **1:**73–74, **2:**466, **5:**1380

Bernini works **1:**97, 98, 99, 100

religious orders **5:**1208

Rome **5:**1234

Thirty Years War **5:**1332, 1333, 1336

Urbina, Juan de **1:**205

Urbino, duke of **3:**701

Ussher, James **1:**110

Uylenburgh, Hendrick van **5:**1212

Uylenburgh, Saskia van **5:**1212, 1214

Uzzanos, the **2:**417, **3:**850

V

Vadislav, king of Bohemia *see* Ulászló II, king of Hungary

Vaenius, Otto *see* Veen, Otto van

Valdor, Johannes **5:***1253*

Valla, Lorenzo **4:**1023

Donation of Constantine forgery **3:**584, 594

Erasmus **2:**358, 359, **3:**591

Latin scholarship **3:**586, 591, 686–687, 688

manuscript analysis **3:**587

overview of **3:**586

Valois dynasty **2:**555, **4:**966

Burgundy **1:**157–164

Catherine de Médicis **1:**197–201

France **2:**433, 436, 438, 451

Francis I **2:**445–450

Henry IV **2:**516–520

Italian wars **2:**421

Valturio, Roberto **5:***1408*

Van Dyck, Anthony **2:***347,* **3:***608,* **4:**993, **5:**1211, 1241, 1243, *1257, 1302*

Van Gogh, Vincent *see* Gogh, Vincent van

van Somer, Paul **1:***81*

Vanson, Adrian **5:**1265

Varano, Giulia **5:**1380

Varcollier, Atala **5:***1179*

Vargas Manrique, Luis de **1:**204

Varro, Marcus **1:**277

Vasa dynasty **5:***1304,* 1305–1310

Christina **1:**227–231

Vasari, Giorgio **1:**34, 42, 148, **2:**485, **3:***649,* 714

on Brunelleschi's dome **1:**150, 156

Michelangelo **5:***1225*

on Palladio **4:**1005

on Raphael **5:**1183, 1185, 1187

Vasily I, grand prince of Muscovy **4:**934

Vasily II (the Blind), grand prince of Muscovy **4:**934

Vasily III, grand prince of Muscovy **3:**652, **4:**935, 936
Vasily Shuysky **4:**939
Vasnezov, Viktor Michailovitch **3:***653*
Vasquez, Daniel **1:***248*
Vecchi, Giovanni da **4:***1025*
Vecchietta, Lorenzo **4:**1090
Veen, Otto van **5:**1236
Vega, Garcilaso de la **3:**726
Vega, Lope de **1:**204, **3:**727, 728, **5:**1284, 1322–1323
  on *Don Quixote* **1:**205
Vega Carpio, Lope Felix de **3:**726
Velázquez, Diego Rodríguez de Silva **4:**993, 994, **5:**1237, 1242, **1384–1391**
Velázquez, Juan **5:**1199
Velde, J. van de **5:***1168*
Velde, Willem van de, II **5:***1347*
Veli, Benedetto **5:***1201*
Venn, John **4:**1068
Vere, Edward de **5:**1276
Vergerio, Piero Paolo **3:**584, **5:**1220
  background of **2:**318
Verhaecht, Tobias **5:**1236
Vermeer, Jan **4:**997, 998, *999*
Vermuyden, Cornelius **1:**276
Vernet, Emile-Jean-Horace **5:***1231*
Veronese **1:***203,* **4:**992, **5:**1388
Verrazano, Giovanni da **2:**382, **4:**914
Verrocchio, Andrea del **3:**706, 707, 708, 709, **4:**985
Verrocchio, Giuliano del **3:**707
Vesalius, Andreas **2:**302, 303, **3:**840, 845, 846, 848, **5:**1250, 1254
Vespignano **2:**487
Vespucci, Amerigo **1:***254,* 255, **2:***374,* 382
Vettori, Francesco **1:**245
Vicente, Gil **4:**1145
Vicentino, Nicola **4:**943

Victoria, Tomás Luis de **4:**956–957
Vierlingh, Andries **1:**274–275, 276, 281
Viète, François **3:**828, 830
Vignola, Giacomo da **1:**34, 38, 40, 44, 45, **3:**667
Vijd, Joos **2:**387
Villiers, George, duke of Buckingham **2:**342–343, 347, **5:**1300, 1301, 1336
Vimercati, Francesco **1:**56
Vincent de Paul **5:**1208
Vincent Ferrer **3:**676, **5:**1160, 1161
Vincenzo II Gonzaga, duke of Mantua and Montferrat **5:**1336
Virgil **1:**112, **3:***594,* 737, **4:**1144, **5:**1219, 1289
  classical languages **3:**682, 683, 687
  English humanism **2:**336
  Petrarch **4:**1052–1053
Vischer, Georg **1:***178*
Visconti, Azzone **5:**1403, 1405
Visconti, Bernabò **1:**216, **3:**741, **5:***1404,* 1405
Visconti, Bianca Maria **3:**742, **5:**1403, 1404
Visconti, Filippo Maria **3:**742, **5:**1403, 1404, 1405
Visconti, Galeazzo I **5:**1403, 1404, 1405
Visconti, Galeazzo II **5:**1402, 1403, 1404, 1405–1406
Visconti, Gian Galeazzo **3:**741, **5:**1402, 1403, 1404, 1405
Visconti, Giovanni Maria **3:**742, **5:**1403
Visconti, Lucchino **5:**1403, 1404
Visconti, Matto I **3:**741, **5:**1405
Visconti, Ottone **3:**741, **5:**1403, 1404–1405
Visconti, Valentina **3:**645, 742
Viscontis, the **1:**213, **3:**638, 645, 740, 741–742, 744, 745, **5:**1394, **1401–1406**
Visigoths **1:**258

Visscher, Jan Claesz **5:***1271, 1328*
Vitruvius **1:***32,* 33–34, 35, 48, 141, **3:**668, 709, **4:**1001, **5:**1321
Vitry, Jacques de **3:**779
Vittoria, Alessandro **4:**1000
Vives, Juan Luis **5:**1282–1283, 1416, 1417
Viviani, Vincenzo **2:**460
Vladislav the Jagiellonian *see* Ulászló II
Volterra, Daniele da **4:**992
Vroom, Hendrik **1:***66*

W

Waghenaer, Lucas Janszoon **2:***376*
Waldo, Peter **2:**531
Waldseemüller, Martin **1:***254,* 255, **2:**382
Walens, Mayses **5:***1327*
Wales, prince of **3:**598, **4:**903
Walker, Anna **5:**1427
Wallace, William **4:**905
Wallenstein, Albrecht von **3:**838–839, **5:**1332, 1333, 1334, 1335, 1337
  overview of **5:**1415
Waller, Edmund **3:**690
Walsingham, Francis **2:**330, 331
Walsingham, Thomas **3:**825
Walter, Johann **4:**943, 952, 954
Walworth, William **4:**1046
Warbeck, Perkin **1:**233
Ward, Mary **5:**1208
Warham, William **1:**106, 235, 240
Warner, William **3:**753
Warwick, earl of *see* Neville, Richard
Watson, Thomas **3:**822, 824
Watzenrode, Lucas **1:**265
Wavrin, Jean de **3:***599,* **4:***1127, 1137*
Webb, John **1:**48, **3:***667,* 668, **4:**1007
Weber, Max **1:**190, **4:**1123
Webster, John **5:**1325, 1329

Weerdt, Abraham van **5:***1172*
Welf family **2:**505
Wells, H. G. **4:**929
Welser family **5:**1344
Wenceslas, Saint **1:**117, *118*
Wenceslas III, king of Bohemia **1:**116, 117
Wenceslas IV, king of Bohemia *see* Wenceslas, Holy Roman emperor
Wenceslas, Holy Roman emperor **1:**118, 119, **3:**741, **5:**1403, 1404, 1405
Wendel, Lupold von **3:**749
Wentworth, Thomas **2:**350
Werner, count of Hapsburg **2:**507
Westfall, James **2:**459
Weyden, Rogier van der **1:**129, *161,* 163, *221,* **2:**316, **4:**982, *1129,* **5:***1357*
Wheldon, James **2:**547
Whichcote, Benjamin **4:**1070
Whistler, James McNeill **5:**1391
Whitehead, Alfred North **4:**1092
Whitgift, John **1:**79
Whitney, Isabella **3:**726
Whittingham, William **1:**107
Wignancourt, Alof de **1:**194
Wildeck, Magdalena **5:**1246
Willaert, Adriaan **4:**947, 951–952
William I (the Conqueror), king of England **2:**403, **3:**749, 751
William III (William of Orange), king of England *see* William and Mary
William and Mary, king and queen of England **1:**24, 262, **2:**346, 499, **4:**906, **5:**1302
William I (William of Orange), stadholder of the Netherlands **2:**331, 453, **4:**1057
William of Norwich (blood libel) **3:**673

William of Ockham *see* Ockham, William of

William of Orange *see* William I; William and Mary

Willoughby, Francis **5:**1422

Willoughby, Hugh **2:**384

Wishart, George **1:**189

Witt, Johannes de **5:***1326*

Wittelsbach family **2:**549, 550

Witzel, George **3:**768

Wladyslaw I, king of Poland **4:**1112

Wladyslaw II, king of Poland **4:**911, 1104, 1105, 1106, 1107

Wladyslaw III, king of Poland **4:**1105

Wladyslaw IV Vasa, king of Poland **4:**1113, 1114, **5:**1308

Wolfgang of Zweibrücken **2:**453

Wolgemut, Michael **2:**311

Wolmar, Melchior **1:**179

Wolsey, Thomas **2:**521, 522, 523, **4:**930, **5:***1273,* 1373
  Hampton Court Palace **2:**334
  Henry VIII **1:**234, **2:**338

Woodroffe, Benjamin **1:**262

Woodward, William Harrison **5:**1219

Wotton, Henry **5:**1223

Wren, Christopher **1:**32, 33, 47, 48–49, 140, **3:**667, 668, 748, *755,* **4:**1007, **5:**1256, *1374, 1375,* **1429–1433**

Wright, Joseph **4:***1072*

Wroth, Mary **3:**725, 737

Wuchters, Abraham **5:***1311*

Wurst, Wider Hans **5:**1191

Würzburg, bishop of **1:**77

Wyatt, Thomas (the Elder) **3:**722–723, 724, 726

Wyatt, Thomas (the Younger) **2:**326–327

Wycliffe, John **1:**102, 103, 110, 232, **2:**536–537, **3:**761

X

Xavier, Francis **4:**894, 1015, **5:**1205–1206

Xenophon **1:**261

Y

Yarranton, Andrew **1:***276*

Yermak Timofeyevich **4:**936

Yonge, Nicholas **4:**943

York, archbishop of **2:**346

Yorks, the **1:**233, **2:**408, **4:**903, 912, **5:**1273

Young, John **5:**1287

Young, Peter **5:**1264

Young, Thomas **4:**879, 880

Yung-lo *see* Chu Ti

Z

Zabarella, Jacopo **1:**57

Zahir-ud-Din, Muhammad *see* Babur

Zeeman, Reinier **4:***1031*

Zeno **4:**1097

Zuccari, Federico **2:***366,* **3:***648,* **5:**1236, 1237

Zuccari, Taddeo **5:***1362*

Zurbarán, Francisco de **4:**994, **5:**1386

Zwingli, Huldrych **1:**178, 181, 184, **2:**483, 539, **3:**761, 762, **4:**952, **5:**1193, 1312, 1314, 1315, 1316

Cultural and Literary Index

A **boldface** number preceding a colon indicates the volume. Numbers in *italics* refer to captions. Numbers entirely in **boldface** refer to a full article.

A

Abduction of Proserpina (Bernini) **1:***98*, 99

Absalom, fili mi (Josquin) **4:**948

Academy of Design (Florence) **2:**469–470

Account of Denmark As It Was in the Year 1692, An (Molesworth) **5:**1311

Account of Virtue, An (More) **4:**1070–1071

Acropolis (Athens) **4:**1095

Acts and Monuments of the Church (Foxe) **1:***187, 232*

Adagia (Adages) (Erasmus) **2:**357, **3:**684, 688

Ad Atticus (Cicero) **3:**584, 589, 682, 683, 684, **4:**1053

Admiral's Men (London theater) **3:**824

Adnotationes novi testamenti (Valla) **3:**586

Adoration of the Magi (Botticelli) **1:**135, 138, **5:***1219*

Adoration of the Mystic Lamb (Eyck) **2:**386, 387, 390, 392

Adoration of the Name of Jesus (El Greco) **4:***1058*

Adoration of the Shepherds (Caravaggio) **1:**194

Adoration of the Shepherds (Rubens) **5:**1238

Adoration of the Shepherds with Saints Lawrence and Francis (Caravaggio) **1:**194

Advancement of Learning (F. Bacon) **1:**80, **3:**775, **4:**1065, 1067–1068, 1072

Adventures of Master F.J. (Gascoigne) **3:**738

Advertisements to the Jurymen of England (Filmer) **3:**803

Aeneas, Anchises, and Ascanius Fleeing Troy (Bernini) **1:**98

Aeneid (Virgil) **4:**1144
  Surrey translation **3:**823

Aeschylus **3:**685

Affected Young Ladies, The (Molière) **4:**899

Africa (Petrarch) **4:***1050*, 1052

Agricola **1:***279*

Akbarnama (Mogul text) **3:**615

Alba Madonna (Raphael) **5:**1185

Alberti, Leon Battista **1:**30–31, 32, 34, 35–36, 37, 139, 154, **2:***418*, **3:**745, 827, 847, **4:**984–985, 987, 989, 1001, **5:**1229
  on Brunelleschi's dome **1:**154

Album amicorum (Walens) **5:***1327*

alexandrine **3:**731

Alhambra Palace **2:***396*

allegory **4:**1094–1095, **5:**1318–1319, 1328

Allegory (Raphael) *see Knight's Dream, The*

Allegory on Charles V as Ruler of the World (Rubens) **5:***1200*

Allegory of Commerce, The (Amman) **5:***1344*

Allegory of Painting (Gentileschi) **2:**472–473

Allegory of Peace and Arts under the English Crown, The (Gentileschi) **2:**474

"Allegro, L'" (Milton) **4:**880

alliterative verse **1:**220

All's Well That Ends Well (Shakespeare) **5:**1272

Almagest (Ptolemy) **1:**265, 267, 269, **3:**728

Altieri Chapel (Ripa) **1:**100

Amadis of Gaul **1:**222–223

Americae tertia pars (Bry) **1:***251*

Amman, Jost **5:**1344

Amoretti (Spenser) **5:**1287, 1289

Amorum emblemata (Veen) **5:**1236

Anabasis (Xenophon) **1:**261

Anatomy Lesson of Doctor Tulp, The (Rembrandt) **5:**1212, 1217

Andromaque (Racine) **3:**730

Anelida and Arcite (Chaucer) **1:**213, 217

Angelico, Fra **2:**428, **5:**1229

Anglo-Saxon literature **1:**214

Annals of the Old and New Testament (Ussher) **1:**110

Annotationes (Valla) **2:**358

Annunciation, The (Leonardo attribution) **3:***706*, 708

Antiquities of Rome (Palladio) **1:**43, **4:**1003

anti-Stratfordians **5:**1276

Antony and Cleopatra (Shakespeare) **5:**1272

Aphorisms (Hippocrates) **5:**1177

Apocalypse Cycle (Dürer) **2:**314

Apollo and Daphne (Bernini) **1:**98

Apollo and Daphne (Pollaiuolo) **2:**425

Apologie for Poesie, An (Spenser) **5:**1287

Aqua Claudia (Rome) **5:***1227*

Aqua Virgo (Rome) **1:**37

Arcadia (Sidney) **3:**725, 737

arches **1:**36

architecture **1:30–49**
  Bernini **1:**97–101
  Bramante **1:**139–143
  Brunelleschi **1:**149–156, **4:**983, 984
  Burgundy **1:**163
  Byzantium **1:**170, 171, 263
  England **2:**334
  Florence **2:**418, 424, 425
  France **2:***436*, 444, 450
  housing **2:**563
  Italian city-states **3:**634, *640*, 641, 642
  Jones **3:**663–668
  London **1:**48–49, **3:**748, *755*
  Medicis **3:**852, 855
  Michelangelo **2:**424–425, **4:**871, 876, 877, **5:***1226*

Palladio **4:**1000–1007

papacy **4:**1025–1026, 1040

Paris **4:**1031, 1034

Portugal **4:**1141, 1144, *1145*

Raphael **5:**1186–1187

Rome **5:**1229, 1231, 1232, 1235

Scotland **5:**1263–1264

Spain **4:**1060, **5:***1277*, 1280

Sweden **5:**1308

theater buildings **5:***1320*, 1321, 1326

Venice **5:**1399

Warsaw **4:**1112

Wren **1:**48–49, **5:***1429*, 1430–1433

Architecture of Triumphal Arches (Harrison) **3:**665

Architettura (Bramante) **1:**140

Arena Chapel (Padua) **2:**485, 486, 487, 488, 490

Areopagitica (Milton) **4:**883

Arianna, L' (Monteverdi) **4:**918, 920–921, 922

Ariosto, Ludovico **1:**125, 223, **3:**721, 733, **5:**1289

Aristotle with a Bust of Homer (Rembrandt) **1:***59*

Armada Portrait **2:***332*

Armada Tapestry **1:**66

Armelina (Rueda) **5:**1323

Arnolfini Portrait (Jan van Eyck) **2:***389*, 390

arsenale (Venice) **5:***1394*

Ars poetica (Horace) **1:**59

art *see* painting and sculpture

Art de l'artillerie, L' (Senftenberg) **5:***1415*

Arte de la pintura (Pacheco) **5:**1384

Arte nuevo de hacer comedias (Vega) **3:**728

Arthurian romances **1:**222, 223, 224

Art of Making New Plays, The (Vega) **3:**728

Art of Raising Children (Galen) **5:**1177

Art of War, The (Machiavelli) **3:**770, 772, 773

Ascent of Mount Carmel (John of the Cross) **5:**1207

Ashton Court (Bristol) **5:**1350

Assayer, The (Galileo) **2:**465, 466

Assumption, Cathedral of the (Moscow) **4:**933, 934, *935*

Assumption of the Virgin, The (Carracci) **1:**193

Assumption of the Virgin, The (Titian) **4:**988

Astrophel and Stella (Sidney) **3:**724, 725, **4:**1052

As You Like It (Shakespeare) **3:**737, **5:**1271, 1274

Aubrey, John **2:**547

Autobiography (Christina) **1:**231

Auto-da-Fé (Berruguete) **2:***397*

Ave regina coelorum (Dufay) **4:**945

B

Babylonian Captivity of the Church (Luther) **1:**232, **5:**1192

Bacchus (Caravaggio) **1:***191*

Bacchus (Michelangelo) **4:**870–871

ballads **3:**726, **4:**960

ballet **4:**943

Banker and His Wife, The (Massys) **1:***84*

Banqueting House (London) **1:**48, **2:**355, **3:**666, 667, **5:**1241

Baptism of Christ, The (Verrocchio) **3:**706–707

Bardi, Donato di Niccolò di Betto *see* Donatello

Bardi Chapel **2:**485, 487

baroque architecture **1:**30, 33, 38, 44–45, 47, 49, 97

Jones **3:***667*, 668

Portugal **4:**1144

baroque music **1:**230, **4:**961

Monteverdi **4:**916, 919, 920, 923

Schütz **5:**1244–1247

baroque painting **4:**980, 981, 990–995, 996, **5:**1213, 1224–1225

Rubens **5:**1236–1243

Velázquez **5:**1387

Bartolomeo, Fra **4:***1077*, **5:**1184

Bartolomeo da Venezio **1:***123*

basilica **1:**152, 154

Basilica (Vicenza) **4:**1004

Basilica of Saint Peter *see* Saint Peter's Basilica

Battista della Porta, Giovanni **4:***1073*

Battle of Ostia (Raphael) **5:**1187

Bayeux tapestry **3:**691

Bazán, Álvaro de **5:***1401*

bearbaiting **1:**92–96

Beheading of Saint John the Baptist (Caravaggio) **1:**194

Beheading of Saint John the Baptist (Verrocchio) **3:**707

Behemoth (Hobbes) **2:**543, 546, 547

Belfagor (Machiavelli) **3:**736

Bellini, Gentile **1:***263*, **3:**618, *635*, **4:***1099*, **5:***1396*, *1399*

Bellini, Giovanni **2:**312, **4:***988*, 989

Belvedere palace (Vatican) *see* Villa del Belvedere

Belvoir Castle (England) **3:**665

Benozzo di Lesse Gozzoli, Francesco **1:***52*

Benvenuto di Giovanni **1:***86*

Berckenrode, Balthasar Florisz van **1:***274*

Berkman, Hendrik **5:***1252*

Bernat, Martin **5:***1279*

Bernini, Gian Lorenzo **1:**97–101, 195, **2:***458*, **3:**668, **4:**1000, **5:**1225

architecture **1:**32, 33, 34, 38, 40, 44–45, 48, 49

Caravaggio as influence **1:**195

Christina **1:**230

painting and sculpture **4:**993, 994

Rome **5:***1234*, 1235

Saint Peter's colonnade **4:***1008*, 1026

Urban VIII **5:**1333

Bernini, Luigi di Pietro **1:**44

Bernini, Pietro **1:**44, 97, 98

Berner Chronik (Schilling) **5:***1313*

Berruguete, Pedro **2:***397*

Bettes, John (the Elder) **5:***1272*

Big Fish Eat Little Fish (Bruegel) **1:**145

Biondo, Flavio **3:**587

Birth of Venus (Botticelli) **1:**135, **2:***424*, 425

Blackfriars (London theater) **3:**748, 749, **5:**1275, 1327

Blaeu, Jan **1:**275

Blaeu Atlas **5:**1251

blank verse **3:**731, 732, 823

Shakespeare **5:**1270, 1274

blood sports **1:**92–96

Boccaccio, Giovanni **1:**111–115, **3:**735, 736, **4:**963, 1051, **5:**1202

Cervantes comparison **1:**205

Chaucer **1:**216–219

Florence **2:**423

vernacular language **1:**217, **3:**694

bodegónes (still lifes) **5:**1385

bonae literae **2:**362, 363

Book of Common Order, The (Knox) **1:**189

Book of Contemplative Life (Meli da Crema) **1:**126

Book of the Courtier (Castiglione) **3:**736

Book of Dede Korkut (Turkish epic) **3:**629

Book of the Duchess, The (Chaucer) **1:**215, 218

book fairs **3:**781, 806, 819

Book of Fiefs, The (treatise) **2:**405

Book of Grand Manners, The (Jacques le Grant) **1:**85

Book of Hours of the Blessed Virgin **4:**1118

Book of Hours of Duchess Mary of Burgundy **4:***1121*

Book of King Arthur and the Knights of the Round Table (Chrétien de Troyes) **4:***1101*

Book of Margery Kempe, The **4:**1081

Book of My Life, The (Cardano) **1:***70*, **3:**830

Book Named the Governor, The (Elyot) **4:**1122

Book of the Order of Chivalry (Lull) **1:**224

Book of Sir Thomas More, The (Munday) **5:**1323

Books of the Memorable Cases (Petrarch) **4:**1051

Borrachos, Los (Velázquez) **5:**1387

Borromini, Francesco **1:**33, 38, 40, 44–45, 49, **5:**1235

Bosch, Hieronymus **1:**127–132

as Bruegel influence **1:***144*, 145, 146, 148

Bosse, Abraham **5:***1423*

Botticelli, Sandro **1:***114*, **133–138, 2:***424–425*, **3:**706, 852, 856, **4:**985, **5:***1219*, 1220, 1230

Bourdon, Sebastien **1:***227*, **2:***300*, **5:***1293*

Bourguignon, Le (Jacques Courtois) **5:***1337*

Bouscal, Guérin de **1:***204*

Bramante (Bruschi) **1:**143

Bramante, Donato **1:**31, 32, 36, 37–38, 39, **139–143**, **3:**710, **4:**873, 878, **5:**1186

Palladio **4:**1002, 1004

Saint Peter's Basilica **1:**140, 142, 143, **4:**1026, **5:**1231

Brancacci Chapel (Florence) **3:**589

Braun, Georg **1:***78*, *281*, **5:***1316*, *1350*

Bregno, Andrea **1:**40, **5:***1230*

Brief Lives (Aubrey) **2:**547

"Brief Notes upon a Late Sermon" (Milton) **4:**886

Bronckhorst, Jan Gerritsz von **5:***1338*

Bronzino, Il **4:**990
Broquière, Bertrandon de la **1:***264*
Bruegel, Pieter (the Elder) **1:**131, **144–148, 4:***1119, 1125*
Brueghel, Pieter, III **2:***405*
Brueghel, Jan **1:**144, **4:***1124*
Brueghel, Pieter (the Younger) **1:**144, **4:***1128*, **5:***1319*
Bruhl, Nikolaus **5:***1191*
Brunelleschi, Filippo **1:**139, **149–156, 3:**668, 856, **4:**876, 878
architecture **1:**32, 34–35, 37, 47
classicism **4:**983
Florence **2:**424
perspective **2:**312, **4:**984
Bruschi, Arnaldo **1:**143
Bry, Theodore de **1:***251*, **5:***1346*
Bucolicum carmen (Petrarch) **1:**115, **4:***1051*
Bueil, Jean de **5:***1410*
Buonarroti, Michelangelo *see* Michelangelo
Buonarroti, Michelangelo (the Younger) **2:***469*
Burghley House (England) **5:***1289*
Burial of the Count of Orgaz, The (El Greco) **5:***1284*
Burial of Saint Lucy (Caravaggio) **1:**194
Burleigh House (London) **3:***749*
Buxtehude, Dietrich **4:***960*
Byrd, William **4:**943, 952
Byron, Lord (George Gordon) **1:**126, **5:***1290*
Byzantine Tradition after the Fall of Constantinople, The (Runciman) **1:**171

C

Cailleau, Hubert **5:***1317*
Calderón de la Barca, Pedro **3:**726, 727, 728, **5:***1284*, 1323
Caliari, Benedetto **1:***58*

Calling of Saint Matthew, The (Caravaggio) **1:**192–193, **4:***997*
Calling of Saint Matthew, The (Carpaccio) **1:***91*
Cambrai, Cathedral of **4:**945
Camerarius, Joachim **5:***1372*
Camerata **2:**567, **5:***1321*, 1322
Camila (Rueda) **5:**1323
Campidoglio (Rome) **5:***1232*
Campion, Edmund **4:**896, **5:**1206, 1323, 1324
Canaletto **4:***1039*, **5:***1433*
Cancelleria (Rome) **1:**30, 39, 40
Canon of Proportions (Leonardo da Vinci) **3:***709*
Canterbury Cathedral **1:**100, 218
Canterbury Tales, The (Chaucer) **1:**113, *212*, 213, 217, 218–219, 220, **3:**694, 801, **4:**931, *1081, 1083*, **5:***1202*
Cantigas de Santa María (manuscript) **3:***693*
Cantiones sacrae (Schütz) **5:***1246*
Canzoniere, Il (Petrarch) **3:**720, 721, **4:**1049, 1050, 1051, 1052
Cape Coast Castle **5:***1349*
Capitol (Washington, DC) **1:**140
Capitoline Hill (Rome) **1:**32, 37, **4:**878, 1003, 1004, **5:**1228
Cappella Giulia (Rome) **4:***955*
Cappella Paolini (Rome) **4:***1040*
Caravaggio **1:191–196, 4:**878, 993, 994, 997, **5:**1235, 1386
Gentileschi **2:**469, 470, 471, 472, 474
as Rembrandt influence **5:**1211
Rubens **5:**1237–1238
Caravaggisti, Dutch **5:**1211
Cardinal Virtues (Raphael) **5:**1186

Cardi Palace (Florence) **3:***702*
Cardsharps (Caravaggio) **1:**191, 192
caricature **1:**195
Carnevale italiano mascherato, Il (Bertelli) **5:***1321*
Carnival and Lent (Bruegel) **1:**146
Caron, Antoine **4:***1102*
Carpaccio, Vittore **1:***87, 91*, **5:***1399*
Carracci, Agostino **1:**195
Carracci, Annibale **1:**41, 193, 195, **4:**993, **5:**1235, 1237–1238
Castagno, Andrea del **1:***216*, **5:***1229*
Castel Durante **5:***1383*
Castello Visconteo **5:***1402*
Castel Sant'Angelo (Rome) **1:**37, 243, **4:***1014*, **5:**1228, 1428
Castle Howard (Yorkshire) **1:**140
castles **2:**410–411, **5:**1409–1411
decline of **5:**1407, 1410–1411
Visconti **5:***1403*
cathedrals **1:**30, **3:***639 see also specific cathedrals by keyword*
Cellini, Benvenuto **1:**243, **2:**450, **3:**767, **4:**989
Cerasi chapel **1:**193, 194, 195
Certain Experiments concerning Fish and Fruite (Taverner) **1:**280
Cervantes, Miguel de **1:202–206, 3:**728, 736, 739, **5:**1221, 1284, 1323
chivalric satire **1:**223–224
Chamberlain's Men (London theater) **5:**1270, 1271, 1272
Chambord, Château of **2:**450
Chanson de Roland, Le **1:**222, **3:***695*
chansons de geste **1:**222, **4:**950
Chant des oyseulx, Le (Janequin) **4:**948

Chapman, George **3:***825*, **5:***1327*
Charles, Duke of Byron (Chapman) **5:***1327*
Charles I, King of England (Van Dyck) **5:***1243*
Charles Quint (Madariaga, ed.) **1:**211
château **2:***436*, 450, 563
Château Steen (Rubens's home) **5:***1237*
Chatsworth House (Derbyshire) **3:***663*
Chaucer, Geoffrey **1:212–220, 3:**801, **4:**931, *1081, 1083*, **5:**1289, 1290
Boccaccio **1:**112, 113
religious orders **5:**1202
vernacular language **3:**694
Chester play cycle **5:**131
Chevensey Palace (Kent) **3:***665*
Chigi, Agostino **1:**39, 40, 41, **5:**1186
Chigi chapel (Rome) **1:**39
Children's Games (Bruegel) **1:**146, 147
chivalry **1:221–226**
Agincourt **1:**18, 20
Burgundy **1:**158, 161–162, 163, 164
courtly love **1:**221, **4:***1101*, 1102
decline of **5:**1313, 1314, 1411, 1413
feudalism **2:**402–403, 408–413
France **2:**451
Hapsburgs **2:**514, 515
Hundred Years War **3:**598
tournaments **1:**162, *224*, *225, 226*, **3:**598
chorales **4:**952, 954, 958
Choralis Constantinus (Isaac) **4:**957
choral music **1:**163, **4:**949, 950, 952
Chrétien de Troyes **1:**222, **4:***1101*
Christ before Pilate (Bosch) **1:**131

Christ Carrying the Cross (Bosch) **1:**128, 130, 131

Christ Church (Oxford) **5:***1373*

Christ Delivering the Keys to Saint Peter (Perugino) **5:***1182*

Christ and Doubting Thomas (Verrocchio) **3:**707

Christ Healing the Sick (the Hundred Guilder Print) (Rembrandt) **5:**1212, 1215

Christ in the House of Martha and Mary (Velázquez) **5:***1384*

Christine de Pisan **5:**1418

Christmas Oratorio (Schütz) **5:**1247

chromaticism **4:**919, 955

Chronica gentis scotorum (John of Fordun) **5:**1260

Chronicles (Froissart) **1:**224

Chronicle of Saint Denis **4:***1042*

Chronicle of Ulrich von Richental **1:***158*

Chronicum Helveticum **5:**1312

Chroniques d'Angleterre, Les (Wavrin) **3:***599,* **4:***1127, 1137*

churches
    arches **1:**36
    architecture **1:**30–39, 43, 44, 46, 48, 49, **3:**667, 668
    Bernini designs **1:**100–101
    Bramante designs **1:**139
    Brunelleschi designs **1:**153, 156
    circular design **1:**32, 37, 141
    Constantinople **1:**263
    Italian city-states **3:**639, 641
    mosques converted from **1:**170, 171, 172
    rood screen **5:***1160*
    Wren designs **5:**1431, 1432
    see also specific churches under keyword

Churrigueresque **1:**47

Cid, Le (Corneille) **3:**730, 731

Cigarrales de Toledo, Los (Molina) **1:**205

Cignani, Carlo **5:***1209*

Cimabue **2:**484, *485,* 488

Cino da Pistoia **5:***1366*

Cinquième Livre (Rabelais) **5:***1178*

circular churches **1:**32, 37, 141

Città di Castello chapel (Perugia) **5:***1182*

Cities of the World see Civitates orbis terrarum

City of God (Augustine) **1:**53, **4:***1055,* **5:***1282*

Civilization of the Renaissance in Italy, The (Burckhardt) **5:***1220*

Civitates orbis terrarum (Braun and Hogenberg) **1:***78, 281,* **4:***1139,* **5:***1316, 1350*

classical orders **1:**30, *31,* 37, 140, 141, 142, **2:***424*

clavichord **4:**959

Cleanness (Pearl Poet) **1:**220

Cleopatra (Gentileschi) **2:**472, 473

Cléopatre captive (Jodelle) **3:**729

Cloth Hall (Warsaw) **4:**1112

Clouet, François **1:***198,* **5:***1262*

Clouet, Jean **3:***590,* **4:**990, **5:***1298*

Cock, Hieronymus **1:**145, 146

Cocq, Frans Banning **5:**1213

Coeck van Aelst, Mayken **1:**144, 146

Coeck van Aelst, Pieter **1:**144, 145, 146

Colin Clouts Come Home Againe (Spenser) **5:**1287, 1289

Collegium Maius (Kraków) **1:***270*

Collegium Musicum **5:***1377*

Colleone, Bartolomeo, monument of **3:**707, 709

Colloquia familiaria (Erasmus) **2:**357

Colosseum (Rome) **1:**39, **4:***1026,* **5:**1326

Colours of Good and Evil (Bacon) **1:**80

Combattimento di Tancredi e Clorinda, Il (Monteverdi) **4:**917, 922

Comédie-Française **4:**902

Comedy of Errors, The (Shakespeare) **3:**732, **5:**1271

commedia dell'arte **3:**734, **4:**899, **5:**1320, *1321,* 1322

Commentaries on Caesar (Palladio) **1:**43

Commentariolus (Copernicus) **1:**265, 269, 272

Compass and Ruler (Dürer) **2:**312

Complaints (Spenser) **5:**1288–1289

Composite order **1:**30, *31*

Comus (Milton) **4:**879, 880, 884, 885

Concerning the Christian Religion (Ficino) **2:**422

Concert of Youths (Caravaggio) **1:**192

Confession of Faith (Lucaris) **1:**263

Confessions (Augustine) **4:**1052

Confutations of Tyndale's Answer (More) **1:**106

Conjurer, The (Bosch) **1:***127,* 128, 129

Consolation of Philosophy (Boethius; Chaucer translation) **1:**213, 217

Constitutions (Ignatius of Loyola) **5:**1206

Contarelli chapel (Rome) **1:**192, 193

contemptus mundi literature **1:**127

continuo **4:**916

Conversation between Women, A (Bosse) **5:***1423*

Conversion of Saint Paul (Caravaggio) **1:**193

Conversion of Saint Paul (Michelangelo) **4:**877

Conversion of Saint Peter (Caravaggio) **1:**193

coralles **3:**727, 728

Corbaccio (Boccaccio) **1:**115

Corelli, Arcangelo **1:**230

Corinthian order **1:**30, *31, 152*

Coriolanus (Shakespeare) **5:**1272

Cornaro, Luigi Alvaro **4:**1001

Corneille, Pierre **3:**729, 730, 731, **4:**898

Coronation of Poppea, The (Monteverdi) **4:**922, 923

Coronation of the Virgin (Raphael) **5:**1181, 1182

Correa, Juan **5:***1199*

Corsini Palace (Rome) *see* Palazzo Corsini

Cortegiano, Il (Castiglione) **5:**1383

Cortile de Belvedere (Vatican) **1:**142, **4:**1040

Corvus, Hans **5:***1373*

Cosmographic Mystery (Kepler) **1:**271, **2:**463

counterpoint **5:**1245

Courtier, The (Castiglione) **5:**1221, 1383

courtly love **1:**221, **2:**402, **4:***1101,* 1102

Courtois, Jacques (Le Bourguignon) **5:***1337*

Coverdale, Miles **1:***106,* 107

Cranach, Lucas (the Elder) **1:***95,* **2:***324,* **3:***704, 705, 760, 762,* **4:***1064, 1066, 1115,* **5:***1163,* 1171, *1188*

Creation (Michelangelo) **4:***1025*

Credi, Lorenzo di **3:**706, 708, **5:***1428*

Cremona, Cathedral of **4:**917

Critias (Plato) **4:**1103

Crivelli, Taddeo **3:**686

Crowning with Thorns (Bosch) **1:**130

crucifix, Byzantine **1:***170*

Crucifixion, The (Raphael) **5:**1181

Crucifixion (Bosch) **1:**130

Crucifixion of Saint Peter (Michelangelo) **4:**877

Crucifixion with Saints Mary the Virgin, Mary

Magdalene, John, and Jerome (Raphael) **5**:1182

Cure of Folly, The (Bosch) **1**:128, 129, 130

Curtain (London theater) **5**:1326, 1327

Cymbeline (Shakespeare) **5**:1271

D

Dafne (Peri) **4**:920, 943

Dafne (Schütz) **5**:1246

Dance of the Nudes (Pollaiuolo) **2**:425

dancing **4**:950

Dante Alighieri **1**:53, **2**:484, **4**:963, 1050, **5**:1249
  Boccaccio **1**:111, 112, 113, 114, 115
  as Chaucer influence **1**:216, 217–218, 219
  overview of **1**:217
  vernacular language **1**:217, **3**:694

Daumier, Honoré **1**:*206*

David (Bernini) **1**:98–99

David (Donatello) **2**:424, **3**:856, **4**:984, 999

David (Michelangelo) **4**:870, 871, 872–873, 986, 990

David (Verrocchio bronze) **3**:707

David, Jacques-Louis **4**:*1093*

De architectura (Vitruvius) **5**:1321

Death and the Miser (Bosch) **1**:128, 129

Death of Socrates (David) **4**:*1093*

Death of the Virgin (Caravaggio) **1**:193, 194

De augmentis scientiarum (Bacon) **1**:80

Debarkation at Marseilles, The (Rubens) **5**:1241

Decameron (Boccaccio) **1**:113, 114, 115, 205, 218, 219, **2**:423, **3**:694, 735, 736, **5**:1202

De casibus virorum illustrium (Boccaccio) **1**:115

Deceived Ones, The (Rueda) **3**:727

De cive (Hobbes) **2**:544

De claris mulieribus (Boccaccio) **1**:115

De corpore (Hobbes) **2**:546

De docta ignorantia (Nicholas of Cusa) **4**:1098

Defence of Poesie, The (Sidney) **3**:724, 725, 737

Defense of Free Will (Erasmus) **3**:767

Defense of the Seven Sacraments, A (Henry VIII) **1**:232, 240, **4**:929

Defense of True Liberty and Antecedent and Extrinsical Necessity (Hobbes) **2**:546

Defensiones (Milton) **4**:879, 884, 886, 887

Defensor pacis (Marsilius of Padua) **1**:53, 257, **2**:367

De historia stirpium (Fuchs) **1**:*29*

De homine (Hobbes) **2**:546

De humani corporis fabrica (Vesalius) **2**:302, **3**:840, 845, 846, **5**:1250

Dekker, Thomas **1**:93, **3**:733, 748, **5**:1326, 1327, 1329

Delaroche, Hippolyte **4**:*1074*

De libero arbitrio (Erasmus) **2**:360–361

Della misura dell'acque correnti (Castelli) **1**:277

Della Robbia, Andrea **1**:*151*

Della Robbia, Luca **1**:*154*, **3**:*682*

De machinis bellicis (Taccola) **5**:*1407*

De magistratibus et republica Venetorum (Contarini) **5**:1400

De monarchia (Dante) **1**:217

Demonstrating the Avarice of Christians (engraving) **2**:382

De naturis rerum (Neckam) **3**:778

Denkwürdigkeiten (Kottannerin) **5**:1418

De pittura (Alberti) **4**:984

Deposition of Christ (Raphael) **5**:1185

De remediis utriusque fortunae (Petrarch) **4**:1054

De re metallica (Agricola) **1**:*279*

De re militari (Valturio) **5**:*1408*

De revolutionibus orbium coelestium (Copernicus) **1**:50, 266, 269, 270, 272, **2**:463, 465, **4**:1109, **5**:1221, *1250*

Descent from the Cross, The (Rubens) **5**:1239–1240

Description of the Churches (Palladio) **4**:1003

De servo arbitrio (Luther) **2**:361

Detto d'amore, Il (Dante) **1**:217

De viris illustribus (Fazio) **2**:389

De viris illustribus (Petrarch) **4**:1052

De vita solitaria (Petrarch) **4**:1054

"Devotions upon Emergent Occasions" (Donne) **5**:1166

De vulgari eloquentia (Dante) **3**:694

Dialogo della musica antica et della moderna (V. Galilei) **4**:961

Dialogue of Comfort against Tribulation (More) **4**:932

Dialogue concerning Heresies and Matters of Religion (More) **4**:930, 931

Dialogue concerning the Two Chief World Systems (Galileo) **1**:*60, 272*, **2**:466, 467, **3**:690

Dialogue concerning Two New Sciences (Galileo) **2**:467, **3**:828, 833

Dialogue on the Dignity of the Pope and King (Ockham) **2**:366

Dialogues, The (Bruni) **1**:55

Dido, Queene of Carthage (Marlowe) **3**:823

Diodati, Charles **4**:879, 880, 882, 883

Dionysius the Areopagite Converting the Pagan Philosophers (Caron) **4**:*1102*

Dioptrics (Descartes) **2**:*297*

Discourse of a Discoverie for a New Passage to Cataia [Cathay] (Gilbert) **2**:383

Discourse on the Method (Discours de la méthode) (Descartes) **2**:295, 296–297, **3**:833

Discourses on Livy, The (Machiavelli) **3**:770, 772

Discourses on Sacred Images (John of Damascus) **3**:604

Discourses on Two New Sciences (Galileo) *see Dialogue concerning Two New Sciences*

Discourse to the Ten on Pisan Affairs (Machiavelli) **3**:779

Discourse of Voyages into the East and West Indies (Linschoten) **5**:*1343*

Discoverer of Witches, The (Hopkins) **5**:*1425*

Discoverie of Witchcraft (Scot) **5**:1425

Disputa, La (Raphael) **5**:1186

Disputation of Saint Catherine of Alexandria (Pinturicchio) **1**:*125*

dissonance, musical **4**:916, 918, 943, 944

dits amoureux **1**:215

Divers Voyages Touching the Discovery of America and the Islands Adjacent unto the Same (Hakluyt) **2**:375

Divine Comedy (Dante) **1**:113, *216*, 217, 218, 220, **2**:484, **3**:694

Doctor Faustus (Marlowe) **2**:335, **3**:732, 822, 824, 826

"Doctrine and Discipline of Divorce, The" (Milton) **4:**879, 883, 884

Doges' Palace (Venice) **5:***1399, 1400*

Dome of Paradise (Menabuoi) **4:***1062*

domes **1:**38, 43, 44, 48, 99, 140, 141

   Florence Cathedral **1:**32, 34, 35, 47, 149, 150–151, 154, *156*

Dominique, Jean **3:***659*

Donatello **1:**35, 36, **3:**856, **4:**871, *874,* 984, 985, **5:***1395*

   Florence **2:**424, 428

   Four Evangelists **1:***152*

Doni Tondo (Michelangelo) **4:***872*

Don Juan (Molière) **4:**897, 901, 902

Donne, John **3:**726, **5:**1166

Don Quixote (Cervantes) **1:**202, 203, *204,* 205, 206, 223–224, **3:**728, 739, **5:**1221, 1284

Don Quixote, the Second Volume of the Ingenious Don Quixote of La Mancha (Fernández de Avellaneda) **1:**206

Doré, Gustave **1:***205*

Doric order **1:**30, *31,* 37, 141

Dorigatti, Niccolò **1:***186,* **4:***1016*

Double Cube Room (Wilton House) **3:***667*

Doubting Thomas (Caravaggio) **1:***193*

Dowland, John **4:***957,* 959

drama *see* theater

Drayton, Michael **3:**755, 824, **5:**1329

"Dreames, Legendes, Courte of Cupide" (Spenser) **5:**1287

Dream of John Ball, A (Morris) **4:**1048

Dream of Philip II (El Greco) **4:***1058*

Drury Lane Theatre (London) **5:**1432

Dryden, John **4:**887

Dubois, François **1:***200, 201,* **4:***1033*

Dufay, Guillaume **4:**943, 944–946

Duke of Lerma on Horseback, The (Rubens) **5:***1238*

Dumonstier, Pierre **2:***469,* 471

Dunstable, John **4:**944

Duo seraphim (Monteverdi) **4:**921

Duran, Diego **5:***1285*

Dürer, Albrecht **2:311–316,** 550, *551,* **3:**828, **4:**983, 993, **5:**1171, *1220,* 1221

Durham House (England) **1:**48

Dutch painting **4:**995–998

Dyck, Anthony van *see* Van Dyck, Anthony

Dyer, Edward **3:**725, **5:**1287

Dying Slave (Michelangelo) **4:**874

E

Ecce homo (Bosch) **1:**129

Ecclesiae militantis (Dufay) **4:**946

Ecclesiastical Builders and Furniture Makers (Borromeo) **1:**32

Ecstasy of Saint Teresa (Bernini) **5:**1235

Edward II (Marlowe) **3:**822, 825

Eglogs, Epytaphs, and Sonettes (Googe) **5:**1288

Eight Plays and Eight Interludes, New and Never Performed (Cervantes) **1:**206

Eikonoklastes (Milton) **4:**884, 886

Electra (Sophocles) **3:**729

Elegances of the Latin Language (Elegantiae linguae Latinae) (Valla) **3:**586, 686, 687

Elements of the Common Laws of England (Bacon) **1:**80

Elements of Law, Natural and Politic (Hobbes) **2:**544

El Greco *see* Greco, El

Ellesmere Chaucer **5:***1202*

Elyot, Thomas **4:**1122

Emblems of Love, The (Veen) **5:**1236

Enchiridion militis christiani (Erasmus) **2:**357

Encomium moriae (Erasmus) *see* Praise of Folly, The

Encyclopédie (Diderot and D'Alembert) **2:**466

Engañados, Los (Rueda) **5:**1323

England's Improvement by Sea and Land (Yarranton) **1:**276

"English Poete, The" (Spenser) **5:**1287

engraving **1:**145, **2:**311, 314–315, **5:**1171

Enneads (Plotinus) **4:**1096

Enquiry concerning Human Understanding (Hume) **4:**1068

Enrico, ovvero Bisanzio acquistato, L' (Gonzaga) **5:**1417

entertainment *see* popular culture; theater

Entombment (Caravaggio) **1:**193

Entzauberung der Welt (Weber) **4:**1123

epic poetry **3:**721

"Epigram on Milton" (Dryden) **4:**887

epiphany **4:**1118

Epistolae familiares (Petrarch) **4:**1053

Epistolae seniles (Petrarch) **4:**1052, 1053

"Epitaphium Damonis" (Milton) **4:**883

Epithalium (Spenser) **5:**1287

Epitome of the Almagest (Regiomontanus) **1:**265, **3:**728

Escorial (Spain) **1:**46, 47, **3:***716,* **4:**1060

Essayes or Counsels, Civil and Morall, The (Bacon) **1:**80

etchings, Rembrandt **5:**1211, 1215

Ethics (Spinoza) **5:**1292, 1294

Euridice (Peri and Caccini) **4:**920

Euripides **3:**688, 729

Everyman (morality play) **5:**1318

Executed Anabaptists (woodcut) **5:**1195

Exemplary Stories (Cervantes) **1:**205, 206

Experiment on a Bird in the Air Pump, An (Wright) **4:***1072*

Eyck, Hubert van **2:**386, **4:**983

Eyck, Jan van **1:**129, 163, **2:**316, **386–392,** **4:**981, 982, 983

Eyck, Lambert van **2:**386, 391

F

fabliaux **1:**214, 219

Faerie Queene (Spenser) **2:**335, **3:**721, **5:**1286, 1289, *1290*

fairs *see* markets and fairs

Falkland Palace (Scotland) **5:**1263, 1264, *1296*

Fall of the Rebel Angels, The (Bruegel) **1:***144,* 145

Fanatic Moderations (Hall) **3:**609

Farnese Gallery **1:**195

Farnese Palace *see* Palazzo Farnese

Favola d'Orfeo, La (Monteverdi) *see* Orfeo

Feast of Bacchus, The (Velázquez) **5:**1387

Feast in the House of Levi (Veronese) **4:**992

Feast of the Rose Garlands, The (Dürer) **2:**313, 314

"Feste Burg ist unser Gott, Ein'" (Luther) **4:**952

Fiefs and Vassals (Reynolds) **2:**405

Filipepi, Alessandro di Moriano *see* Botticelli
Filocolo, Il (Boccaccio) **1:**112, *113*
Filostrato, Il (Boccaccio) **1:**112, 217
Finances of the Commune of Siena, in Time of Peace and in Time of War, The (Benvenuto di Giovanni) **1:***86,* **5:***1411*
Fine Flower of Histories, The (manuscript) **1:**69
Finta pazza Licori, La (Monteverdi) **4:***922*
Fiore, Il (Dante) **1:**217
Fire in the Borgo (Raphael) **5:**1187
First Account (Rheticus) **1:***269*
First and Chief Groundes of Architecture (Shute) **1:***34*
First Blast of the Trumpet against the Monstrous Regiment of Women (Knox) **1:**189, **5:**1267, 1426
First Book of Architecture (Serlio) **1:***31*
First Book of Discipline (Knox) **1:**189
First Map of Australia **2:***385*
Fitzwilliam Virginal Book **4:***943*
Five Books on Fish Ponds (Dubraius) **1:**280
Flagellation of Christ (Caravaggio) **1:**194, *196*
Flemish art **4:**981, 982–983, 990, 993
  Bruegel **1:**144–148
  Burgundy **1:**163
  Eyck **2:**386–392
  Italianate-style painting **1:**145–146
  Rubens **5:**1236–1243
Fletcher, John **3:**733, **5:**1325
Florence, Cathedral of
  baptistery bronze doors **3:**641, **4:**983
  Brunelleschi dome **1:**32, 34, 35, 47, 149, 150–151, *156*

Giotto **2:**487
  Michelangelo **4:**872, 878
Florentine Camerata **4:**920, 961
Florentine Histories (Machiavelli) **3:**772–773
Flower, The (Dante) **1:**217
folklore **5:**1312
Fondaco dei Tedeschi (Venice) **5:**1398
Fontainebleau (France) **1:**45, **4:**990
Fontaine-Henry, Château de **2:***436*
Fontana, Domenico **1:**38, 44, 47
Fontana, Lavinia **4:***1024*
fool, the **5:**1319
Fortitude (Botticelli) **1:**133, 134, 135
Fortune theatre (London) **3:**732
Foundations (Teresa of Ávila) **5:**1207
Fountain of the Four Rivers (Bernini) **1:**98, **5:**1235
Four Apostles, The (Dürer) **2:**312, 316
Four Books of Architecture (Palladio) **1:**34, *42,* 43, **3:**665, **4:**1001, 1002, 1003, 1004, 1007
Four Books of Human Proportion (Dürer) **2:**316
Four Horsemen of the Apocalypse, The (Dürer) **2:**313, *314*
Four Slaves (Michelangelo) **4:**874
Foxe, John **1:***187, 232,* **5:**1325
François, Jean-Charles **4:***1067,* **5:**1295
François, Simon **5:***1208*
Frankfurt Book Fair **3:**781, 819
Frauenberg, Cathedral of **1:**265, *266*
Frescobaldi, Girolamo **4:**960
"Friar's Tale, The" (Chaucer) **5:**1202
Froger, François **5:***1349*

Froissart, Jean **1:***16,* 215, 216, 224, **4:***1045,* **5:***1405*
Fuchs, Leonhard **1:***29*
Fuente ovejuna (Vega) **3:**728

G
Gabrieli, Andrea **4:**952
Gabrieli, Giovanni **4:**952, **5:**1244
Gadio, Bartolomeo **5:***1403*
Gailde, Jean **5:***1160*
Gainsborough, Thomas **5:**1243
Galatea, La (Cervantes) **1:**204
Game at Chess, A (Middleton) **5:**1329
Gammer Gurton's Needle (anon.) **3:**732
Garcia Infanzon, Juan **5:***1323*
Garden of Earthly Delights, The (Bosch) **1:**128, 129, 131
gardens **1:**25, 26, *40,* **3:**751
Gargantua (Rabelais) **3:**436, **5:**1176, 1177, 1178
Gargiulo, Domenico **2:***370,* 474
Gattamelata (Erasmo di Narni) **5:***1395*
Genealogia deorum gentilium (Boccaccio) **1:**111
General Rules of Architecture, The (Serlio) **1:**34
genre painting **5:**1215, *1386*
Gent, Justus van **2:***431*
Gentileschi, Artemisia **2:469–474**
Gentileschi, Orazio **2:**469, 474
Gentle Craft, The (Deloney) **3:**738
Geographia (Ptolemy) **2:**374
Geometry (Descartes) **3:**828
Georgics (Virgil) **3:**594, *683*
Germania (Tacitus) **3:**590
Gerusalemme liberata (Tasso) **1:**223, **3:**721, **4:**922
Gesualdo, Carlo **4:**955
Ghent Altarpiece (Eyck) **2:**386, 387, 390, 392
Ghiberti, Lorenzo **1:**34, **2:**428, **3:**641, **4:**981, 983
  Brunelleschi **1:**149, 150, 151

Ghirlandaio, Domenico **1:**169, *247,* **4:**870, 871, 985, **5:**1230
Gidea Hall (Cooke home) **5:**1419
Giorgio, Francesco di **1:**34, **5:**1379
Giorgione **4:**988, 989, **5:**1389, 1399
Giotto di Bondone **1:**145, *156,* **2:484–492,** **4:**980, 981
Giovanni, Agostino di **5:***1366*
Giovanni, Benvenuto di **1:***86,* **5:***1411*
Globe Theatre (London) **3:**748, 751, **5:**1269, 1270, 1271, *1324,* 1326, *1328,* 1329
Goat Amalthea with the Infant Jupiter and a Faun, The (Bernini) **1:***97*
Gobelin tapestry **2:***372*
Gogh, Vincent van **4:**996
Golden Ass, The (Apuleius) **1:***41*
goldsmiths **1:**149, **2:**311, 314, **3:**632
Goldsmith's Company **3:**750
Gonçalves, Nuno **4:***1138,* 1144
Gonville Hall (Cambridge) **2:**334
Gossaert, Jan (Mabuse) **1:**145
Gothic architecture **1:**30, *32,* 44, 47, 100, 152, 154, **5:**1308
  Bruges **1:**163
  Orvieto **1:***246*
  Scotland **5:**1263
  Venice **5:**1399
Gothic painting **1:**127, 129, **2:**312–313, 316
  international style **4:**981
Gowthwaite Hall (Yorkshire) **5:**1328
Goya, Francisco de **4:***1123,* **5:**1391
Gradualia (Byrd) **4:**943, 953
Gramática de la Lengua Castellana (Nebrija) **3:**694

Granacci, Francesco **2**:*419*
Granada Palace **1**:46
Grand Mosque (Djenné) **3**:*612*
Granen, Blasco de **3**:*695*
Grape and Melon Eaters (Murillo) **5**:*1386*
graphic arts **2**:310–316
Great Art, The (Cardano) **3**:829
Great Model (Wren) **5**:1432
Greco, El **1**:131, **4**:957, *1058*, 1060, **5**:1284
Greek Cross Design (Wren) **5**:1432
Greek revival architecture **1**:49
Greene, Robert **3**:732, 755, 823, 824, **5**:1325
Gregorian chant **4**:957
Guarino da Verona *see* Veronese
Guildhall (London) **3**:751
Guillaume Tell (Rossini) **5**:1312
Guzmán de Alfarache (Alemán) **3**:738

H
Haarlemmermeerboek (Leeghwater) **1**:275
Hackness manor (Yorkshire) **5**:1422
Haft Awrang (Persian manuscript) **4**:1085
Hagia Sophia, Church of (Constantinople) **1**:171–172, *256*, 263
Hakluytus Posthumus, or Purchas his Pilgrimes (Purchas, ed.) **2**:375, 377, 379
Hals, Franz **4**:996, 997, 998
Hamlet (Shakespeare) **5**:1270, 1271, 1275, 1326, 1327
Hammer of Witches, The (text) **3**:802
Hampton Court Palace (England) **2**:334
Handel, George Frideric **5**:1247
harmony **4**:944

harpsichords **4**:959
Harriot, Thomas **3**:825, 830, 831
Haywain, The (Bosch) **1**:128, *129*, 130
Healing of the Madman, The (Carpaccio) **1**:*87*
Hecuba (Euripides) **3**:729
Hendrickje at a Window (Rembrandt) **5**:1217
Henry IV (Shakespeare) **1**:17, **5**:1268, 1271, 1273
Henry V (Shakespeare) **1**:17, 19, **3**:600, *603*, **5**:1272, 1273
Henry VIII (Shakespeare) **5**:1268, 1271, 1273
Henry; or, Byzantium Gained (Gonzaga) **5**:1417
Heptaméron (Margaret of Navarre) **3**:735–736
Heptaplus (Pico) **4**:1074, 1077
Hermetic Corpus (Greek texts) **3**:799
Hero and Leander (Marlowe) **3**:822, 825
Her Protection for Women (Anger) **5**:1420
Het Schilderboeck (van Mander) **1**:144, 148
High Renaissance
architecture **1**:30, 32, 46
Bramante **1**:139, 143
music **4**:946–947
painting **1**:145, **4**:980, 981, 986–989, 990, 991, 992, 995, 999, **5**:1184–1185, 1187, 1237
Rome **5**:1231–1232
Venice **5**:1399
Hilanderas, Las (Velázquez) **5**:1390
Historia Augusta (Mussato) **3**:584
Historia de las Indias (Duran) **5**:*1285*
Historia de las Indias (Las Casas) **1**:253
Historia naturalis (Bacon) **1**:80
Historia vitae et mortis (Bacon) **1**:80

Historie of the Raigne of King Henry the Seventh, The (Bacon) **1**:80
History of Britain (Milton) **4**:887
History of the Council of Trent (Sarpi) **4**:1038
History of Italy, The (Guicciardini) **1**:245
History of the Life of the Petty Thief, The (Quevedo y Villegas) **3**:738–739
history painting **2**:469, **4**:997
Rembrandt **5**:1210, 1212
History of the Reformation (Knox) **5**:1265
History of the Resurrection (Schütz) **5**:1246
History of Richard III (More) **4**:928
History of Rome (Livy) **3**:682, 684
Hogarth, William **4**:*1116*
Hogenberg, Franz **1**:64, *78*, *183*, *184*, *211*, *281*, **2**:*371*, **5**:*1165*, *1301*, *1316*, *1350*
Holbeach House (England) **5**:1301
Holbein, Ambrosius **2**:*318*
Holbein, Hans (the Younger) **1**:*181*, *235*, **2**:*337*, **5**:*1198*, *1223*, *1371*
holidays *see* festivals
Hollar, Wenzel **3**:*749*
Holy Apostles, Church of the (Constantinople) **1**:263, 264
Holy Cross, Church of the (Blesa) **5**:*1279*
Holy Family with Curtain (Rembrandt) **5**:1215
Holyrood Palace (Scotland) **5**:1263
Holy Trinity Church (Stratford-upon-Avon) **5**:*1275*
Holy Wisdom, Church of *see* Hagia Sophia, Church of
Homer **1**:59, 258, 264, **2**:373, **5**:1289

Hope (London theatre) **3**:732
Horace **1**:59
Horace (Corneille) **3**:730
horoscope **1**:70–71, *73*, **3**:830
House of Saint-Cyr (Paris) **5**:*1419*
Hous of Fame (Chaucer) **1**:213, 217
How a Christian Youth Can Benefit from the Study of the Classics (Basil) **1**:257
"How soon hath time" (Milton) **4**:880, 881
Hradschin Palace (Prague) **2**:371
Hudibras (poem) **4**:*1116*
Hundred Guilder Print, The (Rembrandt) **5**:1212, 1215
Hunername (Ottoman manuscript) **4**:*1084*
Hunters in the Snow (Bruegel) **1**:*148*
Hunt in Honor of Charles V (Cranach the Elder) **1**:*95*
Hymnes (Ronsard) **3**:22
hymns **1**:118, **4**:952, 954
Hyperaspistes (Erasmus) **2**:361

I
Iconologica (Ripa) **2**:472
icons **1**:168, 263, **3**:*604*, 605
Idea of a Universal Architecture (Scamozzi) **1**:34
Iliad (Homer) **1**:59, 258
Hobbes translation **2**:546
illusory perspective **1**:145, **2**:312, 316
illustration **5**:1171
Image of Julius II (Michelangelo) **4**:874
images, printed **5**:1171
Imitation of Christ (Thomas à Kempis) **1**:99, **3**:760, **4**:1079
Imperial History (Mussato) **3**:584
Incoronazione di Poppea, L' (Monteverdi) **4**:922, 923
incunabula (printed books) **5**:1169
Ingannati, Gl' (anon.) **3**:727

Inquiry into the Nature and Causes of the Wealth of Nations (Smith) **5:**1349

Inspiration of Saint Matthew (Caravaggio) **1:**194

Instauratio Magna (Bacon) **1:***82*

Institutes of the Christian Religion (Calvin) **1:**179, 185, 188, **3:**607, **5:**1194

Institutio oratoria (Quintillian) **3:**583, 683, **5:**1373

Institutio principii christiani (Erasmus) **2:**357

Instruction (Charles V) **5:**1283

Instruction in Faith (Calvin) **1:**185

Instruction for Measurement with the Compass and Ruler (Dürer) **2:**312, **3:**828

Interior Castle, The (Teresa of Ávila) **5:**1207

intermezzi **3:**734, **5:**1321

international Gothic style **4:**981

Introduction to Christian Life and Virtue (Olier) **5:***1361*

Invincible Armada (Cervantes) **1:**203

Ionic order **1:**30

Isaac, Heinrich **4:**946, 950, 951, 957

isorhythmic motets **4:**945

Italy Liberated from the Goths (Trissino) **4:**1000

Ivan the Terrible and His Son on November 16, 1581 (Repin) **3:***656*

J

Jack Newberie (Deloney) **3:**738

Jacques le Grant **1:***85*

Janequin, Clément **4:**948

Jason and the Agronauts **1:**163, **2:**515

Jáuregui y Aguilar, Juan de **1:***202*

Jerusalem Delivered see Gerusalemme liberata

Jesus Was Born a Jew (Luther) **3:***675*

Jewish Bride, The (Rembrandt) **5:**1217

Jew of Malta, The (Marlowe) **3:**671, 822, 825

Jodelle Étienne **3:**720, 729

John of Fordun **5:**1260

Jones, Inigo **1:**47–48, 49, **3:***663–668*, **4:**1007, **5:***1431*

jongleurs **5:**1319

Jonson, Ben **2:**335, **3:**663, 732, 733, 739, 755, **5:**1325, 1326

Joseph's Bloody Coat Brought to Jacob (Velázquez) **5:***1387*

Josquin des Prez **4:**946–948, 949, 951, 952

Journey to Parnassus (Cervantes) **1:**202, 203

Jouvencel (Bueil) **5:***1410*

Judas Returning the Thirty Pieces of Silver (Rembrandt) **5:***1212*

Judith and Her Maidservant (Gentileschi) **2:**471, 473, *474*

Judith Beheading Holofernes (Gentileschi) **2:**471, 473

Jugement du roy de Behaigne, Le (Machaut) **1:**215

jugglers **5:**1319

Juives, Les (Garnier) **3:**730

Julian II Ordering Work on the Vatican (Vernet) **5:***1231*

Justus of Ghent **4:***1055*, **5:**1181

K

Kalff, Willem **4:***996*, 997

Kalmar Castle **5:***1304*

Kariye Carni (Constantinople) **1:***258*

Kermesse, The (Rubens) **4:***1117*

Kerseboom, Johann **5:**1256

keyboards **4:**959–960

Khadjou barrage bridge **1:***280*

Kieser, Eberhard **3:***836*

Killingworth, John **1:***174*

"Kingdom of Ireland, The" (map) **5:***1287*

King Lear (Shakespeare) **5:**1270, 1271, 1319

King's Book (1543) **2:**527

King's Cabinet Opened, The (Charles I letters) **2:**352

King's Men (London) **5:**1270, 1272, 1275

Kleine geistliche Konzerte (Schütz) **5:**1246

Klementinum (Prague) **1:***120*, 121

Kleyne Chronycke (Leeghwater) **1:**275

Klinkicht, Moritz **5:***1372*

Kneller, Godfrey **5:**1303, *1429*

Knight, Death, and the Devil, The (Dürer) **2:**314–315

knighthood *see* chivalry

Knight's Dream, The (Raphael) **5:**1181, 1183

"Knight's Tale, The" (Chaucer) **1:***213*, 217

Koburger, Anthony **5:***1171*

Kölderer, Jörg **5:***1413*

König, Gustav **5:***1376*

Koster, Laurens Janszoon **5:***1168*

krummhorn **4:**958

Kyd, Thomas **3:**732, 822, 824, **5:**1286, 1325

L

Lambeth Palace (London) **4:**1046

Lances, The (Velázquez) *see Surrender of Breda, The*

landscape design **1:**26

landscape painting **1:**144, 145, 146, 148

Langland, William **1:**220

Lanzani, Bernardino **5:***1402*

Larkin, William **4:***1068*

Lasso, Orlando di **4:**971

Last Judgment, The (Michelangelo) **1:**244, **4:**871, 877, 992, 1025, **5:***1354*

Lastman, Pieter **5:**1210–1211, 1212

Last Supper (Leonardo da Vinci) **2:**425, **3:**709, 710, 712, 713, **5:**1220

Last Supper, The (Veen) **5:***1237*

Lateran Palace (Rome) **1:**257

La Tour, Georges de **4:***995*, 997, *1120*

Laudate pueri (Monteverdi) **4:***921*

Laudatio urbis Florentinae (Bruni) **3:**584

Laura (Petrarch's muse) **4:***1050*, 1051

Laurana, Luciano da **5:**1181, *1378*, 1382

Laws (Plato) **4:**1063

Laws of Ecclesiastical Polity, The (Hooker) **2:**367, 369

Leah (Michelangelo) **4:**874

Legend of Good Women, The (Chaucer) **1:**218–219

Leonardo da Vinci **1:**133, **2:**437, 450, 560, **3:***706–714*, **4:**873

as Bramante influence **1:**139

contributions of **5:**1249

Florence **2:**424, 425

hydraulic engineering **1:**277, 278, 279

machines **3:**775, 782, 783

Medicis **3:**852, 856

painting **4:**986, 987, 988, 999

as Raphael influence **5:**1183, 1184, 1185, 1187

Renaissance **5:**1220, 1224

Leo X with Two Cardinals (Raphael) **5:**1185

Lese Gozzali, Benozzo di **1:***52*

Lesser, Aleksandr **4:***1104*

Letter to the Grand Duchess Christina (Galileo) **2:**467

Letters to Atticus (Cicero) **3:**584, 589, 682, 683, 684

Leviathan (Hobbes) **2:**543, 545–546, **4:**1066

Libro de vita contemplativa (Meli da Crema) **1:**126

Lievens, Jan **5:**1211, 1212

Life and Death of Jack Straw (anon.) **5:**1327

Life in the Countryside, The (Brueghel the Elder) **4:***1124*

Life Is a Dream (Vega) 728

Life of Aristotle (Bruni) **1**:54

Life of Bernini, The
(Baldinucci) **1**:34, 101

Life of Filippo Brunelleschi
(Manetti) **1**:34, *155*

*Life of Gargantua and
Pantagruel, The* (Rabelais)
3:436, **5**:1176, 1177,
1178

*Life of the Admiral Christopher
Columbus, The*
(F. Columbus) **1**:248

linden tree **1**:*29*

Linlithgow Palace (Scotland)
5:1263

Linschoten, Jan Huyghen van
5:*1343*

literature **3**:720–739

as architectural subjects **1**:41

Aristotle **1**:59, 61

blank verse **3**:823

Boccaccio **1**:112, 113

book production **3**:780–783

Borgia patronage **1**:125

Burgundy **1**:163

Cervantes **1**:202–206

chansons de geste **1**:222

Chaucer **1**:212–220

chivalry **1**:222–224

classical languages
3:682–683

Czech **1**:118, 122

drama **3**:731, 732, 823

English **1**:220, **2**:334–336,
337

Erasmus **2**:362–363

Florence **2**:423

French **1**:214–225

humanism **2**:334–337,
3:582, 584, 588, 589,
591, 594, 683, **5**:1218,
1282

Italian **1**:216–217, 223

Jewish portrayals **3**:671

Jonson on **3**:739

London **3**:753, 754, 755

Machiavelli **3**:770

Margaret of Navarre **3**:735

Marlowe **3**:822–826

Medici patronage **3**:852

Michelangelo **4**:870, 877

Milton **4**:879–887

Molière **4**:897–902

More **4**:927–928

nationalism **4**:963

pastoral **3**:737

Petrarch **4**:1049–1055

Polish **4**:1109

Portugal **4**:1144–1145

Rabelais **5**:1176–1179

religious orders **5**:1202–1203

Renaissance **5**:1222–1223,
1225

Shakespeare **4**:916,
5:1268–1276

Spain **5**:1284

Spenser **2**:335, **5**:1286–1290

theater **5**:1322–1323, 1325,
1326, 1329

vernaculars **3**:694, 695

women **5**:1427

Little Dutch Masters **4**:997

Lives (Plutarch) **3**:684, 685

Lives of the Artists (Baglione)
1:192

*Lives of the Modern Painters,
Sculptors and Architects*
(Bellori) **1**:196

*Lives of the Most Eminent
Painters, Sculptors, and
Architects* (Vasari) **1**:34, 143,
148, 150, **5**:1183

Living Flame of Love (John of
the Cross) **5**:120

Livre des bonnes moeurs, Le
(Jacques le Grant) **1**:85

Lochamer Liederbuch
(collection) **4**:942

Loci communes (Melanchthon)
3:767–768

Lockley, Rowland **1**:*62*

Lodge, Thomas **3**:755,
5:1286

Loggia del Capitaniato **4**:1001

Loggia of the Galatea (Villa
Farnese) **1**:41

Loggia of Psyche (Villa
Farnese) **1**:41

London Bridge **3**:*748*, 749,
5:*1324*

Lope de Vega *see* Vega, Lope de

Loqman **1**:*69*, **4**:*1084*, **5**:*1409*

Lorenzetti, Ambrogio **2**:492,
4:980

Lorenzetti, Pietro **2**:488, 492,
4:980

Lotto, Lorenzo **5**:*1420*

Louvre (Paris) **1**:45, 98, **2**:444,
3:708, 709, 712, **4**:1029,
1030, 1031, 1034, 1035

Loves, Matteo **5**:*1206*

Loves of the Gods (Carracci)
1:*195*

Love's Labor's Lost
(Shakespeare) **5**:1271

Love Triumphant (Caravaggio)
1:193

Lucan **3**:590, 649

Lucretia (Gentileschi) **2**:471

Lull, Ramon **1**:224

Lully, Jean-Baptiste **4**:900

Lusiads, The (Camões) **4**:1144

lute **4**:943, 959

"Lycidas" (Milton) **4**:882, 884

Lyon Temple **1**:*185*

M

Mabuse *see* Gossaert, Jan

Macbeth (Shakespeare) **5**:1271,
1274

MacDuff castle (Scotland)
5:*1296*

Machaut, Guillaume de **1**:*214*,
215, **4**:943

Madariaga, Salvador de **1**:211

Maderna, Carlo **1**:38, 40, 44,
99, 100, **4**:1026

Madness of Orlando, The
(Ariosto) *see Orlando furioso*

Madonna and Child **1**:*145*,
2:*398*, 425, **5**:*1220*

Michelangelo **4**:874, 876

Madonna and Child (Raphael)
5:*1180*

*Madonna and Child with Saint
Anne* (Caravaggio) **1**:193,
194

*Madonna and Child with Saint
Anne* (Leonardo da Vinci)
2:425

*Madonna and Child with
Saints and Angels* (della
Francesca) **5**:1379

*Madonna and Child with a
Vase of Flowers* (Leonardo
da Vinci) **3**:708

Madonna di Loreto
(Caravaggio) **1**:193

Madonna of the Goldfinch
(Raphael) **5**:1184

Madonna of the Meadows
(Raphael) **5**:1184, 1185

Madonna of the Rocks
(Leonardo da Vinci) **2**:*425*,
3:709, 714

Madonna of the Stairs
(Michelangelo) **2**:425

*Madrigale dei guerrieri e
amorosi* (Monteverdi) **4**:922

madrigals **4**:918–919, 922,
943, 955, 971, **5**:1244–1245

Maestà (Duccio) **2**:489, 492

Maestro, El (Milán) **4**:959

Mágico prodigioso, El
(Calderón) 728

Magnaura Palace
(Constantinople) **1**:258

magnetite **2**:375

Maids of Honor, The
(Velázquez) *see Meninas,
Las*

majolica **5**:1383

Malade imaginaire, Le
(Molière) **4**:901

Malleus maleficarum (Institoris
and Sprenger) **3**:802

Malory, Thomas **1**:223, 224

Mander, Carel van **1**:144,
146, 148, **5**:*1308*

Mandragola (Machiavelli)
3:733, 772

Manetti, Antonio **1**:34, 155

*Man Holding a Medallion of
Cosimo de' Medici*
(Botticelli) **1**:133, *135*

Man in a Red Turban (Jan van
Eyck) **2**:*386*, 388

mannerism **4**:878, 980, 981,
990, 991, 998, **5**:1284

architecture **1**:30, 32–33, 38,
40, 42

Rubens **5**:1236, 1237

Velázquez **5**:1384, 1385

mansard roof **1**:45

Mansart, François **1:**45, 48
Mantegna, Andrea **1:**139,
    2:312, 314, **3:**642, 745
Manueline architecture
    4:*1141,* 1144, *1145*
Marienburg Castle **4:**1106
Marienkirche (Wolfenbüttel)
    1:49
Mariner's Mirror (Waghenaer)
    2:*376*
markets and fairs **1:***23,* **3:**810,
    813–821
    book fairs **3:**781, 806, 819
    Italian city-states **3:**631, *633*
    trade **5:**1340, 1342, 1348
Marlowe, Christopher
    2:335–336, **3:**671, 726,
    728, 732, **822–826,**
    5:1269, 1270, 1325
Marriage at Cana (Bosch)
    1:129
Martyrdom of Saint Matthew
    (Caravaggio) **1:**192
Martyrdom of Saint Peter
    (Caravaggio) **1:**193
Marvell, Andrew **4:**886
Masaccio **1:**35, **2:***492,* **3:***589,*
    4:984, **5:**1185
Maser chapel (Venice) **3:**667
Maske, A (Milton) *see Comus*
Masque of Blackness (Jonson)
    3:663
Masque of Queens (Jonson)
    3:663
masques **3:**663, 665, 666,
    5:1328
Massacre of Paris, The
    (Marlowe) **3:**822, 825
Massys, Quentin **1:***84*
Master John (artist) **5:***1427*
Mathematical Compilation
    (Ptolemy) *see Almagest*
Mathematical Philosophy
    (Russell) **4:**1068
Mathematical Principles
    (Newton) *see Principia*
    mathematica
Matthew Passion (Schütz)
    5:1247
Maxims of the Law (Bacon)
    1:80

May Day **4:**1118, 1123
maypole dancing **2:**342
Mazzola, Girolamo *see*
    Parmigianino
Measure for Measure
    (Shakespeare) **5:**1272
Mechanick Exercises (1683
    book) **5:***1173*
Meditationes Sacrae (Bacon)
    1:80
Meditation of a Penitent Sinner,
    A (A. Locke) **5:**1423
Meditation XVII (Donne)
    5:1166
Meditations on First Philosophy
    (Descartes) **2:**295,
    297–301, **4:**1069
Medora (Rueda) **5:***1323*
Meistersingers **4:**960
Melancholia I (Dürer) **2:**315
Memoires (Commynes) **1:**163,
    164
Menabuoi, Giusto **4:***1062*
Menaechmi (Plautus) **3:**732
Meninas, Las (Velázquez)
    5:1385, 1390, 1391
Meno (Plato) **4:**1092, 1093
Mercator, Gerardus **2:**384, 385
    5:*1248,* 1250
Mercer Hall (London) **3:**751
Merchant of Venice, The
    (Shakespeare) **3:**671,
    5:1271, 1274
Merian, Matthäus (the Elder)
    1:*75,* **5:***1293, 1310*
Merisi, Michelangelo *see*
    Caravaggio
Merry Wives of Windsor, The
    (Shakespeare) **3:***733,*
    5:1271
Mesquita (Cordoba) **5:***1277*
Messiah (Handel) **5:**1247
Metamorphoses (Ovid) **5:***1321*
Metaphysics (Aristotle) **1:**51,
    261
"Methought I saw my late
    espoused saint" (Milton)
    4:885
Michelangelo **1:**97, 98, 135,
    244, **2:**466, 469, 492,
    3:668, 703, **4:870–878,**

946, 948, 1025, 1026,
    5:*1226,* 1232, 1353, *1354,*
    1387
architecture **1:**32, 36, 38, 42,
    44, 47, **2:**424–425, **4:**871,
    876, 877, **5:***1226*
Bramante **1:**143
Clement VII **1:**241, 242, 244
mannerism **1:**32–33
Medicis **2:**424, 425–426,
    3:852, 856, **4:**870, 871,
    872, 876–877
melancholia of **2:**315
painting and sculpture **4:**986,
    988, 990, 992, 999
Palazzo Farnese **1:**40
Palladio **4:**1000, 1003, 1004
as Raphael influence **5:**1183,
    1184–1185, 1187
Renaissance **5:**1220, 1221,
    1225
Michelazzo **3:***702*
Middleton, Thomas **3:**733,
    5:1323, 1325, 1326, 1329
midsummer festival **4:**1118
Midsummer Night's Dream, A
    (Shakespeare) **5:**1271, 1274
Milan, Cathedral of **1:***32,*
    3:710, *746*
Military Campaigns of
    Süleyman I (Loqman)
    5:*1409*
Milton, John **3:**609, 726, 823,
    4:879–887
minstrels **4:**949
Minute of First Draught of the
    Optiques, A (Hobbes) **2:**544
Miracle of the Cross on the San
    Lorenzo Bridge, The (Bellini)
    5:*1399*
Miracle of the Relic of the True
    Cross on the Rialto Bridge,
    The (Carpaccio) **3:***639*
Misanthrope, Le (Molière)
    4:899, 901
Miscellanea (Poliziano) **3:**585
Miser, The (Molière) **4:**901
Missa pro defunctis (Morales)
    4:957
Mocedades del Cid, Las (Castro
    y Bellvís) **3:**728

Molesworth, Robert **5:**1311
Molière **3:**730, 731,
    4:897–902, 5:1322, 1323
Mona Lisa (Leonardo da
    Vinci) **1:**133, **3:**709, 712,
    714, **4:**986, 999, **5:**1249
Monde, Le (Descartes) **2:**296,
    297
"Monk's Tale, The" (Chaucer)
    5:1202
monody **4:**916, 918, 942, 961
Montaigne, Michel de **1:***80,*
    95, 96
Monteverdi, Claudio **3:**745,
    4:916–923, 943, 961,
    5:1244
Month of January (Rustici)
    5:*1421*
Monument (London fire)
    5:*1433*
Moorish architecture **1:**46–47,
    5:*1277*
morality plays **5:**1318–1319
Moro, Antonio **2:***327,* **5:***1422*
Moroni, Andrea **5:***1370*
Morris, William **4:**1048
Mort de César, La (Grevin)
    3:729
Morte d'Arthur, Le (Malory)
    1:223, 224
mosaics **1:**257
Moses (Michelangelo) **4:**874
motets **4:**917, 920, 945–946,
    947, 956–967
"Mother Hubbard's Tale"
    (Spenser) **5:**1288–1289
Mulder, Joseph **1:***60*
Munday, Anthony **5:**1324,
    1329
Murano glass **5:**1394
Murillo, Bartolomé Esteban
    5:1242, 1386
Musée Charles X (Louvre)
    5:*1231*
music **4:942–961**
    Burgundy **1:**163
    Christina **1:**230
    France **1:**215
    Galileo **2:**460
    households **2:**567
    Hussite hymns **1:**118

music (cont.)
  intermezzi **3:**734, **5:**1321
  Italian theater **3:**734
  Monteverdi **4:**916–923, 943, 961
  Schütz **5:**1244–1247
  Scotland **5:**1264
  shipboard **2:***379*
  theater **5:**1328
  Venice **5:**1399
  see also opera
musical instruments **4:**958–959
Musica transalpina (Yonge) **4:**943
Musicians, College of (London) **5:**1432
music publishing **4:**957
music theory **4:**958
"My Mistress Commanding Me to Return Her Letters" (Carew) **2:**402
My Secret Book (Petrarch) **4:**1052
Mystical Nativity, The (Botticelli) **1:**137–138

N

Narrative of Barents's Last Voyage **2:***384*
Nash, Thomas **3:**738, 823
National Gallery (London) **3:**709, **5:**1389
Natural History (Pliny the Elder) **1:**58, **3:***687*
Navicella (Giotto) **2:**491
neoclassicism **1:**49
New Atlantis (Bacon) **1:**80, **4:**1103, **5:**1251
New Horse Hoeing Husbandry, The (Tull) **1:**27
New Life, The (Dante) **1:**217
New Theory of the Planets (Copernicus and Peurbach) **3:**829
New Year's Day **1:**174, 177
Nicomachean Ethics (Aristotle) **1:**53, 54, 55, 59, 61, **4:**1054, 1102
Nieuwe maniere van sterctebou, door spilsluysen (Stevin) **1:**275

Night Watch, The (Rembrandt) **5:***1212,* 1213
Nigra sum (Monteverdi) **4:**921
northern Renaissance **2:**551–552
  Erasmus **2:**552
  humanism **5:**1370
  painting **1:**128–129, 145, **2:**312, 316
  Paris **4:**1031–1035
  perspective **2:**312
  universities **5:**1376–1377
notation (music) **4:**942
Notes on the New Testament (Valla) **3:**586, 591
Notre Dame, Cathedral of (Paris) **1:***179,* **4:***1028*
Nouveau-né, Le (La Tour) **4:***1120*
Nouvelles, Les (Périers) **3:**736
Novelas ejemplares (Cervantes) **1:**205, 206
Novelle (Bandello) **3:**736
Novum organum (Bacon) **1:**61, 80, 81, 83, **4:**1067, 1068
Nozze d'Enea con Lavinia, Le (Monteverdi) **4:**922
Numancia, La (Cervantes) **1:**204
Nuremberg Chronicle **1:***267*

O

Obedience of the Christian Man (Tyndale) **2:**524
Objections to Aristotle (Ramus) **4:**1064
Objections and Replies (Descartes) **2:**295
"Ode to the West Wind" (Shelley) **1:**113
Odyssey (Homer) **1:**59, **2:**373
  Hobbes translation **2:**546
Of Famous Men (Petrarch) **4:**1052
Of Liberty and Necessity (Hobbes) **2:**546
Ognissanti Madonna (Giotto) **2:**487, 489, 490
oil painting **2:**391, 392
Old Sacristy, Church of San Lorenzo (Florence) **1:**152

Old Woman Frying Eggs (Velázquez) **5:***1385*
O Magnum mysterium (Victoria) **4:**957
On Being and the One (Pico della Mirandola) **4:**1074, 1076
On Citizenship (Hobbes) **2:**544
"On Cruelty" (Montaigne) **1:**96
On Interpretation (Aristotle) **1:**258
On Man (Hobbes) **2:**546
On Mercy (Calvin) **1:**181
On Military Affairs (Valturio) **5:***1408*
On Mills (Stevin) **1:**275
On Monarchy (Dante) **1:**217
On Noble Manners and Liberal Studies (Vergerio) **2:**318
On Perspective in Painting (Piero della Francesca) **3:**827–828
"On Shakespeare" (Milton) **4:**879, 880
"On the Abolition of Images" (Karlstadt) **3:**606
On the Body (Hobbes) **2:**546
On the Bondage of Will (Luther) **3:**767
On the Eloquence of Vernacular (Dante) **1:**217
"On the Late Massacre in Piedmont" (Milton) **4:**885
On the Motion of the Heart (Harvey) **5:**1255
On the Natures of Things (Neckham) **3:**778
On the Nobility and Excellence of Women (Nettesheim) **5:**1417
On the Remedies of Good and Bad Fortune (Petrarch) **4:**1054
On the Revolution of Heavenly Spheres (Copernicus) **1:**50, 266, 269, 270, 272, **2:**463, 465, **4:**1109, **5:**1221, *1250*
On the Roman Penny (Budé) **3:**590

On the Solitary Life (Petrarch) **4:**1054
On the Structure of the Human Body (Vesalius) **5:**1250
On the Threefold Life (Ficinus) **2:**422
On War against the Turk (Luther) **3:**618
On War Machines (Taccola) **5:***1407*
opera **2:**567, **3:**734, **4:**943, 961, **5:**1312, 1321, 1322
  Christina's patronage of **1:**228, 230
  Monteverdi **4:**916, 919–921, 922, 923
  Schütz **5:**1246
Oprichnina **3:**654–656
optical illusion **2:**389–390, 392
Optics (Euclid) **3:**827
Optics (Kepler) **3:**832
Optime pastor (Isaac) **4:**946
oral tradition **3:**669
Oration on the Dignity of Man (Pico della Mirandola) **2:**537, **4:**1064, 1075, 1076, **5:**1220
Oration on the Need to Restore the Republic (Alcionio) **5:**1233
oratorio **5:**1247
Oratory Church (Fermo) **5:**1238
orders, architectural *see* classical orders
Orfeo (Monteverdi) **4:**918, 919–920, 921, 943
organ **4:**960
Orlando furioso (Ariosto) **1:**125, 223, **3:**721, **5:**1289
Orlando innamorato (Boiardo) **1:**223
Orley, Bernard van **1:**145, *207, 242,* **5:***1417*
Orvieto, Cathedral of **1:***246*
Orygynale Cronykil (Andrew of Wyntoun) **5:**1260
Ospedale degli Innocenti (Florence) **1:**35, 37, 151–152

Ospedale di Santo Spirito
(Rome) **5:**1230
Othello (Shakespeare) **5:**1270,
1272, 1274, 1327
ottava rima verse **1:**217
Our Lady of Guadalupe,
Church of (Spain) **4:**1082
Ovid **1:**112, 136, **2:**336,
3:823, **4:**1053, **5:**1321
Oxburghe Hangings **5:***1264*

P

Pacheco, Francisco **5:**1384,
1385
Painter's Book, The (van
Mander) **1:**144, 148
painting and sculpture
4:980–999
architectural ornaments **1:**38,
39, 41, 42, 44
Bernini **1:**44, 97–101
Bosch **1:**127–132
Botticelli **1:**133–138
Bruegel **1:**144–148
Burgundian patrons **1:**163
Caravaggio **1:**191–196
chivalry **1:**224–225
Clement VII **1:**241–242,
244
Constantinople **1:**263
Dürer **2:**311–316
Eastern vs. Western Roman
Empire **1:**257
Eyck **2:**386–392
Florence **2:**418, 424–425
Gentileschi **2:**469–474
Giotto **2:**484–492
Gonzaga patronage **3:**745
Holy Roman Empire **2:**550,
559
iconoclasm **1:**184,
3:604–609
illusory perspective **1:**145,
2:312, 316
Italianate-style **1:**145
Italian city-states **3:**641, 642
Leonardo da Vinci
3:706–714, **5:**1249
Leo X **3:**703
Medici patronage **3:**852,
855, 856

Michelangelo **1:**42,
4:870–878
papal patronage **4:**1025,
5:1230
perspective **3:**827–828
Portugal **4:**1144
Raphael **1:**38, 39, 41,
5:1180–1187
Rembrandt **5:**1210–1217
Renaissance **5:***1219,*
1221–1222, 1224, 1225,
1231, 1235
Rome **5:**1235
Rubens **5:**1236–1243
Scotland **5:**1264–1265
Spain **5:**1284
Velázquez **5:**1384–1391
Venice **5:**1399
Pajou, Augustin **4:***1070*
palaces **1:**36, 37, 39–40, 45
Florence **2:**563
France **2:**444, 450
Italian city-states **3:**642
London **3:**749–750, 751
papacy **5:**1230
Paris **4:**1031
Rome **4:**1025
Venice **5:**1399, *1400*
see also palazzo listings
Palacio del Viso (Spain)
5:*1401*
Palais du Luxembourg (Paris)
5:1240, 1241
Palamon and Arcite (Chaucer)
1:213, 217
Palazzo Barberini (Rome) **1:**40,
44, *231*
Palazzo Borghese (Rome) **1:**40
Palazzo Caprini (Rome) **1:**142
Palazzo Chieracati (Vicenza)
1:43, **4:**1002, 1004, 1007
Palazzo Chigi-Odescalchi
(Rome) **1:**40
Palazzo Corsini (Rome) **1:**230
Palazzo da Porto Festa
(Vincenzo) **4:**1004
Palazzo del Tè (Mantua) **1:***38,*
39, **4:**991
Palazzo Ducale (Mantua)
3:*642*
Palazzo Ducale (Venice) **3:***640*

Palazzo Falconieri (Rome) **1:**40
Palazzo Farnese (Capraola)
5:*1362*
Palazzo Farnese (Rome) **1:**39,
40, 195, *210,* **4:**871, 1002,
1025
Palazzo Farnesina (Rome)
4:1003
Palazzo Iseppo Porto (Vicenza)
3:*668*
Palazzo Massimi (Rome) **1:**39,
40
Palazzo Medici (Rome) **1:**197
Palazzo Piccolomini (Pienza)
4:*1089*
Palazzo Pubblico (Siena)
5:*1421*
Palazzo Spada (Rome) **1:**39,
40, 41
Palazzo Thiene (Vicenza) *see*
Villa Thiene
Palazzo Vecchio (Florence)
3:*851*
Palestrina, Giovanni Pierluigi
da **4:**954, 955–956, 957
Palladianism **1:**45, 47, 49,
3:664, 668
Palladio, Andrea **1:**32, 33, 34,
42–43, 140, *141,* **3:**664,
665, 666, 667, *668,*
4:1000–1007, 5:1399
Palladio, Marc'Antonio **4:**1000
Pallas and the Centaur
(Botticelli) **1:**135
Pampaloni, Luigi **1:***149*
Pandosto (Greene) **3:**732
Panfili, Pio **5:***1356*
Pannini, Giovanni Paolo **1:***39*
Pantagruel (Rabelais) **3:**436,
5:1176, 1177, 1178
Pantheon (Rome) **1:**142,
3:667
dome **1:**34, 47
interior **1:***34*
main body **1:***35*
Paradise Lost (Milton) **4:**879,
880, 881, 885, 886, 887
Paradise Regained (Milton)
4:886–887
Paraphrases (Aristotle) **1:**56
Pareja, Juan de **5:**1389, *1390*

Parlement of Foules (Chaucer)
1:113, 213, 217
Parmigianino **1:***209,* 242
Parnassus (Raphael) **5:**1186
parody, literary **1:**223–224
parody, polyphonic **4:**943
Passion of Christ, The (Dürer)
2:314
Passions of the Soul, The
(Descartes) **2:***296,* 301
pastoralism **3:**725, *726,* 737,
738, 825
Pastoral Songs (Petrarch)
4:1051
Patience (Pearl Poet) **1:**220
patronage **1:**138,
5:1177–1178, 1230, 1231
Bernini **5:***1333*
Burgundian dukes **1:**163
Christina **1:**227, 229
Clement VII **1:**241, 242,
244
France **2:**437, 450
Italian city-states **3:**640–641,
642, 651
Leo X **3:**703
Maximilian I **2:**550
Medicis **3:**852
papacy **4:**1008, 1021–1022,
1023, 1025–1026
Rome **5:**1230, 1231
Rudolf II **2:**559
Urbino **5:**1378–1383
Pauline Chapel (Rome) **1:**97,
98, **4:**871, 877
Paul's Cross (London) **3:**751
Pavia, Cathedral of **1:**139
Pazzi Chapel (Florence) **1:**153,
154
Pearl (Pearl Poet) **1:**220
Pearl Poet **1:**220
Peasant Dance (Bruegel) **1:**147
Penitent Magdalen
(Gentileschi) **2:**470–471,
473
"Penseroso, Il" (Milton) **4:**880
Peri, Jacopo **4:**920, 943,
5:1246, 1321
Pericles, Prince of Tyre
(Shakespeare) **5:**1272
Perkin Warbeck (Ford) **5:**1327

Perrissin, Jean **1**:*185*

perspective **4**:980, 984, 987
  Botticelli **1**:133, 134, 137
  Bramante **1**:139, 142
  Bruegel **1**:*146*
  illusory **1**:145, **2**:312, 316
  mathematics **3**:827–828

Perugino, Pietro **3**:706,
  5:1181, 1182, 1185, 1230

Peruzzi, Baldassare **1**:32, 38,
  40, 41, 281, **4**:1003

Peruzzi Chapel **2**:485, 487,
  490

Petrarch **2**:320, **3**:720, 721,
  722, 724, 725, 726, **4**:963,
  1049–1055, 1072, 1143
  Boccaccio **1**:111, 112, 114,
    115
  Borgia, Lucrezia **1**:125
  Chaucer **1**:216
  humanism **2**:357,
    3:583–584, 585, 589,
    682–683, 684, 686,
    4:1049, 1053–1055,
    1075, **5**:1218
  papacy **4**:1009, 1052
  Rome **5**:1227, 1228
  Spenser translations **2**:335,
    5:1286
  vernacular **3**:694
  Viscontis **5**:1405–1406

Phaedo (Plato) **4**:1094

Phaedrus (Plato) **4**:1097

Phèdre (Racine) **3**:730

Philogia (Petrarch) **4**:1050

*Philosophical and Physical
  Opinions* (Lucas) **5**:1257

Phoenix, The (Middleton)
  5:1329

Piazza Ducale (Vigevano)
  1:139

Piazza Giovanni e Paolo
  (Venice) **3**:707

Piazza Navona (Rome) **5**:1235

Piazza Santa Annunziata
  (Florence) **1**:151

picaresque novel **3**:738–739

Picart, Bernard **5**:*1232*

Pienza, Cathedral of **4**:*1091*

*Pierce Penniless, His Suplication
  to the Divell* (Nash) **3**:738

Piero della Francesca **1**:139,
  3:*630*, 827–828, **4**:985,
  987, 1090, **5**:*1181*, 1379

Pietà (Michelangelo) **4**:871

Pietro de Crescenzi **1**:*25, 26*

Pinturicchio (Betto di Biago)
  1:*125*, **2**:*428*, **4**:*1086,
  1087, 1088*, 1091, **5**:*1183*

Piombo, Sebastiano del **1**:41,
  241, **3**:*650*

Pippi de' Gianuzzi, Giulio *see*
  Romano, Giulio

Pisa, Cathedral of **2**:460

Pisanello, Antonio **1**:*224*,
  2:*428*, **5**:*1416*

Pistoia, Cathedral of **5**:*1366*

pizzicato **4**:922

Place Royale (Paris) **4**:1034

plainsong **4**:957

Planetary Hypotheses (Ptolemy)
  1:268, 271

Plateresque **1**:*46*

*Platonic Theology concerning the
  Immortality of the Soul*
  (Ficino) **2**:422

Plautus, Titus Maccius **3**:683,
  729, 732, 733, **5**:1320

Playne Discourse, A (Dee)
  1:177

Poema del Cid (epic) **3**:695

Poetics (Aristotle) **1**:59, 61,
  5:1321

poetry *see* literature

Poets' Corner (Westminster
  Abbey) **1**:218, *220*

Polish Rider, The (Rembrandt
  attribution) **5**:1217

Political Treatise (Spinoza)
  5:1294

Politics (Aristotle) **1**:53, **3**:684

Poliziano, Angelo **1**:54, **3**:585,
  587, *588*, 687, **4**:1074

Pollaiuolo, Antonio **2**:425,
  4:98

Pollaiuolo, Piero del **1**:133,
  134

polychoral music **4**:951

polyphony **4**:916, 917, 918,
  919, 923, 943, 944, 951,
  952, 954, 957, 961,
  5:1246, 1247

Ponte Sisto (Rome) **5**:1230,
  1231

Pont Neuf (Paris) **4**:1034

Pope, Alexander **5**:1257

popular culture **4**:**1115–1123**
  astrology **1**:67–74
  blood sports **1**:92–96
  as Bruegel subject **1**:144,
    146, 147
  London **3**:751, 753, 754,
    755
  magic **3**:795
  markets and fairs
    3:817–818
  music **4**:948–952, 960
  printing **5**:1174–1175
  theater **5**:1317–1329

Poquelin, Jean-Baptiste *see*
  Molière

Porta, Giacomo della **1**:38, 40,
  47

Porta Pia (Rome) **5**:*1226*

Porta San Paolo (Rome) **1**:37

Portrait of a Woman
  (Bartolomeo da Venezia)
  1:*123*

Portraits of Living Plants
  (Brunfels) **5**:1250

portraiture **4**:980, 985, 996,
  997
  Rembrandt **5**:1210, 1212,
    1214, 1217
  Rubens **5**:*1236*, 1243

Portrait of a Young Man
  (Rubens) **5**:1237

Poussin, Nicolas **4**:994, 995,
  5:1243, 1388

Praetorius, Michael **4**:950,
  955, 958

Praise of Folly, The (Erasmus)
  1:180, **2**:357, 362–363,
  3:762, **4**:925, **5**:1221,
  1319

Praise of the City of Florence
  (Bruni) **3**:584

Précieuses ridicules, Les
  (Molière) **4**:899

Prendas de amor (Rueda)
  5:1323

Prepared Table, The (Caro)
  3:680

Primavera (Botticelli) **1**:135,
  136, **2**:425, **5**:1220

Primo libro de madrigali, Il
  (Schütz) **5**:1246

Prince, The (Machiavelli)
  2:337, 395, 419, **3**:769,
  770, 771, 772, 773,
  4:1011, 1066, **5**:1221

Principall Navigations
  (Hakluyt) **2**:375, 385

Principia mathematica
  (Newton) **3**:828, 834,
  5:1251, 1258, *1292*, 1430

Principles of Philosophy, The
  (Descartes) **2**:295

Pro Archia (Cicero) **3**:684,
  4:1053

*Procession in Saint Mark's
  Square* (Bellini) **3**:635

Prodigal Son, The (Bosch)
  1:131

Prognostico (Cardano) **1**:*70*

Prophet (Michelangelo)
  4:874

"Pro Populo Anglicano
  Defensio" (Milton) **4**:887

prose fiction **3**:735–739

Prospect of Venice (painting)
  1:*277*

*Protestant Ethic and the Spirit
  of Capitalism, The* (Weber)
  1:190

Psalms of David (Schütz)
  5:1245, 1246

Punch and Judy shows **5**:1320

puppet shows **5**:1320

Q

Quart Livre (Rabelais) **5**:1178

quattrocento artists **4**:985

Quattro libri (Palladio) **1**:140

Queen's House (Greenwich)
  1:48, **3**:666–667, 668

Queen's Men (London
  theater) **5**:1328

Querela pacis (Erasmus) **2**:357

*Questions concerning Liberty,
  Necessity and Chance, The*
  (Hobbes) **2**:546

Quirinal Hill (Rome) **4**:*1039*,
  1040

R

Rabelais, François **3:**735, 736, **5:1176–1179**
Racine, Jean **3:**730, 731
Raising of the Cross (Rubens) **5:**1239–1240
Raising of Drusiana, The (Giotto) **2:**487
Raising of Lazarus (Caravaggio) **1:**194
Raising of the Son of Theophilus, The (Masaccio) **3:***589*
Rape of Lucrece (Shakespeare) **5:**1268
Raphael **1:**39, 40, 41, *50,* 97, 242, **3:***700,* **4:**957, 981, 1012, 1061, **5:1180–1187,** 1221, 1224, *1383,* 1387
Bramante **1:**37, 38, 142, *143,* **4:**1002, 1004
Clement VII **1:**242
Dürer **2:**316
High Renaissance **4:**986, 988, 990
Julius II **1:**36, **4:**1025
Leo X **3:**703
Palladio **4:**1002, 1003, 1004
as Rembrandt influence **5:**1213, 1214
Saint Peter's Basilica **1:**48, **4:**1026
Sistine Chapel **1:**135, **5:***1158*
Rathaus (Bremen) **1:**49
Rayman Hall (Norfolk) **3:**665
Reading on the Statute of Uses (Bacon) **1:**80
Rebellious Slave (Michelangelo) **4:**874
recitar cantando **4:**920
Red Bull (London theater) **3:***733*
Redeemer, Church of the (Prague) **1:***120*
Redemption Triptych (van der Weyden) **4:***1129*
Redentore, Il (Venice) **1:**32, 43, **3:**668, **4:**1006, *1007*
Red Lion (London theater) **3:**732

Regulae ad directionem ingenii (Descartes) **2:**295
Reims, Cathedral of **2:***432,* **4:***943*
Charles VII coronation **3:**602, 657, 658–659
Rembrandt **1:***59,* **4:**996, 997, 998, **5:1210–1217,** 1243, 1387
Caravaggio as influence **1:**196
Rembrandt, Titus **5:**1212, 1214, 1217
Rembrandt Research Project **5:**1217
Remedy of Fortune, The (Machaut) **1:**215
Renaissance **5:1218–1226**
architecture **1:**30–49, 97–101, 139–143, 156, **2:**334, **3:**663, 664–668, **5:***1320,* 1399
Brunelleschi **1:**149, 152, 153, 156
chivalry **1:**221, 222, 223
Columbus's worldview **1:**249
Constantinople **1:**256, 258
Counter-Reformation **5:**1226
dams **1:**278–281
Dante **1:**217
education **2:**317–320, 325
England **2:**339, **5:**1286
Florence **2:**414, 418, 421–426
France **2:**437–438, 444, 450
humanism **1:**181, 264, **3:**638, 682–694
Italian city-states **3:**640–642
Judaism **3:**671, 672, 677
limits of **5:**1225
literature **1:**111–115, **3:**720–739
London **3:**754–755
Luther and **3:**767
music **5:**1245, 1247
musical style **4:**916, 919, 920, 922, 945–961
opera **5:**1321
painting and sculpture **1:**101, 127, 133–138, 145, **2:**312–313, 314,

316, 469–474, 484–492, **3:**706–714, **5:**1184–1187, 1221–1222, 1230, 1235, 1236
papacy 1011–1028
Paris **4:**1031–1035
Petrarch **4:**1052, 1053–1055
philosophy **4:**1072, 1076
Poland **4:**1109–1112
Portugal **4:**1139, 1143–1145
preaching **5:**1160–1166
printing **5:**1172–1173
Rome **5:**1231–1235
sack of Rome **1:**243, **2:**523, **4:**986, 1002, 1014, 1023, 1026
science **5:**1248–1259
Scotland **5:**1262–1265, 1296
Spain **5:**1279–1285
Sweden **5:**1308
theater **5:**1323
theatrical architecture **5:***1320*
universities **5:**1365, 1369, 1370–1375
Urbino **5:**1378–1383
Venice **5:**1392–1400, 1399
vernaculars **3:**696–697
Viscontis **5:**1405–1406
warfare changes **5:**1335, 1407–1415
women **5:**1416–1428
René Descartes's Principles of Philosophy, Parts I and II (Spinoza) **5:**1293
Renoir, Pierre-Auguste **5:**1242
Repin, Ilya Efimovich **3:***656*
Republic, The (Plato) **1:**31, **4:**928–929, 1094, 1103
Rerum memorandum libri (Petrarch) **4:**1051
Resurrection (Piero della Francesca) **4:***987*
Return of the Prodigal Son (Rembrandt) **5:**1217
Return to Amsterdam of the Fleet of the Dutch East India Company, The (van Eertvelt) **5:***1351*

revenge plays **3:**732
Revolutions (Copernicus) **3:**829
Reynolds, Joshua **5:**1242
Richard II (Shakespeare) **1:**17, **4:***963,* **5:**1271
Richard III (Shakespeare) **4:**928, **5:**1270, 1271, 1273
Richental, Ulrich von **1:***119, 158,* **4:***1010*
Richia (Ibn Battutah) 611
Richmond Castle **2:***401*
Rider on Rearing Horse (Leonardo da Vinci) **3:***710*
Rievaulx Abbey (Yorkshire) **5:***1203*
Ritorno d'Ulisse in patria, Il (Monteverdi) **4:**922
Roaring Girl, The (Middleton) **5:**1329
Robbia *see* Della Robbia
Rokeby Hall (Yorkshire) **5:***1389*
Rokeby Venus (Velázquez) **5:***1389*
Rolin Virgin, The (Jan van Eyck) **2:***388,* 390–391, 392
Roma instaurata (Biondo) **3:**587
romance literature **1:**214, 219, 220, 222, 223, 224, **5:**1322
Roman de la rose **1:**214–215, 217, 218, 219
Roman de Tristan, Le **1:***222*
Romanists (painting style) **1:**145
Romano, Giulio **1:***38,* 39, 97, 242, **4:**991, 1003, 1004, 1012, **5:**1187
romantic poets **5:**1290
Romeo and Juliet (Shakespeare) **5:***1276*
Rome Restored (Biondo) **3:**587
Ronsard, Pierre de **3:**721, 722, 723, 725, 735
Rose Theatre (London) **3:**732, **5:**1323, 1326
Rossellino, Antonio **5:***1218*
Rossellino, Bernardo **1:***155,* **3:***585,* **4:***1089,* 1090

Rossini, Gioacchino **5:**1312
Rosso, Giovanni Battista *see* Rosso Fiorentino, Il
Rosso Fiorentino, Il **1:**242, **4:**990
Rubenistes **5:**1243
Rubens, Jan **5:**1236
Rubens, Peter Paul **3:**666, **4:**917, 993, 994, 995, *1117,* **5:***1200,* **1236–1243,** *1359*
  Caravaggio **1:**194
  Rembrandt **5:**1210, 1212
  Velázquez **5:**1386–1387, 1388
Rubens and Helana Fourment in the Garden (Rubens) **5:**1242
Rucellai Palace (Florence) **1:**36
"Ruins of Time, The" (Spenser) **5:**1288
Rules for the Direction of the Mind (Descartes) **2:**295
Rules of the Five Orders of Architecture, The (Vignola) **1:**34
Rustici, Cristofano **4:***1421*

S
sackbut **4:**958
Sacrifice of Isaac (Caravaggio) **1:**193
Saggiatore, Il (Galileo) **2:**465, 466
Saint Barnabas, Church of (Milan) **5:**1204
Saint Basil the Blessed, Cathedral of (Moscow) **3:***654*
Saint Bavo's Cathedral (Ghent) **2:**387
Saint Benet's Church (London) **5:***1431*
Saint Catherine's Monastery (Sinai) **5:***1364*
Saint-Étienne-du-Mont, Church of (Paris) **3:***698*
Saint Francis Cycle (Giotto) **2:**488, 489, *491*
Saint Hubert, Chapel of **3:**714
Saint-Inglevert **1:***226*

Saint Jerome (Leonardo da Vinci) **3:**708
Saint Jerome in His Study (Dürer) **2:**315
Saint Jerome in His Study (Jan van Eyck) **2:**391
Saint Jerome and the Lion (Dürer) **2:**312
Saint John, Church of (Ghent) **2:**387
Saint John Lateran Basilica (Rome) **1:**38, **2:**491
Saint Mark's Basilica (Venice) **1:***258,* **4:**922, 951–952, 958, 1006, *1021,* **5:**1399
  library of **3:**664
Saint Martin's, Church of (Ludgate) **1:**49
Saint-Mary-le-Bow, Church of (London) **1:**49
Saint Mary Pammakaristos, Church of (Constantinople) **1:**263
Saint Mary's Church (Warsaw) **4:**1112
Saint Matthew and the Angel (Caravaggio) **1:**194
Saint Paul's Cathedral (London) **1:**32, 48, 140, 212, **3:**665, 667, 668, 748, 754, *755,* **4:***1103,* **5:***1161,* 1166, *1328,* 1430–1433
Saint Peter's Basilica (Rome) **1:**32, 38, *39,* 44, 124, **2:***358,* 491, **3:***855,* **4:**955, 1003, 1037, **5:**1228, 1232, 1234, 1432
  Bernini **1:**98, 99, 100, 101, **5:**1235
  Bramante **1:**140, 142, 143, **5:**1231
  Caravaggio **1:**193
  Charlemagne **1:**264
  Christina's crypt **1:**231
  Clement VI **3:**756, 757
  indulgences **3:**757, **4:**1013, **5:**1190
  Leo X **3:**703, 704
  Michelangelo **1:**32, 38, 98, **4:**871, 873, 878, 1026, **5:**1353

papacy **4:***1008,* 1026, 1037, 1040
  Raphael **1:**48, **3:**703, **5:**1186
  Second Vatican Council **5:***1363*
  see also Sistine Chapel
Saint Sebastian catacombs (Rome) **4:***1027*
Saint Vitus, Cathedral of (Prague) **1:***118*
Saint Wensceslas, Chapel of (Prague) **1:***118*
Salisbury House (London) **3:**749
Salve Deus Rex Judaeorum (Lanier) **5:**1423
Samson Agonistes (Milton) **4:**886, 887
San Andrea, Church of (Mantua) **1:**139
San Carlo alle Quattro Fontane, Church of (Rome) **1:**45, **5:**1235
San Francesco, Church of (Assisi) **2:**487, 488, *529*
San Francesco, Church of (Perugia) **5:**1182
San Francesco, Church of (Ripa) **1:**100
San Francesco Grande, Church of (Milan) **3:**709
Sangallo, Antonio da (the Elder) **1:**38, 39, 44
Sangallo, Antonio da (the Younger) **1:**32, *33,* 38, 40, 44, 47, **4:**1026
San Giorgio dei Fiorentini, Church of (Rome) **1:**44
San Giorgio Maggiore, Church of (Venice) **3:**666, 668, **4:**1006
San Giovanni del Fiorentini **1:**32
San Lorenzo, Church of (Florence) **1:**35, 42, 152, 154, **2:**417, 424, **4:**876
San Luigi dei Francesci, Church of (Rome) **1:**44, 192, 193
San Marco, Church of (Florence) **4:**1077

San Pietro in Montorio, Church of (Rome) **1:**37, **5:**1231
San Sebastiano, Church of (Mantua) **1:**36
Sansovino, Jacopo **1:**43, **3:**664, *690,* **4:**1001, 1002, 1004, 1005, 1006, **5:**1399
San Stephano Rotondo (Rome) **1:**32
Santa Bibiana, Church of (Rome) **1:**98
Santa Croce, Church of (Florence) **1:**35, 153, *155,* **2:**466, 485, 489, **3:***585,* **5:***1225*
Sant'Agnese, Church of (Rome) **1:**45
Sant'Agostino, Church of (Rome) **1:**30, 193
Santa Hermandad (Spain) **2:**395
Santa Maria, Church of (Rome) **5:**1238
Santa Maria, Church of (Vallicella) **1:**193
Santa Maria degli Angeli, Church of (Florence) **1:**156
Santa Maria del Carmine, Church of (Florence) **3:***589,* **4:**984
Santa Maria del Fiore, Cathedral of *see* Florence, Cathedral of
Santa Maria della Assunzione, Church of (Ariccia) **1:**32, 100, 101
Santa Maria della Pace, Church of (Rome) **1:**37, 140, 141
Santa Maria della Salute (Venice) **5:***1392*
Santa Maria della Scala, Church of (Rome) **1:**193, 194
Santa Maria della Vittoria, Church of (Rome) **5:**1235
Santa Maria delle Grazie, Church of (Milan) **1:**139
Santa Maria del Popolo (Rome) **1:**39, 193

Santa Maria di Loreto, Church of (Rome) **1:**32, *33*

Santa Maria Maggiore Basilica (Rome) **1:**42, 44, 97, 98, **4:**1040

Santa Maria Novella, Church of (Florence) **1:**30, 36, **2:***418,* 490

Santa Maria Presso Santo Satiro, Church of (Milan) **1:**139

Sant'Andrea, Church of (Mantua) **1:**36

Sant'Andrea al Quirinale, Church of (Rome) **1:**32, 45, 100, 101, **3:**667

Sant'Angelo Castel (Rome) *see* Castel Sant'Angelo

Santa Susanna, Church of (Rome) **1:**44

Sant'Eligio degli Orefici, Church of (Rome) **1:**38, 40, **5:**1186

San Teodore, Church of (Pavia) **5:***1402*

Sant'Eufemia, Church of (Verona) **3:***676*

Santi, Giovanni **5:**1180, 1181, 1185

Santiago de Compostela, Cathedral of **4:***1072*

Santi Luca e Martina, Church of (Rome) **1:**32

Santissima Annunziata, Church of (Florence) **1:**32

Sant'Ivo chapel (Rome) **1:**45

Santo Spirito, Church of (Florence) **1:**139, 152, 154

Santo Tomé, Church of (Toledo) **5:***1284*

Sanzio, Raffaello *see* Raphael

satire **1:**203, 223–224

Savoy Palace (London) **1:**216, **3:**749, **4:**1047

Scamozzi, Vincenzo **1:**34, **3:**664, 665, 668

Scarlatti, Alessandro **1:**230

Scène Galante at the Gates of Paris **4:***1028*

Sceptical Chymist, The (Boyle) **5:***1256*

Scherzi musicali (Monteverdi) **4:**917

Schilderboeck, Het (van Mander) **1:**148

Schiller, Friedrich von **5:**1312

Scholemaster, The (Ascham) **2:**327

Schöner Dialogus von Martino, Ein (woodcut) **5:***1192*

School of Abuse (Gosson) **3:**725

School of Athens, The (Raphael) **1:**38, *50, 143,* **3:**703, **4:**1025, 1061, **5:**1186

Schütz, Heinrich **4:**952, **5:1244–1247**

Scotichronicon (Bower) **5:**1260

Second and Third Blast of Retrait from Plaies and Theaters (Munday) **5:**1324

Second (Greater) Cloister, Santa Croce (Florence) **1:***155*

Secret of the Universe (Kepler) **3:**832

Secretum meum (Petrarch) **4:**1052

Segni, Bernardo **1:**59

Self-Portrait at the Age of Fifty-two (Rembrandt) **5:**1214

Self-Portrait at Twenty-six (Dürer) **2:**313

Self-Portrait Leaning on a Sill (Rembrandt) **5:**1214

self-portraits
   Dürer **2:***311,* 312, 313
   Rembrandt **5:***1210,* 1214

Seneca **1:**181, **3:**590, 729, 732, 734, **5:**1320

Senfl, Ludwig **4:**950, 951

Serlio, Sebastiano **1:**31, 34, 43, 45, 140, **3:**665, **4:**1001, 1002, 1004

Serrur, Calixte-Joseph **5:***1262, 1426*

Seven Deadly Sins, The (Bosch) **1:**129

Seven Last Words of Christ on the Cross, The (Schütz) **5:**1247

Seven Works of Mercy (Caravaggio) **1:**194

Sforzinda (theoretical city) **1:**31

Shahnama (Persian text) **3:**629

Shakespeare, William **2:**335, **3:**600, *603,* 664, 671, 724–726, 727, 731, 732, 733, 737, **4:**880, 916, 928, **5:1268–1276,** 1322

Aristotelian unities **5:**1321

blank verse **3:**823

English language **1:**108

English theater **5:**1324–1325, 1326, 1328, 1329

fool depiction **5:**1319

history plays **1:**17, 19

Jesuit plays **5:**1323

London **3:**751

Marlowe **3:**826

Middleton collaboration **5:**1329

nationalism **4:**963

religion **5:**1326–1327

Renaissance **5:**1223, 1225

sonnet **4:**1052, **5:**1270

Sonnet 18 **3:**726

Sonnet 130 **3:**725

Shaw, George Bernard **3:**692

Sheep Well, The (Vega) **3:**728

Shelley, Percy Bysshe **1:**113, **5:**1290

Shepheardes Calender, The (Spenser) **3:**737, **5:**1287, 1288

Ship of Fools, The (Bosch) **1:**128, *132*

Shipwreck Caused by Demons (painting) **2:***377*

Short Treatise on God, Man, and His Well-Being (Spinoza) **5:**1292

Shulham 'arukh (Caro) **3:**680

Shute, John **1:**34

Sidereus nuncius (Galileo) **2:**464, *465*

Sidney, Philip **3:**724, 725, 737, 738, 823, **4:**1052, **5:**1287, 1416

Siena, Cathedral of **1:***30,* **4:**872, 1091

Sir Gawain and the Green Knight (Pearl Poet) **1:**220

Sistine Chapel (Rome) **1:**42, 47, **4:***986,* 988, 994, 1022, **5:**1182, 1230, *1354*

Botticelli **1:**133, 135, 138

Byzantine philosopher **1:**169

Michelangelo **1:**135, 244, **4:**870, 871, 873, 874–875, 877, 878, 1025, **5:**1220, 1231

tapestry **5:***1158*

"So Crewell a Prison" (Surrey) **3:**723

soliloquy **5:**1272, 1275

Somerset House (London) **3:**749

Song of Roland, The (romance) **1:**222, **3:**695

sonnet **3:**720, 722, 723, 724–726

Italian **5:**1279

Petrarch **4:**1049, 1050, 1052

Shakespeare **3:**725, 726, **4:**1052, **5:**1270

Sonnets pour Hélène (Ronsard) **3:**722

Sophocles **3:**685, 688, 729

Sorbonne, Church of the (France) **1:**48

Southwell, Robert **4:**896, **5:**1424

Spanish Tragedy (Kyd) **3:**732, **5:***1325*

Spenser, Edmund **2:**335, **3:**721, 725, 726, 737, 754, **5:1286–1290**

Spinners, The (Velázquez) **5:**1390

Spiritual Canticle (John of the Cross) **5:**1207

Spiritual Exercises (Ignatius of Loyola) **1:**99, **5:**1199, 1206

Spozalizio (Raphael) **5:**1182

stained-glass windows **3:***607*

stanza, Spenserian **5:**1290

Stanza della Segnatura (Vatican) **5:**1181, 1186–1187

Stanza dell'Incendio di Borgo (Rome) **5:**1187

Stanza di Eliodoro (Vatican) **5:**1187

Starry Messenger, The (Galileo) **2:**464, **5:**1253

Starry Messenger, The (Lilly) **1:***72*

Stefaneschi altarpiece (Giotto) **2:**490, 491

Stereometrics of Wine Casks (Kepler) **3:**828, 831

Stiatessi, Pierre Antonio **2:**469, 471

Stiatessi, Prudentia **2:**471, 474

Stigmatization of Saint Francis, The (Giotto) **2:**490

Stimmer, Tobias **2:***367,* **4:***1075*

Stirling Castle (Scotland) **5:***1263,* 1264

Stoffels, Hendrickje **5:**1212, 1215, 1217

Stoning of Saint Stephen (Rembrandt) **5:**1212

Struggle between Carnival and Lent, The (Bruegel) **4:***1119*

Study of a Bather (Michelangelo) **4:**873

Summa theologiae (Thomas Aquinas) **1:**52

"Summoner's Tale, The" (Chaucer) **5:**1202

surrealism **1:**131, 132

Surrender of Breda, The (Velázquez) **5:**1385, 1388

Susannah and the Elders (Gentileschi) **2:**470, 471, 473, 474

Swan Theatre (London) **5:**1326

Symbolic Logic (Venn) **4:**1068

symbolism, Dürer's use of **2:**313, 314

Symphoniae sacrae (Schütz) **5:**1246

Symposium (Plato) **4:**1092, 1095, 1102

Syndics of the Clothmakers' Guild, The (Rembrandt) **5:***1216,* 1217

Syntagma musicum (Praetorius) **4:**958

Systema naturae (Linnaeus) **5:**1258

T

Table Talk (Luther) **1:**102

Taccola, Mariano **1:**280, **5:***1407*

Tale of a Tub (Jonson) **3:**663

Tallis, Thomas **4:**953

Tamburlaine the Great (Marlowe) **3:**822, 824

Taming of the Shrew, The (Shakespeare) **5:**1271, 1274

tapestries **1:**163, *242,* **5:**1237

Tartuffe (Molière) **4:**899, 900–901

Tasso, Torquato **1:**223, **3:**721, **4:**922

Taverner, John **1:**280

Tavola Strozzi **4:***1130*

Temperance (Pollaiuolo) **1:***134*

Tempe Restored (Jones masque) **3:**663

Tempest, The (Giorgione) **4:**989

Tempest, The (Shakespeare) **5:**1271, 1275

Tempietto (Rome) **1:**32, 37, 38, 139, 140, 141, **5:**1231

Temptation of Saint Anthony, The (Bosch) **1:***128,* 129

Ten Books on Architecture (Vitruvius) **1:**33, 34, 35, 37, **3:**668, **4:**1001, **5:**1321

tenebrism **4:**994, 997, **5:**1386

"Tenure of Kings and Magistrates, The" (Milton) **4:**884

Terence **3:**683, 687, 729, 732, 733, **5:**1320

Terpsichore (Praetorius) **4:**950

Terra Australis myth **2:**384–385

terza rima **1:**113

Teseida (Boccaccio) **1:**113, 217

Tetrabiblos (Ptolemy) **1:**69

theater **3:**726–733, 735, 737, 748, 772, **5:1317–1329**

England **2:**335–336

festivals **4:**1118, 1119, *1222,* **5:**1317

London **3:**732, 733, 751, 754, 755

Marlowe **3:**822–826

masques **3:**663, 665, 666

Molière **4:**897–902

opera **4:**916, 920

Portugal **4:**1145

Shakespeare **5:**1268–1276, 1322

tournaments **1:**225

Theatre (London playhouse) **3:**732, **5:**1326, 1327

Theater of Marcellus (Rome) **5:**1430

Theatre of the Empire of Great Britain (Speed) **5:***1297*

Theatre Wherein Be Represented As Well the Miseries and Calamities That Follow the Voluptuous Worldlings (van der Noot) **5:**1286

Theologia Platonica (Ficino) **4:***1100*

Theological-Political Treatise (Spinoza) **5:**1292, 1293, 1294, 1295

Theotokópoulos, Doménikos *see* Greco, El

Thomas of Reading (Deloney) **3:**738

Three Graces, The (Raphael) **5:**1181, 1183

Thucydides **2:**542, **3:**588

Tiers Livre (Rabelais) **5:**1178

Timon of Athens (Shakespeare and Middleton) **5:**1329

Tintoretto **1:***259,* **5:**1236, 1387, 1388, 1399

Tirsi e Clori (Monteverdi) **4:**916

Titian **2:***364,* **3:***701,* **4:**981, 986, 988, 989, 994, *1012, 1056,* **5:***1197,* 1222, 1236, 1237, *1352, 1353, 1360,* 1386, 1387, 1388, 1389, 1399

as Rembrandt influence **5:**1213, 1214

Titus Andronicus (Shakespeare) **2:**335

Titus at His Desk (Rembrandt) **5:**1217

toccata **4:**960

Topkapi Palace **3:***625*

"To Posterity" (Petrarch) **4:**1052

Tordinona opera house (Rome) **1:**228, 230

"To the Lord General Cromwell" (Milton) **4:**885

Tottel's Miscellany **3:**723–724

Tower of Belém (Lisbon) **4:**1141, *1145*

towers, Italian *grandi* **3:**634

To the Younger Generation on Making Good Use of Greek Literature (Basil of Caesarea) **3:**665

Trabaios de Persiles y Sigismunda, Los (The Trials of Persiles and Sigismunda) (Cervantes) **1:**203, 206

Tractaet van Dyckague (Vierlingh) **1:**281

tragedy

Aristotelian **4:**920

Greek **5:**1321, 1322

Shakespearean **5:**1271, 1272, 1274

Training in Oratory (Quintilian) **3:**583

Transfiguration (Raphael) **1:**242, **5:**1187

Trastevere (Rome) **1:**40, **5:**1230, 1231

Trato de Argel, El (Cervantes) **1:**204

Trattato dell'architettura (Cornaro) **4:**1001

Travels (Ibn Battutah) 611

Treatise of the Virtues and Properties of Waters . . . (Sitoni) **1:**280

Treatise on Man (Descartes) **5:**1251

Treatise on the Abacus (Piero della Francesca) **3:**827

Treatise on the Astrolabe, A (Chaucer) **1:**213

Treatise on the Emendation of the Intellect (Spinoza) **5:**1292

tremolo **4:**922

Trent, Cathedral of **5:**1353

Trevi fountain (Rome) **1:**37

Trinity Manuscript (Milton) **4:**881

Trionfi (Petrarch) **4:***1053*

Trismegistus (Hermes) **4:***1065*

Triumph of Death, The (Bruegel) **1:**145, **4:***1125*

Triumph of Galatea (Raphael) **1:***41*

Triumph of Saint Thomas Aquinas (Benozzo di Lesse Gazzoli) **1:***52*

Troilus and Criseyde (Chaucer) **1:**112, 113, 213, 217–218, 220

trompe l'oeil **1:**139

troubadours and trouvères **1:**214

Tuscan order **1:**30, *142*

Twelfth Night (Shakespeare) **3:**727, **5:**1271

Two New Sciences (Galileo) **2:**468, **3:**690

U

Uffizi Gallery (Florence) **2:**489, **3:**708

Underweysung der Messung mit dem Zirckel und Richscheyt (Dürer) **2:**312

Unfortunate Traveller; or, The Life of Jacke Wilson (Nash) **3:**738

"Upon the Famous Voyage" (Jonson) **3:**755

Urania (Wroth) **3:**725, 737

Utopia (More) **3:**585, **4:**927–928, 1103, **5:**1173

V

Val-de-Grâce, Church of (France) **1:**48

Valladolid, Cathedral of **1:**47

Valturio, Roberto **5:***1408*

Van de molens (Stevin) **1:**275

Van Dyck, Anthony **2:***347,* **3:***608,* **4:**993, **5:**1211, 1241, 1243, *1257, 1302*

van Eyck, Hubert *see* Eyck, Hubert van

van Eyck, Jan *see* Eyck, Jan van

van Eyck, Lambert *see* Eyck, Lambert van

van Gogh, Vincent *see* Gogh, Vincent van

Vasari, Giorgio **1:**34, 42, 148, **2:**485, **3:***649,* 714, **5:***1225*

on Brunelleschi's dome **1:**150, 156

Michelangelo **5:***1225*

on Palladio **4:**1005

on Raphael **5:**1183, 1185, 1187

Vega, Lope de **1:**204, **3:**727, 728, **5:**1284, 1322–1323

on *Don Quixote* **1:**205

Velázquez, Diego Rodríguez de Silva **4:**993, 994, **5:**1237, *1242,* **1384–1391**

Velázquez, Juan **5:**1199

Velde, J. van de **5:***1168*

Velde, Willem van de, II **5:***1347*

Venus and Adonis (Shakespeare) **5:***1268*

Venus and Cupid (Gentileschi) **2:**472

Venus and Mars (Botticelli) **1:**135

Venus at Her Toilette (Velázquez) *see Rokeby Venus*

Venus of Urbino (Titian) **5:**1389

Vermeer, Jan **4:**997, 998, *999*

Vernet, Emile-Jean-Horace **5:***1231*

Veronese **1:***203,* **4:**992, **5:**1388

Verrocchio, Andrea del **3:**706, 707, 708, 709, **4:**985

Versailles **1:**45, 48, **2:**450, **4:**1007

gardens **1:**26

Vespro della Beata Vergine (Monteverdi) **3:**745, **4:**921, 943

Viaje del Parnaso (Cervantes) **1:**203

Victory (Michelangelo) **4:**874

Vida del Buscón, La (Quevedo y Villegas) **3:**738–779

Vida es sueño, La (Calderón) 728, *1323*

Vie de Gargantua et de Pantagruel, La (Rabelais) *see Gargantua; Pantagruel*

Vier Bücher von Menschlicher Proportion (Dürer) **2:**312, 316

View of Delft (Vermeer) **4:***999*

View of the Present State of Ireland, A (Spenser) **5:**1287, 1289

Vignola, Giacomo da **1:**34, 38, 40, 44, 45, **3:**667

villa **2:**563

Villa Badoer (Vicenza) **4:**1005

Villa Barbaro (Vicenza) **1:**43

Villa Borghese (Rome) **4:***1037*

Villa Chiericati (Vicenza) **3:***666*

Villa Coronaro (Vicenza) **1:**43, **4:**1005

Villa del Belvedere (Vatican) **1:**140, 142, **3:**703, **5:**1231

courtyard **1:**142, **4:**1040

Villa Emo (Vicenza) **4:**1005

Villa Farnesina (Rome) **1:***41*

Villa Foscari (Vicenza) **4:**1001, 1005

Villa Franca, Ana de **1:**204

Village Fair (Brueghel the Younger) **5:***1319*

Villa Godi (Vicenza) **4:**1005

Villa Madama (Rome) **1:**39

Villa Medici (Rome) **5:**1389

Villani Chronicle (Pucci) **2:**484

Villa Pisani (Vicenza) **1:**43, **4:**1005

Villa Poiani (Vicenza) **4:**1005

Villa Polano (Vicenza) **1:**43

Villa Rotunda (Vicenza) **1:***42,* 43, **4:**1005

Villa Thiene (Vicenza) **1:**43, **3:***668,* **4:**1001, 1004, 1005

viol **4:**958

violin **4:**942, 958

Virgil **1:**112, **3:***594,* 737, **4:**1144, **5:**1219, 1289

classical languages **3:**682, 683, 687

English humanism **2:**336

Petrarch **4:**1052–1053

Virgin and Child (Michelangelo) **4:**874, 876

Virgin by a Fountain (Eyck) **2:**390

Vision of Delight (Jonson) **3:**663

Visscher, Jan Claesz **5:***1271, 1328*

Vita nuova, La (Dante) **1:**217

Vitruvian Man (Leonardo da Vinci) **3:**709

Vitruvius **1:***32,* 33–34, 35, 48, 141, **3:***668,* 709, **4:**1001, **5:**1321

Vittoria d'Amore, La (Monteverdi) **4:**919

vocal music **4:**950, 952

Vulcan's Forge (Velázquez) **5:**1387

Vulgari eloquentia, De (Dante) **1:**217

W

Wakefield play cycle **5:***1318*

Waldseemüller, Martin **1:***254,* 255, **2:**382

Walens, Mayses **5:***1327*

Walter, Johann **4:**943, 952, 954

Warrant Design (Wren) **5:***1432*

Wavrin, Jean de **3:***599,* **4:***1127, 1137*

Wawel Castle (Kraków) **4:**1109, 1112

Wawel Cathedral (Kraków) **4:**1112

Way of Perfection, The (Teresa of Ávila) **5:**1207

Way of Reconciliation (Ponet) **5:**1419

Webb, John **1:**48, **3:***667,* 668, **4:**1007

Webster, John **5:**1325, 1329

Well of Moses (Sluter) **4:**981

Werewolf, The (Cranach the Elder) **4:***1115*

Westminster Abbey **1:**30, **5:***1301*

Chaucer's tomb **1:**218, *220*

Newton's tomb **5:**1257

Westminster Abbey (cont.)
Poets' Corner 1:218, *220*
Spenser's tomb 5:1290
Weyden, Rogier van der
1:129, *161,* 163, *221,*
2:316, 4:982, *1129,*
5:*1357*
Whaddon folio 4:*1043*
"What Can Be Called into
Doubt" (Descartes) 2:297
What a Tailor Can Do! (Goya)
4:*1123*
Whetstone of Witte, The
(Recorde) 3:829
Whistler, James McNeill
5:1391
Whore of Babylon, The
(Dekker) 5:1327
Widow and Her Son (Moro)
5:*1422*
Wife of Bath (illustration)
4:*1081*
Wilhelm Tell (Schiller) 5:1312
Willaert, Adriaan 4:947,
951–952
Wilton House (Wiltshire)
1:*47,* 48, 3:*667, 668*
windows 1:31, 36, 40, *46*
stained-glass 3:*607*
Winter's Tale, The
(Shakespeare) 3:732,
5:1271, 1275, 1321
women 5:**1416–1428**
Borgia 1:123–126
chivalry 1:221, *222,* 226
Christina 1:227–231
cities 4:1132
colonialism 5:1285
court society 5:1383, 1427
education 2:319, 322
Florentine artists' portrayal
2:*424,* 425
Gentileschi 2:469–474
household roles 2:562–563,
564–565, 566
humanist education 3:584,
588
inheritance rights
2:404–405, 413
Joan of Arc 3:657–662
Judaism 3:681

literacy 5:1172
London advantages 3:753
marital age 4:1129, 5:1419
Medicis 1:197–202, 232,
246, 3:857
Middleton depictions 5:1329
midwives 3:842
in monarchical succession
3:595, 4:911
as monarchs 1:227–231,
2:326–333, 393–400,
523, 528, 4:1104, 5:1221,
1225, 1267, 1277–1279,
1425–1427
nude paintings 5:1183, 1238
pilgrimage 4:1081
popular culture 4:1116,
1117, *1120*
as preaching audience
5:1161, 1162
religious orders 5:1201,
1202, 1207, 1208
Renaissance status 5:1225
scientific pursuits 5:1257
witchcraft charges 2:534,
3:796, 802, 803, 5:1425
as writers 3:724, 725, 726,
735–736, 737, 5:1427
"Women's War against the
Pope for Stealing Ten Days
from the Calendar, The"
(poem) 1:177
Wonderful Magician, The
(Calderón) 728
woodcuts 2:310, 311, 5:1170,
1171
Dürer 2:311, 312, 313, 314
*Wordes unto Adam, His Owne
Scriveyn* (Chaucer) 1:*213*
Work for Armourers (Dekker)
1:93
Works of Aristotle 3:586
World, The (Descartes) 2:296,
297
*World Turned Upside Down,
The* (pamphlet) 5:*1175*
Wren, Christopher 1:32, 33,
47, 48–49, 140, 3:667,
668, 748, *755,* 4:1007,
5:1256, *1374, 1375,*
1429–1433

Wright, Joseph 4:*1072*
Wyatt, Thomas (the Elder)
3:722–723, 724, 726
Wyatt, Thomas (the Younger)
2:326–327

X
Xenophon 1:261

Y
Yarranton, Andrew 1:*276*
York play cycle 5:1318
Young Man Playing the Lute
(Lievens) 5:1211
Young Woman with a Water Jug
(Vermeer) 4:998
*Youthful Adventures of the Cid,
The* (Castro y Bellvís) 3:728

Z
Zuccari, Federico 2:*366,*
3:*648,* 5:1236, 1237
Zuccari, Taddeo 5:*1362*

Index of Philosophy, Religion, Politics, and Scholarship

A **boldface** number preceding a colon indicates the volume. Numbers in *italics* refer to captions. Numbers entirely in **boldface** refer to a full article.

A

Aberdeen University **5:**1263
Abraham (prophet) **3:**610, **4:**1084, 1085
absolutism *see* divine right
Academy, Plato's **4:**1063, 1090, 1095, **5:**1365
Acalá, University of **5:**1282
Accademia de' Desiosi (Venice) **2:***469,* 471
Accademia dei Lincei **2:**464–465
Accademia dell'Arcadia (Rome) **1:**230, **4:**1068
Accademia Olympica (Vicenza) **4:**1001, 1006–1007
Act of Supremacy (England) **2:**327, 328, 338, 339, 340, 341, 524, **4:**931, 932, **5:**1374
Act of Uniformity (England) **2:**327, 328, 341
Acts of the Apostles **1:**193, **3:***695,* **4:**1102
Adam and Eve **1:**185, **4:**1064, *1066*
Adrian VI, Pope **1:**210, 241, 242, **4:**1023, **5:**1380
adult baptism **1:**178, **5:**1194, 1195, 1314
afterlife **2:**430, 431
Albertus Magnus **1:**52, 56, **3:**797
Albigensian crusade **2:**531
Alcalá, University of **1:**109
aldermen **3:**751, 752
Alexander III, Pope **4:**1137
Alexander IV, Pope **3:**693
Alexander VI, Pope **3:**700, **4:**948, 1011, 1016, **5:**1231, 1279, 1379
  Borgia, Lucrezia **1:**123–124, 126
  exploration **2:**381

heresy **2:**533
missionaries **4:**888–889
Pico della Mirandola **4:**1074, 1077
Alexander VII, Pope **1:**100, 229–230, 231
Alexander VIII, Pope **2:**372
All Saints' Day **2:**387
All Souls' Day **4:**1118
Altdorf, University of **5:**1367, 1377
Ambrosian rite **3:**745
Anabaptists **1:**178, 187, **2:**539, 540, **3:**761, **5:**1191, 1194, 1195, 1200, 1314
  iconoclasm **3:**606
  Peace of Augsburg **1:**76
Anglicans *see* Church of England
Anglo-Norman language **1:**212, 214
Annunciation **4:**1081
anointing **5:**1357
antipopes **4:**1010
Apocrypha **1:**103, 104, 108, **5:**1355
apostolic succession **1:**237
Arabic language **3:**610, 611, 618, 670, 684, 692
Arab scholars **3:**693, **5:**1367
  Aristotelianism **1:**51–52, 54
  astronomy **1:**267, 268, 271
  mathematics **3:**827
  philosophy **4:**1054, 1061, 1064
Aramaic language **3:**695, 696, 697
Arcadian Academy (Rome) **1:**230, **4:**1068
Arezzo, University of **5:**1367
Arianism **4:**1110
Aristotle **1:50–61,** 81, 181, **2:**357, 359, **3:***595, 703,* **4:**1049, 1054–1055, *1061*
  astrology **1:**69
  Byzantine Empire **1:**169, 170, 258
  classical languages **1:**261, **3:**684, 685, 686, 693
  cosmology **1:**265, 267, **5:**1253

dramatic unities **3:**727, 729, **4:**920, **5:**1321
  English translation of **2:**336
  Galileo **2:**460, 461, 463
  Hobbes vs. **2:**543
  humanism **2:**384, **3:**582, 583, *586*
  Luther vs. **3:**761, 763, 767
  on monarchy **4:**903
  philosophy **4:**1061–1066, 1072, 1099, 1102
  Pico della Mirandola **4:**1073, 1074, 1075, 1076
  Platonism **1:**261, **4:**1095
  printed editions **3:**688
  Reformation **1:**181, **2:**320
  science **5:**1248
  Thomas Aquinas **1:**52, 56, 59, **3:**604
  universities **5:**1365, 1367, 1369
Armenian Catholic Church **2:**429, 431
Arminianism **1:**190, **2:**345, 346, **5:**1329
Articles of Religion (England) **1:**104, 109, *237,* 240
Ashkenazim **3:**670, *681*
Assumption **1:**193, **4:**1081, **5:**1317, 1318
astrology **1:67–74,** **2:**422, **3:**679, 800
  almanacs **1:**173
  magic **4:**1065
  mathematics **3:**828, 829, 830
Augsburg, Peace of (1555) **1:75–78,** **2:**365, 370, 371, 372, 482, 556, 557, 558, **3:**767, **5:**1193, 1200, 1221, 1331, 1333
Augsburg Confession **1:**75, 76, 262, **2:**483, 540, 553
Augustine, Saint **1:**182, **3:**606, 696, **5:**1229, 1248, *1284*
  Aristotle vs. **1:**53, **2:**357
  bibles **1:**104, **2:**467
  Erasmus **2:**357
  Lutheranism **3:**758–759, 765, 767
  Petrarch **4:**1052, 1055
  philosophy **4:**1069

Platonism **4:**1098, 1100
  preaching **5:**1158, *1159*
  Vives commentary **5:**1282
Augustinians **2:**482, **3:**756, 758, 762, **5:**1201, 1362
Authorized Version *see* King James Bible
auto-da-fé **2:**530, **5:**1278
autos sacramentales (religious plays) **5:**1322, *1323*
Averroës *see* Ibn Rushd
Averroistic Aristotelianism **1:**52–53
Avignon papacy **2:**366, 491, **3:**756, 854, **4:**913, 1009–1011, 1052, **5:**1227, 1406
  Black Death **2:**306
  Boccaccio **1:**112, 115
  Petrarch **4:**1049–1050, 1051, 1052

B

Babington Plot (1586) **2:**331, **5:**1298–1299
Bacon, Francis **1:79–83,** **2:**542, **3:**775, **4:**929, **5:**1419
  Aristotle **1:**60, 61
  philosophy **4:**1065, 1067–1068, 1069, 1072
  Platonism **4:**1103
  science **5:**1251, 1256
  Shakespeare **5:**1276
Bamberg, University of **5:**1367, 1377
Bancroft Library (California) **2:**383
banking **1:84–91,** **3:**809, **5:**1162
  Bardi family **2:**567
  Florence **2:**414, 415–416, 417, 421
  Italian city-states **3:**630, *632,* 633
  Judaism **3:**671
  Lombardy **3:**740
  London **3:**750, 751
  Medicis **1:**87, 88, **2:**416, 417, **3:**849, 850, 851, 852, 854, **5:**1342

banking (cont.)
  papacy 5:1228
  trade 5:1340, 1341, 1344
baptism 1:184, 3:757, 763,
    764, 4:1121, 5:1357,
    1358–1359
  adult 1:178, 5:1194, 1195,
    1314
  infant 1:178, 5:1314
Barebone's Parliament
    (England) 2:351
Barefoot Trinitarians, Convent
    of the 1:206
Barnabites 5:1204
Basel, Council of 2:537,
    3:679, 4:*1087,* 5:1352,
    1363
  calendar reform 1:174
  Florence, Council of 2:427,
    428, 429
  Pius II 4:1086, 1088
Basil, Saint 1:257, 3:684, 685,
    5:1419
Basil of Caesarea *see* Basil,
    Saint
Basil the Great *see* Basil, Saint
begging 4:1079, 1080–1081
Beghards 3:605
Beguines 3:605
Bembo, Pietro 1:125, 241,
    2:310, 3:703, 721, 5:1383
Benedict, Saint 5:1201
Benedict XIII (anti-pope)
    3:672
Benedictines 5:1201, 1204
  Rabelais 5:1176, 1177, 1178
Bessarion 1:260, 261 3:688,
    690, 728, 829
  humanist learning 2:430,
    431, 4:1023
  Platonism 4:1063,
    1099–1100
Bible of Borso d'Este 1:*102*
bibles 1:**102–110**
  Calvinism 1:178, 180, 183,
    5:1195
  critical analysis 2:538, 3:689
  England 1:107, 232, 238,
    239, 240, 2:339, 369,
    526, 536, 4:931, 5:1221,
    1223

Erasmus 1:181, 2:358, 360,
    538, 3:585, 591, 684,
    688–689, 703, 5:1357
France 2:448
  as Gentileschi source 2:473
Greek Codex B 4:1022
Greek translation 1:103, 104,
    109, 3:695
Gutenberg 3:780–781
heresy 2:538
humanism 1:181, 2:337,
    551, 3:585, 586, 591,
    592, 593, 689, 853,
    5:1177, 1218, 1369
hymns 4:952, 954
iconoclasm 3:607
illumination 3:*686*
interpretations 1:109, 2:538,
    551, 3:853, 5:1356
Judaism 3:669, 671, 672
Koine Greek 3:695, 696
Latin 4:1024, 5:1159, 1160
  see also Vulgate
literacy 2:321
as literally true 2:467, 536,
    539, 5:1194
liturgical drama 5:1318,
    1320
Luther and Lutheranism
    1:180, 2:482, *554,*
    3:758–759, 761, 763,
    764, 765, 767, 5:1189,
    1193, 1201, 1221, 1222,
    1352, 1354, 1356, 1357,
    1371, 1372
marginal notes 1:105, 106,
    110
missals 1:173, 5:1363
multilingualism 3:591
mystery plays 3:729
original texts 5:1357
preaching 5:1159, 1160,
    1162, 1164, 1165
printing 1:178, 3:591, *688,*
    697–699, 5:1169, 1170,
    1171, 1173–1174, 1175,
    1193, 1220
as Protestant sole authority
    1:107, 178, 180, 183,
    232, 240, 5:1352, 1354,
    1356, 1371, 1372

Reformation 5:1173–1174,
    1194, 1417
translations 1:58, 102–108,
    109, 110, 118, 181,
    2:358, 526, 536, 538,
    554, 3:585, 591, 684,
    688–689, 703, 4:892,
    970, 5:1315, 1357
Trent, Council of 5:1354,
    1355–1357
vernacular 2:321, 3:689, 695,
    696, 697–699
Zwingli 5:1315
see also New Testament; Old
    Testament
Bibliothèque du Roi (France)
    5:1375
Bill of Rights (England, 1689)
    2:346, 4:903, 906
bishops 4:1018, 1022
  Church of England 2:368
  Counter-Reformation 5:1197
  preaching 5:1158
Bishops' Bible 1:238
blood libel 3:673, 675
Bohemian Brethren 1:122
Bologna, University of 3:844,
    4:1143, 5:1250, *1365,*
    1367, *1368,* 1371
  Bessarion 1:261
  Petrarch 4:1050, 1051
  science studies 5:1255
  Spanish scholars 5:1279
Boniface VIII, Pope 2:366,
    491, 4:903, *1079,* 1080,
    5:1227, 1235
Book of Common Prayer
    1:108, 188, 236, *237,* 238,
    239, 240, 2:368, 3:609,
    699, 5:1197, 1267
Book of Homilies 1:*237,*
    2:368
Book of Splendor (kabbalistic
    work) 3:*680*
books of hours 1:*21,* 163, *164,*
    173, 4:1030, *1078,* 1118,
    1121, 1131, 5:*1167*
borders and boundaries
    4:964–965
Bracciolini, Poggio *see* Poggio
    Bracciolini

Brethren of the Common Life
    2:356, 3:760
Brethren of the Passion
    5:1318
Bruni, Leonardo 1:125, 264,
    3:640, 855
  Aristotle 1:54, 55
  classical languages 3:684,
    685
  English translation 2:336
  Florence 2:422, 423
  humanism 2:357, 3:584,
    585, 586, 588
  tomb of 1:*155*
Bruno, Saint 4:926
Bruno, Giordano 1:57, 272,
    4:*1019,* 1065, 1071
Burckhardt, Jacob 5:1220
Byzantium 1:**165–172,** 256

C

Caen, University of 5:1371
caesaropapism 1:257, 2:366
California, University of
    (Berkeley) 2:383
caliphate 3:626
Calixtus III, Pope 3:619,
    4:1011, 1086
Calvin, John 1:178, 181, 183,
    184, 185, 186–187, 188,
    189, 2:369, 483, 3:761,
    762, 4:906, 1032
  bibles 1:107, 108
  catechism 5:1174
  Church of Scotland 2:369
  divorce grounds 2:566–567
  education 2:321, 324–325
  France 2:439–440, 5:1191
  Geneva 5:1315–1316, 1423
  humanism 1:190,
    2:324–325, 3:593
  hunting critique 1:96
  iconoclasm 3:607, 608
  interest-bearing loans 1:85,
    5:1316
  on Islam 3:618
  music ban 4:952
  nationalism 2:364
  overview of 1:179
  philosophy 4:1062–1063,
    1064, 1065

preaching **5:**1164, 1165
Puritanism **2:**342
Rabelais **5:**1179
Reformation **5:**1194–1196
religious wars **1:**183
sacraments **5:**1358
Switzerland **5:**1312
witch hunts **2:**535
Calvinism **1:178–190, 2:**483,
   3:837, **4:**881, 906, 975,
   5:1179
astrology **1:**73
Augsburg, Peace of **1:**76
Catherine de Médicis **1:**198,
   199, 200, 201
Church of England **1:**236,
   237, 239, 240, **5:**1329
Eastern church **1:**263
education **2:**321, 324–325
England **1:**236, 237, 239,
   240, **2:**342, 343–346,
   349, 368–369
established church **2:**349,
   353, 369, 371–372
France **2:**439–440, 441,
   442–443, 444, 451–459,
   541, 556, **5:**1179
French civil wars **5:**1331
Geneva **5:**1316
Heidelberg Catechism
   5:1174
Henry IV **2:**516, 517,
   518–519, 520
heresy **1:**187, **2:**539, **5:**1316
Holy Roman Empire **1:**76,
   2:558, 559, **5:**1200
iconoclasm **3:**606–607, 608,
   609
Lutheranism vs. **1:**185,
   3:766, 767, **5:**1377
missionaries **4:**892, 894
monarchy **4:**912
music **4:**952, 954
Netherlands **2:**556
Palatinate **1:**76–77, 122
Poland-Lithuania **4:**1110
preaching **1:**183, **5:**1164,
   1165
Protestant ethic **1:**190
Reformation **5:**1195–1196,
   1198

Scotland **2:**349, 369,
   5:1265–1266, 1267,
   1298, 1301, 1426
Thirty Years War
   5:1331–1332
universities **5:**1377
Waldensians **2:**531
witch hunts **2:**535
women **5:**1423
Zwingli **5:**1315
see also Huguenots;
   Presbyterianism; Puritans
Cambridge Platonists
   4:1070–1071, 1072, 1103
Cambridge University **1:**79,
   100, **5:**1374–1375, 1419
Arabic studies **1:**262, **3:**618
architecture **1:**48, **2:**334
bibles **1:**107
dramatic productions **3:**732,
   5:1328
Elizabeth I **2:**327
founding of **5:**1367
King's College choir **4:**949
Marlowe **3:**822–823
Milton **4:**880, 881, 882
More as chancellor **4:**930
Newton **5:**1256–1257
science studies **5:**1255
Spenser **5:**1286–1287
University Wits **3:**732, 824
Wren **5:**1430, 1432
canonization *see* saints
capitalism **1:**22, **3:**821,
   5:1349
Calvinism **1:**189–190
feudalism **2:**401
Capuchins **5:**1206–1207,
   1209, 1332
cardinal-nephew **4:**1037
cardinals **4:**1008, 1010, 1012,
   1014, 1016, 1022, 1023,
   1025, 1026, 1029
Cardinal's College (Oxford)
   5:1373
Carmelites **5:**1201, 1206,
   1207–1208
Cartesianism *see* Descartes,
   René
Carthusians **2:**370, **4:**925,
   926, 981

Castiglione, Baldassare **1:**48,
   3:685, 736, **5:**1221, 1383
Castilian language **2:**399,
   5:1284
catacombs, Roman **3:**604,
   4:1026, *1027*
Catalan language **1:**123
catechisms **2:**323, **5:**1174
Cathars **2:**530, 531, 532,
   3:605
Catherine, Saint **1:***125,* **3:**657
Catholic Defense League
   5:1191
Catholicism *see* Roman
   Catholic Church
Catholic League **3:**626, 835,
   835–839, 836, 837, 838,
   839, **4:**1033, 1040, 1060,
   5:1331
   army size **5:**1332
cave, allegory of the (Plato)
   4:1094–1095
Cecil, William (Lord Burghley)
   1:81, **5:**1287, 1289, 1419
   Elizabeth I **2:**327, 328, 331
celibacy **1:**229, 230, 235,
   2:569
Celtis, Conradus **2:**550, *551,*
   552, **3:**590
censorship **3:**754, **4:**883,
   900–901, **5:**1197, 1283
   London theater **5:**1322, 1326
chain of being *see* great chain
   of being
Charlier, Jean *see* Gerson, Jean
   de
chinea (ritual papal gift)
   5:1234
Chishti Sufi order **3:**615
Chora monastery
   (Constantinople) **1:***258,*
   263
Christ *see* Jesus of Nazareth
Christ, Order of **1:**33, **2:**380,
   4:1137
Christian Civic Alliance
   5:1315
Christian Prayers (prayer book)
   1:*239*
Christmas **4:**1118, 1119
   festivals **5:**1317, 1320, 1328

Chrysoloras, Manuel **1:**261,
   3:584, 684–685, **5:**1220
   overview of **1:**264
Church of England
   1:232–240
   bibles **1:**104, 106–107, 108
   Calvinism **1:**188, **5:**1267
   Eastern Orthodoxy **1:**262,
     263
   Elizabeth I **1:**235, 236–239,
     240, **2:**326, 328–329,
     331, 341, 343, 368–369,
     4:1015, **5:**1198
   English civil wars **2:**347,
     348, 349, 352, 372
   as established church
     2:342–343, 346, 367,
     368–369, 370, 372,
     4:930–931, **5:**1197
   Henry VIII **1:**178, **2:**326,
     521, 524–527, **528,**
     4:1015
   High Church movement
     5:1325
   iconoclasm **3:**608–609
   missionaries **4:**892
   monarchy **4:**913, 914
   nobility **4:**975
   nonjurors **1:**262
   papacy **4:**1015, 1016
   preaching **5:**1166
   printing **5:**1175
   Puritan conflicts **1:**109,
     2:347, **5:**1198
   Roman Catholicism **1:**263
   Stuarts **5:**1301, 1302,
     1328–1329
   theater **5:**1325, 1328–1329
   Tudors **5:**1325
   universities **5:**1374
   vernacular **3:**698–699
   see also Book of Common
     Prayer
Church of Scotland **1:**190,
   2:369, **5:**1265, 1266,
   1267, 1298, 1300, 1301,
   1303
church-state relations
   absolutism **2:**367, 368
   Aristotle **1:**53
   Calvinism **1:**186–187, **4:**906

church-state relations (cont.)
Constantinople **1:**257
Eastern vs. Western Roman Empire **1:**257, 259
education **2:**317, 321–322, 324
England **1:**235–240, **2:**364–365, 524
English iconoclasm **3:**608–609
France **2:***432*
heresy **2:**530, 533, 539, 541
Hobbes **2:**544
Holy Roman Empire **1:***208,* 209, 210, **2:**510, 556, 557, **5:**1331
investiture controversy **2:**365–366, 368
Islam **3:**612–613, 614
Italian city-states **3:**639
monarchy **4:**903, 905, 912, 913–914, 915, **5:**1331
More **4:**930–932
nationalism **4:**969, 970
Ottoman Empire **3:**623, 627
papacy **1:**156, 257, **3:**594, 686, **4:**1012, 1019–1021, 1037, 1038–1039
Philip II **4:**1057–1058
Reformation **2:**321
religious pluralism **2:**541
taxation **1:**180
Urbino **5:**1382–1383
see also established churches
Cicero **3:**682, 683, 684, *685,* 686, 687, **4:**1102
humanism **2:**336, **3:**583, 584, 588, 589, **5:**1219
Petrarch **4:**1053, 1054
circumcision **3:**671
Cistercians **3:**748, 806
citizenship
London **3:**752, 755
Venice **5:**1397–1398
civic humanism **3:**585, 638, 640
civil servants **3:**638, 640, **4:**913
Clampers **2:**383
classical languages *see* languages, classical

classical revival *see* humanism and learning
Clement V, Pope **4:**905, 1052, 1109, **5:**1227
Clement VI, Pope **1:**174, **3:**757, **5:**1367
Clement VII (antipope) **4:**1010, **5:**1427
Clement VII, Pope **1:241–246, 2:***426,* **4:**930, 1014–1015, 1023, **5:**1196
Catherine de Médicis **1:**197
Charles V **1:***208,* 209, 210, 241, 242, 243, 244
Hapsburgs **2:**513
Henry VIII **1:**234, 242, 244, **2:**523
Italian wars **3:**647, 648, 649
Judaism **3:**677
Machiavelli **3:**773
Medicis **2:**418, 420, 421, 426, **3:**850, 851, *854,* 855
Michelangelo **2:**426
Paul V **4:**1037
Rome **5:**1232, 1233
Urbino **5:**1380
Venice **5:**1400
Clement VIII, Pope **2:**370, 517, 519
Clement IX, Pope **1:**330
Clement XI, Pope **5:**1209
Clement XIV, Pope **5:**1209
Clement of Alexandria **4:**1098
clergy **1:**235, **2:**439, **4:**1008–1009
Poland **4:**1108–1109
seminaries **5:**1361
see also religious orders
Codex Alexandrinus **1:**109
Codex B **4:**1022
Codex Vaticanus **1:**109
Cogito, ergo sum (Descartes statement) **2:**296–297, 299, **4:**1070, **5:**1294
Cognac, League of (1526) **1:**210, 242, *244,* **3:**647, **5:**1232–1233
Coimbra, University of **2:***403,* **4:**1144
Colet, John **2:**337, **4:**879, 1103, **5:**1373

Coligny, Gaspard II de **1:**199, 200, **2:**452–453, 454, 455
colleges **5:**1376
Calvinist **1:**181, 189
colonialism **3:**603, 642
agriculture **1:**24–25, 28, 29
architecture **1:**49
Columbus **1:**251–253
disease **2:**306–309
exploration **2:**373, 375, 381
monarchy **4:**915
Portugal **4:**1137, 1140, 1142–1143, 1145
Spain **2:**399, **5:**1284, 1285
trade **5:**1342, 1346–1347
Commentaries (Pius II) **4:**1087, 1091
Commonwealth (England) **2:**355, **4:**884, 885, 906
communion *see* Eucharist; Holy Communion
Commynes, Philippe de **1:**162, 163, 164
"Concerning the Jews and Their Lies" (Luther) **3:**675
conciliarism **2:**367, **3:**762
condominium system **2:**507, 508, 512
confession **1:**235, **3:**767, **5:**1357
confessionalism **1:**187, **2:**540, 556
Confucianism **4:**895, 1015
Congregationalism **1:**181, 188, 189, **2:**372 *see also* Puritans
conlegium vs. *universitas* **5:**1376
Constance, Council of **1:**119, 264, **3:***696,* **4:**962–963, 969, 1010–1011, **5:**1227, 1352, 1363
calendar reform **1:**174
heresy **2:**537
Constantinople, University of **1:**168, 261
constitutionalism **2:**545, **4:**906
consubstantiation **3:**764, **5:**1194
conversos **2:**396, 397, 398, 399, **3:**676–677, 678, **5:**1278, 1283

Coptic Church **2:**429, 431
Corporation Act of 1660 (England) **1:**240
Corpus Christi, feast of **5:**1318
Corpus Christi plays **5:**1322
Cossa, Baldassare *see* John XXIII
councils, papal **2:**434, **5:**1352
see also specific councils
Counter-Reformation
armada, Spanish **1:**66
Bohemia **1:**122
Descartes **2:**296
education **2:**320
Galileo **2:**467
Greek revival **2:**320
Hapsburg Empire **2:**513, 514–515, 559
Holy Roman Empire **2:**556
Jesuits **5:**1191, 1199
Judaism **3:**679
literature **3:**736–737, 739
music **4:**943, 954–957
overview of **5:**1197
painting **1:**194, **4:**990–991, 992
papacy **3:**703, **4:**1016–1019, 1024, 1036
Paris **4:**1035
Poland **4:**1111
religious orders **5:**1204–1209
Renaissance **5:**1226
Rome **5:**1234–1235
Rubens **5:**1240
Scholasticism **1:**58–59
Scotland **5:**1265
Spain **1:**66, **4:**1058, **5:**1282–1283
Thirty Years War **5:**1332
Trent, Council of **5:**1352, 1364
universities **5:**1365, 1368, 1375, 1377
vernaculars **3:**696
see also Inquisition
Court of Alderman **3:**751
Court of Ashton **5:**1350
Court of Common Council **3:**751

Court of Star Chamber
  5:1328
Covenanters (Scotland) **2:**349,
  350, 351, **5:**1303
covenanting **5:**1267
Coventry mystery plays
  5:*1318*
Cranmer, Oliver **2:**544, **4:***884,*
  887, **5:***1303, 1427*
Cranmer, Thomas **1:**106–107,
  237, **3:***699,* **5:**1267
  Church of England **1:**235,
    236, 237, 238, 240
  Henry VIII **2:**524, 526, 527,
    528, **3:**608, **5:**1197
Cromwell, Thomas **1:**235,
  2:338, 522, 524, 525, 526,
  527
  biblical translation **1:**106,
    2:339
Crucifixion **5:***1163*
Crusades **3:**618, 619, 715
  Burgundy **1:**158, 162
  chivalric orders **1:**223, 226
  Constantinople sacking
    1:168, 259–260, **5:**1393
  Pius II **4:**1086–1088, 1089
  Teutonic Knights **4:**1104,
    1106, 1107
  trade **5:**1341
  Venice **1:**259–260,
    5:1392–1393
crypto-Jews **2:**533
cuius regio, eius religio **5:**1331
curriculum **2:**318, 320, 321,
  322, 325, **3:**582, 584, 588,
  589, 683, 689, **5:**1218,
  1282
  Colet-Erasmus **4:**879
  Constaninople **1:**257
  see also Scholasticism
Czech Bible **1:**118
Czech Confession (1575)
  1:121

D

Dar al-Islam see Islam
Day of Judgment **1:**177,
  2:387
Declaration of Independence
  (United States) **4:**887

Declaration of Rights
  (England) **1:**24
Decree of Reunion (Eastern-
  Western churches)
  2:429–431
deductive logic **1:**50, 81, 82
deism **4:**1071, 1072
democracy **1:**166, **2:**542,
  4:906, **5:**1339
demography *see* population
Descartes, René **1:**60,
  2:294–301, 544, **3:***783,*
  5:1206, 1251
  Christina **1:**228, 229
  dualism **2:**300
  mathematics **2:**294, 295,
    296, 301, **3:**828, 830, 833
  philosophy **4:**1069–1070,
    1071, 1072
  Spinoza **5:**1291–1292, 1293,
    1294
Deuteronomy, book of **1:**233,
  3:607
devil **2:**533, 534
devotio moderna movement
  3:760–761, **4:**1065
devshirme **3:**617, 626
dialectic **2:**357, 362
  rhetoric vs. **5:**1369, 1372
Diaspora, Jewish **3:**669, 679,
  695
dietary laws **3:**669, 671
diets (political bodies) *see*
  parliaments
Diodati, Giovani **4:**882
Dionysius the Areopagite
  4:1102, 1103
diplomacy
  Clement VII **1:**241
  Florence **2:**414
  Leo X **3:**702–703
  Machiavelli **2:**419
  Renaissance **5:**1223
  Rubens **5:**1242
  Venice **5:**1393
dispensations **4:**1080
divine grace **3:**606
  Calvinism **1:**185, 186
  Lutheranism **3:**759, 766
  Paul V **4:**1036
  sacraments **5:**1358

Divine Love, Oratory of
  3:703
divine right **2:**539, 544, 546,
  4:906–907, **5:**1339
  England **1:**239, **2:**344, 345,
    346, 347–348, 367
  France **1:**188, **2:**367, 432,
    442, 443, 449, 517, 519
  Hapsburgs **2:**514
  Muscovy **4:**934, 940
  Russia **3:**652, 656
  state vs. church **2:**367, 368
  Stuarts **1:**239, **5:**1264, 1299,
    1300, 1302–1303
  Westphalia, Peace of **5:**1339
doge **3:**650, **5:***1396,* 1397
Dominic, Saint **2:***398,* **5:**1201
Dominicans **1:**52, 137, **3:**594,
  674, 676, **4:**1036, 1077,
  5:1201, 1204, 1209, 1327
  heresy **2:**532, 533
  missionaries **4:**889, 891, 892,
    895
  preaching **5:**1158
Donation of Constantine
  3:584, 586, 594, 686
Douay-Reims Bible **1:**108, 110
double-truth theory
  4:1054–1055
dualism *see* mind-body dualism
Duns Scotus, John **4:**1075

E

Easter
  dating of **1:**174–175, 176,
    218
  festival **4:**1118, 1119, **5:**1317
Eastern church *see* Orthodox
  Church
East India Company
  British **2:**375, 499, 501,
    5:1342, 1351
  Dutch **2:**383, **5:**1342, *1351*
Eastland Company **2:**500–501
Ecclesiastical Ordinances
  (Calvin) **1:**186
Ecclesiasticus, book of **1:**103,
  5:1355
ecological imperialism **2:**306
economic theory
  5:1348–1351

ecumenical councils *see specific*
  councils
education **2:317–325**
  Constantinople **1:**257
  Counter-Reformation
    4:1018, 1111
  England **5:**1286
  Germany **5:**1372
  households **2:**563, 569
  Islam **3:**614
  Jesuits **2:**294, **5:**1206, 1207,
    1250, 1291
  Latin language **3:**682
  mission schools **4:**892
  music **4:**942
  Poland **4:**1111
  Portugal **4:**1139
  Presbyterianism **1:**189
  religious orders **5:**1357
  school plays **5:**1323
  Scotland **5:**1263
  of women **2:**327,
    5:1416–1418, 1419,
    1424
  see also humanism and
    learning; literacy;
    Scholasticism; universities
efficient cause **4:**1063
elect, the *see* predestination
electors **2:**477, 478, 510, 548,
  551, 553, **4:**909–911, 966
elementary schools
  2:318–319, 320, 321, 322,
  325
Elizabethan Settlement of
  1559 (Elizabethan
  Compromise) **1:**239,
  5:1198
Emmanuel College
  (Cambridge) **5:**1374–1375
English Bible **1:**106–109, 238,
  239, **5:**1175
English Ladies (religious
  order) **5:**1208
English language **5:**1221,
  1222
  biblical translation **1:**108,
    109, 238, **2:**339, **3:***697,*
    698, **5:**1357
  Chaucer **1:**212–213, 217,
    218, 219, 220

English language *(cont.)*
  Latin influence **3**:690
  Spenser **2**:335
  as vernacular **3**:691, 692,
    694, 695
Enlightenment **1**:49, **4**:1072,
  5:1295
epistemological relativism
  2:294
Erasmus, Desiderius
  2:356–363, 439, 482,
  3:762
  Aristotle **1**:58, 59
  biblical interpretation **2**:538
  biblical translation **1**:58,
    104, 109, 181, **2**:358,
    3:585, 591, 684,
    688–689, 697, **5**:1357
  Catholicism **1**:180, **5**:1189
  Colet curriculum **4**:879
  Dürer **2**:316
  on foolery **5**:1221, 1319
  humanism **2**:337, 339, 356,
    423, **3**:585, 589, 590,
    591, 592, 593, **5**:1282,
    1283, 1370, 1371, 1373
  iconoclasm **3**:606
  Latin language **3**:684
  Leo X **3**:703
  Luther vs. **2**:339, 552, **3**:767
  on Margaret of Navarre
    3:735
  on marriage **2**:565
  More **4**:925
  northern Renaissance **2**:552
  papacy **4**:1023
  pilgrimage **4**:1079
  printed works **3**:688
  as Rabelais influence **5**:1176
  Rome **5**:1232
  women's education **2**:322
established churches
  2:364–372
  Calvinism **1**:186–187,
    2:349, 353
  Church of England
    1:235–240, **2**:326, 346,
    368–369
  Eastern Orthodoxy **1**:166,
    170, 257, 259
  Elizabeth I **2**:340–341

England **5**:1197, 1374
  Genevan Calvinism **5**:1316
  Henry VIII **2**:338, 521,
    524–527, 528
  heresy **2**:529–541
  Holy Roman Empire
    2:482–483
  Lutheranism **3**:768
  monarchy **4**:912, 913,
    930–931
  nationalism **2**:364–365,
    4:969, 970
  Scotland **5**:1265–1267
  Sweden **1**:229
  Thirty Years War
    5:1330–1339
  universities **5**:1374
estates (French ranking system)
  2:439
Estates General (France)
  2:407, **4**:913
ethics, Aristotelian **1**:*53,* 54,
  61
Eton (English school) **5**:1323
Eucharist **1**:119, 262, **3**:674,
  696, 698, 710, **5**:1163
  Calvinism **1**:184, 185, 189
  Church of England **1**:235,
    236–237, 240, **2**:341,
    5:1197, 1267
  Decree of Reunion **2**:430
  Eastern-Western doctrinal
    split **1**:259
  heresy **2**:536
  iconoclasm **3**:608
  kneeling for **5**:1267
  as Lord's Supper **1**:181, 183,
    184
  Lutheranism **3**:761, 762,
    764, 766, 767
  missal **1**:173, **5**:1363
  music **4**:943, 946, 954, 955,
    956, 957
  Reformation **1**:178, 181,
    5:1194, 1267
  Roman Catholicism **1**:178,
    180, 184, **5**:1197, 1358
  Trent, Council of **5**:1197,
    1357, 1358, 1363
  Zwingli **5**:1315
  see also transubstantiation

Eudocia, Saint **3**:*605*
Eugenius IV, Pope **3**:672,
  4:946, 1086, *1087,* **5**:1229,
  1379
  Florence, Council of **1**:260,
    2:427, 428, 429, 430
evangelical Protestants **1**:96
Eve *see* Adam and Eve
evil **2**:360
Execrabilis (papal bull) **4**:1086
Exodus, book of **1**:*102,* **3**:607
Expulsion, Edict of (1492)
  2:394
Expulsion, Edict of (1500)
  3:612
extreme unction **5**:1357

F

faith, Islamic **3**:611
faith alone, justification by
  1:58, **2**:341, 343, 369,
  5:1164, 1191, 1197
  bibles **1**:104, 105, 109
  Calvinism **1**:185, 186
  Church of England **1**:232,
    240
  Lutheranism **3**:761–762,
    763–764, 766
  Tridentine doctrine vs.
    5:1354–1355, 1356
fasts and fast days **1**:173,
  2:504, **3**:611, **5**:1341
Fawkes, Guy **1**:*238,* **2**:342,
  343, **5**:1301
feast days **1**:173, 174,
  4:1118
Felix V (antipope) **2**:429,
  4:1086
Feltre, Vittorino da **3**:584,
  5:1220, 1379, 1417
Ferrara, University of **3**:844,
  4:1073, **5**:1367
Festa (Assumption) **5**:1318
feudalism **1**:22, **2**:401–413,
  569, **4**:973
  abolition of **1**:28
  armies **5**:1411
  chivalry **1**:161, 221–226
  households **2**:562, 563, 569
  Hundred Years War **3**:595,
    597

investiture controversy
  2:365–366
Lombardy **3**:744
monarchy **4**:*903,* 904,
  905–906
papacy **5**:1234
peasants' revolts
  4:1041–1048
Ficino, Marsilio **2**:538, **3**:799,
  4:*1075*
Florence **2**:422, 423, 424
  humanism **3**:584, 586, *587,*
    588
  Medicis **3**:852, 855, 856
  philosophy **4**:1063, 1065,
    1068
  Pico della Mirandola **4**:1073,
    1074, 1075, 1076, 1103
  Platonism **1**:57,
    4:1100–1103
Fifth Lateran Council **3**:703,
  756
Filarete **1**:31, 34
filioque **1**:259, **2**:430
First Crusade **1**:223
First Vatican Council **5**:1363,
  1364
Fisher, John **1**:235, **2**:340,
  525
flagellants **2**:307
Florence, Council of **1**:169,
  260, 261, **2**:427–431,
  4:935, 1063, 1073,
  5:1358, 1359 *see also* Basel,
  Council of
Florence, University of **1**:54,
  169, **2**:318
Florentine Academy **4**:1073,
  1075
  Platonism **1**:261, **2**:418,
    3:855, **4**:1068, 1099,
    1100, 1103
Flores, Isabel de *see* Rose of
  Lima
forgeries **2**:383, **3**:584, 594,
  686
forms, Platonic **4**:1092,
  1094–1095, 1097
Forty-two Articles (England,
  1553) **1**:107, *237,* **2**:368
  see also Thirty-nine Articles

Four Evangelists **1:**_152, 154,_
   _2:_316
Four Lands, Council of
   (Poland) **4:**1111
Fourth Crusade **1:**259–260,
   5:1392–1393
Fourth Lateran Council
   3:670–671, **5:**1158
Foxe, John **1:**_187, 232,_ **5:**1325
Foxe, Richard **5:**1373
Francis of Assisi **5:**1162, 1201,
   1206
Francis Xavier _see_ Xavier,
   Francis
Franciscans **1:**126, **2:**485, 488,
   532, **3:**703, **5:**1201, 1204,
   1206, 1332
   Cervantes **1:**206
   missionaries **4:**888, 889–890,
     891–892, 893, 895, 896
   preaching **5:**1158, 1162
   Rabelais **5:**1176, 1177
fratricide, law of **3:**625
free trade **5:**1351
free will **1:**73, **2:**361, 543,
   546, **3:**586, 593, **5:**1195,
   1295
   Erasmus **2:**360–361, 552,
     3:767
   Paul V **4:**1036
   Pico della Mirandola **2:**538,
     4:1076
French Calvinists _see_
   Huguenots
French language
   biblical translation **1:**181
   Calvin **1:**179
   Descartes **2:**296
   nationalism **4:**963
   Rabelais **5:**1179
   as vernacular **1:**214,
     2:432–433, 444, **3:**695,
     696, **5:**1222
friars _see_ religious orders
Friars Minor _see_ Franciscans
Fugger Bank **1:**88, 90

G

Gabriel, archangel **3:**611, 657
Gallicanism **2:**372, **4:**969,
   5:1177, 1178

Garden of Eden **1:**249
Gardiner, Stephen **1:**236,
   3:608
Garter, Order of the **1:**223,
   3:598
Gemistus Plethon, George
   1:261, **4:**1063, 1099, 1100
Genesis, book of **2:**539,
   4:1077, **5:**1425
   Adam and Eve **1:**185,
     4:1064, _1066_
   Ptolemaic cosmos **1:**267
Geneva Bible **1:**105, 107, 108,
   238
Geneva Psalter **4:**942
Gennadius II Scholarios **1:**170,
   261
George, Saint **1:**224
German Bible **1:**104–105,
   107, 180, **2:**316, **5:**1357
German language **2:**548,
   3:699, **4:**963, 970,
   5:1222–1223
   Luther's New Testament
     1:_103,_ 104–105, _180,_
     2:316, **3:**765, **5:**1221,
     1222
   Yiddish **3:**670
Gerson, Jean de (Jean Charlier)
   2:367
ghetto **3:**672, 679
Ghibellines **2:**421, **3:**743, 854,
   5:1378
   Viscontis **5:**1405
Glorious Revolution of 1688
   1:24, **2:**346, **4:**906
Gnosticism **3:**605
God
   Cartesian existence proof
     2:297, 298–300
   election by **1:**185, 189–190
   free will **2:**361
   monotheism **1:**167, **3:**620,
     669
   philosophy **4:**1070,
     1071–1072, 1076,
     1098–1099, 1100, 1101
   theodicy **2:**360
   see also divine grace
Golden Bull (1356) **2:**478,
   549, **4:**910–911

Golden Haggadah **3:**_669_
good works, salvation by
   1:104, 180, 186, 190, 232,
   5:1191, 1197, 1354, 1355,
   1356
Gospels **3:**671
   preaching of **5:**1158, _1159,_
     _1162,_ 1165
   see also John, Gospel of; New
     Testament
government
   condominium system **2:**508
   democracy **1:**166, **2:**542,
     4:906, **5:**1339
   electors **2:**477, 478, 510,
     548, 551, **4:**909–911, 966
   France **2:**439, 440, 451
   Hobbes **2:**542, 543, 544,
     545–546, **4:**1066–1067
   humanism **3:**585, 640
   Italian city-states **3:**630, 634,
     635, 636, 637–639, 641,
     642, 643, 650, 693, 702
   Ivan IV reforms **3:**652
   Machiavelli **3:**769–773,
     4:1066–1067
   Ottoman Empire **3:**625–628
   political philosophy
     4:1066–1067, 1071, 1072
   Renaissance republics **5:**1223,
     1224
   Venice **5:**1392, 1396, 1397,
     1400
   see also absolutism;
     diplomacy; monarchy;
     Parliament; parliaments;
     republics
grace _see_ divine grace
grain trade **5:**1341, 1350
grammar **3:**582, 683, 689,
   5:1218, 1282
grammar schools **2:**319
Grand Remonstrance (1641)
   2:350
Great Bible **1:**107, 238, **2:**339
great chain of being
   2:335–336, 538, **4:**1062,
   1076
Great Schism of 1054 **1:**166,
   259, **2:**427, **3:**854, **4:**1073
   pivotal doctrine **1:**259

Great Schism of 1378–1417
   see Western Schism
Greek Christianity _see_
   Orthodox Church
Greek Codex Alexandrinus
   1:109
Greek language _see_ languages,
   classical
Greek Orthodox Church _see_
   Orthodox Church
Greek philosophy **1:**167, 169,
   181, 261, **2:**334, 422,
   3:685, 730
   Aristotle **1:**50–61
   Platonism **4:**1092–1103
   School of Athens, The
     (Raphael) **1:**_38, 50, 143,_
     3:703, **4:**1025, 1061,
     5:1186
   universities **5:**1368, 1370,
     1376
Gregory I (the Great), Pope
   1:258, 259
Gregory VII, Pope **2:**366,
   529
Gregory IX, Pope **2:**_532_
Gregory X, Pope **3:**673,
   4:1010
Gregory XI, Pope **5:**1227
Gregory XII, Pope **1:**264,
   2:318
Gregory XIII, Pope
   1:175–176, **4:**1024
Gregory XV, Pope **1:**33,
   5:1205
Gregory of Nyssa **4:**1024
Gresham College (London)
   5:1429–1430
Guelfs **1:**156, **2:**421, **3:**743,
   854, **5:**1378, 1405
Guicciardini, Francesco **1:**242,
   _244,_ 245, **3:**856
guilds and companies
   2:493–501
   companies **3:**497–501
   craft guilds **2:**496–497, 499,
     4:983
   Dürer **2:**311
   Florence **1:**151, **2:**415, 417,
     419, **3:**853
   German towns **2:**476, 478

guilds and companies *(cont.)*
  Italian city-states **3:**632, 633, 635, 636, 637, 640, 641, 706
  London **3:**750, 751, 753
  Lutheranism **2:**555
  machines **3:**774
  manufacturing **3:**810–811
  Meistersingers **4:**960
  physicians **3:**843
  theater **5:**1317, 1318
  women members **5:**1421
Gunpowder Plot (1605) **1:***238,* 239, **2:**342, *343,* **4:**880, 1039, **5:**1301
Gutenberg Bible **3:***688,* **5:**1169, *1170*

H

hadith **3:**611
Hagar **4:**1085
Haggadah **3:***669*
hajj **3:**611, 621, **4:**1078, *1084,* 1085
Halacha **3:**669
Hanno (papal elephant) **4:**1012
Hanseatic League **2:**475–476, 481, **502–506, 5:**1340
  Denmark **5:**1304, 1305
Harmensen, Jacob **1:**190, **2:**346
Harvard University **1:**189, **2:***325,* **4:**891
Hasan **3:**620
Havdalah prayer **3:***677*
healing pilgrimage **4:**1078, 1079, 1082
Hebrew Bible *see* Old Testament
Hebrew language
  bibles **3:**688, 697
  education **2:**321
  humanist learning **3:**589, 590, 591, 592, 679, 689
  Judaism **3:**670, 696
Hegel, Georg Wilhelm Friedrich **4:**1072
Heidelberg, University of **1:**77, **2:**324
Heidelberg Catechism **5:**1174

Helena, Saint **5:***1279*
Hellenism **1:**166, 167, 170, 171, 172
Helmstadt, University of **5:**1372, 1377
Heraclitus **4:**1097
heresy **2:529–541, 3:**695, 830, **4:**935, 1038
  Aristotelian questioners **1:**57
  astrology as **1:**73
  biblical translations **1:**103
  Bohemia **1:**119, 212
  Bruno **1:**57
  Calvinist penalty **1:**187, **2:**539, **5:**1316
  Catholic damnation **2:**431
  Charles V **1:**211
  Christian humanism **3:**592
  Church of England **1:**232, 236, 237
  Counter-Reformation **5:**1197, 1226, 1234–1235
  Cranmer **1:**237
  England **2:**522, 526, 527
  Florence **2:**422
  under Ferdinand and Isabella **2:**396
  Galileo **1:**262, **2:**296, 297, 467, 539, **3:**783, 784, **5:**1226, 1234–1235, 1251, 1254, 1256, 1258
  heliocentric universe **1:**272, **2:**539, **4:**1036
  Henry IV **2:**518
  Holy Roman Empire **2:**549
  iconoclasm **3:**605
  Inquisition **4:**1018, 1019, 1026, 1065, **5:**1278, 1283, 1400
  Islam **3:**622
  Joan of Arc **3:**602, 658, 660, 661–662
  Luther **3:**701, 705, 766, 767
  magic **3:**802
  under Mary Tudor **1:**236, 237
  monarchy **5:**1331
  papacy **5:**1333
  Paris **4:**1032
  Pico della Mirandola **4:**1074, 1075, *1076,* 1077

Savonarola **1:**137
science **3:**783, 784
Scotland **5:**1264, 1265
Hexapla **1:**109
hieroglyphs **3:**774, 776
Hieronymites, monastery of (Portugal) **4:**1141
High Church movement **5:**1325
Hinduism **3:**615
history
  English nationalism **2:**339
  humanist studies **1:**180, **2:**336, 339, **3:**582, 584, 587, 588, 590, 682, 683, 686, **5:**1218, 1282
  national **4:**964
  Renaissance **5:**1220
  Scottish writers **5:**1263
  Shakespeare's plays **5:**1273
Hobbes, Thomas **1:**51, 59, **2:542–547, 4:**1066–1067, 1071, 1072
Holy Alliance **4:***967*
Holy Communion **1:**240
Holy League **2:**442, 443, 457, 458, 459, 517, 518, **3:**643, 645, 715–716, 718
Holy Office of the Inquisition *see* Inquisition
Holy Spirit **2:**430, **3:***695,* 757, **5:**1199
  preaching **5:**1165
  Trent doctrine **1:**186
holy war **3:**612, 616, 626
Hooker, Richard **2:**367, 369
Hospitallers *see* Knights Hospitallers
House of Commons **2:**350, 354, 407
House of Lords **2:**354, 355
Hudson's Bay Company **2:**501
Huguenots **1:**188, **2:**332, 371, 440, **5:**1195
  Catherine de Médicis **1:**198, 199, 200, 201
  French civil wars **2:**451–459, **5:**1331
  North America **1:**189
  Paris **4:**1033–1034

Saint Bartholomew's Day Massacre **1:**188, 200, 201, **2:**371, 441, 454, 455, 456, 516, 556, **3:**825, **4:**1033, **5:**1331
Thirty Years War **5:**1336
Huizinga, Johann **5:**1160
humanism and learning **3:582–594**
  Alfonso X **3:**693
  architecture **1:**31–32, 33, 43, 44, 49, 140, 141, 143, 151, *152,* **2:**334, 424, **3:**665, 666, 667, **4:**983
  Aristotle **1:**50–61
  astrology **1:**69
  astronomy **1:**265–269, 270, *271, 272*
  Bessarion **1:**261
  Boccaccio **1:**114–116
  Borgia, Lucrezia **1:**125, 126
  Botticelli **1:**135, 136–137
  Bruegel **1:**145, 152
  Byzantium **1:**166–172
  Calvin **1:**181, 190
  Christina **1:**227, *228,* 229
  classical languages **3:**682–690, 693, 694
  Clement VII **1:**241–242, 244
  Constantinople **1:**256, 258–264, 269, **2:**430
  Descartes **2:**294
  Dürer **2:**311, 312, 314, 316
  education **2:**317–325, 327
  England **1:**262–263, **2:**334–337, **3:**590, 593
  Erasmus **2:**356, 357, 358, 362, **5:**1189
  Florence **2:**414, 421–426
  France **2:**439, 448, 450
  German towns **2:**481, 482
  heresy **2:**538–539
  Holy Roman Empire **2:**551–552
  Hussites **1:**118
  Inquisition **2:**362, **5:**1283
  Italian city-states **3:**638, 640
  James I **5:**1299
  Judaism **3:**674, 679, 693

Leo X **3**:700, 703
literature **2**:334–337, **3**:720, 722, 727, 729, 730, 731–735, 737, 739, 823
Luther vs. **2**:339, **3**:756, 761, 767, **5**:1371
Machiavelli **3**:772
Marlowe **3**:823
mathematics **3**:827, 829
medicine **3**:840, 844–847
Medicis **2**:422, **3**:852, 853, 855, 856
More **4**:925–932
music **4**:916, 920, 942, 946–947, 961
mythology **1**:135, 136–137
painting and sculpture **1**:145, **2**:312, **4**:980–981, 983, 984–985, 986, 990
Palladio **1**:43
papacy **4**:1020, 1021–1023, 1024
Petrarch **2**:320, **4**:1049, 1053–1055, 1075
philosophy **1**:167, 169, 181, 261, **2**:334, 422, **3**:685, 730, **4**:1025, 1064, 1072, **5**:1368, 1370, 1376
Pico della Mirandola **4**:1073–1077
Platonism **1**:57, 181, **3**:605, **4**:1092–1103
Portugal **4**:1143–1145
printed texts **2**:323, **3**:780, 782–783, **5**:1172–1173
Rabelais **5**:1176–1179
Reformation **2**:339–340
Renaissance **5**:1218–1221, 1224, 1240
Roman Catholic Church **5**:1189
Rome **5**:1228, 1229, 1230, 1231–1232, 1235
Scotland **5**:1263
Spain **5**:1279–1283
theater **3**:727, 729–735, **4**:916, 920, **5**:1320–1321, 1322, 1326
universities **5**:1365, 1366, 1368–1370, 1372, 1373, 1376

Venice **5**:1399
vernaculars **3**:694, 696
women **5**:1416, 1417–1418, 1419
Wren **5**:1429–1430
human nature **2**:339, **4**:763, 1064, *1066*, 1072, 1076
opposing views on **4**:1064
Pico della Mirandola **2**:537, 538, **4**:1067
Hume, David **4**:1068, 1070
Hus, Jan **1**:118–119, **2**:549, 550, 557, **5**:1192, 1334
heresy **2**:537
Lutheranism **3**:764, 766
nationalism **4**:969
universities **5**:1367
Husayn **3**:620
Hussites **1**:118–119, 120, 122, **2**:537, **3**:660, 674, 766, **4**:969, **5**:1192

I

Ibn Battutah **3**:611, **4**:1084
Ibn Rushd (Averroës) **1**:51, 52–53, 58, **4**:1054, 1064, *1098,* **5**:1367
Ibn Sina (Avicenna) **5**:1367
Ibrahim (prophet) *see* Abraham
iconoclasm **3:604–609,** **4**:992, 995
Calvinism **1**:183, 184, 185, *5:1165*
Church of England **1**:240
Islam **1**:172, **3**:605
Lutheranism **3**:761, 762
Puritanism **1**:48, **5**:1198
idealism **1**:57, **2**:543, **4**:1070, 1092
nominalism vs. **1**:182
Ignatius of Loyola **1**:59, **4**:894, 955, **5**:1205–1206
Jesuits **4**:1015, *1017*
Spiritual Exercises **1**:99, **5**:1199, 1206
Immaculate Conception **4**:1036
Immaculate Conception, Confraternity of the **3**:708–709
imperialism *see* colonialism

Incarnation **1**:183, **3**:604, 605, 607, **4**:1098
Index of Forbidden Books **2**:465, 466, 467, **4**:1018, 1019, **5**:1178–1179, 1197, 1226, 1234
Copernicus's works **1**:272
Erasmus's works **3**:585, 592
Trent, Council of **5**:1363
inductive logic **1**:81, 82, 83
indulgences
Leo X **2**:421, **3**:704, 855
Luther's critique of **2**:423, **3**:757, 763, **4**:929, 1012–1013, **5**:1190
papacy **4**:1012–1013, **5**:1231, 1232
penance **1**:180
pilgrimage **4**:1079, 1080
printing **5**:1169
Reformation vs. **2**:481, **5**:1189, 1190–1191, 1192
sale of **2**:481, 553, **3**:757, 855
theological basis of **4**:1013
Trent, Council of **5**:1360
infant baptism **1**:178, **5**:1314
inheritance **2**:506, 565, 568
fief **2**:404–405
Huguenots **5**:1331
monarchy **3**:595, 625
Poland **4**:1106, 1107, 1114
primogeniture **1**:235, **2**:512, **3**:625, **4**:911
Salic Law **2**:517, **3**:595
Sweden **5**:1335, 1337
Teutonic Knights **1**:222, 223
Tudor male heir **1**:233
by women **2**:404–405, 413
Inner Temple (London) **1**:213
Innocent III, Pope **1**:260, **2**:531, **5**:1158
Innocent VIII, Pope **3**:700, **4**:1074, 1075, *1076*
Innocent X, Pope **5**:1388, 1389
Inns of Court (London) **1**:79, 213, **3**:752, **5**:1328
Inquisition
Aristotle **1**:57
Black Legend **2**:400

Cardano **1**:70, **3**:830
Erasmus **2**:362
Ferdinand and Isabella **2**:393, 396, 397, 400
Galileo **2**:297, 467, 539, **3**:784, **4**:1036, **5**:1254
heresy **2**:530, 531, 532–535
humanism **2**:362, **3**:586, 592
Islam **3**:613
Judaism **3**:677, 678, **5**:1291
monarchy **4**:907, 912
Paul III **4**:1018, 1019, **5**:1197, 1234
Philip II **4**:1058
popular culture **4**:1120, 1121
Portugal **4**:1139, 1141
Renaissance vs. **5**:1226
Rome **1**:187, **4**:1018, 1019, 1036, 1065, **5**:1226, 1234, 1251
Spain **5**:1278, 1279, 1283
theater **5**:1321
Torquemada **2**:533
Venice **5**:1400
witchcraft **2**:534–535, **3**:801–802, **4**:1019
women **5**:1424
Interregnum (England) **2**:354
investiture controversy **2**:365–366, 368
Islam **3:610–629**
Africa **2**:380
agricultural technology **1**:21
architecture **1**:46–47
Aristotle **1**:51, 52–53
astronomy **1**:267, 268, 271
Byzantium **1**:166, 170
Constantinople **1**:263
Crusades against **1**:223, 259–260
Francis I **2**:448
Hapsburgs **2**:512, 514
iconoclasm **1**:172, **3**:605
Inquisition **5**:1278
Judaism **3**:669, 670, 676
machines **3**:777, 779
mathematics **3**:827
monotheism **3**:620, 669
navigation **5**:1343

Islam *(cont.)*
 papermaking **3:**805
 Philip II **4:**1056–1057
 pilgrimage **4:**1078,
  1084–1085
 Poland **4:**1110
 Portugal **4:**1137, 1138,
  1140, 1141, 1142
 scholarship **3:**693, **4:**1054,
  1061, 1064, **5:**1367
 science and technology
  5:1250
 slave trade **5:**1348
 Spain **2:**393, 394, 396–398,
  408, 533, **3:**612, 613,
  676, 678, **4:**956, 969,
  5:1277, 1278, 1279,
  1322, 1425
 trade **2:**373, 379, 380,
  5:1341, 1344, 1345
 Venice **5:**1392
Ismail **3:**612, 621, 622
Italian language **2:**465, **3:**682,
 694, 696
 Dante **1:**217
 Galileo **5:**1254
 Petrarch **4:**1049, 1050, 1052

J

Jacquerie (1358) **2:**433,
 4:1029, 1042, *1044*
James, Saint **4:**1060, *1078,*
 1080, 1082, **5:**1356
Jena, University of **5:**1377
Jerome, Saint **1:**104, **3:***682,*
 688, 689, 696, **4:**1024,
 5:1357
Jesuits **1:**59, **2:**465, 556,
 3:839, **4:**1036,
 5:1205–1206
 Bohemia **1:***120,* 121
 catechisms **5:**1174
 Christina **1:**229
 Counter-Reformation
  4:1016, **5:**1191, 1199,
  1204
 Descartes **2:**294
 education **2:**294, **4:**1111,
  1139, 1140
 England **1:**238, **5:**1324,
  1326

humanism **2:**324, **3:**593
missionaries **4:**889, 890, 891,
 892, 893, 894–895, 896,
 1015, *1018*
music **4:**955
Paul III **4:**1015, *1017,*
 5:1191, *1197,* 1199,
 1205, 1353
suppression of **5:**1209
Sweden **5:**1307
theater **5:**1323, 1326
Thirty Years War **5:**1332
universities **2:**324, 325
Jesus of Nazareth **1:**99, 105
 Bosch paintings **1:**128, 130,
  131
 Calvinism **1:**183, 184
 Dürer woodcuts **2:**314
 Eucharist **1:**178, 183, **5:**1194
 Gospels on **3:**671
 horoscope of **1:**70, 72, *73,*
  3:830
 iconoclasm **3:**604, 605, 607,
  5:1222
 Islam **3:**610, 618
 Judaism **3:**671
 Last Supper **3:**710, 712, 713
 Michelangelo painting
  5:*1354*
 Neoplatonism **4:**1098–1099
 preaching on **5:**1163–1164,
  1165
 Raphael paintings **5:**1180,
  1182, 1184, 1185, 1187
 religious orders **5:**1201
 religious plays **5:**1317, 1318,
  1319, 1322
 Rembrandt paintings **5:**1213,
  1215
 Rome **5:**1232
 sacraments **1:**184, **5:**1358,
  1359
 Trent, Council of **5:**1360
Jews *see* Judaism
jihad **3:**612, 616
John, Saint **2:**316, 485, 487
John, Gospel of **3:**591, 604,
 605, 607, *697,* **5:***1159*
John Climacus, Saint **1:**168
John of Damascus **1:**168,
 3:604, 761

John of the Cross **5:**1207
John Paul II, Pope **2:**466,
 4:1023, **5:**1226
John the Baptist **2:**485,
 5:1184, 1185
John the Evangelist *see* John,
 Saint
Josephinism **2:**372
Joshua, book of **2:**467, **3:***591*
jubilee year **4:***1079,* 1080
Judaism **3:**669–681
 Aristotelianism **1:**51
 bibles **1:**103, 104, **3:**689
 iconoclasm **3:**605
 Inquisition **2:**532, 533,
  5:1278
 Islam **3:**610, 612, 613
 Kabbalah **1:**57, **3:**677,
  679–680, 689
 Poland **4:**1110–1111,
  1113–1114
 Portugal **4:**1139
 Roman Catholic damnation
  2:431
 scholarship **3:**693
 Spain **5:**1277, 1278, 1279,
  1283
 Spanish conversos
  2:396–397, 399
 Spanish expulsion **2:**393,
  394, 398–399
 Spinoza **5:**1291, 1292, 1293,
  1295
 usury **1:**85
 vernaculars **3:**695
judges **3:**635
Judgment Day **1:**177, **2:**387
Julius II, Pope **1:***50,* 245,
 3:756, 757, **4:**1012, 1025,
 1026, **5:**1420
 architecture **1:**36, 38,
  141–142
 Florence **2:**420
 Henry VIII **1:**232
 Italian wars **3:**643, 645, 648,
  649, 702
 Leo X **3:**700–701, 702
 Medicis **2:**420
 Michelangelo **4:**871,
  873–875, 876
 Raphael **5:**1186, 1187

Rome **5:**1230, 1231–1232
 Urbino **5:**1380
 Venice **5:**1394
Julius III, Pope **3:**648, 672,
 4:*954,* 955
Trent, Council of **5:**1353,
 1357, 1359
Justin Martyr **3:**765

K

Kaaba (Mecca) **3:***611,* **4:**1084,
 1085
Kabbalah **1:**57, **3:**677,
 679–680, 689, **4:**1075,
 1103
Kalmar, Union of (1397)
 4:911, **5:**1304
Kant, Immanuel **4:**1070
Karlstadt, Andreas **3:**606, 758,
 761, **5:**1193
Kempe, Margery **4:**1081,
 5:1427
Kempis, Thomas *see* Thomas à
 Kempis
khanates **3:**653
King James Bible (Authorized
 Version) **1:**106, 108, 109,
 110, 239, *240,* **3:**698, 699,
 5:1221, 1357
King's College (Cambridge)
 1:30, 100, **4:**949
Kirk *see* Church of Scotland
kneeling **5:**1267
Knights Hospitallers **1:**194,
 223, **4:**1046
Knights of the Golden Fleece
 see Golden Fleece, Order of
 the
knowledge, Platonic
 4:1092–1093, 1094
Knox, John **1:**189,
 5:1265–1266, 1267, 1423,
 1424, 1426
Koine Greek **3:**695, 696
Königsberg, University of
 5:1372, 1377
Koran **3:**611, 614, 618, *626*
kosher laws **3:**671
Kraków, University of **1:**265,
 266, *270,* **4:**1109, **5:**1250
Kremlin **4:**939

L

Laetentur caeli **2:***427,* 429, 430

land and land rights
  agriculture **1:**21–29
  enclosure movement **1:**28, **3:**818
  feudalism **2:**401–413
  merchant wealth **5:**1350
  monasteries **5:**1202, 1203
  property law **3:**809
  reclamation **1:**273–276, 277
  Reformation **5:**1332–1333, 1338
  Spain **4:**965–966
  Sweden **5:**1306, 1308
  Venice **5:**1395

languages, classical **3:**640, **682–690,** 691–695, 703, **5:**1219, 1280
  Aristotelian translations **1:**51, 52, 54–56, 57, 58, 59
  bibles **1:**103–105, 109, 110, 181, **2:**358, **3:**591, *682,* 684, 688–690, 696, 697, 703, **4:**1022, 1024, **5:**1159, 1160, 1355, 1357
  see also Vulgate
  Boccaccio **1:**113–114
  Cicero **3:**683
  Constantinople **1:**258, 261, 264
  education **2:**317, 319, 320, 321, 324
  England **2:**334–337
  English language **3:**690
  Erasmus **2:**357, 358, 359
  Eucharist **5:**1363
  Greek translation **1:**57, 261, 264
  humanism **1:**264, **2:**336, **3:**582–594, 640, 693, 694, 703, **5:**1220, 1282
  Latin translations **1:**261, 264
  literary genres **1:**219
  manuscript collection **1:**261
  Middle Ages **3:**682–683
  papacy **4:**1022–1023
  Petrarch **4:**1049, 1050, 1052–1053
  philosophy **4:**1063, 1100

Pico della Mirandola **4:**1073, 1074, 1075
printing **5:**1173
Septuagint **1:**103, 104, 109, **3:**695
text analysis **3:**686–687
universities **1:**261, **5:**1368, 1369, 1373
Valla scholarship **3:**586, 686–687, 688
vernacular texts vs. **3:**696–697, 698, 699
women's education **5:**1417, 1418, 1419

languages, vernacular **3:691–699,** **4:**931
  biblical translations **1:**102–110, *180,* **2:**316, 321, 526, 536, **3:**689, **4:**970, **5:**1173–1174, 1175, 1193, 1221, 1315, 1357
  Calvin **1:**179
  Chaucer **1:**212–213, 217, 218, 219, 220
  Czech **1:**118, 119, 122, **2:**537
  Dante **1:**217
  Descartes **2:**296
  education **2:**319, 321, 323, 325
  Eucharist **5:**1363
  France **1:**214, **2:**432–433, 444, **3:**695, 696, **4:**963, **5:**1222
  Galileo **2:**465, **3:**690, **5:**1254
  Holy Roman Empire **2:**548
  Judaism **3:**670
  literature **2:**335, **3:**720, 721, 723
  nationalism **2:**364, **4:**962, 963–964, 966, 969, 970
  Petrarch **4:**1049, 1050, 1052
  Polish writers **4:**1109
  preaching **5:**1160
  printing press **2:**323
  Rabelais **5:**1179
  Renaissance **5:**1222–1223
  Scotland **5:**1260–1261
  Spain **3:**693–695, **4:**963, **5:**1222, 1282, 1284

Spanish empire **2:**399
  theater **5:**1318
  see also specific languages
Last Judgment **1:**177, **2:**387
Lateran Council, Fifth (1512–1517) **3:**703, 756
Lateran Council, Fourth (1215) **3:**670–671, **5:**1158
Latin language *see* languages, classical
Laud, William **2:**372, **3:***608,* 609, **4:**881, **5:**1267, 1302
  anti-Calvinism **2:**345, 346, 348, 349
  Church of England **1:**239
  execution of **2:**351
  theater **5:**1325, 1329
Laurentian Library (Florence) **1:**33, **4:**876
law
  Bacon **1:**79, 80
  Boccaccio **1:**111
  Chaucer **1:**213
  chivalry **1:**222
  heresy **2:**531
  Islam **3:**612, 614, 623, 625
  Italian city-states **3:**632, 635
  Ivan IV **3:**652
  Judaism **3:**669, 671, *679, 680*
  London **3:**752
  Ottoman Empire **3:**623
  students of **5:**1367, 1371
  urbanization **3:**809
lay orders *see* third orders
learning *see* education; humanism and learning; universities
leather trade **3:**741, **5:**1350
legal studies **5:**1367, 1371
Leibniz, Gottfried Wilhelm **3:**828, 834, **5:**1295
Leiden, University of **2:***323,* **3:**585, 592, **5:**1210, 1292, 1367
Leipzig, University of **5:**1367, *1372*
Lent **4:**1118, 1119, 1123
  preaching **5:**1159
Leo III, Pope **1:**257, 258–259
Leo IV, Pope **5:**1187

Leo IX (Pope) **4:**1073
Leo X, Pope **1:**152, 277, **2:***426,* **3:700–705,** *763,* 765, **4:**929, **5:**1194
  architecture **1:**38, 40
  Charles V **2:**513–514
  Clement VII **1:**241, 242, 245, 246
  Counter-Reformation **5:**1197
  elephant gift **4:**1012, 1037
  Erasmus **2:**357
  France **2:**442, *446,* 447, **3:**701
  Henry VIII **1:**240, **5:**1191, 1196
  hunting **1:**95
  indulgences **2:**421, **3:**704, 855
  Italian wars **3:**646, 648, 649
  Luther **1:**242, **3:**701, 703, 704–705, 757, *763,* 765, **4:**1013, **5:**1192, 1232
  Medicis **2:**418, 420, 421, 426, **3:**850, 851, 853, 855, 857
  Michelangelo **4:**876
  music **4:**946, 949
  Pontine Marshes drainage **1:**277
  Raphael **5:**1186, 1187
  Rome **5:**1232
  Urbino **5:**1380, 1382, 1383
Leo XIII, Pope **4:**932, 1022
letter writing **3:**589, 640, 682
Levant Company **1:**262
Levellers **2:**354
Leviticus, book of **1:**233
libraries **1:**271, **3:**695, 703
  universities **5:**1375
  Vatican **4:**1022
Libreria Vecchia (Venice) **3:***690*
Lisbon Bible **3:***591*
literacy **2:**552–553, 555, **3:**720, 819
  education **2:**323, 325
  Judaism **3:**669
  London **3:**754
  printing **2:**323, **5:**1172, 1174, 1222

literacy *(cont.)*
  rates of **5:**1173
  Reformation **2:**321
  Scotland **5:**1263
  vernaculars **3:**695, 697
  women **5:**1416, 1417
liturgical calendar **1:**173, 174,
  175–177
liturgical drama *see* religious
  drama
Livy **3:**584, 682, 684, 686,
  770, 772
loans *see* usury
Locke, Anne Vaughan
  5:1423–1424
Locke, John **2:**545, **5:**1295,
  1348–1349
logic
  Aristotle **1:**50, 60–61, 81
  Bacon **1:**81–82, 83
  dialectic **2:**357, 362
Lollards **1:**103, 107, 232,
  2:536–537, **3:**605, 761,
  766
Lombard League **3:**740
Long Parliament (1640)
  2:*344*, 349, 351
lord mayor **3:**751, 754
Lord's Prayer **5:**1318
Lord's Supper **1:**181, 183, 184
Louis II, cardinal of Lorraine
  2:456, 517
Louvain, University of **1:**108,
  3:589
Loyola, Ignatius *see* Ignatius of
  Loyola
Lublin, Union of (1569)
  4:911, 1104, 1108, 1109
Lucaris, Cyril, patriarch of
  Constantinople **1:**109, 263
Lucretius **1:**136
Luke, Saint **1:***145*, **2:**380
Luther, Martin **1:**99, 246,
  262, **2:**339, 370, 438, 439,
  448, **3:**756–768, **4:**906,
  929, **5:***1188*, 1189
  alchemy **3:**801
  Aristotle **1:**58, **4:**1065
  biblical authority **1:**104–105,
    106–107, **5:**1352, 1354,
    1356, 1371, 1372

biblical translation **1:**102,
  103, *180,* **2:**316, **3:**698,
  4:931, 970, **5:**1193, 1222,
  1357
calendar reform **1:**175
Calvinism **1:**181, 183, 185
  Charles V vs. **1:**211, 242,
    2:514
  on divorce grounds **2:**566
  doctrine **5:**1192, 1194, 1195,
    1197, 1198
  Dürer **2:**315, 315–316
  Eastern patriarchate **1:**262
  education **2:**321–322, 324
  English Reformation **1:**232,
    240
  Erasmus **2:**339, 356, 357,
    358, 359–362, 552,
    5:1283
  excommunication of **1:**242
  German towns **2:**479, 481,
    482
  Henry VIII **1:**232, **2:**338
  heresy **4:**1032
  Holy Roman Empire **2:**553
  humanism **2:**423, **3:**585, 593
  Hus as forerunner **1:**118
  Hussites **2:**537
  iconoclasm **3:**606
  indulgences critique **2:**423,
    3:757, 763, **4:**929,
    1012–1013, **5:**1360
  Islam **3:**618
  Judaism **3:**675
  Leo X **1:**242, **3:**701, 703,
    704–705, 757, *763,* 765,
    4:1013, **5:**1192, 1232
  on marriage **2:**569
  music **4:**947, 952, 957
  nationalism **2:**364
  Ninety-five Theses **3:**758,
    5:1190–1191, 1221
  papacy **1:**246, **4:**1012–1013,
    5:1400
  peasant revolts **2:**555
  philosophy **4:**1063, 1064,
    1065–1066
  preaching **5:**1163–1165
  Reformation inception **1:**178
  religious orders **5:**1201,
    1203, 1362

  religious wars **1:**183
  Rome **5:**1232
  sacraments **5:**1358
  Shorter Catechism **5:**1174
  Swiss Reformation **5:**1305,
    1315, 1316
  universities **5:**1368, 1371,
    1376
  usury condemnation **1:**85
  witch hunting **2:**535
  women's education **2:**322
Lutheranism **1:**181, 240,
  2:525, 527, **3:**756–768,
  836, 855, **5:**1314
  Augsburg, Peace of **1:**75–78
  biblical authority **1:**104–105,
    106–107, 180
  Calvinism vs. **1:**185
  Christina **1:**227
  church-state separation **4:**906
  Dürer **2:**315–316
  Eastern Orthodox
    patriarchate **1:**262
  England **1:**240, **2:**338, 339
  as established church **2:**365,
    369–370, 371
  German towns **1:**242, **2:**479,
    482, 483, 552–554
  Henry VIII **1:**235
  heresy **2:**539, 540
  Holy Roman Empire **2:**548,
    552–554, 556, 557, 558,
    559, **5:**1200
  iconoclasm **3:**606, 608
  music **4:**957, 958, **5:**1247
  nobility **2:**370
  Poland-Lithuania **4:**1107,
    1110, 1112
  preaching **5:***1162*
  Reformation **5:**1192, 1194,
    1195, 1197, 1198
  religious orders **5:**1201,
    1203, 1209
  Sweden **5:**1305, 1306, 1307
  Thirty Years War **5:**1332
  Trent, Council of **5:**1352
  universities **5:**1377
Luttrell Psalter **1:***92,* **4:***1041*
Lyceum **4:**1095, **5:**1365
Lyons, Second Council of
  (1274) **1:**85, 260, **5:**1358

M

Maccabees 1 and 2 **1:**103,
  5:1355
Machiavelli, Niccolò **1:**164,
  245, **2:**337, 395, 419,
  3:655, **769–773,** 853
  Borgias **4:**1011
  on Ferdinand of Spain **2:**395
  Florence **2:**419
  literature **3:**376, 770, 772
  Medicis **2:**419
  monarchy **2:**337, 419, **3:**771
  political philosophy
    4:1066–1067
  Renaissance **5:**1221, 1224
  theater **3:**733
madrassas **3:**614
Magdalen College (Oxford)
  2:*336*
magic **2:**532–534,
  3:795–803, **4:**1065
  astrology **1:**72, **4:**1065
  popular culture **4:***1115,*
    1120, 1121, 1123
Magna Carta (1215) **4:**906,
  5:1339
Maimonides **3:***678, 679*
Maimonides Synagogue
  (Cairo) **3:***678*
Malta, Order of *see* Knights
  Hospitallers
Malthusian cycle
  4:1127–1128, 1129, 1130
Mamluks **3:**612, 623
Mantua, congress of
  4:1087–1089
manuscripts
  bibles **1:**102
  forgery detection **3:**584, 594,
    686
  humanists' analyses **3:**582,
    583, *584,* 587, 588, 683,
    684, 685, 687, 688, *689,*
    690
  Petrarch's collection **3:**682,
    684, **4:**1053
  printing **5:**1169–1170, 1193
Manutius, Aldus **1:**56, 59,
  2:357, **3:**584, 688, **5:**1399
Marburg, University of
  5:1372, 1377

Marcellus II, Pope **5:**1353, 1355, 1359, 1360

Margaret, Saint **3:**657

Mark, Saint **2:**316
  winged lion of **5:***1400*

Mark of Ephesus **1:**260, **2:**429

Marranos **3:**674, 678, 681, **5:**1291, 1292

Marsilius of Padua **1:**53, 257, **2:**367

Martin V, Pope **2:**428, **4:**1011, 1052, **5:**1162, 1227, 1379

martyrdom **1:***232*, **5:**1201, 1206
  Islam **3:**620, 621
  Joan of Arc **3:**662
  Protestantism **1:***232*

Mary, mother of Jesus *see* Virgin Mary

Mary Magdalene **5:**1160

Mass *see* Eucharist

Massachusetts Institute of Technology **2:**383

materialism **2:**543, 544

Matthew, Saint **1:**193

Matthew, Gospel of **1:**105, 110, **3:**671, **5:**1215

Matthew's Bible **1:**107

Maurice, Saint **1:**224

Mazarin, Cardinal **1:**230, **2:***459*

Mazarin Bible **1:**103

Meaux, conspiracy of **1:**200, **2:**454

Mecca **3:**611, 623, 625, **4:**1078, 1084, 1085

Medici Bank **1:**87, 88

Medici Chapel (Florence) **4:**876

Melanchthon, Philipp **2:**483, 566, **3:**585, 593, 767–768
  educational reform **2:**320, 324
  universities **5:**1371, 1372, 1373, 1377

Mendoza, Pedro González de **5:**1279–1280

mercantilism **1:**25, **5:**1348–1350

messianism **3:**622, 677

Michael, archangel **1:**224

Middle English **1:**213, 214

Middleton cross **3:**815

"Mighty Fortress Is Our God, A" (Luther) **4:**952

millennialism **1:**137

mind-body dualism **2:**300–301, **3:**606, **5:**1294

miracle plays **3:**732, **5:**1318, 1319, 1323, 1328

Mishneh Torah **3:***679*

missals **1:**173, 175, **5:**1363

missionaries **4:888–896**
  Americas **5:**1285
  exploration **2:**379, 380, 382, **5:**1346
  Islam **3:**614
  Jesuits **4:**1015, *1018,* **5:**1199, 1205, 1206
  Jewish converts **3:**676–677
  Leo X **3:**701
  Portugal **4:**1142, *1143*
  religious orders **5:**1204, 1206–1207, 1208

Modena, University of **5:**1370–1371

monarchy **4:903–915**
  absolutism **2:**367, 368, 544, 546, **4:**906–907
  architecture **1:**46
  astrological prediction **1:**71–72
  banking **1:**85, 86, 88, 89, 90
  Bohemia **1:**117, 121, 222
  chivalry **1:**221, 223, 224, 225
  companies **2:**499, 500
  court etiquette **2:**437
  court musicians **4:**949
  court society **4:**978–979
  cuius regio, eius religio principle **5:**1331
  divine right **4:**906, **5:**1299, 1300, 1302–1303, 1339
  England **2:**334–346, 348, 523, **4:**906
  English civil wars **2:**347–355
  English Restoration **1:**240, **2:**351, **4:**886, **5:**1302, 1322, 1329
  established churches **2:**365, 366, 368, 369, 370, 371, 372, **5:**1374

feudalism **2:**406, 407, 408, 409, 412–413

France **2:**432, 433, 436, 437, 438, 444, 445–450, 516–520

French civil wars **2:**440–443, 451–459

Hapsburgs **2:**512

heresy **2:**539
  Hobbes on **2:**542, 544, 546

Holy Roman Empire **2:**555
  as household **2:**569

Hundred Years War **3:**595–603, 658–659, 660

Lutheranism **3:**767, 768

Machiavelli on **2:**337, 419, **3:**771

markets **3:**815

More relationship **4:**926–927, 929–932

Muscovy **4:**934–941

nationalism **4:**903, 914, 915, 966, 970

nobility **2:**407, 408, **5:**1339

Ottoman sultans **3:**625–626, 628

papal relations **4:**1008, 1009, 1012, 1014, 1015, 1017

Paris **4:**1031–1035

Parliament **5:**1302–1303

Poland **4:**1104, 1108, 1111, 1112

Portugal **4:**1137–1138

Renaissance **5:**1218, 1220, 1221, 1223, 1224, 1225

Russia **3:**652–656

Scotland **5:**1261–1264, 1296–1301

Spanish Inquisition **4:**1019

Stuarts **1:**239–240, **5:**1296–1303, 1329

succession rules **3:**595, 625

Sweden **1:**227–231, **5:**1306

tournaments **1:**225

universities **5:**1374

warfare **5:**1414

women rulers **5:**1425–1427

monasteries *see* religious orders

moneylending *see* usury

monotheism **1:**167, **3:**620, 669

Montpellier, University of **5:**1367, 1371

Moors *see* Islam

moral philosophy *see* philosophy

More, Thomas **3:**698, **4:924–932,** 1074, **5:**1319, 1418
  bibles **1:**106
  Erasmus **2:**357, 362, 363
  execution of **1:**235
  Henry VIII **1:**235, **2:**525
  humanism **2:**335, 339–340, **3:**585, 590, 593, **5:**1370, 1371, 1373
  Platonism **4:**1063, 1103
  printing **5:**1173
  Reformation **2:**339–340

Moriscos **2:**396–397, **3:**613, **4:**1056–1057, **5:**1278

morphology **5:**1258

mosques **1:**170, 171, 172

Mount Athos monastery **1:***170,* 171

Muhammad **3:**610, 611, 614, 620, 626
  pilgrimage **4:**1084

Muslims *see* Islam

Musta'rabim Jews **3:**670

mystery plays **3:**729, **5:***1317,* 1318, 1319, 1322

mysticism **3:**760, **5:**1207, 1283
  Islam **3:**614, 620, 621
  Judaism **3:**677, 679–680, 689, **4:**1075, 1103
  women **5:**1427

N

Nantes, Edict of (1598) **1:**198, **2:**443, 454, *457,* 458, 459, 517, 520, 541, **4:**1034

Nantes, Synod of **2:**493

Nantes, University of **5:**1371

Naples, University of **4:**1061, **5:**1367

national churches *see* established churches

National Covenant of 1638 (Scotland) *see* Covenanters

nationalism 4:903, 914, 915, **962–970**
  Bohemia 1:118, 122, 5:1334, 1367
  English arts 2:339, 3:664
  established churches 2:364–372
  France 2:435, 444
  German towns 5:1200
  humanism 3:590
  Hundred Years War 3:603
  monarchy 4:903, 914, 915, 966, 970
  Reformation 2:364–365
  Scotland 5:1260
  technology 3:786
  vernaculars 3:695, 696, 698, 699
naturalism 4:980, 982–983, 985
natural philosophy 4:1065, 1067–1068, 1069, 1070, 1072
Nebrija, Elio Antonio de 2:399, 3:694, 699, 5:1280
Neoplatonism 1:137, 3:696, 4:1061, 1076, 1096–1099, 5:1376
  education 2:320
nepotism 4:1016, 1023, 1037, 1091, 5:1230
Neri, Philip 4:956, 5:1204
New Divinity 1:190
New Learning see humanism and learning
New Testament 1:181, 193, 2:358, 5:1369
  Dürer images 2:314, 316
  English translation 1:240
  Erasmus translation 3:585, 591, 684, 689, 697, 703
  Four Evangelists 2:316
  Greek language 3:688, 5:1355, 1357, 1419
  humanism 5:1218
  Incarnation 3:604, 605
  Luther translation 1:103, 104–105, 180, 2:316, 3:765, 5:1221, 1222
  preaching of 5:1158, 1159, 1162, 1165

Trent, Council of 5:1356, 1357
  vernacular translations 3:695, 698
  Zwingli sermons 1:178
  see also Gospels
Nicaea, Creed of see Nicene Creed
Nicaea, First Council of 5:1364
Nicaea, Second Council of 3:605, 5:1364
Niccolò de' Niccoli 3:583, 584, 585, 587
Nicene Creed 1:259, 2:430, 3:607, 4:953
Nicholas, Saint 2:378
Nicholas I, Pope 1:259
Nicholas IV, Pope 1:44
Nicholas V, Pope 1:34, 39, 142, 4:1022–1023
  Bessarion 1:261
  humanism 3:584, 586
  Rome 5:1228–1229, 1230
Nicholas of Cusa 3:618, 4:1098–1099, 1101
Nieszawa, Privilege of (1454) 4:1108
Nihil Novi constitution (Poland) 4:1108
Nineteen Propositions (1642) 2:351
Ninety-five Theses (1517) 1:178, 2:482, 553, 3:704, 758, 759, 4:929, 5:1189, 1190–1191, 1197, 1221, 1352, 1360
nobility and rank **4:971–979**
  Agincourt 1:18
  architects 1:33
  armies 5:1411, 1414
  astrology 1:71–72
  Bohemia 1:117, 118, 119, 120, 121, 122
  Calvinism 2:442, 453
  chivalry 1:221, 222
  courtiers 5:1383, 1427
  education 2:317, 318–319, 321–322
  English barons 2:407–408, 409, 410

English country homes 2:334
feudal hierarchy 2:401–413
feudalism 1:22, 2:401–413
Florence 2:415, 417, 419
France 2:433, 435, 437, 439, 442, 443, 451
German towns 2:476, 478, 479, 482
households 2:561–569
humanism 3:593, 594
Hundred Years War 2:435
hunting 1:94–95
infant mortality 5:1420–1421
interactions 4:1123
Italian city-states 3:632, 634–636, 638–639, 642, 648, 651
kinship 2:568–569
knighthood 1:221
language 3:691, 692
Lutheranism 2:370, 482, 553–554, 555
manufacturing 3:805, 809, 821
marriage and family life 5:1418–1419, 1420, 1421
monarch relations 4:906, 907, 908, 5:1339
Muscovy 4:934, 937, 938, 939, 940, 941
palaces 1:39–40, 45, 47
papal relations 4:969
peasants' revolt 4:1042–1048
Poland-Lithuania 4:1104, 1106, 1108, 1109, 1110, 1111, 1113
popular culture 4:1115–1123
Renaissance 5:1223, 1224
Russia 3:652, 653, 654, 655, 656
Scotland 5:1260, 1261, 1262, 1265, 1267, 1296, 1298, 1299
sumptuary laws 4:979, 1041
Sweden 1:228, 5:1304, 1307, 1308
universities 5:1368, 1372
Venice 5:1392, 1393, 1395, 1396–1397, 1400
warfare 5:1411, 1414

women 5:1416–1418, 1419, 1422, 1423, 1425–1427
nominalism 4:1062–1063, 1065
  Calvinism 1:181, 182, 184
  iconoclasm 3:606, 607
  Lutheranism 3:759–760, 761
Nonconformist Act of 1665 (England) 1:240
nuns see religious orders
Nuremberg, Diet of (1524) 2:553

O

Oath of Supremacy (England) 2:524
Oberammergau passion play 5:1318
Observants (Franciscans) 5:1162
Ockham, William of 2:366, 367, 3:759, 763
  nominalism 1:181, 4:1062, 1063
Ockham's razor 4:106
Old Believers 4:936
Old Testament 1:167, 233, 235, 3:672, 689, 5:1369
  Apocrypha 1:103–104
  Greek translation 1:103–104, 181, 3:695
  Hebrew language 3:688, 689
  humanist scholarship 3:591, 592
  iconoclasm 3:607
  imagery 2:392
  Kabbalah 1:57
  Ptolemaic cosmos 1:267
  Torah 3:669, 679
  Trent, Council of 5:1355, 1357
  vernacular translation 3:698
Olier, Jean-Jacques 5:1361
oligarchy see republics
Ommegang procession 5:1317
Oratorians 4:956, 5:1204–1205, 1208
oratory see rhetoric
Order of Preachers see Dominicans

orders, religious *see* religious orders
ordination **5:**1357
Origen **1:**109, **4:**1098
original sin **2:**339, **3:**763, **4:**1064, *1066*
Orléans, University of **5:**1371
Orthodox Church **2:**366, **4:**1008, 1023
  Byzantium **1:**166, 170, 172
  calendars **1:**177, **4:**1024
  Constantinople **1:**170, 171, 257, 260, 262–263, **2:**427
  Decree of Reunion **2:**429–431
  Florence, Council of **1:**260, 261, **2:**427–431
  Great Schism **1:**166, 259, **2:**427, **3:**854, **4:**1073
  icons **3:***604,* 605
  Lithuania **4:**1109, 1110
  Lyons, Council of **1:**260
  monasticism **1:**171, **5:**1201
  Muscovy **4:**934–936, 939
  Ottoman Empire **3:**626
  Reformation **1:**262
  Russia **1:**166, **4:**935–936, 1109
  vernaculars **3:***696,* 697
Our Lady of Guadalupe **4:**890
Oxenstierna, Axel **1:**227, 228, **5:**1307, 1309, 1310, 1337
Oxfordians **5:**1276
Oxford Reformers **4:**1103
Oxford University **2:**375, 536, **3:**668, **5:**1368, 1374
  Arabic studies **1:**262, **3:**618
  Church of England **1:**232
  Constantinople **1:**262
  Drake hoax **2:**383
  founding of **5:**1367, 1373
  Hobbes **2:**542, 543
  humanism **2:**336
  Magdalen College **2:***336*
  More **4:**924, 1063
  plays **3:**732, **5:**1328
  science studies **5:**1255, 1256
  Sheldonian Theatre **5:**1430
  University Wits **3:**732, 824
  Wren **5:**1429, 1430, 1431, 1432, 1433

P

Padua, University of **2:**318, 462, **3:**829, **5:**1255, 1367, *1370,* 1371, 1400
  Aristotelianism **1:**56–58, 59
  botanical garden **3:**840, 847
  Copernicus **1:**265
  Galileo **5:**1252
  medical studies **3:**840, 845, 846–847
  philosophy **4:**1064
  Pico della Mirandola **4:**1073, 1074
  Vesalius dissection **2:**302
paganism **2:**431
  Greek philosophy **1:**261
  Hellenism **1:**167
  Poland-Lithuania **4:**1104, 1105, 1107
pantheism **4:**1065, 1071–1072
papacy **1:**178, **4:1008–1027,** 1052
  architecture **1:**39, 40, 141–142
  astrology **1:**72, 73–74
  authority of **1:**257, **5:**1363
  bibles **1:**102–103, 105
  Bramante **1:**142
  calendar **1:**174, 175–177
  Catherine de Médicis **1:**197
  Charles V **1:**209, 210, 230–231, 241, 242, 243, **2:**513–514
  Christina **1:**229, 230–231, 234
  Church of England **1:**232
  Contarini **5:**1400
  councils **2:**430, **5:**1352
  Decree of Reunion **2:**429–431
  Donation of Constantine **3:**584, 586, 594, 686
  Elizabeth I **2:**341
  Erasmus **5:**1189
  established churches **2:**364, 365–367, 368, 370
  feudalism **2:**406, *407,* 412, 413
  Florence **2:**415, 418, 419, 420, 421, 422, 423, 425, 426

Florence, Council of **1:**260, 261, **2:**427–431
France **2:***432,* 438, 453
French civil wars **1:**183
Galileo **2:**465, 466–467, **5:**1226
Giotto **2:**491
Guelfs **1:**156, **3:**743, 854, **5:**1378, 1405
Hapsburgs **2:**479, 481, 507, 513, 514
as head of church **1:**259
Henry IV **2:**366, 517, 518, 519
Henry VIII **1:**232–234, 235, 240, 242, **2:**338, 339, 521, 522, 523, 524, 525, **5:**1191, 1196
heresy **2:**530, 531, 532, 533
Holy Roman emperors **1:**156, *208,* 241, **2:**510, 513–514
humanism **3:**584, 586
indulgences **2:**421, 423, **3:**704, 757, **4:**1080, **5:**1189, 1190–1191, 1231
Italian wars **3:**643–649, 701, 702
Judaism **3:**672, 673, 677
Lombardy **3:**744, 745
Luther vs. **1:**246, **2:**481, 482, **3:**756, 757, 762, 764, 765, 766, 767, 768, **5:**1352
Medici bankers **1:**87
Medicis **2:**416, 418, 420, 421, 426, **3:**850, 851, 852, 853, 854, 855
missionaries **4:**888–889, 1015
monarch relations **2:**365–366, 368, 372, **4:**311, 903, 907, 913, 930–932, 969, 970
music **4:**946, 947, 948, 949
nepotism **4:**1016, 1023, 1037, 1091
Ottoman Empire **3:**626, 715, *717*
painting **1:**133, 135, 257, **2:**428, **4:**992

Paul V **4:**1020, 1021, 1026, 1036–1040
Petrarch **4:**1052
Philip II **4:**1058
Pico della Mirandola **4:**1074, 1075, *1076,* 1077
Pius II **4:**1086–1091
Raphael **5:**1186–1187
Reformation against **1:**183, 232
Renaissance popes (list) **4:**1025
Rome **5:**1227–1235
schism **2:**366, 421, 429, 430, 431, **4:**913, 1009–1011, 1052, **5:**1227, 1406 *see also* Avignon papacy
Spain **5:**1234
spiritual vs. temporal power **1:**257
Swiss Guards **5:**1314
theater **5:**1325
Thirty Years War **5:**1332, 1333, 1334, 1336
Trent, Council of **5:**1352, 1353, 1357, 1359–1360, 1363, 1364
universities **5:**1367, 1368, 1369
Urbino **5:**1378–1383
Venice **5:**1394, 1398–1399, 1400
Viscontis **5:**1404–1405
worldliness **2:**426
see also specific popes
Paris, University of **5:**1199, 1371, 1430
  Aristotelianism **1:**53, 56
  Erasmus **2:**357, 358
  founding of **5:**1367, 1369
  humanism **3:**585, 589, 590, 592
  medical studies **3:**845
  Petrarch **4:**1052
  Pico della Mirandola **4:**1073, 1075
  Rabelais **5:**1177, 1178
  religious orders **5:**1205
  Roman Catholicism **4:**1032
  science studies **5:**1255

Parliament, British **2:**350, 354, 355, 407
Bacon **1:**79, 80, 82
Cromwell **1:**239, **2:**351
English civil wars **2:**347–355, 544
established church **2:**368, 524
feudalism **2:**407
guilds **2:**494–495
Gunpowder Plot **4:**880, 1039, **5:**1301
Hundred Years War **3:**603
London **3:**751
monarchy **2:**344, 346, **4:**906, 911, 912, **5:**1302–1303
More **4:**926–927, 929, 931
Restoration settlement **5:**1302
Rump Parliament **2:***344,* 351, 355
Scotland **5:**1263, 1298
Stuarts **1:**239, **5:**1300, 1302–1303, 1329
theater closure **5:**1322, 1329
parliaments **2:**407, **4:**910, 913
Florence **3:***851*
Hanseatic League **2:**505, 506
Holy Roman Empire **2:**548
Poland **4:**111, 1108, 1113
Russia **3:**652
Scotland **5:**1298, 1299
Sweden **1:**227, **5:**1306, 1308
Parma, University of **5:**1367
Pascal, Blaise **3:**775
pasha **3:**628
passion plays **5:**1317, 1318
Passover **3:***669*
Paul, Saint **3:**605, 689, **4:**1102, **5:**1230
bibles **1:**105, 110
Calvin commentary **1:**179
conversion of **1:**193
Dürer image **2:**316
humanist learning **2:**337
letters of **1:**105, 179, **2:**337, **5:**1356
missionizing **4:**894
preaching **5:***1158,* 1160, 1163

Paul III, Pope **2:**361, **3:**648, 836, **4:***1009, 1025*
astrology **1:**72
Charles V **1:**210
Counter-Reformation **4:**1016, 1017, 1019
Inquisition **5:**1197, 1234
Jesuits **4:**1015, *1017,* **5:**1191, *1197,* 1199, 1205, 1353
Michelangelo **4:**871, 877
overview of **4:**1016
Rome **5:**1232, 1234
Saint Peter's Basilica **4:**1026
Trent, Council of **5:**1352, 1353, 1357
Urbino **5:**1381
Venice **5:**1400
Paul IV, Pope **3:**644, **4:**992, 1058, **5:**1353, 1360, 1363
Inquisition **5:**1197
religious orders **5:**1204
Rome **5:**1233, 1234
Paul V, Pope **1:**97, **2:**465, **4:**921, 1020, 1021, 1026, **1036–1040**
Venice **5:**1400
Paul VI, Pope **5:**1363, 1364
Paulicians **3:**605
pawnbrokers **1:**88–89
Pazzi conspiracy (1478) **1:**24
Pembroke College (Cambridge) **1:**48, **5:**1286–1287, 1430
penance **1:**104, 180, 186, **3:**689, 757, 763, **5:**1190
Calvinist rejection of **1:**183
confession **5:**1357
pilgrimage **4:**1078, 1080
see also indulgences
Pentecost **3:**695
Personal Rule (England) **2:**347–348
Peter, Saint **1:**37, 99, 100, 105, 141, 193, **3:**798, **4:**1026
Dürer image **2:**316
papacy **1:**257
preaching on **5:**1160
Rome **5:**1230, 1231, 1234
Petition of Right of 1628 (England) **2:**347

Petrarch **2:**320, **3:**720, 721, 722, 724, 725, 726, **4:**963, **1049–1055,** 1072, 1143
Boccaccio **1:**111, 112, 114, 115
Borgia, Lucrezia **1:**125
Chaucer **1:**216
humanism **2:**357, **3:**583–584, 585, 589, 682–683, 684, 686, **4:**1049, 1053–1055, 1075, **5:**1218
papacy **4:**1009, 1052
Rome **5:**1227, 1228
Spenser translations **2:**335, **5:**1286
vernacular language **3:**694
Viscontis **5:**1405–1406
Philaret, patriarch of Constantinople **4:**940
philology **3:**586, 587, 594, 686, 690
philosopher's stone **3:**800–801, **4:**1065
philosophy **3:**730, **4:**1025, **1061–1072**
Aristotle **1:**50–61
Bacon **1:**81–82
Byzantium **1:**168–169, 170
Christina **1:**228, 229, 230
Descartes **2:**294–301
education **2:**325
Erasmus **2:**357–363
Florence **2:**422, 422–423
Greek translations **3:**685
Hobbes **2:**542, 543, 544, 545–546
humanism **3:**582, 584, 585, 588, 591, 682, 683, **5:**1219, 1282
Judaism **3:**679
Lutheranism **3:**759–761, 765, 767, 768
Machiavelli **3:**769, 771–773
magic **3:**799, 800
More **4:**927–928
Neoplatonism **4:**1096–1097
nominalism **1:**181, 182, 184
Petrarch **4:**1053–1054
Pico della Mirandola **4:**1073–1075

Platonism **4:**1092–1103, **5:**1376
Scholasticism **2:**357, **4:**1049
Spinoza **5:**1291, 1294–1295
universities **5:**1368, 1370
see also Greek philosophy
Photius, patriarch of Constantinople **1:**259
physical education **2:**318, 319
Piacenza, University of **5:**1367
Piccolomini, Enea Silvio *see* Pius II
Piccolomini, Francesco *see* Pius III
Pico della Mirandola, Giovanni **4:1073–1085**
Florence **2:**422–423, 424
humanism **2:**482, **3:***588,* 589
magic **4:**1065
Medicis **3:**852, 855, 856
More **4:**924
optimism **2:**537, 538, **4:**1064, 1066
Platonism **4:**1100, 1103
Renaissance **5:**1220
Pigafetta, Antonio **3:**789, 791, *792, 793*
pilgrimage **4:1078–1085**
Calvinist rejection **1:**183
Chaucer **1:***212,* 213, 218, 219, **5:**1202
Islam **3:**611, 615, 621, 625
Rome **4:**1026, **5:**1228, *1232*
Pilgrimage of Grace (England, 1536) **1:**187, 235, **2:**340, 526, **4:**1042
Pilgrims (Puritans) **5:**1342
Pisa, Council of (1409) **2:**367
Pisa, University of **3:**700, **5:**1367
botanical garden **3:**840, 847
Galileo **2:**460, 461, **5:**1252
science studies **5:**1255
Pius II, Pope **2:***428,* **3:**619, **4:1086–1091, 5:**1230
Pius III, Pope **4:**1091
Pius IV, Pope **2:**453, **3:**747, **4:**1020, 1024, **5:***1226,* 1353, 1360

Pius V, Pope **3**:715, *717,* **4**:*967,* 975, *1058,* 1059
excommunication of Elizabeth I **1**:238, **2**:330
Pius XI, Pope **4**:932
Platina *see* Sacchi, Bartolomeo
Plato **3**:*703,* **4**:*1054, 1061,* 1092, 1096, 1097, 1098
Academy **4**:1063, 1090, 1095, **5**:1365
English translation **2**:336
Latin translation **1**:264, **2**:422, **3**:685, 687
see also Platonism
Platonic Academy (Florence) *see* Florence, Academy of
platonic love **4**:1092, 1095, 1097, 1102–1103
Platonism **1**:31, 69, 137, *167,* 264, **2**:320, 538, 543, **4**:928–929, 1025, 1061–1062, 1070, 1073, 1075, **1092–1103**
Aristotelianism **1**:50, 57, 60, 181, 261, **4**:1063, 1099
Cambridge Platonists **4**:1070–1071, 1072, 1103
Christianity **1**:258, **3**:696
Constantinople **1**:261
Florence **1**:261, **2**:418, 422, 423, 424, 425
humanism **1**:181, **3**:584, 586, *587*
iconoclasm **3**:605, 606
magic **3**:798, 799, 855, 856
nature **4**:1065
nominalism vs. **1**:182
Petrarch **4**:1049, 1054
Pico della Mirandola **4**:1073, 1074, 1075, 1076
Ptolemaic cosmos **1**:267
universities **1**:261, **5**:1376
see also Neoplatonism
plenary indulgence **4**:1080
Plessis, Armand-Jean du *see* Richelieu, Cardinal
Plethon *see* Gemistus Plethon, George
Pliny the Elder **1**:58, **3**:583, *687*
Pliny the Younger **3**:583

Plotinus **2**:422, 538, **4**:1061, 1063, 1070, 1096–1097, 1098, 1099, 1100, 1101
Plutarch **1**:*59,* **2**:336, **3**:684, 685, 729
podesta **3**:637, 638
Poggio Bracciolini **1**:33, **2**:336, 359, **3**:583, 683, **5**:1229
Poitiers, University of **2**:295, **5**:1371
Pole, Reginald **1**:234, 236, **5**:1355
Polish Brethren **4**:1110
political philosophy **4**:1066–1067
Aristotle **1**:53, **3**:684
Hobbes **2**:542–547
Machiavelli **3**:769–773
Renaissance **5**:1223–1224
see also democracy; government; republics
poll tax **1**:216, **4**:1042–1043, 1047
polytheism **4**:1105
Pomponazzi, Pietro **1**:56, 261, **4**:1064, 1069
Ponce de León, Juan **2**:374, 382, **4**:888–889, 891
Ponsonby, William **5**:1288, *1289*
Poor Clares **5**:1201
population **4**:1124–1136
agriculture **1**:22
Black Death **2**:305, **4**:1048, 1124
France **2**:433, 436
German towns **2**:481
Italian city-states **3**:630–631, 633
London **3**:748
Paris **4**:1028, 1030
Poland **4**:1106
sixteenth-century growth **4**:*1126*
Portuguese Inquisition *see* Inquisition
Portuguese language **5**:1222
Prague, University of **1**:19, 118, **2**:537, **3**:779, **5**:1367
preaching **1**:183, **5**:1158–1166

predestination **1**:185, 189–190, **2**:341, 342, 343, 345, 369, 536, **3**:761, **5**:1195
Presbyterianism **1**:104, 239
Calvinism **1**:178, 181, 188, 189, 190
English civil wars **1**:239, **2**:353
as established church **2**:369
New Divinity **1**:190
Puritanism **2**:342
Scotland **1**:189, 190, **2**:369, **5**:1265–1267, 1298, 1300, 1301, 1303
priest training **5**:1361
primary schools *see* elementary schools
primogeniture **1**:235, **2**:512, **3**:625, **4**:911
princedom **5**:1223
Princeton College **1**:189
Proclus **1**:*271,* **2**:422
propaganda, printed **5**:1174–1175
property law **3**:809 *see also* inheritance
Protestantism *see* Reformation; *specific denominations*
Protestant Union **3**:836, 837, **5**:1331, 1334
Psalms **4**:1077
Pseudo-Dionysius *see* Dionysius the Areopagite
public education **2**:322, 323–325
purgatory **2**:430, 525, **3**:704, 757, **5**:1231, 1232, 1360
indulgences **4**:1013
penance **1**:180
Puritans **1**:108, **2**:328, **4**:892, 894
biblical interpretation **1**:109
Calvinism **1**:178, **5**:1196
Church of England **1**:188, 237, 239, 240, **2**:368–369, **5**:1198
church reform **2**:342
Cromwell **2**:351
Elizabethan Compromise **1**:239, **5**:1198

England **1**:188, 239, **2**:341, 343, 345, **4**:1066
English civil wars **2**:346, 348, **5**:1325, 1336
iconoclasm **1**:48–49, **3**:609, **5**:1198
theater **5**:1326, 1327, 1329
theocracy **1**:187
universities **5**:1374–1375
Putney Debates (1647) **2**:354

Q

quadrivium **2**:357, **5**:1366, 1372
Quetzalcoatl **4**:890
Quintilian **3**:583, 584, 588, 590, 683, 686, **5**:1373
Qum (Shiite shrine) **3**:621

R

Rabelais, François **3**:735, 736, **5**:1176–1179
Radcliffe Camera (Oxford) **1**:140
reading *see* literacy
realism **3**:759–760
reason **3**:761, 766, 767
Aristotelianism **1**:57
humanism **2**:337
reasoning **2**:317
Recollects **4**:889, 893
Reconquista **2**:398, **3**:676, 678, **4**:956, 969, **5**:1322, 1425
Red Book (Sweden) **5**:1307
Reformation **5**:1188–1200
Aristotelianism **1**:58
astrology **1**:73
Augsburg, Peace of **1**:75–78
bibles **1**:102–110, **2**:320, **3**:689
Bohemia **1**:118, 119–122, **5**:1334
calendar **1**:175, 176–177
Calvinism **1**:178–190
Charles V **1**:210–211
church architecture **1**:49
church music **5**:1244, 1246
Church of England **1**:232, 236–240
common themes **1**:178

Reformation (cont.)

Constantinople 1:262–263

Dante 1:217

divorce grounds 2:566–567

Dürer 2:314, 315–316

education 2:317, 320, 321–325

Elizabeth I 2:328–329, 5:1297, 1298, 1301

England 1:62, 232–240, 2:326–333, 334, 338–343, 346, 349, 365, 524, 525, 526, 527, 528, 3:608–609, 4:1015, 5:1300, 1301, 1302, 1325, 1326, 1424, 1426

English chronology 1:240

Erasmus 2:356, 357, 358, 359–362

established churches 1:257, 2:364–372

Florentine humanism 2:423, 426

France 2:432, 438–440, 541

Francis I 2:447–448

Greek revival 2:320

Gregorian calendar 1:175, 176–177

Hapsburg opposition 2:507, 513, 514–515

heliocentric universe 1:272

Henry IV 2:516–520, 541

Henry VIII 2:338–340

heresy 2:535, 537, 539–540

Holy Roman Empire 2:423, 479, 480, 482–483, 548, 552–554, 556, 557–559

households 2:563

humanism 2:324, 339–340, 3:590, 592, 593

iconoclasm 3:605, 606–609

key issues 3:855, 5:1354–1359, 1363–1364

Leo X 3:704–705

literacy 3:720

literature 2:335, 3:739

London 3:748

Luther 5:1352

Lutheranism 3:756–768

Milton 4:882, 883, 885

missionaries 4:892, 895, 896

monarchy 4:906, 907, 912, 913

More 4:929, 930–932

music 4:943, 952–954, 957, 958

nationalism 2:364–365, 4:969, 970

Netherlands 4:1057

painting and sculpture 4:992, 995–996

papacy 4:1012–1013, 1014, 1016, 1018, 1019, 1023, 1026–1027, 1040

Paris 4:1031, 1032–1034

philosophy 4:1064–1066

pilgrimage critics 4:1079, 1083

Poland 4:1110–1111

popular culture 4:1121–1123

preaching 5:1163–1166

printing 1:180–181, 2:323, 5:1173–1174, 1175, 1192, 1193

religious orders 5:1201–1204, 1209, 1362

Renaissance chronology 5:1221

Rome 5:1232

sacraments 5:1358

science 5:1256

Scotland 5:1262, 1263, 1265–1267, 1298, 1300, 1302, 1303, 1426

Spenser 5:1289

Sweden 5:1305, 1306, 1308

Switzerland 5:1312, 1313, 1314–1316

theater 5:1325, 1326–1327, 1329

theodicy 2:360

Thirty Years War 1:227, 3:767, 835–839, 4:1040, 5:1310, 1330–1339

Trent, Council of 1:99, 5:1352–1364

universities 5:1365, 1368, 1369, 1370, 1371, 1372, 1373–1377

usury relaxation 1:85

vernacular languages 2:321, 335, 3:696, 698–699

warfare 5:1408, 1411

women 5:147, 1423–1424, 1426

see also Counter-Reformation

Reformation Parliament (Scotland, 1560) 5:1298

Reformed churches see Calvinism

Regensburg, Diet of (1541) 1:209

regicide 5:1303, 1325

Reichstag (Germany) 2:548, 4:910

relativism 2:294

religious festivals 4:1118, 5:1317

religious guilds 2:493–494, 495, 500

religious orders 2:365, 368, 370, 4:1008–1009, 5:1201–1209

Bavaria 3:839

Byzantium 1:171, 5:1201

Cervantes 1:206

contemplative life 3:585, 586

Eastern Orthodoxy 1:171, 5:1201

England 2:526

English closure 1:235, 236, 2:340, 365, 3:608, 5:1202, 1203

exploration 2:380

fulling mills 3:806

as household model 2:569

Italian city-states 3:639

Ivan IV Vasilyevich 3:655

libraries 5:1375

Lombardy 3:740

London 3:748

Luther 3:756–757, 758, 762, 767, 4:767

manuscripts 3:582, 583, 682, 686

missionaries 4:888–896

nobility and rank 4:975

papacy 4:1038

Paul III 5:1353

preaching 5:1158, 1159

priestly training 5:1361

Rabelais 5:1176, 1177, 1178

Thirty Years War 5:1332

Trent, Council of 5:1362

universities 2:322, 324

waterwheels 3:812

see also specific orders

religious plays 3:727, 728–729, 732, 5:1318–1320, 1322, 1323, 1328

religious poetry 3:726, 735

religious tolerance

Bohemia 1:119, 121

Catherine de Médicis 1:201

Christina 1:230

German towns 2:482, 483

Henry IV (France) 2:517, 520, 541

heresy vs. 2:540–541

Holy Roman Empire 2:441, 556, 558

Islamic Ottomans 1:169, 170, 3:612, 613, 615, 623, 626, 676, 680

James I 5:1301

Levellers 2:354

Milton 4:883

Netherlands 3:681

Poland 4:1110–1111

Spanish Jews 3:676

Venice 5:1398

Westphalia, Peace of 5:1338

republics 4:995, 5:1223, 1224

English civil wars 2:352–353, 355

Florence 2:416–417, 3:585, 702, 4:967

Italian city-states 3:630, 638–639, 641, 642

Italian wars 3:644, 649, 650, 651

Venice 3:668, 5:1392, 1396, 1397, 1400

Restitution, Edict of (1629) 3:839, 5:1333, 1336, 1337

Restoration (England) 1:240, 2:351, 4:886, 5:1302, 1322, 1329

Reuchlin, Johann 3:592, 593, 674, 689

Revelation 1:32, 105, 138

Dürer images 2:314

Eyck images 2:387

Revised Standard Version (1946 Bible) 1:106
Revised Version (1881 Bible) 1:106
rhetoric
  dialectic vs. 5:1369, 1372, 1373
  Erasmus 2:363
  humanist learning 3:582, 584, 588, 589, 683, 5:1218, 1282
Ricci, Matteo 4:894–895, 1015, 5:1206
Richelieu, Cardinal (Armand-Jean du Plessis) 4:882, 908, 1034–1035, 5:1240
  French civil wars 2:458–459
  Thirty Years War 5:1333, 1336, 1337
Rienzo, Cola di 4:1052, 5:1227
Riksbank (Sweden) 1:90
Riksdag (Sweden) 1:227, 5:1306, 1308
Rinuccini, Ottavio 4:920, 5:1321
Roman Catholic Church
  Aristotelianism 1:52, 53, 54, 55, 56, 57, 58–59 see also Scholasticism
  astrology 1:72, 73–74
  astronomy 2:296
  Augsburg, Peace of 1:75–78
  Bernini sculpture 1:97, 99, 100
  bibles 1:104, 105, 108, 110, 3:688, 689
  Bohemia 1:119, 120, 121–122
  calendar 1:173, 174, 175–177
  Calvinism vs. 1:179, 180, 182, 183, 184, 186, 188, 189, 190, 198–200
  catechism 5:1174
  Christina's conversion to 1:228, 229–231, 5:1311
  Church of England 1:235, 237–238, 239, 240, 263
  Decree of Reunion 2:429–431

divorce ban 2:566, 567
education 2:317, 319, 322, 324, 325, 364, 4:1018, 1111
Elizabethan Settlement 2:329, 5:1198
England 1:62, 66, 79, 108, 232, 235–240, 262, 2:326–331, 333, 335, 338–346, 368, 370, 371, 372, 526, 4:896, 929–932, 953, 5:1196–1197, 1198, 1297, 1298–1299, 1301, 1302, 1324, 1325, 1326–1327, 1328, 1374, 1424, 1426
English civil wars 2:347, 348, 350, 352
Erasmus 2:356–363
established churches 2:364–365, 368, 369, 370–372
exploration 2:380
fairs 3:813, 815
fast days 2:504, 5:1341
festivals 4:1118, 1119, 5:1317
France 2:438–440, 441, 516–520, 541, 5:1177, 1178, 1179
French civil wars 2:441–443, 451–459, 516, 517, 518, 519, 520, 5:1331
Galileo 2:464–465, 466–467, 539, 3:783, 784, 5:1254
German towns 2:478, 479, 481, 553, 558
guilds 2:495
Guise family 1:198
Hapsburgs 2:478, 479, 482–483, 507, 512–515
heresy 1:187, 2:529–541
Hobbes critique of 2:544
Holy Roman Empire 2:548, 555, 556, 557, 558, 559, 3:835–839, 5:1189, 1200, 1338
households 2:563
humanism 1:181, 2:421–423, 425, 3:585,

586, 591, 592, 593, 5:1370, 1371
hunting 1:95, 96
iconoclasm 3:604, 606, 607, 609, 761
Ireland 2:333, 350, 352, 5:1303
Italian city-states 3:639, 640
Joan of Arc 3:657, 658, 660, 662
knighthood 1:221
Latin language 3:682, 684, 688–689, 690, 696, 697
legal kinship 2:568
libraries 5:1375
Lithuanian conversion 4:1104, 1106, 1109
Lutheranism vs. 2:423, 3:756, 762, 764–765, 766, 767, 768, 836, 837, 5:1201
Lyons, Council of 1:260
magic 3:796–797, 801
missionaries 4:888–896
monarchy 2:371, 4:905, 906, 907, 912, 913–914
moral reform 5:1360–1362
More 4:925–926, 929, 930–932
music 4:943, 953, 954–957
nationalism 4:969, 970
nobility and rank 4:975
Orthodox schism 1:166, 259, 2:427, 3:854, 4:1073
Ottoman Empire 3:626
painting and sculpture 1:193, 194, 2:387, 4:992–996
Paris 4:1032–1034, 1035
Petrarch 4:1055
Pico della Mirandola 4:1073, 1074, 1075, 1076–1077
pilgrimage 1078–1085
Platonism 4:1098, 1099, 1100–1101
Poland 4:1110, 1111, 1113
popular culture 4:1119, 1120, 1121, 1122–1123
Portugal 4:1137, 1139, 1140
preaching 5:1158–1163
printing 5:1175
Rabelais 5:1176, 1177, 1178

Reformation 5:1188–1193, 1194, 1195, 1221
religious orders 5:1201–1209
Rome 5:1227–1235
science 5:1253
Scotland 5:1262, 1265, 1266, 1267
seven sacraments 5:1357–1359, 1360
Spain 1:62, 66, 2:393, 396, 397, 398, 400, 3:613, 4:1057–1058, 1059, 1060, 5:1277–1279, 1283, 1301
Sweden 5:1305, 1306, 1307, 1308
Switzerland 5:1315, 1316
theater 4:900–901, 5:1317, 1318–1328, 1329
theodicy 2:360
Thirty Years War 2:371, 3:835, 5:1310, 1330–1339
traditional beliefs 1:178–179
Trent, Council of 3:593, 4:1017–1018, 5:1352–1364
universe model 1:272, 2:296, 5:1226
universities 2:322, 324, 5:1365, 1367, 1368, 1369, 1370, 1372–1373, 1375, 1377
usury 1:85, 89
vernaculars 3:695, 696–697, 698, 699
women 5:1424, 1426
see also Counter-Reformation; Inquisition; papacy
Roman Curia 4:1021
Roman Inquisition see Inquisition
Roman Missal 5:1363
Romans, Letter to the 1:105, 179
Rome, University of 3:703, 4:1022, 5:1367
rosary 5:1197
Rose of Lima 5:1209

Royal Academy of France **4**:981, 995, **5**:1243

Royal Academy of Science (London) **3**:695

Royal Academy of Sciences (France) **3**:775, **5**:1256

Royal Academy of Spain **3**:694

Royal College (France) **5**:1176

Royal College of Physicians (England) **5**:1250

Royal Exchange (London) **3**:751, **5**:1432

Royal Hospital (London) **5**:1432

Royal Mint (England) **1**:90

Royal Society of London **3**:775, **4**:1068, **5**:1256, 1257, 1430, 1431

Rule of St. Benedict **5**:1201

Rump Parliament **2**:*344*, 351, 355

Russia Company **2**:501

Russian Orthodox Church **1**:166, **4**:935–936, 1109

S

sabbatarianism **2**:345, **3**:669, 671

Sacchi, Bartolomeo (Platina) **4**:1022, *1023*

sacraments
  bibles **5**:1173
  Calvinism **1**:182
  Florence, Council of **2**:431
  Lutheranism **3**:764
  preaching **5**:1163
  Reformation **5**:1358
  Roman Catholicism **1**:178
  Trent, Council of **1**:186, **5**:1197, 1357–1359, 1360
  see also Eucharist; *other specific sacraments*

Saint Andrews University **5**:1263, 1264, 1267

Saint Bartholomew's Day Massacre (1572) **1**:188, 200, 201, **2**:371, 441, 454, 455, 456, 516, 556, **3**:825, **4**:1033, **5**:1331

Saint Crispin's Day **1**:18, 19, **3**:599

Saint Guinefort, cult of **4**:1120

Saint John, Knights of **1**:223, **3**:619, 624, 626, 715

Saint Paul's Cathedral School **4**:879, **5**:1323

saints **1**:178, **4**:1118
  Bernini depictions **1**:100
  blood libel **3**:673
  canonizations **4**:1036
  iconoclasm **3**:604, 606
  Joan of Arc **3**:657, 658, 662
  miracle plays **5**:1318
  More **4**:932
  patron **5**:1317
  pilgrimage **4**:1078, 1081, 1083
  religious orders **5**:1208, 1209
  sermons on **5**:1160
  Sufi **3**:615
  Trent, Council of **5**:1360

Salamanca, University of **5**:1207, 1367

Salerno, University of **5**:1367

Salic Law **2**:517, **3**:595

Salutati, Coluccio **3**:584, 589, 684, 685

salvation **2**:339, 341, 343, **3**:593, 761, 767, **4**:1064
  Calvinism **1**:178, 180, 181, 182, 183, 185, 186, **5**:1195, 1329
  Lutheranism **5**:1189
  preaching on **5**:1160
  religious orders **5**:1201
  Roman Catholicism **1**:180, 190, **5**:1197, 1198
  Trent, Council of **1**:186, **5**:1354
  Tyndale **1**:232
  see also divine grace; faith alone, justification by; good works; predestination

San Fiorentino, monastery of **3**:707, 714

San Marco, monastery of **2**:417, 423

San Sisto, convent of **1**:123

Santa Lucia, convent of **1**:194

Santa Maria delle Grazie, monastery of **3**:710, 711

Santiago, Order of **5**:1390

Satan **4**:880

Savonarola, Girolamo **1**:137, 138, **2**:422, 423, **3**:707, 769, 855
  Pico della Mirandola **4**:1076–1077
  preaching **5**:1160

Savoy, duke of *see* Felix V

Scaliger, Joseph **3**:585, 592, 594

Schmalkalden, Articles of **3**:763

Schmalkaldic League **1**:121, **2**:555, **3**:767, **5**:1191, 1200

scholarships **2**:322

Scholastic (hermit) **1**:168

Scholastica, Saint **5**:1201

Scholasticism **1**:181, **3**:696
  Aristotelianism **1**:54, 57, 58–59, 61
  Bacon vs. **1**:81
  Cartesianism vs. **2**:294
  Erasmus vs. **2**:357, 359, 362
  humanism vs. **3**:582, 583, 588, 592, 593, **5**:1365, 1368–1369, 1372, 1373
  Luther **5**:1371
  nominalism vs. **1**:181
  overview of **2**:357, 358
  Petrarch vs. **4**:1049, 1054–1055
  Pico della Mirandola vs. **4**:1075
  Platonism vs. **1**:57, 261

schools *see* education

Scots Engagers **2**:354

Scottish Confession **1**:189

scripture *see* bibles

scrofula **2**:*519*

seconda prattica **4**:916, 918, 921

secondary cause **1**:182

secondary schools **2**:319, 320, 321, 322, 325

Second Prayer Book (1551) **1**:189

Second Vatican Council **2**:430, **5**:1363, 1364

Secreta secretorum (treatise) **3**:*595*

secularism, Reformation **5**:1188, 1198 *see also* church-state relations

sedition **5**:1175

Sefer hazohar (kabbalistic text) **3**:*680*

Sefiroth **3**:*680*

Sejm (Polish assembly) **4**:1108, 1111, 1113

seminaries **5**:1357

Sephardim **3**:670

Septuagint **1**:103, 104, 109, **3**:695

Seripando, Girolamo *see* Marcellus II

sermons *see* preaching

Servetus, Michael **1**:187, **2**:539

Servites **4**:1038

sharia **3**:612, 614, 623

Short Parliament **2**:349, 351

shrines **4**:1078–1079, 1082, 1083, 1084, 1085

Shrove Tuesday **4**:*1119*

Siena, University of **4**:1086, 1088, **5**:1367

Siete Partidas **3**:693

signature literacy **5**:1173

simony **4**:1023

sin **4**:1064, *1066*
  Calvinist theocracy **1**:186–187
  Cartesian **2**:300
  Lutheran **3**:757, 759, 762, 763, 765, 766
  Luther vs. Calvin on **1**:185
  Luther vs. Erasmus on **2**:339
  see also original sin

Sisters of Charity **5**:1208

Six Articles of Faith (1539) **1**:235, 240, **2**:527

Sixtus II, Saint **5**:*1221*

Sixtus IV, Pope **1**:133, 277, **3**:673, 852, **4**:907, 975, 1022, *1023*, **5**:1230–1231, 1278, 1379, 1428
  calendar reform **1**:175

Sixtus V, Pope **1**:40, 44, 45, 277, **2**:442, **4**:1022

Sixty-seven Articles (Zwingli) **5**:1315

Smith, Adam **5:**1348–1349

social contract **2:**542, 545

Society of Jesus *see* Jesuits

Socrates **4:**1092–1093, 1094,
1095

Solemn League and Covenant
(1643) **2:**351

solipsism **2:**301

Solomon's Ophir **2:**384–385

Sophia Paleologa **4:**934

Sorbonne *see* Paris, University
of

soul **2:**300

Southwell, Robert **4:**896,
5:1424

souvenirs of pilgrimage
4:*1083*

Spanish Inquisition *see*
Inquisition

Spanish language **3:**670, 693,
694–695, 696, **5:**1222

Speyer, Diet of (1526) **5:**1193

spice trade **5:**1341, 1344
  Columbus **1:**247
  exploration **2:**373, 380, 381
  Italian city-states **3:**630, 633
  Magellan **3:**787, 788
  Netherlands **4:**1141, 1145
  Portugal **4:**1139, 1142,
    5:1344
  Venice **5:**1393

Spinoza, Baruch
4:1071–1072,
5:1291–1295

Star Chamber, Court of
5:1328

state and church *see* church-
state relations; established
churches

Stationers' Company **5:**1170

Stephen, Saint **5:***1284*

Strasbourg, University of
5:1377

studia humanitatis **3:**588, 592,
594

studium generale **5:**1366, 1368,
1371, 1372

Sufism **3:**612, 614–615, 620,
621, 622, 625

Sulpicians **5:***1361*

sultanate **3:**625–626, 628

Sunni Islam **3:**610, 611, 620,
621, 623, 626

Surprise de Meaux see Meaux,
conspiracy of

Susanna and the elders **5:**1355

Swabian League **2:**480, 550

Swiss Brethren **5:**1314

syllogism **1:**50, 81

Sylvester I, Pope **3:**594, 686

synagogues **3:**669, 672, *675,
678,* 679, 681

Syriac language **3:**695

T

Tacitus **3:**588, 590, **4:**923

Talmud **3:**669, 672, 674

Tauler, Johannes **1:**185, **3:**760,
4:1065

taxation **4:**1135
  church-state tensions **1:**180
  English civil wars **2:**347, 352
  feudal levies **2:**407, 408, 409
  Florence **2:**421
  France **2:**456
  households **2:**568–569
  Maximilian I **2:**550
  Ottoman **3:**617, 626
  peasants' revolts **1:**216,
    4:1042–1043, 1047
  Sweden **1:**228

Tell, William **5:**1312

Ten, Council of (Venice)
5:1397, 1400

Ten Articles (1536) **2:**525

Ten Commandments **5:**1158,
1170

Teresa of Ávila **1:**100, **5:**1207,
1427

Tertiary Order of Saint Francis
1:206

Tetzel, Johann **3:***757,* **5:**1189,
1190, 1191

Teutonic Knights, Order of the
1:222, 223, **2:**506
  Hanseatic League **5:**1304,
    1306
  Poland **4:**1104, 1106, 1107

Textus Receptus **1:**109

Theatines **5:**1204

theocracy **1:**186–187

theodicy **2:**360

third orders (lay orders)
5:1209

Thirty-nine Articles (1563,
England) **1:**104, 188,
2:341, 368, **3:**608–609,
5:1374

Thomas à Kempis **1:**99, 185,
3:606, 760, **4:**1079

Thomas Aquinas **2:**398, 461,
3:696, 760, **4:**1075, **5:**1249
  Aristotelianism **1:**52, 56, 59,
    3:604
  astrology **1:**73
  blood-sports critique **1:**96
  divine right **4:**906
  Erasmus vs. **2:**357, 358–359
  Greek translation **1:**261
  iconoclasm **3:**604, 606
  idealism **1:**182
  magic **3:**797
  philosophy **4:**1062, 1064

Thomas the Apostle **2:**380

three estates **2:**406, *407,* 439

Time of Troubles (Russia)
3:656, **4:**938, 940, 1113,
5:1308

Torah **3:**669, *679*

Tordesillas, Treaty of (1494)
2:381, 382, **3:**788, **4:**889,
1142

Torquemada, Tomás de **2:**533,
5:1278

Totenfresser (Protestant
pamphlet) **5:**1192

*To the Councilors of All German
Cities That They Establish
and Maintain Christian
Schools* (Luther) **2:**321–322

Toulouse, University of **5:**1371

Tower of London **1:**218,
2:330, 332, **3:**597, 749,
751, **4:**931–932, 1046,
1047

trade **4:**914, **5:1340–1351**
  agriculture **1:**22, 26
  Americas **3:**719
  ancient Greece **1:**166–167
  banking **1:**84–91
  Bardi family **2:**567
  Black Death **2:**306
  cannon use **3:**775

Columbus **1:**247

companies **2:**498–501

Constantinople **1:**260–261,
263

disease **2:**302–303,
304–305, 306

England **3:**751, 752

exploration **2:**373, 379,
4:1139, 1140–1141

fairs **3:**813–821

Florence **2:**414–415

German towns **2:**480, 481

guilds **2:**494–496, 497, 498

Hanseatic League **2:**475–
476, 502–506, **5:**1306

humanism **3:**588

Hundred Years War **3:**596

Islam **3:**613

Italian city-states **2:**414–415,
3:630–632, 633,
634–635, 636, 640, 642,
5:1401

Judaism **3:**671

Lombardy **3:**740, 741

London guilds **3:**750, 753

Lutheranism **2:**553

machines **3:**774, 776

manufacturing **3:**804, 806,
811, **4:**1135–1136

markets **3:**813–821

Medicis **3:**849

missionaries **4:**892, 895

noble status **4:**977–978

Ottoman Empire **3:**624

pilgrimage **4:**1082, 1085

Portugal **4:**1142, 1143, 1145

ship design **3:**777–778

Silk Road **3:**805

Sweden **5:**1304–1306, 1311

towns **3:**809

Venice **5:**1340, 1341, 1344,
1392–1394, 1395, 1398

transubstantiation **1:**52, 184,
2:536, **3:**608, 764, **5:**1194,
1268

Calvin's rejection **1:**184

Elizabeth I **2:**341

Reformation **1:**178

Trent, Council of **5:**1197,
1358

Zwingli **5:**1315

Trent, Council of **1:**44, 75, 175, *186,* **2:**430, 467, 540, **3:**593, 698, 747, **5:**1226, 1234, **1352–1364**
  Bernini sculpture **1:**97, 99
  bibles **1:**104
  catechism **5:**1174
  Decree of Reunion **2:**431
  Eucharist **5:**1197, 1357, 1358, 1363
  holiness doctrine **1:**186
  missal **1:**175, **5:**1363
  music **4:**943, 954, 955
  painting **4:**992
  Paul III **4:**1016, 1017–1018
  Paul V **4:**1036
  Pius IV **4:**1020, 1024
  Sarpi critique **4:**1038
  status of **5:**1364
  Vulgate **3:**684, 689
Triennial Act of 1641 (England) **2:**349
trinitarianism **3:**610–611, 669, 757
  Decree of Reunion **2:**430
Trinitarian order **1:**204, 206
Trinity College (Cambridge) **1:**262, **5:**1432
  library **5:***1375*
Trissino, Gian Giorgio **1:**43, 125, **4:**1000, 1001, 1002
trivium **2:**357, **5:**1366, 1372
Tübingen, University of **2:**324, **5:**1371, *1372*
Turin, University of **2:**357, **5:**1367
Twelve Apostles **1:***154*
Twelver Shiism **3:**621
Twenty-third Psalm **1:**183
Tyndale, William **1:**232, 234, *240,* **2:**524, **3:***697,* 698
  bibles **1:**103, 105, 106, 107, 110

U

ulema **3:**614
Ulozheniye (law code) **4:**940, *941*
"Unigenitus" (Clement VI) **3:**757

universitas vs. *conlegium* **5:**1376
universities **2:**317, 318, *322, 323*–325, **5:1365–1377,** *1406*
  Arabic studies **3:**618
  Aristotelianism **1:**51, 56–58
  Constantinople **1:**257, 258, 261
  degree holders **4:**973
  dramatic productions **5:**1328
  England **2:**336
  Greek studies **1:**264, **3:**685
  humanism **2:**319, 324, 336, **3:**582, 584, 585, 588–589, 590, 592, 593, 594, 683, **5:**1218–1219, 1220, 1224, 1282
  Jewish students **3:**679
  London law studies **3:**752
  Luther at Wittenberg **3:**672, 758–759
  Marlowe at Cambridge **3:**822–823
  medicine **3:**840, 841, 844, 845, 846–847, 848, **5:**1367
  Ottoman **3:**627
  Platonism **1:**261
  Portugal **4:**1144
  Prague **1:**118, 119, 212
  public **2:**323–325
  Reformation **2:**321, 324, *325*
  religious founders **4:**891
  Roman Catholicism **2:***322,* 324
  Scholasticism **1:**54, 57, 58–59, 261, **2:**294, 357
  science **5:**1255
  Scotland **5:**1263
  specialization **2:**320
  Sweden **5:**1308
  theater **3:**732
University Wits **3:**732, 824
unleavened bread **1:**259
Unmoving Mover **1:**52
Uppsala, University of **5:**1308, 1367
Urban V, Pope **1:**112, 115, **4:**1052

Urban VI, Pope **4:**1010, **5:**1424
Urban VIII, Pope **1:**73–74, **2:**466, **5:**1380
  Bernini works **1:**97, 98, 99, 100
  religious orders **5:**1208
  Rome **5:**1234
  Thirty Years War **5:**1332, 1333, 1336
Ursulines **5:**1353
usury **1:**85, **3:**633, **5:**1316
utopias **4:**1048, 1103, **5:**1251

V

Valentes, University of **5:**1371
Valla, Lorenzo **4:**1023
  Donation of Constantine forgery **3:**584, 594
  Erasmus **2:**358, 359, **3:**591
  Latin scholarship **3:**586, 591, 686–687, 688
  manuscript analysis **3:**587
  overview of **3:**586
Vatican *see* papacy
Vatican archives **4:**1036, 1037
Vatican Council I **5:**1363, 1364
Vatican Council II **2:**430, **5:**1363, 1364
Vatican Library **1:**230, **4:**1022, *1023,* **5:**1230
  Paul III **5:**1353
Vatican Museum **3:**708
Vatican Palaces **3:**703, **4:**1025, **5:**1228, 1229–1232
  Cortile de Belvedere **1:**142, **4:**1040
  Villa del Belvedere **1:**140, 142, **3:**703, **5:**1231
Venus (goddess) **1:**135, **2:***424,* 425
Vera Cruz, College of (Valladolid) **5:**1280
Vergerio, Piero Paolo **3:**584, **5:**1220
  overview of **2:**318
vernaculars *see* languages, vernacular
Vicenza, University of **5:**1371

Vienna, Council of (1312) **1:**85
Vincent de Paul **5:**1208
Vincent Ferrer **3:**676, **5:**1160, 1161
Vincentians **5:**1208
Virginia Company **2:**375
Virgin Kykkotissa **2:**380
Virgin Mary **1:**137, *145,* 178, **2:**425, **3:**689, 709, **4:**890, *1062,* **5:**1222
  Assumption **1:**193, **4:**1081, **5:**1317, 1318
  Dürer paintings **5:***1220*
  iconoclasm **3:**604, *606*
  Immaculate Conception **4:**1036
  prayer to **5:**1160
  Raphael paintings **5:**1180, 1182, 1184, *1221*
  shrines **4:**1081, 1083
Vives, Juan Luis **5:**1282–1283, 1416, 1417
Vulgate **1:**104, 107, 108, 109, **2:**337, **3:**591, *682,* 684, 696, **4:**1024
  Gutenberg Bible **3:**697
  translation errors **3:**688–689
  Trent, Council of **5:**1357

W

Wadham College (Oxford) **5:**1429, 1431
Waldensians **2:**530, 531, **3:**766
Warham, William **1:**106, 235, 240
Washington College **1:**189
Weber, Max **1:**190, **4:**1123
Wenceslas, Saint **1:**117, *118*
Western Schism of 1378–1417 **2:**366, 421, 429, 430, **4:**913, 1010–1011, 1052, **5:**1227, 1406 *see also* Avignon papacy
Westminster Confession **1:**104
"What Can Be Called into Doubt" (Descartes) **2:**297
William and Mary, College of **4:**892

William of Ockham *see* Ockham, William of

Wisdom, book of *see* Wisdom of Solomon

Wisdom of Solomon **1:**103, **5:**1355

witchcraft
  Inquisition **2:**534–535, **3:**801, **4:**1019
  Joan of Arc **3:**661
  magic **3:**795–796, 801–803
  Scotland **5:**1267
  witch hunts **2:**535, **5:**1425

Wittenberg, University of **2:**482, **3:**585, 593, 606, 704, 705, **5:**1189
  Luther **4:**1013, **5:***1352, 1376*
  Melancthon **2:**324

Wolsey, Thomas **1:**234, **2:**334, 338, 521, 522, 523, **4:**930, **5:***1273,* 1373
  Hampton Court Palace **2:**334
  Henry VIII **1:**234, **2:**338

wool trade **5:**1341, 1344, 1350
  Ciompi **2:**415, 419
  cloth **3:**740, 806, *807,* 849, 853
  Italian city-states **3:**630, 636
  Scotland **5:**1260

Worcester College (Oxford) **3:**668

Worms, Diet of (1521) **1:**210–211, **2:**514, 553, **3:**762, 765, 768

Worms, Edict of (1521) **1:**104, **2:**555, **5:**193, 1192, 1200

writing system **3:**774, 776 *see also* literacy

Wycliffe, John **1:**102, 103, 110, 232, **2:**536–537, **3:**761

X

Xavier, Francis **4:**894, 1015, **5:**1205–1206

Y

Yale College **1:**189

Yiddish language **3:**670

Z

Zeno's paradoxes **4:**1097

Zwingli, Huldrych **1:**178, 181, 184, **2:**483, 539, **3:**761, 762, **4:**952, **5:**1193, 1312, 1314, 1315, 1316

Zwinglians **1:**76

Index of Places

This index includes place-names appearing in the articles and captions. For place-names mentioned in the maps, see the Index of Maps.

A **boldface** number preceding a colon indicates the volume. Numbers in *italics* refer to captions. Numbers entirely in **boldface** refer to a full article.

A

Aachen **1:**77
Aar River **4:**507
Adda River **5:**1334
Adrianople **3:**612
Adriatic Sea **1:**276, **2:**414, **3:**715, 741, **5:**1392, 1393, 1394, 1401
Aegean Sea **1:**262, **3:**619
Afghanistan **3:**615
Africa
  Cheng Ho voyage **5:**1342
  Columbus voyage **1:**247
  exploration **2:**373, 374, 379, 380, 381, **4:**914, **5:**1346
  Islam **3:**611, 612, 613
  missionaries **4:**888, 895
  Portugal **4:**1137, 1140–1141, 1142
  slave trade **1:**255, **4:**1141, **5:**1285, 1342, 1345, 1348, 1349
  trade **5:**1341
  warfare **4:***1140*
  see also North Africa; *specific countries*
Albania **1:**170
Alcalá **3:**689
Algeria **1:**202
Algiers **1:**109, 202, 211, **3:**624, **5:**1347
Alicante Dam (Tibi Dam) **1:**280
Almansa Dam **1:**280
Alps **1:**157, **3:**741, **5:**1393, 1394
Alpujarras Mountains **2:**397
Amboise **3:**707, 714
Americas
  agriculture **1:**28
  architecture **1:**46, 49
  Calvinism **1:**178, 189, 190

chartered companies **2:**501
colonial iconoclasm **3:**609
colonial settlements **5:**1342, 1346–1347
Columbus **1:**248, 250–255, **2:**306
  dam designs **1:**280
  disease **1:**255, **2:**306–309, 382
  exploration **2:**374, 375, 381–384, 385, **3:**693, **4:**914, 915, **5:**1220, 1342, 1345
  Holy Roman Empire **2:**511
  Huguenot émigrés **5:**1331
  inventions **3:**776
  Jesuits **4:**1015, **5:**1206
  Magellan voyage **3:**790–791
  missionaries **4:**792, 888–894, 896, 1015
  naturalists **5:**1259
  Philip II **4:**1060
  Portugal **4:**1142
  Puritans **1:**189, **2:**328, **5:**1375
  religious orders **4:**1015, **5:**1206, 1209
  Scholasticism **1:**58
  scientific exploration **5:**1259
  slave trade **5:**1342, 1348, 1349
  Spain **1:**207, **2:**400, **4:**889–890, 966, **5:**1283–1284, 1285, 1345
  trade **2:**481, **3:**633, 719, **5:**1344, 1345–1346, 1348
  universities **2:***325*
  witch hunts **5:**1425
  see also specific countries and place-names
Amiata, Monte **4:**1090
Amsterdam **2:***299*
  banking **1:**90
  dikes **1:**275
  Jewish community **3:**681
  Rembrandt **5:**1211, 1212
  Renaissance map **1:***281*

Spinoza **5:**1291, 1292
  trade **5:**1344
Anatolia **3:**612, 616, 617, 621
Ancona **4:**1088, 1089
Angers **2:**451
Angoulême **2:**453
Anjou **1:**16, **2:**294, **3:**601, 602
  Hundred Years War **1:**16
Antarctica **2:**384
Antioch **1:**260
Antwerp **2:**334, **3:**819
  banking **1:**88
  Bruegel **1:**144, 145, 146
  Rubens **5:**1236, 1237, 1238–1239, 1242
  sack of **4:**1057
  trade **5:**1344
Apennines **3:**744
Appian Way **1:**277
Aquitaine **2:**412–413, **3:**595–596, 597, 598, 603
  Hundred Years War **1:**16
Arabian Peninsula **2:**302, **3:**611, 623, **4:**107
Aragon **2:**445, 513, **4:**903, 905, 965, **5:**1277, 1278–1279
  Charles V **1:**207, 211
  Ferdinand **2:**393–400
  hydraulics **1:**280
  Philip II **1:**211, **4:**1057
Arctic **2:**383, 384
Arezzo **4:**1049, 1051
Argentina **4:**892
Armagnac **1:**159, **2:**437, **3:**600, **4:**1030
Armenia **2:**429
Arno River **1:**276, 278, 279, 280, **3:**706, *708*
Arquà **4:**1051
Artois **1:**157, 164
Asia
  Black Death **2:**306
  disease **2:**302–303
  exploration **2:**373, 380, 381, 382
  missionaries 1015
  religious orders **5:**1204

trade **2:**302–303, **3:**805, **4:**1139, 1141, 1142, **5:**1341
  see also China; India; Japan
Assisi **2:**488, *491,* 492
Astrakhan **3:**653, **4:**936
Atlantic Ocean **2:**374, 379, 381, 383, 399, **4:**1138, 1141
  Columbus voyages **1:**247, 248–249, 251
  trade network **2:**373, 481, **5:**1348, 1349
Augsburg **1:***78,* **2:**475, 476, 478, 482
  banking **1:**88, 90, **5:**1228
  Dürer **2:**315
Aurelian Walls (Rome) **5:**1227
Australia **2:**385, **5:**1258
Austria **2:**372, **3:**837, **4:**966
  anti-Semitism **3:**674
  fishpond dam **1:**280
  Hapsburg Empire **1:**209, **2:**507, 508, 509, 510, 511, 512, 557
  Holy Roman Empire **1:**211, **2:**475
  Ottoman Empire **1:**211, **3:**624, 629, 715, 716
  Poland **4:**1114
  Spain **3:**746
  see also Vienna
Avignon **1:**87, **2:**416, **3:**682
Avon River **5:***1350*
Azerbaijan **3:**620
Azores **1:**247, 251, **2:**379, 381, **4:**1138, 1140

B

Baghdad **4:**1085
Bahamas **1:**248, 250, **2:**308
Balkans
  Hellenic culture **1:**167, 170
  Ottoman Empire **1:**263, **3:**613, 616, 617
Baltic Sea **3:**653, **4:**937, 940
  chartered companies **2:**500–501

fish products **5:**1341
Hanseatic League **2:**502,
503, 505, 506
Russia **5:**1309, 1334
Sweden **5:**1305, 1307, 1310,
1311, 1334, 1335,
1336–1337
trade routes **2:**475
Baltiysk (Pillau) **5:**1334
Barcelona **1:**89–90, **2:**395
Bardas **1:**258
Bardowiek **2:**503
Basel **2:**555
Calvin **1:**179
Erasmus **2:**357, 361, 362
northern Renaissance **2:**311,
312
Reformation **1:**188, **5:**1314,
1315
Bavaria **2:**482–483, 505,
3:387, **5:**1335
Jewish purges **3:**672
Maximilian I **3:**835, 836,
839
Bayonne **3:**596
Béarn **2:**516
Belarus **4:**1109
Belgium *see* Flanders
Belgrade **3:**623
Benin **4:***1140*
Bergamo **3:**638, 744, **5:**1394
Bergen **1:**22
Berlin **5:**1256
Bern **5:**1312, 1314, 1315,
1316
Berwick **5:**1267
Bethlehem **1:**259
Bishopsgate (London) **3:**749
Black Sea **1:**165, 166, 170,
263, **4:**1106
Blekinge **5:**1311
Blois **1:**45, **2:**451
Bobbio **3:**638
Bohemia **1:116–122**
Hapsburgs **2:**438, 507, 509,
510–511
heresy **2:**536–537, 549
Holy Roman Empire **2:**475,
548, 549, 557, 559
Hussites **2:**537, 557, **3:**660,
674, **4:**969

Maximilian I **3:**836, 837,
838
Ottoman Empire **2:**555, 557
Reformation **5:**1191, 1192
Thirty Years War **5:**1301,
1331, 1334, 1335, 1336,
1337, 1338, 1415
university **5:**1367
Bologna **1:**246, **4:**1012,
5:*1356,* 1404
Carraccis **1:**195
Charles V coronation **1:***208,*
209, 210, 244
Italian wars **3:**645
Leo X **3:**701
market **3:***633*
Paul V **4:**1036, 1037
Pico della Mirandola **4:**1073,
1074
public health **4:**1133
Trent, Council of **5:**1357
Viscontis **3:**638
Bordeaux **2:**455, **3:**596, 597
wine production **5:**1341,
1350
Bosporus **1:**165, 263
Bourges **1:**179, *184*
Brabant **1:**144, 146
Brandenburg **2:**548, **5:**1334,
1337
Braxton Moor **5:**1297
Brazil **2:***374,* 381, **3:**790
Jesuits **4:**1015
Portugal **4:**1142, 1145
Breda **1:**144
Bremen **2:**305, 503, 505
Brenta River and Canal **1:**277
Brescia **3:**638, 645
Brindisi **5:**1393
Bristol **5:**1350
British Isles *see* England,
Ireland, Scotland, Wales
Brittany **2:**437, 452, **3:**598
Bruges **1:**22, 160, **2:**387, 391,
392
banking **1:**87, **2:**416
Gothic architecture **1:**163
Bruna River **1:**281
Brunswick **2:**479, 505
Brussels **1:**144, 146, 148, 161,
163, **2:**557

Bulgaria **1:**158, 170, 177, 259,
3:616
Burgundy **1:157–164**
Charles V **1:**207, 208
chivalry **1:**223
England **2:**334
France **2:**413, 434–435, 437,
446, 453
Hapsburgs **2:**509, 511, 515,
550
Holy Roman Empire **4:**966
Hundred Years War **3:**600,
601, 602, **4:**1030
Joan of Arc **3:**658, 661
music **4:**944, 945, 951
nationalism **4:**964–965, 966
Ottoman Empire **3:**616
Paris **4:**1030
sculpture **4:**981
Spain **5:**1278
Switzerland **5:***1313,* 1314
Button Bay **2:**383
Byzantine Empire **1:**256,
2:366, **4:**1073, 1109
architecture **1:**170, 171, 263
Byzantium **1:**165–172
Constantinople **1:**256–264
Florence, Council of
2:427–431
Fourth Crusade **1:**260
iconoclasm **3:**605
Ottoman Empire **3:**586, 616,
618
Venice **5:**1392, 1393
Byzantium **1:165–172,** 256 *see
also* Constantinople

C

Cádiz **1:**63, *64,* 251
Ca' d'Oro (Venice) **5:**1399
Cairo **3:***678,* 680
Calais **1:**16, 20, 65, **2:**435,
3:597
Calicut **5:***1345*
California **2:**383
Camerino **5:**1380, 1381
Canada
exploration **2:**383, **4:**915
Jesuits **4:**1015
missionaries **4:**893, 1896
Presbyterians **1:**190

Canary Current **5:**1348
Canary Islands **1:**248, 251,
2:379
Canterbury **5:**1424
pilgrimage **4:**1083
Cape Blanc **2:**380, **5:**1345
Cape Bojador **2:**380, **4:**1140,
1141, **5:**1345
Cape of Good Hope *see* Good
Hope, Cape of
Cape Palmas **5:**1345
Cape Verde **1:**247, **2:**379,
381, **3:**794, **4:**1138, 1141,
1142
Cape Vert **5:**1345
Caribbean region
Columbus **1:**247, 248,
250–254, **2:**399
disease **2:**306, 307
missionaries **4:**889, 891, 892
piracy **5:**1347
Spanish conquests **1:**62, 207
Carinthia **2:**509, 557
Carniola **2:**509
Castile **2:**445, 515, **3:**598,
693, **4:**965, **5:**1277, 1280,
1281, 1282
Alfonso X **3:**693
anti-Jewish violence **3:**672,
674
Charles V **1:**207, 211
Isabella **2:**393–400
John of Gaunt **4:**1047
monarchy **4:**903, 905
Philip II **1:**211, **4:**1056
Portugal **4:**1137
Castres **2:**453
Catalonia **2:**394, **4:**965, 1145,
5:1277, 1278, 1279, 1285
Certaldo **1:**112, 115
Certosa di Pavia **3:***740*
Ceuta **2:**380, **4:**1137
Chambord **1:**45, **2:**444
Chenonceaux **1:**45, **2:**444
Cher River **2:**444
China
crafts **3:**804
disease **2:**302–303, 305
exploration **2:**373, 376, 380,
381, 382, **5:**1341, 1342,
1343

China *(cont.)*
  inventions **3:**774, 775, 778, 804, 805
  Jesuits **4:**1015
  Judaism **3:**669
  missionaries **4:**894–895, 1015
  Portugal **4:**1142
  printing **5:**1168, 1193
  religious orders **5:**1206
  ships **5:**1343
  technology **5:**1343
  trade **2:**302–303, **5:**1346
Chinon **3:**657
Cognac **2:**454
Colmar **2:**311
Cologne **1:**77, **2:**548, 557, 558, **3:**672
  archbishop-elector of **1:**77
  Jewish purges **3:**672
Como **3:**638
Compiègne **3:**658, 661
Concordia **4:**1073
Condé **2:**456
Connecticut **1:**189, **2:**372
Constantinople **1:**256–264, **4:**1073
  Byzantium **1:**165–172
  Christianity **1:**170–171
  Crusade of Nicopolis **1:**158
  crusader sacking of **1:**168, 260, **5:**1393
  Florence, Council of **1:**260, **2:**427, 428, 430
  Greek manuscripts **1:**269, **2:**430, **3:**685, 688
  Greek-speaking refugees **1:**55, **2:**320
  Hagia Sophia **1:**171–172
  Jewish settlements **3:**680
  Ottoman siege of **1:***264*, **5:**1410
  Ottoman takeover of **1:**158, 166, 169, 170, 171, 172, 263–264, **2:**320, 427, 429, 430, **3:**612, 616, 618, 619, 623, 625, 685, **4:**935
  philosophy **4:**1063
  scholarship **4:**1063
Copenhagen **5:**1246, 1311

Corbie **5:**1338
Corfu **1:**202
Corinth, Gulf of **3:**715
Cork, County (Ireland) **5:**1288, 1290
Corsignano **4:**1086, 1090
Crema **3:**744
Cremona **3:**638, 743, **4:**916, 917, 921, 923
Crete **4:**1073, **5:**1393
Crimea **3:**653, 655, **5:**1337
Cuba **1:**250, **4:**892
Cyprus **2:**304, **3:**626, 715, 718, **5:**1393
Czech Republic *see* Bohemia

D

Danube River **1:**158, 169, **2:**611, **3:**835
Danube valley **5:**1330
Danzig **2:**503, **4:**1106
Denmark
  divorce law **2:**568
  established church **2:**370, 372
  guilds **2:**493
  Hanseatic League **2:**503, 504, 505, 506
  Hapsburgs **2:**480
  Lutheranism **2:**370, **3:**768
  monarchy **4:**903, 911
  Reformation **5:**1191
  Russia **3:**653
  Schütz **5:**1246
  science and technology **5:**1251
  Sweden **5:**1304–1306, 1307, *1308,* 1309, 1310, 1311, 1338
  Thirty Years War **5:**1330, 1333, 1335–1336, 1338, 1415
Deventer **2:**356
Dijon **1:**157, 163
Dolomite Mountains **1:**276
Dominican Republic **1:**250, 253, *255*
Domrémy **3:**657, 658
Donauworth **1:**78, **3:**836
Dordrecht **1:**274
Dresden **5:**1246, 1247

Dublin **5:**1288
Durance River **1:**280

E

East Africa **2:**374, 381, **5:**1342
East Anglia **1:**188
eastern Europe
  Black Death **2:**305
  Jews **3:**670, 675
East Indies **4:**1139, 1145
Edessa **1:**260
Edirne (Adrianople) **3:**612
Egypt
  ancient calendars **1:**173
  ancient Christianity **1:**57
  Judaism **3:***678,* 680
  Mamluks **3:**612, 623
  Ottoman Empire **3:**623
Elbe River **2:**505, **5:**1335
Emden **1:**188
England **2:334–346**
  African slave trade **5:**1348
  Agincourt **1:**16–20
  agriculture **1:**24, 27, 28, 47–49
  architecture **1:**30, 32, 33, 43, 140, **2:**334, **3:**664–668, **5:**1429, 1430–1433
  armada, Spanish **1:**62–66, 204, 238, **2:**331, 332, **4:**1058, 1060, 1145, **5:**1412
  astrology **1:**71–73
  Bacon **1:**79–83
  banking **1:**90
  bibles **1:**104, 105, 106–110, **5:**1357
  Black Death **2:**304, 305
  blood sports **1:**92–93, 95, 96
  Burgundy **1:**158, 159, 160
  calendars **1:**173, 176–177, **4:**1024
  Calvinism **1:**178, 188, 189
  Chaucer **1:**212–220
  chivalry **1:**221–222, 223, 225
  coal **3:**784–785, 811
  colonialism **2:**501, **3:**754, **5:**1284, 1342
  colonial missions **4:**892, 894, 896

  colonial settlements **5:**1342, 1346
  companies **2:**497–498, 499, 500, 501
  Cyprus **3:**718
  dams and drainage **1:**276
  diplomacy **5:**1223
  dual monarchy **3:**601
  East India Company **5:**1342
  education **2:**322, 323
  Elizabeth I **2:**326–333, **5:**1221, 1225
  Erasmus **2:**357, 362
  established church **1:**232–240, **2:**346, 368–369, 370, 371, 372, **4:**913, 969, 975, **5:**1198, 1374
  exploration **2:**375, 382, **4:**914, 915
  feudalism **2:**403, 406, 407, 408, 409, 410, 412–413
  football **4:**1122
  France **2:**434–435
  garden design **1:**26
  Gentileschi **2:**470, 474
  Greek culture **1:**262–263
  guilds **2:**494–495, 496
  Henry VIII **1:**232–235, **2:**521–528, **5:**1220
  heresy **2:**536
  Hobbes **2:**542–547
  Huguenot émigrés to **5:**1331
  humanism **2:**335, 336–337, **3:**590, 593
  Hundred Years War **3:**595–603, 657–662, **4:**968
  iconoclasm **3:**608–609
  interest loans **1:**85
  Joan of Arc **3:**661–662
  Jones **3:**663–668
  Judaism **3:**672, 673
  literature **1:**220, 223, **2:**334–336, **3:**721–726, 737–739, 753–755, 823
  Lord Protector **2:**351
  machines **3:**785, 786
  magic **3:**800
  manufacturing **3:**786, 806, 808

markets and fairs **3**:813–814, 815, 816–817, 818–821

Marlowe **3**:822–826

mathematics **3**:829, 834

mercenaries **5**:1411

Milton **4**:879–887

missions to **4**:896

monarchy **4**:904, 906, 907, 912, 914, **5**:1218, 1220, 1221, 1224, 1225

monarchy's restoration **1**:240, **2**:351, **4**:886, **5**:1302, 1322, 1329

More **4**:924–932, **5**:1371

music **4**:942, 943, 944, 948, 951, 952, 953, 954, 959, 961

nationalism **4**:962, 963, 966, 968

naval power **5**:1412

nobility and rank **4**:971, 975, 977

painting **1**:223, **5**:1242, 1243

Palladianism **3**:668, **4**:1007

papacy **4**:1014–1015

Peasants' Revolt (1381) **1**:216, **3**:598, **4**:1041, 1042–1048

Philip II **4**:1056, *1057,* 1058, 1059, 1060

philosophy **4**:1067–1068, 1070–1071, 1072, 1103

pilgrimage **4**:1079, 1081, 1083

Pilgrimage of Grace **1**:187, 235, **2**:340, 526, **4**:1042

piracy **5**:1347

poetry **3**:721, 722–726, 737, 739, 753, 754, 755, 823

Portugal **4**:1137, 1139

printing **3**:819, **5**:1170, 1175

prose fiction **3**:737–738

Puritanism **1**:188, **5**:1196, 1198

Reformation **1**:62, 66, 107, 232, **2**:338–349, 364, 365, **4**:953, **5**:1191, 1196–1198, 1221, 1265

Reformation chronology **1**:240

religious conflict **1**:187

religious orders **5**:1202, 1203, 1206, 1208

Roman Catholicism **1**:187, 238, **2**:340, 371, 372, **4**:894, 896, 906, 929–932, 953, 969, 1039, **5**:1198, 1267, 1424

Russia **3**:654

school plays **5**:1323

science **4**:1068, **5**:1250, 1256–1257, 1258

Scotland **4**:904, 905, **5**:1261–1267, 1296, 1297, 1300, 1426

Shakespeare **5**:1268–1276

Spain **5**:1283

Spenser **5**:1286–1290

Stuarts **5**:1296–1303, 1426

technology **5**:1259

textiles **3**:849

theater **3**:729, 731–733, 735, 737, 748, 751, 754, 755, 822–826, **5**:*1317,* 1318, 1319, 1320, 1321, 1322, 1323, 1324–1329

Thirty Years War **5**:1330, 1334, 1335, 1336

trade **5**:1341, 1344, 1350–1351, 1393

universities **5**:1367, 1373–1375

widow remarriage **5**:1422

witch trials **3**:802, 803, **5**:1425

women's status **5**:1416, 1418, 1419, 1420, 1422, 1423–1424, 1426–1427

Wren **5**:1429–1433

see also London

English Channel **2**:408, **3**:595, **5**:1344

Spanish armada **1**:62, 63, 64, 66, **2**:332

Estonia **2**:503, 505, **3**:653, **5**:1307

Euphrates River **1**:169

Eyüb (Islamic holy place) **3**:625

F

Ferrara **2**:413, 419, **3**:637, 642, 648, 650, 681, 853, **4**:947, 949, **5**:1381

Borgias **1**:124, 125–126, **5**:1427

Fersina River **1**:279

Fiammetta **1**:111

Fife **5**:*1296*

Finland **2**:370, **3**:768, **5**:1305

Flanders

architecture **1**:49

Bruegel **1**:144–148

Burgundy **1**:157, 158, 160, 162, 163, 164

dikes and drainage **1**:273–276

Eyck **2**:386–392

humanism **3**:585, 589, 590, 592

Hundred Years War **1**:16, **3**:595, 596

mathematics **5**:1250

Rubens **5**:1236–1243

trade **5**:1341, 1344

Florence **1**:169, 261, **2**:414–426, *427,* 538, **3**:630, 742

architecture **1**:30, 32, 33, 35, 36, 49

banking **1**:84, 87, 88, **3**:740, 850, 854, **5**:1228, 1342

Bardis **2**:567

Black Death **2**:305, **4**:1131

Boccaccio **1**:111, 112, 113, 114, 115

Botticelli **1**:133–138

Brunelleschi **1**:149–156

Charles V **1**:208

Chaucer **1**:216

Ciompi revolt **3**:636–637

Clement VII **1**:241, 242

fall of republic **3**:649

famines **4**:1131

Galileo **2**:460, **5**:1252

Gentileschi **2**:469–471

Giotto **2**:484, 487, 489, 490, 491, 492

government **3**:635, 636–637, 638, 643, 649, 702

humanism **2**:320, **3**:584, 585, 586, 587, 588, 589, 640, 684–685, 687, 700, 703, **5**:1220

Italian wars **1**:208, **2**:*420,* 421, **3**:643, 647, 648–649

Leonardo da Vinci **3**:706, 707, 708

Machiavelli **3**:769–773, **4**:1066

May carnival **4**:951

Medicis **1**:137, 197, 208, 242, 243, 244, **2**:413, 477, **3**:*587,* 588, 641, 700, 702, 703, 705, 708, 849–857, **5**:1224

Michelangelo **4**:870, 871, 872–873, 876–877

Milanese rivalry **5**:1401, 1404, 1405

Milton **4**:882, 883

music **4**:951, 961

opera **4**:920, **5**:1321, 1322

painting and sculpture **2**:312, **3**:641, 706, 707, **4**:981, 983–984, 985, 986, 988, **5**:1236–1237

palaces **2**:563

Petrarch **3**:682

Pico della Mirandola **4**:1073, 1074, 1075, 1076–1077

Platonism **1**:57, 137, **2**:320

Portugal **4**:1143, 1144

Raphael **5**:1181, 1183–1185

republic **4**:967

Savonarola **1**:137

theater **3**:734

trade **2**:475

Florida **2**:374, 382, **3**:609, **4**:891–892

missions **4**:891–892

Forlì **5**:1427, 1428

France **2**:432–444

Agincourt **1**:16–20

architecture **1**:45, 48, 49

astrology **1**:70, 71, 73

bibles **1**:108

Black Death **2**:304, 305, **4**:1126

France *(cont.)*

Burgundy **1:**157, 158, 159–161, 162–163, 164

Calvin **1:**179, 188

Calvinism **1:**188, **2:**371

Catherine de Médicis **1:**197–201, 242, **5:**1426

Champagne fairs **3:**816

charivari **4:**1116

Charles V **1:**208, 209, 210, 211, 242, 243, 244

châteaus **2:**436, 450, 563

Chaucer **1:**214–215, 216

chivalry **1:**221

Church Latin **3:**689

Clement VII **1:**242

colonial settlements **5:**1284, 1342, 1346

companies **2:**500

dams and drainage **1:**273, 276, 280

Descartes **2:**294–301

dual monarchy **3:**601

Elizabeth I **2:**327, 329, 332

England **2:**521, 522, 527, **4:**927

established church **2:**370, 371, 372

exploration **4:**896, 914, **5:**1342

feudalism **2:**404, 406, 407, 410, 412–413

Florence **2:**419, 420, 421

Francis I **2:**445–450

Gregorian calendar **1:**176

Hapsburgs **2:**480, 512, 555

Henry IV **2:**516–520, 541

heresy **2:**531, 532

Hobbes **2:**543, 544

Holy Roman Empire **2:**558, 560

humanism **3:**585, 589, 590, 592, **5:**1176–1177, 1178, 1370

Hundred Years War **3:**595–603, 657–662, **4:**968

interest loans **1:**85

Italian wars **1:**221, 241, **2:**437–438, 550, **3:**630, 639, 642, 643–651, 701,

702–703, 742–743, 745, 746, 853, **5:**1220, 1231, 1233

Jesuits **5:**1206

Jewish expulsion **3:**672

Joan of Arc **3:**657–662

language **4:**963

Leo X **3:**701

Leonardo da Vinci **3:**707, 714

libraries **5:**1375

literature **1:**214–216

manufacturing **3:**808, 809

Mary, Queen of Scots **2:**327, 330

Maximilian I **3:**839

mercenaries **5:**1411

missionaries **4:**893–894, 896

Molière **4:**897–902

monarchy **3:**660, **4:**907, 908, 909, 913, 914, **5:**1218, 1224

music **4:**944–947, 948, 949, 954

nationalism **4:**963, 964, 965

nobility and rank **4:**971, 974, 975, 976, 977

Ottoman alliance **3:**616, 619, 624, 715

painting and sculpture **4:**990, 994–995, 997

Palladianism **4:**1007

papacy **4:**913, 1008, 1009, 1010, 1039

Paris **4:**1028–1035

peasants' revolts **2:**433, 456, **4:**1029, 1042, *1044*

Philip II **4:**1059

poetry **3:**721–722, 725, 735

printing **3:**819, **5:**1169

prose fiction **3:**735–736

Rabelais **5:**1176–1179

Reformation **5:**1191, 1194–1195, 1196, 1198

Roman Catholicism **4:**969, **5:**1177, 1178, 1179

Rome **5:**1233, 1234

Rubens **5:**1243

science **5:**1256

Scotland **5:**1261, 1262, 1264–1267, 1296

Spain **5:**1279, 1284

Stuarts **5:**1296, 1302

Switzerland **5:**1314

theater **3:**728–731, 733, **5:**1319, 1320

Thirty Years War **5:**1310, 1330, 1331–1334, 1336, 1337–1338

trade **5:**1341, 1350

universities **5:**1367, 1369, 1370, 1371

vernaculars **3:**695

wars of religion **1:***184,* 198–200, **2:**371, **4:**912, 914

women **5:**1418, 1426, 1427

Franche-Comté **1:**157

Franconia **2:**310

Frankfurt **2:**475, 506, **5:**1267, 1337

Frankish empire **1:**157

Freiburg **2:**357, 361

Fribourg **5:**1314

Friesland **1:**274

G

Gallipoli **3:**715

Gambia River **2:**380, **5:**1345

Gascony *see* Aquitaine

Gdańsk **4:**1106

Geneva

banking **1:**87, **2:**416

Calvinism **1:**179, 186–187, 188, 189, **2:**324, 440, 539, **4:**952, **5:**1195–1196, 1265, 1267, 1315–1316, 1423

humanism **3:**585

iconoclasm **3:**607

Puritanism **2:**342

Roman Catholicism **1:**188

Genoa **1:**216, **2:**414, **3:**626, 632

banking **1:**84, 88, **5:**1228

Columbus **1:**247, 248

Constantinople **1:**260–261

Italian wars **3:**643, 647, 650, 651

Ottoman expansion **3:**715

silk manufacture **3:**805

trade **2:**475, **5:**1340, 1393, 1401

Venice **5:**1395

German towns **2:475–483,** 498, 549, 558

agriculture **1:**21

architecture **1:**49

Augsburg, Peace of **1:**75–78

banking **1:**88, **5:**1344

bibles **1:**103, 104–105

Black Death **2:**305

Bohemia **1:**118, 119, 120, 121

calendar **1:**176, 177

Calvinism **1:**178, 188

Charles V **1:**209, 210–211

dams **1:**279

Descartes **2:**294, 295

Dürer **2:**311–316

education **2:**322, 324, **5:**1372

elected monarchs **4:**909–911

established churches **2:**365, 369–370

Florence **2:**419

Hanseatic League **2:**475–476, 481, 502–506

Hapsburgs **2:**438, 509, 514

heresy **2:**531

humanism **2:**552–553, **3:**590, 592, 593

iconoclasm **3:**605, 606, *607,* 609

infantry **3:**651

interest loans **1:**85

Judaism **3:**672–673, 674–675

language **4:**963, 970

Luther **1:**178, **5:**1352

Lutheranism **1:**181, 242, **2:**479, 482, 483, 552–554, 558, **3:**767, 768, 836, **5:**1352

mercenaries **5:**1411

music **4:**950, 951, 952, 954, 958, 960

nationalism **2:**364, **4:**970

nobility and rank **4:**971

papacy **4:**1013

peasants' revolts 1:187, 2:*475*, 479, 480
Poland-Lithuania 4:1104, 1106, 1107, 1110
popular culture 4:1122–1123
preaching 5:1164
printing press 3:687, 775, 780–781, 819, 5:1168, 1169, *1170*, 1193
Reformation 1:178, 181, 183, 4:970, 5:1189–1192, 1193, 1195, 1196, 1198, 1200, 1221, 1267
Roman Catholicism 3:835–839
Schütz 5:1240–1247
science and technology 5:1250, 1256
Thirty Years War 1:183, 228, 2:560, 5:1331, 1332, 1335, 1336–1337, 1415
tournaments 1:225
trade 5:1340, 1344, 1393
universities 5:1367, 1371, 1372, 1373, 1376, 1377
witch hunts 3:802
see also specific place-names
Geto Nuovo (Venice) 3:672
Ghana 4:1141, 5:*1349*
Ghent 1:160, 207, 209, 2:386
Gibraltar, Straits of 2:380
Giume Giuliano canal 1:277
Glarus 5:1312, 1314
Goa 4:894, 1142
Gobi Desert 2:303
Gold Coast 5:*1349*
Golden Horn 1:256
Good Hope, Cape of 2:374, 381, 4:1138, 1139, 5:1341, 1342, 1345
Gorizia 2:509
Goslar 2:505
Göteborg 5:1305
Gotland 5:1310, 1338
Gouda 2:356
Granada 2:408, 4:956, 5:1277, 1279
Alhambra Palace 2:*396*
fall to Spain 2:397, 5:1277, 1279, 1322

Ferdinand and Isabella 2:393, 394, 396, *400*
Philip II 4:1056–1057
Grand Canal (Venice) 5:*1392*, 1398
Grand Canyon (United States) 2:382
Graubünden 5:1334
Great Yarmouth 1:262
Greece 1:177, 262, 3:626, 715
calendar 1:177
war of independence 1:262
Greenwich 1:48, 3:666–667, 668
Grisons *see* Graubünden
Groningen 1:176
Grünwald 4:1107
Guam 3:792
Guinea, Gulf of 2:379
Guyenne *see* Aquitaine

H

Haarlem Lake 1:275
Hague, The 5:1294
Haiti 1:250
Halland island 5:1310, 1338
Hamburg 2:305, 475, 504–505, 506
  Black Death 2:305
  Hanseatic League 2:475, 504–505, 506
Hapsburg Empire 1:88, **2:507–515, 4:**1113, 5:1302
  Bohemia 1:120–122
  Burgundy 1:164
  Charles V 1:207, 209, 2:445–446, 476
  Florence 2:420, 421
  France 2:438, 449, 451, 555
  German towns 2:475–482
  Hanseatic League 2:481
  Holy Roman Empire 2:475–478, 507–515, 549, 550–551, 556, 557
  Italian wars 2:420, 421, 3:647
  land holdings 4:966
  Lombardy 3:740, 745, 746
  Netherlands revolt 2:331
  Ottoman Empire 3:624, 625, 626, 715

primogeniture 4:911
religious wars 4:914
Switzerland 5:1312, 1313, 1314, 1315
Thirty Years War 1:227, 5:1310, 1330–1339
Venice 5:1394
Harfleur 3:599
Härjedalen 5:1310, 1338
Harwood Dale (Yorkshire farm) 5:1422
Harz Mountains 1:279
Hellespont 1:263
Hesse 5:1267
Hispaniola 1:250–251, 252–253, 254
  disease effects 2:307
  missionaries 4:889, 892
Holland *see* Netherlands
Holy Land
  Crusades 1:223, 259–260, 5:1392–1393
  Islam 3:623, 625
  trade 5:1341
Holy Roman Empire 1:156, 180, 2:421, **548–560,** 3:693, 4:904, 1066
  Alfonso X 3:693
  architecture 1:39, 46
  Augsburg, Peace of 1:75–78
  Bohemia 1:117–122
  Burgundy 1:157, 158, 160, 161, 162
  Charles V 1:207–211, 241, 243, 244, 2:446, 448, 513–514, 523
  Clement VII 1:241, 244
  dissolution of 2:512
  electors 4:910–911
  established churches 2:364, 365, 366, 370, 371
  feudalism 2:413
  Florence 2:419, 421, 423
  France 2:444, 448, 451
  German-speaking lands 4:964
  German towns 2:475–483
  Ghibellines 3:743, 5:1378, 1405
  Hanseatic League 2:503, 505

Hapsburg Empire 2:507–515
humanism 2:423
Hundred Years War 4:1136
Italian wars 3:643, 644, 646, 647, 648, 649, 650, 702
Jewish protection 3:673, 674
libraries 5:1375
Lombardy 3:743, 744, 745
Lutheranism 1:210–211, 3:765, 766–767, 836, 855
Maximilian I 3:835
Ommegang procession 5:1317
papacy 1:156, 3:686, 4:1008, 1013, 1014, 1015, 1017, 1023, 1040, 1086, 1088, 5:1227
peasants' revolt 2:555, 558, 4:1042
Reformation 2:482–483, 514, 537, 539, 541, 5:1189, 1200, 1221
religious wars 4:914
Roman Catholicism 3:836, 837, 838, 839, 5:1338, 1365
Rome 5:1232
Thirty Years War 1:227, 5:1330–1339, 1415
Trent, Council of 5:1352, 1353, 1357, 1359
universities 5:1365, 1368
Venice 5:1394
Viscontis 5:1403, 1404, 1405
Hudson River 5:1342
Hungary
  Bohemia 1:120
  crusade of Nicopolis 1:158
  Hapsburgs 2:438, 507, 509, 510–511, 557
  nobility 4:971
  Ottoman Empire 1:242, 2:555, 557, *558*, 3:616, 618, 623, 624, 629, 715
  peasant revolt 4:1042
  Poland 4:1112
  Reformation 2:559
  Thirty Years War 5:1335

I

Iberian Peninsula *see* Portugal, Spain
Imola **5:**1427, 1428
Incisa (Tuscany) **4:**1049
India
  exploration **2:**373, 374, 380, 381, **5:**1342, 1345
  Islam **3:**612, 613, 614, 615, 629
  Judaism **3:**669
  missionaries **4:**894
  Portugal **4:**1142, 1144
  religious orders **5:**1204, 1206
  trade **2:**302, **5:**1341
Indian Ocean **2:**379, 381, **3:**624, 787, 788, 793, 794, **4:**1138, 1142
  shipping **2:**302
  trade **5:**193, 1342
Indonesia **2:**373, **3:**612, 613, **4:**1139
  Islam **3:**612, 613
Ingria **5:**1309, 1334
Iran *see* Persia
Ireland **4:**904, **5:**1265
  Elizabeth I **2:**326, 327, 332, 333
  England **2:**343, 344
  English civil wars **2:**348, 350, 352, 354
  patron saint **5:**1317
  Scotch Protestants **1:**189
  Spenser **5:**1287–1288, 1289, 1290
  Stuarts **5:**1300, 1302, 1303
  trade **5:**1350
Isfahan **1:***280,* **3:**622
Istanbul *see* Byzantium, Constantinople
Italian city-states **3:630–642**
  architecture **1:**30–45, **3:**663, 664, 665, 666, 667
  banking **1:**84, 87–88
  Black Death **2:**304, 305, 306
  Borgias **1:**123–126
  Bruegel **1:**144, 145
  Chaucer **1:**216–217
  Church Latin **3:**689
  classical languages **3:**682
  conflict among **3:**853, 854

Counter-Reformation **5:**1198
dams and drainage **1:**276–277, 278, 279, 280, 281
Dürer **2:**311, 312–313
feudalism **2:**412
Florence **2:**414–426
Graubünden **5:**1334
Greek philosophy **1:**169
Gregorian calendar **1:**176
Hapsburgs **2:**511, **3:**715
humanism **2:**320, **3:**583–589, 591, 592, 638, 640, **5:**1370
Judaism **3:**670, 673, 679, 681
Leonardo da Vinci **3:**706–714
literature **1:**206–207, **3:**720–724, 735, 736–737, 770
Machiavelli **4:**1066–1067
manufacturing **3:**740, 741, *743,* 805
medical studies **3:**840, 841, 844, 845, 846–847
Monteverdi **4:**916–923
music **4:**944, 951–952, 954–956, 958–959, 960, 961
nationalism **4:**966
nobility **4:**974, 977
Ottoman Empire **3:**715
painting and sculpture **1:**144, 145, **2:**312–313, **4:**980, 981, 983–993
papacy **4:**1008, 1011, 1019–1023, 1089–1090
Petrarch **4:**1049–1055
Pico della Mirandola **4:**1073–1085
Platonic academies **2:**320
poetry **3:**720–721, 722–723, 724, 770
printing **5:**1169
prose fiction **3:**735, 736–737
Raphael **5:**1180–1187
religious orders **5:**1204
Renaissance **5:**1218–1226
republics **5:**1224
Rubens **5:**1237, 1238

science and technology **5:**1249, 1250–1254, 1256
territorial battles **2:**419
theater **3:**729, 733–735, 772, **5:**1320–1321, 1322
trade **5:**1341, 1401
universities **5:***1365,* 1367, *1368,* 1370–1371
Urbino **5:**1378–1383
Velázquez **5:**1387, 1388–1389
vernaculars **3:**693, 694, **4:**963
villas **2:**563
Viscontis **5:**1401–1406
women **5:**1420, 1422, 1424, 1427, 1428
see also Florence; Mantua; Milan; Naples; Padua; Rome; Venice
Italy *see* Italian city-states

J

Jamestown colony **5:**1342
Jämtland **5:**1310, 1338
Janiculum Hill (Rome) **1:**141
Japan
  Jesuit missionaries **4:**894, 896, 1015, *1018*
  Portugal **4:**1142, *1143*
  scientific exploration **5:**1259
Jerusalem **2:**399
  Crusades **1:**259, 260
  Ottoman conquest **3:**623
  pilgrimage **4:**1080, 1083
  temple **3:**695
Judea **3:**695
Jülich, duchy of **5:**1338
Jutland **5:**1335, 1338

K

Kabul **3:**612
Kaliningrad (Königsberg) **4:**1106
Kara Sea **2:**384
Karelia **5:**1309, 1334
Kasimov **4:**934
Kassel **5:**1245
Kattegat Strait **5:**1338
Kazan **3:**653, *654,* **4:**936
Kazimierz **3:***675*

Kilcolman **5:**1288
Kilcullen **5:**1288, 1290
Kildare, County (Ireland) **5:**1288
King's Lynn **4:**1081
Klaipeda (Memel) **5:**1334
Königsberg (Kaliningrad) **4:**1106
Köstritz **5:**1244
Kraków **3:***675,* **4:**1106, 1109, 1112

L

La Flèche **2:**294, **5:**1206
La Haye **2:**294, 295
La Isabela **1:**252, 253, 254
La Navidad **1:**251, 252
Languedoc **2:**440, 455
Lanzelin **2:**507
Latvia **2:**503, 505, **3:**653 *see also* Livonia
Lausanne **5:**1312, 1314
Le Havre **2:**453
Leiden **5:**1210, 1211, 1212
Leipzig **1:**88, 279, **2:**506, 553
  Thirty Years War **5:***1310*
Lepini Mountains **1:**277
Levant **2:**501
Liberia **5:**1345
Liège **2:**386
Ligurian Sea **2:**414, **5:**1401
Lille **1:**157, **2:**387
Lima **1:**49, **5:**1209
Lincolnshire **1:**235
Lisbon **1:**205, 251, **4:**1139
  earthquake **4:**1141, *1145*
  Renaissance map **4:***1139*
Lithuania
  Judaism **3:**675
  monarchy **4:**911
  Muscovy **4:**933, 934
  Poland **4:**1104, 1105, 1107, 1108, 1109
  Russia **3:**653
  Teutonic Knights **1:**223
Livonia
  Hanseatic League **2:**503, 504, 505
  Ivan IV Vasilyevich **3:**653, 654, 656
  Poland **4:**1112

Sweden **5:**1307, 1309
Thirty Years War **5:**1334, 1335
Lodi **3:**638
Loire River **1:**45, 276, **3:**657, 659, 660
Loire valley **2:**438
Lombardy **3:740–747**
  agriculture **5:**1401, 1402
  Bramante **1:**139, 140
  feudalism **2:**405
  Italian wars **3:**646, 647, 651
  Viscontis **5:**1401–1406
London **3:748–755**
  agriculture **1:**22
  architecture **1:**32, 48–49, 140, **3:**663, 665, 666, 667, 668
  banking **1:**87, **2:**416
  Chaucer **1:**212, 213, 214
  Covent Garden **3:**820
  Essex rebellion **2:**332, 333
  map (c. 1588) **5:***1324*
  More **4:**924, 927
  peasants' revolt **1:**216, **4:**1043, 1044–1045, 1046–1047
  plague **4:**886
  preaching **5:***1161,* 1166
  printing **3:**819
  Shakespeare **5:**1268, 1269, 1270, 1271, 1275
  Spenser **5:**1286, 1287
  theater **3:**732, 733, 751, 755, 823, 824–825, **5:**1322, 1323, *1324,* 1326–1327, 1328
  Wren's rebuilding plan **1:**48–49, **5:**1431–1432, 1433
Lorraine **5:**1338
Low Countries *see* Flanders, Netherlands
Lübeck **1:**22, **5:**1307
  Hanseatic League **2:**475, 502, 503, 504, 506
Lüneburg **2:**505
Lyons **2:**451, **3:**819, **5:**1176, 1177
  banking **1:**87, 88

M

Macao **4:**894, 1015, 1142
Macedonia **1:**167
Mactan Island **3:**793
Madagascar **5:**1347
Madeira **1:**247, **2:**379, **4:**1140
Madrid
  Cervantes **1:**202
  Philip II **4:**1056, 1060
  Velázquez **5:**1384, 1385, 1386, 1388, 1390
Magdeburg **1:**77, **2:**475, 480–481, **5:**1337
Magellan, Straits of **3:**788, 790–791
Maine (France) **3:**601, 602
Mainz **2:**548, 550, **3:**687
Malacca **3:**787, **4:**1142, 1143
Malaya **4:**1142
Mali **3:**612
Malta **1:**194, 223, **3:**612, 626
Mantua **2:**419, **3:**637, 642, 853, **4:**1087, **5:***1416*
  architecture **1:**36, *38,* 39
  Caravaggio **1:**194
  humanism **5:**1220
  Lombardy **3:**741, 744, 745
  Monteverdi **4:**917–918, 919
  opera **3:**734
  Thirty Years War **5:**1336
  Urbino **5:**1379
Marche **5:**1378, 1380
Marciana (Venice) **1:**261
Marmara, Sea of **1:**165, 256, 263
Marseilles (Renaissance map) **4:***1132*
Maryland **3:**609, **4:**893, 894, 895
Massachusetts **1:**189, **3:**609, **5:**1342
  established church **2:**372
  missionaries **4:**892
  Puritans **1:**189
  university **2:***325*
Mauritania **5:**1345
Meaux **1:**17
Mecklenburg **5:**1334
Medina **3:**623, 625
Mesopotamia **2:**302
Messina **1:**194, **3:**715

Meuse River **5:**1334
Mexico
  dams **1:**280
  disease **2:**307
  exploration **2:**374, 382
  gold **5:**1345
  missionaries **4:**889–890, 891
  Spain **2:**306, **5:**1285
Mexico City **1:**49
Milan **2:**555, **3:**630, 775, 853, **4:**947, 965, 1090, **5:**1413
  architecture **1:***32,* 36, 139
  banking **1:**87, **2:**416
  Black Death **2:**306
  Bramante **1:**139, 140, 141
  canals **3:**741
  Clement VII **1:**242
  description of **3:**631
  feudalism **2:**403, 413
  Florence **2:**414, 417
  Francis I **2:**445, 446, 449
  government **3:**637, 638, 641, 650
  Hapsburgs **2:**509, 511
  humanism **3:**586
  Italian wars **1:**208, 221, 241, 242, **3:**642, 643, 645–647, 648, 650
  Leonardo da Vinci **2:**425, **3:**707, 708–710
  Lombardy **3:**740, 741, 743, 744, 745
  manufacturing **3:**740, 741, *743*
  nobility **3:**638
  Spain **5:**1224
  Switzerland **5:**1314
  territorial battles **2:**419
  Thirty Years War **5:**1336
  Venice **5:**1394
  view of **5:***1401*
  Viscontis **3:**740, 741, 742, **5:**1401–1406
Mincio River **3:**741
Mississippi River **2:**382
Modena **2:**413, 419, **3:**648, 853, **4:**1073
Mogul Empire **3:**612, 615, 629, **4:**1142
Molucca Islands **3:**788, 792, 793, 794, **4:**1142

Mondovì **4:**1091
Monferrato **3:**744
Mongolia **2:**303
Monte Mario (Rome) **1:**39
Montereau **1:**159
Montmorency **2:**456
Montpellier **2:**452, **5:**1176, 1177, 1422
Moorgate (London) **3:**749
Moravia **1:**116, 119, 122, **5:**1335
Morocco 611, **4:**1137, 1140
Moscow **3:***654,* **4:**933, 934, 935, 936, 1109, **5:**1337
  Ivan IV Vasilyevich **3:**653, 655
  Orthodox Church **1:**166
  Poland **5:**1308, 1309
Moselle River **5:**1338
Mozambique **3:**787
Münster **5:**1195, 1338
Muscovy **3:**652–653, **4:933–941**

N

Naples **3:**743, 853, **4:**905, *1130,* **5:**1256
  agriculture **1:**22
  Boccaccio **1:**111, 112, 115
  Borgia, Lucrezia **1:**123
  Caravaggio **1:**191, 194, 195
  charivari **4:**1116
  Charles V **1:**208, 210, 243
  Christina **1:**230
  Gentileschi **2:**470, 472, 474
  Giotto **2:**487, 491
  Hapsburgs **2:**445, 446, 511, 513
  humanism **3:**586, 594
  Italian wars **1:**244, **2:**310, 412, 438, **3:**642, 643, 644–645, 647, 648, 650, 702
  Judaism **3:**679
  markets **3:**818
  nationalism **4:**965, 966
  as papal fief **2:**412
  Pius II **4:**1089–1090
  population **4:**1131, 1132
  Spain **5:**1224, 1234, 1278
  syphilis **2:**310

Naples *(cont.)*
  territorial battles **2:**419
  Venice **5:**1393, 1394
Narva **3:**653, **5:**1307
Navarino **1:**202
Navarre **1:**199, **2:**437, 456,
  516, **5:**1278, 1279
Nazareth **1:**259
Nemi, Lake **1:**37
Netherlands **1:**200, **3:**716
  architecture **1:**49
  Baltic traders **2:**506
  banking **1:**90
  Bosch **1:**127–132
  Bruegel **1:**144, 148
  Burgundy **1:**160, 164
  Calvinism **1:**178, 188, 190,
    2:371, **3:**767
  Charles V **1:**207, 210, 211
  colonialism **5:**1284, 1342,
    1346
  companies **2:**383, 500,
    5:1342, *1351*
  Descartes **2:**294, 295, 296,
    299
  dikes and drainage
    1:273–276, 279
  divorce law **2:**568
  Dürer **2:**316
  Elizabeth I **2:**331, 332
  Erasmus **2:**356, 357
  exploration **2:**384, 385
  Gregorian calendar **1:**176
  Holy Roman Empire **2:**555,
    556, **3:**838
  Huguenots **5:**1331
  humanism **3:**585, 589, 590,
    592
  Hundred Years War **1:**16,
    3:596
  iconoclasm **3:**605, **5:***1165*
  interest-bearing loans **1:**85
  Judaism **3:**681, **4:**1139
  market **5:***1340*
  monarchy **4:**912, 914
  music **4:**944, 949, 951
  naval power **5:**1412
  painting **2:**391, 392,
    4:995–998, **5:**1264–1265
  Philip II **1:**211, **4:**1056,
    1057, 1058, 1060

  preaching **5:**1164
  Reformation **5:**1195, 1196
  Rembrandt **5:**1210–1217
  science **5:**1252, 1256, 1258
  Spain/Spanish wars **1:**176,
    200, 279, **2:**331, 371,
    454, **3:**746, 767, **4:**914,
    966, 1057, 1058, 1060,
    5:1281, 1282, 1283,
    1332, 1333, 1334, 1336,
    1338, 1344
  Spanish armada **1:**62, 66,
    2:331
  Spanish Hapsburgs **2:**438,
    445, 453, 510, 511
  spice trade **4:**1141, 1145
  Spinoza **5:**1291–1295
  Sweden **5:**1306, 1311
  Thirty Years War **5:**1333,
    1334, 1335, 1337, 1338
  trade **5:**1393
  tulips **1:**26
  universities **2:***323,* **5:**1367
  wind power **3:**777
  women regents **5:**1426
Neuberg **5:**1334
Neuchâtel **5:**1314
Neva River **4:**933
Nevers **1:**157
New Abbey **5:**1288
New Amsterdam **5:**1342
Newark **2:**352
New England
  architecture **1:**49
  Calvinism **1:**178
  witch hunts **5:**1425
New Exchange (London)
  3:665
New Holland (Australia)
  2:385
Newmarket (Suffolk) **3:**665,
  666
New Spain *see* Mexico
New World *see* Americas;
  Caribbean region
New York **5:**1342
New Zealand **2:**385
Nicaea **1:**168, 261
Nicaragua **4:**892
Nîmes **2:**452
Normandy **2:**440, 456

Hundred Years War **1:**16, 17,
  3:599–601, 602–603
  university **5:**1371
North Africa
  exploration **2:**379, 380
  Islam **3:**612, 613, 624, 626
  Judaism **2:**399, **3:**670, *678,*
    679
  Ottoman Empire **3:**624, 626,
    715
  piracy **1:**208, 209, 211,
    3:626, *627,* 716, **5:**1347
  slave trade **5:**1348
  Spanish Jews and Muslims
    5:1277, 1279
  see also specific countries
North America *see* Americas;
  Canada; Mexico; United
  States
North Carolina **2:**382
Northeast Passage **2:**374, 384
northern Ireland **1:**189
North Petherton **1:**218
North Sea **1:**273–274, **5:**1305
  dikes **1:**273–274
  trade **5:**1341, 1344
Northwest Passage **2:**374, 383,
  4:888
Norway
  Black Death **2:**305
  Denmark **5:**1304, 1305
  exploration **2:**384
  fishing trade **5:**1341
  guilds **2:**493
  Hanseatic League **2:**503, 505,
    506
  Lutheranism **3:**768
  monarchy **4:**903, 911
  Sweden **5:**1310
Nottingham **2:**351
Novara **3:**638
Novgorod **4:**933, 940
Nuremberg **2:**475, *476,* 482,
  506, 554
  Dürer **2:**311, 312, 314, 316
  Lutheranism **2:**316

O

Oder River **2:**505
Oesel (Saaremaa) Island
  5:1310, 1338

Ontígola, Sea of **1:**280
Oran **1:**204
Ore Mountains **1:**279
Orkney Isles **5:**1296
Orléans **1:**179, **2:**451, 452
  dike **1:***273*
Osnabrück **1:**77, **5:**1338
Otranto **3:**619
Ottoman Empire **2:**427,
  4:935
  Byzantium **1:**165, 167,
    3:586, 685
  cannon **5:***1409,* 1410
  Cervantes **1:**202
  Charles V **1:**75, 208, 209,
    210, 211, 242–243
  Christianity **1:**169, 170–171
  Constantinople **1:**55, 158,
    162, 165, 166, 169–172,
    260, 263–264, **2:**429,
    430, **4:**1063
  crusade of Nicopolis **1:**158
  Francis I **2:**448
  Holy Roman Empire
    2:512–513, 514, 515,
    548, 553, 555, 556, 557,
    558, 559
  Islam **3:**612, 613, 616–619,
    622–628, 629
  Judaism **3:**670, 679, 680,
    681
  Lepanto, Battle of
    3:715–719
  Mehmed II **1:**169
  Philip II **4:***1058,* 1059–1060
  Pius II crusade
    4:1087–1088, 1089
  Poland **4:**1113, 1114
  Thirty Years War
    5:1330–1331, 1337
  Venice **5:**1393, 1398
Oxford **2:**352

P

Pacific Ocean **2:**373, 382,
  383, 385, **3:**788, 790–791,
  794, **5:**1258–1259
Paderborn **1:**77
Padua
  Giotto frescoes **2:**485, 486,
    487, 488, 489

humanism **3**:583
Italian wars **3**:647
Medicis **2**:420
painting **2**:312
Palladio **4**:1001
Petrarch **4**:1051
Venice **1**:277, **5**:1394, 1395
waterways **1**:277
Palatinate **1**:76–77, 122,
    2:548, 558, **3**:837
Thirty Years War **5**:1301,
    1302, 1334, 1335, 1336
Palestine *see* Holy Land,
    Jerusalem
Palos **1**:248, 251
Pamlico Sound **2**:382
Panama **1**:254, **2**:374, 382,
    4:892
Papal States **1**:124, 246,
    3:756, **4**:1009, 1011–1012,
    1016, **5**:1231, 1357
Charles V **1**:210, 242
Italian wars **3**:644, 648
Leo X **3**:701
Medicis **3**:853
Paul V **4**:1036, 1037
Pius II **4**:1090
territorial battles **2**:419
Urbino **5**:1378–1383
Venice **5**:1393, 1394,
    1398–1399
Paris **4:1028–1035**
agriculture **1**:22
architecture **1**:45, **2**:444
banking **1**:87
Black Death **2**:305
Calvin **1**:179
Christina **1**:*229*
Descartes **2**:296
England **1**:160
famines **4**:1124
as French governmental seat
    2:451
French monarchy **2**:438,
    446, 447
Hobbes **2**:544
humanism **4**:1023
Hundred Years War **1**:160,
    3:600, 658, 660, *661*
indoor theater **5**:1318
literature **3**:725

Molière **4**:897–902
nominalism **1**:182
plague **2**:433
population **4**:1028, 1030,
    1131, 1132, 1133
printing **3**:819
Renaissance map **1**:*179,*
    4:*1029*
Saint Bartholomew's Day
    Massacre **2**:371, 441, 454,
    4:*1033*
wars of religion **2**:456, 457,
    458, 517, 519
Parma **3**:638, 644, 648, 743,
    744
Patras, Gulf of **3**:*718*
Pavia **3**:643, 646, 743, **5**:*1402*
Pennsylvania **1**:189
Persia
    astronomy **1**:271
    dams **1**:278, *280*
    education **2**:*317*
    Islam **3**:612, 617, 620–621,
        622–623, 626, 628, *629*
    shipping **2**:302
Peru
    disease **2**:307, **5**:1285
    exploration **2**:374
    missionaries **4**:892
    religious orders **5**:1209
    Spanish control **2**:306
Perugia **4**:1012, **5**:1181, 1182,
    1183, 1404
Philippines **3**:788, 792–793,
    4:892, 1060
Piacenza **3**:648, 743, 744
Piedmont **3**:643, 644
Pienza **4**:*1089,* 1090
Pillau (Baltiysk) **5**:1334
Pisa **2**:414, *461,* **3**:632, 637,
    638, 649, 770
    banking **1**:87, **2**:416
    Black Death **2**:305
    Galileo **5**:1252
    Viscontis **5**:1401, 1404
Poitou **2**:440
Poland **4:1104–1114, 5**:1330
    Bohemia **1**:120
    Catherine de Médicis **1**:200
    Christina **1**:230
    Copernicus **1**:265–272

Judaism **3**:675
Lithuanian Commonwealth
    4:911
Muscovy **4**:934, 937,
    938–939, 940
nobility **4**:971
Russia **3**:653, 654, 656,
    5:1337
Sweden **5**:1306, 1307–1308,
    1309, 1310, 1311,
    1334–1335
Teutonic Knights **1**:223
Thirty Years War **1**:228,
    4:1113
Polotsk **4**:1112
Pomerania **5**:1332, 1338
Pontine Marshes **1**:277
Po River **1**:276, 280, **3**:638,
    740, 741, **5**:1336
Porte Neuve (Paris) **4**:*1034*
Portugal **2**:399, **3**:775, **4**:905,
    961, **1137–1145**
    African slave trade **5**:1348
    Columbus **1**:247, 248, 251
    exploration **2**:373, 379–381,
        382, 385, **4**:888–889,
        914, **5**:1284, 1343, 1344,
        1346
    feudalism **2**:403
    Gregorian calendar **1**:176
    humanism **3**:693
    Judaism **2**:399, **3**:677, 679,
        681
    Magellan voyage **3**:787, 788,
        789, 792, 793, 794
    missionaries **4**:889, 891, 894,
        895, 896
    monarchy **5**:1224
    Ottoman Empire **3**:624
    shipping **5**:1343
    Spain **4**:1058, 1060, **5**:1277,
        1284
    trade **3**:633, **5**:1341, 1342,
        1344, 1350, 1393
Poznań **2**:506
Prague **1**:117–119, *120,*
    121–122, **2**:559, **3**:836,
    837, 838
Thirty Years War **2**:371,
    5:1337
Provence **1**:157, **2**:437, 456

Q
Quebec **3**:609, **4**:893, **5**:1342

R
Ravenna **1**:258, 264, **5**:1393,
    1394
Red Square (Moscow) **3**:*654*
Regensburg **3**:673, **5**:1337
Reims **3**:602, 657, 658–659,
    660
Rethel **1**:157
Reval (Tallinn) **2**:503,
    5:1307
Rhineland **5**:1196, 1198
Rhine River **2**:304–305, 506,
    507, **3**:836, **4**:965, 1139,
    5:1344
Rhodes **1**:223, **3**:624
Rhône River **4**:965
Rhône valley **2**:456
Riga **2**:503, **5**:1309, 1334
Rijnsburg **5**:1292
Rimini **4**:1090
rivers **3**:741, 749, 751, *754,*
    804, 809
    dikes and drainage
        1:276–277, 278
Roman Empire
    architecture **1**:30, 33, 34, 40,
        47, 140, 141, 142, **2**:334,
        424, **3**:665, 667
    bull baiting **1**:94
    Burgundy **1**:157
    Byzantium **1**:165, 258
    Christianity **3**:604, 696
    dams **1**:278
    disease **2**:303
    Donation of Constantine
        3:584, 586, 594, 686
    education **2**:318, 319
    Greek language **3**:684, 691
    Hapsburg Empire **2**:512,
        513, 514
    Hellenic culture **1**:167
    heresy law **2**:531
    humanism **3**:582–589, 756,
        5:1219
    Judaism **3**:669, 695
    Latin language **3**:682, 691
    literature **2**:334–335
    Ottoman Empire **1**:169

Roman Empire (cont.)
  Rome 5:1227, 1228, 1232
  sculpture 1:98
  theater 3:732, 733,
      5:1320–1321, 1322, 1326
  see also Byzantine Empire
Roman Republic 3:769, 772
Rome 5:1227–1235
  architecture 1:30, 32, 33, 34,
      35, 36–40, 43, 44–45, 47,
      139, 140, 141, 4:1025–
      1026, 1040, 5:1235
  banking 1:87, 88, 2:416
  Bernini 1:97
  Borgia, Lucrezia 1:123, 124,
      125
  Bramante 1:41, 140, 141
  Bruegel 1:149
  Byzantium as "New Rome"
      1:172
  Caravaggio 1:191, 192, 194,
      195
  Catherine de Médicis 1:197
  Catholicism 1:166
  Christina 1:227, 228,
      229–231
  Galileo 3:699, 5:1253
  Gentileschi 2:470, 471, 472
  Giotto 2:487, 491
  Greek philosophy 1:169
  humanism 3:586, 587, 703,
      756, 4:1023
  Inquisition 1:187, 4:1018,
      1019, 1036, 1065,
      5:1226, 1234, 1251
  Jones 3:663, 668
  Leo X 3:700, 703, 704
  Michelangelo 2:425–426,
      4:870–871, 873–875,
      876–878, 986, 5:1231,
      1232
  Milton 4:882
  Moscow as "third" Rome
      4:935–936
  music 4:954, 955, 956
  painting and sculpture
      1:145, 4:986–988, 992,
      5:1236–1237
  Palladio 4:1001, 1002–1003
  papacy 4:1008, 1009–1010,
      1011, 1019, 1020, 1022,

  1025–1026, 1037, 1040,
      1052
  Petrarch 4:1052
  Pico della Mirandola 4:1074,
      1075
  pilgrimages 4:1079, 1080,
      1083
  Pontine Marshes drainage
      1:277
  Porta Pia 5:1226
  Raphael 5:1181, 1183, 1185,
      1186–1187
  sack of (1527) 1:209, 210,
      243, 2:523, 3:643, 647,
      649, 773, 4:986, 1002,
      1014, 1023, 1026,
      5:1232, 1233
  Velázquez 5:1387,
      1388–1389
Rostock 5:1334
Rotterdam 1:274, 275, 2:356,
      362
Rouen 1:17, 2:451, 455, 457,
      3:661, 662
Roussillon 5:1279
Rumania 1:170
Russia
  architecture 1:49
  Black Death 2:305
  calendar 1:177, 4:1024
  exploration 2:384
  German towns 4:1107
  Hanseatic League 2:503
  icons 1:168, 3:604
  Ivan IV Vasilyevich
      3:652–656
  Lithuanian wars 4:1109
  Muscovy 4:933–941
  Orthodox Church 1:166,
      4:935–936, 1109
  Poland 4:1112, 1113, 1114
  puppet show 5:1320
  Sweden 5:1306–1307, 1308,
      1309, 1311, 1334, 1337
  trade 2:501
  see also Moscow
Ryazan 4:936

S

Safed (Galilee) 3:680
Sagres 5:1345

Sahara Desert 2:379, 4:1137,
      1142
Saint Augustine (Florida)
      4:891, 892
Saint Gall 1:279
Saint Lawrence River 4:893,
      896
Saint Mark's Square (Venice)
      1:277, 4:1021
Saint Marys City (Maryland)
      4:894
Saint Petersburg 4:941
Saint Peter's Square (Rome)
      4:1026, 1040, 5:1190
Salisbury Plain 3:665
Salzburg 2:475, 476
San Gimignano 3:635
San Salvador 1:248, 250,
      4:889
Santa Cruz 4:889
Santa María de Belén 1:254
Santiago de Compostela
      4:1060, 1078, 1079, 1080,
      1082, 1083
Santo Domingo 1:248, 253,
      254, 2:307, 5:1342
Saône River 4:965
Sardinia 1:207, 208, 2:511
Saudi Arabia see Arabian
      Peninsula
Savoy 2:449, 3:715,
      5:1315–1316
Saxony 2:505, 5:1335, 1337
  education 2:324
  Holy Roman Empire 2:548,
      553, 556
  Luther 4:1013
  Schütz 5:1244–1247
  vernaculars 5:1222–1223
Schaffhausen 5:1314
Scheldt River 5:1344
Schermer polder (Holland)
      1:275
Schipol airport 1:275
Schleswig, duchy of 2:506
Schleswig-Holstein 5:1338
Schwyz 5:1312
Scotland 5:1260–1267, 1330
  Calvinism 1:189, 190, 2:346,
      349, 5:1196, 1198,
      1265–1267, 1298

Charles I 1:239, 2:344
  divorce law 2:568
  education 2:323
  Elizabeth I 2:327, 330–331,
      332
  England 2:343, 344, 346,
      5:1296, 1297, 1300,
      1413
  English civil wars 2:348,
      349, 351, 352, 353, 354,
      372
  established church 2:349,
      353, 369, 372
  Henry VIII 2:522, 527–528
  Hundred Years War 3:595,
      597
  Mary, Queen of Scots 2:327,
      330–331
  monarchy 2:342, 4:904,
      905, 5:1224
  Reformation Parliament
      5:1298
  Spanish armada 2:331
  Stuarts 5:1297–1303, 1426
Seine River 1:16, 3:662, 809,
      4:1034, 1035
Senigallia (Sinigaglia) 4:1091,
      5:1383
Serbia 1:170, 263, 3:616
Seville
  Columbus's funerary
      monument 1:255
  Murillo 5:1386
  Velázquez 5:1384, 1385
Shetland Islands 5:1296
Shottery 5:1269
Siberia 3:656, 4:933,
      936–937, 938, 940
Sicily 2:511, 3:684
  Byzantine jurisdiction 1:259
  Charles V 1:207, 208
  plague 2:304
  Spain 5:1278, 1279
Siena 2:413, 419, 3:637, 638,
      701, 853
  dam project 1:281
  Italian wars 3:643, 644, 649
  painting 2:492
  theater 3:734
  Viscontis 5:1404
Sierra Leone 2:380

Signoria (Florence) **3:**851

Silesia **1:**116, **5:**1335, 1337

Sinigaglia *see* Senigallia

Skåne **5:**1311

Slovenia **4:**1042

Smolensk **4:**936, 940, **5:**1337

Somme River **1:**17

Songhay Empire **3:**612

South America *see* Americas;
   specific countries

Southeast Asia **5:**1341

South Pacific **5:**1258–1259

Spain **5:1277–1285**
  agriculture **1:**21
  architecture **1:**46–47, 141
  armada **1:**62–66, 238, **2:**331,
    332, **4:**1060, 1145
  baroque art **4:**994
  Black Legend **2:**400
  Bosch paintings **1:**131, 132
  Catherine de Médicis **1:**198,
    199, 200
  Cervantes **1:**202–206
  Charles V **1:**207, 208, 209,
    211, 241
  colonial settlements **1:**242
  Columbus **1:**247–248,
    250–255
  Counter-Reformation
    5:1199
  dams **1:**279, 280
  Elizabeth I **2:**331, 332–333
  English Catholics **2:**342,
    5:1301
  established church **2:**370
  exploration **2:**306, 307–308,
    373, 381, 382, **3:**788,
    4:888–889, 1138, 1142,
    5:1283–1284, 1285,
    1342, 1345, 1346
  Ferdinand and Isabella
    2:393–400, *411,*
    5:1425–1426
  feudalism **2:**408
  France **2:**442, 453, 458
  Gregorian calendar **1:**176
  Hapsburgs **1:**164, **2:**438,
    445, 507, 510, 511, 512,
    515, 556, 557, **3:**715
  Holy Roman Empire **2:**558,
    560

humanism **3:**590, 591, 592

Hundred Years War **3:**598

infantry **3:**651

Islam **3:**612, 613, 676, 678

Italian city-states **1:**208,
    5:1224, 1231, 1234

Italian wars **3:**630, 642, 643,
    644–651, 702, 703, **4:**966

Judaism **3:**669, 670, 671,
    672, 674, 676–679, 680,
    4:1139

land holdings **4:**965–966

loans **1:**88

Lombardy **3:**746–747

Magellan voyage **3:**788–794

missionaries **4:**888–892, 895,
    896

monarchy **4:**904–905, 907,
    5:1218, 1220, 1224, 1225

music **4:**956–957, 959

Naples **3:**743

nationalism **4:**963, 965

nobility **4:**971

Ottoman Empire **3:**626, 715,
    716

papacy **5:**1234

Philip II **4:**1056–1060

pilgrimage **4:**1060, *1078,*
    1079, 1080, 1082

poetry **3:**726

Portugal **4:**1138, 1141, 1142,
    1145

prose fiction **3:**738–739

Reconquista **2:**398, **3:**676,
    678, **4:**956, 969, **5:**1322,
    1425

religious orders
    5:1205–1206, 1207

Roman Catholic Church
    2:370

Rome **5:**1232–1234

Rubens **5:**1237, 1242

Stuarts **5:**1301, 1336

theater **3:**726–727, 729, 731,
    5:1317, 1318, 1319,
    1320, 1321, 1322–1323

Thirty Years War **5:**1336,
    1337–1338

trade **3:**633, **5:**1341, 1344,
    1347, 1350

universities **5:**1367

Urbino **5:**1381

Velázquez **5:**1384–1391

vernaculars **3:**693, 694–695,
    4:963, **5:**1222, 1282,
    1284

Spanish Netherlands *see*
  Netherlands

Spanish road **3:**746

Spice Islands **2:**373, **3:**787,
  789
  missionaries **4:**894, 1015

Spoleto **1:**124, **5:**1379

Steinau **5:**1337

Stockholm **1:**228, **5:**1304,
  1307, 1309
  Descartes **2:**301

Stonehenge **3:**665

Stralsund **2:**503, **5:**1164, 1334

Strasbourg **1:**77, 179, 188,
  2:475, 482, 507, 558,
  5:1169

Stratford-upon-Avon **5:**1268,
  1269, 1271, 1274–1275,
  1322

Styria **2:**557

Sumatra **4:**1142

Sweden **5:1304–1311**
  banking **1:**90
  Christina **1:**227–231
  Descartes **2:**301
  established church **2:**370,
    372
  guilds **2:**493
  Hanseatic League **2:**503, 505,
    506
  Hapsburgs **2:**480
  literacy **2:**323
  Lutheranism **2:**370
  Maximilian I **3:**839
  monarchy **4:**909, 911
  Muscovy **4:**933, 934, 937,
    939, 940, 941
  Poland **4:**1111, 1112–1113,
    1114
  Reformation **5:**1191
  Russia **3:**653
  Thirty Years War **1:**228,
    2:371, 372, **5:**1330,
    1332–1338, 1415
  trade **5:**1341
  university **5:**1367

Switzerland **2:**509, **3:**742,
  5:1312–1316
  Black Death **2:**305
  Burgundy **1:**163
  Calvinism **1:**178, 188
  dams **1:**279, 280
  education **2:**322, 324
  humanism **2:**312, **3:**585
  iconoclasm **3:**606–607, 609
  infantry **3:**651
  Italian wars **3:**645, 646
  markets **3:**819
  national history **4:**964
  Reformation **1:**178, 179,
    181, 188, **5:**1193, 1195,
    1196, 1198
  Reformation music **4:**952
  warfare **5:**1313, 1315, 1411,
    1413
  witch hunts **5:**1425
  see also Geneva; Zurich

Syria **1:**260, **2:**429, **3:**623
  Islam **3:**612, 617, 623

T

Tagus River **1:**280, **4:**1141

Tallinn (Reval) **2:**503, **5:**1307

Tenochtitlán **2:**307

Thames River **3:**749, *750,*
  751, *754, 755,* 820,
  4:1047, **5:***1324,* 1326,
  1328

Theobalds (Hertfordshire)
  5:1289

Thessaloníki (Thessalonica)
  1:258, *262,* **3:**680

Thrace **1:**165

Tiber River **1:**38, 40, 41, 100,
  140, **5:**1227, 1228, 1230,
  1231
  bridge **4:**1025

Ticino River **3:**647, 688

Tierra del Fuego **3:**791

Tilbury **2:**331

Toledo **3:**693, **5:**1207

Tordesillas **5:**1280, 1281

Torre de la Parada (Madrid)
  5:1241

Torre delle Tilzie (Rome) **1:**39

Torun **1:**265, 266

Toulon **3:**624

Toulouse **2**:455
Touraine **2**:294, **5**:1176, 1177
Tours **2**:451
Transylvania **2**:555, **5**:1335, 1337
  Gregorian calendar **1**:176
Trent (Trento) **1**:279, **5**:*1352*, 1357
Treviso **3**:647, **5**:1394
Trier **2**:548
Tsaritsyn *see* Volgograd
Tuileries **4**:1031
Tunis **1**:202, 209, 211, **3**:624, **5**:1347
Turkey, Republic of **1**:172 *see also* Ottoman Empire
Tuscany **3**:*635,* **4**:1091
  Galileo **2**:464
  government **3**:637, 642
  Italian wars **3**:642, 649
  Petrarch **4**:1049
  see also Florence
Tyrol **1**:88, **2**:508, 509, 511
Tyrrhenian Sea **1**:277

U

Ukraine **4**:1109, 1113–1114, **5**:1337
Ulm **2**:295, 475, *476,* 482
Ulster **2**:350
United Provinces *see* Netherlands
United States
  architecture **1**:140
  disestablishment **2**:367, 372
  see also Americas; *specific states*
Unterwalden **5**:1312
Ural Mountains **3**:656
Urbino **1**:139, 140, **2**:444, **3**:701, **5**:**1378–1383**
  Raphael **5**:1180, 1181, 1183
Uri **5**:1312

V

Valencia **1**:205, **2**:396, 397, **4**:965, **5**:1277
Valladolid **1**:205, 206, 248, 255, **2**:396, **4**:1056, 1058, **5**:1280
Valtellina **5**:1337

Varmia **1**:265, 266
Venezuela **1**:249
Venice **2**:414, **3**:630, 668, 853, **5**:1336, **1392–1400**
  architecture **1**:32, 33, 42–43, **3**:*640,* 641, 642, 666, 667, 668
  banking **1**:87, 91, **2**:416
  Black Death **2**:305, 306
  Charles V **1**:210
  Constantinople **1**:168, 260–261
  dams and drainage **1**:276–277
  France **2**:447
  government **3**:637, 638–639, 642, 651, 668
  Greek texts **1**:261, **2**:320, 430, **3**:688
  Italian wars **1**:242, 244, **3**:545, 643, 647, 648
  Jewish ghetto **3**:672, 679
  Lepanto, Battle of **3**:715, 716, 718, *719*
  Lombardy **3**:744, 745
  Milan **5**:1404
  Monteverdi **4**:922
  music **4**:951–952, 958–959, **5**:1244–1245, 1246
  nationalism **4**:966–967, 969
  nobility **4**:974, 977
  opera **3**:734
  Ottoman Empire **3**:616, 618–619, 626, 715, 716, 718
  painting **2**:312, 313, **4**:981, 986, 988, 989, **5**:1236
  Palladio **3**:664, *668,* **4**:1000, 1006–1007, **5**:1399
  papacy **4**:1012, 1020–1021, 1037, 1038–1039
  Petrarch **4**:1051
  printing **3**:819
  silk manufacture **3**:805
  telescope **5**:1252
  territorial battles **2**:419
  theater **3**:734
  trade **2**:475, **3**:740, 741, **5**:1340, 1341, 1344, 1392–1394, 1395, 1398, 1401

Urbino **5**:1380, 1381
Velázquez **5**:1388, 1389
Verona **5**:1394
Via della Lungara (Rome) **5**:1231
Via Giulia (Rome) **1**:40, 141, **5**:1231
Vicenza **3**:789
  Palladio **1**:42–43, **2**:563, **3**:664, 666, *668,* **4**:1000, 1002, 1004, 1005 1006–1007
  university **5**:1371
  Venice **4**:966, **5**:1394
Vienna **2**:556, 557
  Black Death **2**:305
  Jewish purges **3**:672
  Ottoman sieges (1529, 1683) **1**:209, **2**:555, **3**:612, 624, **4**:1114
Virginia **3**:609, **4**:892, 894, **5**:1342
Vistula River **4**:*1105*
Volga River **3**:653, **4**:933
Volgograd **4**:933
Voorburg **5**:1292, 1293
Vorarlberg **2**:509

W

Wales **1**:17, **3**:596, **4**:904, **5**:1416
Wallachia **3**:616
Warsaw **4**:1105, 1112
Wartburg **3**:765
Warwickshire **2**:351
Weissenfels **5**:1247
Wendish towns **2**:506
Weser River **2**:506, **5**:1335
Western Isles **5**:1296
West Indies *see* Caribbean region
Westphalia **5**:1236, 1237
Whitehall (London) **2**:355, **3**:*666,* 668, 749, 751
White Sea **4**:933
Wight, Isle of **2**:353
Wismar **5**:1334
Wittenberg
  altarpiece **5**:*1163*
  bibles **1**:105

church door **1**:178, **5**:*1189,* 1191
indulgences **5**:1190
Luther **3**:*756,* 758–759, 762, 765, **4**:929, **5**:1190
Worms **2**:557

Y

Yorkshire **1**:235, **2**:351
Yucatán *see* Mexico
Yuste **1**:209, 211

Z

Zayandeh River **1**:*280*
Zuider Zee **1**:274
Zurich
  Black Death **2**:304, 305
  public education **2**:322
  Reformation **1**:188, **5**:1193, 1267, 1312, 1314, 1315, 1316
  Renaissance map **5**:*1316*
Zwingli **1**:181

Index of Science, Technology, and Exploration

A **boldface** number preceding a colon indicates the volume. Numbers in *italics* refer to captions. Numbers entirely in **boldface** refer to a full article.

A

adding machine **3:**775
agriculture **1:21–29, 3:**710, **4:***1121*
 astrological prediction **1:**68
 Black Death **2:**306
 calendar **1:**177
 city provisions **4:**1132, 1134
 Columbian exchange **1:**255
 dams and drainage **1:**28, 273–277, 280, **3:**741, **5:**1402
 festivals **4:**1118
 food shortages **2:**479, **4:**1027, 1174
 France **2:**433, 456
 households **2:**562
 Lombardy **3:**740, 741
 markets **3:**813, 814, 818, 821
 peasants' revolts **4:**1041–1048
 population **4:**1114, 1124, 1126, 1127, 1134–1135
 Scotland **5:**1260
 trade **5:**1340, 1341, 1346, 1348, 1401
 Viscontis **5:**1401, 1402
Alembert, Jean d' **2:**466, 516
algebra **3:**827, 829–830, 833, 834
almanacs **1:**68, 173, 174–175
anatomical theaters **3:**847
anatomy **3:**845–846, 847, 848, **5:**1250, 1251, 1254, 1255
 disease **2:**309–310
 dissection **2:**302, 303, *320,* **3:**845, 846, 848, **5:**1254
 illusory perspective **2:**312, 316
 Wren **5:**1429
Archimedean Point **2:**297, 300
astrolabe **2:**377, **3:**775, 779, 790, **5:**1250

astrology **1:67–74, 2:**422, **3:***679,* 800
astronomy **1:**60, **2:**559, **3:**693, 699, **4:**1109, **5:**1249–1254
 astrology **1:**67, 74
 calendars **1:**174, 175, **4:**1024
 celestial chart **1:***67, 69*
 Copernicus **1:**265–267, **5:**1221, 1226, 1250
 Descartes **2:**296, 297
 education **2:**319, 320
 Galileo **1:**271, **2:**296, 297, 460, 462, 465–467
 heresy **2:**539, **5:**1226, 1234–1235, 1251
 inventions **3:**774, 775, 779–780, 783
 mathematics **3:**827, 828, 830–831, 832
 Ptolemy **1:**266–267, **5:**1249–1250
 revolutionary thought **3:**783
 Wren **5:**1429, 1430
 see also telescope
atmospheric pressure **5:**1433

B

bacteria **2:**302, 303, 310
barometer **3:**775, **5:**1429, 1433
biology **5:**1258
bird movement **3:**709
blast furnaces **3:**812
blood circulation **3:**840–841, **5:**1251, 1255
blue dye (woad) **5:**1350, 1402
body snatching **3:**848
book production *see* printing
botany **1:**29, **5:**1250, 1258–1259
 medical **3:**840, 846–847
Brahe, Tycho **1:**121, *268,* 271, 272, **2:**559, **3:***831,* 832, **5:**1251
Brunfels, Otto **3:**840, **5:**1250

C

Cabot, John **4:**888, 914, 915, **5:***1350*
Cabot, Sebastian **2:**383

Cabral, Pedro Álvares **2:**374, 381
calculus **3:**783, 827, 833, 834, **4:**1072
calendars **1:173–177,** **4:**1024–1025
 festivals **5:**1317
caravels **2:**373, **4:**1138, **5:**1343, *1346,* 1412
 Columbus's voyages **1:**248
Cardano, Girolamo **1:**70, 71, 72, *73,* **3:**828, 829, 830
carrack **2:**373
cartography **5:***1248,* 1250
 Columbus's worldview **1:**249
 exploration **2:**374, 378, 379, 380, 382, 383, 384, *385*
 Portugal **4:**1138
 Spain **5:**1284
 world map **1:***254*
cast iron **3:**812
celestial chart **1:***67, 69*
Cheng Ho **2:**373, **5:**1342, *1343*
circumnavigation **2:**373, 374, 382, 384, **3:**787, 788, 789, 793–794, **5:**1250
clinical medicine **3:**847
clocks **3:**775, 779–780
clog calendars **1:**173
cog (vessel) **2:**506
Columbian exchange **1:**255
Columbus, Christopher **1:**46, **247–255, 3:**693, 782, 788, 829, **4:**1138, 1142, **5:**1345
 armed trade **3:**775
 disease **2:**306, 308
 exploration **1:**247–251, **2:**373, 374, 381–382, **4:**914, 915, **5:**1220
 Ferdinand and Isabella **2:**393, 394, 399
 missions **4:**888, 889, 891, 895
 writings of **1:**253
compass **2:**376, 384, **3:**778–779, **5:**1343
compass needle **3:**790
conquistadores **1:**207, **2:**307–308, **5:**1285, 1345
constellations **1:***67,* 68, *69*

Cook, James **2:**384, **5:**1258–1259
Copernicus, Nicolaus **1:***57, 60,* **265–272, 2:**539, **3:**699, 783, 827, 829, 831, 832, **4:**1036, 1069, **5:**1221, 1251
 circular planetary path **1:**31, 60, 265, 270
 Descartes **2:**296
 Galileo **2:**463, 465, 466, 467, **5:**1226
 Polish Renaissance **4:**1109
 universe model **1:**265, **2:**296, **4:**1109, **5:**1226, 1250, 1252–1253
Coronado, Francisco Vásquez de **2:**382
Cortés, Hernán **2:**307, **2:**374, 382, **4:**890, **5:**1285, 1345
cosmology *see* astronomy; heliocentric universe
crop rotation **1:**27, **4:**1134

D

dams and drainage **1:**28, **273–282, 2:**461, 462, **3:**741
decimal system **3:**828, **5:**1250
Dee, John **1:**72, 176, 177, **2:**384, **3:**800, 801, **4:**1065
Descartes, René **1:**60, **2:294–301,** 544, **3:**783, **5:**1206, 1251
 mathematics **2:**294–296, 301, **3:**828, 830, 833
Dias, Bartolomeu **2:**374, 381, **4:**1138, 1142, **5:**1341
differential calculus **3:**833
disease **2:302–310,** **3:**843–844, 848 *see also* medicine
dissection **2:**302, **3:**845, 846, 848, **5:**1254
doctors *see* medicine
Drake, Francis **2:**331, **3:**751, **5:**1374
 armada, Spanish **1:**62, 63, 64
 exploration **2:**374, 382, 383, 385, **3:**791

drills, seed **1:**27
dyes **5:**1344, 1350, 1402

E

Elcano, Juan Sebastián de
 2:374, **3:**793–794
equal sign **3:**829, 833
equant **1:**271
Euclid **1:***143,* **3:**827, **5:**1294
Eustachian tubes **3:**840, 846
evolution theory **1:**110
exploration **2:373–385,** 399,
 3:776, **5:**1220
 books on **3:**782
 Columbus **1:**247–255
 disease **2:**306–308
 England **3:**751, 754
 humanism **3:**693
 Magellan **3:**787–794
 missionaries **4:**888–896
 monarchy **4:**914–915
 navies **5:**1412
 Portugal **4:**1137–1138,
  1139, 1140–1142, 1144
 science **5:**1258–1259
 ship design **3:**777–778
 Spain **1:**207, **2:**307, 308,
  394, 399, 400,
  5:1283–1284, 1285
 technology **5:**1250,
  1283–1284, 1343
 trade **5:**1341, 1342,
  1345–1346, 1351
 worldview **1:**249

F

fallopian tubes **3:**840, 846
Fermat, Pierre de **3:**833–834
flood control **1:**28, 273–276,
 279
flying machine **3:**709, **5:**1249
fonts **3:**819
forestry **1:**25–26
free fall, law of **2:**295, 462
frigates **5:**1412
fulling mills **3:**806, *807*
Fust, Johann **3:**781, **5:**1169

G

Galen **3:**840, 844–845, 846,
 5:1177

Galilei, Galileo **1:**262,
 2:460–468, 539, 543,
 3:828, **4:**882, 917, 961
 Aristotelianism **1:**57, 60, 61
 Copernicus **1:***272,* **4:**1109
 Descartes **2:**296, 297
 disease **2:**309
 heresy trial **2:**296, 297,
  3:783, 784, **5:**1226,
  1234–1235, 1251, 1254,
  1256, 1258
 Inquisition **4:**1036
 inventions **1:**271, **2:**309,
  3:775, 783, **5:**1252
 mathematics **3:**831, 833
 philosophy **4:**1068–1069
 rehabilitation **2:**466
 vernacular language **2:**465,
  3:690, **5:**1254
 water dynamics **1:**277
galleons **1:**63, **4:**1138, *1143,*
 5:1412
galleys **3:**715, 716, 717,
 5:1393, 1394, 1412
Gama, Vasco da **2:**374, 381,
 3:782, **4:**1139, 1142, 1144,
 5:1342, *1345*
geocentric universe **1:**265, 268,
 2:296, **5:**1249–1250, 1253
geography **2:**379, 384–385,
 4:1137
geology **1:**110
geometry **3:**827, 830, 833, 834
 architecture **1:**30–31, 36, 44
 education **2:**319
 perspective **2:**312
 Spinoza **5:**1294
gravitation **3:**783, 827, 834
Gregorian calendar **1:**173,
 175–177, **4:**1024–1025
Gutenberg, Johannes **1:**102,
 103, **3:***688,* 697, 775,
 780–781, 783, 805,
 5:1168, 1169, 1193, 1218,
 1220

H

Hakluyt, Richard **2:**375, 384,
 385
Harvey, William **3:**840,
 5:1251, 1255

heat **1:**83, **3:**786, 811
heliocentric universe **1:**60, 74,
 3:699, **5:**1249, 1250–1254
 Copernicus **1:**265, 269,
  270–271, 272, **4:**1109,
  5:1226, 1250
 Descartes **2:**296, 297
 Galileo **2:**464, 465, **4:**1036,
  1069
 heresy **1:**272, **2:**539, **4:**1036
 Kepler **1:**271
Hippocrates **3:**840, 844,
 5:1177
Hooke, Robert **5:**1258, 1433
hospitals **3:**842
Hudson, Henry **2:**374, 383,
 5:1342
hydrostatics **2:**461, 462

I

immunity **2:**302, 303, 306,
 307, 308
indigenous peoples
 Columbus **1:**250–251,
  252–253, 254, 255
 disease **1:**255, **2:**307, 308,
  382
 missionaries **4:**890–891, 892,
  893, 1015, **5:**1285
indigo **5:**1348
industrial revolution **3:**784,
 785–786, **5:**1259
inertia **2:**295
infinitesimals **3:**831, 832, 833
iron **3:**812
 cannon **5:**1408–1409
irrigation **1:**273, 276, 277,
 280, **3:**741, **5:**1402

J

Julian calendar **1:**174–175,
 176, 177, **4:**1024
junk (vessel) **5:***1343*
Jupiter (planet) **2:**464, **5:**1253

K

Kepler, Johannes **1:**121,
 2:463, 559, **3:**783, 828,
 4:1109
 astronomy **3:**1250,
  1251–1252

Copernicus **1:**271, 272
 mathematics **3:**828, 831,
  832

L

Las Casas, Bartolomé de
 1:*253,* **2:**400, **4:**891
latitude **2:**377
lead line **2:**376
leap year **1:**174, 176
Leeuwenhoek, Antoni van
 5:1258
Leonardo da Vinci **1:**133,
 2:437, 450, 560,
 3:706–714, 4:873
 contributions of **5:**1249
 hydraulic engineering **1:**277,
  278, 279
 machines **3:**775, 782, 783
 Renaissance **5:**1220, 1224
Leoniceno, Niccolò **3:**840,
 844
light rays **5:**1250
Lilly, William **1:**70, *72,* 73
Linnaeus, Carolus (Carl von
 Linné) **5:**1258, *1259*
Little Ice Age **2:**303
logarithms **3:**831
longitude **2:**376
lunar year **1:**173–174

M

machines **3:774–786,** 819
Magellan, Ferdinand **2:**373,
 374, 382, **3:787–794,**
 4:888, **5:**1250
man-of-war (ship) **3:**778, *786*
manufacturing **3:804–812,**
 4:1135–1136, **5:**1259
 books **3:**806
 cloth **3:**740, 741, 750, *753,*
  805
 factories **3:**786, 809
 German towns **2:**476, 477
 guilds **2:**497
 households **2:**562
 Italian city-states **3:**630, 632,
  633
 London **3:**750, *753*
 markets **3:**813
 Milan **3:**740, 741, *743*

trade **5:**1340, 1402
Venice **5:**1394
mapmaking *see* cartography
Maragha observatory (Persia)
  1:271
mathematics **3:**783, **827–834,**
  5:1250, 1251–1252
  architecture **1:**36
  Descartes **2:**294, 295, 296,
    301, **3:**828, 830, 833
  education **2:**319, *321*
  Galileo **2:**460, 461, 462,
    464, 465, 467, **3:**699
  Gregorian calendar **1:**174,
    175
  Hobbes **2:**542, 543, 544,
    546
  machines **3:**774, 775, **4:**776
  Newton **5:**1256–1257
  perspective **2:**312
  philosophy **4:**1063, 1068,
    1069, 1072, 1103
  Wren **5:**1430
Medicean stars **2:**464
medicine **3:**776, 829,
  840–848
  anatomy **2:**302, 303, 309
  astrology **1:**68–69
  Black Death **2:**306, 309
  Descartes **2:***196,* 301
  disease **2:**306, 309,
    3:843–844, 848
  guilds **3:**843
  Judaism **3:**671, 679
  plague **4:**1125
  public health **2:**305–306,
    4:1131–1132
  Rabelais **5:**1176, 1177, 1178
  science and technology
    5:1250, 1251, 1254, 1255
  syphilis **2:**310
  universities **5:**1367
Mercator, Gerardus **2:**384,
  385, **5:**1250
mercury **2:**310
Mersenne, Marin **2:**294, *295,*
  544
metalworking **2:**311, **3:**654,
  5:1284
Sweden **5:**1306, 1309, 1341
microbes *see* pathogens

microscope **2:**309–310, **3:**775,
  783, **5:**1254
mills **1:**24, 273, 279, 280,
  3:806, 807–808
  waterwheels **1:***278,*
    3:776–777, 809, 812
  wind power **1:**24, 275, 277,
    278, **3:**777–778, 804,
    807–808
moon **1:**268, **5:**1252–1253
  calendar **1:**173–174
  movement **1:**271
  surface **2:**463, 464
motion, theories of **2:**461–462
movable type *see* printing
Müller, Johann *see*
  Regiomontanus

N

National Edition of Galileo's
  Works **2:**466
naturalists **5:**1259
navigation **3:**693, 754, 775,
  4:914, *1065,* **5:**1250, 1283
  Columbus **1:**249, 251
  compass **2:**376, 384,
    3:778–779, **5:**1343
  exploration **2:**376–377, 378,
    380, 381
  Magellan **3:**787, 790
  Portugal **4:**1138, **5:**1345
  trade **5:**1340, 1341, 1343,
    1344–1345, 1349
Navigliaccio Canal **5:**1402
Newcomen, Thomas **3:**785
Newcomen engine **3:**785
Newton, Isaac **1:**262, **2:**467,
  3:783, 801, **4:**1072
  calculus **3:**827, 828, 833,
    834
  Cambridge University
    5:*1375*
  science **5:**1251, 1256–1257,
    1258, 1259
  Wren **5:**1430
Niña (Columbus ship) **1:**240,
  248, 251, **4:**1138
notebooks (Leonardo da Vinci)
  3:709–710, *711*
Núñez de Balboa, Vasco **2:**374,
  382

O

observatories **5:**1251
optics **2:**544, **3:**827, 831, 832

P

paper **3:**780, 805–806, **5:**1168
parachute **3:**775, **5:**1249
pathogens **2:**302, 306, 310
pendulum **2:**460, **5:**1433
Philosophical Transactions
  (journal) **5:**1256
physicians *see* medicine
physics **3:**830–831, **5:**1250,
  1256, 1257
  Descartes **2:**295, *297*
  Hooke **5:**1433
  Wren **5:**1429
physiology **5:**1251
Pinta (Columbus ship) **1:**248,
  250, 251, **4:**1138
Pinzón, Martín Alonso **1:**248,
  250, 251, 252
piston **3:**785
Pizarro, Francisco **2:**374,
  4:892
planetary motion **3:**783, 831,
  832, **5:**1249, 1251–1252
  Copernicus **1:**31, 60, 265,
    270
  Ptolemy **1:**266–267, 268
Pléiade, the **3:**721, 722, 723,
  725, 729, 730, **5:**1287
plow **1:**25, 27, 28, **4:**1134
polestar **2:**377
Polo, Marco **2:**373, **3:**804,
  5:1341
portolan charts **2:**376
predictions *see* astrology
press *see* printing
printing **3:**780–783, 805,
  5:1167–1175**
  Aristotle's works **1:**56, 58, 59
  bibles **1:**102, 103, 106–110,
    178, 180, **3:**591, 688,
    698–699, 761, **5:**1220
  Bohemia **1:**118, 122
  book fairs **3:**806, 819
  calendars **1:**173
  China **3:**774
  classical languages
    3:687–688, 690

education **2:**323
German towns **2:**482, 548,
  553
Greek texts **2:**320
humanism **2:**423, **3:**586,
  588, 591, 684, **5:**1218
literacy **2:**323, **5:**1172, 1174,
  1222
literature **1:**223, **3:**720, 739,
  754, **5:**1222
movable type **3:**775,
  780–781, 805, 806
music texts **4:**957
papacy **4:**1024
Paris **4:**1031
Portugal **4:**139
Rabelais **5:**1176
Reformation **1:**180–181,
  3:704, **5:**1173–1174,
  1175, 1192, 1193
Scotland **5:**1263
Shakespeare **5:**1271
Venice **5:**1394, 1399
vernaculars **3:**696, 697–699
women **5:**1421
probability **3:**829
Protagoras **5:**1368
Ptolemy, Claudius **1:***60*
  astrology **1:**69, **3:**830
  Columbus's worldview **1:**249
  Copernicus vs. 2, **1:**265,
    268–269, 270, 271,
    2:463, **3:**825.272
  exploration **2:**373, 374, 384
  Galileo **2:**466, **3:**699
  mathematics **3:**829, 830
  universe model **1:**266–269,
    2:296, **5:**1249–1250
Purchas, Samuel **2:**375, 377,
  379
Pythagoras **2:**334

Q

quadrant **2:**377, **3:**790,
  5:1250

R

Raleigh, Walter **3:**726, 751,
  825, **5:**1288
Regiomontanus **1:**174–175,
  265, 269, **3:**828, 829, 831

resistance theory **5:**1299
Roman calendar **1:**173–174
Rudolphine Tables **3:***831,* 832

S

Sagres observatory **3:**693
sailing ships **2:**373, **3:**777–778
Santa María (Columbus ship)
  1:248, 250, 251, 252
science and technology **2:**559,
  3:782–783, 784,
  5:1248–1259
  agriculture **1:**21, 24, 25,
    26–27, 28, 29, **4:**1134
  Aristotle **1:**53, 57, 59,
    60–61, 81
  astrology **1:**74
  Bacon **1:**80–82, 83
  Brunelleschi **1:**156
  Copernicus **1:**265–272
  dams and drainage
    1:273–281
  Descartes **2:**294, 295, 296,
    297
  education **2:**319, 325
  Galileo **2:**460–468, **3:**690,
    699
  Greek studies **2:**320
  heresy **2:**539
  Hobbes **2:**542, 543, 544,
    546
  Hooke **5:**1433
  Leonardo da Vinci **3:**709,
    710
  machines **3:**774–786, 819
  manufacturing **3:**804–812
  mathematics **3:**827,
    830–831, 832
  natural philosophy **4:**1065,
    1067–1068, 1069, 1070,
    1072
  Renaissance **5:**1221, 1226
  seafaring **5:**1343, 1347
  vernaculars **3:**693, 696, 699
  warfare **5:**1309, 1407–1415
  Wren **5:**1429–1430
  see also medicine; printing
scientific method **1:**60, **2:**468,
  532, 546
Seven Golden Cities of Cibola
  2:382

sextant **5:**1250
solar year **1:**174
Soto, Hernando de **2:**382,
  4:888
stars **1:***67,* 68, *69,* 266, 271
steam engine **3:**775, 785, 786,
  812, **5:**1259
Stevin, Simon **1:**275, **3:**831,
  5:1250
Stjerneborg observatory **5:**1251
sun **2:**464, 465, 467 *see also*
  heliocentric universe
supernova **1:**50, **2:**463
surgeons **2:**302, **3:**840, 841,
  843
sweating sickness **3:**841

T

tangents **3:**833
telescope **1:**60, **2:**539, **3:**699,
  775, 783, **4:**1069, **5:**1250,
  1251, 1252, 1253, 1258
  Descartes **2:***297*
  Galileo **1:**271, **2:**460, 463,
    464, **3:**774
thermometer **3:**775
tidal mills **3:**808
timekeeping **3:**775, 779–780,
  790
Tordesillas, Treaty of (1494)
  2:381, 382, **3:**788, **4:**889,
  1142
trigonometry **3:**728, 828, 829,
  831, 834

U

universe **2:**463, 464, 465, 467,
  539
Uraniborg observatory **5:**1251

V

vacuum pump **3:**775
Venus (planet) **2:**464
vernal equinox **1:**174, 176
Verrazano, Giovanni da **2:**382,
  4:914
Vesalius, Andreas **2:**302, 303,
  3:840, 845, 846, 848,
  5:1250, 1254
Vespucci, Amerigo **1:***254,* 255,
  2:*374,* 382

Vierlingh, Andries **1:**274–275,
  276, 281
viruses **2:**302, 310

W

weather forecasts **1:**68
weather gauge **1:**66
wheel lock **3:**782
woad (blue dye) **5:**1350, 1402

Index of Wars and Battles

A **boldface** number preceding a colon indicates the volume. Numbers in *italics* refer to captions. Numbers entirely in **boldface** refer to a full article.

A

Adrianopolis, Peace of (1568) **2:**557

Agincourt, Battle of (1415) **1:16–20,** 159, **2:**434–435, **3:**599–600, *603,* **4:**1030, **5:***1412,* 1413
- nationalism **4:**968
- Shakespeare **5:**1272

Agnadello, Battle of (1509) **3:**647

Alais, Peace of (1629) **2:**458

Aljubarrota, Battle of (1385) **4:**1137

Alte Veste, Battle of (1632) **5:**1415

Altmark, Truce of (1629) **5:**1334–1335

Amalfi, Battle of (1528) **3:**645

Amboise, Peace of (1563) **2:**453, 454

American Revolution **1:**28

Ankara, Battle of (1402) **3:**617

Arbedo, Battle of (1422) **5:**1413

archers **1:***16, 17,* 18, 19, 20, **2:**435, **3:**596, *597,* 600, 653, **5:**1412–1413

archery butts **3:**751

armada, Spanish **1:62–66,** 238, **4:**909, 1145, **5:**1347, 1412
- Cervantes **1:**204
- Elizabeth I **2:**331, 332
- Philip II **4:**1058

armor **1:**221, 226, **3:***743,* 793

Arras, Treaty of (1435) **1:**160, **3:**602, 660

artillery **2:***435,* **3:**651, **5:**1335

artillery towers **5:**1410

Austrian War **3:**628

B

Bannockburn, Battle of (1314) **4:**905, **5:**1413

Barnet, Battle of (1471) **2:**408

Barwalde, Treaty of (1631) **5:**1337

Basel, Peace of (1499) **5:**1313

Basinghouse, siege of (1645) **3:**668

battles *see keywords*

Billericay, Battle of (1381) **4:**1047

Bishops' Wars (1639) **2:**349, 350, **5:**1267

Bobâlna Revolt (Hungary) **4:**1042

Bologna, Concordat of (1516) **2:**447, **3:**701

Bosworth Field, Battle of (1485) **1:**233

Breisach, Battle of (1638) **5:**1338

Breitenfeld, Battle of (1631) **3:**839, **5:**1137, 1310, 1338

Bretigny, Treaty of (1360) **3:**597, 598

Brömsebro, Peace of (1645) **5:**1338

Brunkeberg, Battle of (1471) **5:**1304

Brussels, Treaty of (1522) **2:**510

C

Cambrai, Treaty of (1529) **3:**643, 647

Cambrai, War of the League of **5:**1394, 1400

cannon **3:**618, 775, **5:**1341, 1407–1409, 1411, 1415
- armada, Spanish **1:**63, 65, 66
- Hundred Years War **3:**596
- Lepanto, Battle of **3:**717
- naval **5:**1412
- standardization **5:**1408

catapult **5:***1249, 1407,* 1408, 1409

Cateau-Cambrésis, Peace of (1559) **2:***420,* 421, **3:**643, 644, 649, **4:**1058, 1059, **5:**1221, 1233, 1265

cavalry **2:***409,* **3:**597, 651
- chivalry **1:**221
- English civil wars **2:***352*

firearms **5:**1414, 1415
- pikemen vs. **5:**1309, 1313, 1314, 1413
- warfare **5:**1411, 1412, 1414

Chaldiran, Battle of (1514) **3:**623

Cherasco, Treaty of (1631) **5:**1336

Cherbourg, surrender of (1450) **3:**603

Chioggia, War of **5:**1395

Chmiehicki massacres (1648) **3:**675

Ciompi revolt (1378) **2:**415, 417, 419, **3:**636–637

civil war *see* English civil wars; French civil wars

Coligny, Gaspard II de **1:**199, 200, **2:**452–453, 454, 455

condottieri *see* mercenaries

Cornish Rebellion (1497) **4:**1042

corsairs *see* piracy and privateering

Cossacks **3:**675, **4:**936, 938, 1113–1114, **5:**1337

Crécy, Battle of (1346) **1:**117, **2:**434, 435, **3:**596–597, 598, **5:***1412,* 1413

Crépy, Peace of (1544) **1:**209

Croquants rebellion **2:**456

crossbow **2:**435

cross-staff **5:**1343

Crusades **3:**618, 619, 715
- Burgundy **1:**158, 162
- chivalric orders **1:**223, 226
- Constantinople sacking **1:**168, 259–260, **5:**1393
- Pius II **4:**1086–1088, 1089
- Teutonic Knights **4:**1104, 1106, 1107
- trade **5:**1341
- Venice **1:**259–260, **5:**1392–1393

Czech civil war **1:**119

D

Danish War **5:**1335–1336

Deulino, Truce of (1618) **4:**940

Diu, Battle of (1509) **4:**1142

Dreux, Battle of (1562) **2:**452, **5:**1411

E

earthworks **5:**1407, 1410

Edgehill, Battle of (1642) **2:**351, **4:**883

Edinburgh, Treaty of (1560) **5:**1266

English civil wars **1:**73, 109, 239, **2:**328, 346, **347–355,** 372, **4:**1048, 1066, **5:**1256
- Hobbes **2:**543, 544, 545, 546
- iconoclasm **3:**609
- Jones **3:**668
- longbow **5:**1413
- Milton **4:**883, 884, 886
- monarchy **4:**904, 906, 912
- Scotland **5:**1262, 1265, 1267
- Stuarts **5:**1302, 1303
- theater closures **5:**1325, 1329

Thirty Years War **5:**1336

Esztergom, siege of (1604) **5:**1415

F

Falkirk, Battle of (1297) **4:**905

Ferrara, War of **3:**741

field artillery **5:**1335

firearms **1:**226, **3:**717, **5:**1407, 1411, 1413–1414, 1415
- gunpowder **3:**774, 775
- musket **5:**1335, 1413
- wheel lock **3:**782
- *see also* cannon

First Crusade **1:**223

Flodden, Battle of (1513) **5:**1261, 1297

fortifications **2:**410–411, **3:**651, **5:**1335, 1407, 1409–1411
- chivalric laws **1:**222

Fourth Crusade **1:**259–260, **5:**1392–1393

Freiburg, Battle of (1638) **5:**1338

French and Swedish War
  5:1137–1138
French civil wars **1**:279,
  2:440–443, 448, **451–459**,
  556, **3**:707, **5**:1331
  Calvinism **1**:183, *184*
  Catherine de Médicis
    1:198–200
  Francis I **2**:448
  Henry IV **2**:516–520, 540
  Hundred Years War **3**:599,
    600
  mercenaries **5**:1411
  Paris **4**:1031–1034
  Spain **4**:1058, 1060
French Revolution **1**:28, **4**:887

G

Garigliano, Battle of (1503)
  3:644–645
Granada, Treaty of (1500)
  3:644
Granson, Battle of (1476)
  5:*1313*, 1314
Great Northern War **4**:941
Greenwich, Treaty of (1543)
  2:528
gunpowder **3**:774, 775,
  5:1309, 1335, 1407–1409,
  1408 *see also* cannon;
  firearms
Gustavus II Adolphus, king of
  Sweden **5**:1309, 1332

H

Hague, Treaty of (1625)
  5:1335
Hannibal **4**:1052
Harfleur, siege of (1415) **1**:16,
  17
Heilbronn, Treaty of (1632)
  5:1337
holy war **3**:612, 616, 626
Hundred Years War **1**:160,
  2:434–435, 445,
  3:595–603, **4**:1136,
  5:*1412*, 1413
  Agincourt **1**:16–20,
    3:599–600
  Aquitaine **2**:413
  Burgundy **1**:158, 160, 162

Joan of Arc **3**:602, 657–662,
  5:1427
  monarchy **4**:911
  nationalism **4**:965, 968
  Paris **4**:1029–1030
  peasants' revolts **4**:1042,
    1047
Hussite wars **2**:549

I

infantry **1**:226, **3**:651
  tactics **5**:1309, 1313, 1314
Italian wars **1**:279, **2**:550,
  3:630, 633, 639, 642,
  643–651, 853, **4**:986,
  5:1220
  Charles V **1**:208, 210, 241,
    242–243, **2**:413, 421,
    555, **3**:702
  Florence **2**:419, 420, 421
  France **2**:437–438, 444
  Francis I **1**:221, **2**:445, 446,
    555
  Leo X **3**:701, 702–703
  Lombardy **3**:742–743, 745,
    746
  Naples **1**:244, **2**:412
  nationalism **4**:966
  Rome **5**:1231, 1233
  syphilis **2**:310

J

Jam-Zapolski, Peace of (1582)
  see Yam Zapolsky, Truce of
janissaries **3**:617, 622, 626,
  629
Jankov, Battle of (1645)
  5:1338
Jarnac, Battle of (1569) **2**:452
Jasna Góra siege (1655)
  4:1114
Joan of Arc **1**:160, **2**:435,
  3:602, **657–662**, **4**:968,
  5:1427
Joinville, Treaty of (1584)
  2:457
Jülich Succession, War of the
  2:560, **5**:1334
just-war theory **2**:357
Jüterbog, Battle of (1645)
  5:1338

K

Kappel, Battle of (1531)
  5:1194, 1315
Kosovo, Battle of (1444) **1**:263
Ksar al-Kebir, Battle of (1578)
  4:1140
Kulikovo Field, Battle of
  (1380) **4**:934

L

La Bicocca, Battle of (1522)
  3:646, 650
La-Charité-sur-Loire, siege of
  (1429) **2**:454, **3**:658
Ladies, Peace of the (1529)
  2:446, 448
Landshut War **2**:549
La Rochelle, siege of (1627)
  2:454, 458, *459*, **5**:1336
Lech, Battle of the **3**:839
Lepanto, Battle of (1571)
  1:63, **3**:626, **715–719**,
  4:*1058*, 1060
  Cervantes **1**:202, 203, 206
Livonian war **4**:937
London, Treaty of (1518)
  2:522
longbow **1**:*16*, 18, **2**:435,
  5:1412–1413
Longjumeau, Peace of (1568)
  2:454
Lutter am Barenberge, Battle
  of (1626) **5**:1335
Lützen, Battle of (1632)
  1:227, **5**:1310, 1337, 1415

M

Madrid, Treaty of (1526)
  1:242, **2**:446, **3**:647
Mantuan Succession, War of
  the **3**:745, **5**:1336
Marignano, Battle of (1515)
  1:221, **2**:445, **3**:646
Marston Moor, Battle of
  (1644) **2**:351, *353*
Meaux, siege of (1422) **3**:601
mercenaries **2**:409, **3**:651,
  5:1181, 1395, 1403, 1411,
  1413
Milan, Peace of (1639) **5**:1334
military tank **5**:1249

Militia Ordinance (1641)
  2:350
Mirandola fortress **3**:650
Mohács, Battle of (1526)
  1:243, **3**:618, 623
Moncontour, Battle of (1569)
  5:*1414*
Monsieur, Peace of (1576)
  2:456, 457
Montcontour, Battle of (1569)
  2:452
Morat, Battle of (1477)
  5:1314
Mühlberg, Battle of (1547)
  1:75, 211, **2**:554
Münster, siege of (1534,
  1535) **2**:540
musket **5**:1335, 1413
musketeers **5**:1309, 1415

N

Najéra, Battle of (1367) **3**:598
Nancy, Battle of (1477) **1**:163,
  5:1314, 1413
Naseby, Battle of (1645)
  2:352
naval warfare **5**:1347, 1412
  armada, Spanish **1**:62–66
  Italian wars **3**:650
  Lepanto, Battle of
    3:715–719
  ship design **3**:778, 786,
    5:1412
Nérac, Treaty of **1**:200
Nevel, Battle of (1562) **3**:654
Neville's Cross, Battle of
  3:597
*New Manner of Fortification
  by Sluices* (Stevin) **1**:275
New Model Army **2**:351–352,
  353, 354
Nicopolis, Battle of (1396)
  1:158, **3**:616–617
Nijmegen, Treaty of (1678)
  2:512
Nike Revolt **1**:172
Nine Years War **5**:1290
Nonsuch, Treaty of (1585)
  2:327
Nördlingen, Battle of (1634)
  5:1310, 1337

Norman Conquest (1066) **2**:403, 494, 496, **3**:595, 691

Northern Seven Years War **4**:*1113*

Novara, Battle of (1513) **3**:645

O

Öland, Battle of (1564) **4**:*1113*

Orléans, siege of (1429) **3**:601, 602, 657, 658, 660

Orsha, Battle of (1514) **4**:1109

P

Palatine War **5**:1334

Passau, Treaty of (1552) **1**:75, 76

Patay, Battle of (1429) **3**:659

Pavia, Battle of (1525) **2**:446, 555, **3**:643, 646, 647
    Charles V **1**:208, *242*
    Peace of *see keywords*

Peasants' Revolt of 1381 (England) **1**:216, **3**:598, **4**:1041, 1042–1048

peasants' revolts **1**:216, **3**:762, 767, **4:1041–1048**
    France **2**:433, 456, **4**:1029, 1042, *1044*
    German towns **1**:187, **2**:*475*, 479, 480
    Holy Roman Empire **2**:555, 558, **4**:1042
    Paris **4**:1029
    preaching **5**:1162
    Sweden **5**:1305

Peasants' War **1**:187, **2**:475, 479, 480, **4**:1042

pikes and pikemen **5**:1412, 1413
    Sweden **5**:1309
    Switzerland **5**:1313–1314, 1413
    Thirty Years War **5**:1335

piracy and privateering **2**:502, 505, **5**:1394, 1412
    Barbary coast **1**:208, 209, 211, **3**:626, *627,* 716, **5**:1347

Cervantes as captive **1**:202, 204
    England **2**:331

Pisan Wars **1**:279

pistol **5**:1414

Poitiers, Battle of (1356) **1**:157, **2**:434, 435, **3**:597, 598, **4**:1029

Porta Camollia, Battle of (1555) **3**:649

Prague, Peace of (1635) **5**:1337

Prayer Book Rebellion (1637) **5**:1262

Preveza, Battle of (1538) **3**:715

Pride's Purge (1648) **2**:354

privateers *see* piracy and privateering

Puritan Revolution *see* English civil wars

R

ransom **1**:222, 225

Ravenna, Battle of (1512) **3**:643, 645

religious wars *see* French civil wars; Thirty Years War

Remençes, Rebellion of the **4**:1042

Rheinfelden, Battle of (1638) **5**:1338

Rhodes, siege of (1480) **3**:619, **5**:1408

Roosebeke, Battle of (1382) **1**:157

Roses, Wars of the **1**:17, 233, **2**:408, **4**:911, 912, **5**:1271, 1411

Rostock, Battle of (1636) **5**:1338

Runnymede, Battle of (1215) **4**:906

Ruthven Raiders **5**:1262

S

Saint-Germain, Peace of (1570) **1**:200, **2**:454

Saint-Pierre-le-Moutier, Battle of (1429) **3**:658

Saint Quentin, Battle of (1557) **4**:1056, 1059

Sankt Jakob an der Birs, Battle of (1444) **5**:1314

San Quentin, Battle of (1557) **4**:1060

Sauchieburn, Battle of (1488) **5**:1261, 1296

Schmalkalden, Battle of (1547) **5**:1336

sea battles *see* naval warfare

Second Bishops' War **2**:349

Second Schmalkaldic War **1**:75

Senta, Battle of (1697) **2**:513

shields **2**:*410*

Shrewsbury, Battle (1403) **1**:17

Sluys, Battle of (1340) **3**:596

Smolensk, War of **5**:1337

Solway Moss, Battle of (1542) **2**:527, **5**:1261, 1297

Stalingrad, Battle of (1942) **4**:1107

Stångebro, Battle of (1598) **5**:1308

Stolbova, Peace of (1617) **4**:940, **5**:1309, 1334

Swedish-Polish War **5**:1309, 1334–1335

T

Tannenberg, Battle of (1410) **1**:223, **4**:1106, 1107

Tannenberg, Battle of (1914) **4**:1107

Thionville, Battle of (1638) **5**:1338

Third Crusade **2**:505

Thirty Years War **1**:46, 183, **3**:767, **4**:911, 914, 1040, 1057, **5**:1191, 1225, 1246, **1330–1339**, 1415
    Augsburg, Peace of **1**:77, 78
    Bohemia **1**:121–122
    dams and drainage **1**:279
    established churches **2**:371–372
    German towns **2**:476, 477, 478, 480, 514, *540,* 541
    Holy Roman Empire **2**:476, 480, 481, 483, 514, 558, 560
    James I **2**:343
    Maximilian I **3**:835–839

Poland **1**:228, **4**:1113

printed propaganda **5**:1174

Stuarts **5**:1301, 1302, 1336

Sweden **1**:227, 228, **5**:1307, 1310, 1330, 1333–1338

Swiss neutrality **5**:1315
    see also Westphalia, Peace of

Three Henrys, War of the **2**:454, 458

Tilly, count of *see* Tserclaes, Johann

Toro, Battle of (1476) **5**:1277

Tours, Truce of (1444) **3**:602

Troyes, Treaty of (1420) **1**:17, 160, **3**:601, **4**:1030

Tserclaes, Johann, count of Tilly **3**:835, 836, 837, 838, 839, **5**:1333, 1334, 1335, 1337, 1415

V

Varna, Battle of (1444) **3**:618

Vervins, Peace of (1598) **2**:458, **4**:1058, 1060

W

Wallenstein, Albrecht von **3**:838–839, **5**:1332, 1333, 1334, 1335, 1337
    overview of **5**:1415

warfare **5:1407–1415**
    Agincourt **1**:16–20
    archers **3**:596, *597,* 600
    armada, Spanish **1**:62–66
    chivalric laws **1**:221, 222, 224, 226
    chivalric orders **1**:223
    dams and drainage **1**:279
    feudalism **2**:402–403, 408–412
    France **2**:433, 449, 451, 458, 520
    Gustavus II Adolphus **5**:1309, 1332
    Henry VIII **2**:521, 522, 527
    Holy Roman Empire **2**:554, 555
    Hundred Years War **2**:435, **3**:596, 597
    Islam **3**:612, 616, 617, 618, 628–629

warfare (cont.)
Italian soldiers **3:**651
Italy **3:**632, 651
Japan **4:**1142
Joan of Arc **3:**658, 659,
660–661
knighthood **1:**221, 225
Leonardo innovations **3:**710,
711, **5:**1249
Lepanto **3:**715–719
Machiavelli **3:**770, 772, 773
mercantilism **5:**1351
mercenaries **5:**1395, 1403,
1411
monarchy **4:**908–909, 912
Muscovy **4:**936–937, 938,
939, 940, 941
nationalism **4:**967–968, 970
naval forces **3:**650, 715–719,
778, 786, **5:**1347, 1412
Ottoman Turks **3:**617, 618,
622, 623, 624, 626, 628,
629, 717, 719
papacy **4:**1090
pikes **5:**1309, 1313–1314,
1335, 1412, 1413
Poland-Lithuania **4:**1104,
1106, 1107, 1109,
1112–1114
political philosophy **4:**1066
population effects **4:**1136
Portugal **4:**1142
Renaissance changes **5:**1335
Russia **3:**653, 654
Safavids **3:**628–629
Spain **4:**1145
Sweden **5:**1309
Switzerland **5:**1313–1314,
1315
technology **3:**774, 775, 782,
786
Thirty Years War **5:**1335
tournaments **1:**225
trade **5:**1341
Venice **5:**1395
Viscontis **5:**1403, 1404,
1406
see also cannon; firearms;
specific battles and wars
wars of religion *see* French civil
wars; Thirty Years War

Westphalia, Peace of (1648)
1:46, **2:**511, *540,* 541,
3:836, 839, **4:**914, **5:**1191,
1200, 1234, 1246, 1330,
1333, 1338
Christina **1:**228
German towns **2:**478, 480,
483
religious toleration **5:**1339
Sweden **5:**1307, 1310, 1311,
1330
White Mountain, Battle of
(1620) **1:**122, **3:**836, 838,
4:1040, **5:**1192, 1334,
1335, 1336
World War I **2:**512, **3:**629,
4:1107
World War II **4:**1107, 1112,
5:1312

X
Xanten, Treaty of (1614)
5:1334

Y
Yam Zapolsky, Truce of (1582)
3:656, **4:**1112

Comprehensive Index

A **boldface** number preceding a colon indicates the volume. Numbers in *italics* refer to captions. Numbers entirely in **boldface** refer to a full article.

A

Aachen **1:**77
Aar River **4:**507
abacists **3:**827
abacus schools **2:**319
Abbas I, shah of Persia **3:**612, 622
Abbas II, shah of Persia **1:***280*
Abduction of Proserpina (Bernini) **1:***98*, 99
Aberdeen University **5:**1263
Abraham (prophet) **3:**610, **4:**1084, 1085
Absalom, fili mi (Josquin) **4:**948
absolutism
  Hobbes **2:**544, 546
  monarchy **4:**906–907
  state vs. church **2:**367, 368
  see also divine right
Abulafia, Abraham **3:**680
Academy, Plato's **4:**1063, 1090, 1095, **5:**1365
Academy of Design (Florence) **2:**469–470
Academy of Geneva **5:**1195
Accademia de' Desiosi (Venice) **2:***469*, 471
Accademia degli Intornati (Siena) **3:**734
Accademia dei Lincei **2:**464–465
Accademia dell'Arcadia (Rome) **1:**230, **4:**1068
Accademia Olympica (Vicenza) **1:**43, **4:**1001, 1006–1007
Accession Day Tilts (England) **1:**225
Account of Denmark As It Was in the Year 1692, An (Molesworth) **5:**1311
Account of Virtue, An (More) **4:**1070–1071

Acqua Paola (Travastere) **4:**1040
Acquaviva y Aragon, Giulio **1:**202
Acropolis (Athens) **4:***1095*
Act in Restraint of Appeals to Rome (England) **5:**1197
Act of Six Articles (England) **3:**608
Act of Succession (England) **4:**931
Act of Supremacy (England) **2:**327, 328, 338, 339, 340, 341, 524, **4:**931, 932, **5:**1374
Act of Uniformity (England) **2:**327, 328, 341
actors *see* theater
Acts and Monuments of the Church (Foxe) **1:***187, 232*
Acts of the Apostles **1:**193, **3:***695,* **4:**1102
Adagia (Adages) (Erasmus) **2:**357, **3:**684, 688
Adam and Eve **1:**185, **4:**1064, *1066*
Adams, John **4:**887
Ad Atticus (Cicero) **3:**584, 589, 682, 683, 684, **4:**1053
Adda River **5:**1334
adding machine **3:**775
Admiral's Men (London theater) **3:**824
Adnotationes novi testamenti (Valla) **3:**586
Adolf II of Schauenburg **2:**503
Adoration of the Magi (Botticelli) **1:**135, 138, **5:***1219*
Adoration of the Mystic Lamb (Eyck) **2:**386, 387, 390, 392
Adoration of the Name of Jesus (El Greco) **4:***1058*
Adoration of the Shepherds (Caravaggio) **1:**194
Adoration of the Shepherds (Rubens) **5:**1238
Adoration of the Shepherds with Saints Lawrence and Francis (Caravaggio) **1:**194

Adorno, Antoniotto **3:**650
Adorno, Giuliano **5:**1420
Adramyttenus, Emanuel **4:**1073
Adrian VI, Pope **1:**210, **4:**1023, **5:**1380
  Clement VII **1:**241, 242
Adrianople **3:**612
Adrianopolis, Peace of (1568) **2:**557
Adriatic Sea **1:**276, **2:**414, **3:**715, 741, **5:**1392, 1393, 1394, 1401
adult baptism **1:**178, **5:**1194, 1195, 1314
adultery **2:**326, 566, 568
Advancement of Learning (F. Bacon) **1:**80, **3:**775, **4:**1065, 1067–1068, 1072
Adventures of Master F. J. (Gascoigne) **3:**738
Advertisements to the Jurymen of England (Filmer) **3:**803
Aegean Sea **1:**262, **3:**619
Aeken, Anthonis van **1:**127, 128
Aeken, Goossen van **1:**128
Aeneas, Anchises, and Ascanius Fleeing Troy (Bernini) **1:**98
Aeneid (Virgil) **4:**1144
  Surrey translation **3:**823
Aeschylus **3:**685
Affair of the Placards **5:**1177, 1178
Affected Young Ladies, The (Molière) **4:**899
Afghanistan **3:**615
Afonso V, king of Portugal **4:**1144, **5:**1277
Africa
  Cheng Ho voyage **5:**1342
  Columbus voyage **1:**247
  exploration **2:**373, 374, 379, 380, 381, **4:**914, **5:**1346
  Islam **3:**611, 612, 613
  missionaries **4:**888, 895
  Portugal **4:**1137, 1140–1141, 1142
  slave trade **1:**255, **4:**1141, **5:**1285, 1342, 1345, 1348, 1349

  trade **5:**1341
  warfare **4:***1140*
  see also North Africa; *specific countries*
Africa (Petrarch) **4:***1050,* 1052
afterlife **2:**430, 431
Age of Exploration *see* exploration
Agincourt, Battle of (1415) **1:16–20, 3:**599–600, *603,* **4:**1030
  Burgundy **1:**159
  France **2:**434–435
  longbow **5:***1412,* 1413
  nationalism **4:**968
  Shakespeare **5:**1272
Agnadello, Battle of (1509) **3:**647
Agricola **1:***279*
agriculture **1:21–29, 4:***1121*
  astrological prediction **1:**68
  Black Death **2:**306
  calendar **1:**177
  city provisions **4:**1132, 1134
  Columbian exchange **1:**255
  dams and drainage **1:**28, 273–277, 280
  festivals **4:**1118
  food shortages **2:**479, **4:**1028, 1124
  France **2:**433, 456
  households **2:**562
  irrigation **1:**273, 276, 277, 280, **3:**741, **5:**1402
  Italian city-states **3:**630
  Leonardo sketches **3:**710
  Lombardy **3:**740, 741
  markets and fairs **3:**813, 814, 818, 821
  Muscovy **4:**937
  peasants' revolts **4:**1041–1048
  population **4:**1114, 1124, 1126, 1127, 1134–1135
  Scotland **5:**1260
  trade **5:**1340, 1341, 1346, 1348, 1401
  Viscontis **5:**1401, 1402
  see also famine
Agrippa, Marsilio **3:**799
agronomy **1:**25

Ahnlund, Nils **5:**1339

Aix-en-Provence, University of **5:**1371

Akbar, Mogul emperor **1:***71,* **3:**615

Akbarnama (Mogul text) **3:***615*

Alais, Peace of (1629) **2:**458

Alba, duke of **1:***190,* **2:**454, 556, **4:**1057, 1060, **5:**1233

Alba Madonna (Raphael) **5:**1185

Albania **1:**170

Albergati, Niccolò **4:**1086

Albert III, archduke of Austria **2:**507, 508

Albert IV, archduke of Austria **2:**508

Albert V, archduke of Austria **2:**508

Albert I, king of Germany **2:**509

Albert II, king of Germany **2:**509

Albert, archduke of Spain **5:**1241

Alberti, Leon Battista **1:**139, 154, **3:**847, **4:**984–985, 987, 989, 1001

  architecture **1:**30–31, 32, 34, 35–36, 37

  Florence **2:***418*

  Lombardy **3:**745

  mathematics **3:**827

  Rome **5:**1229

Albert of Brandenburg **3:**704, **4:**1107, **5:**1190

Albertoni, Ludovica **1:**100

Albertus Magnus **1:**52, 56, **3:**797

Albigensian crusade **2:**531

Albigensians *see* Cathars

Albizzi, Rinaldo **2:**417, 420

Albizzis, the **2:**417, **3:**850

Albornoz, Gil Álvarez Carillo de **5:**1378

Albret, Charles d' **1:**17, 18

Album amicorum (Walens) **5:***1327*

Albuquerque, Afonso de **4:**1143

Alcalá **3:**689

Alcalá, duke of **2:**471

Alcalá, University of **1:**109, **5:**1282

Alcalá de Henares **1:**202, 203, 204

alchemy **2:**296, **3:**800–801

Alciati, Andrea **1:**179

Alcionio, Pietro **5:**1233

Alderman, Court of **3:**751

aldermen **3:**751, 752

Aldine Press **5:**1399

Aldus Manutius *see* Manutius, Aldus

Alemán, Mateo **3:**738, 739

Alembert, Jean d' **2:**466, 516

Alençon, duke of **2:**456, 457, 517

Alexander III, Pope **4:**1137

Alexander IV, Pope **3:**693

Alexander VI, Pope **4:**948, 1011, 1016, **5:**1231, 1279

  Borgia, Lucrezia **1:**123–124, 126

  exploration **2:**381

  heresy **2:**533

  Leo X **3:**700

  missionaries **4:**888–889

  Pico della Mirandola **4:**1074, 1077

  Urbino **5:**1379

Alexander VII, Pope **1:**100, 229–230, 231

Alexander VIII, Pope **2:**372

Alexander II (the Great), king of Macedonia **1:***59,* 167, 224, **3:***595*

Alexander Nevsky **4:**933

Alexander of Aphrodisias **1:**56

alexandrine **3:**731

Alexis I, emperor of Russia **4:**940, *941,* 1113

Alfonso V (the Magnanimous), king of Aragon **2:**412, **3:**619, **4:**1091, **5:**1279

Alfonso VI, king of Castile and León **4:**1137

Alfonso X (the Wise), king of Castile **3:**693

Alfonso III, duke of Mantua **5:***1206*

Alfonso I, king of Naples *see* Alfonso V, king of Aragon

Alfonso II, king of Naples **3:**644

Alfonso V, king of Portugal *see* Afonso V

Alfonso of Aragon **1:**124

Alfonso of Cartagena **1:**54

Alfonso of Castile **2:**393

algebra **3:**827, 829–830, 833, 834

Algeria **1:**202

Algiers **1:**109, 202, 211, **3:**624, **5:**1347

Alhambra Palace **2:***396*

Alicante Dam (Tibi Dam) **1:**280

Ali ibn Abi Talib **3:**620, 621

Aljubarrota, Battle of (1385) **4:**1137

Allde, John **5:**1324

allegory **4:**1094–1095, **5:**1318–1319, 1328

Allegory (Raphael) *see Knight's Dream, The*

Allegory of Commerce, The (Amman) **5:***1344*

Allegory of Painting (Gentileschi) **2:**472–473

Allegory of Peace and Arts under the English Crown, The (Gentileschi) **2:**474

Allegory on Charles V as Ruler of the World (Rubens) **5:***1200*

Allegretti, Allegretto **1:**281

"Allegro, L'" (Milton) **4:**880

Alleyne, Edward **3:**824, **5:**1268

alliterative verse **1:**220

All Saints' Day **2:**387

All Souls' Day **4:**1118

All's Well That Ends Well (Shakespeare) **5:**1272

Almagest (Ptolemy) **1:**265, 267, 269, **3:**728

almanacs **1:**68, 173, 174–175

Almansa Dam **1:**280

Almeida, Francisco de **3:**787, **4:**1142

Almonry School (Saint Paul's Cathedral) **1:**212

Alps **1:**157, **3:**741, **5:**1393, 1394

Alpujarras Mountains **2:**397

altarpieces **3:**709, **5:***1163, 1279*

  Caravaggio **1:**194, 195, *196*

  Carracci **1:**195

  Dürer **2:**313

  Eyck **2:**386, 387, 390, 392

  Giotto **2:**490, 491, *492*

  Raphael **5:**1182

  Rubens **5:**1238

  seven sacraments **5:***1357*

Altdorf, University of **5:**1367, 1377

Altenberg abbey (Germany) **3:***607*

Alte Veste, Battle of (1632) **5:**1415

Altieri Chapel (Ripa) **1:**100

Altmark, Truce of (1629) **5:**1334–1335

alumbrados (mystics) **5:**1283

Álvarez, duke of Toledo **5:**1164

Alviano, Bartolomeo Liviano d' **3:**651

Amadis of Gaul **1:**222–223

Amalfi, Battle of (1528) **3:**645

Amati, Andrea **4:**943, 958

Amboise **3:**707, 714

Amboise, Peace of (1563) **2:**453, 454

Ambrose, Saint **3:**745

Ambrosian rite **3:**745

American Indians *see* indigenous peoples

American Revolution **1:**28

Americas

  agriculture **1:**28

  architecture **1:**46, 49

  Calvinism **1:**178, 189, 190

  chartered companies **2:**501

  colonial iconoclasm **3:**609

  Columbus **1:**248, 250–255, **2:**306

  dam designs **1:**280

  disease **1:**255, **2:**306–309, 382

established churches **2**:367
exploration **2**:374, 375,
    381–384, 385, **3**:693,
    4:914, 915, **5**:1220,
    1342, 1345
  Holy Roman Empire **2**:511
  Huguenot émigrés **5**:1331
  inventions **3**:776
  Jesuits **4**:1015, **5**:1206
  Magellan voyage **3**:790–791
  missionaries **3**:792, **4**:888–
    896, 891, 892, 1015
  naturalists **5**:1259
  Philip II **4**:1060
  Portugal **4**:1142
  Puritans **1**:189, **2**:328,
    5:1375
  religious orders **4**:1015,
    5:1206, 1209
  Scholasticism **1**:58
  scientific exploration **5**:1259
  settlement colonies **5**:1342,
    1346–1347
  slave trade **5**:1342, 1348,
    1349
  Spain **1**:207, **2**:400,
    4:889–890, 966,
    5:1283–1284, 1285, 1345
  trade **2**:481, **3**:633, 719,
    5:1344, 1345–1346, 1348
  universities **2**:325
  witch hunts **5**:1425
  see also specific countries
Americae Tertia Pars (Bry)
    1:251
Amiata, Monte **4**:1090
Amman, Jost **5**:1344
Amoretti (Spenser) **5**:1287,
    1289
Amorum emblemata (Veen)
    5:1236
ampullae **4**:1082
Amsterdam **2**:299
  banking **1**:90
  dikes **1**:275
  Jewish community **3**:681
  Rembrandt **5**:1211, 1212
  Renaissance map **1**:281
  Spinoza **5**:1291, 1292
  trade **5**:1344
Amy, Pierre **5**:1177

Anabaptists **1**:178, 187, **2**:539,
    540, **3**:761, **5**:1191, 1194,
    1195, 1200, 1314
  iconoclasm **3**:606
  Peace of Augsburg **1**:76
Anabasis (Xenophon) **1**:261
Anatolia **3**:612, 616, 617, 621
Anatomical Exercises on the
    Movement of the Heart and
    Blood (Harvey) **5**:1251
anatomical theaters **3**:847
anatomy **3**:845–846, 847, 848,
    5:1250, 1251, 1254, 1255
  disease **2**:309–310
  dissection **2**:302, 303, **3**:845,
    846, 848, **5**:1254
  education **2**:320
  illusory perspective **2**:312,
    316
  Wren **5**:1429
Anatomy Lesson of Doctor Tulp,
    The (Rembrandt) **5**:1212,
    1217
ancient Greece see Greek
    culture
ancient Rome see Roman
    Empire
Ancona **4**:1088, 1089
Ancona, Ciriaco d' **3**:587
Andrea del Castagno **1**:111
Andrew, Saint **5**:1230
Andrewes, Lancelot **2**:346
Andrew of Wyntoun **5**:1260
Andromaque (Racine) **3**:730
Andronicus IV, Byzantine
    emperor **1**:262
Anelida and Arcite (Chaucer)
    1:213, 217
Angelico, Fra **2**:428, **5**:1229
Angelos, Christopher **1**:262
Anger, Jane **5**:1420
Angers **2**:451
Angers, University of **5**:1371
Angevins, the **3**:596, 655,
    4:965, 1090
  Naples **2**:412
Anglicans see Church of
    England
Anglo-Norman language
    1:212, 214
Anglo-Saxon literature **1**:214

Angoulême **2**:453, 437
Angus, earl of **5**:1261, 1262
animals
  Black Death **2**:306
  blood sports **1**:92–96
  Bosch portrayals **1**:128, 132
  Columbian exchange **1**:255
  domestication **1**:25
  plague transmission **2**:303
  see also horses; livestock
Anjou **2**:294, **3**:601, 602
  Hundred Years War **1**:16
Anjou, duke of see Henry III,
    king of France
Ankara, Battle of (1402) **3**:617
Anna, princess of Saxony
    5:1236
Annals of the Old and New
    Testament (Ussher) **1**:110
Anne, Saint **5**:1220
Anne, countess of Arundel
    5:1424
Anne of Bohemia **1**:217
Anne of Brittany **3**:644
Anne of Cleves, queen consort
    of England **2**:522, 527
Anne of Denmark, queen
    consort of England **3**:663,
    665
Anne of Hungary **2**:510
Anne of Montmorency **2**:452
Annibaldis **1**:39
Annius of Viterbo **3**:594
Annotationes (Valla) **2**:358
Annunciation, The (Leonardo
    attribution) **3**:706, 708
Annunciation **4**:1081
anointing **5**:1357
Antarctica **2**:384
Anthony, Saint **5**:1201
Antioch **1**:260
antipopes **4**:1010
Antiquities of Rome (Palladio)
    1:43, **4**:1003
antiquity see classical antiquity,
    Greek culture, Roman
    Empire, languages, classical
anti-Semitism **3**:671, 672,
    673–674, 675, **5**:1202
  Poland **4**:1111, 1114
  Spain **2**:397, 398–399

anti-Stratfordians **5**:1276
António of Crato **4**:1140,
    1145
Antony and Cleopatra
    (Shakespeare) **5**:1272
Antwerp **2**:334, **3**:819
  banking **1**:88
  Bruegel **1**:144, 145, 146
  Rubens **5**:1236, 1237,
    1238–1239, 1242
  sack of **4**:1057
  trade **5**:1344
Apennines **3**:744
Aphorisms (Hippocrates)
    5:1177
Apocalypse Cycle (Dürer)
    2:314
Apocrypha **1**:103, 104, 108,
    5:1355
Apollo and Daphne (Bernini)
    1:98
Apollo and Daphne
    (Pollaiuolo) **2**:425
Apologie for Poesie, An
    (Spenser) **5**:1287
Apology for the Church of
    England (Jewel) **1**:238
Apostles, Church of the **1**:258
apostolic succession **1**:237
Appeal to the Christian
    Nobility of the German
    Nation (Luther) **2**:370
Appian Way **1**:277
apple tree **1**:29
apprentices
  Brunelleschi **1**:149
  Dürer **2**:311
  London **3**:753
  manufacturing **3**:810
  minstrels **4**:949
  see also guilds and companies
Apuleius **1**:41
Aqua Claudia (Rome) **5**:1227
Aqua Virgo (Rome) **1**:37
aqueducts **4**:1026, 1040,
    5:1227
Aquitaine **2**:412–413,
    3:595–596, 597, 598, 603
  Hundred Years War **1**:16
Arabian Peninsula **2**:302,
    3:623

Arabic language **1:**51–52, 54, **3:**610, 611, 618, 670, 684, 692

Arab scholars **3:**693, **5:**1367
astronomy **1:**267, 268, 271
mathematics **3:**827
philosophy **4:**1054, 1061, 1064
see also Islam

Aragon **2:**445, 513, **4:**903, 905, 965, **5:**1277, 1278–1279
Charles V **1:**207, 211
Ferdinand **2:**393–400
hydraulics **1:**280
Philip II **1:**211, **4:**1057

Aramaic language **3:**695, 696, 697

Arawaks (people) **4:**891

Arbedo, Battle of (1422) **5:**1413

Arcadia (Sidney) **3:**725, 737

Arcadian Academy (Rome) **1:**230, **4:**1068

archers **1:***17*, 18, 19, 20, **3:**596, *597*, 600, 653
longbow **1:***16*, 18, **2:**435, **5:**1412–1413

archery butts **3:**751

arches **1:**36

Archias **3:**682

Archimedean Point **2:**297, 300

Archimedes **2:**297, 461, 462, **3:**831

architecture **1:30–49**
Bernini **1:**97–101
Bramante **1:**139–143
Brunelleschi **1:**149–156, **4:**983, 984
Burgundy **1:**163
Byzantium **1:**170, 171, 263
England **2:**334
Florence **2:**418, 424, 425
France **2:***436*, 444, 450
housing **2:**563
Italian city-states **3:**634, *640*, 641, 642
Jones **3:**663–668
London **1:**48–49, **3:**748, *755*
Medicis **3:**852, 855

Michelangelo **2:**424–425, **4:**871, 876, 877, **5:***1226*
Palladio **4:**1000–1007
papacy **4:**1025–1026, 1040
Paris **4:**1031, 1034
Portugal **4:**1141, 1144, *1145*
Raphael **5:**1186–1187
Romano **4:**991
Rome **5:**1229, 1231, 1232, 1235
Scotland **5:**1263–1264
Spain **4:**1060, **5:***1277*, 1280
Sweden **5:**1308
theater buildings **5:***1320*, 1321, 1326
Venice **5:**1399
Warsaw **4:**1112
Wren **1:**48–49, **5:**1429, 1430–1433

Architecture of Triumphal Arches (Harrison) **3:**665

Architettura (Bramante) **1:**140

Arcimboldo, Giuseppe **2:**559

Arctic **2:**383, 384

Arena Chapel (Padua) **2:**485, 486, 487, 488, 490

Areopagitica (Milton) **4:**883

Areopagus **5:**1287

Aretino, Pietro **3:**733

Arezzo **4:**1049, 1051

Arezzo, University of **5:**1367

Argentina **4:**892

Argonauts **2:**515

Arguin **5:**1345

Argyropoulos, Johannes **1:**55, 169

Arianism **4:**1110

Arianna, L' (Monteverdi) **4:**918, 920–921, 922

Ariosto, Ludovico **1:**125, 223, **3:**721, 733, **5:**1289

Aristarchus of Samos **1:**265

Aristotelian Institutes (Ramus) **4:**1064

Aristotle **1:50–61, 3:***595, 703*, **4:***1055, 1061*
astrology **1:**69
Byzantine Empire **1:**169, 170, 258
classical languages **3:**684, 686

cosmology **1:**265, 267, **5:**1253
dramatic unities **3:**727, 729, **5:**1321
English translation of **2:**336
exploration **2:**384
Galileo **2:**460, 461, 463
Hobbes vs. **2:**543
humanism **3:**582, 583, *586*
Latin translation of **1:**261, **3:**685, 693
Luther vs. **3:**761, 763, 767
on monarchy **4:**903
philosophy **4:**1061–1062, 1063, 1064, 1065, 1066, 1072, 1099, 1102
Pico della Mirandola **4:**1073, 1074, 1076
Platonism **1:**261, **4:**1095
printed editions **3:**688
Reformation **1:**181, **2:**320
Scholasticism **1:**54, 57, 58–59, 61, 81, 181, 261, **2:**357, 359, **4:**1049, 1054–1055, 1075
science **5:**1248
Thomas Aquinas **1:**52, 56, 59, **3:**604
on tragedy **4:**920
universities **5:**1365, 1367, 1369
see also philosophy

Aristotle with a Bust of Homer (Rembrandt) **1:***59*

armada, Spanish **1:62–66**, 238, **4:**909, 1145, **5:**1347, 1412
Cervantes **1:**204
Elizabeth I **2:**331, 332
Philip II **4:**1058

Armada Portrait **2:***332*

Armada Tapestry **1:***66*

Armagnac **1:**159, **2:**437, **3:**600, **4:**1030

Armelina (Rueda) **5:**1323

Armenia **2:**429

Armenian Catholic Church **2:**429, 431

armies *see* warfare

Arminianism **1:**190, **2:**345, 346, **5:**1329

Arminius, Jacobus **1:**190, **2:**346

armor **1:**221, 226, **3:***743*, 793

Arms of the Nobility of Scotland (manuscript) **5:***1297*

Arnolfini, Giovanni **2:***389*, 390

Arnolfini Portrait (Jan van Eyck) **2:***389*, 390

Arno River **1:**276, 278, 279, 280, **3:**706, *708*

Arquà **4:**1051

Arran, earl of *see* Hamilton, James

Arras, Treaty of (1435) **1:**160, **3:**602, 660

arsenale (Venice) **5:***1394*

Arsenius, Saint **1:***168*

ars nova **4:**945

Ars poetica (Horace) **1:**59

art *see* painting, sculpture

Art de l'artillerie, L' (Senftenberg) **5:***1415*

Arte de la pintura (Pacheco) **5:***1384*

Arte nuevo de hacer comedias (Vega) **3:**728

Arthur, Prince of Wales **1:**232, **2:**521, 522, 523

Arthurian romances **1:**222, 223, 224

Articles of Religion (England) **1:**104, 109, *237*, 240

artillery **2:***435*, **3:**651, **5:**1335

artillery towers **5:**1410

artisans
guilds **2:**496–497, 499
Italian city-states **3:**632, 635, 636, 641, 849
manufacturing **3:**804, 810–811
markets **3:**813

Art of Artillery, The (Senftenberg) **5:***1415*

Art of Raising Children (Galen) **5:***1177*

Art of War, The (Machiavelli) **3:**770, 772, 773

Artois **1:**157, 164

Artusi, Giovanni Maria **4:**918

Arundel, earl of **1**:83
Ascent of Mount Carmel (John of the Cross) **5**:1207
Ascham, Roger **2**:327
Ashkenazim **3**:670, *681*
Ashton Court (Bristol) **5**:1350
Asia
Black Death **2**:306
disease **2**:302–303
exploration **2**:373, 380, 381, 382
missionaries 1015
religious orders **5**:1204
trade **2**:302–303, **3**:805, **4**:1139, 1141, 1142, **5**:1341
see also China; India; Japan; spice trade
Aske, Robert **1**:235, **2**:340, 526
Asper, Hans **5**:*1315*
Assayer, The (Galileo) **2**:465, 466
Assisi **2**:488, *491, 492*
Assumption **1**:193, **4**:1081, **5**:1317, 1318
Assumption, Cathedral of the (Moscow) **4**:933, 934, *935*
Assumption of the Virgin (Carracci) **1**:193
Assumption of the Virgin, The (Titian) **4**:*988*
Astrakhan **3**:653, **4**:936
astrolabe **2**:377, **3**:775, 779, 790, **5**:1250
astrology **1**:67–74, **2**:422, **3**:679, 800
almanacs **1**:173
magic **4**:1065
mathematics **3**:828, 829, 830
astronomy **1**:60, **2**:559, **3**:693, 699, **4**:1109, **5**:1249–1254
astrology **1**:67, 74
calendars **1**:174, 175, **4**:1024
celestial chart **1**:*67, 69*
Copernicus **1**:265–267, **5**:1221, 1226, 1250
Descartes **2**:296, 297
education **2**:319, 320
Galileo **1**:271, **2**:296, 297, 460, 462, 465–467

heresy **2**:539, **5**:1226, 1234–1235, 1251
inventions **3**:774, 775, 779–780, 783
mathematics **3**:827, 828, 830–831, 832
Ptolemy **1**:266–267, **5**:1249–1250
revolutionary thinking **3**:783
Wren **5**:1429, 1430
see also telescope
Astrophel and Stella (Sidney) **3**:724, 725, **4**:1052
As You Like It (Shakespeare) **3**:737, **5**:1271, 1274
Athens *see* Greek culture
Atlantic Ocean **2**:374, 379, 381, 383, 399, **4**:1138, 1141
Columbus's voyages **1**:247, 248–249, 251
trade network **2**:373, 481, **5**:1348, 1349
see also circumnavigation
atmospheric pressure **5**:1433
Atticus **3**:584, 589, 682, 683, 684
Aubrey, John **2**:547
Augsburg **2**:475, 476, 478, 482
banking **1**:88, 90, **5**:1228
Dürer **2**:315
Renaissance map **1**:*78*
Augsburg, Peace of (1555) **1**:75–78, **2**:365, 370, 371, 372, 482, 556, 557, 558, **3**:767, **5**:1193, 1200, 1221, 1331, 1333
Augsburg Confession **1**:262, **2**:483, 540, 553
Augustine, Saint **3**:606, 696, **5**:1229, 1248, *1284*
Aristotle vs. **1**:53, **2**:357
bibles **1**:104, **2**:467
Erasmus **2**:357
ideas **1**:182
Lutheranism **3**:758–759, 765, 767
Petrarch **4**:1052, 1055
philosophy **4**:1069
Platonism **4**:1098, 1100

preaching **5**:1158, *1159*
Vives commentary **5**:1282
Augustine of Hippo *see* Augustine, Saint
Augustinians **2**:482, **3**:756, 758, 762, **5**:1201, 1362
Auld Alliance **5**:1297
Aurelian Walls (Rome) **5**:1227
Aurispa, Giovanni **3**:685
Australia **2**:385, **5**:1258
Austria **2**:372, **3**:837, **4**:966
anti-Semitism **3**:674
Hapsburg Empire **1**:209, **2**:507, 508, 509, 510, 511, 512, 557
Holy Roman Empire **1**:211, **2**:475
Ottoman Empire **1**:211, **3**:624, 629, 715, 716
Poland **4**:1114
Spain **3**:746
Austrian War **3**:628
Authorized Version *see* King James Bible
Autobiography (Christina) **1**:231
auto-da-fé **2**:530, **5**:1278
Auto-da-Fé (Berruguete) **2**:*397*
autos sacramentales (religious plays) **5**:1322, *1323*
Ave regina coelorum (Dufay) **4**:945
Averroës *see* Ibn Rushd
Averroistic Aristotelianism **1**:52–53
Avignon **1**:87, **2**:416, **3**:682
Avignon papacy **2**:366, 491, **3**:756, 854, **4**:913, 1009–1011, 1052, **5**:1227, 1406
Black Death **2**:306
Boccaccio **1**:112, 115
Petrarch **4**:1049–1050, 1051, 1052
Aviz dynasty **4**:1137–1140
Avon River **5**:*1350*
Azaro, Ambrosio Mariano **1**:280
Azerbaijan **3**:620
Azores **1**:247, 251, **2**:379, 381, **4**:1138, 1140

Aztecs **2**:382, **3**:788, **5**:1345
disease **2**:307–308
missionaries **4**:889, 890, 891
Azzolino, Decio **1**:230, 231

B

Babington, Anthony **2**:330, 331, **5**:1298, 1299
Babington Plot (1586) **2**:331, **5**:1298–1299
Babur (Muhammad Zahir ud-Din), king of India **3**:612, 615
Baburen, Dirck van **4**:997
Babylonian Captivity of the Church (Luther) **1**:232
Bacchus (Caravaggio) **1**:*191*
Bacchus (Michelangelo) **4**:870–871
Bach, Johann Sebastian **4**:960
Bacon, Anthony **5**:1419
Bacon, Francis **1**:79–83, **2**:542, **3**:775, **4**:929, **5**:1419
Aristotle **1**:60, 61
philosophy **4**:1065, 1067–1068, 1069, 1072
Platonism **4**:1103
science **5**:1251, 1256
Shakespeare **5**:1276
Bacon, Nicholas **1**:79, **5**:1419
Bacon, Roger **1**:174
bacteria **2**:302, 303, 310
badges **2**:*410*
Baghdad **4**:1085
Baglione, Giovanni **1**:192, 194
Baglioni, Grifoneto **5**:1185
Bahamas **1**:248, 250, **2**:308
Balboa *see* Núñez de Balboa, Vasco
Baldinucci, Filippo **1**:34, 101, 230
Baldung, Hans Grien **4**:*1080*
Balkans
Hellenic culture **1**:167, 170
Ottoman Empire **1**:263, **3**:613, 616, 617
Ball, John **4**:1044, 1045, 1047, 1048
ballads **3**:726, **4**:960

ballet 4:943

Baltellina 5:1334

Balten, Pieter 4:*1122*

Baltic lands
Poland 4:1104–1114
Sweden 5:1306–1310, 1311, 1333
Teutonic Knights 1:223
see also Hanseatic League

Baltic Sea 3:653, 4:937, 940
chartered companies 2:500–501
fish products 5:1341
Hanseatic League 2:502, 503, 505, 506
Russia 5:1309, 1334
Sweden 5:1305, 1307, 1310, 1311, 1334, 1335, 1336–1337
trade routes 2:475

Baltimore, Lord *see* Calvert, George

Baltiysk (Pillau) 5:1334

Bamberg, University of 5:1367, 1377

Bancroft Library (Berkeley, CA) 2:383

Bandello, Matteo 3:711, 736

Banér, Johan 5:1338

Banister, John 5:*1254*

Banker and His Wife, The (Massys) 1:*84*

banking 1:84–91, 5:1162
Bardi family 2:567
Florence 2:414, 415–416, 417, 421
Italian city-states 3:630, 632, 633
Judaism 3:671
Lombardy 3:740
London 3:750, 751
manufacturing 3:809
Medicis 2:416, 417, 3:849, 850, 851, 852, 854, 5:1342
papacy 5:1228
towns 3:809
trade 5:1340, 1341, 1344

Bank of England 1:90, 2:499

Bannockburn, Battle of (1314) 4:905, 5:1413

Banqueting House (London) 1:48, 2:355, 3:666, 667, 5:1241

baptism 1:184, 3:757, 763, 764, 4:1121, 5:1357, 1358–1359
adult 1:178, 5:1194, 1195, 1314
infant 1:178, 5:1314

Baptism of Christ, The (Verrocchio) 3:706–707

Barbara, Saint 5:*1221*

Barbaro, Daniele 1:33, 4:1001

Barbaro, Ermolao 1:56, 4:1075

Barbaro, Marc'Antonio 4:1001

Barbary pirates 1:208, 209, 211, 3:626, *627*, 716, 5:1347

Barberini, Francesco 4:882

Barberini, Maffeo *see* Urban VIII

Barbosa, Duarte 3:793

Barcelona 1:89–90, 2:395

Barcilon, Pinin Brambilla 3:713

Bardas 1:258

Bardi, Donato di Niccolò di Betto *see* Donatello

Bardi, Giovanni 2:567, 4:920

Bardi Chapel 2:485, 487

Bardis, the 2:567

Bardowiek 2:503

Barebone's Parliament 2:351

Barefoot Trinitarians, Convent of the 1:206

Barents, Willem 2:374, 384

Barezzi, Stefano 3:713

Barnabites 5:1204

Barnet, Battle of (1471) 2:408

Barocci, Federico 5:*1380, 1381*

barometer 3:775, 5:1429, 1433

Baron, Hans 3:585

Baronio, Cesare 5:1205

barons *see* nobility

baroque architecture 1:30, 33, 38, 44–45, 47, 49, 97
Jones 3:*667,* 668
Portugal 4:1144

baroque music 1:230, 4:961
Monteverdi 4:916, 919, 920, 923
Schütz 5:1244–1247

baroque painting 4:980, 981, 990–995, 996, 5:1213, 1224–1225
Rubens 5:1236–1243
Velázquez 5:1387

Barozzi, Giacomo *see* Vignola, Giacomo da

Barrow, Isaac 3:833

barter 5:1340, 1342

Bartolomeo, Fra 4:*1077,* 5:1184

Bartolomeo da Venezio 1:*123*

Baruch, book of 5:1355

Barwalde, Treaty of (1631) 5:1337

Bascio, Matteo da 5:1206

Basel 2:555
Calvin 1:179
Erasmus 2:357, 361, 362
northern Renaissance 2:311, 312
Reformation 1:188, 5:1314, 1315

Basel, Council of 2:537, 3:679, 4:*1087,* 5:1352, 1363
calendar reform 1:174
Florence, Council of 2:427, 428, 429
Pius II 4:1086, 1088

Basel, Peace of (1499) 5:1313

Basel, University of 5:1220

Basil, Saint 1:257, 3:684, 685, 5:1419

Basil, Simon 3:665

basilica 1:152, 154

Basilica (Vicenza) 4:1004

Basilica of Saint Peter *see* Saint Peter's Basilica

Basilikon doron (James VI) 5:1299

Basil of Caesarea *see* Basil, Saint

Basil the Great *see* Basil, Saint

Basinghouse, siege of (1645) 3:668

bastard feudalism 2:410, 412

Bastard of Vaurus 4:1115

Bastille (Paris) 4:1030

Bastwick, John 2:346

Báthory, Stephen *see* Stephen Báthory, king of Poland

Battista della Porta, Giovanni 4:*1073*

Battle of Ostia (Raphael) 5:1187

battles *see* warfare, *specific battles by keyword*

Bauer, Georg *see* Agricola

Bautista de Toledo, Juan 1:*46,* 47, 4:1060

Bavaria 2:482–483, 505, 3:387, 5:1335
Jewish purges 3:672
Maximilian I 3:835, 836, 839

Bavaria, duke of 1:78

Bayart, Pierre de 1:221

Bayeux tapestry 3:*691*

Bayezid I, Ottoman sultan 3:616, 617

Bayezid II, Ottoman sultan 3:619

Baynard's Castle (London) 3:749

Bayonne 3:596

Bayonne meetings (1565) 2:454

Bazán, Álvaro de 5:*1401*

bearbaiting 1:92–96

Bear Garden 5:*1324*

Béarn 2:516

Beatrice del Sera 1:112–113

Beaufort, Henry 1:17

Beaufort, Thomas 1:17

Beaumont, Francis 3:733, 5:1325

Becerra, Francisco 1:279

Becket, Thomas 1:218, 4:1083

Bedford, duke of 3:601, 602

Bedford, earl of *see* Russell, Francis

Beeckman, Isaac 2:294, 295

begging 4:1079, 1080–1081

Beghards 3:605

Beguines 3:605

Behain, Martin 3:775

Beheading of Saint John the Baptist (Caravaggio) **1:**194

Beheading of Saint John the Baptist (Verrocchio) **3:**707

Behemoth (Hobbes) **2:**543, 546, 547

Béjar, duke of **1:**205

Béjart, Armande **4:**900

Béjart, Madeleine **4:**898, 899, 900, 901

Béjarts, the **4:**897, 898

Belarus **4:**1109

Belfagor (Machiavelli) **3:**736

Belgium *see* Flanders

Belgrade **3:**623

Belisarius **1:***166*

Belknap, Robert **4:**1043

Bellarmine, Robert **2:**465, **5:**1253

Bellay, Jean du **5:**1176, 1177–1178

Bellay, Joachim du **3:**729, **5:**1286

Bellini, Gentile **1:***263,* **3:**618, *635,* **4:***1099,* **5:***1396, 1399*

Bellini, Giovanni **2:**312, **4:**988, 989

Bellori, Giovanni Pietro **1:**196

Belskys, the **3:**652

Belvedere palace (Vatican) *see* Villa del Belvedere

Belvoir Castle (England) **3:**665

Bembo, Pietro **1:**125, 241, **2:**310, **3:**703, 721, **5:**1383

Benavente **5:**1323

Bendido, Lucrezia **3:**721

Benedict, Saint **5:**1201

Benedict XIII (antipope) **3:**672

Benedictines **5:**1201, 1204

Rabelais **5:**1176, 1177, 1178

Benin **4:***1140*

Bening, Simon **4:**1134

Benozzo di Lesse Gozzoli, Francesco **1:***52*

Bentheim, Luder von **1:***49*

Bentivoglios, the **3:**701

Benvenuto di Giovanni **1:***86*

Berckenrode, Balthasar Florisz van **1:***274*

Bérenger, Jean **2:**557

Bergamo **3:**638, 744, **5:**1394

Bergen **1:**22

Berkman, Hendrik **5:***1252*

Berlin **5:**1256

Berlin, University of **5:**1220

Bern **5:**1312, 1314, 1315, 1316

Bernáldez, Andrés **3:***678*

Bernard, count of Armagnac **1:**159

Bernardino of Siena **5:**1160, 1162, 1163

Bernat, Martín **5:***1279*

Bernhard of Saxe-Weimar **3:**839, **5:**1337–1338

Bernini, Gian Lorenzo **1:97–101,** 195*,* **2:***458,* **3:**668, **4:**1000, **5:**1225

architecture **1:**32, 33, 34, 38, 40, 44–45, 48, 49

Caravaggio as influence **1:**195

Christina **1:**230

painting and sculpture **4:**993, 994

Rome **5:***1234,* 1235

Saint Peter's colonnade **4:***1008,* 1026

Urban VIII **5:**1333

Bernini, Luigi di Pietro **1:**44

Bernini, Pietro **1:**44, 97, 98

Berner Chronik (Schilling) **5:***1313*

Beroaldo, Filippo (the Younger) **1:**41

Berruguete, Pedro **2:***397*

Bertendona, Martín de **1:**64

Berthelot, René **4:**897

Berthold of Henneberg **2:**550

Bérulle, Pierre de **2:**296, **5:**1205, 1208

Berwick **5:**1267

Bessarion **1:**260, **3:**688, *690,* 728, 829

humanist learning **2:**430, *431,* **4:**1023

overview of **1:**261

Platonism **4:**1063, 1099–1100

Bethlehem **1:**259

Bethlehem Chapel (Prague) **1:**118

Bethlen, Gábor von **5:**1335

Bettes, John (the Elder) **5:***1272*

Bèze, Théodore de **1:**107, 108, **2:**369, 566–567

Bible moralisée **1:**104

Bible of Borso d'Este **1:***102*

bibles **1:102–110**

Apocrypha **1:**103, 104, 108

Calvinism **1:**178, 180, 183, **5:**1195

Church of England **1:**107, 232, 238, 239, 240, **2:**369

critical analysis **2:**538, **3:**689

England **1:**238, *240,* **2:**339, 526, 536, **4:**931, **5:**1221, 1223

Erasmus **1:**181, **2:**358, 360, 538, **3:**585, 591, 684, 688–689, 703, **5:**1357

France **2:**448

as Gentileschi source **2:**473

Greek Codex B **4:**1022

Greek translation **1:**103, 104, 109, **3:**695

Gutenberg **3:**780–781

heresy **2:**538

humanism **1:**181, **2:**337, 551, **3:**585, 586, 591, 592, 593, 689, 853, **5:**1177, 1218, 1369

hymns **4:**952, 954

iconoclasm **3:**607

illumination **3:***686*

Indian translation **4:**892

interpretations **1:**109, **2:**538, 551, **3:**853, **5:**1356

Judaism **3:**669, 671, 672

Koine Greek **3:**695, 696

Latin **4:**1024, **5:**1159, 1160

see also Vulgate

literacy **2:**321

as literal **2:**467, 536, 539, **5:**1194

liturgical drama **5:**1318, 1320

Luther and Lutheranism **1:**180, **2:**482, *554,* **3:**758–759, 761, 763,

764, 765, 767, **5:**1189, 1193, 1201, 1221, 1222, 1352, 1354, 1356, 1357, 1371, 1372

marginal notes **1:**105, 106, 110

missals **1:**173, **5:**1363

multilingualism **3:**591

mystery plays **3:**729

original texts **5:**1357

preaching **5:**1159, 1160, *1162,* 1164, 1165

printing **1:**178, **3:**591, *688, 697–699,* **5:**1169, 1170, *1171,* 1173–1174, 1175, 1193, 1220

as Protestant sole authority **1:**107, 178, 180, 183, 232, 240, **5:**1352, 1354, 1356, 1371, 1372

Reformation **5:**1173–1174, 1194, 1417

translations **1:**58, 102–108, 109, 110, 118, 181, **2:**358, 526, 536, 538, *554,* **3:**585, 591, 684, 688–689, 703, **4:**970, **5:**1315, 1357

Trent, Council of **5:**1354, 1355–1357

vernaculars **2:**321, **3:**689, 695, 696, 697–699

Zwingli **5:**1315

see also New Testament; Old Testament

Bibliothèque du Roi (France) **5:**1375

bigamy **2:**569

Big Fish Eat Little Fish (Bruegel) **1:**145

Bigordi, Domenico di Tommaso *see* Ghirlandaio, Domenico

Bilhères-Lagrulas, Jean de **4:**871

Bill, John **1:***82*

Billericay, Battle of (1381) **4:**1047

Bill of Rights of 1689 (England) **2:**346, **4:**903, 906

Binchois, Gilles **4**:944

biology **5**:1258

Biondo, Flavio **3**:587

bird movements **3**:709

Birth of Venus (Botticelli) **1**:135, **2**:*424,* 425

birthrates **4**:1128, 1129, **5**:1419, 1420

bishops **4**:1018, 1022
  Church of England **2**:368
  Counter-Reformation **5**:1197
  preaching **5**:1158

Bishops' Bible **1**:238

Bishop's Book (1537) **2**:527

Bishopsgate (London) **3**:749

Bishops' Wars (1639) **2**:349, 350, **5**:1267

Bisticci, Vespasiano da **5**:1229

Black Death **2**:303–306, 307, 309, 310, **3**:818, **4**:980–981, 1083
  anti-Semitism **3**:673
  Boccaccio **1**:112, 113, 114, **2**:423
  cities **4**:1130–1131
  flagellants **2**:307
  France **2**:432, 433, 434, 436
  German towns **2**:481
  Italian city-states **2**:306, **3**:632–633
  Paris **4**:1029
  peasants' revolts **1**:216, **4**:1041, 1042, 1048
  population decline **4**:1048, 1124, 1125, 1129, 1134
  Scotland **5**:1260
  social consequences **2**:306, **3**:692–693
  transmission **2**:303, 309, 310
  treatment **2**:306, 309, 310

Blackfriars (London theater) **3**:748, 749, **5**:1275, 1327

Black Legend **2**:400, **4**:1059

Black Prince *see* Edward, the Black Prince

Black Sea **1**:165, 166, 170, 263, **4**:1106

Blaeu, Jan **1**:*275*

Blaeu Atlas **5**:*1251*

Blanche of Lancaster **1**:215, **4**:1047

blank verse **3**:731, 732, 823
  Shakespeare **5**:1270, 1274

blast furnaces **3**:812

Blekinge **5**:1311

Blois **1**:45, **2**:451

Blomberg, Barbara **3**:716

blood circulation **3**:840–841, **5**:1251, 1255

blood libel **3**:673, 675

blood sports **1**:92–96

blood taint **3**:671

blue dye (woad) **5**:1350, 1402

Boabdil **2**:397–398

Bobadilla, Francisco de **1**:254

Bobâlna Revolt (Hungary) **4**:1042

Bobbio **3**:638

Boccaccio, Giovanni **1**:111–115, **3**:735, 736, **4**:963, 1051
  Cervantes comparison **1**:205
  Chaucer **1**:216, 217, 218–219
  Florence **2**:423
  religious orders **5**:1202
  vernacular **1**:217, **3**:694

bodegónes (still lifes) **5**:1385

Bodenehr, Gabriel **4**:1114

body
  disease **2**:302–310
  dualism **2**:300–301, **3**:606, **5**:1294
  Florentine art **2**:424, 425
  see also anatomy

body snatching **3**:848

Boethius, Anicius Manlius Severinus **1**:213, 217

Bogomils **3**:605

Bohemia **1**:116–122
  Hapsburgs **2**:438, 507, 509, 510–511
  heresy **2**:536–537, 549
  Holy Roman Empire **2**:475, 548, 549, 557, 559
  Hussites **2**:537, 557, **3**:660, 674, **4**:969
  Maximilian I **3**:836, 837, 838
  Ottoman Empire **2**:555, 557

Reformation **5**:1191, 1192
  Thirty Years War **5**:1301, 1331, 1334, 1335, 1336, 1337, 1338, 1415
  university **5**:1367

Bohemian Brethren **1**:122

Bohemian Cycle of Months **2**:*402*

Bohíos (people) **1**:250

Boiardo, Matteo Maria **1**:223

Bojador, Cape **2**:380, **5**:1345

Boleyn, Anne **3**:735, **4**:931, 1014, 1015, 1123, **5**:1297
  Elizabeth I **1**:236, **2**:326
  Henry VIII **1**:233, 234, 235, 240, **2**:338, 522, 523, 524, 525, 527

Boleyn, Thomas **1**:234

Bolingbroke, Henry *see* Henry IV, king of England

Bologna **1**:246, **4**:1012, **5**:*1356,* 1404
  Carraccis **1**:195
  Charles V coronation **1**:*208,* 209, 210, 244
  Italian wars **3**:645
  Leo X **3**:701
  market **3**:*633*
  Paul V **4**:1036, 1037
  Pico della Mirandola **4**:1073, 1074
  public health **4**:1133
  Trent, Council of **5**:1357
  Viscontis **3**:638

Bologna, Concordat of (1516) **2**:447, **3**:701

Bologna, University of **3**:844, **4**:1143, **5**:1250, *1365,* 1367, *1368,* 1371
  Bessarion **1**:261
  Petrarch **4**:1050, 1051
  science studies **5**:1255
  Spanish scholars **5**:1279

Bolton, Herbert Eugene **2**:383

Bolton, Robert **3**:663

bonae literae **2**:362, 363

Bona of Savoy **3**:742

Bonaventure **3**:760, **4**:1062

Boniface VIII, Pope **2**:366, 491, **4**:903, *1079,* 1080, **5**:1227, 1235

Bonvesin de la Riva **3**:631

Booker, John **1**:70

book fairs **3**:781, 806, 819

Book Named the Governor, The (Elyot) **4**:1122

Book of Common Order, The (Knox) **1**:189

Book of Common Prayer **1**:108, 188, 236, *237,* 238, 239, 240, **2**:368, **3**:609, 699, **5**:1197, 1267

Book of Contemplative Life (Meli da Crema) **1**:126

Book of Dede Korkut (Turkish epic) **3**:629

Book of Fiefs, The (treatise) **2**:405

Book of Grand Manners, The (Jacques le Grant) **1**:*85*

Book of Homilies **1**:*237,* **2**:368

Book of Hours of Duchess Mary of Burgundy **4**:*1078, 1121*

Book of Hours of the Blessed Virgin **4**:1118

Book of King Arthur and the Knights of the Round Table (Chrétien de Troyes) **4**:*1101*

Book of Margery Kempe, The **4**:1081

Book of My Life, The (Cardano) **1**:*70,* **3**:830

Book of Sir Thomas More, The (Munday) **5**:1323

Book of Splendor (kabbalistic work) **3**:*680*

Book of the Courtier (Castiglione) **3**:736

Book of the Duchess, The (Chaucer) **1**:215, 218

Book of the Order of Chivalry (Lull) **1**:224

book production *see* printing

booksellers **3**:754

books of hours **1**:*21,* 173, **4**:*1078,* 1118, *1121, 1131,* **5**:*1167*
  Burgundy **1**:163, *164, 173*
  Paris **4**:1030

Books of the Memorable Cases (Petrarch) **4**:1051

book trade **3**:754, 780–783, 805, 806, 819

Bora, Katharina von **3**:762, **5**:1201

Bordeaux **2**:455, **3**:596, 597
  wine production **5**:1341, 1350

Bordeaux, University of **5**:1371

borders and boundaries **4**:964–965

Borghese, Camillo *see* Paul V

Borghese, Marcantonio **4**:1037

Borghese, Scipione **1**:97, **4**:1037

Borgia, Cesare **1**:123, 124, 126, **3**:707, 769, **4**:1011, **5**:1379, 1428

Borgia, Juan **1**:123

Borgia, Lucrezia **1**:**123–126**, **5**:1427, 1428

Borgia, Rodrigo *see* Alexander VI

Borgias, the **4**:1011, **5**:1231

Boris Godunov *see* Godunov, Boris

Borja, Alfonso de *see* Calixtus III

Borluut, Elizabeth **2**:387

Borrachos, Los (Velázquez) **5**:1387

Borromeo, Carlo **1**:32, **3**:747, **4**:1036, **5**:1197

Borromini, Francesco **1**:33, 38, 40, 44–45, 49, **5**:1235

Boscán Almogáver, Juan **3**:726, **5**:1284

Bosch, Hieronymus **1**:**127–132**
  as Bruegel influence **1**:*144,* 145, 146, 148

Bosporus **1**:165, 263

Bosse, Abraham **5**:*1423*

Bossuet, Jacques-Bénigne **2**:372

Bosworth Field, Battle of (1485) **1**:233

botanical gardens **3**:840, 847

botany **1**:29, **5**:1250, 1258–1259
  medical **3**:840, 846–847

Bothwell, earl of *see* Hepburn, James

Botticelli, Sandro **1**:*114,* **133–138, 2**:*424,* **3**:706, 852, 856, **4**:985, **5**:*1219,* 1220, 1230
  Florence **2**:424–425

Boucicaut *see* Meingre Boucicaut, Jean II le

Bourbon, Antoine de **1**:199, **2**:516

Bourbon, Antoinette de **1**:198

Bourbon, Armand de, prince of Conti **4**:898

Bourbon, François de **1**:198

Bourbon dynasty **2**:437, 443
  Henry IV **2**:516–520
  Thirty Years War **5**:1330, 1333

Bourbon-Vendôme, Louis de **1**:199

Bourchier, John **1**:224

Bourdon, Sebastien **1**:*227,* **2**:*300,* **5**:*1293*

Bourgeois, Louis **4**:954

Bourges **1**:179, *184*

Bourges, University of **5**:1371

Bourguignon, Le (Jacques Courtois) **5**:*1337*

Bouscal, Guérin de **1**:*204*

Bouts, Dirck **4**:982

Bower, Walter **5**:1260

boyars
  Ivan IV Vasilyevich **3**:652, 653, 654, 655
  Muscovy **4**:934, 937, 938, 939, 940, 941

Boyle, Elizabeth **5**:1289

Boyle, Richard, earl of Cork **5**:1289

Boyle, Robert **5**:1256

Brabant **1**:144, 146

Bracciolini, Poggio **1**:33, **2**:359, **3**:583, 683, **5**:1229
  English translation **2**:336

Bradamante (Garnier) **3**:730

Bradley, Humphrey **1**:276

Bradley, William **3**:824

Bragança, the **4**:1145

Brahe, Per **1**:229

Brahe, Tycho **1**:121, *268,* 271, 272, **2**:559, **3**:*831,* 832, **5**:1251

Bramante (Bruschi) **1**:143

Bramante, Donato **1**:**139–143,** **3**:710, **4**:873, 878, **5**:1186
  architecture **1**:31, 32, 36, 37–38, 39
  Palladio **4**:1002, 1004
  Saint Peter's Basilica **1**:140, 142, 143, **4**:1026, **5**:1231

Bramhall, John **2**:543, 546

Brancacci Chapel (Florence) **3**:*589*

Brandenburg **2**:548, **5**:1334, 1337

Brandenburg, elector of **1**:76

Brant, Isabella **5**:1238–1239, 1241–1242

Brask, Hans, bishop of Linköping **5**:1305

Braun, Georg **1**:*78, 281,* **5**:1316, *1350*

Braxton Moor **5**:1297

Brazil **2**:*374,* 381, **3**:790
  Jesuits **4**:1015
  Portugal **4**:1142, 1145

breast-feeding **5**:1420

Breda **1**:144

Bregno, Andrea **1**:40, **5**:*1230*

Breisach, Battle of (1638) **5**:1338

Breitenfeld, Battle of (1631) **3**:839, **5**:1137, 1310, 1338

Bremen **2**:305, 503, 505

Brenta River and Canal **1**:277

Brescia **3**:638, 645

Breslau, University of **5**:1377

Brethren, Bohemian **1**:122

Brethren, Polish **4**:1110

Brethren, Swiss **5**:1314

Brethren of the Common Life **2**:356, **3**:760

Brethren of the Passion **5**:1318

Bretigny, Treaty of (1360) **3**:597, 598

Breton, Gilles le **1**:45

Bridgewater, earl of *see* Egerton, John

Brief Lives (Aubrey) **2**:547

"Brief Notes upon a Late Sermon" (Milton) **4**:886

Brindisi **5**:1393

Bristol **5**:1350

British East India Company **2**:375, 499, 501, **5**:1342, 1351

British Isles *see* England, Scotland, Ireland

Brittany **2**:437, 452, **3**:598

Brömsebro, Peace of (1645) **5**:1338

Bronckhorst, Arnold van **5**:1265

Bronckhorst, Jan Gerritsz von **5**:*1338*

Bronzino, Il **4**:990

Broquière, Bertrandon de la **1**:*264*

Brotherhood of Our Lady **1**:128

Bruegel, Pieter (the Elder) **1**:131, **144–148, 4**:*1119, 1125*

Brueghel, Pieter, III **2**:*405*

Brueghel, Jan **1**:144, **4**:*1124*

Brueghel, Pieter (the Younger) **1**:144, **4**:*1128,* **5**:*1319*

Bruges **1**:22, 160, **2**:387, 391, 392
  banking **1**:87, **2**:416
  Gothic architecture **1**:163

Bruhl, Nikolaus **5**:*1191*

Bruna River **1**:281

Brunelleschi, Filippo **1**:139, **149–156, 3**:668, 856, **4**:876, 878
  architecture **1**:32, 34–35, 37, 47
  classicism **4**:983
  Florence **2**:424
  perspective **2**:312, **4**:984

Brunfels, Otto **3**:840, **5**:1250

Bruni, Leonardo **1**:125, *155* **3**:640, 855
  Aristotle **1**:54, 55
  Chrysoloras **1**:264
  classical languages **3**:684, 685
  English translation **2**:336

Bruni, Leonardo *(cont.)*
Florence **2**:422, 423
humanism **2**:357, **3**:584,
585, 586, 588
tomb of **1**:*155*
Brunkeberg, Battle of (1471)
5:1304
Bruno, Saint **4**:926
Bruno, Giordano **1**:57, 272,
4:*1019,* 1065, 1071
Brunswick **2**:479, 505
Brus, Anton **1**:121
Bruschi, Arnaldo **1**:143
Brussels **1**:144, 146, 148, 161,
163, **2**:557
Brussels, Treaty of (1522)
2:510
Bry, Theodore de **1**:*251,*
5:*1346*
bubonic plague *see* Black
Death
Bucer, Elizabeth **5**:1423
Bucer, Martin **5**:1423
Buchanan, George **5**:1263,
1264, 1299
Buckingham, duke of *see*
Villiers, George
Bucolicum carmen (Petrarch)
1:115, **4**:1051
Budé, Guillaume **1**:179,
3:590, **5**:1176
Bueil, Jean de **5**:*1410*
buffoons **5**:1319
Buil, Bernado **4**:895
Bulgaria **1**:158, 170, 177,
3:616
Christian conversion **1**:259
bull baiting **1**:94, 95
Bullinger, Henry **2**:369
Buonacorsi, Filippo de
(Callimachus) **4**:1109
Buonarroti, Michelangelo *see*
Michelangelo
Buonarroti, Michelangelo (the
Younger) **2**:469
Buoninsegna *see* Duccio di
Buoninsegna
Buontalenti, Bernado Timante
1:276
Burbage, James **5**:1270,
1326

Burbage, Richard **5**:1270,
1271
Burckhardt, Jacob **5**:1220
Bure, Idelette de **1**:179
Bürgermeister **2**:478
Burghley, Lord *see* Cecil,
William
Burghley House (England)
5:1289
Burgundy **1**:**157–164**
Charles V **1**:207, 208
chivalry **1**:223
England **2**:334
France **2**:413, 434–435, 437,
446, 453
Hapsburgs **2**:509, 511, 515,
550
Holy Roman Empire **4**:966
Hundred Years War **3**:600,
601, 602, **4**:1030
Joan of Arc **3**:658, 661
music **4**:944, 945, 951
nationalism **4**:964–965, 966
Ottoman Empire **3**:616
Paris **4**:1030
sculpture **4**:981
Spain **5**:1278
Switzerland **5**:*1313,* 1314
Burial of Saint Lucy
(Caravaggio) **1**:194
Burial of the Count of Orgaz,
The (El Greco) **5**:*1284*
Burke, Thomas **5**:*1290*
Burleigh House (London)
3:749
Burley, Simon **4**:1043
Burlington, Lord **3**:668,
4:1007
Burton, Henry **2**:346
Busenello, Giovanni **4**:923
Busnois, Antoine **4**:946
Busti, Agostino **3**:*645*
Butler, James, earl of Ormond
2:353
Button Bay **2**:383
Buxtehude, Dietrich **4**:960
Byrd, William **4**:943, 952
Byron, Lord **1**:126, **5**:1290
Byzantine Empire **1**:256,
4:1073, 1109
architecture **1**:170, 171, 263

Byzantium **1**:165–172
Constantinople **1**:256–264
established church **2**:366
Florence, Council of
2:427–431
Fourth Crusade **1**:260
iconoclasm **3**:605
Ottoman Empire **3**:586, 616,
618
Venice **5**:1392, 1393
see also Orthodox Church
Byzantine Tradition after the
Fall of Constantinople, The
(Runciman) **1**:171
Byzantium **1**:**165–172**, 256 *see*
also Constantinople

C

Cabot, John **4**:888, 914, 915,
5:*1350*
Cabot, Sebastian **2**:383
Cabral, Pedro Álvares **2**:374,
381
Caccini, Giulio **4**:920
Cade, Jack **4**:1042
Cádiz **1**:63, *64,* 251
Ca' d'Oro (Venice) **5**:1399
Caen, University of **5**:1371
Caesar, Julius **1**:174, **4**:1024,
5:1232
caesaropapism **1**:257, **2**:366
Caffarelli, Scipione *see*
Borghese, Scipione
Cailleau, Hubert **5**:*1317*
Cairo **3**:*678, 680*
Calais **1**:16, 20, 65, **2**:435,
3:597
calculus **3**:783, 827, 833, 834,
4:1072
Calderón de la Barca, Pedro
3:726, 727, 728, **5**:1284,
1323
calendars **1**:**173–177,**
4:1024–1025
festivals **5**:1317
Caliari, Benedetto **1**:58
Caliari, Paolo **5**:1399
Calicut **5**:*1345*
California **2**:383
California, University of
(Berkeley) **2**:383

California Historical Society
2:383
caliphate **3**:626
Calixtus III, Pope **3**:619,
4:1011, 1086
Callimachus (Filippo de
Buonacorsi) **4**:1109
Calling of Saint Matthew, The
(Caravaggio) **1**:192–193,
4:*997*
Calling of Saint Matthew, The
(Carpaccio) **1**:*91*
Calvert, George (Lord
Baltimore) **4**:894
Calvin, Gerard **1**:179
Calvin, John **1**:178, 181, 183,
184, 185, 186–187, 188,
189, **2**:369, 483, **3**:761,
762, **4**:906, 952, 1032
bibles **1**:107, 108
catechism **5**:1174
Church of Scotland **2**:369
divorce grounds **2**:566–567
education **2**:321, 324–325
France **2**:439–440, **5**:1191
Geneva **5**:1315–1316, 1423
humanism **1**:190,
2:324–325, **3**:593
hunting critique **1**:96
iconoclasm **3**:607, 608
interest-bearing loans **1**:85,
5:1316
on Islam **3**:618
nationalism **2**:364
overview of **1**:179
philosophy **4**:1062–1063,
1064, 1065
preaching **5**:*1164,* 1165
Puritanism **2**:342
Rabelais **5**:1179
Reformation **5**:1194–1196
religious wars **1**:183
sacraments **5**:1358
Switzerland **5**:1312
witch hunts **2**:535
Calvinism **1**:**178–190, 2**:483,
3:837, **4**:881, 975, **5**:1179
astrology **1**:73
Augsburg, Peace of **1**:76
Catherine de Médicis **1**:198,
199, 200, 201

Church of England **1:**236, 237, 239, 240, **5:**1329
church-state relations **1:**186–187, **4:**906
Eastern Orthodoxy **1:**263
education **2:**321, 324–325
England **1:**236, 237, 239, 240, **2:**342, 343, 344, 345, 346, 349, 368–369
established church **2:**349, 353, 369, 371–372
France **2:**439–440, 441, 442–443, 444, 451–459, 541, 556, **5:**1179
French civil wars **5:**1331
Geneva **5:**1316
Heidelberg Catechism **5:**1174
Henry IV **2:**516, 517, 518–519, 520
heresy **1:**187, **2:**539, **5:**1316
Holy Roman Empire **1:**76, **2:**558, 559, **5:**1200
iconoclasm **3:**606–607, 608, 609
Lutheranism vs. **1:**185, **3:**766, 767, **5:**1377
missionaries **4:**892, 894
monarchy **4:**912
music **4:**952, 954
Netherlands **2:**556
Palatinate **1:**76–77, 122
Poland-Lithuania **4:**1110
preaching **1:**183, **5:**1164, 1165
Protestant ethic **1:**190
Reformation **5:**1195–1196, 1198
Scotland **2:**349, 369, **5:**1265–1266, 1267, 1298, 1301, 1426
Thirty Years War **5:**1331–1332
universities **5:**1377
Waldensians **2:**531
witch hunts **2:**535
women **5:**1423
Zwingli **5:**1315
see also Huguenots; Presbyterianism; Puritans
Cambrai, bishop of **2:**356

Cambrai, League of **3:**643, 648
war of the **5:**1394, 1400
Cambrai, Treaty of (1529) **3:**643, 647
Cambrai Cathedral **4:**945
Cambridge Platonists **4:**1070–1071, 1072, 1103
Cambridge University **1:**79, 100, **5:**1374–1375, 1419
Arabic studies **1:**262, **3:**618
architecture **1:**48, **2:**334
bibles **1:**107
dramatic productions **3:**732, **5:**1328
Elizabeth I **2:**327
founding of **5:**1367
King's College choir **4:**949
Marlowe **3:**822–823
Milton **4:**880, 881, 882
More as chancellor **4:**930
Newton **5:**1256–1257
science studies **5:**1255
Spenser **5:**1286–1287
University Wits **3:**732, 824
Wren **5:**1430, 1432
Camden, William **5:**1290
Camerarius, Joachim **5:***1372*
Camerata **2:**567, **5:**1321, 1322
Camerino **5:**1380, 1381
Camila (Rueda) **5:**1323
Camões, Luíz Vaz de **2:**385, **4:**1144
Campanella, Tommaso **1:**31, **4:**1103
Campbell, Colin **4:**1007
Campidoglio (Rome) **5:**1232
Campion, Edmund **4:**896, **5:**1206, 1323, 1324
Campofregoso, Ottaviano **3:**650
Canada
exploration **2:**383, **4:**915
Jesuits **4:**1015
missionaries **4:**893, 1896
Presbyterians **1:**190
Canaletto **4:***1039,* **5:***1433*
canals **1:**275, *276, 277,* 278, **3:**741
irrigation **5:**1402
Venice **1:**277

Canary Current **5:**1348
Canary Islands **1:**248, 251, **2:**379
Cancelleria (Rome) **1:**30, 39, 40
Canigiani, Sandra di Matteo di Giovanni **5:**1185
cannon **3:**618, 775, **5:**1341, 1407–1409, 1411, 1415
armada, Spanish **1:**63, 65, 66
Hundred Years War **3:**596
Lepanto, Battle of **3:**717
naval **5:**1412
standardization **5:**1408
see also weaponry
canonization see saints
Canon of Proportions (Leonardo da Vinci) **3:**709
Canossa, Lodovico da **5:**1383
Canterbury **5:**1424
pilgrimage **4:**1083
Canterbury, archbishop of **1:**237, **2:**338, 341, 345, 348, 349
Henry VIII **1:**106–107, 240, **5:**1197
Canterbury Cathedral **1:**100, 218
Canterbury Tales, The (Chaucer) **1:**113, *212,* 213, 217, 218–219, 220, **3:**694, 801, **4:**931, *1081, 1083*
Prologue **1:**219
religious orders **5:**1202
Cantigas de Santa María (manuscript) **3:***693*
Cantiones sacrae (Schütz) **5:**1246
Canzoniere, Il (Petrarch) **3:**720, 721, **4:**1049, 1050, 1051, 1052
Cape Blanc **2:**380, **5:**1345
Cape Bojador **4:**1140, 1141
Cape Coast Castle **5:***1349*
Cape of Good Hope **2:**374, 381, **4:**1138, 1139, **5:**1341, 1342, 1345
Cape Verde **1:**247, **2:**379, 381, **3:**794, **4:**1138, 1141, 1142

capitalism **1:**22, **3:**821, **5:**1349
Calvinism **1:**189–190
feudalism **2:**401
Capitol (Washington, DC) **1:**140
Capitoline Hill (Rome) **1:**32, 37, **4:**878, 1003, 1004, **5:**1228
Cappella Giulia (Rome) **4:**955
Cappella Paolini (Rome) **4:**1040
Capponis, the **2:**417, **3:**850
Capranica, Domenico **4:**1086, 1088
Capuchins **5:**1206–1207, 1209, 1332
Carafa, Gian Pietro see Paul IV
Carafa, Olivero **1:***140*
Caravaggio (Michelangelo Merisi) **1:191–196, 4:**878, 993, 994, 997, **5:**1235, 1386
Gentileschi **2:**469, 470, 471, 472, 474
as Rembrandt influence **5:**1211
Rubens **5:**1237–1238
Caravaggisti, Dutch **5:**1211
caravels **2:**373, **4:**1138, **5:**1343, *1346,* 1412
Columbus voyages **1:**248
Carda, Bernardino della **5:**1379
Cardano, Girolamo **1:**70, 71, 72, *73,* **3:**828, 829, 830
overview of **1:**70, **3:**830
Cardano's Rule **3:**829
cardinal-nephew **4:**1037
cardinals **4:**1008, 1010, 1012, 1014, 1016, 1022, 1025, 1026, 1029
humanism **4:**1023
Cardinal's College (Oxford) **5:**1373
Cardinal Virtues (Raphael) **5:**1186
Cardsharps (Caravaggio) **1:**191, 192
Carew, Thomas **2:**402

Caribbean region
  Columbus **1**:247, 248,
    250–254, **2**:399
  disease **2**:306, 307
  missionaries **4**:889, 891, 892
  piracy **5**:1347
  Spanish conquests **1**:62, 207
Caribs (people) **4**:891
caricature **1**:195
Carinthia **2**:509, 557
Carlos, Don, prince of Spain
  4:1059
Carmelites **5**:1201, 1206,
  1207–1208
*Carnevale italiano mascherato,
  Il* (Bertelli) **5**:*1321*
Carniola **2**:509
Carnival **4**:1119, 1123
Carnival and Lent (Bruegel)
  1:146
Caro, Joseph **3**:680
Caroline divines **1**:239
Carolingian capitularies **2**:493
Caron, Antoine **4**:*1102*
Carpaccio, Vittore **1**:*87, 91,*
  5:*1399*
Carpio, marquess del **5**:1389
Carr, Robert **5**:1300
Carracci, Agostino **1**:195
Carracci, Annibale **1**:41, 193,
  195, **4**:993, **5**:1235,
  1237–1238
carrack **2**:373
Carrara, princes of **2**:318
cartels **1**:86
Cartesianism *see* Descartes,
  René
Carthusians **2**:*370,* **4**:925,
  926, 981
cartography **5**:*1248,* 1250
  Columbus's worldview
    1:249
  exploration **2**:374, 378, 379,
    380, 382, 383, 384, *385*
  Portugal **4**:1138
  Spain **5**:1284
  world map **1**:*254*
Casaubon, Isaac **1**:58
Casillas II Dam **1**:279
Casimir, John *see* John II, king
  of Poland

Casimir III (the Great), king of
  Poland **3**:675, **4**:1104
Cassotti, Marsilio and Faustina
  5:*1420*
Castagno, Andrea del **1**:*216,*
  5:*1229*
Castel Durante **5**:1383
Castellar Dam **1**:280
Castelli, Benedetto **1**:277
Castello Visconteo **5**:*1402*
Castel Sant'Angelo (Rome)
  1:37, 243, **4**:1014, **5**:1228,
  1428
Castiglione, Baldassare **1**:48,
  3:685, 736, **5**:1221, 1383
Castile **2**:445, 515, **3**:598,
  693, **4**:965, **5**:1277, 1280,
  1281, 1282
  Alfonso X **3**:693
  anti-Jewish violence **3**:672,
    674
  Charles V **1**:207, 211
  Isabella **2**:393–400
  John of Gaunt **4**:1047
  monarchy **4**:903, 905
  Philip II **1**:211, **4**:1056
  Portugal **4**:1137
Castilian language **2**:399,
  5:1284
Castillo, Juan del **5**:1386
cast iron **3**:812
Castle Howard (Yorkshire)
  1:140
castles **2**:410–411,
  5:1409–1411
  decline of **5**:1407,
    1410–1411
  Visconti **5**:*1403*
Castres **2**:453
Castro del Rio jail **1**:203
Castro y Bellvís, Guillén de
  3:728, 730, 731
Castro y Velasco, Antonio
  Palomino de **5**:1384–1391
catacombs, Roman **3**:604,
  4:1026, *1027*
Catalan language **1**:123
Catalonia **2**:394, **4**:965, 1145,
  5:1277, 1278, 1279, 1285
catapult **5**:*1249, 1407,* 1408,
  1409

Cateau-Cambrésis, Peace of
  (1559) **2**:*420,* 421, **3**:643,
  644, 649, **4**:1058, 1059,
  5:1221, 1233, 1265
catechisms **2**:323, **5**:1174
Cathars **2**:530, 531, 532,
  3:605
cathedrals **1**:30, **3**:639 *see also
  specific cathedrals by
  keyword*
Catherine, Saint **1**:*125,* **3**:657
Catherine de Médicis
  1:197–201, **3**:722, 827,
  5:1426
  astrological prediction **1**:73
  Clement VII **1**:242, 245
  France **2**:440–441
  French civil wars **2**:452, 454
  Paris **4**:1031
  Thirty Years War **5**:1333,
    1334
Catherine of Aragon **4**:930,
  1014–1015, 1123, **5**:1297,
  1417
  Ferdinand and Isabella
    5:1280
  Henry VIII **1**:232–233, 234,
    235, 240, 242, 244,
    2:338, 340, 521,
    522–523, 524
  Mary Tudor **1**:236, 240
  Reformation **5**:1196, 1197
Catherine of France **3**:601
Catherine of Siena **5**:1424
Catherine of Valois **1**:17
Catholic Defense League
  5:1191
Catholicism *see* Roman
  Catholic Church
Catholic League **3**:626, 835,
  836, 837, 838, **4**:1033,
  1040, 1060, **5**:1331
  army size **5**:1332
Cattanei, Vannozza **1**:123
cattle *see* livestock
Cauchon, Peter **3**:661–662
Caulery, Louis de **4**:*1021*
causality **4**:1063
Cavalieri, Bonaventura **3**:833
Cavalieri, Tommaso de' **4**:877
Cavalli, Marino **2**:447

Cavallini, Pietro **2**:491
Cavallino, Bernardo **2**:474
cavalry **2**:*409,* **3**:597, 651
  chivalry **1**:221
  English civil wars **2**:352
  firearms **5**:1414, 1415
  pikemen vs. **5**:1309, 1313,
    1314, 1413
  warfare **5**:1411, 1412, 1414
Cavazza, Bartolomeo **4**:1000
cave, allegory of the (Plato)
  4:1094–1095
Cavenaghi, Luigi **3**:713
Cavendish family **2**:542
Caxes, Eugenio **5**:*1322*
Caxton, William **1**:223
Cecil, Robert **2**:333, **3**:665
Cecil, William (Lord
  Burghley) **1**:81, **5**:1287,
  1289, 1419
  Elizabeth I **2**:327, 328, 331
celestial chart **1**:*67, 69*
celibacy **1**:229, 230, 235,
  2:569
Cellini, Benvenuto **1**:243,
  2:450, **3**:767, **4**:989
Celtis, Conradus **2**:550, *551,*
  552, **3**:590
Cenami, Giovanna **2**:*389*
Cennini, Cennino **2**:490
censorship **3**:754, **4**:883,
  900–901, **5**:1197, 1283
  London theater **5**:1322,
    1326
Cento Dam **1**:280
Cerasi, Tiberio **1**:193, 194
Cerasi chapel **1**:193, 194,
  195
*Certain Experiments concerning
  Fish and Fruite* (Taverner)
  1:280
Certaldo **1**:112, 115
Certosa di Pavia (Lombardy)
  3:*740*
Cervantes, Catalina de **1**:203
Cervantes, Miguel de
  1:202–206, **3**:728, 736,
  739, **5**:1221, 1284, 1323
  chivalry **1**:223–224
Cervantes, Rodrigo de **1**:202
Cestius, Caius **1**:37

Charles I, King of England (van Dyke) **5:**1243

Charles Quint (Madariaga, ed.) **1:**211

Charlier, Jean (Jean de Gerson) **2:**367

Charron, Pierre **4:**1071

chartered companies **2:**500–501

Chastillon, Odet de **5:**1178

château **2:**436, 450, 563

Château Steen (Rubens's home) **5:**1237

Chatsworth House (Derbyshire) **3:**663

Chaucer, Geoffrey **1:212–220**, **3:**801, **4:**931, *1081, 1083,* **5:**1289, 1290

  Boccaccio **1:**112, 113

  religious orders **5:**1202

  vernacular language **3:**694

Chaucer, Philippa **1:**213, 214

Chávez Alvardo, Diego de **1:**280

Cheng Ho **2:**373, **5:**1342, *1343*

Chenonceaux **1:**45, **2:**444

Cherasco, Treaty of (1631) **5:**1336

Cherbourg, surrender of (1450) **3:**603

Cherbury, Lord *see* Herbert, Edward

Cher River **2:**444

Cherubin de Centelles, Juan **1:**123

Chester play cycle **5:**1318

Chevensey Palace (Kent) **3:**665

chicken pox **1:**255, **2:**307

Chieracati, Girolamo **4:**1004

Chigi, Agostino **1:**39, 40, 41, **5:**1186

Chigi chapel (Rome) **1:**39

childbirth **3:**842, **4:**1117, *1120*

  deaths **5:**1420

  see also infant mortality; motherhood

Childe, Maccabaeus **5:**1287

childhood disease **2:**307

child rearing **5:**1418, 1421

Children's Games (Bruegel) **1:**146, 147

China

  crafts **3:**804

  disease **2:**302–303, 305

  exploration **2:**373, 376, 380, 381, 382, **5:**1341, 1342, 1343

  inventions **3:**774, 775, 778, 804, 805

  Jesuit missionaries **4:**1015

  Judaism **3:**669

  missionaries **4:**894–895

  Portugal **4:**1142

  printing **5:**1168, 1193

  religious orders **5:**1206

  ships **5:**1343

  technology **5:**1343

  trade **2:**302–303, **5:**1346

chinea (ritual papal gift) **5:**1234

Chinon **3:**657

Chioggia, War of **5:**1395

chip log **2:**376

Chishti Sufi order **3:**615

chivalry **1:221–226**

  Agincourt **1:**18, 20

  Burgundy **1:**158, 161–162, 163, 164

  courtly love **1:**221, **4:**1101, 1102

  decline of **5:**1313, 1314, 1411, 1413

  feudalism **2:**402–403, 408–413

  France **2:**451

  Hapsburgs **2:**514, 515

  Hundred Years War **3:**598

  tournaments **1:**162, *224, 225, 226,* **3:**598

  see also Crusades

Chmiehicki massacres (1648) **3:**675

chocolate **5:**1346

choirs **4:**949

chorales **4:**952, 954, 958

Choralis Constantinus (Isaac) **4:**957

choral music **1:**163, **4:**949, 950, 952

Chora monastery (Constantinople) **1:**258, 263

Chrétien de Troyes **1:**222, **4:**1101

Christ *see* Jesus of Nazareth

Christ, Order of **1:**33, **2:**380, **4:**1137

Christ and Doubting Thomas (Verrocchio) **3:**707

Christ before Pilate (Bosch) **1:**131

Christ Carrying the Cross (Bosch) **1:**128, 130, 131

Christ Church (Oxford) **5:**1373

Christ Delivering the Keys to Saint Peter (Perugino) **5:**1182

Christ Healing the Sick (the Hundred Guilder Print) (Rembrandt) **5:**1212, 1215

Christian I, prince of Anhalt-Bernburg **3:**838

Christian I, king of Denmark and Norway **5:**1304

Christian II, king of Denmark, Norway, and Sweden **5:**1305

Christian IV, king of Denmark and Norway **3:**665, **5:**1246, 1251, 1308, 1335, 1338

Christian Civic Alliance **5:**1315

Christianity

  bibles **1:**102–110

  Byzantium **1:**166, 167, 168, 169, 270–272

  Constantinople **1:**256, 258

  Crusades **1:**223

  defining doctrine **1:**183

  heliocentric universe **1:**272

  humanism **3:**590, 591, 592, 593

  iconoclasm **3:**604–609

  Islam **3:**610–611, 612, 613, 616, 618, 621, 626, 715–719

  Judaism **3:**669, 670–671, 672–679, 689

  missionaries **4:**888–896

Ottoman Empire **1:**169

Petrarch **4:**1054–1055

philosophy **1:**168, **4:**1061, 1064–1065

Platonism **1:**57, 258, 261, **2:**320

popular culture **4:**1119, 1120

Ptolemaic cosmos **1:**267, 268

vernaculars **3:**695–697, 699

see also Orthodox Church; Reformation; Roman Catholic Church; *specific denominations and sects*

Christian of Brunswick (Mad Christian) **5:**1335

Christian Prayers (prayer book) **1:**239

Christina, queen of Sweden **1:227–231**, **4:**1068

  abdication of **1:**229–230, **5:**1311

  Descartes **1:**228, **2:**301

  Oxenstierna **5:**1307, 1310

Christine de Pisan **5:**1418

Christ in the House of Martha and Mary (Velázquez) **5:**1384

Christmas **4:**1118, 1119

  festivals **5:**1317, 1320, 1328

Christmas Oratorio (Schütz) **5:**1247

Christopher III, king of Denmark, Norway, and Sweden **2:**506, **5:**1304

Christopher, duke of Württemberg **1:**75

Christus, Petrus **4:**982

chromaticism **4:**919, 955

Chronica gentis scotorum (John of Fordun) **5:**1260

Chronicle of Saint Denis **4:**1042

Chronicle of Ulrich von Richental **1:**158

Chronicles (Froissart) **1:**224

Chronicum Helveticum **5:**1312

Chroniques d'Angleterre, Les (Wavrin) **3:**599, **4:**1127, 1137

Chrysoloras, Manuel **1:**261, **3:**584, 684–685, **5:**1220
overview of **1:**264
Chukchis (people) **4:**937
church and state *see* church-state relations
churches
  arches **1:**36
  architecture **1:**30–39, 43, 44, 46, 48, 49, **3:**667, 668
  Bernini designs **1:**100–101
  Bramante designs **1:**139
  Brunelleschi designs **1:**153, 156
  circular design **1:**32, 37, 141
  Constantinople **1:**263
  Italian city-states **3:**639, 641
  mosques converted from **1:**170, 171, 172
  rood screen **5:***1160*
  Wren designs **5:**1431, 1432
  see also specific churches under keyword
Church of England **1:232–240, 2:**338
  bibles **1:**104, 106–107, 108
  Calvinist ideas **1:**188, **5:**1267
  Eastern Orthodox patriarchate **1:**262, 263
  Elizabeth I **1:**235, 236–239, 240, **2:**326, 328–329, 331, 341, 343, 368–369, **4:**1015, **5:**1198
  English civil wars **2:**347, 348, 349, 352, 372
  as established church **2:**342–343, 346, 367, 368–369, 370, 372, **4:**930–931, **5:**1197
  Henry VIII **1:**178, **2:**326, 521, 524–527, 528, **4:**1015
  High Church movement **5:**1325
  iconoclasm **3:**608–609
  missionaries **4:**892
  monarchy **4:**913, 914
  nobility and rank **4:**975
  nonjurors **1:**262
  papacy **4:**1015, 1016
  preaching **5:**1166

printing **5:**1175
  Puritan conflicts **1:**109, **2:**347, **5:**1198
  Roman Catholic Church **1:**263
  Stuarts **5:**1301, 1302, 1328–1329
  theater **5:**1325, 1328–1329
  Tudors **5:**1325
  universities **5:**1374
  vernacular language **3:**698–699
  see also Book of Common Prayer
Church of Scotland **1:**190, **2:**369, **5:**1265, 1266, 1267, 1298, 1300, 1301, 1303
church-state relations
  absolutism **2:**367, 368
  Aristotle **1:**53
  Calvinism **1:**186–187, **4:**906
  Church of England **1:**235–240
  Constantinople **1:**257
  Eastern vs. Western Roman Empire **1:**257, 259
  education **2:**317, 321–322, 324
  England **2:**364–365, 524
  English iconoclasm **3:**608–609
  France **2:***432*
  heresy **2:**530, 533, 539, 541
  Hobbes **2:**544
  Holy Roman Empire **1:***208, 209, 210,* **2:**510, 556, 557, **5:**1331
  investiture controversy **2:**365–366, 368
  Islam **3:**612–613, 614
  Italian city-states **3:**639
  monarchy **4:**903, 905, 912, 913–914, 915, **5:**1331
  More **4:**930–932
  nationalism **4:**969, 970
  Ottoman Empire **3:**623, 627
  papacy **1:**156, 257, **3:**594, 686, **4:**1012, 1019–1021, 1037, 1038–1039
  Philip II **4:**1057–1058
  Reformation **2:**321

religious pluralism **2:**541
taxation **1:**180
Urbino **5:**1382–1383
see also Holy Roman Emperor; established churches
Churrigueresque **1:**47
Chu Ti, emperor of China **5:**1342
Cicero **4:**1102
  classical languages **3:**682, 683, 684, *685,* 686, 687
  English humanism **2:**336
  humanism **3:**583, 584, 588, 589, **5:**1219
  Petrarch **4:**1053, 1054
Cid, El **3:**695, 728
Cid, Le (Corneille) **3:**730, 731
Cigarrales de Toledo, Los (Molina) **1:**205
Cignani, Carlo **5:***1209*
Cimabue **2:**484, *485,* 488
Cino dei Sighibuldi (Cino da Pistoia) **1:**111, **5:***1366*
Cinquième Livre (Rabelais) **5:**1178
Ciompi, the **2:**415, **3:**849, 853
Ciompi revolt (1378) **2:**415, 417, 419, **3:**636 637
circular design (church) **1:**32, 37, 141
circumcision **3:**671
circumnavigation **2:**373, 374, 382, 384, **3:**787, 788, 789, 793–794, **5:**1250
Cistercians **3:**748, 806
cities and towns
  agricultural products **1:**22
  biconfessional **1:**78
  Black Death **2:**305, **3:**633, **4:**1130–1131
  education **2:**321
  France **2:**432, 436, 439, 457
  French Calvinism **2:**440, 442
  German towns **2:**475–483
  guilds **2:**495
  Hanseatic League **2:**475–476, 502, 503, 504–505, 506
  Holy Roman Empire **2:**476, 478

housing **2:**563
  insurgencies **4:**1042
  Italian city-states 630–642
  Jewish ghettos **3:**672, 679
  Lombardy **3:**743–744
  Lutheranism **2:**552–554
  machines **3:**774
  manufacturing **3:**808–809, 810
  markets and fairs **3:**815, 817, 818, 819
  population **4:**1124, 1126, 1130–1133
  printing presses **3:**819
  Reformation **5:**1193, 1200
  trade **3:**774, **4:**1136, **5:**1340
  waterworks **1:**273
Cities of the World see Civitates orbis terrarum
citizenship
  London **3:**752, 755
  Venice **5:**1397–1398
Città di Castello chapel (Perugia) **5:**1182
City of God (Augustine) **1:**53, **4:**1055
City of the Sun (utopia) **1:**31
Civedati, Marco **5:***1403*
civic humanism **3:**585, 638, 640
Civilization of the Renaissance in Italy, The (Burckhardt) **5:**1220
civil servants **3:**638, 640, **4:**913
civil war, Czech **1:**119
civil war, English *see* English civil wars
Civitas solis (Campanella) **4:**1103
Civitates orbis terrarum (Braun and Hogenberg) **1:***78, 281,* **4:***1139,* **5:***1316, 1350*
Clampers **2:**383
Clare of Assisi **5:**1201
class *see* nobility and rank, social class
classical antiquity
  architecture **1:**49, 151, *152,* **2:**334, **4:**983
  Calvin **1:**181

classical antiquity (cont.)
  Constantinople 1:258, 261, 264
  drama with music 4:916, 920
  education 2:320, 324
  England 2:334–335, 336, 337
  Erasmus 2:357
  literature 3:720, 722, 727, 739
  Machiavelli 3:772
  Marlowe 3:823
  mathematics 3:827, 829
  medicine 3:840
  More 4:925, 928–929, 930
  music 4:942, 961
  painting and sculpture 1:145, 4:980–981, 983, 986, 990
  pastoral 3:737
  philosophy 1:167, 169, 181, 261, 2:334, 422, 3:685, 730, 4:1025, 5:1368, 1370, 1376
  theater 3:727, 729, 730, 731, 732, 733, 734–735, 5:1320–1321, 1322, 1326
  universities 5:1366, 1373
  see also Greek culture; philosophy; humanism and learning; Roman Empire
classical languages see languages, classical
classical orders 1:30, 31, 37, 140, 141, 142, 2:424
classical revival see humanism and learning
Claude, duchess of Lorraine 1:198
Claudian 1:112
clavichord 4:959
Clavius, Christoph 1:175
Cleanness (Pearl Poet) 1:220
Clement V, Pope 4:905, 1052, 1109, 5:1227
Clement VI, Pope 1:174, 3:757, 5:1367
Clement VII (antipope) 4:1010, 5:1427

Clement VII, Pope 1:241–246, 2:426, 4:930, 1014–1015, 1023, 5:1196
  Catherine de Médicis 1:197
  Charles V 1:208, 209, 210, 241, 242, 243, 244
  Hapsburgs 2:513
  Henry VIII 1:234, 242, 244, 2:523
  Italian wars 3:647, 648, 649
  Judaism 3:677
  Machiavelli 3:773
  Medicis 2:418, 420, 421, 426, 3:850, 851, 854, 855
  Michelangelo 2:426
  Paul V 4:1037
  Rome 5:1232, 1233
  Urbino 5:1380
  Venice 5:1400
Clement VIII, Pope 2:370, 517, 519
Clement IX, Pope 1:330
Clement XI, Pope 5:1209
Clement XIV, Pope 5:1209
Clement of Alexandria 4:1098
Cleopatra (Gentileschi) 2:472, 473
Cléopatre captive (Jodelle) 3:729
clergy 4:1008–1009
  Church of England 1:235
  France 2:439
  Poland 4:1108–1109
  seminaries 5:1361
  see also religious orders
Clermont, Collège de 4:897
Cleves, duke of 4:1088
Clifford, Anne, countess of Dorset 5:1290, 1427
clinical medicine 3:847
Clinton family 2:542
clocks 3:775, 779–780
clog calendars 1:173
cloth see textiles, wool trade
Cloth Hall (Warsaw) 4:1112
clothing
  Jews 3:671
  pilgrimage 4:1081
  Polish Jews 4:1111
  Puritans 2:342
  sumptuary laws 4:979, 1041

cloth manufacture see textiles
Cloth of Gold, Field of the 2:522, 4:927
Clouet, François 1:198, 5:1262
Clouet, Jean 3:590, 4:990, 5:1298
Clough, Richard 5:1164
clowns 5:1319
Clubmen (English civil wars) 2:352
coal 3:784–785, 811, 812
coats of arms 1:226, 2:410, 3:598
Cock, Hieronymus 1:145, 146
cockfighting 1:92, 96
Cocq, Frans Banning 5:1213
cod 5:1341
Codex Alexandrinus 1:109
Codex B 4:1022
Codex Vaticanus 1:109
Coeck van Aelst, Mayken 1:144, 146
Coeck van Aelst, Pieter 1:144, 145, 146
cofferdam 1:279
cog (vessel) 2:506
Cogito, ergo sum (Descartes) 2:296–297, 299, 4:1070, 5:1294
Cognac 2:454
Cognac, League of (1526) 1:210, 242, 244, 3:647, 5:1232–1233
Coimbra, University of 2:403, 4:1144
coins 1:84–85, 90, 245, 264, 2:416
coke 3:811
Coke, Edward 1:79
Colantonio, Niccolò 2:391
Coles, Isaac 4:1007
Colet, John 2:337, 4:879, 1103, 5:1373
Coligny, Gaspard II de 1:199, 200, 2:452–453, 454, 455
Colin Clouts Come Home Againe (Spenser) 5:1287, 1289
Coliseum (Rome) 5:1326

Collectanea satis copiosa (document) 2:524
colleges 5:1376
  Calvinist 1:181, 189
Collegium Maius (Kraków) 1:270
Collegium Musicum 5:1377
Colleone, Bartolomeo, monument of 3:707, 709
Colloquia familiaria (Erasmus) 2:357
Colmar 2:311
Cologne 2:548, 557, 558
  archbishop-elector of 1:77
  Jewish purges 3:672
Cologne, University of 3:689
Colombo, Domenico 1:247
colonialism 3:603, 642
  agriculture 1:24–25, 28, 29
  architecture 1:49
  Columbus 1:251–253
  disease 2:306–309
  exploration 2:373, 375, 381
  monarchy 4:915
  Portugal 4:1137, 1140, 1142–1143, 1145
  Spain 2:399, 5:1284, 1285
  trade 5:1342, 1346–1347
  see also Americas
Colonna, Ascanio 5:1238
Colonna, Caterina 5:1379
Colonna, Giovanni 4:1051, 1052, 1053, 5:1228
Colonna, Oddo see Martin V
Colonna, Prospero 3:651
Colonna, Sciarra 5:1227
Colonna, Vittoria 4:877
Colosseum (Rome) 1:39, 4:1026
Colours of Good and Evil (Bacon) 1:80
Columbian exchange 1:255
Columbus, Bartolomé 1:255
Columbus, Christopher 1:46, 247–255, 3:693, 782, 788, 829, 4:1138, 1142, 5:1345
  armed trade 3:775
  disease 2:306, 308

exploration **1:**247–251,
  2:373, 374, 381–382,
  4:914, 915, **5:**1220
  Ferdinand and Isabella
    2:393, 394, 399
  missionizing **4:**888, 889,
    891, 895
  writings of **1:**253
Columbus, Diego **1:**248
Columbus, Ferdinand **1:**248
Columella, Lucius **1:**277
*Combattimento di Tancredi e
  Clorinda, Il* (Monteverdi)
  4:917, 922
Comédie-Française **4:**902
comedy **3:**731, 732, 733, 734
  Shakespeare **5:**1271, 1272,
    1274
  theater **5:**1323
comedy-ballet **4:**900
Comedy of Errors, The
  (Shakespeare) **3:**732,
  5:1271
commedia dell'arte **3:**734,
  4:899, **5:**1320, *1321*, 1322
Commentaries (Pius II)
  4:1087, 1091
Commentaries on Caesar
  (Palladio) **1:**43
Commentariolus (Copernicus)
  1:265, 269, 272
commerce *see* trade
Common Council, Court of
  3:751
common-law companies
  2:500
Common Penny (tax) **2:**550
Commonwealth (England)
  2:355, **4:**884, 885, 906
communion *see* Eucharist,
  Holy Communion
community life **4:**1116–1117
Commynes, Philippe de
  1:162, 163, 164
Como **3:**638
companies *see* guilds and
  companies
compass **2:**376, 384,
  3:778–779, **5:**1343
Compass and Ruler (Dürer)
  2:312

compass needle **3:**790
Compiègne **3:**658, 661
Complaints (Spenser)
  5:1288–1289
Complutensian Polyglot **1:**109
Composite (order) **1:**30, *31*
Comus (Milton) **4:**879, 880,
  884, 885
Comyn, John **4:**905
*Concerning the Christian
  Religion* (Ficino) **2:**422
"Concerning the Jews and
  Their Lies" (Luther) **3:**675
Concert of Youths (Caravaggio)
  1:192
conciliarism **2:**367, **3:**762
Concordia **4:**1073
concrete **1:**47
Condé **2:**456
Condé *see* Louis, prince of
  Condé
Condé, prince of *see* Bourbon-
  Vendôme, prince of
condominium system **2:**507,
  508, 512
condottieri *see* mercenaries
Condulmer, Gabriele *see*
  Eugenius IV
Confessio Bohemica (1609)
  1:121
confession **1:**235, **3:**767,
  5:1357
confessionalism **1:**187, **2:**540,
  556
Confession of Augsburg **1:**75,
  76
Confession of Faith (Lucaris)
  1:263
Confessions (Augustine)
  4:1052
Confucianism **4:**895, 1015
Confutations of Tyndale's Answer
  (More) **1:**106
Congregationalism **1:**181, 188,
  189, **2:**372 *see also* Puritans
Conjurer, The (Bosch) **1:**127,
  128, 129
conjuring **3:**800
conlegium vs. *universitas*
  5:1376
Connecticut **1:**189, **2:**372

conquistadores **1:**207,
  2:307–308, **5:**1285, 1345
  disease **2:**307
Conrad of Mazowsze **4:**1107
Consiglio delle Provvisioni
  (Milan) **5:**1403
Consolation of Philosophy
  (Boethius), Chaucer
  translation **1:**213, 217
Constance, Council of **1:**119,
  264, **3:**696, **4:**962–963,
  969, 1010–1011, **5:**1227,
  1352, 1363
  calendar reform **1:**174
  heresy **2:**537
Constance of Castile **1:**214
Constantine I (the Great),
  emperor of Rome **1:**38, 99,
  2:366, 512, **3:**594, 686,
  4:1026, **5:**1201
  Byzantium **1:**165, 166, 172
Constantinople **1:**256, 257
Constantine IX, Byzantine
  emperor **1:**258
Constantine X, Byzantine
  emperor **1:**258
Constantine XI, Byzantine
  emperor **1:**263
Constantinople **1:256–264,**
  4:1073
  Byzantium **1:**165–172
  Christianity **1:**170–171
  Crusade of Nicopolis **1:**158
  crusader sacking of **1:**168,
    260, **5:**1393
  Florence, Council of **1:**260,
    2:427, 428, 430
  Greek manuscripts **1:**269,
    2:430, **3:**685, 688
  Greek-speaking refugees **1:**55,
    2:320
  Hagia Sophia **1:**171–172
  Jewish settlements **3:**680
  Ottoman seige of **1:***264,*
    5:1410
  Ottoman takeover of **1:**158,
    166, 169, 170, 171, 172,
    263–264, **2:**320, 427,
    429, 430, **3:**612, 616,
    618, 619, 623, 625, 685,
    4:935

philosophy **4:**1063
scholarship **4:**1063
Constantinople, University of
  1:168, 261
Constantius, emperor of
  Rome **1:**172
constellations **1:***67,* 68, *69*
constitutional government
  2:545
constitutional monarchy
  4:906
Constitution of the United
  States **2:**372
Constitutions (Ignatius of
  Loyola) **5:**1206
consubstantiation **3:**764,
  5:1194
Contarelli chapel (Rome)
  1:192, 193
Contarini, Gasparo **5:**1400
contemptus mundi literature
  1:127
continuo **4:**916
Convenole de Prato **4:**1050
*Conversation between Women,
  A* (Bosse) **5:***1423*
Conversion of Saint Paul
  (Caravaggio) **1:**193
Conversion of Saint Paul
  (Michelangelo) **4:**877
Conversion of Saint Peter
  (Caravaggio) **1:**193
conversos (Jewish converts)
  2:396, 397, 398, 399,
  3:676–677, 678, **5:**1278,
  1283
Cook, James **2:**384,
  5:1258–1259
Cooke, Anne **1:**79
Cooke, Anthony **1:**79,
  5:1419, 1427
Cooke sisters **5:**1418, 1419,
  1422, 1427
Cooper, Samuel **2:***351,* **3:***663*
Cop, Nicholas **4:**1032
Copenhagen **5:**1246, 1311
Copernicus, Nicolaus **1:***57,
  60,* **265–272, 2:**539,
  3:699, 783, 827, 829, 831,
  832, **4:**1036, 1069,
  5:1221, 1251

Copernicus, Nicolaus *(cont.)*
  circular planetary path **1:**31,
    60, 265, 270
  Descartes **2:**296
  Galileo **2:**463, 465, 466,
    467, **5:**1226
  Polish Renaissance **4:**1109
  universe model **1:**265, **2:**296,
    4:1109, **5:**1226, 1250,
    1252–1253
Coptic Church **2:**429, 431
Coptic language **3:**695
coralles **3:**727, 728
Corbaccio (Boccaccio) **1:**115
Corbie **5:**1338
Cordier, Mathurin **1:**179
Cordovero, Moses **3:**680
Corelli, Arcangelo **1:**230
Corfu **1:**202
Corinth, Gulf of **3:**715
Corinthian order **1:**30, *31,*
  152
Coriolanus (Shakespeare)
  5:1272
Cork, County (Ireland)
  5:1288, 1290
Cork, earl of *see* Boyle,
  Richard
Corkine, William **3:**825
corn (maize) **1:**28, **5:**1346
Cornaro, Luigi Alvise **4:**1001
Corneille, Pierre **3:**729, 730,
  731, **4:**898
Cornish Rebellion (1497)
  4:1042
Cornyshe, William **4:**948
Coronado, Francisco Vásquez
  de **2:**382
Coronation of Poppea, The
  (Monteverdi) **4:**922, 923
Coronation of the Virgin
  (Raphael) **5:**1181, 1182
corporal punishment **2:**319
Corporation Act of 1660
  (England) **1:**240
Corpus Christi, feast of
  5:1318
Corpus Christi College
  (Oxford) **5:**1373
Corpus Christi plays **5:**1322
Correa, Juan **5:***1199*

corsairs *see* piracy
Corsignano **4:**1086, 1090
Corsini Palace (Rome) *see*
  Palazzo Corsini
Cortegiano, Il (Castiglione)
  5:1383
Cortés, Hernán **4:**890, **5:**1285,
  1345
  disease **2:**307
  exploration **2:**374, 382
Cortile de Belvedere (Vatican)
  1:142, **4:**1040
Cortona, Pietro da **1:**32
Corvus, Hans **5:***1373*
Cosmographic Mystery (Kepler)
  1:271, **2:**463
cosmology *see* astronomy,
  heliocentric universe
Cossa, Baldassare *see* John
  XXIII
Cossacks **3:**675, **4:**936, 938,
  1113–1114, **5:**1337
cotton textiles **3:**808
councils, papal **2:**434, **5:**1352
  *see also specific councils by
    keyword*
counterpoint **5:**1245
Counter-Reformation
  armada, Spanish **1:**66
  Bohemia **1:**122
  Descartes **2:**296
  education **2:**320
  Galileo **2:**467
  Greek revival **2:**320
  Hapsburg Empire **2:**513,
    514–515, 559
  Holy Roman Empire **2:**556
  Jesuits **5:**1191, 1199
  Judaism **3:**679
  literature **3:**736–737, 739
  music **4:**943, 954–957
  overview of **5:**1197
  painting **1:**194, **4:**990–991,
    992
  papacy **3:**703, **4:**1016–1019,
    1024, 1036
  Paris **4:**1035
  Poland **4:**1111
  religious orders **5:**1204–1209
  Renaissance **5:**1226
  Rome **5:**1234–1235

Rubens **5:**1240
Scholasticism **1:**58–59
Scotland **5:**1265
Spain **1:**66, **4:**1058,
  5:1282–1283
Thirty Years War **5:**1332
Trent, Council of **5:**1352,
  1364
universities **5:**1365, 1368,
  1375, 1377
vernaculars **3:**696
see also Inquisition
country houses, English **2:**334
Courbet, Gustave **5:**1391
Courtier, The (Castiglione)
  5:1221, 1383
courtiers **2:***411,* **5:**1383, 1427
courtly love **1:**221, **2:**402,
  4:*1101,* 1102
Court of Alderman **3:**751
Court of Ashton **5:**1350
Court of Star Chamber **5:**1328
Courtois, Jacques (Le
  Bourguignon) **5:***1337*
court society **4:**978–979
  chivalry **1:**221
  etiquette **2:**437
  musicians **4:**948, 949
  Scotland **5:**1296
  tournaments **1:**225
  Urbino **5:**1383
  women **5:**1383, 1427
  see also courtiers
Covenanters (Scotland) **2:**349,
  350, 351, **5:**1303
covenanting **5:**1267
Covent Garden (London)
  3:820
Coventry mystery plays
  5:*1318*
Coverdale, Miles **1:***106,* 107
Covilhã, Pero da **2:**381
craft guilds **2:**496–497, 499,
  4:983
crafts *see* artisans
Cranach, Lucas (the Elder)
  1:95, **2:***324,* **3:***704, 705,*
  760, 762, **4:***1064, 1066,*
  1115, **5:***1163,* 1171, *1188*
Cranmer, Thomas
  bibles **1:**106–107, 237

Book of Common Prayer
  5:1267
Church of England **1:**235,
  236, 237, 238, 240
English vernacular **3:***699*
established church **2:**338
Henry VIII **2:**524, 526, 527,
  528, **3:**608, **5:**1197
Craponne, Adam de **1:**280
Creation (Michelangelo)
  4:1025
Crécy, Battle of (1346) **1:**117,
  2:434, 435, **3:**596–597,
  598, **5:***1412,* 1413
Credi, Lorenzo di **3:**706, 708,
  5:*1428*
credit *see* banking
Crema **3:**744
Cremona **3:**638, 743, **4:**916,
  917, 921, 923
Cremona, Cathedral of **4:**917
Cremonini, Cesare **1:**57
Crépy, Peace of (1544) **1:**209
Crescas, Hasdai **3:**679
Crete **4:**1073, **5:**1393
crime **2:**565, **3:**753
Crimea **3:**653, 655, **5:**1337
Critias (Plato) **4:**1103
critical thinking **2:**317
Crivelli, Taddeo **3:***686*
Croatian peasants' revolt
  4:1042
Crocyn, William **5:**1373
Cromwell, Oliver **2:**544,
  4:*884,* 887, **5:***1303,* 1427
  English civil wars **1:**239,
    2:351–352, *353,* 354
Cromwell, Richard **2:**351
Cromwell, Thomas
  biblical translation **1:**106,
    2:339
  Henry VIII **1:**235, **2:**338,
    522, 524, 525, 526, 527
crop rotation **1:**27, **4:**1134
crops *see* agriculture
Croquants rebellion **2:**456
Crosby, Alfred **1:**255, **2:**306
crossbow **2:**435
cross-staff **5:**1343
Crowning with Thorns (Bosch)
  1:130

crown of Saint Wenceslas
1:117
crucifix, Byzantine **1:***170*
Crucifixion **5:***1163*
Crucifixion, The (Raphael)
5:*1181*
Crucifixion (Bosch) **1:***130*
Crucifixion of Saint Peter
(Michelangelo) **4:**877
*Crucifixion with Saints Mary
the Virgin, Mary Magdalene,
John, and Jerome* (Raphael)
5:1182
Crusades **3:**618, 619, 715
Burgundy **1:**158, 162
chivalric orders **1:**223, 226
Constantinople sacking
1:168, 259–260, **5:**1393
Pius II **4:**1086–1088, 1089
Teutonic Knights **4:**1104,
1106, 1107
trade **5:**1341
Venice **1:**259–260,
5:1392–1393
Cruzada, Council of **1:**202
crypto-Jews **2:**533
Cuba **1:**250, **4:**892
Cudworth, Ralph **4:**1070
cuius regio, eius religio principle
5:1331
Culverwell, Nathaniel **4:**1070
Cure of Folly, The (Bosch)
1:128, 129, 130
currency *see* money
curriculum **2:**318, 320, 321,
322, 325
Aristotelian **1:**57
Colet-Erasmus 7, 879
Constaninople **1:**257
humanist **3:**582, 584, 588,
589, 683, 689, **5:**1218,
1282
see also Scholasticism
Curtain (London theater)
5:1326, 1327
Custom House (London)
5:1431, 1432
customs dues **5:**1350
Cuylenborch, Abraham van
4:*1037*
Cydones, Demitrius **1:**261

Cymbeline (Shakespeare)
5:1271
Cyprus **2:**304, **3:**626, 715,
718, **5:**1393
czar, as title **4:**934
Czech Bible **1:**118
Czech civil war **1:**119
Czech Confession (1575)
1:121
Czech culture *see* Bohemia
Czech Republic *see* Bohemia

D

Dafne (Peri) **4:**920, 943
Dafne (Schütz) **5:**1246
Dakin, Margaret (later Hoby)
3:749, **5:**1416, 1422
dams and drainage **1:**28,
273–281, 3:741, 808
Dance of the Nudes (Pollaiuolo)
2:425
dancing **4:**950
Daniel, book of **5:**1355
Daniel, grand prince of
Muscovy **4:**933
Danish War **5:**1335–1336
Dansereye (Susato) **4:**950
Dante Alighieri **1:**53, **2:**484,
4:963, 1050, **5:**1249
Boccaccio **1:**111, 112, 113,
114, 115
as Chaucer influence **1:**216,
217–218, 219
overview of **1:**217
vernacular **1:**217, **3:**694
Danti, Ignatio **1:***175*
Danube River **1:**158, 169,
2:611, **3:**835
Danube valley **5:**1330
Danzig **2:**503, **4:**1106
Dar al-Islam see Islam
Darby, Abraham **3:**811
Dardanelles **1:**165, **3:**715
Darnley, Henry (Lord Darnley)
2:330, **5:**1298
Darwin, Charles **1:**110
Dati, Carlo **4:**883
Dati, Gregorio **5:**1420
Daumier, Honoré **1:***206*
David II, king of Scotland
3:597

David (Bernini) **1:**98–99
David (Donatello) **2:**424,
3:856, **4:**984, 999
David (Michelangelo) **4:**870,
871, 872–873, 986, 990
David (Verrocchio) **3:**707
David, Jacques-Louis **4:***1093*
Davis, Natalie **2:**459
Day of Judgment **1:**177, **2:**387
Day of the Barricades (Paris)
4:1033
De architectura (Vitruvius)
5:1321
De asse (Budé) **3:**590
death
disease **2:**307
magic **3:**798–799, 801–802
popular culture **4:**1117, 1121
preaching **5:**1161, 1166
see also mortality rates
Death and the Miser (Bosch)
1:128, 129
Death of Socrates (David)
4:1093
Death of the Virgin
(Caravaggio) **1:**193, 194
death penalty *see* executions
De augmentis scientiarum
(Bacon) **1:**80
Debarkation at Marseilles, The
(Rubens) **5:**1241
Decameron (Boccaccio) **1:**113,
114, 115, 205, 218, 219,
3:694, 735, 736
Florence **2:**423
religious orders **5:**1202
De casibus virorum illustrium
(Boccaccio) **1:**115
Deceived Ones, The (Rueda)
3:727
decimal system **3:**828, **5:**1250
De cive (Hobbes) **2:**544
Declaration of Independence
(United States) **4:**887
Declaration of Rights
(England) **1:**24
*Declaration of the Use and
Fabrication of Water
Instruments, Mills and
Other Things* (Giraba)
1:280

De claris mulieribus
(Boccaccio) **1:**115
De corpore (Hobbes) **2:**546
Decree of Reunion (Eastern-
Western churches)
2:429–431
De docta ignorantia (Nicholas
of Cusa) **4:**1098
deductive logic **1:**50, 81, 82
Dee, John **2:**384, **4:**1065
astrology **1:**72, **3:**800, 801
calendar **1:**176, 177
overview of **3:**800
Defence of Poesie, The (Sidney)
3:724, 725, 737
Defender of Peace (Marsilius of
Padua) **1:**53, 257, **2:**367
Defenestration of Prague
(1419) **1:**119, 122
Defenestration of Prague
(1618) **1:**121–122, **5:**1334
Defense of Free Will (Erasmus)
3:767
*Defense of the Seven
Sacraments, A* (Henry VIII)
1:232, 240, **2:**522, **4:**929
*Defense of True Liberty and
Antecedent and Extrinsical
Necessity* (Hobbes) **2:**546
Defensiones (Milton) **4:**879,
884, 886, 887
Defoe, Daniel **4:**1108
De historia stirpium (Fuchs)
1:*29*
De homine (Hobbes) **2:**546
De humani corporis fabrica
(Vesalius) **2:**302, **3:**840,
845, 846, **5:**1250
deism **4:**1071, 1072
Dekker, Thomas **1:**93, **3:**733,
748, **5:**1326, 1327, 1329
Delaroche, Hippolyte **4:***1074*
Delhi Sultanate **3:**613, 615,
629
De libero arbitrio (Erasmus)
2:360–361
Del Lama, Guaspare di
Zenobio **1:**138
Della misura dell'acque correnti
(Castelli) **1:**277
Della Robbia, Andrea **1:***151*

Della Robbia, Luca **1**:*154,* **3**:*682*

Della Rovere, Federico Ubaldo **5**:1381

Della Rovere, Felice **5**:1420

Della Rovere, Francesco Maria I **3**:701, **5**:1379, 1380–1381, 1382, 1383

Della Rovere, Francesco Maria II **5**:1381, 1383

Della Rovere, Giovanni **5**:1379, 1380

Della Rovere, Giuliano *see* Julius II

Della Rovere, Guidobaldo II **5**:1380, 1381, 1382–1383

Della Rovere, Livia **5**:1381

Della Rovere, Vittoria **5**:1380, 1381

Della Roveres, the **5**:1380–1381, 1420

Della Torres, the **3**:741, **5**:1403

Deloney, Thomas **3**:738

Delumeau, Jean **5**:1160

De machinis bellicis (Taccola) **5**:*1407*

De magistratibus et republica Venetorum (Contarini) **5**:1400

democracy **1**:166, **2**:542, **4**:906, **5**:1339

demography *see* population

De monarchia (Dante) **1**:217

Demonstrating the Avarice of Christians (engraving) **2**:382

De motu cordis (Harvey) **5**:1251

De naturis rerum (Neckam) **3**:778

Denkwürdigkeiten (Kottannerin) **5**:1418

Denmark
  divorce law **2**:568
  established church **2**:370, 372
  guilds **2**:493
  Hanseatic League **2**:503, 504, 505, 506
  Hapsburgs **2**:480

Lutheranism **2**:370, **3**:768
monarchy **4**:903, 911
Reformation **5**:1191
Russia **3**:653
Schütz **5**:1246
science and technology **5**:1251
Sweden **5**:1304–1306, 1307, *1308,* 1309, 1310, 1311, 1338
Thirty Years War **5**:1330, 1333, 1335–1336, 1338, 1415

De pittura (Alberti) **4**:984

Deposition of Christ (Raphael) **5**:1185

De remediis utriusque fortunae (Petrarch) **4**:1054

De re metallica (Agricola) **1**:*279*

De re militari (Valturio) **5**:*1408*

De revolutionibus orbium coelestium (Copernicus) **1**:50, 266, 269, 270, 272, **2**:463, 465, **4**:1109, **5**:1221, *1250*

Dering, Edward **5**:1419, 1424

dervishes **3**:*620*

Descartes, René **1**:60, **2**:**294–301,** 544, **3**:783, **5**:1206, 1251
  Christina **1**:228, 229
  mathematics **2**:294, 295, 296, 301, **3**:828, 830, 833
  philosophy **4**:1069–1070, 1071, 1072
  Spinoza **5**:1291–1292, 1293, 1294

Descent from the Cross, The (Rubens) **5**:1239–1240

Deschamps, Eustache **1**:215

Description of the Churches (Palladio) **4**:1003

De servo arbitrio (Luther) **2**:361

Detto d'amore, Il (Dante) **1**:217

Deulino, Truce of (1618) **4**:940

Deuteronomy, book of **1**:233, **3**:607

Deventer **2**:356

de Vere, Edward *see* Vere, Edward de

Devereux, Robert, earl of Essex **1**:79, 93, **2**:332–333, **5**:1290, 1416

Devereux, Walter **5**:1416

devil **2**:533, 534

De viris illustribus (Fazio) **2**:389

De viris illustribus (Petrarch) **4**:1052

De vita solitaria (Petrarch) **4**:1054

devotio moderna movement **3**:760–761, **4**:1065

"Devotions upon Emergent Occasions" (Donne) **5**:1166

dévots **2**:459

devshirme **3**:617, 626

De vulgari eloquentia (Dante) **3**:694

dialectic **2**:357, 362
  rhetoric vs. **5**:1369, 1372

Dialogo della musica antica et della moderna (V. Galilei) **4**:961

Dialogue concerning Heresies and Matters of Religion (More) **4**:930, 931

Dialogue concerning the Two Chief World Systems (Galileo) **1**:60, *272,* **2**:466, 467, **3**:690

Dialogue concerning Two New Sciences (Galileo) **2**:467, **3**:828, 833

Dialogue of Comfort against Tribulation (More) **4**:932

Dialogue on the Dignity of the Pope and King (Ockham) **2**:366

Dialogues, The (Bruni) **1**:55

Dias, Bartolomeu **2**:374, 381, **4**:1138, 1142, **5**:1341

Diaspora, Jewish **3**:669, 679, 695

Diderot, Denis **2**:466

Dido, Queene of Carthage (Marlowe) **3**:823

Diefendorf, Barbara **2**:459

Diego, Juan **4**:890

dietary laws **3**:669, 671

diets (nutrition) *see* food supply

diets (political bodies) *see* parliaments

differential calculus **3**:833

Dijon **1**:157, 163

dikes *see* dams and drainage

Diodati, Charles **4**:879, 880, 882, 883

Diodati, Giovanni **4**:882

Dionigi da Sansepolcro **1**:111

Dionysius the Areopagite **4**:1102, 1103

Dionysius the Areopagite Converting the Pagan Philosophers (Caron) **4**:*1102*

Dioptrics (Descartes) **2**:*297*

Diotima **4**:1092, 1095

diphtheria **3**:843

diplomacy
  Clement VII **1**:241
  Florence **2**:414
  Leo X **3**:702–703
  Machiavelli **2**:419
  Renaissance **5**:1223
  Rubens **5**:1242
  Venice **5**:1393

Discours de la méthode (Descartes) **2**:295, 296–297, **3**:833

Discourse of a Discoverie for a New Passage to Cataia [Cathay] (Gilbert) **2**:383

Discourse of Voyages into the East and West Indies (Linschoten) **5**:*1343*

Discourse on the Method (Descartes) **2**:295, 296–297, **3**:833

Discourses on Livy, The (Machiavelli) **3**:770, 772

Discourses on Sacred Images (John of Damascus) **3**:604

Discourses on Two New Sciences (Galileo) *see* *Dialogue concerning Two New Sciences*

Discourse to the Ten on Pisan Affairs (Machiavelli) **3**:779

Discoverer of Witches, The (Hopkins) **5:***1425*
Discoverie of Witchcraft (Scot) **5:**1425
disease **2:302–310,** **3:**843–844, 848
    African slave trade **5:**1349
    agriculture **1:**22, 29
    cities **4:**1131, 1133
    Columbian exchange **1:**255
    exploration **2:**382, **4:**1143
    indigenous peoples **5:**1285
    London **3:**755
    naming of **3:**841
    peasants **4:**1115
    pilgrimage **4:**1078, 1079, 1082
    population effects **4:**1124, 1125, 1127, 1128, 1129, 1134, 1135
    seafaring **2:**378, 379, 382
    technology **5:**1254
    Trent, Council of **5:**1357
    see also Black Death; medicine; *specific diseases*
dispensations **4:**1080
Disputa, La (Raphael) **5:**1186
Disputation of Saint Catherine of Alexandria (Pinturicchio) **1:**125
dissection **2:**302, **3:**845, 846, 848, **5:**1254
    body snatching **3:**848
    disease **2:**302
dissonance, musical **4:**916, 918, 943, 944
dits amoureux **1:**215
Diu, Battle of (1509) **4:**1142
Divers Voyages Touching the Discovery of America and the Islands Adjacent unto the Same (Hakluyt) **2:**375
Divina commedia (Dante) *see Divine Comedy*
divination **3:**795
Divine Comedy (Dante) **1:**113, *216,* 217, 218, 220, **2:**484, **3:**694
divine grace **3:**606
    Calvinism **1:**185, 186
    Lutheranism **3:**759, 766

Paul V **4:**1036
    sacraments **5:**1358
    see also free will
Divine Love, Oratory of **3:**703
divine right **2:**539, **4:**906, 907, **5:**1339
    England **1:**239, **2:**344, 345, 346, 347, 347–348, 348, 367
    France **1:**188, **2:**367, 432, 442, 443, 449, 517, 519
    Hapsburgs **2:**514
    Muscovy **4:**934, 940
    Russia **3:**652, 656
    state vs. church **2:**367, 368
    Stuarts **1:**239, **5:**1264, 1299, 1300, 1302–1303
    Westphalia, Peace of **5:**1339
    see also absolutism
divorce **2:**566, 567–568, **4:**913, 930
    Henry VIII **1:**232–235, 240, **2:**338, 340, 523, 524, **4:**1015, **5:**1196, 1197, 1297
    Milton **4:**883, 884
Dmitry, prince of Russia **4:**937, 938–939
Dmitry Donskoi **4:**934
Doctor Faustus (Marlowe) **2:**335, **3:**732, 822, 824, 826
doctors *see* medicine
"Doctrine and Discipline of Divorce, The" (Milton) **4:**879, 883, 884
doge **3:**650, **5:***1396,* 1397
Doges' Palace (Venice) **5:**1399, *1400*
dogfighting **1:**92
dogma statements **2:**540
Dolet, Étienne **5:**1177
Dolomite Mountains **1:**276
Dome of Paradise (Menabuoi) **4:***1062*
domes **1:**38, 43, 44, 48, 99, 140, 141
    Florence Cathedral **1:**32, 34, 35, 47, 149, 150–151, 154, *156*
Dominic, Saint **2:***398,* **5:**1201

Dominican Republic **1:**250, 253, *255*
Dominicans **1:**52, 137, **3:**594, 674, 676, **4:**1036, 1077, **5:**1201, 1204, 1209, 1327
    heresy **2:**532, 533
    missionaries **4:**889, 891, 892, 895
    preaching **5:**1158
Dominique, Jean **3:***659*
Domrémy **3:***657,* 658
Domzlice Agreement (1318) **1:**117
Donatello **1:**35, 36, **3:**856, **4:**871, *874,* 984, 985, **5:***1395*
    Florence **2:**424, 428
    Four Evangelists **1:***152*
Donation of Constantine **3:**584, 586, 594, 686
Donatus **3:***682*
Donauworth **1:**78, **3:**836
Doni Tondo (Michelangelo) **4:***872*
Don John *see* John of Austria
Don Juan (Molière) **4:**897, 901, 902
Donne, John **3:**726, **5:**1166
Don Quixote (Cervantes) **1:**202, 203, *204,* 205, 206, **3:**728, 739, **5:**1221, 1284
    as chivalric parody **1:**223–224
Don Quixote, the Second Volume of the Ingenious Don Quixote of La Mancha (Fernández de Avellaneda) **1:**206
Dordrecht **1:**274
Doré, Gustave **1:***205*
Doria, Andrea **3:**650
Doric order **1:**30, *31,* 37, 141
Dorigatti, Niccolò **1:***186,* **4:***1016*
Douay-Reims Bible **1:**108, 110
Double Cube Roome (Wilton House) **3:***667*
double-truth theory **4:**1054–1055

Doubting Thomas (Caravaggio) **1:***193*
Dowland, John **4:***957,* 959
drainage *see* dams and drainage
Drake, Francis
    armada, Spanish **1:**62, 63, 64
    Elizabeth I **2:**331
    exploration **2:**374, 382, 383, 385, **3:**791
    London **3:**751
    privateering **5:**1347
drama *see* theater
Drayton, Michael **3:**755, 824, **5:**1329
"Dreames, Legendes, Courte of Cupide" (Spenser) **5:**1287
Dream of John Ball, A (Morris) **4:**1048
Dream of Philip II (El Greco) **4:***1058*
Dresden **5:**1246, 1247
Dreux, Battle of (1562) **2:**452, **5:**1411
drills, seed **1:**27
Drost, Willem **5:**1217
Drury, William **5:**1287
Drury Lane Theatre (London) **5:**1432
Dryden, John **4:**887
dualism *see* mind-body dualism
Dublin **5:**1288
Dubois, François **1:***200, 201,* **4:***1033*
Duccio di Buoninsegna **2:**489, 492
Dudley, Robert, earl of Leicester **2:**329, 331, **5:**1287
dueling **1:**226, **4:**977
Dufay, Guillaume **4:**943, 944–946
Duke of Lerma on Horseback, The (Rubens) **5:***1238*
Dumas, Alexandre **1:**126
Dumonstier, Pierre **2:***469,* 471
Dunn, Alastair **4:**1047
Duns Scotus, John **4:**1075

Dunstable, John **4**:944

Duo seraphim (Monteverdi) **4**:921

Du Parc **4**:897

Duran, Diego **5**:*1285*

Durance River **1**:280

Dürer, Albrecht **2**:*311–316,* 550, *551,* **3**:828, **4**:983, 993, **5**:*1220,* 1221

printing **5**:1171

Durham House (England) **1**:48

Dutch East India Company **2**:383, **5**:1342, *1351*

Dutch painting **4**:995–998

Dyck, Anthony van *see* Van Dyck, Anthony

Dyer, Edward **3**:725, **5**:1287

dyes **5**:1344, 1350, 1402

Dying Slave (Michelangelo) **4**:874

E

Eanes, Gil **2**:380, **4**:1140

earth-centered universe *see* geocentric universe

earthquake, Lisbon **4**:1141, *1145*

earthworks **5**:1407, 1410

East Africa **2**:374, 381, **5**:1342

East Anglia **1**:188

Easter

dating of **1**:174–175, 176, 218

festival **4**:1118, 1119, **5**:1317

Eastern church *see* Orthodox Church

eastern Europe

Black Death **2**:305

Jews **3**:670, 675

Eastern Kreuz Dam **1**:279

Eastern Roman Empire *see* Byzantine Empire, Constantinople

East India Company

British **2**:375, 499, 501, **5**:1342, 1351

Dutch **2**:383, **5**:1342, *1351*

East Indies **4**:1139, 1145

Eastland Company **2**:500–501

Eastminster abbey **3**:748

Ecce Homo (Bosch) **1**:129

Ecclesiae militantis (Dufay) **4**:946

Ecclesiastical Builders and Furniture Makers (Borromeo) **1**:32

Ecclesiastical Ordinances (Calvin) **1**:186

Ecclesiasticus, book of **1**:103, **5**:1355

École des Beaux Arts (France) **1**:49

ecological imperialism **2**:306

economic classes *see* social class

economic theory **5**:1348–1351

Ecstasy of Saint Teresa (Bernini) **5**:1235

ecumenical councils **5**:1364 *see also* Constance, Council of; Florence, Council of

Edessa **1**:260

Edgehill, Battle of (1642) **2**:351, **4**:883

Edinburgh, Treaty of (1560) **5**:1266

Edinburgh riots (1637) **2**:*348,* 349

Edirne (Adrianople) **3**:612

education **2**:317–325

Catholic clergy **5**:1357

Constantinople **1**:257

Counter-Reformation **4**:1018, 1111

Elizabeth I **2**:327

England **5**:1286

Germany **5**:1372

households **2**:563, 569

Islam **3**:614

Jesuits **2**:294, **5**:1206, 1207, 1250, 1291

Latin language **3**:682

mission schools **4**:892

music **4**:942

Plato's Academy **4**:1095

Poland **4**:1111

Portugal **4**:1139

Presbyterianism **1**:189

school plays **5**:1323

Scotland **5**:1263

women **5**:1416–1418, 1419, 1424

see also humanism and learning; literacy; Scholasticism; universities

Edward I, king of England **4**:905, **5**:*1301*

Edward II, king of England **3**:825, **4**:903

Edward III, king of England **1**:16, 89, **2**:433, 497, 567, **4**:1047, **5**:*1412*

Chaucer **1**:213, 214, 216

chivalry **1**:161, 223, 224

feudalism **2**:406, 410

Florentine debt default **2**:416

Hundred Years War **3**:595, 596, 597, 598, 603

nationalism **4**:965, 968

Edward IV, king of England **1**:162–163, **2**:408

Edward VI, king of England **1**:71, 79, **2**:340, 514, **4**:954

bibles **1**:107

Calvinism **1**:188, 189

Church of England **1**:236, 237, 240, **2**:326, 368

Elizabeth I **2**:326, 327

Henry VIII **2**:522, 527, 528

humanism **5**:1419

iconoclasm **3**:608

mercenaries **5**:1411

papacy **4**:1015

printing **5**:1175

Reformation **5**:1197, 1267, 1325

Scotland **5**:1262

Edward, duke of York **1**:18

Edward, the Black Prince (England) **3**:597, 598

Edward of Woodstock *see* Edward, the Black Prince

Edward II (Marlowe) **3**:822, 825

Eertvelt, Andries van **5**:*1351*

efficient cause **4**:1063

Egerton, John, earl of Bridgewater **4**:880–881

Egerton, Thomas **3**:749

Eglogs, Epytaphs, and Sonettes (Googe) **5**:1288

Egypt

ancient calendars **1**:173

ancient Christianity **1**:57

Judaism **3**:*678,* 680

Mamluks **3**:612, 623

Ottoman Empire **3**:623

Eight Plays and Eight Interludes, New and Never Performed (Cervantes) **1**:206

Eikonoklastes (Milton) **4**:884, 886

Elbe River **2**:505, **5**:1335

Elcano, Juan Sebastián de **2**:374, **3**:793–794

Elche **5**:1318

Eleanor (daughter of Joan I) **1**:208, **5**:1281

Eleanor of Aquitaine **3**:596

elect, the *see* predestination

electors **2**:477, 478, 510, 548, 551, 553, **4**:909–911, 966

Electra (Sophocles) **3**:729

Elegantiae linguae Latinae (Elegances of the Latin Language) (Valla) **3**:586, 686, 687

elementary schools **2**:318–319, 320, 321, 322, 325

Elements of Law, Natural and Politic (Hobbes) **2**:544

Elements of the Common Laws of England (Bacon) **1**:80

elephant, papal **4**:1012

El Greco *see* Greco, El

Eliot, John **4**:892

elite magic **3**:798–799

Elizabeth I, queen of England **1**:*189,* **2**:326–333, **4**:894, 906, 909, **5**:1419

armada, Spanish **1**:62, **2**:331

astrological prediction **1**:71–72, **3**:800

Bacon **1**:79–80

bearbaiting **1**:93

bibles **1**:105, 107

calendar **1**:176

Catherine de Médicis **1**:198, 201

Christina compared with **1:**227, 229

Church of England **1:**235, 236–239, 240, **2:**326, 328–329, 331, 341, 343, 368–369, **4:**1015, **5:**1198

companies **2:**499, 501

courtiers **5:**1427

established church **2:**368–369, 370, 371, 372

excommunication of **1:**238, **2:**330

exploration **2:**382

Henry VIII **2:**524, 527, 528

humanist education **5:**1418

iconoclasm **3:**608–609

literature **2:**335, **3:**724, 725, 732, 733, 735, 737

London **3:**748, 750

Marlowe **3:**823

nationalism **4:**963, 966

Philip II **4:**1059, 1060

printing **5:**1175

Puritans **1:**188

Reformation **1:**176, 187, 188, *189, 237,* **2:**340–341, 342, 343, 345, 365, **5:**1198, 1325, 1424, 1426

religious music **4:**953

Renaissance **5:**1221, 1225

Scotland **5:**1262, 1263

Shakespeare **5:**1269, 1271, 1272

Spain **5:**1283

Spenser **5:**1285, 1287, 1289, 1290

Stuarts **5:**1297, 1298, 1300, 1301, 1426

theater **2:**335, **5:**1322, 1324–1325, 1328

tournaments **1:**225

universities **5:**1371

Elizabeth, princess of England (wife of Frederick V of Palatinate) **5:**1336

Elizabeth, queen consort of Bohemia **1:**117

Elizabeth, queen consort of Spain *see* Elizabeth of Valois

Elizabeth of Spain **2:**454, 466

Elizabeth of Valois **1:**198, 199, 202, 203, **4:**1059

Elizabeth of York **2:**521

Elizabethan Age **2:**333, **3:**664

Elizabethan Settlement (Elizabethan Compromise, 1559) **1:**239, **5:**1198

Ellesmere Chaucer **5:***1202*

Elsheimer, Adam **5:**1211

Elyot, Thomas **4:**1122

emblem books **5:**1236

Emblems of Love, The (Veen) **5:**1236

Emden **1:**188

Emmanuel College (Cambridge) **5:**1374–1375

Empoli, Jacopo Chimenti **1:***197*

Enchiridion militis christiani (Erasmus) **2:**357

Encina, Juan del **4:**956

enclosure movement **1:**28, **3:**818

Encomium moriae (Erasmus) *see Praise of Folly, The*

Encyclopédie (Diderot and D'Alembert) **2:**466

Enden, Franciscus van den **5:**1291

Enders, Ernst Ludwig **5:***1192*

energy sources **3:**777–778, 804, 805, 807, 811–812

coal **3:**784–785, 811, 812

dams **1:**279

water **1:**24, **3:**741, 776–777, 805, 806, *807,* 808, 809, 812

Engañados, Los (Rueda) **5:**1323

Engelbrekt (Swedish rebel) **5:**1304

England **2:334–346**

African slave trade **5:**1348

Agincourt **1:**16–20

agriculture **1:**24, 27, 28, 47–49

architecture **1:**30, 32, 33, 43, 140, **2:**334, **3:**664–668, **5:**1429, 1430–1433

armada, Spanish **1:**62–66, 204, 238, **2:**331, 332,

4:1058, 1060, 1145, **5:**1412

astrology **1:**71–73

Bacon **1:**79–83

banking **1:**90

bibles **1:**104, 105, 106–110, **5:**1357

Black Death **2:**304, 305

blood sports **1:**92–93, 95, 96

Burgundy **1:**158, 159, 160

calendars **1:**173, 176–177, **4:**1024

Calvinism **1:**178, 188, 189

Chaucer **1:**212–220

chivalry **1:**221–222, 223, 225

coal **3:**784–785, 811

colonialism **2:**501, **3:**754, **5:**1284, 1342

colonial missions **4:**892, 894, 896

colonial settlements **5:**1342, 1346

companies **2:**497–498, 499, 500, 501

Cyprus **3:**718

dams and drainage **1:***276*

diplomacy **5:**1223

dual monarchy **3:**601

East India Company **5:**1342

education **2:**322, 323

Elizabeth I **2:**326–333, **5:**1221, 1225

Erasmus **2:**357, 362

established church **1:**232–240, **2:**346, 368–369, 370, 371, 372, **4:**913, 969, 975, **5:**1198, 1374

exploration **2:**375, 382, **4:**914, 915

feudalism **2:**403, 406, 407, 408, 409, 410, 412–413

football **4:**1122

France **2:**434–435

garden design **1:**26

Gentileschi **2:**470, 474

Greek culture **1:**262–263

guilds **2:**494–495, 496

Henry VIII **1:**232–235, **2:**521–528, **5:**1220

heresy **2:**536

Hobbes **2:**542–547

Huguenot émigrés to **5:**1331

humanism **2:**335, 336–337, **3:**590, 593

Hundred Years War **3:**595–603, 657–662, **4:**968

iconoclasm **3:**608–609

interest loans **1:**85

Joan of Arc **3:**661–662

Jones **3:**663–668

Judaism **3:**672, 673

literature **1:**220, 223, **2:**334–336, **3:**721–726, 737–739, 753, 754, 755, 823

Lord Protector **2:**351

machines **3:**785, 786

magic **3:**800

manufacturing **3:**786, 806, 808

markets and fairs **3:**813–814, 815, 816–817, 818–821

Marlowe **3:**822–826

mathematics **3:**829, 834

mercenaries **5:**1411

Milton **4:**879–887

missions to **4:**896

monarchy **4:**904, 906, 907, 912, 914, **5:**1218, 1220, 1221, 1224, 1225

monarchy's restoration **1:**240, **2:**351, **4:**886, **5:**1302, 1322, 1329

More **4:**924–932, **5:**1371

music **4:**942, 943, 944, 948, 951, 952, 953, 954, 959, 961

nationalism **4:**962, 963, 966, 968

naval power **5:**1412 *see also* armada, Spanish

nobility and rank **4:**971, 975, 977

painting **1:**223, **5:**1242, 1243

Palladianism **3:**668, **4:**1007

papacy **4:**1014–1015

Peasants' Revolt (1381) **1:**216, **3:**598, **4:**1041, 1042–1048

England *(cont.)*
Philip II **4:**1056, *1057,* 1058, 1059, 1060
philosophy **4:**1067–1068, 1070–1071, 1072, 1103
pilgrimage **4:**1079, 1081, 1083
Pilgrimage of Grace **1:**187, 235, **2:**340, 526, **4:**1042
piracy **5:**1347
poetry **3:**721, 722–726, 737, 739, 753, 754, 755, 823
Portugal **4:**1137, 1139
printing **3:**819, **5:**1170, 1175
prose fiction **3:**737–738
Puritanism **1:**188, **5:**1196, 1198
Reformation **1:**62, 66, 107, 232, **2:**338–349, 364, 365, **4:**953, **5:**1191, 1196–1198, 1221, 1265
Reformation chronology **1:**240
religious orders **5:**1202, 1203, 1206, 1208
Roman Catholicism **1:**187, 238, **2:**340, 371, 372, **4:**894, 896, 906, 929–932, 953, 969, 1039, **5:**1198, 1267, 1424
Russia **3:**654
school plays **5:**1323
science **4:**1068, **5:**1250, 1256–1257, 1258
Scotland **4:**904, 905, **5:**1261–1267, 1296, 1297, 1300, 1426
Shakespeare **5:**1268–1276
Spain **5:**1283
Spenser **5:**1286–1290
Stuarts **5:**1296–1303, 1426
technology **5:**1259
textiles **3:**849
theater **3:**729, 731–733, 735, 737, 748, 751, 754, 755, 822–826, **5:***1317,* 1318, 1319, 1320, 1321, 1322, 1323, 1324–1329
Thirty Years War **5:**1330, 1334, 1335, 1336

trade **5:**1341, 1344, 1350–1351, 1393
universities **5:**1367, 1373–1375
widow remarriage **5:**1422
witch trials **3:**802, 803, **5:**1425
women's status **5:**1416, 1418, 1419, 1420, 1422, 1423–1424, 1426–1427
Wren **5:**1429–1433
see also Church of England; English civil wars; London
England's Improvement by Sea and Land (Yarranton) **1:***276*
English Bible **1:**106–109, 238, 239, **5:**1175
English Channel **2:**408, **3:**595, **5:**1344
Spanish armada **1:**62, 63, 64, 66, **2:**332
English civil wars **1:**73, 109, **2:**328, 346, **347–355,** **4:**1048, 1066, **5:**1256
Church of England **1:**239
established churches **2:**372
Hobbes **2:**543, 544, 545, 546
iconoclasm **3:**609
Jones's allegiance **3:**668
longbow **5:**1413
Milton **4:**883, 884, 886
monarchy **4:**904, 906, 912
Scotland **5:**1262, 1265, 1267
Stuarts **5:**1302, 1303
theater closures **5:**1325, 1329
Thirty Years War **5:**1336
English College **1:**108
English Ladies (religious order) **5:**1208
English language **5:**1221, 1222
biblical translation **1:**108, 109, 238, **2:**339, **3:***697,* 698, **5:**1357
Chaucer **1:**212–213, 217, 218, 219, 220
Latin influence **3:**690
Spenser **2:**335
as vernacular **3:**691, 692, 694, 695
"English Poete, The" (Spenser) **5:**1287

English Roman Life, The (publication) **5:**1324
engraving
Bruegel **1:**145
Dürer **2:**311, 314–315, **5:**1171
printing **5:**1171
Enlightenment **1:**49, **4:**1072, **5:**1295
Enneads (Plotinus) **4:**1096
Enquiry concerning Human Understanding (Hume) **4:**1068
Enrico, ovvero Bisanzio acquistato, L' (Gonzaga) **5:**1417
Enrique IV *see* Henry IV, king of Castile
Enriquez, Joan **5:**1278
Enriquez de Arana, Beatriz **1:**248
entertainment *see* popular culture
Entombment (Caravaggio) **1:**193
Entzauberung der Welt (Weber) **4:**1123
epic poetry **3:**721
epidemics *see* Black Death, disease
"Epigram on Milton" (Dryden) **4:**887
epiphany **4:**1118
epistemological relativism **2:**294
Epistolae familiares (Petrarch) **4:**1053
Epistolae seniles (Petrarch) **4:**1052, 1053
"Epitaphium Damonis" (Milton) **4:**883
Epithalium (Spenser) **5:**1287
Epitome of the Almagest (Regiomontanus) **1:**265, **3:**728
equal sign **3:**829, 833
equant **1:**271
Erasmus, Desiderius **2:356–363,** 482, **3:**762
Aristotle **1:**58, 59
biblical interpretation **2:**538

biblical translation **1:**58, 104, 109, 181, **2:**358, **3:**585, 591, 684, 688–689, 697, **5:**1357
Colet curriculum **4:**879
Dürer **2:**316
on foolery **5:**1221, 1319
French Protestant Reformation **2:**439
humanism **2:**337, 339, 356, 423, **3:**585, 589, 590, 591, 592, 593, **5:**1282, 1283, 1370, 1371, 1373
iconoclasm **3:**606
Latin language **3:**684
Leo X **3:**703
Luther vs. **2:**339, 552, **3:**767
Margaret of Navarre **3:**735
on marriage **2:**565
More **4:**925
northern Renaissance **2:**552
papacy **4:**1023
pilgrimage **4:**1079
printed works **3:**688
as Rabelais influence **5:**1176
Roman Catholic Church **1:**180, **5:**1189
Rome **5:**1232
women's education **2:**322
Erastus, Thomas **2:**367
Erik VII, king of Demnark **5:**1304
Erik XIV, king of Sweden **5:***1306,* 1307, 1308
Erik of Pomerania **2:**506, **4:**911
Erpingham, Thomas **1:**18
Erri, Bartolomeo degli **3:***676*
Escorial (Spain) **1:**46, 47, **3:***716,* **4:**1060
Espinel, Vicente **1:**205
Essayes or Counsels, Civil and Morall, The (Bacon) **1:**80
Essex, earl of *see* Devereux, Robert
Essex peasants' revolt **4:**1043, 1045, 1047
established churches **2:364–372**
Calvinism **1:**186–187, **2:**349, 353

Church of England
1:235–240, **2**:326, 346,
368–369
Eastern Orthodoxy **1**:166,
170, 257, 259
Elizabeth I **2**:340–341
England **5**:1197, 1374
Genevan Calvinism **5**:1316
Henry VIII **2**:338, 521,
524–527, 528
heresy **2**:529–541
Holy Roman Empire
2:482–483
Lutheranism **3**:768
monarchy **4**:912, 913,
930–931
nationalism **2**:364–365,
4:969, 970
Scotland **5**:1265–1267
Sweden **1**:229
Thirty Years War
5:1330–1339
universities **5**:1374
estates (French ranking
system) **2**:439
Estates General (France)
2:407, **4**:913
Este, Alfonso d' **1**:124–125,
126
Este, Ercole d' 124, **1**:125
Este, Isabella d' **1**:125, **3**:745,
5:*1383*
Este, Lucrezia d' **5**:1381
Estes, the **2**:413
Estienne, Henri II **3**:585,
592
Estoile, Pierre de l' **1**:179
Estonia **2**:503, 505, **3**:653,
5:1307
Esztergom, siege of (1604)
5:1415
etchings, Rembrandt **5**:1211,
1215
Ethics (Spinoza) **5**:1292, 1294
ethics, Aristotelian **1**:*53*, 54,
61
ethnic hatred **3**:671
etiquette, court **2**:437
Eton (English school) **5**:1323
Eucharist **1**:119, 262, **3**:674,
696, 698, 710, **5**:1163

Calvinism **1**:184, 185, 189
Church of England **1**:235,
236–237, 240, **2**:341,
5:1197, 1267
Decree of Reunion **2**:430
Eastern-Western doctrinal
split **1**:259
heresy **2**:536
iconoclasm **3**:608
kneeling for **5**:1267
as Lord's Supper **1**:181, 183,
184
Lutheranism **3**:761, 762,
764, 766, 767
missal **1**:173, **5**:1363
music **4**:943, 946, 954, 955,
956, 957
Reformation **1**:178, 181,
5:1194, 1267
Roman Catholic Church
1:178, 180, 184, **5**:1197,
1358
Trent, Council of **5**:1357,
1358, 1363
Zwingli **5**:1315
see also transubstantiation
Euclid **1**:*143*, **3**:827, **5**:1294
Eudocia, Saint **3**:*605*
Eudocia, Byzantine empress
1:257
Eugene of Savoy **2**:512–513
Eugenius IV, Pope **3**:672,
4:946, 1086, *1087*, **5**:1229,
1379
Florence, Council of **1**:260,
2:427, 428, 429, 430
Euphrates River **1**:169
Euridice (Peri and Caccini)
4:920
Euripides **3**:688, 729
Eustachi, Bartolomeo **3**:840,
846
Eustachian tubes **3**:840, 846
evangelical Protestants **1**:96
Eve *see* Adam and Eve
Evelyn, John **3**:667
Everyman (morality play)
5:1318
evil **2**:360
evolution theory **1**:110
Execrabilis (papal bull) **4**:1086

Executed Anabaptists (woodcut)
5:1195
executions **3**:751
heresy **5**:1316
Exemplary Stories (Cervantes)
1:205, 206
Exodus, book of **1**:*102*, **3**:607
*Experiment on a Bird in the Air
Pump, An* (Wright) **4**:*1072*
exploration **2**:373–385, 399,
3:776, **5**:1220
books on **3**:782
Columbus **1**:247–255
cultural exchanges **1**:255
disease **2**:306–308
England **3**:751, 754
humanism **3**:693
Magellan **3**:787–794
missionaries **4**:888–896
monarchy **4**:914–915
navies **5**:1412
Portugal **4**:1137–1138, 1139,
1140–1142, 1144
science **5**:1258–1259
ship design **3**:777–778
Spain **1**:207, **2**:307, 308,
394, 399, 400,
5:1283–1284, 1285
technology **5**:1250,
1283–1284, 1343
trade **5**:1341, 1342,
1345–1346, 1351
Treaty of Tordesillas **3**:788
worldview **1**:249
Expulsion, Edict of (1492)
2:394, **3**:612
extended family **2**:561–562
extreme unction **5**:1357
Eyck, Bartélemy d' **2**:391
Eyck, Hubert van **2**:386, **4**:983
Eyck, Jan van **1**:129, 163,
2:316, **386–392**, **4**:981,
982, 983
Eyck, Lambert van **2**:386, 391
Eyck, Margaret van (Jan's wife)
2:391
Eyck, Marguerite van (Jan's
sister) **2**:386
Eyüb (Islamic holy place)
3:625
Ezpeleta, Gaspar de **1**:205

F

fabliaux **1**:214, 219
factories **3**:786, 809
Faerie Queene (Spenser) **2**:335,
3:721, **5**:1286, 1289, *1290*
Fairfax, Thomas **2**:352
fairs *see* markets and fairs
faith, Islamic **3**:611
faith alone, justification by
1:58, **2**:341, 343, 369,
5:1164, 1191, 1197
bibles **1**:104, 105, 109
Calvinism **1**:185, 186
Church of England **1**:232,
240
Lutheranism **3**:761–762,
763–764, 766
Trent doctrine vs.
5:1354–1355, 1356
Falconetto, Giovanni Maria
4:1001
falconry **1**:92
Faleiro, Rui **3**:788, 789
Falkirk, Battle of (1297) **4**:905
Falkland Palace (Scotland)
5:1263, 1264, *1296*
Fall of the Rebel Angels, The
(Bruegel) **1**:*144*, 145
Fallopian tubes **3**:840, 846
Falloppio, Gabriele **3**:840,
846
fallowing **1**:26, 27
False Dmitrys **4**:938–939
family life *see* households
famine **4**:*1127*, 1128, 1134
cities **4**:1131
France **2**:433, 456
Paris **4**:1028, 1124
peasant life **4**:1115
plague **2**:304
population effect **4**:1127,
1128, 1129, 1135
Russia **3**:656, **4**:938, 939
Fanatic Moderations (Hall)
3:609
Farel, Guillaume **1**:179,
5:1315
farming *see* agriculture
Farnese, Alessandro *see* Paul III
Farnese, Ottavio **1**:210, **3**:644,
648, **5**:*1362*

Farnese, Pierluigi **3:**644, 648

Farnese, Ranuccio II **1:**195, **2:**470

Farnese Gallery **1:**195

Farnese Palace *see* Palazzo Farnese

Farneses, the **1:**40, *41,* **3:***648,* 744, **5:**1353

fasts and fast days **1:**173, **3:**611, **5:**1341

Favola d'Orfeo, La (Monteverdi) *see Orfeo*

Fawkes, Guy **1:***238,* **2:***342, 343,* **5:**1301

Fazio, Bartolommeo **2:**389

feast days **1:**173, 174

Feast in the House of Levi (Veronese) **4:**992

Feast of Bacchus, The (Velázquez) **5:**1387

Feast of Fools **4:**1119

Feast of the Pheasant **1:**226

Feast of the Rose Garlands, The (Dürer) **2:**313, 314

Fedele, Cassandra **5:**1417

Federigo II, duke of Mantua **4:**991

Federigo II, king of Naples *see* Ferdinand II (Ferrandino), king of Naples

Federigo II, duke of Urbino **5:**1181

Felix V (antipope) **2:**429, **4:**1086

Felton, John **2:**343

Felton, Nicholas **4:**880

Feltre, Vittorino da **3:**584, **5:**1220, 1379, 1417

Fenelon, François **2:**372

Fenizi, Ascania **1:**277

Ferdinand II (the Catholic), king of Aragon *see* Ferdinand and Isabella

Ferdinand, archduke of Austria **1:**209, 211, **3:**624

Ferdinand I, Holy Roman emperor **2:***365,* **5:**1281
  Bohemia **1:**120, 121, **2:**510–511
  Hapsburg Empire **2:**555, 556, 557

Maximilian I **3:**837, 838, 839

Ferdinand II, Holy Roman emperor **2:**371
  Bohemia **1:**120, 121, 122, **3:**837
  Counter-Reformation **2:**514
  German towns **2:**477–478, 560
  Thirty Years War **5:**1330, 1332, 1333, 1336, 1337, 1339, 1415

Ferdinand III, Holy Roman emperor **2:**371, 514, **5:**1330, 1338

Ferdinand I, king of Naples **1:**123, 124, **4:**1088, 1089–1090

Ferdinand II (Ferrandino), king of Naples **3:**643, 644

Ferdinand I, king of Portugal **4:**1137

Ferdinand and Isabella, king and queen of Spain **2:**393–400, *411,* 510, **5:**1394, 1425
  Bramante commission **1:**141
  Catherine of Aragon **1:***233*
  Charles V **1:**207, 209
  Christian conversions **3:**613
  Columbus's voyages **1:**247, 248, 250, 253, 254
  exploration **4:**914
  heirs **1:**207, **5:**1280–1283
  heresy **2:**532, 533
  holdings **4:**965–966
  humanism **5:**1280, 1417
  Inquisition **5:**1278
  Italian wars **3:**643, 645
  Jewish expulsion **3:***670,* 678–679
  knight in livery **2:***411*
  missionizing **4:**889
  monarchy **4:**907
  Renaissance **5:**1220, 1225
  Rome **5:**1231
  Spain **5:**1277–1279, 1285
  theater **5:**1322

Fermat, Pierre de **3:**833–834

Fernández de Avellaneda, Alonso **1:**206

Fernel, Jean **1:**197

Ferrandino *see* Ferdinand II, king of Naples

Ferrara **2:**413, 419, **3:**637, 642, 648, 650, 681, 853, **4:**947, 949, **5:**1381
  Borgias **1:**124, 125–126, **5:**1427

Ferrara, University of **3:**844, **4:**1073, **5:**1367

Ferrara, War of **3:**741

Ferrari, Benedetto **4:**917

Ferrari, Defendente **1:**182

Ferrari, Ettore **4:***1019*

Fersina River **1:**279

fertilizers **1:**27, 28

Festa (Assumption) **5:**1318

"Feste Burg ist unser Gott, Ein'" (Luther) **4:**952

festivals **4:**1118, 1119, *1222,* **5:**1317

feudalism **1:**22, **2:**401–413, 569, **4:**973
  abolition of **1:**28
  armies **5:**1411
  chivalry **1:**161, 221–226
  households **2:**562, 563, 569
  Hundred Years War **3:**595, 597
  investiture controversy **2:**365–366
  Lombardy **3:**744
  monarchy **4:***903,* 904, 905–906
  papacy **5:**1234
  peasants' revolts **4:**1041–1048

Fiammetta **1:**111

Ficino, Marsilio **2:**538, **3:**799, **4:***1075*
  Florence **2:**422, 423, 424
  humanism **3:**584, 586, *587, 588*
  Medicis **3:**852, 855, 856
  philosophy **4:**1063, 1065, 1068
  Pico della Mirandola **4:**1073, 1074, 1075, 1076, 1103
  Platonism **1:**57, **4:**1100–1103

fief *see* feudalism

Fiefs and Vassals (Reynolds) **2:**405

field artillery **5:**1335

Field of the Cloth of Gold **2:**522, **4:**927

Fieschi, Catherine **5:**1420

Fife **5:***1296*

Fifth Lateran Council **3:**756

Figueroa, Francisco de **1:**204

Figueroa, Lope de **1:**203

Filarete **1:**31, 34

filioque (theological dispute) **1:**259, **2:**430

Filipepi, Alessandro di Moriano *see* Botticelli

Filmer, Robert **3:**803

Filocolo, Il (Boccaccio) **1:**112, *113*

Filostrato, Il (Boccaccio) **1:**112, 217

Filz Dam **1:**279

Final Quest concerning the Rectification of Principles, The (al-Shatir) **1:**271

Finances of the Commune of Siena, in Time of Peace and in Time of War, The (Benvenuto di Giovanni) **1:**86, **5:***1411*

Fine Flower of Histories, The (manuscript) **1:***69*

Finland **2:**370, **3:**768, **5:**1305

Finta pazza Licori, La (Monteverdi) **4:**922

Fiore, Il (Dante) **1:**217

firearms **1:**226, **3:**717, **5:**1407, 1411, 1413–1414, 1415
  gunpowder **3:**774, 775
  musket **5:**1335, 1413
  wheel lock **3:**782
  see also cannon

Fire in the Borgo (Raphael) **5:**1187

First Account (Rheticus) **1:**269

First Amendment of United States Constitution **2:**372

First and Chief Groundes of Architecture (Shute) **1:**34

First Blast of the Trumpet against the Monstrous

Regiment of Women (Knox)
  1:*189,* **5:**1267, 1426
First Book of Architecture
  (Serlio) **1:***31*
First Book of Discipline (Knox)
  1:189
First Crusade **1:**223
first estate (France) **2:**439
First Map of Australia **2:***385*
First Vatican Council **5:**1363,
  1364
Fisher, John **1:**235, **2:**340, 525
fishing
  dams **1:**280
  Hanseatic League **2:**504
  trade **5:**1341
  Venice **5:**1392
fishpond dams **1:**280
Fitzjames, bishop of London
  1:232
Fitzroy, Henry, duke of
  Richmond **3:***723*
Fitzwilliam Virginal Book
  4:*943*
Five Books on Fish Ponds
  (Dubraius) **1:**280
flagellants **2:**307
Flagellation of Christ
  (Caravaggio) **1:**194, *196*
Flanders
  architecture **1:**49
  Bruegel **1:**144–148
  Burgundy **1:**157, 158, 160,
    162, 163, 164
  dikes and drainage
    1:273–276
  Eyck **2:**386–392
  humanism **3:**585, 589, 590,
    592
  Hundred Years War **1:**16,
    3:595, 596
  mathematics **5:**1250
  Rubens **5:**1236–1243
  trade **5:**1341, 1344
  see also Flemish art
fleas, plague-carrying **2:**303 *see
  also* Black Death
Flemish art **4:**981, 982–983,
  990, 993
  Bruegel **1:**144–148
  Burgundy **1:**163

Eyck **2:**386–392
  Italianate-style painting
    1:145–146
  Rubens **5:**1236–1243
Fletcher, John **3:**733, **5:**1325
Flicke, Gerlach **3:***699*
Flodden, Battle of (1513)
  5:1261, 1297
flood control **1:**28, 273–276,
  279
Florence **1:**169, 261,
  2:*414–426,* *427,* 538,
  3:630, 742
  architecture **1:**30, 32, 33, 35,
    36, 49
  banking **1:**84, 87, 88, **3:**740,
    850, 854, **5:**1228, 1342
  Bardis **2:**567
  Black Death **2:**305, **4:**1131
  Boccaccio **1:**111, 112, 113,
    114, 115
  Botticelli **1:**133–138
  Brunelleschi **1:**149–156
  Charles V **1:**208
  Chaucer **1:**216
  Ciompi revolt **3:**636–637
  Clement VII **1:**241, 242
  fall of republic **3:**649
  famines **4:**1131
  Galileo **2:**460, **5:**1252
  Gentileschi **2:**469–471
  Giotto **2:**484, 487, 489, 490,
    491, 492
  government **3:**635, 636–637,
    638, 643, 649, 702
  humanism **2:**320, **3:**584,
    585, 586, 587, 588, 589,
    640, 684–685, 687, 700,
    703, **5:**1220
  Italian wars **1:**208, **2:***420,*
    421, **3:**643, 647, 648–649
  Leonardo da Vinci **3:**706,
    707, 708
  Machiavelli **3:**769–773,
    4:1066
  May carnival **4:**951
  Medicis **1:**137, 197, 208,
    242, 243, 244, **2:**413,
    477, **3:***587,* 588, 641,
    700, 702, 703, 705, 708,
    849–857, **5:**1224

Michelangelo **4:**870, 871,
    872–873, 876–877
  Milanese rivalry **5:**1401,
    1404, 1405
  Milton **4:**882, 883
  music **4:**951, 961
  opera **4:**920, **5:**1321, 1322
  painting and sculpture **2:**312,
    3:641, 706, 707, **4:**981,
    983–984, 985, 986, 988,
    5:1236–1237
  palaces **2:**563
  Petrarch **3:**682
  Pico della Mirandola **4:**1073,
    1074, 1075, 1076–1077
  Platonism **1:**57, 137, **2:**320
  Portugal **4:**1143, 1144
  Raphael **5:**1181, 1183–1185
  republic **4:**967
  Savonarola **1:**137
  theater **3:**734
  trade **2:**475
  see also Florentine Academy
Florence, Cathedral of (Santa
  Maria del Fiore)
  baptistery bronze doors
    3:641, **4:**983
  Brunelleschi dome **1:**32, 34,
    35, 47, 149, 150–151,
    156
  Giotto **2:**487
  Michelangelo **4:**872, 878
Florence, Council of **1:**169,
  260, 261, **2:***427–431,*
  4:935, 1063, 1073, **5:**1358,
  1359
  see also Basel, Council of
Florence, University of **1:**54,
  169, **2:**318
Florentine Academy **4:**1073,
  1075
  Platonism **1:**261, **2:**418,
    3:855, **4:**1068, 1099,
    1100, 1103
Florentine Camerata **4:**920,
  961
Florentine Codex **2:**308
Florentine Histories
  (Machiavelli) **3:**772–773
Flores, Isabel de *see* Rose of
  Lima

Florida **2:**374, 382, **3:**609
  missions **4:**891–892
Flower, The (Dante) **1:**217
flying machine **3:**709, **5:**1249
Foix, Gaston de **3:**645
folklore **5:**1312
Fondaco dei Tedeschi (Venice)
  5:1398
Fontainebleau (France) **1:**45,
  4:990
Fontaine-Henry, Château de
  2:*436*
Fontana, Domenico **1:**38, 44,
  47
Fontana, Lavinia **4:***1024*
Fontanarossa, Susanna **1:**247
fonts **3:**819
food supply **1:**28–29,
  4:1028, 1124, *1131*
  Holy Roman Empire **2:**479
  population effects **4:**1114,
    1127, 1128, 1129,
    1134–1135
  see also famine
fool, the **5:**1319
football **4:**1122
Foppa, Vincenzo **3:**685
Ford, John **5:**1327
forestry **1:**25–26
forgeries **2:**383, **3:**584, 594,
  686
Forlì **5:**1427, 1428
forms, Platonic **4:**1070, 1092,
  1094–1095
Forster, George **4:**947
fortifications **2:**410–411,
  3:651, **5:**1335, 1407,
  1409–1411
  chivalric laws **1:**222
Fortitude (Botticelli) **1:**133,
  134, 135
Fortune theatre (London)
  3:732
Forty-two Articles (England,
  1553) **1:**107, *237,* **2:**368
  see also Thirty-nine Articles
Foscari, Francesco **5:***1396*
Foscarini, Paolo Antonio
  5:1253
Foundations (Teresa of Ávila)
  5:1207

preaching **5:**1158, 1162
Rabelais **5:**1176, 1177
François, Jean-Charles **4:***1067,*
5:*1295*
François, Simon **5:***1208*
Franconia **2:**310
Frangipanes, the **1:**39
Frankfurt **2:**475, 506, **5:**1267
Thirty Years War **5:**1337
Frankfurt Book Fair **3:**781,
819
Frankish empire **1:**157
Franklin, Benjamin **4:**887
fratricide, law of **3:**625
Frauenberg, Cathedral of
1:265, *266*
Fray, Agnes **2:**312
Frederick I (Barbarossa), Holy
Roman emperor **2:**505,
509, **3:**740
Frederick II, Holy Roman
emperor **3:**743
Frederick III, Holy Roman
emperor **2:**508, 509, **3:**673,
4:1086, 1088
Burgundy **1:**161, 162
Frederick III, elector of the
Palatinate **1:**76, 77, **2:**453
Frederick IV, elector of the
Palatinate **2:**508, **3:**836,
837, 838
Frederick V, elector of the
Palatinate **5:**1301, 1302,
1334, 1335, 1336
Bohemia **1:**122, **3:**837, 838
Frederick II (the Great), king
of Prussia **3:**773
Frederick III (the Wise),
elector of Saxony **2:**370,
553, **3:**705, **4:**1013,
5:1190, 1191
Frederick, duke of
Württemberg **3:**753
Frederick William (the Great),
elector of Brandenburg
5:1332
free fall, law of **2:**295, 462
free trade **5:**1351
free will **1:**73, **2:**361, 543,
546, **3:**586, 593, **5:**1195,
1295

Erasmus **2:**360–361, 552,
3:767
Paul V **4:**1036
Pico della Mirandola **2:**538,
4:1076
see also predestination
Freiburg **2:**357, 361
Freiburg, Battle of (1638)
5:1338
French Academy of Science *see*
Academy of Sciences
(France)
French and Swedish War
5:1137–1138
French Calvinists *see*
Huguenots
French civil wars **2:**440–443,
448, **451–459, 3:**707
Calvinism **1:**183, *184*
Catherine de Médicis
1:198–200
dams and drainage **1:**279
Francis I **2:**448
Henry IV **2:**516–520, 540
Holy Roman Empire **2:**556
Hundred Years War **3:**599,
600
mercenaries **5:**1411
Paris **4:**1031–1034
Spain **4:**1058, 1060
Thirty Years War **5:**1331
French language
biblical translation **1:**181
Calvin **1:**179
Descartes **2:**296
nationalism **4:**963
Rabelais **5:**1179
as vernacular **1:**214,
2:432–433, 444, **3:**695,
696, **5:**1222
French Revolution **1:**28,
4:887
French Royal Academy *see*
Royal Academy of France
Frescobaldi, Girolamo **4:**960
frescoes
Carracci brothers **1:**195
Raphael **1:***80,* **5:**1186, 1187
Rome **5:**1230
friars *see* religious orders
Friars Minor *see* Franciscans

"Friar's Tale, The" (Chaucer)
5:1202
Fribourg **5:**1314
Frick, Henry Clay **5:**1217
Frick Collection **5:**1217
Friesland **1:**274
frigates **5:**1412
Frizer, Ingram **3:**822, 825
Frobisher, Martin **1:**63
Froger, François **5:***1349*
Froissart, Jean **1:***16,* 215, 216,
224, **4:***1045,* **5:***1405*
Fronde **2:**444
Fucecchio Dam **1:**280
Fuchs, Leonhard **1:***29*
fuel *see* energy sources
Fuente ovejuna (Vega) **3:**728
Fugger, Anton **2:**477
Fugger, Hans **2:**477
Fugger, Jacob (the Rich) **2:**477
Fugger, Jacob II **2:***478*
Fugger, Raimond **2:**477
Fugger Bank **1:**88, 90
Fuggers, the **2:**476, 477, 478,
5:1344
fulling mills **3:**806, *807*
fur trade **5:**1348
Fust, Johann **3:**781, **5:**1169
Fyodor I, emperor of Russia
3:656, **4:**937, 938

G

Gabriel, archangel **3:**611, 657
Gabrieli, Andrea **4:**952
Gabrieli, Giovanni **4:**952,
5:1244
Gadio, Bartolomeo **5:***1403*
Gaelic culture **5:**1260
Gaeta **3:**645
Gailde, Jean **5:***1160*
Gainsborough, Thomas
5:1243
Galatea, la (Cervantes) **1:**204
Galen **3:**840, 844–845, 846,
5:1177
Galilei, Galileo **1:**262,
2:460–468, 539, 543,
3:828, **4:**882, 917, 961
Aristotelianism **1:**57, 60, 61
Copernicus **1:***272,* **4:**1109
Descartes **2:**296, 297

disease **2:**309
heresy trial **2:**296, 297,
3:783, 784, **5:**1226,
1234–1235, 1251, 1254,
1256, 1258
Inquisition **4:**1036
inventions **1:**271, **2:**309,
3:775, 783, **5:**1252
mathematics **3:**831, 833
philosophy **4:**1068–1069
rehabilitation chronology
2:466
vernacular language **2:**465,
3:690, **5:**1254
water dynamics **1:**277
Galilei, Vincenzo **2:**460, 462,
4:882, 961
galleons **1:**63, **4:**1138, *1143,*
5:1412
galleys **3:**715, 716, 717,
5:1393, 1394, 1412
Gallicanism **2:**372, **4:**969,
5:1177, 1178
Gallipoli **3:**715
Galluzzi, Tarquinio **1:**59
Gama, Vasco da **2:**374, 381,
3:782, **4:**1139, 1142,
1144, **5:**1342, *1345*
Gamba, Marina **2:**462–463,
468
Gambia River **2:**380, **5:**1345
Game at Chess, A (Middleton)
5:1329
game parks **1:**95
Gammer Gurton's Needle
(anon.) **3:**732
Garcia Infanzon, Juan **5:***1323*
Garden of Earthly Delights, The
(Bosch) **1:**128, 129, 131
Garden of Eden **1:**249
gardens **1:**25, 26, *40*
London **3:**751
Gardiner, Stephen **1:**236,
3:608
Gargantua (Rabelais) **3:**436,
5:1176, 1177, 1178
Gargiulo, Domenico **2:***370,*
474
Garigliano, Battle of (1503)
3:644–645
Garnier, Robert **3:**730

Garovo, Leone **1**:44

Garter, Order of the **1**:223, **3**:598

Gascoigne, George **3**:738

Gascony *see* Aquitaine

Gaston, duke of Orléans **4**:899

Gattamelata (Erasmo di Narni) **5**:*1395*

Gattinara, Mercurino da **1**:209, **2**:555

Gaul **1**:157

Gaulli, Giovanni **1**:100

Gavari, Domenico **5**:1182

Gaveston, Piers **3**:825

Gdańsk **4**:1106

Geiler von Kayserberg, Johann **5**:1159

Gemistus Plethon, George **1**:261, **4**:1063, 1099, 1100

Genealogia deorum gentilium (Boccaccio) **1**:111

General Rules of Architecture, The (Serlio) **1**:34

Genesis, book of **2**:539, **4**:1077, **5**:1425

Adam and Eve **1**:185, **4**:1064, *1066*

Ptolemaic cosmos **1**:267

Geneva

banking **1**:87, **2**:416

Calvinism **1**:179, 186–187, 188, 189, **2**:324, 440, 539, **4**:952, **5**:1195–1196, 1265, 1267, 1315–1316, 1423

humanism **3**:585

iconoclasm **3**:607

Puritanism **2**:342

Roman Catholicism **1**:188

Geneva Bible **1**:105, 107, 108, 238

Geneva Psalter **4**:942

Genghis Khan **3**:617, *692*

Gennadius II Scholarios **1**:170, 261

Genoa **1**:216, **2**:414, **3**:626, 632

banking **1**:84, 88, **5**:1228

Columbus **1**:247, 248

Constantinople **1**:260–261

Italian wars **3**:643, 647, 650, 651

Ottoman expansion **3**:715

silk manufacture **3**:805

trade **2**:475, **5**:1340, 1393, 1401

Venice **5**:1395

genre painting **5**:*1386*

Rembrandt **5**:1215

Gent, Justus van **2**:*431*

Gentile **5**:1399

Gentileschi, Artemisia **2**:**469–474**

Gentileschi, Orazio **2**:469, 474

Gentle Craft, The (Deloney) **3**:738

gentry **4**:971

geocentric universe **1**:265, 268, **2**:296, **5**:1249–1250, 1253

Geoffroy d'Estissac **5**:1177

Geographia (Ptolemy) **2**:374

geography **2**:379, 384–385, **4**:1137

geology **1**:110

geometry **3**:827, 830, 833, 834

architecture **1**:30–31, 36, 44

education **2**:319

perspective **2**:312

Spinoza **5**:1294

Geometry (Descartes) **3**:828

George, Saint **1**:*224*

George Dósza **4**:1042

George of Podebrady **1**:120, 121

George of Trebizond **1**:261

George William, prince of Brandenburg **5**:1337

Georgics (Virgil) **3**:*594, 683*

Gerardino, Antonio and Alessandro **5**:1281

Gerard of Cremona **3**:728

German Bible **1**:104–105, 107, 180, **2**:316, **5**:1357

Germania (Tacitus) **3**:590

German language **2**:548, **4**:963, 970, **5**:1222–1223

Luther's New Testament **1**:103, 104–105, *180,* **2**:316, **3**:765, **5**:1221, 1222

as vernacular **3**:699

Yiddish **3**:670

see also German Bible

German Theology (Luther) **3**:760

German towns **2**:**475–483,** 498, 549, 558

agriculture **1**:21

architecture **1**:49

Augsburg, Peace of **1**:75–78

banking **1**:88, **5**:1344

bibles **1**:103, 104–105

Black Death **2**:305

Bohemia **1**:118, 119, 120, 121

calendar **1**:176, 177

Calvinism **1**:178, 188

Charles V **1**:209, 210–211

dams **1**:279

Descartes **2**:294, 295

Dürer **2**:311–316

education **2**:322, 324, **5**:1372

elected monarchs **4**:909–911

established churches **2**:365, 369–370

Florence **2**:419

Hanseatic League **2**:475–476, 481, 502–506

Hapsburgs **2**:438, 509, 514

heresy **2**:531

humanism **2**:552–553, **3**:590, 592, 593

iconoclasm **3**:605, 606, *607,* 609

infantry **3**:651

interest loans **1**:85

Judaism **3**:672, 672–673, 674–675

language **4**:963, 970

Luther **1**:178, **5**:1352

Lutheranism **1**:181, 242, **2**:479, 482, 483, 552–554, 558, **3**:767, 768, 836, **5**:1352

mercenaries **5**:1411

music **4**:950, 951, 952, 954, 958, 960

nationalism **2**:364, **4**:970

nobility and rank **4**:971

papacy **4**:1013

peasants' revolts **1**:187, **2**:*475,* 479, 480

Poland-Lithuania **4**:1104, 1106, 1107, 1110

popular culture **4**:1122–1123

preaching **5**:1164

printing press **3**:687, 775, 780–781, 819, **5**:1168, 1169, *1170,* 1193

Reformation **1**:178, 181, 183, **4**:970, **5**:1189–1192, 1193, 1195, 1196, 1198, 1200, 1221, 1267

Roman Catholicism **3**:835–839

Schütz **5**:12440–12447

science and technology **5**:1250, 1256

Thirty Years War **1**:183, 228, **2**:560, **5**:1331, 1332, 1335, 1336–1337, 1415

tournaments **1**:225

trade **5**:1340, 1344, 1393

universities **5**:1367, 1371, 1372, 1373, 1376, 1377

witch hunts **3**:802

see also Holy Roman Empire; Prussia; *specific place-names*

Gerónimo *see* John of Austria

Gerson, Jean de (Jean Charlier) **2**:367

Gerusalemme liberata (Tasso) **1**:223, **3**:721, **4**:922

Gessler (Austrian baliff) **5**:1312

Gesualdo, Carlo **4**:955

Geto Nuovo (Venice) **3**:672

Ghana **4**:1141, **5**:*1349*

Ghent **1**:160, 207, 209, **2**:386

Ghent Altarpiece (Eyck) **2**:386, 387, 390, 392

ghetto **3**:672, 679

Ghibellines **2**:421, **3**:743, 854

Montefeltros **5**:1378

Viscontis **5**:1405

Ghiberti, Lorenzo **1**:34, **2**:428, **3**:641, **4**:981, 983

Brunelleschi **1**:149, 150, 151

Ghirlandaio, Domenico
1:169, *247,* 4:870, 871,
985, 5:1230
Ghirlandaio, Ridolfo del
5:1185
ghosts 4:1121
Giacomo da Vignola *see*
Vignola, Giacomo da
Gianuzzi, Giulio *see* Romano,
Giulio
Gibbs, James 1:140
Gibraltar, Strait of 2:380
Gidea Hall (Cooke home)
5:1419
Giessen, University of 5:1377
Gilbert, Humphrey 2:383
Giocando, Francesco del 3:714
Giorgio, Francesco di 1:34,
5:1379
Giorgione 4:988, 989, 5:1389,
1399
Giotto di Bondone 1:145,
156, **2:484–492,** 4:980,
981
Giovanni, Agostino di 5:*1366*
Giovanni, Benvenuto di
5:*1411*
Giovanni, Bertoldo di 4:870
Giovanni di Bicci 2:417
Giovio, Paolo 4:875
Giraba, Jerónimo 1:280
Girard, Albert 3:830
Giume Giuliano canal 1:277
Giunta, Tommaso 1:58
Giustiniani, Vincenzo 1:194
Glamorgan, earl of 2:352
Glarus 5:1312, 1314
Glasgow University 5:1263
Glendower, Owen 1:17
Glinskaya, Yelena 3:652, 653,
4:933
Globe Theatre (London)
3:748, 751, 5:1269, 1270,
1271, *1324,* 1326, *1328,*
1329
Glorious Revolution of 1688
1:24, 2:346, 4:906
Gloucester, duke of *see*
Humphrey, duke of
Gloucester
Gnosticism 3:605

Goa 4:894, 1142
*Goat Amalthea with the Infant
Jupiter and a Faun, The*
(Bernini) 1:97
Gobelin tapestry 2:*372*
Gobi Desert 2:303
God
Cartesian existence proof
2:297, 298–300
election by 1:185, 189–190
free will 2:361
monotheism 1:167, 3:620,
669
philosophy 4:1070,
1071–1072, 1076,
1098–1099, 1100, 1101
theodicy 2:360
see also divine grace
Godunov, Boris 4:937,
938–939
Goes, Hugo van der 4:982
Gogh, Vincent van 4:996
gold 2:379, 380, 381, 382,
384–385, 4:1137, 5:1284,
1285
Columbus 1:252
currency of Constantinople
1:264
florin 2:*416*
Milanese ducat 5:*1404*
ten-ducat piece 1:*245*
trade 5:1342, 1345, 1347,
1349, 1393
Gold Coast 5:*1349*
Golden Ass, The (Apuleius)
1:41
Golden Bull (1356) 2:478,
549, 4:910–911
Golden Fleece, Order of the
1:*221,* 1663, 2:514, 515,
4:948, 950
Burgundy 1:161, 163, 164,
165, 223
Charles V 1:*207, 211*
Golden Haggadah 3:*669*
Golden Horde 3:653
Golden Horn 1:256
Golden House 1:34
goldsmiths 1:149, 2:311, 314,
3:632
Goldsmith's Company 3:750

Gombert, Nicholas 4:921, 949
Gonçalves, Nuno 4:*1138,*
1144
Gonville Hall (Cambridge)
2:334
Gonzaga, Cecilia 5:*1416,* 1417
Gonzaga, Elisabetta 5:1383
Gonzaga, Federico 3:744, 745
Gonzaga, Gianfrancesco 3:745,
5:*1416*
Gonzaga, Ludovico 3:745
Gonzaga, Ludovico II 3:745
Gonzaga, Vincenzo I 3:745,
4:917, 919, 921, 5:1238
Gonzaga, Vincenzo II 3:745
Gonzaga de Nevers, Carlo
3:745
Gonzagas, the 1:*224,* 3:642,
744, 745
overview 3:745
Good Hope, Cape of *see* Cape
of Good Hope
Goodman, Christopher 5:1267
good works, salvation by
1:104, 180, 186, 190, 232,
5:1191, 1197, 1354, 1355,
1356
Googe, Barnaby 5:1288
Gorhambury (Bacon estate)
1:83
Gorizia 2:509
Goslar 2:505
Gospels 3:671
preaching of 5:1158, *1159,
1162,* 1165
see also New Testament
Gossaert, Jan (Mabuse) 1:145
Gosson, Stephen 3:725
Göteborg 5:1305
Gothic architecture 1:30, *32,*
44, 47, 100, 152, 154,
5:1308
Bruges 1:163
Orvieto 1:*246*
Scotland 5:1263
Venice 5:1399
Gothic painting 1:127, 129,
2:312–313, 316
international style 4:981
Gotland 5:1310, 1338
Gouda 2:356

Goudimel, Claude 4:954
government
condominium system 2:508
democracy 1:166, 2:542,
4:906, 5:1339
electors 2:477, 478, 510,
548, 551, 4:909–911,
966
France 2:439, 440, 451
Hobbes 2:542, 543, 544,
545–546, 4:1066–1067
humanism 3:585, 640
Italian city-states 3:630, 634,
635, 636, 637–639, 641,
642, 643, 650, 693, 702
Ivan IV reforms 3:652
Machiavelli 3:769–773,
4:1066–1067
Ottoman Empire 3:625–628
political philosophy
4:1066–1067, 1071,
1072
Renaissance republics
5:1223, 1224
Venice 5:1392, 1396, 1397,
1400
see also absolutism;
diplomacy; monarchy;
Parliament; parliaments;
republics
Gowrie, earl of 5:1262
Gowthwaite Hall (Yorkshire)
5:1328
Goya, Francisco de 4:*1123,*
5:1391
Gozzolo, Benozzo 1:*262*
grace *see* divine grace
Gracián, Juan 1:204
Gradualia (Byrd) 4:943, 953
grain trade 5:1341, 1350
Gramani, Dominico 2:357
*Gramática de la Lengua
Castellana* (Nebrija) 3:694
grammar, humanist
curriculum 3:582, 683,
689, 5:1218, 1282
grammar schools 2:319
Granacci, Francesco 2:*419*
Granada 2:408, 4:956,
5:1277, 1279
Alhambra Palace 2:*396*

Granada *(cont.)*
  fall to Spain **2**:397, **5**:1277, 1279, 1322
  Ferdinand and Isabella **2**:393, 394, 396, *400*
  Philip II **4**:1056–1057
Granada, Treaty of (1500) **3**:644
Granada Palace **1**:46
Grand Canal (Venice) **5**:*1392*, 1398
Grand Canyon (United States) **2**:382
grandi (merchant nobles) **3**:634–635, 636
Grandi, Alessandro **5**:1246
Grand Mosque (Djenné) **3**:*612*
Grand Remonstrance (1641) **2**:350
Granen, Blasco de **3**:*695*
Granson, Battle of (1476) **5**:*1313*, 1314
Grape and Melon Eaters (Murillo) **5**:*1386*
graphic arts **2**:310–316
Graubünden **5**:1334
gravitation **3**:783, 827, 834
gravity dams **1**:278, 280
Grays Inn **1**:79
Great Art, The (Cardano) **3**:829
Great Bible **1**:107, 238, **2**:339
great chain of being **2**:335–336, 538, **4**:1062, 1076
great fire of London (1666) **1**:*72*, **2**:546, **3**:667, 748, 755, 820, **4**:886
  Hooke Monument **5**:1433
  rebuilding plan **5**:1431–1432, 1433
Great Level (England) **1**:276
Great Model (Wren) **5**:1432
Great Northern War **4**:941
Great Schism of 1054 **1**:166, 259, **2**:427, **3**:854, **4**:1073
  pivotal doctrine **1**:259
Great Schism of 1378–1417 *see* Western Schism
Great Yarmouth **1**:262

Greco, El **1**:131, **4**:957, *1058, 1060*, **5**:1284
Greece **3**:626, 715
  calendar **1**:177
  war of independence **1**:262
  see also classical antiquity; Greek culture
Greek Christianity *see* Orthodox Church
Greek Codex Alexandrinus **1**:109
Greek Cross Design (Wren) **5**:1432
Greek culture
  architecture **1**:49, **2**:334
  Aristotle **1**:50–61
  astrology **1**:69
  astronomy **1**:265–269, 270, *271, 272*
  Byzantium **1**:166–167, 169, 170, 172
  Constantinople **1**:256, 258 264, 269
  drama **4**:920, **5**:1321, 1322
  education **2**:318, 319, 320, 324
  England **1**:262–263
  Florence **2**:422, 423, 424
  Hellenism **1**:166, 167, 170, 171, 172
  humanism **3**:582, 583, 584, 586, 588, 589, 591, 682
  literature **2**:334–335, 336, 337
  mythology **1**:135, 136–137
  Platonism **1**:57, 181, **3**:605, **4**:1092–1103
  see also Greek language; Greek philosophy
Greek independence (1830) **1**:262
Greek language **1**:258, **3**:682, 684–685, 687, 688–689, 690, 691, 695, 696, 697, 703
  bibles **1**:181, **5**:1355, 1357
  education **2**:317, 320, 321
  humanism **1**:264, **2**:336, **3**:584, 585, 586, 588, 589, 590, **5**:1220, 1282
  Latin translations **1**:261, 264

manuscript collection **1**:261
  philosophy **4**:1063
  Pico della Mirandola **4**:1073, 1074
  Septuagint **1**:103, 104, 109, **3**:695
  universities **1**:261, **5**:1373
  women's education **5**:1417, 1418, 1419
Greek Orthodox Church *see* Orthodox Church
Greek philosophy **1**:167, 169, 181, 261, **2**:334, 422, **3**:685, 730
  Aristotle **1**:50–61
  Platonism **4**:1092–1103
  School of Athens, The (Raphael) **1**:38, *50, 143*, **3**:703, **4**:1025, 1061, **5**:1186
  universities **5**:1368, 1370, 1376
Greek revival architecture **1**:49
Greene, Robert **3**:732, 755, 823, 824, **5**:1325
Greenhill, John **5**:*1273*
Greenwich **1**:48, **3**:666–667, 668
Greenwich, Treaty of (1543) **2**:528
Gregorian calendar **1**:173, 175–177, **4**:1024–1025
Gregorian chant **4**:957
Gregorian reforms **2**:529
Gregory I (the Great), Pope **1**:258
Gregory VII, Pope **2**:366, 529
Gregory IX, Pope **2**:*532*
Gregory X, Pope **3**:673, **4**:1010
Gregory XI, Pope **5**:1227
Gregory XII, Pope **1**:264, **2**:318
Gregory XIII, Pope **1**:175–176, **4**:1024
Gregory XV, Pope **1**:33, **5**:1205
Gregory, James **3**:828, 833
Gregory of Nyssa **4**:1024
Gregory of Valencia **4**:906
Gresham, Thomas **3**:750, 762

Gresham College (London) **5**:1429–1430
Grevenbroek, Jan van **1**:*89*
Greville, Fulke **3**:725
Grevin, Jacques **3**:729, 730
Grey, Arthur (Lord Grey of Wilton) **5**:1287
Grey, Lady Jane **1**:236, **2**:326
Grey, William, bishop of Ely **2**:336
Grimald, Nicholas **3**:723
Grindal, Edmund **2**:341
Grindal, William **2**:327
Grisons *see* Graubünden
Grocers' Hall (London) **3**:751
Groningen **1**:176
Grosseteste, Robert **2**:529
Grünewald, Matthias **2**:316
Grünwald **4**:1107
Guacanagari (Taino chief) **1**:250–251
Guam **3**:792
Guangzhou **4**:1142
Guarini, Guarino **5**:1229
Guarino da Verona *see* Veronese
guayacao **2**:*309*
Guelfs **1**:156, **2**:421, **3**:743, 854, **5**:1378, 1405
Guercino, Il **4**:*993*
Guericke, Otto von **3**:775
Guerrero, Francisco **4**:949
Guevara, Antonio de **1**:204
Guicciardini, Francesco **1**:242, *244*, 245, **3**:856
Guienne, duke of **5**:1277
Guildhall (London) **3**:751
guild merchant **2**:494–496
guilds and companies **2**:493–501
  companies **3**:497–501
  craft guilds **2**:496–497, 499, **4**:983
  Dürer **2**:311
  Florence **1**:151, **2**:415, 417, 419, **3**:853
  German towns **2**:476, 478
  Italian city-states **3**:632, 633, 635, 636, 637, 640, 641, 706
  London **3**:750, 751, 753

Lutheranism 2:555
  machines 3:774
  manufacturing 3:810–811
  Meistersingers 4:960
  physicians 3:843
  theater 5:1317, 1318
  women members 5:1421
  see also apprentices
Guillaume de Lorris 1:214,
  5:1202
Guillaume Tell (Rossini)
  5:1312
Guinea, Gulf of 2:379
Guise, Charles de 1:198
Guise, Claude de 1:198
Guise, Henry de 1:201,
  2:517
Guise, Marie de *see* Mary of
  Guise
Guise family 2:440, 442
  Catherine de Médicis 1:198,
    199, 201
  French civil wars 2:452, 453,
    454, 455
  Stuarts 5:1264, 1265, 1266,
    1297, 1298, 1426
gunpowder 3:774, 775,
  5:1309, 1335, 1407–1409,
  see also cannon; firearms
Gunpowder Plot (1605)
  1:*238*, 239, 2:342, *343*,
  4:880, 1039, 5:1301
guns *see* firearms
Guntram the Rich 2:507
Gustav I Vasa, king of Sweden
  4:1112, 5:*1304,*
  1305–1306, 1307,
  1308–1309
Gustavus II Adolphus, king of
  Sweden 2:371, 3:839,
  5:1307, 1308–1309, 1339
  Christina 1:227, 228
  military tactics 5:1309
  Thirty Years War 5:1332,
    1333, 1336–1337, 1415
Gutenberg, Johannes 1:102,
  103, 3:*688*, 697, 775,
  780–781, 783, 805, 5:1168,
  1169, 1193, 1218, 1220
Gutenberg Bible 3:*688,*
  5:1169, *1170*

Guyenne *see* Aquitaine
Guzmán, Gaspar de
  5:1384–1385
Guzmán de Alfarache (Alemán)
  3:738
Gyllenstierna, Christina
  5:1305
gymnasium 5:1372

H

Haarlem Lake 1:275
Haarlemmermeerboek
  (Leeghwater) 1:275
Hackness manor (Yorkshire)
  5:1422
Haddon, Walter 5:1419
hadith 3:611
Haft Awrang (Persian
  manuscript) 4:1085
Hagar 4:1085
Haggadah 3:*669*
Hagia Sophia, Church of
  (Constantinople)
  1:171–172, *256*, 263
Hague, The 5:1294
Hague, Treaty of (1625)
  5:1335
Haiti 1:250
hajj 3:611, 621, 4:1078, *1084,*
  1085
Hakluyt, Richard 2:375, 384,
  385
Hakluyt Society 2:375
*Hakluytus Posthumus, or
  Purchas his Pilgrimes*
  (Purchas, ed.) 2:375, 377,
  379
Halacha 3:669
Hales, Robert 4:1046
Hall, Joseph 3:609
Halland island 5:1310, 1338
Halloween 4:1118
Hals, Franz 4:996, 997, 998
Hamas *see* Hanseatic League
Hamburg
  Black Death 2:305
  Hanseatic League 2:475,
    504–505, 506
Hameel, Alart du 1:131
Hamilton, James, earl of Arran
  5:1426

Hamlet (Shakespeare) 5:1270,
  1271, 1275, 1326, 1327
Hammer of Witches, The (text)
  3:802
Hampton Court Conference
  (1604) 1:108
Hampton Court Palace
  (England) 2:334
Handel, George Frideric
  5:1247
Hannibal 4:1052
Hanno (papal elephant)
  4:1012
Hanseatic League 2:475–476,
  481, **502–506**, 5:1340
  Denmark 5:1304, 1305
Hapsburg Empire 1:88,
  2:507–515, 4:1113, 5:1302
  Bohemia 1:120–122
  Burgundy 1:164
  Charles V 1:207, 209,
    2:445–446, 476
  Florence 2:420, 421
  France 2:438, 449, 451, 555
  German towns 2:475–482
  Hanseatic League 2:481
  Holy Roman Empire
    2:475–478, 507–515,
    549, 550–551, 556, 557
  Italian wars 2:420, 421,
    3:647
  land holdings 4:966
  Lombardy 3:740, 745, 746
  Netherlands revolt 2:331
  Ottoman Empire 3:624, 625,
    626, 715
  primogeniture 4:911
  religious wars 4:914
  Switzerland 5:1312, 1313,
    1314, 1315
  Thirty Years War 1:227,
    5:1310, 1330–1339
  Venice 5:1394
Hardouin-Mansart, Jules
  4:1007
Hardwick, Elizabeth 3:753,
  5:1420
Hardwick, Henry 5:1420
Hardwick, Mary 5:1420
harems 3:625
Harfleur 3:599

Harfleur, siege of (1415) 1:16,
  17
Härjedalen 5:1310, 1338
Harmensen, Jacob 1:190,
  2:346
harmony 4:944
Haro, Luis Méndez de 5:1284
harpsichords 4:959
Harriot, Thomas 3:825, 830,
  831
Harris, Henry 5:*1273*
Harrison, Stephen 3:665
Hart, James D. 2:383
Hartmann, Adam Samuel
  1:122
Hartog, Dirk 2:385
Harvard University 1:189,
  2:*325*, 4:891
Harvey, Anne 5:1329
Harvey, Gabriel 5:1286–1287
Harvey, Thomas 5:1329
Harvey, William 3:840,
  5:1251, 1255
Harwood Dale (Yorkshire
  farm) 5:1422
Harz Mountains 1:279
Hasan 3:620
Hathaway, Anne 5:1268,
  1269
Hatzfeldt, Melchior von
  5:1338
Havdalah prayer 3:*677*
Hawkins, John 1:63, 2:378
Hawksmoor, Nicholas 1:140
Haywain, The (Bosch) 1:128,
  129, 130
Haywood, Thomas 5:1325
Healing of the Madman, The
  (Carpaccio) 1:*87*
healing pilgrimage 4:1078,
  1079, 1082
heat 3:786, 811
  Bacon study 1:83
Hebrew Bible *see* Old
  Testament
Hebrew language
  bibles 3:688, 697
  education 2:321
  humanist learning 3:589,
    590, 591, 592, 679, 689
  Judaism 3:670, 696

Bohemia **1**:119, 212
Bruno **1**:57
Calvinist penalty **1**:187,
 2:539, **5**:1316
Catholic damnation **2**:431
Charles V **1**:211
Christian humanism **3**:592
Church of England **1**:232,
 236, 237
Counter-Reformation
 5:1197, 1226, 1234–1235
Cranmer **1**:237
England **2**:522, 526, 527
Ferdinand and Isabella
 2:396
Florence **2**:422
Galileo **1**:262, **2**:296, 297,
 467, 539, **3**:783, 784,
 5:1226, 1234–1235,
 1251, 1254, 1256, 1258
heliocentric universe **1**:272,
 2:539, **4**:1036
Henry IV **2**:518
Holy Roman Empire **2**:549
iconoclasm **3**:605
Inquisition **4**:1018, 1019,
 1026, 1065, **5**:1278,
 1283, 1400
Islam **3**:622
Joan of Arc **3**:602, 658, 660,
 661–662
Luther **3**:701, 705, 766, 767
magic **3**:802
Mary Tudor **1**:236, 237
monarchy **5**:1331
papacy **5**:1333
Paris **4**:1032
Pico della Mirandola **4**:1074,
 1075, *1076*, 1077
Savonarola **1**:137
science **3**:783, 784
Scotland **5**:1264, 1265
Hermes **4**:1065
Hermes Trismegistus **3**:799
Hermetic Corpus (Greek texts)
 3:799
Hero and Leander (Marlowe)
 3:822, 825
Herodotus **3**:688
Her Protection for Women
 (Anger) **5**:1420

Herrera, Francisco de (the
 Elder) **5**:1384
Herrera, Juan de **1**:*46*, 47,
 4:1060
herring **2**:504, 505
Hertford, earl of *see* Seymour,
 Edward
Hesse **5**:1267
Het Schilderboeck (van Mander)
 1:144, 148
Hexapla **1**:109
Heyden, Jakob van der **5**:*1377*
Heywood, Thomas **3**:733
Hideyoshi Toyotomi **4**:896
hieroglyphs **3**:774, 776
Hieronymites, monastery of
 the (Portugal) **4**:1141
High Church movement
 5:1325
High Renaissance
 architecture **1**:30, 32, 46
 Bramante **1**:139, 143
 music **4**:946–947
 painting **1**:145, **4**:980, 981,
 986–989, 990, 991, 992,
 995, 999, **5**:1184–1185,
 1187, 1237
 Rome **5**:1231–1232
 Venice **5**:1399
Hilanderas, Las (Velázquez)
 5:1390
Hilliard, Nicholas **5**:*1269*
Hinduism **3**:615
Hippocrates **3**:840, 844,
 5:1177
Hispaniola **1**:250–251,
 252–253, 254
 disease **2**:307
 missionaries **4**:889, 892
Historia Augusta (Mussato)
 3:584
Historia de las Indias (Duran)
 5:*1285*
Historia de las Indias (Las
 Casas) **1**:253
Historia naturalis (Bacon) **1**:80
Historia vitae et mortis (Bacon)
 1:80
*Historie of the Raigne of King
 Henry the Seventh, The*
 (Bacon) **1**:80

history
 English nationalism **2**:339
 humanist studies **1**:180,
 2:336, 339, **3**:582, 584,
 587, 588, 590, 682, 683,
 686, **5**:1218, 1282
 national **4**:964
 Renaissance **5**:1220
 Scottish writers **5**:1263
 Shakespeare's plays **5**:1273
History of Britain (Milton)
 4:887
History of Italy, The
 (Guicciardini) **1**:245
History of Richard III (More)
 4:928
History of Rome (Livy) **3**:682,
 684
History of the Council of Trent
 (Sarpi) **4**:1038
History of the Indies (Las Casas)
 1:253
*History of the Life of the Petty
 Thief, The* (Quevedo y
 Villegas) **3**:738–739
History of the Reformation
 (Knox) **5**:1265
History of the Resurrection
 (Schütz) **5**:1246
history painting **2**:469, **4**:997
 Rembrandt **5**:1210, 1212
hoaxes **2**:383
Hobart, John **4**:886
Hobbes, Thomas **1**:51, 59,
 2:**542–547**, **4**:1066–1067,
 1071, 1072
Hoby, Margaret Dakin **3**:749,
 5:1416, 1422
Hoby, Thomas **5**:1419, 1422
Hogarth, William **4**:*1116*
Hogenberg, Franz **1**:*64, 78,
 183, 184, 211, 281*, **2**:*371,*
 5:*1165, 1301, 1316, 1350*
Hohenstaufens, the **2**:505
hoist **1**:156
Holbeach House (England)
 5:1301
Holbein, Ambrosius **2**:*318*
Holbein, Hans (the Younger)
 1:*181, 235*, **2**:*337*, **5**:*1198,
 1223, 1371*

holidays *see* festivals
Holland *see* Netherlands
Hollar, Wenzel **3**:*749*
Holy Alliance **4**:*967*
Holy Apostles, Church of the
 (Constantinople) **1**:263,
 264
Holy Communion **1**:240 *see
 also* Eucharist
Holy Cross, Church of the
 (Blesa) **5**:*1279*
Holy Family with Curtain
 (Rembrandt) **5**:1215
Holy Land
 Crusades **1**:223, 259–260,
 5:1392–1393
 Islam **3**:623, 625
 trade **5**:1341
Holy League **2**:442, 443, 457,
 458, 459, 517, 518, **3**:643,
 645, 715–716, 718
Holy Office of the Inquisition
 see Inquisition
Holy Roman Empire **1**:156,
 180, **2**:421, **548–560,**
 3:693, **4**:904, 1066
 Alfonso X **3**:693
 architecture **1**:39, 46
 Augsburg, Peace of **1**:75–78
 Bohemia **1**:117–122
 Burgundy **1**:157, 158, 160,
 161, 162
 Charles V **1**:207–211, 241,
 243, 244, **2**:446, 448,
 513–514, 523
 Clement VII **1**:241, 244
 dissolution of **2**:512
 electors **4**:910–911
 established churches **2**:364,
 365, 366, 370, 371
 feudalism **2**:413
 Florence **2**:419, 421, 423
 France **2**:444, 448, 451
 German-speaking lands
 2:475–483, **4**:964
 Ghibellines **3**:743, **5**:1378,
 1405
 Hanseatic League **2**:503, 505
 Hapsburg Empire **2**:507–515
 humanism **2**:423
 Hundred Years War **4**:1136

Holy Roman Empire *(cont.)*
  Italian wars **3:**643, 644, 646, 647, 648, 649, 650, 702
  Jewish protection **3:**673, 674
  libraries **5:**1375
  Lombardy **3:**743, 744, 745
  Lutheranism **1:**210–211, **3:**765, 766–767, 836, 855
  Maximilian I **3:**835
  Ommegang procession **5:**1317
  papacy **1:**156, **3:**686, **4:**1008, 1013, 1014, 1015, 1017, 1023, 1040, 1086, 1088, **5:**1227
  peasants' revolt **2:**555, 558, **4:**1042
  Reformation **2:**482–483, 514, 537, 539, 541, **5:**1189, 1200, 1221
  religious wars **4:**914
  Roman Catholicism **3:**836, 837, 838, 839, **5:**1338, 1365
  Rome **5:**1232
  Thirty Years War **1:**227, **5:**1330–1339, 1415
  Trent, Council of **5:**1352, 1353, 1357, 1359
  universities **5:**1365, 1368
  Venice **5:**1394
  Viscontis **5:**1403, 1404, 1405
Holyrood Palace (Scotland) **5:**1263
Holy Spirit **2:**430, **3:**695, 757, **5:**1199
  preaching **5:**1165
  Trent doctrine **1:**186
Holy Trinity Church (Stratford-upon-Avon) **5:***1275*
holy war **3:**612, 616, 626
Holy Wisdom, Church of *see* Hagia Sophia, Church of
Homer **1:**59, 258, 264, **2:**373, **5:**1289
Honthorst, Gerrit van **4:**997
Hood, Thomas **1:***67*
Hooke, Robert **5:**1258, 1433

Hooker, Richard **2:**367, 369
Hope (London theater) **3:**732
Hopkins, Matthew **3:**802, **5:***1425*
Horace **1:**59
Horace (Corneille) **3:**730
Horning Ceremony **3:**818–819
horoscope **1:**70–71, *73,* **3:**830
horses **4:**1134
  harness **1:**25
  knighthood **1:**221, *225*
  see also cavalry
horticulture **1:**25, 26
Hospitallers *see* Knights Hospitallers
hospitals **3:**842
hourglass **3:**790
households **2:561–569**
  marriage age **4:**1129–1130
  peasant life **4:**1116–1117
  women's role **5:**1416–1424
House of Commons (Britain) **2:**350, 354, 407
House of Lords (Britain) **2:**354, 355
House of Saint-Cyr (Paris) **5:***1419*
housing
  architecture **3:**665, 666
  country houses **1:**43, 45, *47,* **2:**334
  France **2:***436*
  Italian city-states **3:**634
  Jewish ghetto **3:**672
  Rome **1:**40, 43
  villas **2:**563
Hous of Fame (Chaucer) **1:**213, 217
How a Christian Youth Can Benefit from the Study of the Classics (Basil) **1:**257
Howard, Catherine **2:**522, 527
Howard, Charles (2nd Baron Howard of Effingham) **1:***62,* 63, *66*
Howard, Henry, earl of Surrey **3:**723, 724, 823
Howard, Thomas, earl of Arundel **3:**665
Howard, Thomas, duke of Norfolk **2:**330, 331, 527

"How soon hath time" (Milton) **4:***880,* 881
Hoyos, López de **1:**202
Hradčany Castle (Prague) **5:**1334
Hradschin Palace (Prague) **2:**371
Hudibras (poem) **4:***1116*
Hudson, Henry **2:**374, 383, **5:**1342
Hudson River **5:**1342
Hudson's Bay Company **2:**501
Hugo, Victor **1:**126
Huguenots **1:**188, **2:**332, 371, 440, **5:**1195
  Catherine de Médicis **1:**198, 199, 200, 201
  French civil wars **2:**451–459, **5:**1331
  North America **1:**189
  Paris **4:**1033–1034
  Saint Bartholomew's Day Massacre **1:**188, 200, 201, **2:**371, 441, 454, 455, 456, 516, 556, **3:**825, **4:**1033, **5:**1331
  Thirty Years War **5:**1336
Huizinga, Johann **5:**1160
humanism and learning **1:**169, 264, **3:582–594**
  Alfonso X translation school **3:**693
  architecture **1:**31–32, 33, 43, 44, 140, 141, 143, **2:**424, **3:**665, 666, 667
  Aristotelian translation **1:**54–56, 58
  astrology **1:**69
  Bessarion **1:**261
  Boccaccio **1:**114–116
  Borgia, Lucrezia **1:**125, 126
  Botticelli **1:**135, 136–137
  as Bruegel influence **1:**145, 152
  Calvinism **1:**181, 190
  Christina **1:**227, *228,* 229
  classical drama **3:**729
  classical languages **3:**682–690, 693, 694
  Clement VII **1:**241–242, 244

  Constantinople **1:**258–259, 260, **2:**430
  Descartes **2:**294
  Dürer **2:**311, 312, 314, 316
  education **2:**317–325, 327
  England **2:**335, 336–337, **3:**590, 593
  Erasmus **2:**356, 357, 358, 362, **5:**1189
  Florence **2:**414, 421–423, 424, 425, 426
  France **2:**439, 448, 450
  German towns **2:**481, 482
  heresy **2:**538–539
  Holy Roman Empire **2:**551–552
  Hussites **1:**118
  Inquistion **2:**362, **5:**1283
  Italian city-states **3:**638, 640
  James I **5:**1299
  Judaism **3:**674, 679, 693
  Leo X **3:**700, 703
  literature **3:**720, 722, 727, 729, 730, 731, 732, 733, 734–735, 737, 739, 823
  Luther vs. **2:**339, **3:**756, 761, 767, **5:**1371
  Machiavelli **3:**772
  mathematics **3:**827, 829
  medicine **3:**840, 844–847
  Medicis **2:**422, **3:**852, 853, 855, 856
  More **4:**925–932
  music **4:**946–947, 961
  painting and sculpture **1:**145, **2:**312, **4:**984–985
  Palladio **1:**43
  papacy **4:**1020, 1021–1023, 1024
  Petrarch **2:**320, **4:**1049, 1053–1055, 1075
  philosophy **4:**1064, 1072
  Pico della Mirandola **4:**1073–1077
  Portugal **4:**1143–1145
  printed texts **2:**323, **3:**780, 782–783, **5:**1172–1173
  Rabelais **5:**1176–1179
  Reformation **2:**339–340
  Renaissance **5:**1218–1221, 1224, 1240

Roman Catholic Church
5:1189
Rome **5:**1228, 1229, 1230,
1231–1232, 1235
Scotland **5:**1263
Spain **5:**1279–1283
universities **5:**1365,
1368–1370, 1372, 1373,
1376
Venice **5:**1399
vernaculars **3:**694, 696
women **5:**1416, 1417–1418,
1419
Wren **5:**1429–1430
see also classical antiquity;
Greek culture; Latin
culture
human nature **2:**339, **4:**763,
1064, *1066,* 1072, 1076
opposing views of **4:**1064
Pico della Mirandola **2:**537,
538, **4:**1067
Hume, David **4:**1068, 1070
humor *see* comedy
humors, four **1:**68, **3:**840
Humphrey, duke of Gloucester
2:336, **3:**601
Hundred Guilder Print, The
(Rembrandt) **5:**1212, 1215
Hundred Years War
3:595–603, **4:**1136,
5:*1412,* 1413
Agincourt **1:**16–20,
3:599–600
Aquitaine **2:**413
Burgundy **1:**158, 160, 162
France **2:**434–435, 445
Joan of Arc **3:**602, 657–662,
5:1427
monarchy **4:**911
nationalism **4:**965, 968
Paris **4:**1029–1030
peasants' revolts **4:**1042,
1047
second stage **1:**16
turning point **1:**160
Hunername (Ottoman
manuscript) **4:***1084*
Hungary
Bohemia **1:**120
crusade of Nicopolis **1:**158

Hapsburgs **2:**438, 507, 509,
510–511, 557
nobility **4:**971
Ottoman Empire **1:**242,
2:555, 557, *558,* **3:**616,
618, 623, 624, 629, 715
peasant revolt **4:**1042
Poland **4:**1112
Reformation **2:**559
Thirty Years War **5:**1335
Hunters in the Snow (Bruegel)
1:*148*
hunting **1:**92, 94–95
Huntingdon, earl of **5:**1416
Hunt in Honor of Charles V
(Cranach the Elder) **1:***95*
Hurons (people) **4:**893
Hurtado de Mendoza, Diego
3:649
Hus, Jan
Bohemia **1:**118–119
heresy **2:**537
Holy Roman Empire **2:**549,
550, 557
Lutheranism **3:**764, 766
nationalism **4:**969
Reformation **5:**1192
Thirty Years War **5:**1334
universities **5:**1367
see also Hussites
Husayn **3:**620
Hussites **3:**660, 674, 766
Bohemia **1:**118–119, 120,
122
heresy **2:**537
nationalism **4:**969
reformation **5:**1192
Hussite wars **2:**549
Hutten, Ulrich von **2:**552
Huygens, Christiaan (son)
3:775
Huygens, Constantijn (father)
5:1211
hydraulic technology *see* dams
and drainage
hydrostatics **2:**461, 462
hygiene *see* public health
Hymnes (Ronsard) **3:**22
hymns **4:**952, 954
Hussite **1:**118
Hyperaspistes (Erasmus) **2:**361

I

Iberian Peninsula *see* Portugal,
Spain
Ibn Battutah **3:**611, **4:**1084
Ibn Rushd (Averroës) **1:**51,
52–53, 58, **4:**1054, 1064,
1098, **5:**1367
Ibn Sina (Avicenna) **5:**1367
Ibrahim (prophet) *see* Abraham
iconoclasm **3:**604–609, **4:**992,
995
Calvinism **1:**183, 184, 185,
5:*1165*
Church of England **1:**240
Islam **1:**172, **3:**605
Lutheranism **3:**761, 762
Puritanism **1:**48–49, **5:**1198
iconography **1:**48–49
Iconologica (Ripa) **2:**472
icons **1:***168, 263,* **3:***604, 605*
idealism **2:**543, **4:**1070
nominalism vs. **1:**182
Platonism **1:**57, **4:**1092
Idea of a Universal Architecture
(Scamozzi) **1:**34
Ignatius, patriarch of
Constantinople **1:**259
Ignatius of Loyola **1:**59, **4:**894,
955, **5:**1205–1206
Jesuits **4:**1015, *1017*
Spiritual Exercises **1:**99,
5:1199, 1206
Iliad (Homer) **1:**59, 258
Hobbes translation **2:**546
illusory perspective **1:**145,
2:312, 316
illustration **5:**1171
Illustre-Théâtre, L' **4:**898
Image of Julius II
(Michelangelo) **4:**874
images, printed **5:**1171
images, rejection of *see*
iconoclasm
Imitation of Christ (Thomas à
Kempis) **1:**99, **3:**760,
4:1079
Immaculate Conception
4:1036
Immaculate Conception,
Confraternity of the
3:708–709

immunity, disease **2:**302, 303,
306, 307, 308
Imola **5:**1427, 1428
imperial circles **2:**550
Imperial History (Mussato)
3:584
imperialism *see* colonialism,
exploration
Incarnation **1:**183, **3:**604,
605, 607, **4:**1098
Incas **2:**374, 382, **3:**776, 788,
4:892
Incisa (Tuscany) **4:**1049
Incoronazione di Poppea, L'
(Monteverdi) **4:**922, 923
incunabula (printed books)
5:1169
indentures **2:**410
Independents **2:**353
Index of Forbidden Books
2:465, 466, 467, **4:**1018,
1019, **5:**1178–1179, 1197,
1226, 1234
Copernicus's *De
revolutionibus* **1:**272
Erasmus's works **3:**585, 592
Trent, Council of **5:**1363
India
exploration **2:**373, 374, 380,
381, **5:**1342, 1345
Islam **3:**612, 613, 614, 615,
629
Judaism **3:**669
missionaries **4:**894
Portugal **4:**1142, 1144
religious orders **5:**1204,
1206
trade **2:**302, **5:**1341
Indian College **4:**892
Indian Ocean **2:**379, 381,
3:624, 787, 788, 793, 794,
4:1138, 1142
shipping **2:**302
trade **5:**193, 1342
indigenous peoples
Columbus **1:**250–251,
252–253, 254, 255
disease **1:**255, **2:**307, 308,
382
missionaries **4:**890–891,
892, 893, 1015, **5:**1285

indigo **5**:1348

individualism **2**:542

Indonesia **2**:373, **4**:1139
 Islam **3**:612, 613

inductive logic **1**:81, 82, 83

indulgences
 Leo X **2**:421, **3**:704, 855
 Luther's critique of **2**:423,
  3:757, 763, **4**:929,
  1012–1013, **5**:1190
 papacy **4**:1012–1013,
  5:1231, 1232
 penance **1**:180
 pilgrimage **4**:1079, 1080
 printing **5**:1169
 Reformation vs. **2**:481,
  5:1189, 1190–1191,
  1192
 sale of **2**:481, 553, **3**:757,
  855
 theological basis of **4**:1013
 Trent, Council of **5**:1360

industrial revolution **3**:784,
 785–786, **5**:1259

inertia **2**:295

infant baptism **1**:178, **5**:1314

infant mortality **3**:843,
 4:1121, 1131,
 5:1420–1421

infantry **1**:226, **3**:651
 tactics **5**:1309, 1313, 1314

infinitesimals **3**:831, 832, 833

influenza **3**:841, 843
 Americas **1**:255, **2**:308

Ingegneri, Marc'Antonio
 4:917

Inglis, Esther **5**:1427

Ingram, Lady **2**:*342*

Ingria **5**:1309, 1334

inheritance **2**:565, 568
 fief **2**:404–405
 monarchy **3**:595, 625
 primogeniture **1**:235, **2**:512,
  3:625, **4**:911
 Salic Law **2**:517, **3**:595
 Tudor male heir **1**:233
 by women **2**:404–405, 413

Inner Temple (London) **1**:213

Innocent III, Pope **1**:260,
 2:531, **5**:1158

Innocent VII, Pope **2**:318

Innocent VIII, Pope **3**:700,
 4:1074, 1075, *1076*

Innocent X, Pope **5**:1388,
 1389

Innocent XI, Pope **2**:372

innovation *see* science;
 technology

Innsbruck, University of
 5:1377

Inns of Court (London) **1**:79,
 213, **3**:752, **5**:1328

*Inquiry into the Nature and
 Causes of the Wealth of
 Nations* (Smith) **5**:1349

Inquisition
 Aristotle **1**:57
 Cardano **1**:70, **3**:830
 Erasmus **2**:362
 Galileo **2**:297, 467, 539,
  3:784, **4**:1036, **5**:1254
 heresy **2**:530, 531, 532–535
 humanism **3**:586, 592
 Jewish converts **3**:677, 678,
  5:1291
 monarchy **4**:907, 912
 Muslim converts **3**:613
 papacy **4**:1018, 1019
 Paul III **5**:1197, 1234
 popular culture **4**:1120, 1121
 Portugal **4**:1139, 1141
 Renaissance vs. **5**:1226
 Rome **1**:187, **4**:1018, 1019,
  1036, 1065, **5**:1226,
  1234, 1251
 theater **5**:1321
 Venice **5**:1400
 witchcraft **2**:534–535,
  3:801–802, **4**:1019
 women **5**:1424
 see also Spanish Inquisition

inscriptions **3**:587

Inspiration of Saint Matthew
 (Caravaggio) **1**:194

Instauratio Magna (Bacon)
 1:*82*

Institoris, Henricus **3**:802

Institute of the Blessed Virgin
 see English Ladies

Institutes of Oratory
 (Quintilian) **3**:583, 683,
 5:1373

*Institutes of the Christian
 Religion* (Calvin) **1**:179,
 185, 188, **3**:607, **5**:1194

Institutio oratoria (Quintillian)
 3:583, 683, **5**:1373

Institutio principii christiani
 (Erasmus) **2**:357

Instruction (Charles V) **5**:1283

*Instruction for Measurement
 with the Compass and Ruler*
 (Dürer) **2**:312, **3**:828

Instruction in Faith (Calvin)
 1:185

insurance **1**:91

Inter caetera (Alexander VI)
 2:381

interest-bearing loans *see* usury

Interior Castle, The (Teresa of
 Ávila) **5**:1207

interior decoration **2**:564

intermezzi **3**:734, **5**:1321

international banking **1**:86–87

international Gothic style
 4:981

Interregnum (England) **2**:*354*

*Introduction to Christian Life
 and Virtue* (Olier) **5**:*1361*

inventions *see* machines,
 technology

investiture controversy
 2:365–366, 368

Invincible Armada (Cervantes)
 1:203

Ionic order **1**:30

Iran *see* Persia

Ireland **4**:904, **5**:1265, 1317
 Elizabeth I **2**:326, 327, 332,
  333
 England **2**:343, 344
 English civil wars **2**:348, 350,
  352, 354
 Scotch Protestants **1**:189
 Spenser **5**:1287–1288, 1289,
  1290
 Stuarts **5**:1300, 1302, 1303
 trade **5**:1350

Irene, empress of Byzantium
 3:605

Ireton, Henry **2**:352

iron **3**:812
 cannon **5**:1408–1409

Iroquois (people) **4**:893

irrigation **1**:273, 276, 277,
 280, **3**:741, **5**:1402

Isaac, Heinrich **4**:946, 950,
 951, 957

Isabella I, queen of Castile *see*
 Ferdinand and Isabella

Isabella, Holy Roman empress
 and regent of Spain **1**:209,
 4:1056, 1139, **5**:1281

Isabella, princess of Spain
 5:1237, 1241, 1280, 1426

Isabella of Portugal (wife of
 Charles V) *see* Isabella,
 Holy Roman empress and
 regent of Spain

Isabella of Portugal (wife of
 John II of Castile and
 León) **2**:387, **5**:1277

Isabelle of France (daughter of
 Charles VI) **3**:599

Isabelle of France (daughter of
 Philip IV) **3**:595

Isfahan **1**:*280*, **3**:622

Islam **3**:610–629
 Africa **2**:380
 agricultural technology
  1:21
 architecture **1**:46–47
 Aristotle **1**:51, 52–53
 astronomy **1**:267, 268, 271
 Byzantium **1**:166, 170
 Constantinople **1**:263
 Crusades against **1**:223,
  259–260
 Francis I **2**:448
 Hapsburgs **2**:512, 514
 iconoclasm **1**:172, **3**:605
 Inquisition **5**:1278
 Judaism **3**:669, 670, 676
 machines **3**:777, 779
 mathematics **3**:827
 monotheism **3**:620, 669
 navigation **5**:1343
 papermaking **3**:805
 Philip II **4**:1056–1057
 pilgrimage **4**:1078,
  1084–1085
 Poland **4**:1110
 Portugal **4**:1137, 1138,
  1140, 1141, 1142

scholarship **3:**693, **4:**1054, 1061, 1064, **5:**1367

science and technology **5:**1250

slave trade **5:**1348

Spain **2:**398, **3:**676, 678, **4:**956, 969, **5:**1277, 1278, 1279, 1322, 1425

Spanish converts **2:**396–398, 408

Spanish expulsion **2:**393, 394, 533, **3:**612, 613, 676, 678

trade **2:**373, 379, 380, **5:**1341, 1344, 1345

Venice **5:**1392

see also Ottoman Empire

Ismail **3:**612, 621, 622

isorhythmic motets **4:**945

Istanbul *see* Byzantium; Constantinople

Italian city-states **3:630–642**

architecture **1:**30–45, **3:**663, 664, 665, 666, 667

banking **1:**84, 87–88

Black Death **2:**304, 305, 306

Borgias **1:**123–126

Bruegel **1:**144, 145

Chaucer **1:**216–217

Church Latin **3:**689

classical languages **3:**682

conflict among **3:**853, 854

Counter-Reformation **5:**1198

dams and drainage **1:**276–277, 278, 279, 280, 281

Dürer **2:**311, 312–313

feudalism **2:**412

Florence **2:**414–426

Graubünden **5:**1334

Greek philosophy **1:**169

Gregorian calendar **1:**176

Hapsburgs **2:**511, **3:**715

humanism **2:**320, **3:**583–589, 591, 592, 638, 640, **5:**1370

Judaism **3:**670, 673, 679, 681

Leonardo da Vinci **3:**706–714

literature **1:**206–207, **3:**720–724, 735, 736–777, 770

Machiavelli **4:**1066–1067

manufacturing **3:**740, 741, *743,* 805

medical studies **3:**840, 841, 844, 845, 846–847

Monteverdi **4:**916–923

music **4:**944, 951–952, 954–956, 958–959, 960, 961

nationalism **4:**966

nobility **4:**974, 977

Ottoman Empire **3:**715

painting and sculpture **1:**144, 145, **2:**312–313, **4:**980, 981, 983–993

papacy **4:**1008, 1011, 1019–1023, 1089–1090

Petrarch **4:**1049–1055

Pico della Mirandola **4:**1073–1085

Platonic academies **2:**320

poetry **3:**720–721, 722–723, 724, 770

printing **5:**1169

prose fiction **3:**735, 736–737

Raphael **5:**1180–1187

religious orders **5:**1204

Renaissance **5:**1218–1226

republics **5:**1224

Rubens **5:**1237, 1238

science and technology **5:**1249, 1250–1254, 1256

territorial battles **2:**419

theater **3:**729, 733–735, 772, **5:**1320–1321, 1322

trade **5:**1341, 1401

universities **5:***1365,* 1367, *1368,* 1370–1371

Urbino **5:**1378–1383

Velázquez **5:**1387, 1388–1389

vernaculars **3:**693, 694, **4:**963

villas **2:**563

Viscontis **5:**1401–1406

women **5:**1420, 1422, 1424, 1427, 1428

see also Florence; Italian wars; Lombardy; Mantua; Milan; Naples; Padua; Rome; Venice

Italian language **2:**465, **3:**682, 694, 696

Dante **1:**217

Galileo **5:**1254

Petrarch **4:**1049, 1050, 1052

Italian masters **2:**312–313

Italian wars **2:**550, **3:**630, 633, 639, 642, **643–651,** 853, **4:**986, **5:**1220

Charles V **1:**208, 210, 241, 242–243, **2:**413, 421, 555, **3:**702

dams **1:**279

Florence **2:**419, 420, 421

France **2:**437–438

Francis I **1:**221, **2:**445, 446, 555

as French architectural influence **2:**444

Leo X **3:**701, 702–703

Lombardy **3:**742–743, 745, 746

Naples **1:**244, **2:**412

nationalism **4:**966

Rome **5:**1231, 1233

syphilis **2:**310

see also Cateau-Cambrésis, Peace of

Italy *see* Italian city-states

Italy Liberated from the Goths (Trissino) **4:**1000

Ivan I, grand prince of Moscow **4:**933

Ivan III (the Great), emperor of Russia **4:**934, 936, 1109

Ivan IV Vasilyevich (the Terrible), emperor of Russia **3:652–656**

Muscovy **4:**934, 936, 937, 940

Poland **4:**1109, 1112

Sweden **5:**1306–1307

Ivan Ivanovich **3:**653, 656

Ivan the Terrible and His Son on November 16, 1581 (Repin) **3:***656*

ivory **2:**379, 380, **5:**1345

J

Jackman, Charles **2:**384

Jack Newberie (Deloney) **3:**738

Jacquerie (1358) **2:**433, **4:**1029, 1042, *1044*

Jacques le Grant **1:**85

Jadwiga, queen of Poland **4:**1104–1105

Jagiello, grand duke of Lithuania *see* Wladyslaw II

Jagiellonian dynasty **1:**120, **4:**911, 1105, 1109, 1111, 1112

Jagiellonka, Anna **4:**1112

James, Saint **4:**1060, *1078, 1080,* 1082, **5:**1356

James I, king of England

architecture **1:**47, **3:**663, 664–665, 666

astrological prediction **1:**72

Bacon **1:**80

bibles **1:**104, 108, 109, **3:**698

Calvinism **1:**189, **2:**328, 343, 345, 349

Church of England **1:**239, **5:**1166, 1329

cockfighting **1:**96

divine right **1:**239

Elizabeth I **2:**330, 332, 333

Gunpowder Plot **4:**880, 1039

iconoclasm **3:**609

as James VI of Scotland **1:**189, **5:**1299–1301

Marlowe **3:**825

monarchy **2:**335, 342–343, 344–347, **4:**907

Paul V **4:**1039

Reformation **2:**342–343

Scotland **5:**1260, 1262, 1263, 1264, *1265*

Shakespeare **3:**732, 737, **5:**1269, 1272

Spenser **5:**1289

Stuarts **5:**1296, 1298, 1299–1301

theater **3:**755, **5:**1324

Thirty Years War **5:**1336

women **5:**1425, 1427

James II, king of England **5:**1302
  Church of England
    nonjurors **1:**262
  divine right **1:**239
  Glorious Revolution **1:**24,
    2:346, **4:**906
James I, king of Scotland
  5:1296
James III, king of Scotland
  5:1261, 1264, 1296
James IV, king of Scotland
  4:927, **5:**1296–1297
James V, king of Scotland
  1:198, **2:**527, **3:**722,
  5:1262, 1263–1264, 1265,
  1296, 1297, 1299, 1426
James VI, king of Scotland *see*
  James I, king of England
Jamestown colony **5:**1342
Jämtland **5:**1310, 1338
Jam-Zapolski, Peace of (1582)
  see Yam Zapolsky, Truce of
Janequin, Clément **4:**948
Janiculum Hill (Rome) **1:**141
janissaries **3:**617, 622, 626,
  629
Jan Kazimierz *see* John II
  Casimir Vasa
Jankov, Battle of (1645)
  5:1338
János Zázpolya **2:**511
Janssen, Zacharias **3:**775
Japan
  Jesuit missionaries **4:**894,
    896, 1015, *1018*
  Portugal **4:**1142, *1143*
  scientific exploration **5:**1259
Jarnac, Battle of (1569) **2:**452
Jasna Góra siege (1655)
  4:1114
Jason and the Argonauts
  1:163, **2:**515
Jáuregui y Aguilar, Juan de
  1:*202*
Jean de Gerson *see* Charlier,
  Jean
Jean de Meun **1:**214, **5:**1202
Jean de Venette **4:**1029
Jeanne of France **3:**595
Jean of Luxembourg **1:**215

Jefferson, Thomas **2:**545,
  4:887
Jem (Ottoman) **3:**619
Jena, University of **5:**1377
Jeremias II, patriarch of
  Constantinople **1:**262
Jeremias III, patriarch of
  Constantinople **1:**262
Jerome, Saint **1:**104, **3:***682,*
  688, 689, 696, **4:**1024,
  5:1357
Jerome of Prague **2:**549
Jerusalem **2:**399
  Crusades **1:**259, 260
  Ottoman conquest **3:**623
  pilgrimage **4:**1080, 1083
  temple **3:**695
Jerusalem Delivered (Tasso)
  1:223, **3:**721, **4:**922
jesters **5:**1319
Jesuits **1:**59, **2:**465, 556,
  3:839, **4:**1036,
  5:1205–1206
  Bohemia **1:***120,* 121
  catechisms **5:**1174
  Christina **1:**229
  Counter-Reformation
    4:1016, **5:**1191, 1199,
    1204
  Descartes **2:**294
  education **2:**294, **4:**1111,
    1139, 1140
  England **1:**238, **5:**1324,
    1326
  humanism **2:**324, **3:**593
  missionaries **4:**889, 890, 891,
    892, 893, 894–895, 896,
    1015, *1018*
  music **4:**955
  Paul III **4:**1015, *1017,*
    5:1191, *1197,* 1199,
    1205, 1353
  suppression of **5:**1209
  Sweden **5:**1307
  theater **5:**1323, 1326
  Thirty Years War **5:**1332
  universities **2:**324, 325
Jesus of Nazareth **1:**99, 105
  Bosch paintings **1:**128, 130,
    131
  Calvinism **1:**183, 184

  Dürer woodcuts **2:**314
  Eucharist **1:**178, 183, **5:**1194
  Gospels on **3:**671
  horoscope of **1:**70, 72, *73,*
    3:830
  iconoclasm **3:**604, 605, 607,
    5:1222
  Islam **3:**610, 618
  Judaism **3:**671
  Last Supper **3:**710, 712, 713
  Madonna and Child
    paintings **1:***145,* **2:***398,*
    425, **5:***1220*
  Michelangelo painting
    5:*1354*
  Neoplatonism **4:**1098–1099
  preaching on **5:**1163–1164,
    1165
  Raphael paintings **5:**1180,
    1182, 1184, 1185, 1187
  religious orders **5:**1201
  religious plays **5:**1317, 1318,
    1319, 1322
  Rembrandt paintings **5:**1213,
    1215
  Rome **5:**1232
  sacraments **1:**184, **5:**1358,
    1359
  Trent, Council of **5:**1360
Jesus Was Born a Jew (Luther)
  3:675
Jewel, John **1:**238
jewels **2:**373
Jewish Bridge, The
  (Rembrandt) **5:**1217
Jew of Malta, The (Marlowe)
  3:671, 822, 825
Jews *see* Judaism
jihad **3:**612, 616
Jimenez, Miguel **5:***1279*
Jiménez de Cisneros, Francisco
  5:1282
Joan I (the Mad), queen of
  Castile **2:**510, 515, **5:**1277,
  1280
  Charles V **1:**207
  overview of **5:**1281
Joan of Arc **1:**160, **2:**435,
  3:602, **657–662,** **4:**968,
  5:1427
Joan of Kent **4:**1046

João II *see* John II (the
  Perfect), king of Portugal
Jodelle Étienne **3:**720, 729
Jogues, Isaac **4:**893
Johannes (artist) **5:***1341*
John, Saint **2:**316, 485, 487
  see also John, Gospel of
John XXII, Pope **4:**905
John XXIII (antipope) **1:**87
John II, king of Aragon **2:**393,
  394, 395, **5:**1278–1279
  peasants' revolt **4:**1042
John, duke of Bedford **3:**601,
  602
John, king of Bohemia *see*
  John of Luxembourg
John, duke of Brittany **2:**406
John VII Palaeologus,
  Byzantine emperor **1:***262*
John VIII Palaeologus,
  Byzantine emperor **1:**169,
  260, 261, **2:**429
John I, king of Castile and
  León **4:**1137, 1145
John II, king of Castile and
  León **2:**393, **5:**1277, 1279
John I, king of Denmark and
  Norway *see* John II, king of
  Sweden
John, king of England **4:**906
John II (the Good), king of
  France **1:**157, **2:**433,
  3:597, **4:**1029, 1042
John II Casimir Vasa, king of
  Poland **1:**230, **2:**453,
  4:1114
John III Sobieski, king of
  Poland **4:**1114
John I, king of Portugal **2:**380
John II (the Perfect), king of
  Portugal **1:**247, **2:**380,
  403, **4:**1138–1139, 1140
John III, king of Portugal
  4:1139, 1140, 1144
John IV, king of Portugal
  4:1145
John, elector of Saxony **2:**370
John II, king of Sweden
  5:1304, 1305
John III, king of Sweden
  5:1307, 1308

John, Gospel of **3**:591, 604, 605, 607, *697,* **5**:*1159*

John of Austria (Don John) **3**:626, 716, 717, 718
Cervantes **1**:202

John of Aviz **4**:1137

John of Bavaria **2**:388

John of Burgundy (doctor) **4**:1125

John of Capistrano **5**:1160, 1163

John of Damascus **1**:168, **3**:604, 761

John of Fordun **5**:1260

John of Gaunt, duke of Lancaster **1**:214, 215, 216, **2**:410, **4**:963, 1043, 1046, 1047

John of Holywood *see* Sacrobosco, Johannes de

John of Luxembourg **1**:117, 118, **3**:598, **4**:943

John of the Cross **5**:1207

John the Baptist **2**:485, **5**:1184, 1185

John the Evangelist *see* John, Saint

John the Fearless, duke of Burgundy **1**:158, 159, 160, 162, **3**:600, 601, **4**:1030

John Climacus, Saint **1**:168

John Frederick (the Magnanimous), elector of Saxony **5**:*1188*

John George I, elector of Saxony **5**:1245, 1246, 1247, 1332, 1337

John George II, elector of Saxony **5**:1247

John Paul II, Pope **2**:466, **4**:1023, **5**:1226

Johnson, Paul **5**:1179

joint-stock companies **2**:498–499, 500, **5**:1346–1347

Joinville, Treaty of (1584) **2**:457

Jones, Inigo **1**:47–48, 49, **3**:*663–668,* **4**:1007, **5**:*1431*

Jonghelinck, Nicolaes **1**:146

jongleurs **5**:1319

Jonson, Ben **2**:335, **3**:663, 732, 733, 739, 755, **5**:1325, 1326

Joseph II, emperor of Austria **2**:372

Joseph I, patriarch of Constantinople **1**:260

Joseph II, patriarch of Constantinople **2**:429

Josephinism **2**:372

Joseph's Bloody Coat Brought to Jacob (Velázquez) **5**:1387

Joshua, book of **2**:467, **3**:*591*

Josquin des Prez **4**:946–948, 949, 951, 952

journeymen **2**:498, **3**:810

Journey to Parnassus (Cervantes) **1**:202, 203

jousting *see* tournaments

Jouvencel (Bueil) **5**:*1410*

Juana the Mad *see* Joan I

Juan de Flandes **5**:*1281*

Juan of Austria *see* John of Austria

jubilee year **4**:*1079,* 1080

Judaism **3**:**669–681**
Aristotelianism **1**:51
bibles **1**:103, 104, **3**:689
iconoclasm **3**:605
Inquisition **2**:532, 533, **5**:1278
Islam **3**:610, 612, 613
Kabbalah **1**:57, **3**:677, 679–680, 689
Poland **4**:1110–1111, 1113–1114
Portugal **4**:1139
Roman Catholic damnation **2**:431
scholarship **3**:693
Spain **5**:1277, 1278, 1279, 1283
Spanish conversos **2**:396–397, 399
Spanish expulsion **2**:393, 394, 398–399
Spinoza **5**:1291, 1292, 1293, 1295
usury **1**:85
vernaculars **3**:695
see also anti-Semitism

Judas Returning the Thirty Pieces of Silver (Rembrandt) **5**:1212

Judea **3**:695

judges **3**:635

Judgment Day **1**:177, **2**:387

Judgment of the King of Bohemia, The (Machaut) **1**:215

Judith, book of **5**:1355

Judith and Her Maidservant (Gentileschi) **2**:471, 473, *474*

Judith Beheading Holofernes (Gentileschi) **2**:471, 473

Jugement du roy de Behaigne, Le (Machaut) **1**:215

jugglers **5**:1319

Juives, Les (Garnier) **3**:730

Julian II, Pope **1**:232

Julian calendar **1**:174–175, 176, 177, **4**:1024

Julian II Ordering Work on the Vatican (Vernet) **5**:*1231*

Jülich, duchy of **5**:1338

Jülich Succession, War of the **2**:560, **5**:1334

Julius II, Pope **1**:*50,* 245, **3**:756, 757, **5**:1420
architecture **1**:36, 38, 141–142
Florence **2**:420
Henry VIII **1**:232
Italian wars **3**:643, 645, 648, 649, 702
Leo X **3**:700–701, 702
Medicis **2**:420
Michelangelo **4**:871, 873–875, 876
papacy **4**:1012, 1025, 1026
Raphael **5**:1186, 1187
Rome **5**:1230, 1231–1232
Urbino **5**:1380
Venice **5**:1394

Julius III, Pope **3**:672, **4**:*954,* 955
Italian wars **3**:648
Trent, Council of **5**:1353, 1357, 1359

junk (vessel) **5**:*1343*

Jupiter (planet) **2**:464, **5**:1253

Justinian I, emperor of Rome **1**:*166,* 171, 172, *256,* **4**:1095

Justin Martyr **3**:765

Justus of Ghent **4**:*1055,* **5**:1181

just-war theory **2**:357

Jüterbog, Battle of (1645) **5**:1338

Jutland **5**:1335, 1338

K

Kaaba (Mecca) **3**:*611,* **4**:1084, 1085

Kabbalah **1**:57, **3**:677, 679–680, 689, **4**:1075, 1103

Kabul **3**:612

Kalff, Willem **4**:*996,* 997

Kaliningrad (Königsberg) **4**:1106

Kalm, Pehr **5**:1259

Kalmar, Union of (1397) **4**:911, **5**:1304

Kalmar Castle **5**:*1304*

Kant, Immanuel **4**:1070

Kappel, Battle of (1531) **5**:1194, 1315

Kara Sea **2**:384

Karelia **5**:*1309,* 1334

Kariye Carni (Constantinople) **1**:*258*

Karl Gustav *see* Charles X Gustav, king of Sweden

Karlstadt, Andreas **3**:606, 758, 761, **5**:1193

Kasimov **4**:934

Kassel **5**:1245

Kattegat Strait **5**:1338

Kazan **3**:653, *654,* **4**:936

Kazimierz **3**:*675*

Keats, John **5**:1290

Kelley, Edward **3**:800, 801

Kempe, Margery **4**:1081, **5**:1427

Kempis, Thomas *see* Thomas à Kempis

Ken, Thomas **1**:262–263

Kent peasants' revolt (1381) **4**:1043, 1045

Kent uprising (1830s) **4**:1048

Kepler, Johannes **1:**121, **2:**463, 559, **3:**783, 828, **4:**1109
  astronomy **3:**1250, 1251–1252
  Copernicus **1:**271, 272
  mathematics **3:**828, 831, 832
Kermesse, The (Rubens) **4:***1117*
Kerseboom, Johann **5:***1256*
Ketelhodt, Christian **5:***1164*
keyboards **4:**959–960
Khadjou barrage bridge **1:***280*
khanates **3:**653
Khmelnytsky, Bohdan **4:**1113
Kiefuss, Johann **3:**782
Kieser, Eberhard **3:***836*
Kilcolman **5:**1288
Kilcullen **5:**1288, 1290
Kildare, County (Ireland) **5:**1288
Killigrew, Henry **5:**1419
Killingworth, John **1:***174*
"Kingdom of Ireland, The" (map) **5:***1287*
kingdoms *see* monarchy; *specific kingdoms*
King James Bible (Authorized Version) **1:**106, 108, 109, 110, 239, *240,* **3:**698, 699, **5:**1221, 1357
King Lear (Shakespeare) **5:**1270, 1271, 1319
King's Book (1543) **2:**527
King's Cabinet Opened, The (Charles I letters) **2:**352
King's College (Cambridge)
  architecture **1:**30
  chapel **1:**100
  choir **4:**949
King's Lynn **4:**1081
King's Men (London) **5:**1270, 1272, 1275
kinship **2:**568–569
Kirk *see* Church of Scotland
Klaipeda (Memel) **5:**1334
Kleine geistliche Konzerte (Schütz) **5:***1246*
Klementinum (Prague) **1:***120,* 121

Kleyne Chronycke (Leeghwater) **1:***275*
Klinkicht, Moritz **5:***1372*
Knaben Dam **1:**279
kneeling **5:**1267
Kneller, Godfrey **5:***1303, 1429*
Knight, Gowin **3:**779
Knight, Death, and the Devil, The (Dürer) **2:**314–315
knighthood *see* chivalry, Crusades
Knight's Dream, The (Raphael) **5:**1181, 1183
Knights Hospitallers **1:**194, 223, **4:**1046
Knights of the Golden Fleece *see* Golden Fleece, Order of the
"Knight's Tale, The" (Chaucer) **1:***213,* 217
knowledge, Platonic **4:**1092–1093, 1094
Knox, John **1:**189, **5:**1265–1266, 1423, 1424, 1426
  overview of **5:**1267
Knutsson, Karl *see* Charles VIII, king of Sweden
Kobila Dam **1:**279
Koburger, Anthony **5:***1171*
Kochanowski, Jan **4:**1109
Koine Greek **3:**695, 696
Kölderer, Jörg **5:***1413*
König, Gustav **5:***1376*
Königsberg (Kaliningrad) **4:**1106
Königsberg, University of **5:**1372, 1377
Koran **3:**611, 614, 618, *626*
kosher laws **3:**671
Kosovo, Battle of (1444) **1:**263
Koster, Laurens Janszoon **5:***1168*
Köstritz **5:**1244
Kottannerin, Helene **5:**1418
Kraków **3:***675,* **4:**1106, 1109, 1112
Kraków, University of **1:**265, 266, *270,* **4:**1109, **5:**1250
Kraus, Martin **1:**262
Kremlin **4:**939

krummhorns **4:**958
Ksar al-Kebir, Battle of (1578) **4:**1140
Kulikovo Field, Battle of (1380) **4:**934
Kurbsky, Andrey Mikhailovich **3:**654
Kyd, Thomas **3:**732, 822, 824, **5:**1286, 1325
Kykko Monastery **2:**380

L

La Bicocca, Battle of (1522) **3:**646, 650
La-Charité-sur-Loire, siege of (1429) **2:**454, **3:**658
Ladies, Peace of the (1529) **2:**446, 448
Ladino dialect **3:**670
Ladislaus Postumus **2:**508, 509
Ladislav, king of Bohemia *see* László V, king of Hungary
Laetentur caeli **2:***427,* 429, 430
La Flèche **2:**294, **5:**1206
La Haye **2:**294, 295
La Isabela **1:**252, 253, 254
Lajos, king of Hungary **3:**623
Lalaing, Yolanda de **1:**164
Lambeth Palace (London) **4:**1046
Lampsonius, Dominic **5:**1236
La Navidad **1:**251, 252
Lancaster, James **2:**379
Lancasters, the **1:**17, **2:**408, **4:**903, 912, **5:**1273
  John of Gaunt **1:**214, 215, 216, **2:**410, **4:**963, 1043, 1046, 1047
Lances, The (Velázquez) *see Surrender of Breda, The*
land and land rights
  agriculture **1:**21–29
  feudalism **2:**401–413
  merchant wealth **5:**1350
  monasteries **5:**1202, 1203
  property law **3:**809
  reclamation **1:**273–276, 277
  Reformation **5:**1332–1333, 1338
  Spain **4:**965–966

Sweden **5:**1306, 1308
Venice **5:**1395
Landi family **3:**744
Landriano, Lucrezia **5:**1428
landscape design **1:**26
landscape painting **1:**144, 145, 146, 148
Landshut War **2:**549
Langland, William **1:**220
Langley, Francis **5:***1326*
languages, classical **3:682–690**
  Aristotelian translations **1:**51, 52, 54–56, 57, 58, 59
  bibles **1:**103–105, 109, 110, **4:**1022, 1024
  Boccaccio **1:**113–114
  Constantinople **1:**258, 264
  education **2:**317, 321
  humanism **2:**336, **3:**582–594, 640, 693, 694, 703
  papacy **4:**1022–1023
  Petrarch **4:**1049, 1050, 1052–1053
  philosophy **4:**1063, 1100
  Pico della Mirandola **4:**1073, 1074, 1075
  universities **5:**1368, 1369
  women's education **5:**1417, 1418, 1419
  see also Greek language; Hebrew language; Latin language
languages, vernacular **2:**537, **3:691–699, 4:**931
  biblical translations **1:**102–110, *180,* **2:**316, 321, 526, 536, **3:**689, **4:**970, **5:**1173–1174, 1175, 1193, 1221, 1315, 1357
  Calvin **1:**179
  Chaucer **1:**212–213, 217, 218, 219, 220
  Czech **1:**118, 119, 122
  Dante **1:**217
  Descartes **2:**296
  education **2:**319, 321, 323, 325

France **1**:214, **2**:432–433, 444, **3**:695, 696, **4**:963, **5**:1222

Galileo **2**:465, **3**:690, **5**:1254

Holy Roman Empire **2**:548

Judaism **3**:670

literature **2**:335, **3**:720, 721, 723

Mass **5**:1363

nationalism **2**:364, **4**:962, 963–964, 966, 969, 970

Petrarch **4**:1049, 1050, 1052

Polish writers **4**:1109

preaching **5**:1160

printing press **2**:323

Rabelais **5**:1179

Renaissance **5**:1222–1223

Scotland **5**:1260–1261

Spain **3**:693, 694–695, **4**:963, **5**:1222, 1282, 1284

Spanish Empire **2**:399

theater **5**:1318

Languedoc **2**:440, 455

Lanier, Emilia **5**:1423

Lannoy, Charles de **1**:243

Lanyer, Aemilia **3**:726

Lanzani, Bernardino **5**:1402

Lanzelin **2**:507

La Ramée, Pierre de see Ramus, Petrus

Larkin, William **4**:1068

La Rochelle, siege of (1627) **2**:454, 458, 459, **5**:1336

Lascaris, John **1**:261

Las Casas, Bartolomé de **1**:253, **2**:400, **4**:891

Lasso, Orlando di **4**:971

Last Judgment **1**:177, **2**:387

Last Judgment, The (Michelangelo) **1**:244, **4**:871, 877, 992, 1025, **5**:1354

Lastman, Pieter **5**:1210–1211, 1212

Last Supper (Leonardo da Vinci) **2**:425, **3**:709, 710, 712, **5**:1220

restoration of **3**:713

Last Supper, The (Veen) **5**:1237

László V, king of Hungary **1**:120

La Taille, Jean de **3**:730

Lateran Council, Fifth (1512–1517) **3**:703

Lateran Council, Fourth (1215) **3**:670–671, **5**:1158

Lateran Palace (Rome) **1**:257

Latimer, Hugh **1**:187

Latin language **1**:258, **2**:548, **3**:691, 692, 695

bibles **2**:358, **3**:591, 682, 684, 688–690, 696, 697, 703, **4**:1024, **5**:1159, 1160, 1357

Cicero **3**:683

Constantinople **1**:261

education **2**:317, 319, 321, 324

English language **3**:690

Erasmus **2**:357, 358, 359

Greek translation **1**:57, 261, 264

humanist learning **2**:334–335, 336, 337, **3**:582–583, 586, 588–589, 591, 592, 593, 594, 640, 683, 684, 685, 687, 693, 694, **5**:1219, 1280, 1282

literary genres **1**:219

Mass **5**:1363

Middle Ages **3**:682–683

Petrarch **4**:1049, 1052–1053

Pico della Mirandola **4**:1073, 1074, 1075

printing **5**:1173

text analysis **3**:686–687

universities **1**:261, **5**:1368, 1369

Valla scholarship **3**:586, 686–687, 688

vernacular texts vs. **3**:696–697, 698, 699

women's education **5**:1417, 1418, 1419

latitude **2**:377

La Tour, Georges de **4**:995, 997, 1120

Latvia **2**:503, 505, **3**:653 see also Livonia

Laud, William **2**:372, **3**:608, 609, **4**:881, **5**:1267, 1302

anti-Calvinism **2**:345, 346, 348, 349

Church of England **1**:239

execution of **2**:351

theater **5**:1325, 1329

Laudate pueri (Monteverdi) **4**:921

Laudatio urbis Florentinae (Bruni) **3**:584

Laura (Petrarch's muse) **4**:1050, 1051

Laurana, Luciano da **5**:1181, 1378, 1382

Laurentian Library (Florence) **1**:33, **4**:876

Lausanne **5**:1312, 1314

law

Bacon **1**:79, 80

Boccaccio **1**:111

Chaucer **1**:213

chivalry **1**:222

heresy **2**:531

Islam **3**:612, 614, 623, 625

Italian city-states **3**:632, 635

Ivan IV **3**:652

Judaism **3**:669, 671, 679, 680

London **3**:752

Ottoman Empire **3**:623

students of **5**:1367, 1371

urbanization **3**:809

Lawes, Henry **4**:880

Laws (Plato) **4**:1063

Laws of Ecclesiastical Polity, The (Hooker) **2**:367, 369

lay orders see third orders

lead line **2**:376

League of Cambrai, War of the **5**:1394, 1400

Leah (Michelangelo) **4**:874

leap year **1**:174, 176

learning see education; humanism and learning; universities

leather trade **3**:741, **5**:1350

Lech, Battle of the **3**:839

Leeghwater, Jan Adriaanszoon **1**:275

Leeuwenhoek, Antoni van **5**:1258

Lefèvre d'Étaples, Jacques **1**:108

Le Gallois de Grimarest, Jean **4**:897

legal studies **5**:1367, 1371

Legend of Good Women, The (Chaucer) **1**:218–219

Le Havre **2**:453

Leibniz, Gottfried Wilhelm **3**:828, 834, **5**:1295

Leicester, earl of see Dudley, Robert

Leiden **5**:1210, 1211, 1212

Leiden, University of **2**:323, **3**:585, 592, **5**:1210, 1292, 1367

Leipzig **1**:88, 279, **2**:506, 553

Thirty Years War **5**:1310

Leipzig, University of **5**:1367, 1372

Lely, Peter **5**:1243

Lemercier, Jacques **1**:48

Le Nain, Louis **4**:995

Lent **4**:1118, 1119, 1123

preaching **5**:1159

Leo III, Pope **1**:257, 258–259

Leo IV, Pope **5**:1187

Leo IX, Pope **4**:1073

Leo X, Pope **1**:95, 152, 277, **2**:426, **3**:700–705, 763, 765, **4**:929, **5**:1194

architecture **1**:38, 40

Charles V **2**:513–514

Clement VII **1**:241, 242, 245, 246

Counter-Reformation **5**:1197

elephant gift **4**:1012, 1037

Erasmus **2**:357

France **2**:442, 446, 447, **3**:701

Henry VIII **1**:240, **5**:1191, 1196

indulgences **2**:421, **3**:704, 855

Italian wars **3**:646, 648, 649

Luther **1**:242, **3**:701, 703, 704–705, 757, 763, 765, **4**:1013, **5**:1192, 1232

Leo X, Pope *(cont.)*
  Medicis **2:**418, 420, 421,
    426, **3:**850, 851, 853,
    855, 857
  Michelangelo **4:**876
  music **4:**946, 949
  Pontine Marshes drainage
    1:277
  Raphael **5:**1186, 1187
  Rome **5:**1232
  Urbino **5:**1380, 1382, 1383
Leo XIII, Pope **4:**932, 1022
Leo III (the Isaurian),
    Byzantium emperor **3:**605
León, Isaac de **3:**679
Leonardo da Vinci **1:**133,
    2:437, 450, 560,
    3:706–714, 4:873
  as Bramante influence **1:**139
  contributions of **5:**1249
  Florence **2:**424, 425
  hydraulic engineering **1:**277,
    278, 279
  machines **3:**775, 782, 783
  Medicis **3:**852, 856
  painting **4:**986, 987, 988,
    999
  as Raphael influence **5:**1183,
    1184, 1185, 1187
  Renaissance **5:**1220, 1224
Leoniceno, Niccolò **3:**840,
    844
Leopold I, Holy Roman
    emperor **2:**513
Leopold III, margrave of
    Styria, Tyrol, and Carinthia
    2:507
Leo the Philosopher,
    archbishop of Thessalonica
    1:258
Leo X with Two Cardinals
    (Raphael) **5:**1185
Lepanto, Battle of (1571)
    1:63, **3:**626, **715–719,**
    4:*1058,* 1060
  Cervantes **1:**202, 203, 206
Lepini Mountains **1:**277
Lerma, duke of **5:**1284
Lescot, Pierre **1:**45
Lese Gozzali, Benozzo di **1:***52*
Lesser, Aleksandr **4:***1104*

Letters to Atticus (Cicero)
    3:584, 589, 682, 683, 684
*Letter to the Grand Duchess
    Christina* (Galileo) **2:**467
letter writing **3:**589, 640, 682
Levant **2:**501
Levant Company **1:**262
Le Vau, Louis **4:**1007
Levellers **2:**354
Leviathan (Hobbes) **2:**543,
    545–546, **4:**1066
Leviticus, book of **1:**233
Leyden, Jan van **5:**1195
Lezceno, Juan Gabrielle de
    4:892
Liberia **5:**1345
libraries **3:**695, 703
  Maratha observatory **1:**271
  universities **5:**1375
  Vatican **4:**1022
Libreria Vecchia (Venice)
    3:*690*
Libri feudorum (treatise) **2:**405
Libro de vita contemplativa
    (Meli da Crema) **1:**126
Licensing Order of June 16,
    1643 **4:**883
Liceti, Fortunio **2:**461
Lichfield, Richard **3:***738*
Liège **2:**386
Lievens, Jan **5:**1211, 1212
Life and Death of Jack Straw
    (anon.) **5:**1327
Life in the Countryside, The
    (Brueghel the Elder)
    4:*1124*
Life Is a Dream (Vega) 728
Life of Aristotle (Bruni) **1:**54
Life of Bernini, The
    (Baldinucci) **1:**34, 101
Life of Filippo Brunelleschi
    (Manetti) **1:**34, *155*
*Life of Gargantua and
    Pantagruel, The* (Rabelais)
    see Gargantua, Pantagruel
*Life of the Admiral Christopher
    Columbus, The* (F.
    Columbus) **1:**248
life span **4:**1131
light rays **5:**1250
Ligurian Sea **2:**414, **5:**1401

Lilio, Antonio **1:**175
Lilio, Luigi **1:**175
Lille **1:**157, **2:**387
Lilly, William **1:**70, *72, 73*
Lima **1:**49, **5:**1209
Linacre, Thomas **4:**924,
    5:1373
Lincolnshire **1:**235
linden tree **1:***29*
Linlithgow Palace (Scotland)
    5:1263
Linnaeus, Carolus (Carl von
    Linné) **5:**1258, *1259*
Linschoten, Jan Huyghen van
    5:*1343*
Lionel of Ulster **1:**213
Lippershey, Hans **2:**464,
    5:1252
Lippi, Filippo **1:**133, 135
Lisbon **1:**205, 251, **4:**1139
  earthquake **4:**1141, *1145*
  Renaissance map **4:***1139*
Lisbon Bible **3:***591*
literacy **2:**323, 325, 552–553,
    555, **3:**720, 754, 819
  Judaism **3:**669
  printing press **2:**323, **5:**1172,
    1174, 1222
  rates of **5:**1173
  Reformation **2:**321
  Scotland **5:**1263
  vernaculars **3:**695, 697
  women **5:**1416, 1417
literature **3:720–739**
  as architectural subject **1:**41
  Aristotle **1:**59, 61
  Boccaccio **1:**111–115
  book production **3:**780–783
  Burgundy **1:**163
  Cervantes **1:**202–206
  Chaucer **1:**212–220
  chivalry **1:**222–224
  classical languages
    3:682–683
  Czech language **1:**118, 122
  England **2:**334–336, 337
  Erasmus **2:**362–363
  Florence **2:**423
  humanist learning
    2:334–337, **3:**582, 584,
    588, 589, 591, 594, 683

Jewish portrayals **3:**671
London **3:**753, 754, 755
Marlowe **3:**822–826
Medici patronage **3:**852
Milton **4:**879–887
Molière **4:**897–902
More **4:**927–928
nationalism **4:**963
Petrarch **4:**1049–1055
Poland **4:**1109
Portugal **4:**1144–1145
Rabelais **5:**1176–1179
religious orders
    5:1202–1203
Renaissance **5:**1222–1223,
    1225
Shakespeare **4:**916,
    5:1268–1276
Spain **5:**1284
Spenser **5:**1286–1290
theater **5:**1322–1323, 1325,
    1326, 1329
vernacular **3:**694, 695
women **5:**1427
see also poetry
Lithuania
  Judaism **3:**675
  monarchy **4:**911
  Muscovy **4:**933, 934
  Poland **4:**1104, 1105, 1107,
    1108, 1109
  Russia **3:**653
  Teutonic Knights **1:**223
Little Dutch Masters **4:**997
Little Ice Age **2:**303
Littleton, Elizabeth **5:**1422
liturgical calendar **1:**173, 174,
    175–177
liturgical drama *see* religious
    drama
livery **2:**410, 411
Lives (Plutarch) **3:**684, 685
Lives of the Artists (Baglione)
    1:192
*Lives of the Modern Painters,
    Sculptors and Architects*
    (Bellori) **1:**196
*Lives of the Most Eminent
    Painters, Sculptors, and
    Architects* (Vasari) **1:**34,
    143, 148, 150, **5:**1183

livestock **1**:21, 25, 26–27, **3**:818–820, 821
  storage dams **1**:280
Living Flame of Love (John of the Cross) **5**:1207
Livonia
  Hanseatic League **2**:503, 504, 505
  Ivan IV Vasilyevich **3**:653, 654, 656
  Poland **4**:1112
  Sweden **5**:1307, 1309
  Thirty Years War **5**:1334, 1335
Livonian Knights **3**:653
Livonian war **4**:937
Livre des bonnes moeurs, Le (Jacques le Grant) **1**:*85*
Livres du Graunt Caam, Li (manuscript) **5**:*1341*
Livy **3**:584, 682, 684, 686, 770, 772
Lloyd's of London **1**:91
loans **1**:85, **3**:633, **5**:1316
Lobkowitz, Wenzel Eusebius von **2**:559
Lochamer Liederbuch (song collection) **4**:942
Loci communes (Melanchthon) **3**:767–768
Locke, Anne Vaughan **5**:1423–1424
Locke, John **2**:545, **5**:1295, 1348–1349
Lockley, Rowland **1**:*62*
lodestone **2**:375
Lodge, Thomas **3**:755, **5**:1286
Lodi **3**:638
Lodowick Bryskett **5**:1287
logarithms **3**:831
Loggia del Capitaniato **4**:1001
Loggia of Psyche (Villa Farnese) **1**:*41*
Loggia of the Galatea (Villa Farnese) **1**:*41*
logic
  Aristotle **1**:50, 60–61, 81
  Bacon **1**:81–82, 83
  dialectic **2**:357, 362
Loire River **1**:45, 276, **3**:657, 659, 660

Loire River valley **2**:438
Lollards **1**:103, 107, 232, **2**:536–537, **3**:605, 761, 766
Lombard League **3**:740
Lombards **1**:89
Lombardy **3**:740–747
  agriculture **5**:1401, 1402
  Bramante **1**:139, 140
  feudalism **2**:405
  Italian wars **3**:646, 647, 651
  Viscontis **5**:1401–1406
Lomi, Prudentia **2**:471
London **3**:748–755
  agriculture **1**:22
  architecture **1**:32, 48–49, 140, **3**:663, 665, 666, 667, 668
  banking **1**:87, **2**:416
  Chaucer **1**:212, 213, 214
  Covent Garden **3**:820
  Essex rebellion **2**:332, 333
  map (c. 1588) **5**:*1324*
  More **4**:924, 927
  peasants' revolt **1**:216, **4**:1043, 1044–1045, 1046–1047
  plague **4**:886
  preaching **5**:*1161*, 1166
  printing **3**:819
  Shakespeare **5**:1268, 1269, 1270, 1271, 1275
  Spenser **5**:1286, 1287
  theater **3**:732, 733, 751, 755, 823, 824–825, **5**:1322, 1323, *1324*, 1326–1327, 1328
  Wren's rebuilding plan **1**:48–49, **5**:1431–1432, 1433
London, Treaty of (1518) **2**:522
London Bridge **3**:*748*, 749, **5**:*1324*
longbow **1**:*16*, 18, **2**:435, **5**:1412–1413
Longhi, Martino (the Elder) **1**:*40*
longitude **2**:376
Longjumeau, Peace of (1568) **2**:454

Long Parliament (1640) **2**:*344*, 349, 351
Lope de Vega *see* Vega, Lope de
Loqman **1**:*69*, **4**:*1084*, **5**:*1409*
lord mayor **3**:751, 754
Lord's Prayer **5**:1318
Lord's Supper **1**:181, 183, 184
Lorenzetti, Ambrogio **2**:492, **4**:980
Lorenzetti, Pietro **2**:488, 492, **4**:980
Lorenzo the Magnificent *see* Medici, Lorenzo de'
Lorrain, Claude **4**:994–995
Lorraine **5**:1338
Lotto, Lorenzo **5**:*1420*
Louis, duke of Bavaria **1**:112
Louis, prince of Condé **2**:451, 452, 453, 454
Louis II de Male, count of Flanders **1**:157
Louis IX, king of France **2**:517, 531, **3**:601
Louis X, king of France **3**:595
Louis XI, king of France **2**:406, **3**:735, **4**:965
  Burgundy **1**:162, 163–164, **2**:413
  Spain **5**:1277
Louis XII, king of France **1**:124, **2**:429, 445, 555, **3**:742, 853, **4**:965, **5**:1394
  Florence **2**:419
  Italian wars **3**:643, 644, 645, 646
Louis XIII, king of France **2**:371, 443, 458, 519, **4**:882, 897, 908, 1034–1035, **5**:1240
Louis XIV, king of France **1**:48, **2**:367, 444, 450, 519, 541, **5**:1256, 1390, *1419*
  absolutism **2**:367, **4**:907
  Aristotle **1**:59
  Bernini portrait bust **1**:97, 98
  established church **1**:257, **2**:372
  gardens **1**:26
  Molière **4**:899, 900, 901, 902, 911

Louis I, king of Hungary **4**:1104
Louis II, king of Hungary **2**:510
Louis II, cardinal of Lorraine **2**:456, 517
Louis, duke of Orléans **1**:159, **4**:1030
Louis of Nassau **2**:453
Louise of Savoy **2**:446
Loukaris, Kyrillis *see* Lucaris, Cyril
Louvain, University of **1**:108, **3**:589
Louvre (Paris) **1**:45, 98, **2**:444, **3**:708, 709, 712, **4**:1029, *1030*, 1031, 1034, 1035
love
  courtly **1**:221, **2**:402, **4**:*1101*, 1102
  platonic **1**:261, **4**:1092, 1095, 1097, 1102–1103
Loves, Matteo **5**:*1206*
Love's Labor's Lost (Shakespeare) **5**:1271
Loves of the Gods (Carracci) **1**:*195*
Love Triumphant (Caravaggio) **1**:*193*
Low Countries *see* Flanders; Netherlands
Loyola, Ignatius *see* Ignatius of Loyola
Lübeck **1**:22, **5**:1307
  Hanseatic League **2**:475, 502, 503, 504, 506
Lublin, Union of (1569) **4**:911, 1104, 1108, 1109
Lubomirska, Katarzyna **4**:*1108*
Lucan **3**:590, 649
Lucaris, Cyril, patriarch of Constantinople **1**:109, 263
Lucas, Margaret **5**:1257
Lucca **3**:634, 642
Lucca Dam **1**:280
Lucena, Vasco Fernández de **4**:1143–1144
Lucian **4**:925

Madonna of the Goldfinch (Raphael) **5:**1184
Madonna of the Meadows (Raphael) **5:**1184, 1185
Madonna of the Rocks (Leonardo da Vinci) **2:***425,* **3:**709, 714
Madonna of the Stairs (Michelangelo) **2:**425
madrassas **3:**614
Madrid
　Cervantes **1:**202
　Philip II **4:**1056, 1060
　Velázquez **5:**1384, 1385, 1386, 1388, 1390
Madrid, Treaty of (1526) **1:**242, **2:**446, **3:**647
Madrigale dei guerrieri e amorosi (Monteverdi) **4:**922
madrigals **4:**918–919, 922, 943, 955, 971, **5:**1244–1245
Maestà (Duccio) **2:**489, 492
Maestro, El (Milán) **4:**959
Magdalen College (Oxford) **2:***336*
Magdeburg **1:**77, **2:**475, 480–481, **5:**1337
Magellan, Ferdinand **2:**373, 374, 382, **3:**787–794, **4:**888, **5:**1250
Magellan, Straits of **3:**788, 790–791
magic **2:**532–534, **3:**795–803
　astrology **1:**72, **4:**1065
　philosophy **4:**1065
　popular culture **4:***1115,* 1120, 1121, 1123
Magical Universe **3:**796
Mágico prodigioso, El (Calderón) 728
Magna Carta (1215) **4:**906, **5:**1339
Magnaura Palace (Constantinople) **1:**258
magnetite **2:**375
Mahdi **3:**620–621, 622
Maiano, Giuliano di **1:***153*
Maids of Honor, The (Velázquez) see *Meninas, Las*

Maimonides **3:***678, 679*
Maimonides Synagogue (Cairo) **3:***678*
Maine (France) **3:**601, 602
Mainprinting **5:**1169
Maintenon, Madame de **5:***1419*
Mainz **2:**548, 550, **3:**687
Mainz, archbishopric of **3:**704
maize (corn) **1:**28, **5:**1346
majolica **5:**1383
Major, John **1:**182
Malacca **3:**787, **4:**1142, 1143
Malade imaginaire, Le (Molière) **4:**901
malarial fevers **3:**741
Malatesta, Sigismondo **4:**1090, 1091
Malatestas, the **5:**1379
Malatesti, Antonio **4:**882
Malaya **4:**1142
Mali **3:**612
Malleus maleficarum (Institoris and Sprenger) **3:**802
Malory, Thomas **1:**223, 224
Malta **1:**194, 223, **3:**612, 626
Malta, Order see Knights Hospitallers
Maltby, William **2:**551
Malthus, Thomas Robert **4:**1127, 1128, 1129
Malthusian cycle **4:**1127–1128, 1129, 1130
Mami, Arnaute **1:**202
Mamluks **3:**612, 623
Mander, Carel van **1:**144, 146, 148, **5:***1308*
Mandragola (Machiavelli) **3:**733, 772
Manelli, Francesco **4:**917
Manet, Édouard **4:**996
Manetti, Antonio di Tuccio **1:**155
Manfredi, Bartolomeo **4:**997
Man Holding a Medallion of Cosimo de' Medici (Botticelli) **1:**133, *135*
Man in a Red Turban (Jan van Eyck) **2:***386,* 388
mannerism **4:**878, 980, 981, 990, 991, 998, **5:**1284

architecture **1:**30, 32–33, 38, 40, 42
　Rubens **5:**1236, 1237
　Velázquez **5:**1384, 1385
Manners family **3:**665
Mannetti, Antonio **1:**34
man-of-war (ship) **3:**778, *786*
manorialism **1:**21–22, 23
manors **2:**562, 563
mansard roof **1:**45
Mansart, François **1:**45, 48
Mansfeld, Peter Ernst von **5:**1335
Mantegna, Andrea **1:**139, **2:**312, 314, **3:**642, 745
Mantua **2:**419, **3:**637, 642, 853, **4:**1087, **5:***1416*
　architecture **1:**36, *38, 39*
　Caravaggio **1:**194
　humanism **5:**1220
　Lombardy **3:**741, 744, 745
　Monteverdi **4:**917–918, 919
　opera **3:**734
　Thirty Years War **5:**1336
　Urbino **5:**1379
Mantua, congress of **4:**1087–1089
Mantuan Succession, War of the **3:**745, **5:**1336
Manuel II Palaeologus, Byzantine emperor **1:***260,* 261, *262*
Manuel I, king of Portugal **4:**1012, 1139, 1141, 1144, 1145
Manueline architecture **4:***1141,* 1144, *1145*
manufacturing **3:**804–812, **4:**1135–1136
　books **3:**806
　cloth **3:**740, 741, 750, *753,* 805
　factories **3:**786, 809
　German towns **2:**476, 477
　guilds **2:**497
　household **2:**562
　Italian city-states **3:**630, 632, 633
　London **3:**750, *753*
　markets **3:**813
　Milan **3:**740, 741, *743*

technology **5:**1259
trade **5:**1340, 1402
Venice **5:**1394
manuscripts
　bibles **1:**102
　forgery detection **3:**584, 594, 686
　humanists' analyses **3:**582, 583, *584,* 587, 588, 683, 684, 685, 687, 688, *689, 690*
　Petrarch's collection **3:**682, 684, **4:**1053
　printing **5:**1169–1170, 1193
Manutius, Aldus **1:**56, 59, **2:**357, **3:**584, 688, **5:**1399
Manuzio, Paolo **4:**1024
Maontalcino **3:**649
mapmaking see cartography
Maragha observatory (Persia) **1:**271
Maratti, Carlo **5:***1204*
Marburg, University of **5:***1372, 1377*
Marcello, Magdalucia **5:**1420
Marcellus II, Pope **5:**1353, 1355, 1359, 1360
Marche **5:**1378, 1380
Marciana (Venice) **1:**261
Mare magnum (1476 papal bull) **5:**1231
Marenzio, Luca **4:**918
Margaret, Saint **3:**657
Margaret I, queen of Denmark and Norway **4:**911
Margaret of Angoulême **3:**735–736, **5:**1176, 1177, 1178, *1179*
Margaret of Anjou **3:***601*
Margaret of Austria **1:**131, 210, **3:**648, **4:**912, 1057, **5:**1281, *1362, 1417,* 1426
Margaret of Flanders **1:**157, 207, *242*
Margaret of Navarre see Margaret of Angoulême, Margaret of Valois
Margaret of Parma see Margaret of Austria
Margaret of Savoy **2:**446

Margaret of Valois **1:**198, 200, **2:***455,* 517

Margaret Tudor, queen consort of Scotland 1298, **5:**1261, 1297, 1298

Margarita, princess of Spain **5:**1391

Margolin, Jean-Claude **5:**1179

Marguerite of Valois *see* Margaret of Valois

Maria of Hungary **5:**1281, 1426

Maria of Portugal **4:**1058, 1059, **5:**1280

Maria Anna of Austria **3:**836

Maria d'Aquino **1:**111

Maria Eleonora of Brandenburg **1:**227

Maria Maddalena of Austria **2:**471

Mariana, queen consort of Spain **5:**1390, 1391

María Teresa, queen consort of France **5:**1390

Marie Célèste (Galileo's daughter) **2:**468

Marienburg Castle **4:**1106

Marienkirche (Wolfenbüttel) **1:**49

Marieschi, Michele **5:***1392*

Marignano, Battle of (1515) **1:**221, **2:**445, **3:**646

Marillac, Louise de **5:**1208

Mariner's Mirror (Waghenaer) **2:***376*

maritime products **5:**1305

Mark, Saint **2:**316
 winged lion of **5:***1400*

markets and fairs **1:***23,* **3:813–821**
 book fairs **3:**781, 806, 819
 Italian city-states **3:**631, *633*
 manufacturing **3:**810, 813
 trade **5:**1340, 1342, 1348

Mark of Ephesus **1:**260, **2:**429

Marlowe, Christopher **2:**335–336, **3:**671, 726, 728, 732, **822–826,** **5:**1269, 1270, 1325

Marmara, Sea of **1:**165, 256, 263

Marot, Clément **2:**450, **5:**1176, 1177

Marprelate, Martin (pamphleteer) **5:**1175

Marranos **3:**674, 678, 681, **5:**1291, 1292

marriage
 age at **4:**1129–1130, **5:**1419
 Christina **1:**228, 229
 Elizabeth I **1:**229, **2:**329
 Erasmus on **2:**565
 French royalty **2:**437
 Hapsburg expansion through **2:**509, 510, 511, 550
 Henry VIII **2:**326, 522, 523, 524, 525, 527, **5:**1197
 households **2:**562–563, 564, 565, 566
 Luther on **2:**569
 popular culture **4:**1116, 1117
 remarriage **5:**1422
 as sacrament **5:**1357
 Trent, Council of **5:**1362
 women **5:**1416, 1418–1419, 1422
 see also divorce

Marriage at Cana (Bosch) **1:**129

Marseilles (map) **4:***1132*

marshes *see* dams and drainage

Marsilius of Padua **1:**53, 257, **2:**367

Marston, John **3:**733

Marston Moor, Battle of (1644) **2:**351, *353*

Martellus, Henricus **1:***249*

Martin V, Pope **2:**428, **4:**1011, 1052, **5:**1162, 1227, 1379

Martin, Gregory **1:**108

Martinelli, Caterina de Cattaneis **4:**918

Martini, Francesco di Giorgio **1:**280, **5:**1181

Martini, Simone **2:**488, 491, 492

Martin of Arles **3:**798

martyrdom **1:***232,* **5:**1201, 1206
 Islam **3:**620, 621
 Joan of Arc **3:**662
 Protestantism **1:***232*

Martyrdom of Saint Matthew (Caravaggio) **1:**192

Martyrdom of Saint Peter (Caravaggio) **1:**193

martyrium **1:**37

Martyrologium Romanum **4:**1024

Marvell, Andrew **4:**886

Mary, mother of Jesus *see* Virgin Mary

Mary I (Mary Tudor), queen of England **1:**62, 107, **5:**1225, 1325, 1374, 1424, *1427*
 Elizabeth I **1:**237, **2:**326–327, 328
 Henry VIII **1:**233, **2:**522, 524, 527, 528
 humanist education **5:**1417, 1418
 iconoclasm **3:**608, 609
 Philip II **1:**209, 236, **2:**327, 328, **4:**1056, *1057,* 1059
 printing **5:**1170, 1175
 Protestant martyrs **1:***232*
 Roman Catholicism **1:**187, 188, 189, 236, 237, 238, 239, 240, **2:**340, 342, **5:**1198, 1265, 1267, 1426

Mary II, queen of England *see* William and Mary

Mary, Queen of Scots **1:**62, 79, **2:**527–528, **3:**722, **5:**1289, 1426
 Calvinism **1:**189
 Elizabeth I **1:**238, **2:**327, 330–331, 332
 Francis II **1:**198, **2:**452
 James I **2:**332
 Reformation **5:**1266
 Scotland **5:**1262, 1264
 Stuarts **5:**1297–1298

Mary of Burgundy **1:**163–164, **2:**509, 511, 515, 550, **4:**966, **5:**1426

Mary of Guise **1:**198, **5:**1264, 1265, 1266, 1297, 1298, 1426

Maryland **3:**609, **4:**893, 894, 895

Mary Magdalene **5:**1160

Masaccio (Tommaso Guidi) **1:**35, **2:**492, **3:***589,* **4:**984, **5:**1185

Maser chapel (Venice) **3:**667

Mashhad (Shiite shrine) **3:**621

Masi, Antonia **5:**1420

Maske, A (Milton) see *Comus*

masonry dams **1:**278

Masque of Blackness (Jonson) **3:**663

Masque of Queens (Jonson) **3:**663

masques **3:**663, 665, 666, **5:**1328

Mass *see* Eucharist

Massachusetts **1:**189, **3:**609, **5:**1342
 established church **2:**372
 missionaries **4:**892
 Puritans **1:**189
 university **2:***325*

Massachusetts Institute of Technology **2:**383

Massacre of Paris, The (Marlowe) **3:**822, 825

Massimi, Piero **1:**40

Massys, Quentin **1:***84*

Master John (artist) **5:***1427*

masters **3:**810–811

Mästlin, Michael **3:**832

Matejko, Jan **4:***1107*

material goods **3:**754

materialism **2:**543, 544

maternal mortality **5:**1420

Mathematical Compilation (Ptolemy) *see Almagest*

Mathematical Philosophy (Russell) **4:**1068

Mathematical Principles (Newton) *see Principa mathematica*

mathematics **3:**783, **827–834,** **5:**1250, 1251–1252
 architecture **1:**36
 Descartes **2:**294, 295, 296, 301, **3:**828, 830, 833
 education **2:**319, *321*
 Galileo **2:**460, 461, 462, 464, 465, 467, **3:**699
 Gregorian calendar **1:**174, 175

Medicis, the *(cont.)*
  tomb sculptures **3:**707
  Viscontis **5:**1404, 1405
  see also specific family members
Medina **3:**623, 625
Medina Sidonia, duke of **1:**53, 65, 66
Meditationes Sacrae (Bacon) **1:**80
Meditation of a Penitent Sinner, A (A. Locke) **5:**1423
Meditation XVII (Donne) **5:**1166
Meditations on First Philosophy (Descartes) **2:**295, 297–301, **4:**1069
Mediterranean Sea **1:**166, **3:**717, **4:**1139
  Constantinople **1:**263
  Hellenistic culture **1:**170
  Italian trade **3:**630
  Ottoman expansion **3:**624, 626, 715
  Roman Empire **1:**167
  shipping **2:**302, 305
  trade routes **2:**373, 475
  Venice **5:**1392–1394
Medora (Rueda) **5:**1323
Mehmed I, Ottoman sultan **3:**617, 680
Mehmed II (the Conqueror), Ottoman sultan **4:**1089, **5:**1408
  Byzantium **1:**170, 171, 172, 269
  Constantinople **1:**263
  Islam **3:**617, 618–619, 625
  overview of **1:**169
Meingre Boucicaut, Jean II le **1:**224
Meistersingers **4:**960
Melancholia I (Dürer) **2:**315
Melanchthon, Philipp **2:**483, 566, **3:**585, 593, 767–768
  educational reform **2:**320, 324
  universities **5:**1371, 1372, 1373, 1377
Meli da Crema, Antonio **1:**126
Melozzo da Forlì **4:***1023*

Memel (Klaipeda) **5:**1334
Memling, Hans **4:**982, *985*
Memoires (Commynes) **1:**163, 164
Menabuoi, Giusto **4:***1062*
Menaechmi (Plautus) **3:**732
Mendes, Francisco **3:**681
Mendoza, Iñigo López de **5:**1279
Mendoza, Pedro de **4:**892
Mendoza, Pedro González de **5:**1279–1280
Meninas, Las (Velázquez) **5:**1385, 1390, 1391
Meno (Plato) **4:**1092, 1093
mercantilism **1:**25, **5:**1348–1350
Mercator, Gerardus **2:**384, 385, **5:***1248,* 1250
mercenaries **2:**409, **3:**651, **5:**1181, 1395, 1403, 1411, 1413
Mercer Hall (London) **3:**751
Merchant Adventurers of England **2:**499
Merchant of Venice, The (Shakespeare) **3:**671, **5:**1271, 1274
merchants *see* trade
Merchant Taylors' School **5:**1286
Mercoeur, duke of **2:**458
mercury **2:**310
Merian, Matthäus (the Elder) **1:***75,* **5:***1293, 1310*
Merisi, Michelangelo *see* Caravaggio
Merry Wives of Windsor (Shakespeare) **3:***733,* **5:**1271
Mersenne, Marin **2:**294, *295,* 544
Mervenne, Aleyt van der **1:**128
Mesopotamia **2:**302
Mesquita (Cordoba) **5:***1277*
Messiah (Handel) **5:**1247
messianism
  Islam **3:**622
  Judaism **3:**677
Messina **1:**194, **3:**715
metallurgy **3:**654, **5:**1284

metalworking **2:**311
  Sweden **5:**1306, 1309, 1341
Metamorphoses (Ovid) **5:**1321
Metaphysics (Aristotle) **1:**51, 261
Meteren, Emanuel van **5:**1286
"Methought I saw my late espoused saint" (Milton) **4:**885
Metropolitan See **4:**933
Meulen, Steven van der **5:***1306*
Meuse River **5:**1334
Mexico
  dams **1:**280
  disease **2:**307
  exploration **2:**374, 382
  gold **5:**1345
  missionaries **4:**889, 890, 891
  Spain **2:**306, **5:**1285
Mexico City **1:**49
Michael, archangel **1:**224
Michael III, Byzantine emperor **1:**258, 259
Michael V, Byzantine emperor **1:**258
Michael VII, Byzantine emperor **1:**258
Michael VIII Palaeologus, Byzantine emperor **1:**258, 260
Michael I, emperor of Russia **4:**940, **5:**1309
Michael Constantine Psellus **1:**168, 258
Michelangelo **1:**97, **2:***315,* 466, 469, 492, **3:**668, 703, **4:870–878,** 946, 948, **5:***1226,* 1232, *1354,* 1387
  architecture **1:**36, 42, 44, 47, **2:**424–425, **4:**871, 876, 877, **5:***1226*
  Bramante **1:**143
  Clement VII **1:**241, 242, 244
  mannerism **1:**32–33
  Medicis **2:**424, 425–426, **3:**852, 856, **4:**870, 871, 872, 876–877
  painting and sculpture **4:**986, 988, 990, 992, 999
  Palazzo Farnese **1:**40

Palladio **4:**1000, 1003, 1004
papal patron **4:**1025
  as Raphael influence **5:**1183, 1184–1185, 1187
  Renaissance **5:**1220, 1221, 1225
  Saint Peter's Basilica **1:**32, 38, 98, **4:**871, 873, 878, 1026, **5:**1353
  Sistine Chapel **1:**135, 244, **4:**870, 871, 873, 874–875, 877, 878, 1025, **5:**1220, 1231
Michelazzo **3:***702*
Michel de Marillac **2:**459
Michieli, Giovanni **1:**200
microbes *see* pathogens
microscope **2:**309–310, **3:**775, 783, **5:**1254
Middle Ages **1:**178, 181, 184, 190, **5:**1218
  anti-Semitism **3:**671, 672
  chivalry **1:**221, 222
  feudalism **2:**401–413
  humanism **3:**582–583, 585, 587, 588, 591
  Hundred Years War **3:**596–599
  Islam **3:**612–613
  Latin language **3:**682–683, 694
  papacy **4:**1009–1010
  Paris **4:**1028–1030
  participation notion **3:**607
  preaching 1158–1163
  Roman Catholic Church **1:**178, 180
  Scholasticism **2:**357
  universities **5:**1365, 1366, 1367, 1368, 1370
  warfare **5:**1409–1411
  women's learning during **5:**1418
  worldview **1:**249
Middle English **1:**213, 214
middle passage **5:**1349
Middleton, Thomas **3:**733, **5:**1323, 1325, 1326, 1329
Middleton cross **3:**815
midsummer festival **4:**1118

Midsummer Night's Dream, A (Shakespeare) **5:**1271, 1274
midwives **3:**842, 843, **4:**1117
"Mighty Fortress Is Our God, A" (Luther) **4:**952
migration **4:**1129, 1130, 1132, 1134
    Huguenots **5:**1331
    Jews **3:**671, 680
    Puritans **2:**328
    settlement colonies **1:**242, **5:**1342, 1346–1347
    see also exploration
Mikulas of Kadan **3:**779
Mila, Adriana de **1:**123
Milan **2:**555, **3:**630, 775, 853, **4:**947, 965, 1090, **5:**1413
    architecture **1:***32*, 36, 139
    banking **1:**87, **2:**416
    Black Death **2:**306
    Bramante **1:**139, 140, 141
    canals **3:**741
    Clement VII **1:**242
    description of **3:**631
    feudalism **2:**403, 413
    Florence **2:**414, 417
    Francis I **2:**445, 446, 449
    government **3:**637, 638, 641, 650
    Hapsburgs **2:**509, 511
    humanism **3:**586
    Italian wars **1:**208, 221, 241, 242, **3:**642, 643, 645–647, 648, 650
    Leonardo da Vinci **2:**425, **3:**707, 708–710
    Lombardy **3:**740, 741, 743, 744, 745
    manufacturing **3:**740, 741, *743*
    nobility **3:**638
    Spain **5:**1224
    Switzerland **5:**1314
    territorial battles **2:**419
    Thirty Years War **5:**1336
    Venice **5:**1394
    view of **5:***1401*
    Viscontis **3:**740, 741, 742, **5:**1401–1406
Milan, Cathedral of **1:***32*, **3:**710, *746*

Milan, dukes of **3:**740, 741, 742–743
Milán, Luis **4:**959
Milan, Peace of (1639) **5:**1334
Mildmay, Walter **5:***1374*
military *see* warfare
Military Campaigns of Süleyman I (Loqman) **5:***1409*
military orders **1:**223
military tank **5:**1249
Militia Ordinance (1641) **2:**350
millennialism **1:**137
mills **1:**24, 273, 279, 280, **3:**806, 807–808
    waterwheels **1:***278*, **3:**776–777, 809, 812
    wind power **1:**24, 275, 277, 278, **3:**777–778, 804, 807–808
Milton, Christopher **4:**879, 887
Milton, Elizabeth Minshull **4:**886, 887
Milton, John **3:**609, 726, 823, **4:**879–887
Milton, Mary Powell **4:**879, 883, 884, 885, 887
Mincio River **3:**741
mind-body dualism **2:**300–301, **3:**606, **5:**1294
Ming dynasty **2:**373, **5:**1342
Minin, Kuzma **4:**939
mining
    dams **1:**279, 280
    Sweden **5:**1304, 1305, 1306
    see also gold
Minshull, Elizabeth **4:**886, 887
minstrels **4:**949
Minute of First Draught of the Optiques, A (Hobbes) **2:**544
Miracle of the Cross on the San Lorenzo Bridge, The (Bellini) **5:***1399*
Miracle of the Relic of the True Cross on the Rialto Bridge, The (painting) **3:***639*
miracle plays **3:**732, **5:**1318, 1319, 1323, 1328

Mirandola fortress **3:**650
Mir-i-Arab madrassa (Bukhara) **3:**614
Mirk, John **5:**1159
Misanthrope, Le (Molière) **4:**899, 901
Miscellanea (Poliziano) **3:**585
Miser, The (Molière) **4:**901
Mishneh Torah **3:***679*
missals **1:**173, 175, **5:**1363
missionaries **4:888–896**
    Americas **5:**1285
    exploration **2:**379, 380, 382, **5:**1346
    Islam **3:**614
    Jesuits **4:**1015, *1018*, **5:**1199, 1205, 1206
    Jewish converts **3:**676–677
    Leo X **3:**701
    Portugal **4:**1142, *1143*
    religious orders **5:**1204, 1206–1207, 1208
Mississippi River **2:**382
Misso pro defunctis (Morales) **4:**957
Mocedades del Cid, Las (Castro y Bellvís) **3:**728
Mocenigo, doge of Venice **4:***1058*
Modena **2:**413, 419, **3:**648, 853, **4:**1073
Modena, University of **5:**1370–1371
Mogul Empire **3:**612, 615, 629, **4:**1142
Mohács, Battle of (1526) **1:**243, **3:**618, 623
molasses **5:**1348
Molcho, Solomon **3:**677
Molesworth, Robert **5:**1311
Molière **3:**730, 731, **4:897–902**, **5:**1322, 1323
Molina, Luis de **1:**205
Molina, Tirso de **1:**205
Molucca Islands **3:**788, 792, 793, 794, **4:**1142
Monaldeschi, Gian Rinaldo **1:**230
Mona Lisa (Leonardo da Vinci) **1:**133, **3:**709, 712, 714, **4:**986, 999, **5:**1249

monarchy **4:903–915**
    absolutism **2:**367, 368, 437, 544, 546, **4:**906–907
    architecture **1:**46
    astrological prediction **1:**71–72
    banking **1:**85, 86, 88, 89, 90
    Bohemia **1:**117, 121, 222
    chivalry **1:**221, 223, 224, 225
    companies **2:**499, 500
    court musicians **4:**949
    court society **4:**978–979
    cuius regio, eius religio principle **5:**1331
    divine right **4:**906, **5:**1299, 1300, 1302–1303, 1339
    England **2:**334–346, 348, 523, **4:**906
    English civil wars **2:**347–355
    English Restoration **1:**240, **2:**351, **4:**886, **5:**1302, 1322, 1329
    established churches **2:**365, 366, 368, 369, 370, 371, 372, **5:**1374
    feudalism **2:**406, 407, 408, 409, 412–413
    France **2:**432, 433, 436, 437, 438, 444, 445–450, 516–520
    French civil wars **2:**440–443, 451–459
    Hapsburgs **2:**512
    heresy **2:**539
    Hobbes **2:**542, 544, 546
    Holy Roman Empire **2:**555
    as household **2:**569
    Hundred Years War **3:**595–603, 658–659, 660
    Lutheranism **3:**767, 768
    Machiavellianism **2:**337, 419, **3:**771
    male heir **1:**233
    markets **3:**815
    More relationship **4:**926–927, 929–932
    Muscovy **4:**934–941
    nationalism **4:**903, 914, 915, 966, 970

monarchy *(cont.)*
nobility **2:**407, 408, **5:**1339
Ottoman sultans **3:**625–626, 628
papal relations **4:**1008, 1009, 1012, 1014, 1015, 1017
Paris **4:**1031–1035
Parliament **5:**1302–1303
Poland **4:**1104, 1108, 1111, 1112
Portugal **4:**1137–1138
Renaissance **5:**1218, 1220, 1221, 1223, 1224, 1225
Russia **3:**652–656
Scotland **5:**1261–1264, 1296–1301
Spanish Inquisition **4:**1019
Stuarts **1:**239–240, **5:**1296–1303, 1329
succession rules **3:**595, 625
Sweden **1:**227–231, **5:**1306
tournaments **1:**225
universities **5:**1374
warfare **5:**1414
women rulers **5:**1425–1427
see also specific monarchs
monasteries **2:**365, 368
Bavaria **3:**839
Byzantium **1:**171
contemplative life **3:**585, 586
Eastern Orthodoxy **1:**171, **5:**1201
England **2:**526
English closure **1:**235, 236, **2:**340, 365, **3:**608, **5:**1202, 1203
fulling mills **3:**806
as household model **2:**569
Italian city-states **3:**639
Ivan IV Vasilyevich **3:**655
libraries **5:**1375
Lombardy **3:***740*
London **3:**748
Luther **3:**756–757, 758, 762, **4:**767
manuscripts **3:**582, 583, 682, 686
waterwheels **3:**812
see also religious orders
Moncontour, Battle of (1569) **5:***1414*

Monde, Le (Descartes) **2:**296, 297
Mondovì **4:**1091
money
coins **1:**84–85, *90, 245, 264,* **2:***416*
trade **5:**1342, 1351
see also banking
money changers *see* banking
moneylending *see* usury
Monferrato **3:**744
Mongolia **2:**303
Mongols **5:**1342
Islam **3:**612, 613, 617
language **3:**692
see also Tatars
monkey baiting **1:**93
monks *see* religious orders, monasteries
"Monk's Tale, The" (Chaucer) **5:**1202
Monmouth, Henry *see* Henry V
monody **4:**916, 918, 961
monophonic music **4:**942
monopoly, printing **5:**1170
monotheism **1:**167, **3:**620, 669
Monsieur, Peace of (1576) **2:**456, 457
Monstrelet, Enguerrand de **1:***159*
Montagu, Richard **2:**346
Montaigne, Michel de **1:***80,* 95, 96
Montauban **2:**453, 454
Montcontour, Battle of (1569) **2:**452
Monte, Francesco Maria del **1:**191, 192
Monte, Giovanni Battista da **3:**847
Montecavallo, Antonio da **1:**40
Montefeltro, Antonio da **5:**1378
Montefeltro, Federigo da **1:**139, **5:**1379, 1382
Montefeltro, Giovanna da **5:**1379
Montefeltro, Guidantonio da **5:**1378–1379

Montefeltro, Guidobaldo da **5:**1379, 1380, 1383
Montefeltro, Oddantonio da **5:**1379, 1382
Montefeltros, the **5:**1378–1379
Monte Mario (Rome) **1:**39
Montereau **1:**159
Monteverdi, Claudio **3:**745, **4:916–923,** 943, 961, **5:**1244
Monteverdi, Julio Cesare **4:**918
Montezuma, Aztec ruler **2:**307, **4:**890
Month of January (Rustici) **5:***1421*
Montmorency **2:**456
Montmors, The **1:**179
Montpellier **2:**452, **5:**1176, 1177, 1422
Montpellier, University of **5:**1367, 1371
Montrose, earl of **2:**351
Monument (London fire) **5:**1433
moon **1:**268, **5:**1252–1253
calendar **1:**173–174
movement **1:**271
surface **2:**463, 464
Moorgate (London) **3:**749
Moorish architecture **1:**46–47, **5:***1277*
Moors *see* Islam
Morales, Cristóbal de **4:**956, 957
morality plays **5:**1318–1319
moral philosophy *see* philosophy
Morandi, Orazio **1:***74*
Morat, Battle of (1477) **5:**1314
Moravia **1:**116, 119, 122, **5:**1335
Moray, earl of **1:**189
More, Anne **5:**1166
More, Henry **4:**1070–1071
More, Margaret **5:**1418
More, Thomas **3:**698, **4:924–932,** 1074, **5:**1319, 1418
bibles **1:**106

Erasmus **2:**357, 362, 363
execution of **1:**235
Henry VIII **1:**235, **2:**525
humanism **2:**335, 339–340, **3:**585, 590, 593, **5:**1370, 1371, 1373
Platonism **4:**1063, 1103
printing **5:**1173
Reformation **2:**339–340
Moriscos (Muslim converts) **2:**396–397, **3:**613, **4:**1056–1057, **5:**1278
Moritz, landgrave of Hessen-Kassel **5:**1244, 1245
Moro, Antonio **2:***327,* **5:***1422*
Morocco 611, **4:**1137, 1140
Morone, Giovanni **5:**1355
Moroni, Andrea **5:***1370*
morphology **5:**1258
Morris, William **4:**1048
mortality rates **4:**1124–1125, 1127, 1128, 1129
city **4:**1131–1132
infant **3:**843, **4:**1121, 1131, **5:**1420–1421
maternal **5:**1420
Mort de César, La (Grevin) **3:**729
Morte d'Arthur, Le (Malory) **1:**223, 224
Mortimer, Edmund **1:**17
Morton, John **4:**924
mosaics **1:**257
Mosca, Giovanni il **4:**112
Moscow **3:***654,* **4:**933, 934, 935, 936, 1109, **5:**1337
Ivan IV Vasilyevich **3:**653, 655
Orthodox Church **1:**166
Poland **5:**1308, 1309
Moselle River **5:**1338
Moses (Michelangelo) **4:**874
mosques **1:**170, 171, 172
motets **4:**917, 920, 945–946, 947, 956–967
motherhood **5:**1418, 1419, 1420–1421
childbirth **3:**842, **4:**1117, *1120*
"Mother Hubbard's Tale" (Spenser) **5:**1288–1289

motion, theories of **2**:461–462
Motteux, Peter **1**:205
Mount Athos monastery **1**:*170*, 171
Mountjoy, Lord **2**:333
Mouton, Jean **4**:949
movable type *see* printing
Mozambique **3**:787
Muezzinade Ali Pasha **3**:715, 717, 718
Muhammad **3**:610, 611, 614, 620, 626, **4**:1084
Mühlberg, Battle of (1547) **1**:75, 211, **2**:554
Mulcaster, Richard **5**:1286
Mulder, Joseph **1**:*60*
Müller, Johann *see* Regiomontanus
Mumford, Lewis **3**:775, 779–780
mumps **2**:307
Munday, Anthony **5**:1324, 1329
Munk, Jens **2**:383
Münster **5**:1195, 1338
Munster, Sébastien **1**:179
Münster, siege of (1534, 1535) **2**:540
Münzer, Thomas **1**:178, **5**:1193
Murad I, Ottoman sultan **3**:616
Murad II, Ottoman sultan **3**:618, 627
Murano glass **5**:1394
Murillo, Bartolomé Esteban **5**:1242, 1386
Murray, Margaret **3**:803
Mus, Decius **5**:1237
Muscovy **3**:652–653, **4**:**933–941**
Musée Charles X (Louvre) **5**:*1231*
music **4**:**942–961**
  baroque **1**:230, **4**:916, 919, 920, 923, 961, **5**:1245
  Burgundy **1**:163
  France **1**:215
  Galileo **2**:460
  households **2**:567
  Hussite hymns **1**:118

intermezzi **3**:734, **5**:1321
Italian theater **3**:734
Monteverdi **4**:916–923, 943, 961
Schütz **5**:1244–1247
Scotland **5**:1264
shipboard **2**:*379*
theater **5**:1328
Venice **5**:1399
see also opera
musical instruments **4**:958–959
Musica transalpina (Yonge) **4**:943
music publishing **4**:957
music theory **4**:958
musket **5**:1335, 1413
musketeers **5**:1309, 1415
Muslims *see* Islam
Mussato, Albertino **3**:584
Musta'rabim Jews **3**:670
"My Mistress Commanding Me to Return Her Letters" (Carew) **2**:402
My Secret Book (Petrarch) **4**:1052
mystery plays **3**:729, **5**:*1317*, 1318, 1319, 1322
Mystical Nativity, The (Botticelli) **1**:137–138
mysticism **3**:760, **5**:1283
  Islam **3**:614, 620, 621
  Judaism **3**:677, 679–680, 689, **4**:1075, 1103
  religious orders **5**:1207
  women **5**:1427
mythology
  ancient Greece **1**:135, 136–137
  Columbus's worldview **1**:249
  Romanist painting **1**:145

N

Najéra, Battle of (1367) **3**:598
Nancy, Battle of (1477) **1**:163, **5**:1314, 1413
Nanni, Giovanni *see* Annius of Viterbo
Nantes, Edict of (1598) **1**:198, **2**:443, 454, *457*, 458, 459, 517, 520, 541, **4**:1034

Nantes, Synod of **2**:493
Nantes, University of **5**:1371
Napier, John **3**:831
Naples **3**:743, 853, **4**:905, *1130*, **5**:1256
  agriculture **1**:22
  Boccaccio **1**:111, 112, 115
  Borgia, Lucrezia **1**:123
  Caravaggio **1**:191, 194, 195
  charivari **4**:1116
  Charles V **1**:208, 210, 243
  Christina **1**:230
  Gentileschi **2**:470, 472, 474
  Giotto **2**:487, 491
  Hapsburgs **2**:445, 446, 511, 513
  humanism **3**:586, 594
  Italian wars **1**:244, **2**:310, 412, 438, **3**:642, 643, 644–645, 647, 648, 650, 702
  Judaism **3**:679
  markets **3**:818
  nationalism **4**:965, 966
  as papal fief **2**:412
  Pius II **4**:1089–1090
  population **4**:1131, 1132
  Spain **5**:1224, 1234, 1278
  syphilis **2**:310
  territorial battles **2**:419
  Venice **5**:1393, 1394
Naples, University of **4**:1061, **5**:1367
Napoléon I, emperor of the French **2**:512, **3**:773
Narrative of Barents's Last Voyage **2**:*384*
Narva **3**:653, **5**:1307
Naseby, Battle of (1645) **2**:352
Nash, Thomas **3**:738, 823
Nasi, Gracia **3**:681
Nasi, Lorenzo **5**:1185
Nasiruddin Mahmud Chiragh-i Dihii **3**:615
national banks **1**:90–91
national churches *see* established churches
National Covenant of 1638 (Scotland) *see* Covenanters
National Edition of Galileo's Works **2**:466

National Gallery (London) **3**:709, **5**:1389
nationalism **4**:903, 914, 915, **962–970**
  Bohemia **5**:1334, 1367
  Czech **1**:118, 122
  English arts **3**:664
  established churches **2**:364–372
  France **2**:435, 444
  German towns **5**:1200
  humanism **3**:590
  Hundred Years War **3**:603
  monarchy **4**:903, 914, 915, 966, 970
  Reformation **2**:364–365
  Scotland **5**:1260
  technology **3**:*786*
  vernaculars **3**:695, 696, 698, 699
Native Americans *see* indigenous peoples
Natural History (Pliny the Elder) **1**:58, **3**:*687*
naturalism **4**:980, 982–983, 985
naturalists **5**:1259
natural philosophy **4**:1065, 1067–1068, 1069, 1070, 1072
nature **5**:1295
naval warfare **5**:1412
  armada, Spanish **1**:62–66
  Italian wars **3**:650
  Lepanto, Battle of **3**:715–719
  ship design **3**:778, 786, **5**:1412
  trade **5**:1347
Navarino **1**:202
Navarre **1**:199, **2**:437, 456, 516, **5**:1278, 1279
Navicella (Giotto) **2**:491
navies *see* naval warfare
navigation **3**:693, 754, 775, **4**:914, *1065*, **5**:1250, 1283
  Columbus **1**:249, 251
  compass **2**:376, 384, **3**:778–779, **5**:1343
  exploration **2**:376–377, 378, 380, 381

navigation *(cont.)*
Magellan **3:**787, 790
Portugal **4:**1138, **5:**1345
trade **5:**1340, 1341, 1343,
1344–1345, 1349
Navigliaccio Canal **5:**1402
Nazareth **1:**259
Nebrija, Elio Antonio de
2:399, **3:**694, 699, **5:**1280
Neckham, Alexander
3:778–779
necromancy **3:**798–799,
801–802
Neile, Richard **2:**346
Nemi, Lake **1:**37
neoclassicism **1:**49
Neoplatonism **1:**137, **3:**696,
4:1061, 1076, 1096–1099,
5:1376
education **2:**320
Florence **2:**422, 423, 424,
425
magic **3:**798, 799, 855, 856
nepotism **4:**1016, 1023, 1037,
1091, **5:**1230
Nérac, Treaty of **1:**200
Neri, Philip **4:**956, **5:**1204
Netherlands **1:**200, **3:**716
architecture **1:**49
Baltic traders **2:**506
banking **1:**90
Bosch **1:**127–132
Bruegel **1:**144, 148
Burgundy **1:**160, 164
Calvinism **1:**178, 188, 190,
2:371, **3:**767
Charles V **1:**207, 210, 211
colonialism **5:**1284, 1342,
1346
companies **2:**383, 500,
5:1342, *1351*
Descartes **2:**294, 295, 296,
299
dikes and drainage
1:273–276, 279
divorce law **2:**568
Dürer **2:**316
Elizabeth I **2:**331, 332
Erasmus **2:**356, 357
exploration **2:**384, 385
Gregorian calendar **1:**176

Holy Roman Empire **2:**555,
556, **3:**838
Huguenots **5:**1331
humanism **3:**585, 589, 590,
592
Hundred Years War **1:**16,
3:596
iconoclasm **3:**605
iconoclast riots **5:***1165*
interest-bearing loans **1:**85
Judaism **3:**681, **4:**1139
market **5:***1340*
monarchy **4:**912, 914
music **4:**944, 949, 951
naval power **5:**1412
painting **2:**391, 392,
4:995–998, **5:**1264–1265
Philip II **1:**211, **4:**1056,
1057, 1058, 1060
preaching **5:**1164
Reformation **5:**1195, 1196
Rembrandt **5:**1210–1217
science **5:**1252, 1256, 1258
Spain/Spanish wars **1:**176,
200, 279, **2:**331, 371,
454, **3:**746, 767, **4:**914,
966, 1057, 1058, 1060,
5:1281, 1282, 1283,
1332, 1333, 1334, 1336,
1338, 1344
Spanish armada **1:**62, 66,
2:331
Spanish Hapsburgs **2:**438,
445, 453, 510, 511
spice trade **4:**1141, 1145
Spinoza **5:**1291–1295
Sweden **5:**1306, 1311
Thirty Years War **5:**1333,
1334, 1335, 1337, 1338
trade **5:**1393
tulips **1:**26
universities **2:***323,* **5:**1367
wind power **3:**777
women regents **5:**1426
Nettesheim, Cornelius Agrippa
von **5:**1417
Neuberg **5:**1334
Neuchâtel **5:**1314
Neva River **4:**933
Nevel, Battle of (1562) **3:**654
Nevers **1:**157

Neville, Richard, earl of
Warwick **2:**408
Neville's Cross, Battle of **3:**597
Nevsky, Alexander *see*
Alexander Nevsky
New Abbey **5:**1288
New Amsterdam **5:**1342
Newark **2:**352
New Atlantis (Bacon) **1:**80,
4:1103, **5:**1251
Newcomen, Thomas **3:**785
Newcomen engine **3:**785
New Divinity **1:**190
New England
architecture **1:**49
Calvinism **1:**178
witch hunts **5:**1425
New Exchange (London)
3:665
New Holland (Australia) **2:**385
New Horse Hoeing Husbandry,
The (Tull) **1:**27
new husbandry **1:**26–27
New Learning *see* humanism
and learning
New Life, The (Dante) **1:**217
New Manner of Fortification by
Sluices (Stevin) **1:**275
Newmarket (Suffolk) **3:**665,
666
New Model Army **2:**351–352,
353, 354
New Science *see* science;
technology
New Spain **4:**889–890
newspapers **5:**1175
New Testament **1:**181, 193,
240, **2:**358, **5:**1369
Dürer images **2:**314, 316
Erasmus translation **3:**585,
591, 684, 689, 697, 703
Four Evangelists **2:**316
Gospels **3:**671 *see also specific*
gospels
Greek language **3:**688,
5:1355, 1357, 1419
humanism **5:**1218
Incarnation **3:**604, 605
Luther translation **1:**103,
104–105, *180,* **2:**316,
3:765, **5:**1221, 1222

preaching of **5:**1158, *1159,*
1162, 1165
Trent, Council of **5:**1356,
1357
vernacular translations
3:695, 698
Zwingli sermons **1:**178
New Theory of the Planets
(Copernicus and Peurbach)
3:829
Newton, Isaac **1:**262, **2:**467,
3:783, 801, **4:**1072
calculus **3:**827, 828, 833,
834
Cambridge University
5:*1375*
science **5:**1251, 1256–1257,
1258, 1259
Wren **5:**1430
New World *see* Americas;
Caribbean region
New Year's Day **1:**174, 177
New Zealand **2:**385
Nicaea **1:**168, 261
Nicaea, Creed of *see* Nicene
Creed
Nicaea, First Council of
5:1364
Nicaea, Second Council of
3:605, **5:**1364
Nicaragua **4:**892
Niccoli, Niccolò **3:**583, 584,
585, 587
Nicene Creed **1:**259, **2:**430,
3:607, **4:**953
Nicholas, Saint **2:**378
Nicholas I, Pope **1:**259
Nicholas IV, Pope **1:**44
Nicholas V, Pope **1:**34, 39,
142, **4:**1022–1023
Bessarion **1:**261
humanism **3:**584, 586
Rome **5:**1228–1229, 1230
Nicholas of Cusa **3:**618,
4:1098–1099, 1101
Nicolls, Allen **3:**825
Nicomachean Ethics (Aristotle)
1:53, 54, 55, 59, 61,
4:1054, 1102
Nicopolis, Battle of (1396)
1:158, **3:**616–617

Nieszawa, Privilege of (1454) **4:**1108

Nieuwe maniere van sterctebou, door spilsluysen (Stevin) **1:**275

Night Watch, The (Rembrandt) **5:**1212, 1213

Nigra sum (Monteverdi) **4:**921

Nihil Novi constitution (Poland) **4:**1108

Nijmegen, Treaty of (1678) **2:**512

Nike Revolt **1:**172

Nikon, patriarch of Constantinople **4:**936

Nîmes **2:**452

Niña (Columbus ship) **1:**240, 248, 251, **4:**1138

Nineteen Propositions (1642) **2:**351

Ninety-five Theses (1517) **1:**178, **2:**482, 553, **3:**704, 758, *759,* **4:**929, **5:**1189, 1190–1191, 1197, 1221, 1352, 1360

Nine Years War **5:**1290

Nobili, Roberto de **5:**1206

nobility and rank **4:971–979**
  Agincourt **1:**18
  architects **1:**33
  astrological prediction **1:**71–72
  Bohemia **1:**117, 118, 119, 120, 121, 122
  Calvinism **2:**442, 453
  chivalry **1:**221, 222
  courtiers **5:**1383, 1427
  education **2:**317, 318–319, 322
  English barons **2:**407–408, 409, 410
  English country homes **2:**334
  feudalism **1:**22, **2:**401–413
  France **2:**433, 435, 437, 439, 442, 443, 451
  German towns **2:**476, 482
  households **2:**561, 563, 564, 565, 566, 569
  Hundred Years War **2:**435
  hunting **1:**94–95

Italian city-states **3:**632, 634–636, 638–639, 642, 648, 651
  kinship **2:**568–569
  Lutheranism **2:**370, 482, 555
  monarch relations **4:**906, 907, 908, **5:**1339
  Muscovy **4:**934, 937, 938, 939, 940, 941
  Netherlands revolt **4:**1057
  palaces **1:**39–40, 45, *47*
  papal relations **4:**969
  peasants' revolts **4:**1042
  Poland-Lithuania **4:**1104, 1106, 1108, 1109, 1110, 1111, 1113
  popular culture **4:**1123
  Renaissance **5:**1223, 1224
  Russia **3:**652, 653, 654, 655, 656
  Scotland **5:**1260, 1261, 1262, 1265, 1267, 1296, 1298, 1299
  Sweden **1:**228, **5:**1304, 1307, 1308
  universities **5:**1368, 1372
  Venice **5:**1392, 1393, 1395, 1396–1397, 1400
  warfare **5:**1411, 1414
  women **5:**1427

nominalism **4:**1062–1063, 1065
  Calvinism **1:**181, 182, 184
  iconoclasm **3:**606, 607
  Lutheranism **3:**759–760, 761

Nonconformist Act of 1665 (England) **1:**240

Nonsuch, Treaty of (1585) **2:**327

Noort, Adam van **5:**1236

Noot, Jan van der **5:**1286

Norden, John **3:**751

Nordic Union **2:**506

Nördlingen, Battle of (1634) **5:**1310, 1337

Norfolk, duke of **2:**330, 331, 527

Norman Conquest (1066) **2:**403, 494, 496, **3:**595, 691

Normandy **2:**440, 456
  Hundred Years War **1:**16, 17, **3:**599–601, 602–603
  university **5:**1371

Norris, Thomas **5:**1290

North Africa
  exploration **2:**379, 380
  Islam **3:**612, 613, 624, 626
  Judaism **2:**399, **3:**670, *678,* 679
  Ottoman Empire **3:**624, 626, 715
  piracy **1:**208, 209, 211, **3:**626, *627,* 716, **5:**1347
  slave trade **5:**1348
  Spanish Jews and Muslims **5:**1277, 1279
  see also specific countries

North America *see* Americas; Mexico; Canada; United States

North Carolina **2:**382

Northeast Passage **2:**374, 384

northern Ireland **1:**189

northern Renaissance **2:**551–552
  Erasmus **2:**552
  humanism **5:**1370
  painting **1:**128–129, 145, **2:**312, 316
  Paris **4:**1031–1035
  perspective **2:**312
  universities **5:**1376–1377

Northern Seven Years War **4:***1113*

North Petherton (Somerset) **1:**218

North Sea **1:**273–274, **5:**1305
  dikes **1:**273–274
  trade **5:**1341, 1344

Northumberland, earl of *see* Percy, Henry

Northwest Passage **2:**374, 383, **4:**888

Norton, Thomas **3:**823

Norway
  Black Death **2:**305
  Denmark **5:**1304, 1305
  exploration **2:**384
  fishing trade **5:**1341
  guilds **2:**493

Hanseatic League **2:**503, 505, 506
  Lutheranism **3:**768
  monarchy **4:**903, 911
  Sweden **5:**1310

Nostredame, Michel de (Nostradamus) **1:**70, 71, 73

notaries **3:**635

notation **4:**942

notebooks (Leonardo da Vinci) **3:**709–710, *711*

Notes on the New Testament (Valla) **3:**586, 591

Notre Dame, Cathedral of (Paris) **1:***179,* **4:***1028*

Nottingham **2:**351

Nouveau-né, Le (La Tour) **4:***1120*

Nouvelles, Les (Périers) **3:**736

Novara **3:**638
  battle (1513) **3:**645

Novelas ejemplares (Cervantes) **1:**205, 206

Novelle (Bandello) **3:**736

Noves, Laura de **4:**1051

Novgorod **4:**933, 940

Novum organum (Bacon) **1:**61, 80, 81, 83, **4:**1067, 1068

Nowell, Robert **5:**1286

Nozze d'Enea con Lavinia, Le (Monteverdi) **4:**922

nuclear family **2:**561

Numancia, La (Cervantes) **1:**204

Núñez de Balboa, Vasco **2:**374, 382

nuns *see* religious orders

Nuremberg **2:**475, *476,* 482, 506, 554
  Dürer **2:**311, 312, 314, 316
  Lutheranism **2:**316

Nuremberg, Diet of (1524) **2:**553

Nuremberg Chronicle **1:***267*

O

Oath of Supremacy (England) **2:**524

Obedience of the Christian Man (Tyndale) **2:**524

Oberammergau Passion play
5:1318

Objections and Replies
(Descartes) **2:**295

Objections to Aristotle (Ramus)
4:1064

Obrecht, Jacob **4:**949

Observants (Franciscans)
5:1162

observatories **5:**1251

Ochino, Bernardino **5:**1209

Ockham, William of **2:**366,
367, **3:**759, 763, **4:**1063
nominalism **1:**181, **4:**1062,
1063

Oder River **2:**505

"Ode to the West Wind"
(Shelley) **1:**113

Odyssey (Homer) **1:**59, **2:**373
Hobbes translation **2:**546

Oesel (Saaremaa) island
5:1310, 1338

Of Famous Men (Petrarch)
4:1052

Of Liberty and Necessity
(Hobbes) **2:**546

"Of Reformation Touching
Church Discipline in
England" (Milton) **3:**609

Of the City of God (Augustine)
5:1282

Oghuz Turks **3:**629

Ognissanti Madonna (Giotto)
2:487, 489, 490

oil painting **2:**391, 392

Ojibwas (people) **4:**893

Okeghem, Jean d' **4:**946

Öland, Battle of (1564)
4:*1113*

Old Believers **4:**936

Old Sacristy, Church of San
Lorenzo (Florence) **1:**152

Old Slavonic **4:**935

Old Testament **1:**167, 233,
235, **3:**672, 689, **5:**1369
Apocrypha **1:**103–104
Greek translation
1:103–104, 181, **3:**695
Hebrew language **3:**688, 689
humanist scholarship **3:**591,
592

iconoclasm **3:**607

imagery **2:**392

Kabbalah **1:**57

Ptolemaic cosmos **1:**267

Torah **3:**669, *679*

Trent, Council of **5:**1355,
1357

vernacular translation
3:698

Old Woman Frying Eggs
(Velázquez) **5:***1385*

Olier, Jean-Jacques **5:***1361*

oligarchy *see* republics

Olivétan, Pierre-Robert **1:**108,
181

O magnum mysterium
(Victoria) **4:**957

Oman, Charles **4:**1044–1045

Ommegang procession **5:**1317

On Architecture (Vitruvius)
5:1321

On Being and the One (Pico)
4:1074, 1076

On Citizenship (Hobbes) **2:**544

"On Cruelty" (Montaigne)
1:96

O'Neill, Hugh **5:**1290

"On Holy Water and Sacred
Salt" (Karlstadt) **3:**606

On Interpretation (Aristotle)
1:258

On Man (Hobbes) **2:**546

On Mercy (Calvin) **1:**181

On Military Affairs (Valturio)
5:*1408*

On Mills (Stevin) **1:**275

On Monarchy (Dante) **1:**217

*On Noble Manners and Liberal
Studies* (Vergerio) **2:**318

On Perspective in Painting
(Piero della Francesca)
3:827–828

"On Shakespeare" (Milton)
4:879, 880

"On the Abolition of Images"
(Karlstadt) **3:**606

On the Body (Hobbes) **2:**546

On the Bondage of the Will
(Luther) **3:**767

On the Eloquence of Vernacular
(Dante) **1:**217

On the Immortality of the Soul
(Pomponazzi) **4:**1064

"On the Late Massacre in
Piedmont" (Milton) **4:**885

*On the Measurement of
Running Water* (Castelli)
1:277

On the Motion of the Heart
(Harvey) **5:**1255

On the Natures of Things
(Neckham) **3:**778

*On the Nobility and Excellence
of Women* (Nettesheim)
5:1417

*On the Remedies of Good and
Bad Fortune* (Petrarch)
4:1054

*On the Revolution of Heavenly
Spheres* (Copernicus) **1:**50,
266, 269, 270, 272, **2:**463,
465, **4:**1109, **5:**1221, *1250*

On the Roman Penny (Budé)
3:590

On the Solitary Life (Petrarch)
4:1054

*On the Structure of the Human
Body* (Vesalius) **5:**1250

On the Threefold Life (Ficinus)
2:422

Ontígola, Sea of **1:**280

On War against the Turk
(Luther) **3:**618

On War Machines (Taccola)
5:*1407*

opera **2:**567, **3:**734, **4:**943,
961, **5:**1321, 1322
Christina's patronage **1:**228,
230
Monteverdi **4:**916, 919–921,
922, 923
Schütz **5:**1246
William Tell legend **5:**1312

*Operation of Geometric and
Military Compasses, The*
(Galileo) **4:***1069*

Oprichnina **3:**654–656

optical illusion **2:**389–390,
392

optics **2:**544, **3:**827, 831, 832

Optics (Euclid) **3:**827

Optics (Kepler) **3:**832

Optime pastor (Isaac) **4:**946

oral tradition **3:**669

Oran **1:**204

Oration on the Dignity of Man
(Pico della Mirandola)
2:537, **4:**1064, 1075,
1076, **5:**1220

*Oration on the Need to Restore
the Republic* (Alcionio)
5:1233

Oratorians **4:**956,
5:1204–1205, 1208

oratorio **5:**1247

oratory *see* rhetoric

Oratory Church (Fermo)
5:1238

Order of Preachers *see*
Dominicans

orders, architectural *see*
classical orders

orders, religious *see* religious
orders

ordination **5:**1357

Ore Mountains **1:**279

Orfeo (Monteverdi) **4:**918,
919–920, 921, 943

organs **4:**960

Origen **1:**109, **4:**1098

original sin **2:**339, **3:**763,
4:1064, *1066*

Orkhan, emir of Anatolia
3:616

Orkney Isles **5:**1296

Orlando furioso (Ariosto)
1:125, 223, **3:**721, **5:**1289

Orlando innamorato (Boiardo)
1:223

Orléans **1:**179, **2:**451, 452
dike **1:***273*

Orléans, siege of (1429)
3:601, 602, 657, 658, 660

Orléans, University of **5:**1371

Orléans family **2:**434, 437

Orley, Bernard van **1:**145,
207, 242, **5:***1417*

Orloj **3:**779

Ormond, earl of *see* Butler,
James

Orsha, Battle of (1514)
4:1109

Orsini, Alfronsina **1:**194

Orsini, Clarice **3:**700, 857
Orsinis, the **5:**1227
Orsis, the **5:**1428
Orte, Juan de la **1:***208*
Orthodox Church **2:**366,
    4:1008, 1023
  Byzantium **1:**166, 170, 172
  calendars **1:**177, **4:**1024
  Constantinople **1:**170, 171,
    257, 260, 262–263, **2:**427
  Decree of Reunion
    2:429–431
  Florence, Council of **1:**260,
    261, **2:**427–431
  Great Schism **1:**166, 259,
    2:427, **3:**854, **4:**1073
  icons **3:***604*, 605
  Lithuania **4:**1109, 1110
  Lyons, Council of **1:**260
  monasticism **1:**171, **5:**1201
  Muscovy **4:**934–936, 939
  Ottoman Empire **3:**626
  Reformation **1:**262
  Russia **1:**166, **4:**935–936,
    1109
  vernaculars **3:***696*, 697
Orvieto, Cathedral of **1:***246*
Orygynale Cronykil (Andrew
  of Wyntoun) **5:**1260
Osiander, Andreas **1:**269
Osman I, emir of Anatolia
  3:616
Osnabrück **1:**77, **5:**1338
Ospedale degli Innocenti
  (Florence) **1:**35, 37,
  151–152
Ospedale di Santo Spirito
  (Rome) **5:**1230
Ostrogski, Janusz **4:**1108
Othello (Shakespeare) **5:**1270,
  1272, 1274, 1327
Otranto **3:**619
Otrepev, Gregory **4:**938
ottava rima verse **1:**217
Otto IV, Holy Roman
  emperor **2:**505
Ottoman Empire **2:**427, **4:**935
  Byzantium **1:**165, 167,
    3:586, 685
  cannon **5:***1409*, 1410
  Cervantes **1:**202

Charles V **1:**75, 208, 209,
  210, 211, 242–243
  Christianity **1:**169, 170–171
  Constantinople **1:**55, 158,
    162, 165, 166, 169–172,
    260, 263–264, **2:**429,
    430, **4:**1063
  crusade of Nicopolis **1:**158
  Francis I **2:**448
  Holy Roman Empire
    2:512–513, 514, 515,
    548, 553, 555, 556, 557,
    558, 559
  Islam **3:**612, 613, 616–619,
    622–628, 629
  Judaism **3:**670, 679, 680,
    681
  Lepanto, Battle of **3:**715–719
  Mehmed II **1:**169
  Philip II **4:***1058*, 1059–1060
  Pius II crusade **4:**1087–1088,
    1089
  Poland **4:**1113, 1114
  Thirty Years War
    5:1330–1331, 1337
  Venice **5:**1393, 1398
Oudin, César **1:**203
Oughtred, William **3:**830, 831
Our Lady of Guadalupe **4:**890
Our Lady of Guadalupe,
  Church of (Spain) **4:**1082
Ovid **1:**112, 136, **2:**336,
  3:823, **4:**1053, **5:**1321
Oxburghe Hangings **5:***1264*
Oxenstierna, Axel **1:**227, 228,
  5:1307, 1309, 1310, 1337
Oxenstierna family **5:**1304
Oxford **2:**352
Oxford, earl of *see* Vere,
  Edward de
Oxfordians **5:**1276
Oxford Reformers **4:**1103
Oxford University **2:**375, 536,
  3:668, **5:**1368, 1374
  Arabic studies **1:**262, **3:**618
  Church of England **1:**232
  Constantinople **1:**262
  Drake hoax **2:**383
  founding of **5:**1367, 1373
  Hobbes **2:**542, 543
  humanism **2:**336

Magdalen College **2:***336*
  More **4:**924, 1063
  plays **3:**732, **5:**1328
  science studies **5:**1255, 1256
  Sheldonian Theatre **5:**1430
  University Wits **3:**732, 824
  Wren **5:**1429, 1430, 1431,
    1432, 1433

P

Pacheco, Francisco **5:**1384,
  1385
Pacheco, Juana **5:**1384, 1385
Pachomius **5:**1201
Pacific Ocean **2:**373, 382, 383,
  385, **3:**788, 790–791, 794,
  5:1258–1259
  see also circumnavigation
Pacino, Al **3:**671
Pacioli, Luca **3:**828
Paderborn **1:**77
Padovano, Annibale **4:**960
Padua
  Giotto frescoes **2:**485, 486,
    487, 488, 489
  humanism **3:**583
  Italian wars **3:**647
  Medicis **2:**420
  painting **2:**312
  Palladio **4:**1001
  Petrarch **4:**1051
  Venice **1:**277, **5:**1394, 1395
  waterways **1:**277
Padua, University of **2:**318,
  462, **3:**829, **5:**1367, *1370*,
  1371, 1400
  Aristotelianism **1:**56–58, 59
  botanical garden **3:**840, 847
  Copernicus **1:**265
  Galileo **5:**1252
  medical studies **3:**840, 845,
    846–847
  philosophy **4:**1064
  Pico della Mirandola **4:**1073,
    1074
  science studies **5:**1255
  Vesalius dissection **2:**302
paganism **2:**431, **4:**1104,
  1105, 1107
  Greek philosophy **1:**261
  Hellenism **1:**167

pageantry *see* theater
Painter's Book, The (van
  Mander) **1:**144, 148
painting **2:**428, **4:980–999**
  architecture **1:**38, 39, 41, 42
  baroque **4:**980, 981,
    990–995, 996, **5:**1213,
    1224–1225
  Bosch **1:**127–132
  Botticelli **1:**133–138
  Bruegel **1:**144–148
  Burgundian patrons **1:**163
  Caravaggio **1:**191–196
  chivalry **1:**224–225
  Clement VII **1:**241–242,
    244
  Constantinople **1:**263
  Dürer **2:**311–316
  Eastern vs. Western Roman
    Empire **1:**257
  Eyck **2:**386–392
  Florence **2:**418, 424–425
  Gentileschi, **2:**469–474
  Giotto **2:**484–492
  Gonzaga patrons **3:**745
  Holy Roman Empire **2:**550,
    559
  iconoclasm **1:**184,
    3:604–609
  illusory perspective **1:**145,
    2:312, 316
  Italianate-style **1:**145
  Italian city-states **3:**641,
    642
  Leonardo da Vinci
    3:706–714, **5:**1249
  Medici patronage **3:**852,
    855, 856
  Michelangelo **1:**42,
    4:870–878
  papal patronage **4:**1025,
    5:1230
  perspective **3:**827–828
  Portugal **4:**1144
  Raphael **1:**38, 39, 41,
    5:1180–1187
  Rembrandt **5:**1210–1217
  Renaissance **5:***1219*,
    1221–1222, 1224, 1231,
    1235
  Rubens **5:**1236–1243

painting *(cont.)*
  Scotland **5:**1264–1265
  Spain **5:**1284
  Velázquez **5:**1384–1391
  Venice **5:**1399
Paiva, Alfonso de **2:**381
Pajou, Augustin **4:***1070*
palaces **1:**36, 37, 39–40, 45
  Florence **2:**563
  France **2:**444, 450
  Italian city-states **3:**642
  London **3:**749–750, 751
  papacy **5:**1230
  Paris **4:**1031
  Rome **4:**1025
  Venice **5:**1399, *1400*
  see also individual palazzo
   listings
Palacio del Viso (Spain)
  5:*1401*
Palaeologus dynasty **1:**166,
  169, 172, **3:**744
Palais du Luxembourg (Paris)
  5:1240, 1241
Palamon and Arcite (Chaucer)
  1:213, 217
Palatinate **1:**76–77, 122,
  2:548, 558, **3:**837
  Thirty Years War **5:**1301,
   1302, 1334, 1335, 1336
Palatine War **5:**1334
Palazzo Barberini (Rome)
  1:40, 44, *231*
Palazzo Borghese (Rome) **1:**40
Palazzo Caprini (Rome) **1:**142
Palazzo Chieracati (Vicenza)
  1:43, **4:**1002, 1004, 1007
Palazzo Chigi-Odescalchi
  (Rome) **1:**40
Palazzo Corsini (Rome) **1:**230
Palazzo da Porto Festa
  (Vicenza) **4:**1004
Palazzo del Tè (Mantua) **1:***38,*
  39, **4:**991
Palazzo Ducale (Mantua)
  3:*642*
Palazzo Ducale (Venice) **3:***640*
Palazzo Falconieri (Rome)
  1:40
Palazzo Farnese (Capraola)
  5:*1362*

Palazzo Farnese (Rome) **1:**39,
  40, 195, *210,* **4:**871, 1002,
  1025
Palazzo Farnesina (Rome)
  4:1003
Palazzo Iseppo Porto (Vicenza)
  3:*668*
Palazzo Massimi (Rome) **1:**39,
  40
Palazzo Medici (Rome) **1:**197
Palazzo Piccolomini (Pienza)
  4:*1089*
Palazzo Pubblico (Siena)
  5:*1421*
Palazzo Spada (Rome) **1:**39,
  40, 41
Palazzo Thiene (Vicenza) *see*
  Villa Thiene
Palazzo Vecchio (Florence)
  3:*851*
Palestine *see* Holy Land,
  Jerusalem
Palestrina, Giovanni Pierluigi
  da **4:**954, 955–956, 957
palisade dams **1:**279
Palladianism **1:**45, 47, 49,
  3:664, 668
Palladio, Andrea **1:**32, 33, 34,
  42–43, 140, *141,* **3:**664,
  665, 666, 667, 668,
  4:1000–1007
  Venice **3:**664, 668, **4:**1000,
   1006–1007, **5:**1399
Palladio, Leonida **4:**1000
Palladio, Marc'Antonio **4:**1000
Pallas and the Centaur
  (Botticelli) **1:**135
Pallavicino, Benedetto **4:**918
Palmas, Cape **5:**1345
Palmieri, Matteo **5:***1218,* 1219
Palos **1:**248, 251
Pamlico Sound **2:**382
Pampaloni, Luigi **1:***149*
pamphlets **5:**1174–1175
Panama **1:**254, **2:**374, 382,
  4:892
Pandosto (Greene) **3:**732
Panfili, Pio **5:***1356*
Pannini, Giovanni Paolo **1:***39*
Pantagruel (Rabelais) **3:**436,
  5:1176, 1177, 1178

pantheism **4:**1065, 1071–1072
Pantheon (Rome) **1:**142,
  3:667
  dome **1:**34, 47
  interior **1:***34*
  main body **1:***35*
Paolo de Perugia **1:**111, 114
papacy **1:**178, **4:1008–1027,**
  1052
  architecture **1:**39, 40,
   141–142
  astrology **1:**72, 73–74
  authority of **1:**257, **5:**1363
  Avignon **4:**1009–1011, 1052
  bibles **1:**102–103, 105
  Bramante **1:**142
  calendar **1:**174, 175–177
  Catherine de Médicis **1:**197
  Charles V **1:**209, 210,
   230–231, 241, 242, 243,
   2:513–514
  Christina **1:**229, 230–231,
   234
  Church of England **1:**232
  Contarini **5:**1400
  councils **2:**430, **5:**1352
  Decree of Reunion
   2:429–431
  Donation of Constantine
   3:584, 586, 594, 686
  Elizabeth I **2:**341
  Erasmus **5:**1189
  established churches **2:**364,
   365–367, 368, 370
  feudalism **2:**406, *407,* 412,
   413
  Florence **2:**415, 418, 419,
   420, 421, 422, 423, 425,
   426
  Florence, Council of
   2:427–431
  France **2:***432,* 438, 453
  French civil wars **1:**183
  Galileo **2:**465, 466–467,
   5:1226
  Giotto **2:**491
  Guelfs **1:**156, **3:**743, 854,
   5:1378, 1405
  Hapsburgs **2:**479, 481, 507,
   513, 514
  as head of church **1:**259

Henry IV **2:**366, 517, 518,
  519
Henry VIII **1:**232–234, 235,
  240, 242, **2:**338, 339,
  521, 522, 523, 524, 525,
  5:1191, 1196
heresy **2:**530, 531, 532, 533
Holy Roman emperors
  1:156, *208,* 241, **2:**510,
  513–514
humanism **3:**584, 586
indulgences **2:**421, 423,
  3:704, 757, **4:**1080,
  5:1189, 1190–1191,
  1231
Italian wars **3:**643–649, 701,
  702
Judaism **3:**672, 673, 677
Lombardy **3:**744, 745
Luther vs. **1:**246, **2:**481,
  482, **3:**756, 757, 762,
  764, 765, 766, 767, 768,
  5:1352
Medici bankers **1:**87
Medicis **2:**416, 418, 420,
  421, 426, **3:**850, 851,
  852, 853, 854, 855
missionaries **4:**888–889,
  1015
monarch relations
  2:365–366, 368, 372,
  4:903, 907, 913,
  930–932, 969, 970
music **4:**946, 947, 948, 949
nepotism **4:**1016, 1023,
  1037, 1091
Ottoman Empire **3:**626,
  715, *717*
painting **1:**133, 135, 257,
  2:428, **4:**992
Paul V **4:**1020, 1021, 1026,
  1036–1040
Petrarch **4:**1052
Philip II **4:**1058
Pico della Mirandola **4:**1074,
  1075, *1076,* 1077
Raphael **5:**1186–1187
Reformation vs. **1:**183, 232
Renaissance popes (list)
  4:1025
Rome **5:**1227–1235

schism 2:366, 421, 429, 430, 431, 4:913, 1010–1011, 1052, 5:1227, 1406 *see also* Avignon papacy
Spain 5:1234
spiritual vs. temporal power 1:257
Swiss Guards 5:1314
theater 5:1325
Thirty Years War 5:1332, 1333, 1334, 1336
Trent, Council of 5:1352, 1353, 1357, 1359–1360, 1363, 1364
universities 5:1367, 1368, 1369
Urbino 5:1378–1383
Venice 5:1394, 1398–1399, 1400
Viscontis 5:1404–1405
worldliness 2:426
see also specific popes
Papal States 1:124, 246, 3:756, 4:1009, 1011–1012, 1016, 5:1231, 1357
Charles V 1:210, 242
Italian wars 3:644, 648
Leo X 3:701
Medicis 3:853
Paul V 4:1036, 1037
Pius II 4:1090
territorial battles 2:419
Urbino 5:1378–1383
Venice 5:1393, 1394, 1398–1399
paper 3:780, 805–806, 5:1168
Papin, Denis 3:785
Paracelsus 3:*843*
parachute 3:775, 5:1249
parades 5:1317
Paradise Lost (Milton) 4:879, 880, 881, 885, 886, 887
Paradise Regained (Milton) 4:886–887
Paraphrases (Aristotle) 1:56
Paré, Ambroise 3:840
Pareja, Juan de 5:1389, *1390*
Paris 4:**1028–1035**
agriculture 1:22
architecture 1:45, 2:444
banking 1:87

Black Death 2:305
Calvin 1:179
Christina 1:*229*
Descartes 2:296
England 1:160
famines 4:1124
as French government seat 2:451
French monarchy 2:438, *446* 447
Hobbes 2:544
humanism 4:1023
Hundred Years War 1:160, 3:600, 658, 660, *661*
indoor theater 5:1318
literature 3:725
map 1:*179,* 4:*1029*
Molière 4:897–902
nominalism 1:182
plague 2:433
population 4:1028, 1030, 1131, 1132, 1133
printing 3:819
Saint Bartholomew's Day Massacre 2:371, 441, 454, 4:1033
wars of religion 2:456, 457, 458, 517, 519
Paris, University of 5:1199, 1371, 1430
Aristotelianism 1:53, 56
Erasmus 2:357, 358
founding of 5:1367, 1369
humanism 3:585, 589, 590, 592
medical studies 3:845
Petrarch 4:1052
Pico della Mirandola 4:1073, 1075
Rabelais 5:1177, 1178
religious orders 5:1205
Roman Catholicism 4:1032
science studies 5:1255
Paris Académie des Sciences 3:695
Parker, Matthew 1:237, 3:822
Parlement of Foules (Chaucer) 1:113, 213, 217
Parliament (Britain)
Bacon 1:79, 80, 82
Cromwell 1:239, 2:351

English civil wars 2:347–355, 544
established church 2:368, 524
feudalism 2:407
guilds 2:494–495
Gunpowder Plot 4:880, 1039, 5:1301
House of Commons 2:350, 354, 407
House of Lords 2:354, 355
Hundred Years War 3:603
London 3:751
monarchy 2:344, 346, 4:906, 911, 912, 5:1302–1303
More 4:926–927, 929, 931
Restoration settlement 5:1302
Rump Parliament 2:*344,* 351, 355
Scotland 5:1263, 1298
Stuarts 1:239, 5:1300, 1302–1303, 1329
theater closure 5:1322, 1329
parliaments 2:407, 4:910, 913
Florence 3:*851*
Hanseatic League 2:505, 506
Holy Roman Empire 2:548
Russia 3:652
Scotland 5:1298, 1299
Sweden 5:1306, 1308
Parma 2:470, 3:638, 644, 648, 743, 744
Parma, University of 5:1367
Parmenides 4:1097
Parmigianino 1:*209,* 242
Parnassus (Raphael) 5:1186
parody, literary 1:223–224
parody, polyphonic 4:943
Parr, Catherine 2:522, 527, 3:735
Paruta, Paolo 3:719
Pascal, Blaise 3:775
pasha 3:628
Passau, Treaty of (1552) 1:75, 76
Passion of Christ, The (Dürer) 2:314
passion plays 5:1317, 1318
Passions of the Soul, The (Descartes) 2:*296,* 301

Passover 3:*669*
Pastor, Ludwig von 1:243
pastoral, the 3:*725, 726, 737, 738,* 825
Pastoral Songs (Petrarch) 4:1051
Patay, Battle of (1429) 3:*659*
Pater Noster guild 5:1318
pathogens 2:302, 306, 310
Patience (Pearl Poet) 1:220
Patras, Gulf of 3:*718*
patronage 1:138, 5:1177–1178, 1230, 1231
Bernini 5:1333
Burgundian dukes 1:163
Christina 1:227, 229
Clement VII 1:241, 242, 244
France 2:437, 450
Italian city-states 3:640–641, 642, 651
Leo X 3:703
Maximilian I 2:550
Medicis 3:852
papacy 4:1008, 1021–1022, 1023, 1025–1026
Rome 5:1230, 1231
Rudolf II 2:559
Urbino 5:1378–1383
Paul, Saint 3:605, 689, 4:1102, 5:1230
bibles 1:105, 110
Calvin commentary 1:179
conversion of 1:193
Dürer image 2:316
humanist learning 2:337
letters of 2:337, 5:1356
missionizing 4:894
preaching 5:*1158,* 1160, 1163
Paul III, Pope 2:361, 3:648, 836, 4:*1009,* 1016, *1025*
astrology 1:72
Charles V 1:210
Counter-Reformation 4:1016, 1017, 1019
Inquisition 5:1197, 1234
Jesuits 4:1015, *1017,* 5:1191, *1197,* 1199, 1205, 1353
Michelangelo 4:871, 877

Paul III, Pope *(cont.)*
  Rome **5:**1232, 1234
  Saint Peter's Basilica **4:**1026
  Trent, Council of **5:**1352, 1353, 1357
  Urbino **5:**1381
  Venice **5:**1400
Paul IV, Pope **4:**992, 1058, **5:**1353, 1360, 1363
  Inquisition **5:**1197
  Italian wars **3:**644
  religious orders **5:**1204
  Rome **5:**1233, 1234
Paul V, Pope **1:**97, **2:**465, **4:**921, 1020, 1021, 1026, **1036–1040**
  Venice **5:**1400
Paul VI, Pope **5:**1363, 1364
Paul, Epistles of **2:**337, **5:**1356
Paulet, Amias **1:**79
Paulicians **3:**605
Pauline Chapel (Rome) **1:**97, 98, **4:**871, 877
Paul of Thebes **5:**1201
Paul's Cross (London) **3:**751
Pavia **3:**643, 646, 743, **5:***1402*
Pavia, Battle of (1525) **2:**446, 555, **3:**643, 646, 647
  Charles V **1:**208, *242*
Pavia, Cathedral of **1:**139
Pavia, University of **5:**1406
pawnbrokers **1:**88–89
Pazzi, Andrea di Guglielmo **1:**153
Pazzi Chapel (Florence) **1:**153, *154*
Pazzi conspiracy (1478) **1:**241
Pazzis, the **3:**852
Peace of *see keywords*
Peake, Robert **4:***1071*
Pearl (Pearl Poet) **1:**220
Pearl Poet **1:**220
pearls **2:**373
Peasant Dance (Bruegel) **1:**147
peasants
  agriculture **1:**21, 28
  as Bruegel subject **1:**144, 146, 147
  feudalism **2:***402, 405*
  France **2:**433, 439
  German towns **2:**480

hardships **4:**1115
households **2:**561, 562, 563
Inquisition **1:**187
Joan of Arc **3:**657, 658
Lutheranism **3:**765
Muscovy **4:**937, 938, 940
popular culture **4:**1115–1123
population **4:**1134–1135
Reformation **4:**1121–1123
Russia **3:**656
Scotland **5:**1260
Sweden **1:**228
see also serfdom
Peasants' Revolt of 1381 (England) **1:**216, **3:**598, **4:**1041, 1042–1048
peasants' revolts **1:**216, **3:**762, 767, **4:1041–1048**
  France **2:**433, 456, **4:**1029, 1042, *1044*
  German towns **1:**187, **2:***475,* 479, 480
  Holy Roman Empire **2:**555, 558, **4:**1042
  Paris **4:**1029
  preaching **5:***1162*
  Sweden **5:**1305
Peasants' War **1:**187, **2:***475,* 479, 480, **4:**1042
Pedemuro, Giovanni da **4:**1000
Pedro (the Cruel), king of Castile **3:**598
Peele, George **3:**732, 824
Pellicioli, Mauro **3:**713
Pembroke, countess of *see* Sidney, Mary
Pembroke College (Cambridge) **1:**48, **5:**1286–1287, 1430
penance **1:**104, 186, **3:**689, 757, 763, **5:**1190
  Calvinist rejection of **1:**183
  confession **5:**1357
  indulgences **1:**180
  pilgrimage **4:**1078, 1080
  purgatory **1:**180
pendulum **2:**460, **5:**1433
Penitent Magdalen (Gentileschi) **2:**470–471, 473

Pennsylvania **1:**189
"Penseroso, Il" (Milton) **4:**880
Pentecost **3:***695*
Percy, Henry (Hotspur) **1:**17
Percy, Henry, earl of Northumberland **3:**825
Pereira, Nuno Álvares **4:**1137
Perestrello e Moniz, Felipa **1:**247, 248
Perez, Martin **4:**890
Peri, Jacopo **4:**920, 943, **5:**1246, 1321
Pericles, Prince of Tyre (Shakespeare) **5:**1272
Périers, Bonaventure des **3:**736
Peringer, Dietrich **2:***479*
Perkin Warbeck (Ford) **5:**1327
Perkunas (Lithuanian god) **4:**1105
Perrissin, Jean **1:***185*
Persia
  astronomy **1:**271
  dams **1:**278, *280*
  education **2:***317*
  Islam **3:**612, 617, 620–621, 622–623, 626, 628, *629*
  shipping **2:**302
Persian language **3:**692
Personal Rule (England) **2:**347–348
Persons, Robert **4:**906
perspective **4:**980, 984, 987
  Botticelli **1:**133, 134, 137
  Bramante **1:**139, 142
  Bruegel **1:***146*
  illusory **1:**145, **2:**312, 316
  mathematics **3:**827–828
Peru
  disease **2:**307, **5:**1285
  exploration **2:**374
  missionaries **4:**892
  religious orders **5:**1209
  Spanish control **2:**306
Perugia **4:**1012, **5:**1181, 1182, 1183, 1404
Perugia, University of **5:**1367
Perugino, Pietro **3:**706, **5:**1181, 1182, 1185, 1230
Peruzzi, Baldassare **1:**32, 38, 40, 41, 281, **4:**1003

Peruzzi Chapel **2:**485, 487, *490*
Pesaro **5:**1380, 1382
Pet, Arthur **2:**384
Peter, Saint **1:**37, 99, 100, 105, 141, 193, **3:**798, **4:**1026
  Dürer image **2:**316
  papacy **1:**257
  preaching on **5:**1160
  Rome **5:**1230, 1231, 1234
Peter I (the Great), emperor of Russia **1:**49, **4:**941, **5:**1311
Peters, Edward **2:**398
Peterzano, Simone **1:**191
Petition of Right of 1628 (England) **2:**347
Petrarch **3:**720, 721, 722, 724, 725, 726, **4:**963, **1049–1055,** 1072, 1143
  Boccaccio **1:**111, 112, 114, 115
  Borgia, Lucrezia **1:**125
  Chaucer **1:**216
  Greek studies **2:**320
  humanism **2:**357, **3:**583–584, 585, 589, 682–683, 684, 686, **4:**1049, 1053–1055, 1075, **5:**1218
  papacy **4:**1009, 1052
  Rome **5:**1227, 1228
  Spenser translations **2:**335, **5:**1286
  vernacular **3:**694
  Viscontis **5:**1405–1406
Petrarch, Giovanni (son) **4:**1051
Petrucci, Alfonso **3:**701
Petrucci, Ottaviano **5:**1399
Peurbach, Georg **3:**828, 829
Pfefferkorn, Johann **3:**674
Phaedo (Plato) **4:**1094
Phaedrus (Plato) **4:**1097
Phèdre (Racine) **3:**730
Philaret, patriarch of Constantinople **4:**940
Philip, archduke of Austria *see* Philip I, king of Spain

Philip (the Bold), duke of
    Burgundy **1:**157–158, 159,
    4:944, 981
Philip (the Good), duke of
    Burgundy **1:**160–162, 163,
    223, 226, **2:**388, 515,
    3:602, 661, **4:**944
Philip (the Handsome), duke
    of Burgundy **1:**207, **2:**399,
    400, **5:**1280, 1281
Philip I, king of Castile *see*
    Philip (the Handsome),
    duke of Burgundy
Philip III, king of France
    2:433
Philip IV (the Fair), king of
    France **2:**366, **3:**595,
    4:911, 913, **5:**1227
Philip V, king of France **3:**595
Philip, landgrave of Hesse
    3:768
Philip II, king of Macedonia
    1:167
Philip I, king of Portugal *see*
    Philip II, king of Spain
Philip I, king of Spain **1:**131,
    2:510, 515
Philip II, king of Spain **1:**46,
    203, **2:**420, 442, 453, 511,
    515, 556, **4:**892, 956,
    1056–1060
  Bosch collection **1:**131
  Charles V **1:**208, 209, 211,
    2:413
  Elizabeth I **2:**328, 331, 332
  Elizabeth of Valois **1:**198,
    199, 203
  England **1:**238
  established church **2:**370
  Fugger loan default **1:**88
  Italian wars **3:**647, 648, 649,
    650
  Mary Tudor **1:**209, 236,
    2:327, 328, **4:**1056,
    1057, 1059
  military tactics **5:**1414
  Netherlands revolt **2:**331
  Ottoman expansion **3:**715,
    718
  papacy **4:**1036, 1037, **5:**1234
  Portugal **4:**1140, 1145

Spanish armada **1:**62, 66,
    238, **2:**331
Spanish empire **5:**1283–1284
  theater **5:**1322, 1323
  waterworks **1:**280
Philip III, king of Spain
    5:1238, 1284
Philip IV, king of Spain **2:**471,
    3:837, **4:**994, **5:**1284
  Rubens **5:**1237, 1242
  Thirty Years War **5:**1333
  Velázquez **5:**1385, 1387,
    1388, 1390, 1391
Philip of Évereux (Philip
    Valois) **2:**433
Philip of Hesse **2:**569
Philip Julius, duke of Stettin-
    Pomerania **3:**751
Philippa of Hainaut, queen
    consort of England **1:**214,
    224, **3:**598
Philippa of Lancaster, queen
    consort of Portugal **2:**380,
    4:1137
Philippines **3:**788, 792–793,
    4:892, 1060
Philogia (Petrarch) **4:**1050
philology **3:**586, 587, 594,
    686, 690
philosopher's stone **3:**800–801,
    4:1065
*Philosophical and Physical
    Opinions* (Lucas) **5:**1257
Philosophical Transactions
    (scientific journal) **5:**1256
philosophy **3:**730, **4:**1025,
    1061–1072
  Aristotle **1:**50–61
  Bacon **1:**81–82
  Byzantium **1:**168–169, 170
  Christina **1:**228, 229, 230
  Descartes **2:**294–301
  education **2:**325
  Erasmus **2:**357–363
  Florence **2:**422–423
  Greek translations **3:**685
  Hobbes **2:**542, 543, 544,
    545–546
  humanism **3:**582, 584, 585,
    588, 591, 682, 683,
    5:1219, 1282

Judaism **3:**679
Lutheranism **3:**759–761,
    765, 767, 768
Machiavelli **3:**769, 771–773
magic **3:**799, 800
More **4:**927–928
Neoplatonism **4:**1096–1097
nominalism **1:**181, 182, 184
Petrarch **4:**1053–1054
Pico della Mirandola
    4:1073–1075
Platonism **4:**1092–1103,
    5:1376
Scholasticism **2:**357, **4:**1049
Spinoza **5:**1291, 1294–1295
universities **5:**1368, 1370
see also Greek philosophy
Phocas, Byzantine emperor
    1:258
Phoenix, The (Middleton)
    5:1329
Photius, patriarch of
    Constantinople **1:**259
physical education **2:**318, 319
physicians *see* medicine
Physicians, College of
    (London) **5:**1432
physics **3:**830–831, **5:**1250,
    1256, 1257
  Descartes **2:**295, *297*
  Hooke **5:**1433
  Wren **5:**1429
physiology **5:**1251
Pia, Emilia **5:**1383
Piacenz **3:**743
Piacenza **3:**648, 744
Piacenza, University of **5:**1367
Piasts, the **4:**1104, 1108, 1112
Piazza Ducale (Vigevano)
    1:139
Piazza Giovanni e Paolo
    (Venice) **3:**707
Piazza Navona (Rome) **5:**1235
Piazza Santa Annunziata
    (Florence) **1:**151
picaresque novel **3:**738–739
Picart, Bernard **5:***1232*
Piccolomini, Andrea **4:**1091
Piccolomini, Antonio **4:**1091
Piccolomini, Enea Silvio *see*
    Pius II, Pope

Piccolomini, Francesco *see*
    Pius III, Pope
Piccolomini, Jacopo **4:**1091
Piccolomini, Octavio **5:**1338
Piccolomini, Silvius **4:**1009
Pico, Giovanni Francesco
    (nephew) **4:**1074
Pico della Mirandola,
    Giovanni **4:1073–1077**
  Florence **2:**422–423, 424
  humanism **2:**482, **3:***588,*
    589
  magic **4:**1065
  Medicis **3:**852, 855, 856
  More **4:**924
  optimism **2:**537, 538,
    4:1064, 1066
  Platonism **4:**1100, 1103
  Renaissance **5:**1220
Piedmont **3:**643, 644
Pienza **4:***1089,* 1090
Pienza, Cathedral of **4:***1091*
Pierce, Mark **1:**28
*Pierce Penniless, His
    Suplication to the Divell*
    (Nash) **3:**738
Piero della Francesca **1:**139,
    3:*630,* 827–828, **4:**1090,
    5:*1181*
Pierre, Jean-Baptiste **4:**1067
Pierre de Beauveau **1:***112*
Pietà (Michelangelo) **4:**871
Pietro de Crescenzi **1:***25, 26*
Pigafetta, Antonio **3:**789, 791,
    792, 793
pikes and pikemen **5:**1412,
    1413
  Sweden **5:**1309
  Switzerland **5:**1313–1314,
    1413
  Thirty Years War **5:**1335
Pilate, Pontius **5:**1232
pilgrimage **4:1078–1085**
  Calvinist rejection **1:**183
  Chaucer **1:***212,* 213, 218,
    219, **5:**1202
  Islam **3:**611, 615, 621, 625
  Rome **4:**1026, **5:**1228, *1232*
Pilgrimage of Grace (England,
    1536) **1:**187, 235, **2:**340,
    526, **4:**1042

Pilgrims (Puritans) **5:**1342

Pillau (Baltiysk) **5:**1334

Pindar **4:**1092

Pine, John **1:***66*

Pinta (Columbus ship) **1:**248, 250, 251, **4:**1138

Pinturicchio (Betto di Biago) **1:***125*, **2:***428*, **4:***1086, 1087, 1088,* 1091, **5:**1183

Pinzón, Martín Alonso **1:**248, 250, 251, 252

Pinzón, Vicente Yañez **1:**248

Piombo, Sebastiano del **1:**41, *241,* **3:***650*

Pippi de' Gianuzzi, Giulio *see* Romano, Giulio

piracy and privateering **2:**502, 505, **5:**1394, 1412

   Barbary coast **1:**208, 209, 211, **3:**626, *627,* 716, **5:**1347

   Cervantes as captive **1:**202, 204

   England **2:**331

Pirkheimer, Willibald **2:**339

Pisa **2:**414, *461,* **3:**632, 637, 638, 649, 770

   banking **1:**87, **2:**416

   Black Death **2:**305

   Galileo **5:**1252

   Viscontis **5:**1401, 1404

Pisa, Cathedral of **2:**460

Pisa, Council of (1409) **2:**367

Pisa, University of **3:**700, **5:**1367

   botanical garden **3:**840, 847

   Galileo **2:**460, 461, **5:**1252

   science studies **5:**1255

Pisanello, Antonio **1:***224,* **2:**428, **5:***1416*

Pisan Wars **1:**279

Pistoia, Cathedral of **5:***1366*

pistol **5:**1414

piston **3:**785

Pittoni, Girolamo **4:**1000

Pius II, Pope **2:***428,* **3:**619, **4:1086–1091, 5:**1230

Pius III, Pope **4:**1091

Pius IV, Pope **2:**453, **3:**747, **4:**1020, 1024, **5:***1226,* 1353, 1360

Pius V, Pope **3:**715, *717,* **4:***967,* 975, *1058,* 1059

   excommunication of Elizabeth I **1:**238, **2:**330

Pius XI, Pope **4:**932

Pizarro, Francisco **2:**374, **4:**892

pizzicato **4:**922

Place Royale (Paris) (Place des Vosgues) **4:**1034

plague **3:**843, 848, **4:**886, 980

   anti-Semitism **3:**673

   France **2:**432, 433, 434, 436, 456

   German towns **2:**481

   Italian city-states **3:**632–633

   London **3:**755, **5:**1269, 1270

   Milan **3:**745

   social effects **3:**692–693

   theater closures **5:**1322, 1328

   see also Black Death

plainsong **4:**957

Planetary Hypotheses (Ptolemy) **1:**268, 271

planetary motion **3:**783, 831, 832, **5:**1249, 1251–1252

   Copernicus **1:**31, 60, 265, 270

   Ptolemy **1:**266–267, 268

plantations **1:**25

Plateresque **1:**46

Platiensis, Michael **1:**261, **2:**304

Platina *see* Sacchi, Bartolomeo

Plato **3:***703,* **4:***1054, 1061,* 1092, 1096, 1097, 1098

   Academy **4:**1063, 1090, 1095, **5:**1365

   English translation **2:**336

   Latin translation **1:**264, **2:**422, **3:**685, 687

   see also Platonism

Platonic Academy (Florence) *see* Florentine Academy

platonic love **4:**1092, 1095, 1097, 1102–1103

   Constantinople **1:**261

Platonic Theology concerning the Immortality of the Soul (Ficino) **2:**422

Platonism **1:**31, 137, *167,* 264, **2:**320, 538, 543,

4:928–929, 1025, 1061–1062, 1070, 1073, 1075, **1092–1103**

   Aristotelianism **1:**50, 57, 60, 181, 261, **4:**1063, 1099

   astrology **1:**69

   Cambridge Platonists **4:**1070–1071, 1072, 1103

   Christianity **1:**258, **3:**696

   education **2:**320

   Florence **1:**261, **2:**418, 422

   humanism **1:**181, **3:**584, 586, *587*

   iconoclasm **3:**605, 606

   nature **4:**1065

   nominalism vs. **1:**182

   Petrarch **4:**1049, 1054

   Pico della Mirandola **4:**1073, 1074, 1075, 1076

   Ptolemaic cosmos **1:**267

   universities **1:**261, **5:**1376

   see also Neoplatonism

Platter, Thomas **3:**753

Plautus, Titus Maccius **3:**683, 729, 732, 733

   Italian stage revival **5:**1320

Playne Discourse, A (Dee) **1:**177

playwrights *see* theater

Pléiade, the **3:**721, 722, 723, 725, 729, 730, **5:**1287

plenary indulgence **4:**1080

Plessis, Armand-Jean du *see* Richelieu, Cardinal

Plethon *see* Gemistus Plethon, George

Pliny the Elder **1:**58, **3:**583, *687*

Pliny the Younger **3:**583

Plotinus **2:**422, 538, **4:**1061, 1063, 1070, 1096–1097, 1098, 1099, 1100, 1101

plow **1:**25, 27, 28, **4:**1134

Plutarch **1:***59,* **3:**684, 685, 729

   English translation **2:**336

pneumonic plague **4:**1124–1125

podesta **3:**637, 638

Poema del Cid (epic) **3:**695

Poetics (Aristotle) **1:**59, 61, **5:**1321

poetry **3:**720–726

   Aristotle **1:**59, 61

   blank verse **3:**823

   Boccaccio **1:**112, 113

   Borgia patronage **1:**125

   chansons de geste **1:**222

   Chaucer **1:**214, 216–217, 220

   chivalry **1:**222, 223

   drama **3:**731, 732, 823

   England **1:**220

   France **1:**214–225

   humanist learning **3:**582, 588, 589, 683, **5:**1218, 1282

   Italy **1:**216–217

   Jonson on **3:**739

   London **3:**753, 754, 755

   Machiavelli **3:**770

   Margaret of Navarre **3:**735

   Marlowe **3:**824, 825

   Michelangelo **4:**870, 877

   Milton **4:**879–887

   pastoral **3:**737

   Petrarch **4:**1049, 1050–1052

   Shakespeare **5:**1268, 1270, 1274

   Spenser **2:**335, **5:**1286, 1287, 1288–1290

   Spenserian stanza **5:**1290

Poets' Corner (Westminster Abbey) **1:**218, *220*

Poissy, Colloquy of (1561) **1:**188

Poitiers, Battle of (1356) **1:**157, **2:**434, 435, **3:**597, 598, **4:**1029

Poitiers, Diane de **1:**198

Poitiers, University of **2:**295, **5:**1371

Poitou **2:**440

Poland **4:1104–1114, 5:**1330

   Bohemia **1:**120

   Catherine de Médicis **1:**200

   Christina **1:**230

   Copernicus **1:**265–272

   Judaism **3:**675

   Lithuanian Commonwealth **4:**911

   Muscovy **4:**934, 937, 938–939, 940

nobility **4:**971
partition **4:**1114
Russia **3:**653, 654, 656,
5:1337
Sweden **5:**1306, 1307–1308,
1309, 1310, 1311,
1334–1335
Teutonic Knights **1:**223
Thirty Years War **1:**228,
4:1113
Pole, Reginald **1:**234, 236,
5:1355
polestar **2:**377
Polish Brethren **4:**1110
Polish Rider, The (Rembrandt
attribution) **5:**1217
political philosophy
4:1066–1067
Aristotle **1:**53, **3:**684
Hobbes **2:**542–547
Machiavelli **3:**769–773
Renaissance **5:**1223–1224
see also democracy;
government; republics
Political Treatise (Spinoza)
5:1294
Politics (Aristotle) **1:**53, **3:**684
Poliziano, Angelo **1:**54, **3:**585,
587, *588,* 687, **4:**1074
Pollaiuolo, Antonio **2:**425,
4:985
Pollaiuolo, Piero del **1:**133,
134
poll tax **1:**216, **4:**1042–1043,
1047
Polo, Marco **2:**373, **3:**804,
5:1341
Polotsk **4:**1112
polychoral music **4:**951
polygamy **2:**540
polyphony **4:**916, 917, 918,
919, 923, 943, 944, 951,
952, 954, 957, 961,
5:1246, 1247
polytheism **4:**1105
Pombal, Marqués de **4:**1141
Pomerania **5:**1332, 1338
Pomponazzi, Pietro **1:**56, 261,
4:1064, 1069
Ponce de León, Juan **2:**374,
382, **4:**888–889, 891

Ponet, John **5:**1419
Ponsonby, William **5:**1288,
1289
Ponte Alto Dam **1:**279
Ponte Sisto (Rome) **5:**1230,
1231
Pontine Marshes **1:**277
Pont Neuf **4:**1034
Pontormo, Jacopo **4:**989, 998
Poor Clares **5:**1201
Poor Robin (almanac) **1:**68
Pope, Alexander **5:**1257
popolo (merchants and
artistans) **3:**635, 636
popular culture **4:1115–1123**
astrology **1:**67–74
blood sports **1:**92–96
as Bruegel subject **1:**144,
146, 147
London **3:**751, 753, 754,
755
magic **3:**795
markets and fairs **3:**817–818
music **4:**948–952, 960
printing **5:**1174–1175
theater **5:**1317–1329
population **4:1124–1136**
agriculture **1:**22
Black Death **2:**305, **4:**1048,
1124
France **2:**433, 436
German towns **2:**481
Italian city-states **3:**630–631,
633
London **3:**748
Paris **4:**1028, 1030
Poland **4:**1106
sixteenth-century growth
4:*1126*
Poquelin, Jean-Baptiste *see*
Molière
Porcari, Stefano **5:**1229
porcelain **3:**804
Po River **1:**276, 280, **3:**638,
740, 741, **5:**1336
Porphyry **4:**1098
Porta, Giacomo della **1:**38, 40,
47
Porta Camollia, Battle of
(1555) **3:**649
Porta Pia (Rome) **5:***1226*

Porta San Paolo (Rome) **1:**37
Porte Neuve (Paris) **4:***1034*
portolan charts **2:**376
Portrait of a Woman
(Bartolomeo da Venezia)
1:*123*
Portrait of a Young Man
(Rubens) **5:**1237
Portraits of Living Plants
(Brunfels) **5:**1250
portraiture **4:**980, 985, 996,
997
Rembrandt **5:**1210, 1212,
1214, 1217
Rubens **5:***1236,* 1243
Portugal **2:**399, **4:**905, 961,
1137–1145
African slave trade **5:**1348
armed trade **3:**775
Columbus **1:**247, 248, 251
exploration **2:**373, 379–381,
382, 385, **4:**888–889,
914, **5:**1284, 1343, 1344,
1346
feudalism **2:**403
Gregorian calendar **1:**176
humanism **3:**693
Judaism **2:**399, **3:**677, 679,
681
Magellan voyage **3:**787, 788,
789, 792, 793, 794
missionaries **4:**889, 891, 894,
895, 896
monarchy **5:**1224
Ottoman Empire **3:**624
shipping **5:**1343
Spain **4:**1058, 1060, **5:**1277,
1284
trade **3:**633, **5:**1341, 1342,
1344, 1350, 1393
Portuguese Inquisition **4:**1139,
1141
Portuguese language **5:**1222
potatoes **1:**28
Pourbus, Frans **1:***234*
Poussin, Nicolas **4:**994, 995,
5:1243, 1388
Poussinistes **5:**1243
poverty
Italian city-states **3:**635
London **3:**753, 755

Powell, Mary (later Mary
Milton) **4:**879, 883, 884,
885, 887
Powell, Richard **4:**880, 883,
887
Pozhansky, Prince Dmitry
4:939
Poznán **2:**506
Praetorius, Michael **4:**950,
955, 958
Prague **1:**117–119, *120,*
121–122, **2:**559, **3:**836,
837, 838
Thirty Years War **2:**371,
5:1337
Prague, Peace of (1635)
5:1337
Prague, University of **1:**19,
118, **2:**537, **3:**779,
5:1367
Praise of Folly, The (Erasmus)
1:180, **2:**357, 362–363,
3:762, **4:**925, **5:**1221,
1319
Praise of the City of Florence
(Bruni) **3:**584
Pramzimas (god) **4:**1105
prayer
Calvinism **1:**183
Islam **3:**611
Prayer Book rebellion (1637)
5:1262
preaching **1:**183,
5:1158–1166
Précieuses ridicules, Les
(Molière) **4:**899
predestination **1:**185,
189–190, **2:**341, 342, 343,
345, 369, 536, **3:**761,
5:1195
predictions *see* astrology
Predis, Ambrogio da **3:**709
pregnancy *see* childbirth
*Prelude on the Babylonian
Captivity of the Church*
(Luther) **5:**1192
Přemyslids, the **1:**116–117
Prendas de amor (Rueda)
5:1323
Prepared Table, The (Caro)
3:680

Presbyterianism **1**:104, 239
Calvinism **1**:178, 181, 188,
189, 190
English civil wars **1**:239,
2:353
as established church **2**:369
New Divinity **1**:190
Puritanism **2**:342
Scotland **1**:189, 190, **2**:369,
5:1265–1267, 1298,
1300, 1301, 1303
press *see* printing
Prester John **2**:380, **4**:1140
Prete, El **1**:125
Preveza, Battle of (1538)
3:715
Pride, Thomas **2**:354
Pride's Purge (1648) **2**:354
priests, training of **5**:1361
primary schools *see* elementary
schools
Primaticcio, Francesco **4**:990
Primavera (Botticelli) **1**:135,
136, **2**:425, **5**:1220
primogeniture **1**:235, **2**:512,
3:625, **4**:911
Primo libro de madrigali, Il
(Schütz) **5**:1246
Prince, The (Machiavelli)
2:337, 395, 419, **3**:769,
770, 771, 772, 773,
4:1011, 1066, **5**:1221
princedom **5**:1223
Princeton College **1**:189
Principall Navigations
(Hakluyt) **2**:375, 385
Principia mathematica
(Newton) **3**:828, 834,
5:1251, 1258, *1292,* 1430
Principles of Philosophy, The
(Descartes) **2**:295
printing **3**:780–783, 805,
5:1167–1175
Aristotle's works **1**:56, 58, 59
bibles **1**:102, 103, 106–110,
178, 180, **3**:591, 688,
698–699, 761, **5**:1220
Bohemia **1**:118, 122
book fairs **3**:806, 819
calendars **1**:173
China **3**:774

classical languages
3:687–688, 690
education **2**:323
German towns **2**:482, 548,
553
Greek texts **2**:320
humanism **2**:423, **3**:586,
588, 591, 684, **5**:1218
literacy **2**:323, **5**:1172, 1174,
1222
literature **1**:223, **3**:720, 739,
754, **5**:1222
movable type **3**:775,
780–781, 805, 806
music texts **4**:957
papacy **4**:1024
Paris **4**:1031
Portugal **4**:139
Rabelais **5**:1176
Reformation **1**:180–181,
3:704, **5**:1173–1174,
1175, 1192, 1193
Scotland **5**:1263
Shakespeare **5**:1271
Venice **5**:1394, 1399
vernaculars **3**:696, 697–699
women **5**:1421
privateers *see* piracy and
privateering
Pro Archia (Cicero) **3**:684,
4:1053
probability **3**:829
*Procession in Saint Mark's
Square* (Bellini) **3**:635
processions **5**:1317, 1318
Procida, Gasparo de **1**:123
Proclus **1**:*271,* **2**:422
Prodigal Son, The (Bosch)
1:131
Prognostico (Cardano) **1**:*70*
propaganda, printed
5:1174–1175
property law **3**:809 *see also*
inheritance
Prophet (Michelangelo) **4**:874
"Pro Populo Anglicano
Defensio" (Milton) **4**:887
prose fiction **3**:735–739
Prospect of Venice (unattributed)
1:*277*
prostitutes **4**:979

Protagoras **5**:1368
*Protestant Ethic and the Spirit
of Capitalism, The* (Weber)
1:190
Protestant Evangelical Union
3:836
Protestantism *see* Reformation;
specific denominations
Protestant Reformation *see*
Reformation
Protestant Union **3**:836, 837,
5:1331, 1334
Provence **1**:157, **2**:437, 456
Prowse, Anne Locke **3**:724
Prussia **2**:506
Huguenots **5**:1331
Poland **4**:1106, 1107, 1114
Sweden **5**:1335, 1337
Teutonic Knights **1**:222,
223
Prynne, William **2**:346
Psalms of David (Schütz)
5:1245, 1246
Psellus, Michael Constantine
see Michael Constantine
Psellus
Pseudo-Dionysius *see*
Dionysius the Areopagite
Ptolemy, Claudius **1**:*60*
astrology **1**:69, **3**:830
Columbus's worldview
1:249
Copernicus vs. **1**:265,
268–269, 270, 271, 272,
2:463, **3**:825
exploration **2**:373, 374, 384
Galileo **2**:466, **3**:699
mathematics **3**:829, 830
universe model **1**:266–269,
2:296, **5**:1249–1250
public education **2**:322,
323–325
public health **4**:1131–1132
Black Death **2**:305–306
Pucci, Antonio **2**:484
Punch and Judy shows **5**:1320
puppet shows **5**:1320
Purchas, Samuel **2**:375, 377,
379
purgatory **2**:430, 525, **3**:704,
757, **5**:1231, 1232, 1360

indulgences **4**:1013
penance **1**:180
Puritan Revolution *see* English
civil wars
Puritans **1**:108, **2**:328, **4**:892,
894
biblical interpretation **1**:109
Calvinism **1**:178, **5**:1196
Church of England **1**:188,
237, 239, 240,
2:368–369, **5**:1198
church reform **2**:342
Cromwell **2**:351
Elizabethan Compromise
1:239, **5**:1198
England **1**:188, 239, **2**:341,
343, 345, **4**:1066
English civil wars **2**:346,
348, **5**:1325, 1336
iconoclasm **1**:48–49, **3**:609,
5:1198
theater **5**:1326, 1327, 1329
theocracy **1**:187
universities **5**:1374–1375
Putney Debates (1647) **2**:354
Puttenham, George **3**:723
Pym, John **2**:350, 351
Pythagoras **2**:334
Pythagorean system **4**:1075

Q

quadrant **2**:377, **3**:790,
5:1250
quadrivium **2**:357, **5**:1366,
1372
quarantine **2**:306, **3**:843
Quarr Abbey **3**:806
Quart Livre (Rabelais) **5**:1178
quattrocento artists **4**:985
Quattro libri (Palladio) **1**:140
Quebec **3**:609, **4**:893, **5**:1342
Queen's Dramatic Ballet, The
4:943
Queen's House (Greenwich)
1:48, **3**:666–667, 668
Queen's Men (London
theater) **5**:1328
Querela pacis (Erasmus) **2**:357
*Questions concerning Liberty,
Necessity and Chance, The*
(Hobbes) **2**:546

Quetzalcoatl (deity) **4**:890

Quevedo y Villegas, Francisco de **3**:738–779

Quintilian **3**:583, 584, 588, 590, 683, 686, **5**:1373

Quirinal Hill (Rome) **4**:*1039,* 1040

Qum (Shiite shrine) **3**:621

R

Rabelais, François **3**:735, 736, **5:1176–1179**

Racine, Jean **3**:730, 731

Radboto, Count **2**:507

Radcliffe Camera (Oxford) **1**:140

Raising of Drusiana, The (Giotto) **2**:487

Raising of Lazarus (Caravaggio) **1**:194

Raising of the Cross (Rubens) **5**:1239–1240

Raising of the Son of Theophilus, The (Masaccio) **3**:*589*

Raleigh, Walter **3**:726, 751, 825, **5**:1288

Ramus, Petrus **4**:1064

rank *see* nobility and rank

ransom **1**:222, 225

Rape of Lucrece (Shakespeare) **5**:1268

Raphael **1**:39, 40, 41, *50,* 97, 242, **3**:*700,* **4**:957, 981, 1012, 1061, **5:1180–1187,** 1221, 1224, *1383,* 1387

Bramante **1**:37, 38, 142, *143,* **4**:1002, 1004

Clement VII **1**:242

Dürer **2**:316

High Renaissance **4**:986, 988, 990

Julius II **1**:36, **4**:1025

Leo X **3**:703

Palladio **4**:1002, 1003, 1004

as Rembrandt influence **5**:1213, 1214

Saint Peter's Basilica **1**:48, **4**:1026

Sistine Chapel **1**:135, **5**:*1158*

rat fleas **2**:303, **4**:1124

Rathaus (Bremen) **1**:49

Ravaillac, François **2**:*457,* 520

Ravenna **1**:258, 264, **5**:1393, 1394

Ravenna, Battle of (1512) **3**:643, 645

Rayman Hall (Norfolk) **3**:665

reading *see* literacy

Reading on the Statute of Uses (Bacon) **1**:80

Reales Sitios (Aranjuez) **1**:280

realism **3**:759–760

reason **3**:761, 766, 767

Aristotelianism **1**:57

humanism **2**:337

reasoning **2**:317

Rebellious Slave (Michelangelo) **4**:874

Recamati, Franco **1**:279

recitar cantando **4**:920

Recollects (Augustinians) **4**:889, 893

Reconquista **2**:398, **3**:676, 678, **4**:956, 969, **5**:1322, 1425

Recorde, Robert **3**:829

Red Book (Sweden) **5**:1307

Red Bull (London theater) **3**:*733*

Redeemer, Church of the (Prague) **1**:*120*

Redemption Triptych (van der Weyden) **4**:*1129*

Redentore, il (Venice) **1**:32, 43, **3**:668, **4**:1006, *1007*

Red Lion (London theater) **3**:732

Redon, Concordat of (1441) **4**:969

Red Square (Moscow) **3**:*654*

Reformation **5:1188–1200**

Aristotelianism **1**:58

astrology **1**:73

Augsburg, Peace of **1**:75–78

bibles **1**:102–110, **2**:320, **3**:689

Bohemia **1**:118, 119–122, **5**:1334

calendar **1**:175, 176–177

Calvinism **1**:178–190

Charles V **1**:210–211

church architecture **1**:49

church music **5**:1244, 1246

Church of England **1**:232, 236–240

common themes **1**:178

Constantinople **1**:262–263

Dante **1**:217

divorce grounds **2**:566–567

Dürer **2**:314, 315–316

education **2**:317, 320–325

Elizabeth I **2**:328–329, **5**:1297, 1298, 1301

England **1**:62, 232–240, **2**:326–333, 334, 338–343, 346, 349, 365, 524, 525, 526, 527, 528, **3**:608–609, **4**:1015, **5**:1300, 1301, 1302, 1325, 1326, 1424, 1426

English chronology **1**:240

Erasmus **2**:356, 357, 358, 359–362

established churches **1**:257, **2**:364–372

Florentine humanism **2**:423, 426

France **2**:432, 438–440, 541

Francis I **2**:447–448

Greek revival **2**:320

Gregorian calendar **1**:175, 176–177

Hapsburg opposition **2**:507, 513, 514–515

heliocentric universe **1**:272

Henry IV **2**:516–520, 541

Henry VIII **2**:338–340

heresy **2**:535, 537, 539–540

Holy Roman Empire **2**:423, 479, 480, 482–483, 548, 552–554, 556, 557–559

households **2**:563

humanism **2**:324, 339–340, **3**:590, 592, 593

iconoclasm **3**:605, 606–609

key issues **3**:855, **5**:1354–1359, 1363–1364

Leo X **3**:704–705

literacy **3**:720

literature **2**:335, **3**:739

London **3**:748

Luther **5**:1352

Lutheranism **3**:756–768

Milton **4**:882, 883, 885

missionaries **4**:892, 895, 896

monarchy **4**:906, 907, 912, 913

More **4**:929, 930–932

music **4**:943, 952–954, 957, 958

nationalism **2**:364–365, **4**:969, 970

Netherlands **4**:1057

painting and sculpture **4**:992, 995–996

papacy **4**:1012–1013, 1014, 1016, 1018, 1019, 1023, 1026–1027, 1040

Paris **4**:1031, 1032–1034

philosophy **4**:1064–1066

pilgrimage critics **4**:1079, 1083

Poland **4**:1110–1111

popular culture **4**:1121–1123

preaching **5**:1163–1166

printing **1**:180–181, **2**:323, **5**:1173–1174, 1175, 1192, 1193

religious orders **5**:1201–1204, 1209, 1362

Renaissance chronology **5**:1221

Rome **5**:1232

sacraments **5**:1358

science **5**:1256

Scotland **5**:1262, 1263, 1265–1267, 1298, 1300, 1302, 1303, 1426

Spenser **5**:1289

Sweden **5**:1305, 1306, 1308

Switzerland **5**:1312, 1313, 1314–1316

theater **5**:1325, 1326–1327, 1329

theodicy **2**:360

Thirty Years War **1**:227, **3**:767, 835–839, **4**:1040, **5**:1310, 1330–1339

Trent, Council of **1**:99, **5**:1352–1364

universities **5**:1365, 1368, 1369, 1370, 1371, 1372, 1373–1377

Reformation (cont.)
  usury relaxation 1:85
  vernacular languages 2:321,
    335, 3:696, 698–699
  warfare 5:1408, 1411
  women 5:147, 1423–1424,
    1426
  see also Counter-Reformation
Reformation Parliament
  (1560, Scotland) 5:1298
Reformed Church see
  Calvinism
Reformed churches see
  Calvinism
Regensburg 3:673, 5:1337
Regensburg, Diet of (1541)
  1:209
Reggio nell'Emilia, University
  of 5:1370–1371
regicide 5:1303, 1325
Regiomontanus 1:174–175,
  265, 269, 3:828, 829, 831
Regulae ad directionem ingenii
  (Descartes) 2:295
Reichstag (Germany) 2:548,
  4:910
Reims 3:602, 657, 658–659,
  660
Reims, Cathedral of 2:432,
  4:943
    Charles VII coronation
      3:602, 657, 658–659
Reinhard, Anna 5:1315
Rej, Mikolaj 4:1109
Relation of a Voyage . . . under
  the Command of M. de
  Gennes (Froger) 5:1349
relativism 2:294
religious festivals 4:1118,
  5:1317
religious guilds 2:493–494,
  495, 500
religious orders 2:370, 380,
  4:1008–1009, 5:1201–1209
  Byzantium 1:171, 5:1201
  Cervantes 1:206
  contemplative life 3:585, 586
  Luther 3:756–757, 758, 762,
    767
  missionaries 4:888–896
  nobility and rank 4:975

papacy 4:1038
Paul III 5:1353
preaching 5:1158, 1159
priestly training 5:1361
Rabelais 5:1176, 1177, 1178
Thirty Years War 5:1332
Trent, Council of 5:1362
universities 2:322, 324
see also monasteries; specific
  orders
religious plays 3:727, 728–
  729, 732, 5:1318–1320,
  1322, 1323, 1328
religious poetry 3:726, 735
religious tolerance
  Bohemia 1:119, 121
  Catherine de Médicis 1:201
  Christina 1:230
  German towns 2:482, 483
  Henry IV (France) 2:517,
    520, 541
  heresy vs. 2:540–541
  Holy Roman Empire 2:441,
    556, 558
  Islamic 3:676
  Islamic Ottomans 1:169,
    170, 3:612, 613, 615,
    623, 626, 680
  James I 5:1301
  Levellers 2:354
  Milton 4:883
  Netherlands 3:681
  Poland 4:1110–1111
  Spanish Jews 3:676
  Venice 5:1398
  Westphalia, Peace of 5:1338
religious wars see French civil
  wars; Thirty Years War
Rembrandt 1:59, 4:996, 997,
  998, 5:1210–1217, 1243,
  1387
  Caravaggio as influence
    1:196
Rembrandt, Titus 5:1212,
  1214, 1217
Rembrandt Research Project
  5:1217
Remedy of Fortune, The
  (Machaut) 1:215
Remences, Rebellion of the
  4:1042

Remole weir 1:280
Renaissance 5:1218–1226
  architecture 1:30–49,
    97–101, 139–143, 156,
    2:334, 3:663, 664–668,
    5:1399
  Brunelleschi 1:149, 152, 153,
    156
  chivalry 1:221, 222, 223
  Columbus's worldview 1:249
  Constantinople 1:256, 258
  Counter-Reformation 5:1226
  dams 1:278–281
  Dante 1:217
  education 2:317–320, 325
  England 2:339, 5:1286
  Florence 2:414, 418,
    421–426
  France 2:437–438, 444, 450
  humanism 1:181, 264,
    3:582–594, 638
  Italian city-states 3:640–642
  Judaism 3:671, 672, 677
  limits of 5:1225
  literature 1:111–115,
    3:720–739
  London 3:754–755
  Luther and 3:767
  music 5:1245, 1247
  musical style 4:916, 919,
    920, 922, 945–961
  opera 5:1321
  painting and sculpture 1:101,
    127, 133–138, 145,
    2:312–313, 314, 316,
    469–474, 484–492,
    3:706–714, 5:1184–1187,
    1221–1222, 1230, 1235,
    1236
  papacy 1011–1028
  Paris 4:1031–1035
  Petrarch 4:1052, 1053–1055
  philosophy 4:1072, 1076
  Poland 4:1109–1112
  Portugal 4:1139, 1143–1145
  preaching 5:1160–1166
  printing 5:1172–1173
  Rome 5:1231–1235
  sack of Rome 1:243, 2:523,
    4:986, 1002, 1014, 1023,
    1026

science 5:1248–1259
Scotland 5:1262–1265,
  1296
Spain 5:1279–1285
Sweden 5:1308
theater 5:1323
theatrical architecture
  5:1320
universities 5:1365, 1369,
  1370–1375
Urbino 5:1378–1383
Venice 5:1392–1400
vernaculars 3:696–697
Viscontis 5:1405–1406
warfare changes 5:1335,
  1407–1415
women 5:1416–1428
see also High Renaissance;
  northern Renaissance
Renata, Elisabeth 3:836
René Descartes's Principles of
  Philosophy, Parts I and II
  (Spinoza) 5:1293
René of Anjou 4:1088, 1089
Reni, Guido 4:1040
Renoir, Pierre-Auguste 5:1242
Repin, Ilya Efimovich 3:656
Republic, The (Plato) 1:31,
  4:928–929, 1094, 1103
republics 4:995, 5:1223, 1224
  English civil wars
    2:352–353, 355
  Florence 2:416–417, 3:585,
    702, 4:967
  Italian city-states 3:630,
    638–639, 641, 642
  Italian wars 3:644, 649, 650,
    651
  Venice 3:668, 5:1392, 1396,
    1397, 1400
Rerum memorandum libri
  (Petrarch) 4:1051
resistance theory 5:1299
Restitution, Edict of (1629)
  3:839, 5:1333, 1336, 1337
Restoration (England) 1:240,
  2:351, 4:886, 5:1302,
  1322, 1329
Resurrection (Piero della
  Francesca) 4:987
Rethel 1:157

Return of the Prodigal Son (Rembrandt) **5:**1217

Return to Amsterdam of the Fleet of the Dutch East India Company, The (van Eertvelt) **5:***1351*

Reubeni, David **3:**677

Reuchlin, Johann **3:**592, 593, 674, 689

Reval (Tallinn) **2:**503, **5:**1307

Revelation **1:**32, 105, 138

Dürer images **2:**314

Eyck images **2:**387

revenge plays **3:**732

Revised Standard Version (1946 Bible) **1:**106

Revised Version (1881 Bible) **1:**106

Revolutions (Copernicus) **3:**829

Reynolds, Joshua **5:**1242

Reynolds, Susan **2:**405

Reza, Imam **3:***621*

Rhaw, Georg **4:**957

Rheinfelden, Battle of (1638) **5:**1338

Rhenanus, Beatus **3:**590

Rheticus, Georg Joachim **1:**266, 269

rhetoric

dialectic vs. **5:**1369, 1372, 1373

Erasmus **2:**363

humanist learning **3:**582, 584, 588, 589, 683, **5:**1218, 1282

Rhineland **5:**1196, 1198

Rhine River **2:**506, 507, **3:**836, **4:**965, 1139, **5:**1344

Black Death **2:**304–305

Rhodes **1:**223, **3:**624

Rhodes, siege of (1480) **3:**619, **5:**1408

Rhône River **4:**965

Rhône valley **2:**456

Riario (Rome) **1:**230

Riario, Girolamo **5:**1427, 1428

Riario, Pietro **5:**1230

Riario, Rafaello **1:**40, **4:**870

Ribera, José de **4:**994

Riccardi Palace (Florence) **3:***702*

Ricci, Matteo **4:**894–895, 1015, **5:**1206

Ricci, Ostilio **2:**460

rice **3:**741

ricercar **4:**960

Richard II, king of England **1:**17, **2:***378,* 499

Chaucer **1:**216, 217, 218

Hundred Years War **3:**599

Peasants' Revolt **4:**1043, 1046–1047, 1048

Richard III, king of England **1:**233

Richard, 3rd duke of York **2:**408, **3:***601*

Richard of Wallingford **3:**780

Richard II (Shakespeare) **1:**17, **4:**963, **5:**1271

Richard III (Shakespeare) **4:**928, **5:**1270, 1271, 1273

Richelieu, Cardinal (Armand-Jean du Plessis) **4:**882, 908, 1034–1035, **5:**1240

French civil wars **2:**458–459

Thirty Years War **5:**1333, 1336, 1337

Richental, Ulrich von **1:***119, 158,* **4:***1010*

Richia (Ibn Battutah) 611

Richmond, duke of *see* Fitzroy, Henry

Richmond Castle **2:***401*

Rider on Rearing Horse (Leonardo da Vinci) **3:***710*

Ridley, Nicholas **1:***187*

Ridolfi, Roberto **2:**331

Rienzo, Cola di **4:**1052, **5:**1227

Rievaulx Abbey (Yorkshire) **5:***1203*

Riga **2:**503, **5:**1309, 1334

Rijnsburg **5:**1292

Riksbank (Sweden) **1:**90

Riksdag (Sweden) **1:**227, **5:**1306, 1308

Riley, John **5:***1255*

Rimini **4:**1090

Rinuccini, Ottavio **4:**920, **5:**1321

Ripa, Cesare **2:**472

Ritorno d'Ulisse in patria, Il (Monteverdi) **4:**922

rivers **3:**741, 749, 751, *754,* 804, 809

dikes and drainage **1:**276–277, 278

Rizzio, David **5:**1298

Roaring Girl, The (Middleton) **5:**1329

Robbia *see* Della Robbia

Robert, king of Naples **1:**111, 112, **2:**487

Robert I (the Bruce), king of Scotland **4:**904, 905

Robert II, king of Scotland **5:**1296

Robert of Anjou *see* Robert, king of Naples

Robert of Artois **3:**595

Robert de Sorbon **5:***1369*

Robertello, Francesco **1:**59

Robles, Francisco de **1:**205

Robsart, Amy **2:**329

Roche, Lord **5:**1288, 1289

Rodriguez Juarez, Juan **5:***1205*

Roet, Gilles de **1:**213–214

Roet, Philippa de (later Chaucer) **1:**213–214

Rogers, Daniel **5:**1287

Rogers, John **1:**107

Rokeby Hall (Yorkshire) **5:**1389

Rokeby Venus (Velázquez) **5:**1389

Roland **1:**222, 223

Rolin, Nicholas **2:***388*

Rolin Virgin, The (Jan van Eyck) **2:***388,* 390–391, 392

Roma instaurata (Biondo) **3:**587

Romana, Francesca **4:**1036

Roman calendar **1:**173–174

Roman Catholic Church

Aristotelianism **1:**52, 53, 54, 55, 56, 57, 58–59

astrology **1:**72, 73–74

astronomy **2:**296

Augsburg, Peace of **1:**75–78

Bernini sculpture **1:**97, 99, 100

bibles **1:**104, 105, 108, 110, **3:**688, 689

Bohemia **1:**119, 120, 121–122

calendar **1:**173, 174, 175–177

Calvinism vs. **1:**179, 180, 182, 183, 184, 186, 188, 189, 190, 198–200

catechism **5:**1174

Christina's conversion to **1:**228, 229–231, **5:**1311

Church of England **1:**235, 237–238, 239, 240, 263

Decree of Reunion **2:**429–431

divine right of kings **4:**906

divorce ban **2:**566, 567

education **2:**317, 319, *322,* 324, 325, 364, **4:**1018, 1111

Elizabeth I **1:**237, 238, **2:**328, 330–331, 333

Elizabethan Settlement **2:**329, **5:**1198

England **1:**62, 66, 79, 108, 232, 235–240, 262, **2:**326–327, 328, 329–330, 333, 335, 338, 339, 340, 341, 342–343, 344, 345, 346, 368, 370, 371, 372, 526, **4:**896, 929–932, 953, **5:**1198, 1297, 1298–1299, 1301, 1302, 1324, 1325, 1326–1327, 1328, 1374, 1424, 1426

English civil wars **2:**347, 348, 350, 352

Erasmus **2:**356–363

established churches **2:**364–365, 368, 369, 370–372

exploration **2:**380

fairs **3:**813, 815

fast days **2:**504, **5:**1341

Ferdinand and Isabella **2:**393, 396, 397, 398, 400, **5:**1279

festivals **4:**1118, 1119, **5:**1317

Roman Catholic Church
(cont.)
Florence, Council of 1:260,
261, 2:427–431
France 2:438–440, 441,
516–520, 541, 5:1177,
1178, 1179
French civil wars 2:441–443,
451–459, 5:1331
Galileo 2:464–465,
466–467, 539, 3:783,
784, 5:1254
German towns 2:478, 479,
481, 553, 558
guilds 2:495
Guise family 1:198
Hapsburgs 2:478, 479,
482–483, 507, 512–515
heliocentric universe 1:272,
5:1226
Henry IV 2:516, 517, 518,
519, 520
Henry VII 3:608
Henry VIII 1:232, 2:338,
5:1196–1197
heresy 1:187, 2:529–541
Hobbes critique of 2:544
Holy Roman Empire 2:548,
555, 556, 557, 558, 559,
5:1189, 1200, 1338
households 2:563
humanism 1:181,
2:421–423, 425, 3:585,
586, 591, 592, 593,
5:1370, 1371
hunting 1:95, 96
iconoclasm 3:604, 606, 607,
609, 761
indulgences 3:704, 5:1189,
1190–1191, 1231
intermediaries system 1:186
Ireland 2:333, 350, 352,
5:1303
Italian city-states 3:639, 640
Joan of Arc 3:657, 658, 660,
662
knighthood 1:221
Latin language 3:682, 684,
688–689, 690, 696, 697
legal kinship 2:568
libraries 5:1375

Lithuanian conversion
4:1104, 1106, 1109
Luther 5:1201
Lutheranism vs. 2:423,
3:756, 762, 764–765,
766, 767, 768, 836, 837
Lyons, Council of 1:260
magic 3:796–797, 801
Maximilian I 3:835–839
Middle Ages 1:178, 184, 190
missionaries 4:888–896
monarchy 2:371, 4:905, 906,
907, 912, 913–914
moral reform 5:1360–1362
More 4:925–926, 929,
930–932
music 4:943, 953, 954–957
nationalism 4:969, 970
nobility and rank 4:975
Orthodox Church 2:427–431
Orthodox schism 1:166, 259,
4:1073
Ottoman Empire 3:626
Ottoman schism 1:166, 259,
2:427, 3:854, 4:1073
painting and sculpture 1:193,
194, 2:387, 4:992–995,
996
Paris 4:1032–1034, 1035
pawn operations 1:89
Petrarch 4:1055
Philip II 4:1057–1058, 1059,
1060
Pico della Mirandola 4:1073,
1074, 1075, 1076–1077
pilgrimage 1078–1085
Platonism 4:1098, 1099,
1100–1101
Poland 4:1110, 1111, 1113
popular culture 4:1119,
1120, 1121, 1122–1123
Portugal 4:1137, 1139, 1140
preaching 5:1158–1163
printing 5:1175
Rabelais 5:1176, 1177, 1178
Reformation 5:1188–1193,
1194, 1195, 1221
religious orders 5:1201–1209
Rome 5:1227–1235
Scholasticism 4:1052,
1054–1055

science 5:1253
Scotland 5:1262, 1265,
1266, 1267
seven sacraments
5:1357–1359, 1360
Spain 1:62, 66, 3:613,
5:1277–1279, 1283, 1301
Sweden 5:1305, 1306, 1307,
1308
Switzerland 5:1315, 1316
theater 4:900–901, 5:1317,
1318–1320, 1321, 1322,
1323
theodicy 2:360
Thirty Years War 2:371,
3:835, 5:1310,
1330–1339
traditional beliefs 1:178–179
Trent, Council of 3:593,
4:1017–1018,
5:1352–1364
universe model 2:296
universities 2:322, 324,
5:1365, 1367, 1368,
1369, 1370, 1372–1373,
1375, 1377
usury laws 1:85
vernaculars 3:695, 696–697,
698, 699
women 5:1424, 1426
see also Counter-Reformation;
Inquisition; papacy
romance literature 1:214, 219,
220, 222, 223, 224, 5:1322
Roman Curia 4:1021
Roman de la rose 1:214–215,
217, 218, 219
Roman de Tristan, Le 1:222
Roman Empire
architecture 1:30, 33, 34, 40,
47, 140, 141, 142, 2:334,
424, 3:665, 667
bull baiting 1:94
Burgundy 1:157
Byzantium 1:165, 258
Christianity 3:604, 696
dams 1:278
disease 2:303
Donation of Constantine
3:584, 586, 594, 686
education 2:318, 319

Greek language 3:684, 691
Hapsburg Empire 2:512,
513, 514
Hellenic culture 1:167
heresy law 2:531
humanism 3:582–589, 756,
5:1219
Judaism 3:669, 695
Latin language 3:682, 691
literature 2:334–335
Ottoman Empire 1:169
Rome 5:1227, 1228, 1232
sculpture 1:98
theater 3:732, 733, 5:1320–
1321, 1322, 1326
see also Byzantine Empire;
humanism; Latin
language
Roman Inquisition see
Inquisition
Romanists (painting style)
1:145
Roman law 2:531
Roman Martyrology 4:1024
Roman Missal 5:1363
Romano, Giulio 1:38, 39, 97,
242, 4:991, 1003, 1004,
1012, 5:1187
Romanov, Michael see Michael
I, emperor of Russia
Romanov dynasty 1:166,
4:940–941, 5:1309
Roman Republic 3:769, 772
Romans, Letter to the (Paul)
1:105, 179
romantic poets 5:1290
Romanus II, Byzantine
emperor 1:257
Rome 5:1227–1235
architecture 1:30, 32, 33, 34,
35, 36–40, 43, 44–45, 47,
139, 140, 141, 4:1025–
1026, 1040, 5:1235
banking 1:87, 88, 2:416
Bernini 1:97
Borgia, Lucrezia 1:123, 124,
125
Bramante 1:41, 140, 141
Bruegel 1:149
Byzantium as "New Rome"
1:172

Caravaggio **1:**191, 192, 194, 195

Catherine de Médicis **1:**197

Catholicism **1:**166

Christina **1:**227, 228, 229–231

Galileo **3:**699, **5:**1253

Gentileschi **2:**470, 471, 472

Giotto **2:**487, 491

Greek philosophy **1:**169

humanism **3:**586, 587, 703, 756, **4:**1023

Inquisition **1:**187, **4:**1018, 1019, 1036, 1065, **5:**1226, 1234, 1251

Jones **3:**663, 668

Leo X **3:**700, 703, 704

Michelangelo **2:**425–426, **4:**870–871, 873–875, 876–878, 986, **5:**1231, 1232

Milton **4:**882

Moscow as "third" **4:**935–936

music **4:**954, 955, 956

painting **1:**145, **4:**986–988, 992, **5:**1236–1237

Palladio **4:**1001, 1002–1003

papacy **4:**1008, 1009–1010, 1011, 1019, 1020, 1022, 1025–1026, 1037, 1040, 1052

Petrarch **4:**1052

Pico della Mirandola **4:**1074, 1075

pilgrimages **4:***1079,* 1080, 1083

Pontine Marshes drainage **1:**277

Porta Pia **5:***1226*

Raphael **5:**1181, 1183, 1185, 1186–1187

sack of (1527) **1:**209, 210, 243, **2:**523, **3:**643, 647, 649, 773, **4:**986, 1002, 1014, 1023, 1026, **5:**1232, 1233

Velázquez **5:**1387, 1388–1389

Rome, University of **3:**703, **4:**1022, **5:**1367

Romeo and Juliet (Shakespeare) **5:***1276*

Rome Restored (Biondo) **3:**587

Romier, Lucien **2:**459

Ronsard, Pierre de **3:**721, 722, 723, 725, 735

Roosebeke, Battle of (1382) **1:**157

rosary **5:**1197

Rosenblatt, Wibrandis **5:**1423

Rose of Lima **5:**1209

Roses, Wars of the **1:**17, 233, **2:**408, **4:**911, 912, **5:**1271, 1411

Rose Theatre (London) **3:**732, **5:**1323, 1326

Rosselli, Cosimo **3:***588*

Rossellino, Antonio **5:***1218*

Rossellino, Bernardo **1:***155,* **3:***585,* **4:***1089,* 1090

Rossi, Luigi di **2:***426*

Rossi family **3:**744

Rossini, Gioacchino **5:**1312

Rosso, Franco dei **3:***686*

Rosso, Giovanni Battista *see* Rosso Fiorentino, Il

Rosso Fiorentino, Il **1:**242, **4:**990

Rostock **5:**1334

Rostock, Battle of (1636) **5:**1338

Rotterdam **1:***274,* 275, **2:**356, *362*

Roubillac, Louis-François **1:***79*

Rouen **1:**17, **2:**451, 455, 457, **3:**661, 662

Round Table, knights of the **1:**222, 223

Roussillon **5:**1279

Rovere *see* Della Rovere

Rowlett, Ralph **5:**1419

Royal Academy of France **4:**981, 995, **5:**1243

Royal Academy of Science (London) **3:**695

Royal Academy of Sciences (France) **3:**775, **5:**1256

Royal College (France) **5:**1176

Royal College of Physicians (England) **5:**1250

Royal Exchange (London) **3:**751, **5:**1432

Royal Hospital (London) **5:**1432

Royal Mint (England) **1:**90

Royal Society of London **3:**775, **4:**1068, **5:**1256, 1257, 1430, 1431

Roydon, Matthew **3:**824

Rubenistes **5:**1243

Rubens, Jan **5:**1236

Rubens, Peter Paul **3:**666, **4:**917, 993, 994, 995, *1117,* **5:***1200,* **1236–1243,** *1359*

Caravaggio **1:**194

Rembrandt **5:**1210, 1212

Velázquez **5:**1386–1387, 1388

Rubens and Helana Fourment in the Garden (Rubens) **5:**1242

Rucellai, Giovanni **1:**36

Rucellai Palace (Florence) **1:**36

Rudolf I, king of Bohemia **1:**117

Rudolf II, king of Bohemia **3:**801

Rudolf IV, king of Bohemia **2:**507

Rudolf I, king of Germany **2:**509

Rudolf II, Holy Roman emperor **1:**121, **2:**556, 558, 559, 560, **4:**990, **5:**1334, 1415

Rudolphine Tables **3:***831,* 832

Rue, Pierre de la **4:**951

Rueda, Lope de **3:**727, **5:**1323

Ruggieri, Michele **4:**895

"Ruins of Time, The" (Spenser) **5:**1288

Rule of Saint Benedict **5:**1201

Rules for the Direction of the Mind (Descartes) **2:**295

Rules of the Five Orders of Architecture, The (Barozzi) **1:**34

Rumania **1:**170

Rump Parliament **2:***344,* 351, 355

Runciman, Steven **1:**171

Runnymede, Battle of (1215) **4:**906

rural areas *see* agriculture; peasants; popular culture

Russell, Bertrand **4:**1068

Russell, Elizabeth **5:**1419, 1427

Russell, Francis, earl of Bedford **3:**820

Russell, John **5:**1419, 1427

Russia
  architecture **1:**49
  Black Death **2:**305
  calendar **1:**177, **4:**1024
  exploration **2:**384
  German towns **4:**1107
  Hanseatic League **2:**503
  icons **1:***168,* **3:***604*
  Ivan IV Vasilyevich **3:**652–656
  Lithuanian wars **4:**1109
  Muscovy **4:**933–941
  Orthodox Church **1:**166, **4:**935–936, 1109
  Poland **4:**1112, 1113, 1114
  puppet show **5:**1320
  Sweden **5:**1306–1307, 1308, 1309, 1311, 1334, 1337
  trade **2:**501

Russia Company **2:**501

Russian Orthodox Church **1:**166, **4:**935–936, 1109

Rustici, Cristofano **5:***1421*

Ruthven Raiders **5:**1262

Ryabushkin, Andreii Petrovich **3:***655*

Ryazan **4:**936

S

Saavedra, Isabel de **1:**204, 205

Sabbatarianism **2:**345, **3:**669, 671

Sacchi, Bartolomeo (Platina) **4:**1022, *1023*

Sachs, Hans **4:**960

sackbut **4:**958

Sackville, Thomas **3:**823

sacraments
  bibles **5:**1173
  Calvinism **1:**182

sacraments (cont.)
Florence, Council of **2:**431
Lutheranism **3:**764
preaching **5:**1163
Reformation **5:**1358
Roman Catholicism **1:**178
Trent, Council of **1:**186,
5:1197, 1357–1359, 1360
see also Eucharist; other
specific sacraments
Sacrifice of Isaac (Caravaggio)
1:193
Sacrobosco, Johannes de **1:**174
Sadoleto, Jacopo **1:**179, **3:**703
Safavid dynasty **3:**612,
620–621, 622–623, 626,
628–629
Safed (Galilee) **3:**680
Safi al-Din **3:**612, 620
Saggiatore, Il (Galileo) **2:**465,
466
Sagres **5:**1345
astronomical observatory
3:693
Sahagun, Bernardino **2:**308
Sahara Desert **2:**379, **4:**1137,
1142
sailing ships **2:**373, **3:**777–778
Saint-André, marshal of **2:**452
Saint Andrews University
5:1263, 1264, 1267
Saint Augustine (Florida)
4:891, 892
Saint Barnabas, Church of
(Milan) **5:**1204
Saint Bartholomew's Day
Massacre (1572) **1:**188,
200, 201, **2:**371, 441, 454,
455, 456, 516, 556, **3:**825,
4:1033, **5:**1331
Saint Basil the Blessed,
Cathedral of (Moscow)
3:*654*
Saint Bavo's Cathedral (Ghent)
2:387
Saint Benet's Church
(London) **5:***1431*
Saint Catherine's Monastery
(Sinai) **5:***1364*
Saint Crispin's Day **1:**18, 19,
3:599

Saint-Étienne-du-Mont,
Church of (Paris) **3:***698*
Saint Francis Cycle (Giotto)
2:488, 489, *491*
Saint Gall **1:**279
Saint-Germain, Peace of **1:**200,
2:454
Saint Guinefort, cult of **4:**1120
Saint Hubert, Chapel of **3:**714
Saint-Inglevert **1:***226*
Saint Jerome (Leonardo da
Vinci) **3:**708
Saint Jerome and the Lion
(Dürer) **2:**312
Saint Jerome in His Study
(Dürer) **2:**315
Saint Jerome in His Study
(Eyck) **2:**391
Saint John, Church of (Ghent)
2:387
Saint John, Knights of **1:**223,
3:619, 624, 626, 715
Saint John Lateran Basilica
(Rome) **1:**38, **2:**491
Saint John's College
(Cambridge) **5:**1367
Saint John's Night **4:**1118
Saint Lawrence River **4:**893,
896
Saint Leonard's College (Saint
Andrews University)
5:1264
Saint Mark's Basilica (Venice)
1:*258,* **4:**922, 951–952,
958, 1006, *1021,* **5:**1399
library of **3:**664
Saint Mark's Square (Venice)
1:*277,* **4:***1021*
Saint Martin's, Church of
(Ludgate) **1:**49
Saint-Mary-le-Bow, Church of
(London) **1:**49
Saint Mary Pammakaristos,
Church of (Constantinople)
1:263
Saint Mary's Church (Warsaw)
4:1112
Saint Marys City (Maryland)
4:894
Saint Matthew and the Angel
(Caravaggio) **1:**194

Saint Paul's Cathedral
(London) **1:**32, 48, 140,
212, **3:**665, 667, 668, 748,
755, **4:***1103,* **5:***1161,* 1166,
1328, 1430, 1431–1432,
1433
churchyard **3:**754
Saint Paul's Cathedral School
4:879, **5:**1323
Saint Peter's Basilica (Rome)
1:32, 38, *39,* 44, 124,
2:*358,* 491, **3:***855,* **4:**955,
1003, 1037, **5:**1228, 1232,
1234, 1432
Bernini **1:**98, 99, 100, 101,
5:1235
Bramante **1:**140, 142, 143,
5:1231
Caravaggio **1:**193
Charlemagne **1:**264
Christina's crypt **1:**231
Clement VI **3:**756, 757
indulgences **3:**757, **4:**1013,
5:1190
Leo X **3:**703, 704
Michelangelo **1:**32, 38, 98,
4:871, 873, 878, 1026,
5:1353
papacy **4:***1008,* 1026, 1037,
1040
Raphael **1:**48, **3:**703, **5:**1186
Second Vatican Council
5:*1363*
see also Sistine Chapel
Saint Petersburg **4:**941
Saint Peter's Square (Rome)
4:1026, 1040, **5:***1190*
Saint-Pierre-le Moutier, Battle
of (1429) **3:**658
Saint Quentin, Battle of
(1557) **4:**1056, 1059
saints **1:**178
Bernini depictions **1:**100
blood libel **3:**673
canonizations **4:**1036
feast days **4:**1118
iconoclasm **3:**604, 606
Joan of Arc **3:**657, 658, 662
miracle plays **5:**1318
More **4:**932
patron **5:**1317

pilgrimage **4:**1078, 1081,
1083
religious orders **5:**1208,
1209
sermons on **5:**1160
Sufi **3:**615
Trent, Council of **5:**1360
Saint Sebastian catacombs
(Rome) **4:***1027*
Saint Vitus, Cathedral of
(Prague) **1:**118
Saint Wenceslas, Chapel of
(Prague) **1:**118
Salamanca, University of
5:1207, 1367
Salazar y Palacios, Catalina de
1:204
Salerno, University of **5:**1367
Salic Law **2:**517, **3:**595
Salisbury House (London)
3:749
Salisbury Plain **3:**665
Salmon, Pierre **4:***1050*
salt **2:**504–505, **5:**1341
salt herring **5:**1341
Salutati, Coluccio **3:**584, 589,
684, 685
salvation **2:**339, 341, 343,
3:593, 761, 767, **4:**1064
Calvinism **1:**178, 180, 181,
182, 183, 185, 186,
5:1195, 1329
Lutheranism **5:**1189
preaching on **5:**1160
religious orders **5:**1201
Roman Catholic Church
1:180, 190, **5:**1197, 1198
Trent, Council of **1:**186,
5:1354
Tyndale **1:**232
see also faith alone,
justification by; good
works, salvation by;
predestination
Salve Deus Rex Judaeorum
(Lanier) **5:**1423
Salviati, Francesco **4:***1009*
Salviati, Giovanni **1:**246
Salviati, Jacopo **1:**246
Salviati, Lucrezia de' Medici
1:246

Salvini, Antonio **5**:*1403*

Salzburg **2**:475, *476*

Sambucus, Johannes **1**:*54*

Samson Agonistes (Milton)
    4:886, 887

San Ambrogio monastery
    (Milan) **1**:139

San Andrea, Church of
    (Mantua) **1**:139

San Carlo alle Quattro
    Fontane, Church of (Rome)
    1:45, **5**:1235

Sánchez Coello, Alonso **1**:*121*

Sandomierz Agreement (1570)
    4:1110

Sandoval y Rojas, Francisco de
    5:*1238*

San Fiorentino, monastery of
    3:707, 714

San Francesco, Church of
    (Assisi) **2**:487, 488, *529*

San Francesco, Church of
    (Perugia) **5**:1182

San Francesco, Church of
    (Ripa) **1**:100

San Francesco Grande,
    Church of (Milan) **3**:709

Sangallo, Antonio da (the
    Elder) **1**:38, 39, 44

Sangallo, Antonio da (the
    Younger) **1**:32, *33*, 38, 40,
    44, *47*, **4**:1026

Sangallo, Giuliano da **1**:44

San Gimignano **3**:*635*

San Giorgio dei Fiorentini,
    Church of (Rome) **1**:44

San Giorgio Maggiore,
    Church of (Venice) **3**:666,
    668, **4**:1006

San Giovanni del Fiorentini
    1:32

sanitation **2**:305–306

Sankt Jakob an der Birs, Battle
    of (1444) **5**:1314

San Lorenzo, Church of
    (Florence) **1**:35, 42, 152,
    154, **2**:417, 424, **4**:876
    Old Sacristy **1**:152

San Luigi dei Francesci,
    Church of (Rome) **1**:44,
    192, 193

San Marco, Church of
    (Florence) **4**:1077

San Marco, monastery of
    (Florence) **2**:417, 423

Sanmicheli, Michele **4**:1002,
    1004

San Pietro in Montorio, Church
    of (Rome) **1**:37, **5**:1231

San Quentin, Battle of (1557)
    4:1060

San Salvador **1**:248, 250,
    4:889

San Sebastiano, Church of
    (Mantua) **1**:36

San Sisto convent (Rome)
    1:123

Sansovino, Jacopo **1**:*43*, **3**:664,
    690, **4**:1001, 1002, 1004,
    1005, 1006, **5**:1399

San Stephano Rotondo (Rome)
    1:32

Santa Bibiana, Church of
    (Rome) **1**:98

Santa Croce, Church of
    (Florence) **1**:35, 153, *155*,
    2:466, 485, 489, **3**:*585*,
    5:*1225*

Santa Cruz **4**:889

Santa Fe Capitulations **1**:248

Sant'Agnese, Church of
    (Rome) **1**:45

Sant'Agostino, Church of
    (Rome) **1**:30, 193

Santa Hermandad (Spain)
    2:395

Santa Lucia, convent of **1**:197

Santa María (Columbus ship)
    1:248, 250, 251, 252

Santa Maria, Church of
    (Rome) **5**:1238

Santa Maria, Church of
    (Vallicella) **1**:193

Santa María de Belén **1**:254

Santa Maria degli Angeli,
    Church of (Florence) **1**:156

Santa Maria del Carmine,
    Church of (Florence) **3**:*589*,
    4:984

Santa Maria del Fiore,
    Cathedral of *see* Florence,
    Cathedral of

Santa Maria della Assunzione,
    Church of (Ariccia) **1**:32,
    100, 101

Santa Maria della Pace,
    Church of (Rome) **1**:37,
    140, 141

Santa Maria della Salute
    (Venice) **5**:*1392*

Santa Maria della Scala,
    Church of (Rome) **1**:193,
    194

Santa Maria della Vittoria,
    Church of (Rome) **5**:1235

Santa Maria delle Grazie,
    Church of (Milan) **1**:139

Santa Maria delle Grazie,
    monastery of **3**:710, 711

Santa Maria del Popolo,
    Church of (Rome) **1**:39,
    193

Santa Maria di Loreto, Church
    of (Rome) **1**:32, *33*

Santa Maria Maggiore Basilica
    (Rome) **1**:42, 44, 97, 98,
    4:1040

Santa Maria Novella, Church
    of (Florence) **1**:30, 36,
    2:*418*, 490

Santa Maria Presso Santo
    Satiro, Church of (Milan)
    1:139

Sant'Andrea, Church of
    (Mantua) **1**:36

Sant'Andrea al Quirinale,
    Church of (Rome) **1**:32, 45,
    100, 101, **3**:667

Santángel, Luis de **1**:251, 253

Sant'Angelo Castel (Rome) *see*
    Castel Sant'Angelo

Santa Susanna, Church of
    (Rome) **1**:44

Sant'Eligio degli Orefici,
    Church of (Rome) **1**:38, 40,
    5:1186

San Teodoro, Church of
    (Pavia) **5**:*1402*

Sant'Eufemia, Church of
    (Verona) **3**:*676*

Santi, Giovanni **5**:1180, 1181,
    1185

Santiago, Order of **5**:1390

Santiago de Compostela
    4:1060, *1078*, 1079, 1080,
    1082, 1083

Santiago de Compostela,
    Cathedral of **4**:*1072*

Santi Luca e Martina, Church
    of (Rome) **1**:32

Santissima Annunziata,
    Church of (Florence) **1**:32

Sant'Ivo chapel (Rome) **1**:45

Santo Domingo **1**:248, 253,
    254, **5**:1342

smallpox **2**:307

Santo Spirito, Church of
    (Florence) **1**:139, 152, 154

Santo Tomé, Church of
    (Toledo) **5**:*1284*

Sanzio, Raffaello *see* Raphael

Saône River **4**:965

Saraceni, Carlo **1**:194

Sardinia **1**:207, 208, **2**:511

Sarpi, Paolo **4**:1038

Satan **4**:880

satire **1**:203

Sauchieburn, Battle of (1488)
    5:1261, 1296

Saudi Arabia **3**:611, **4**:1078

Saule (goddess) **4**:1105

Savery, Thomas **3**:775

savings and loan societies
    5:1162

Savonarola, Girolamo **1**:137,
    138, **3**:707, 769, 855
    Florence **2**:422, 423
    Pico della Mirandola
        4:1076–1077
    preaching **5**:1160

Savoy **2**:449, **3**:715,
    5:1315–1316

Savoy, duke of *see* Felix V
    (antipope)

Savoy Palace (London) **1**:216,
    3:749, **4**:1047

Saxony **2**:505, **5**:1335, 1337
    education **2**:324
    Holy Roman Empire **2**:548,
        553, 556
    Luther **4**:1013
    Schütz and **5**:1244, 1245,
        1246, 1247
    vernaculars **5**:1222–1223

Scaliger, Joseph **3:**585, 592, 594

Scamozzi, Vincenzo **1:**34, **3:**664, 665, 668

Scarlatti, Alessandro **1:**230

Scène Galante at the Gates of Paris **4:***1028*

Sceptical Chymist, The (Boyle) **5:***1256*

Sceve, Maurice **4:**1051

Schaffhausen **5:**1314

Scheldt River **5:***1344*

Schermer polder (Holland) **1:***275*

Schertlin, Sebastian **1:**243

Scherzi musicali (Monteverdi) **4:**917

Schilderboeck, Het (van Mander) **1:**148

Schiller, Friedrich von **5:**1312

Schilling, Diebold **5:***1313*

Schipol (airport) **1:**275

Schleswig, duchy of **2:**506

Schleswig-Holstein **5:**1338

Schmalkalden, Articles of **3:**763

Schmalkalden, Battle of (1547) **5:**1336

Schmalkaldic League **1:**121, **2:**555, **3:**767, **5:**1191, 1200

Schöffer, Peter **5:**1169

scholarships **2:**322

Scholastic (hermit) **1:**168

Scholastica, Saint **5:**1201

Scholasticism **1:**181, **3:**696
Aristotle **1:**54, 57, 58–59, 61
Bacon vs. **1:**81
Cartesianism vs. **2:**294
Erasmus vs. **2:**357, 359, 362
humanism vs. **3:**582, 583, 588, 592, 593, **5:**1365, 1368–1369, 1372, 1373
Luther **5:**1371
nominalism vs. **1:**181
overview of **2:**357, 358
Petrarch vs. **4:**1049, 1054–1055
Pico della Mirandola vs. **4:**1075
Platonism vs. **1:**57, 261

Scholemaster, The (Ascham) **2:**327

Schöner Dialogus von Martino, Ein (woodcut) **5:***1192*

Schongauer, Martin **2:**311, 314

School of Abuse (Gosson) **3:**725

School of Athens, The (Raphael) **1:**38, *50, 143,* **3:**703, **4:**1025, 1061, **5:**1186

School of Night **3:**825

schools *see* education

Schooten, Joris van **5:**1211

Schütz, Heinrich **4:**952, **5:1244–1247**

Schwyz **5:**1312

science **2:**559, **3:**782–783, 784, **5:1248–1259**
Aristotle **1:**53, 57, 59, 60–61, 81
astrology **1:**74
Bacon **1:**80–82, 83
Copernicus **1:**265–272
Descartes **2:**294, 295, 296, *297*
education **2:**319, 325
Galileo **2:**460–468, **3:**690, 699
Greek studies **2:**320
heresy **2:**539
Hobbes **2:**542, 543, 544, 546
Hooke **5:**1433
Leonardo da Vinci **3:**709, 710
mathematics **3:**827, 830–831, 832
natural philosophy **4:**1065, 1067–1068, 1069, 1070, 1072
printing **5:**1173
Renaissance **5:**1221, 1226
Spain **5:**1284
vernaculars **3:**693, 696, 699
Wren **5:**1429–1430
see also medicine; technology

scientific method **1:**60, **2:**468, 532, 546

scientific revolution *see* science

Scipio **4:**1052

Scot, John **5:**1425

Scotch-Irish **1:**189

Scotichronicon (Bower) **5:**1260

Scotland **5:1260–1267,** 1330
Calvinism **1:**189, 190, **2:**346, 349, **5:**1196, 1198, 1265–1267, 1298
Charles I **1:**239, **2:**344
divorce law **2:**568
education **2:**323
Elizabeth I **2:**327, 330–331, 332
England **2:**343, 344, 346, **5:**1296, 1297, 1300, 1413
English civil wars **2:**348, 349, 351, 352, 353, 354, 372
established church **2:**349, 353, 369, 372
Henry VIII **2:**522, 527–528
Hundred Years War **3:**595, 597
Mary, Queen of Scots **2:**327, 330–331
monarchy **2:**342, **4:**904, 905, **5:**1224
Reformation Parliament **5:**1298
Spanish armada **2:**331
Stuarts **5:**1296–1303, 1426
see also Church of Scotland

Scots Engagers **2:**354

Scottish Confession **1:**189

scripture *see* bibles

scrofula **2:***519*

Scrovegni, Enrico **2:**486, *487*

Scrovegni, Reginaldo **2:**486

Scudéry, Madeleine de **4:**898

sculpture **4:980–999**
architectural ornaments **1:**38, 42, 44
Bernini **1:**44, 97–101
Florence **2:**418, 424, 425
iconoclasm **3:**604–609
Italian city-states **3:**641
Leonardo da Venci **3:**707, 709–710
Leo X **3:**703
Medicis **3:**855, 856
Michelangelo **1:**42, **4:**870–878
Renaissance **5:**1225
Rome **5:**1235
Venice **5:**1399

Scuole (charities) **3:**640–641

scurvy **2:**379

scutage **2:**409

sea battles *see* naval warfare

seafaring *see* ships and shipping

Seager, Jane **5:**1427

sea monster **2:***375, 380*

Sebastian, king of Portugal **4:**1140

Second (Greater) Cloister, Santa Croce (Florence) **1:***155*

Second and Third Blast of Retrait from Plaies and Theaters (Munday) **5:**1324

seconda prattica **4:**916, 918, 921

secondary cause **1:**182

secondary schools **2:**319, 320, 321, 322, 325

Second Bishops' War **2:**349

second estate (France) **2:**439

Second Prayer Book (1551) **1:**189

Second Schmalkaldic War **1:**75

Second Vatican Council **2:**430, **5:**1363, 1364

Secreta secretorum (treatise) **3:**595

Secret of the Universe (Kepler) **3:**832

Secretum meum (Petrarch) **4:**1052

secularization **5:**1188, 1198

sedition **5:**1175

Sefer hazohar (kabbalistic text) **3:***680*

Sefiroth **3:***680*

Segni, Bernardo **1:**59

Seine River **1:**16, **3:**662, 809, **4:**1034, 1035

Sejm (Polish assembly) **4:**1108, 1111, 1113

Self-Portrait at the Age of Fifty-Two (Rembrandt) **5:**1214

Self-Portrait at Twenty-six (Dürer) **2:**313

Self-Portrait Leaning on a Sill (Rembrandt) **5:**1214

self-portraits
Dürer 2:*311*, 312, 313
Rembrandt 5:*1210*, 1214
Selim I, Ottoman sultan 2:555, 3:622–623
seminaries 5:1357
Seneca 3:590, 729, 732, 734
Calvin's commentary 1:181
Italian stage revivals 5:1320
Senfl, Ludwig 4:950, 951
Senftenberg, Veit Wolff von 5:*1415*
Senigallia (Sinigaglia) 4:1091, 5:1383
Senta, Battle of (1697) 2:513
Sephardim 3:670
Septuagint 1:103, 104, 109, 3:695
Serbia 1:170, 263, 3:616
serfdom 1:21, 28, 3:655, 656, 4:937, 940
Poland 4:1108
Seripando, Girolamo *see* Marcellus II, Pope
Serlio, Sebastiano 1:31, 34, 43, 45, 140, 3:665, 4:1001, 1002, 1004
Sermoneta 1:*124*
sermons *see* preaching
Serrur, Calixte-Joseph 5:*1262, 1426*
servants 3:635, 636
Servetus, Michael 1:187, 2:539
Servites 4:1038
Seven Deadly Sins, The (Bosch) 1:129
Seven Golden Cities of Cibola 2:382
Seven Last Words of Christ on the Cross, The (Schütz) 5:1247
Seventy-five Theses (Erastus) 2:367
Seven Works of Mercy (Caravaggio) 1:194
Seville
Columbus's funerary monument 1:*255*
Murillo 5:1386
Velázquez 5:1384, 1385

Sevillian Academy of Fine Arts 5:1386
sextant 5:1250
Seymour, Edward 2:528, 3:608, 5:1411
Calvinism 1:188, 236
Seymour, Jane 1:236, 2:522, 524, 527, 528
Sforza, Ascanio 1:123
Sforza, Bianca 2:509, 4:1087
Sforza, Bona 4:1109
Sforza, Caterina 5:1427, 1428
Sforza, Francesco 2:417, 3:709, 742, 4:1087, 1088, 1090, 5:1403, 1404
Sforza, Francesco II 1:208, 3:646, 647, 743
Sforza, Galeazzo Maria 3:742, 5:1428
Sforza, Giangaleazzo Maria 3:742
Sforza, Giovanni 1:123, 124
Sforza, Ludovico 1:36, 139, 278, 3:645, 710, 742
Sforza, Massimiliano 3:645, 646, 742–743
Sforzas, the 1:31, 42, 141, 3:638, 641, 645, 646, 5:1382, 1427, 1428
Charles V 1:208
Lombardy 3:742–743, 744, 745
Venice 5:1394
Viscontis 5:1403, 1406
Sforzinda (theoretical city) 1:31
Shahnama (Persian text) 3:629
Shakespeare, Hamnet 5:1269
Shakespeare, Judith 5:1269, 1275
Shakespeare, Susanna 5:1269, 1275
Shakespeare, William 2:335, 3:600, *603*, 664, 671, 724–726, 727, 731, 732, 733, 737, 4:880, 916, 928, **5:1268–1276**, 1322
Aristotelian unities 5:1321
blank verse 3:823
English language 1:108

English theater 5:1324–1325, 1326, 1328, 1329
fool depiction 5:1319
history plays 1:17, 19
Jesuit plays 5:1323
London 3:751
Marlowe 3:826
Middleton collaboration 5:1329
nationalism 4:963
religion 5:1326–1327
Renaissance 5:1223, 1225
sonnet 4:1052, 5:1270
Sonnet 18 3:726
Sonnet 130 3:725
sharia 3:612, 614, 623
Shatir, Ibn al- 1:271
Shaw, George Bernard 3:692
Sheep Well, The (Vega) 3:728
Sheldonian Theatre (Oxford) 5:1430
Shelley, Percy Bysshe 1:113, 5:1290
Shelton, Thomas 1:205
Shepheardes Calender, The (Spenser) 3:737, 5:1287, 1288
Shetland Islands 5:1296
Shia Islam 3:611, 620–622
shields 2:*410*
Ship of Fools, The (Bosch) 1:128, *132*
ships and shipping 1:63, 2:506
Black Death 2:306
canal transport 5:1402
design 3:773, 777–778, 786, 4:1138, 5:1412
disease 2:302, 304–305, 306
exploration 2:373–385
Hanseatic League 2:502, 505
insurance 1:91
Portugal 4:1138, *1143*, 1145, 5:*1342*, 1345
shipbuilding 3:811, 5:1283
technology 5:1343, 1347
trade 5:1340–1341, 1342, 1344–1345, 1347, 1349, 1350–1351, 1393
Venice 5:1393–1394
warfare 5:1412
see also navigation

Shipwreck Caused by Demons (unattributed) 2:*377*
Short Parliament 2:349, 351
Short Treatise on God, Man, and His Well-Being (Spinoza) 5:1292
Shottery 5:1269
Shrewsbury, Battle (1403) 1:17
Shrewsbury, earl of *see* Talbot
shrines 4:1078–1079, 1082, 1083, 1084, 1085
Shrove Tuesday 4:*1119*
Shuisky, Andrew 3:652, 653
Shuisky family 3:652
Shulham 'arukh (Caro) 3:680
Shute, John 1:34
Shuysky, Vasily *see* Vasily Shuysky
Siberia 3:656, 4:933, 936–937, 938, 940
Sicily 2:511, 3:684
Byzantine jurisdiction 1:259
Charles V 1:207, 208
plague 2:304
Spain 5:1278, 1279
Sidereus nuncius (Galileo) 2:464, *465*
Sidney, Mary 3:725, 726, 738
Sidney, Philip 3:724, 725, 737, 738, 823, 4:1052, 5:1287, 1416
Sidney, Robert 3:824, 5:1422
Sidney, Thomas 5:1416
Siena 1:281, 2:413, 419, 3:637, 638, 701, 853
Italian wars 3:643, 644, 649
painting 2:492
theater 3:734
Viscontis 5:1404
Siena, Cathedral of 1:*30*, 4:872, 1091
Siena, University of 4:1086, 1088, 5:1367
Sierra Leone 2:380
Siete Partidas 3:693
Sigismund, Holy Roman emperor 1:119, 2:318, 508, 509, 549, 3:745, 4:1073
Sigismund, king of Hungary 1:158, 3:616

Sigismund I, king of Poland **4:**1109, 1110, **5:**1307, 1308, 1310

Sigismund II, king of Poland **1:**200, **3:**654, **4:**1109, 1110, 1112

Sigismund III Vasa, king of Poland **4:**939, 1112–1113

signature literacy **5:**1173

Signoria (Florence) **3:**851

Silesia **1:**116, **5:**1335, 1337

Silk Road **2:**302, **3:**805, **5:**1341

silks **2:**373, 380, **3:**633, 740, 805

trade **5:**1344, 1393, 1394

silver **5:**1284, 1285

Antwerp **5:**1344

exploration **5:**1345

trade **5:**1344, 1349

Simeon, grand prince of Moscow and Vladimir **4:**933

Simmons, Samuel **4:**879

Simonetta, Cicco **3:**742

Simon of Trent (blood libel) **3:**673

Simons, Menno **5:**1195

simony **4:**1023

sin **4:**1064, *1066*

Calvinist theocracy **1:**186–187

Cartesian **2:**300

Lutheran **3:**757, 759, 762, 763, 765, 766

Luther vs. Calvin on **1:**185

Luther vs. Erasmus on **2:**339

see also original sin

Sinan Bey **3:***618*

Sindel, Jan **3:**779

Sinigaglia *see* Senigallia

Sir Gawain and the Green Knight (Pearl Poet) **1:**220

Sisters of Charity **5:**1208

Sistine Chapel (Rome) **1:**42, 47, **4:***986,* 988, 994, 1022, **5:**1182, 1230, *1354*

Botticelli **1:**133, 135, 138

Byzantine philosopher **1:**169

Michelangelo **1:**135, 244, **4:**870, 871, 873,

874–875, 877, 878, 1025, **5:**1220, 1231

tapestry **5:***1158*

Sitoni, Giovanni Francesco **1:**280

Six Articles of Faith (1539) **1:**235, 240, **2:**527

Sixtus II, Saint **5:***1221*

Sixtus IV, Pope **1:**133, 277, **3:**673, 852, **4:**907, 975, 1022, *1023,* **5:**1230–1231, 1278, 1379, 1428

calendar reform **1:**175

Sixtus V, Pope **1:**40, 44, 45, 277, **2:**442, **4:**1022

Sixty-seven Articles (Zwingli) **5:**1315

Skála, Jan **1:**280

Skåne **5:**1311

slavery

African trade **1:**255, **4:**1141, **5:**1285, 1342, 1345, 1348, 1349

Columbus voyages **1:**252, 253, 254, 255

exploration **2:**380, **5:**1285

missionaries **4:**891, 892, 895

Ottoman Empire **3:**617, 622, 625

Venetian trade **5:**1393

Slavs **1:**170

Slovenia **4:**1042

Sluter, Claus **4:**981

Sluys, Battle of (1340) **3:**596

smallpox **1:**255, **2:**307, 308, **3:**755, 843

smelting **3:**811

Smith, Adam **5:**1348–1349

Smith, Cyril Stanley **2:**383

Smith, J. C. **5:***1429*

Smolensk **4:**936, 940, **5:**1337

Smolensk, War of **5:**1337

Smythe, John **5:**1350

Snellick, Jan **5:***1414*

Snyders, Frans **5:**1241

social class

armies **5:**1411, 1414

education **2:**317, 318–319, 321–322

feudal hierarchy **2:**401–413

Florence **2:**415, 417, 419

French three estates **2:**439

German towns **2:**478, 479

households **2:**561–569

humanism **3:**593, 594

infant mortality **5:**1420–1421

interactions **4:**1123

Italian city-states **3:**634–635

knighthood **1:**221

language **3:**691, 692

Lutheranism **2:**553–554

manufacturing **3:**805, 809, 821

marriage and family life **5:**1418–1419, 1420, 1421

peasants' revolt **4:**1042–1048

Polish Jews **4:**1111

popular culture **4:**1115–1123

sumptuary laws **4:**979, 1041

women's status **5:**1416–1418, 1419, 1422, *1423,* 1425–1427

see also nobility and rank; peasants

social contract **2:**542, 545

social life *see* popular culture

Society of Jesus *see* Jesuits

Socrates **4:**1092–1093, 1094, 1095

"So Crewell a Prison" (Surrey) **3:**723

Soderini, Pietro **4:**872

Sodo, Hernando de **2:**382

Solander, Daniel **5:**1258

solar year **1:**174

Solemn League and Covenant (1643) **2:**351

soliloquy **5:**1272, 1275

solipsism **2:**301

Solomon's Ophir **2:**384–385

Solothurn **5:**1314

Solway Moss, Battle of (1542) **2:**527, **5:**1261, 1297

Somerset, duke of *see* Seymour, Edward

Somerset House (London) **3:**749

Somme River **1:**17

Songhay Empire **3:**612

Song of Roland, The (romance) **1:**222, **3:**695

sonnet **3:**720, 722, 723, 724–726

Italian **5:**1279

Petrarchan **4:**1049, 1050, 1052

Shakespearean **3:**725, 726, **4:**1052, **5:**1270

Sonnets pour Hélène (Ronsard) **3:**722

Sonni Ali **3:**612

Sophia Palaeologa **4:**934

Sophocles **3:**685, 688, 729

Sorbonne *see* Paris, University of

Sorbonne, Church of the (France) **1:**48

sorcerers **2:**533, 534

Soto, Hernando de **2:**382, **4:**888

soul **2:**300

South America *see* Americas; *specific countries*

Southeast Asia **5:**1341

South Pacific **5:**1258–1259

Southwell, Robert **4:**896, **5:**1424

souvenirs of pilgrimage **4:***1083*

Spadas, the **1:**40, 41

Spain **5:**1277–1285

agriculture **1:**21

architecture **1:**46–47, 141

armada **1:**62–66, 238, **2:**331, 332, **4:**1060, 1145

baroque art **4:**994

Black Legend **2:**400

Bosch paintings **1:**131, 132

Catherine de Médicis **1:**198, 199, 200

Cervantes **1:**202–206

Charles V **1:**207, 208, 209, 211, 241

colonial settlements **1:**242

Columbus **1:**247–248, 250–255

Counter-Reformation **5:**1199

dams **1:**279, 280

Elizabeth I **2:**331, 332–333

English Catholics **2:**342, **5:**1301

Spain (cont.)
established church **2:**370
exploration **2:**306, 307–308,
373, 381, 382, **3:**788,
4:888–889, 1138, 1142,
5:1283–1284, 1285,
1342, 1345, 1346
Ferdinand and Isabella
2:393–400, *411,*
5:1425–1426
feudalism **2:**408
France **2:**442, 453, 458
Gregorian calendar **1:**176
Hapsburgs **1:**164, **2:**438,
445, 507, 510, 511, 512,
515, 556, 557, **3:**715
Holy Roman Empire **2:**558,
560
humanism **3:**590, 591, 592
Hundred Years War **3:**598
infantry **3:**651
Inquisition *see* Spanish
Inquisition
Islam **3:**612, 613, 676, 678
Italian city-states **1:**208,
5:1224, 1231, 1234
Italian wars **3:**630, 642, 643,
644–651, 702, 703,
4:966
Judaism **3:**669, 670, 671,
672, 674, 676–679, 680,
4:1139
land holdings **4:**965–966
loans **1:**88
Lombardy **3:**746–747
Magellan voyage **3:**788–794
missionaries **4:**888–892, 895,
896
monarchy **4:**904–905, 907,
5:1218, 1220, 1224, 1225
music **4:**956–957, 959
Naples **3:**743
nationalism **4:**963, 965
nobility **4:**971
Ottoman Empire **3:**626,
715, 716
papacy **5:**1234
Philip II **4:**1056–1060
pilgrimage **4:**1060, *1078,*
1079, 1080, 1082
poetry **3:**726

Portugal **4:**1138, 1141, 1142,
1145
prose fiction **3:**738–739
Reconquista **2:**398, **3:**676,
678, **4:**956, 969, **5:**1322,
1425
religious orders
5:1205–1206, 1207
Roman Catholic Church
2:370
Rome **5:**1232–1234
Rubens **5:**1237, 1242
Stuarts **5:**1301, 1336
theater **3:**726–727, 729, 731,
5:1317, 1318, 1319,
1320, 1321, 1322–1323
Thirty Years War **5:**1336,
1337 1338
trade **3:**633, **5:**1341, 1344,
1347, 1350
universities **5:**1367
Urbino **5:**1381
Velázquez **5:**1384–1391
vernaculars **3:**693, 694–695,
4:963, **5:**1222, 1282,
1284
see also Netherlands
Spanish Inquisition **2:**362,
532, **3:**592, **4:**1139,
5:1278, 1279, 1283
Black Legend **2:**400
Ferdinand and Isabella **2:**393,
396, 397, 400
humanism **2:**362
Islam **3:**613
Judaism **3:**677, 678, **5:**1291
Paul III **4:**1018, 1019
Philip II **4:**1058
Torquemada **2:**533
women **5:**1424
Spanish language **3:**670, 693,
694–695, 696, **5:**1222
Spanish Netherlands *see*
Netherlands
Spanish road **3:**746
Spanish Royal Academy **3:**694
Spanish Tragedy (Kyd) **3:**732,
5:*1325*
Sparrman, Anders
5:1258–1259
Speed, John **5:***1297*

Spenser, Edmund **2:**335,
3:721, 725, 726, 737, 754,
5:1286–1290
Spenserian stanza **5:**1290
Speusippus **4:**1095
Speyer, Diet of (1526) **5:**1193
Spice Islands **2:**373, **3:**787,
789, **4:**894, 1015
spice trade **5:**1341, 1344
Columbus **1:**247
exploration **2:**373, 380, 381
Italian city-states **3:**630, 633
Magellan **3:**787, 788
Netherlands **4:**1141, 1145
Portugal **4:**1139, 1142,
5:1344
Venice **5:**1393
Spinners, The (Velázquez)
5:1390
Spinoza, Baruch **4:**1071–1072,
5:1291–1295
spirits **4:**1121
Spiritual Canticle (John of the
Cross) **5:**1207
Spiritual Exercises (Ignatius of
Loyola) **1:**99, **5:**1199, 1206
Spoleto **1:**124, **5:**1379
Spozalizio (Raphael) **5:**1182
Spranger, Bartholomeus **2:**559,
4:990
Sprenger, Jacob **3:**802
Squadrone Volante **1:**230
Stafford, Edward **2:**375
stained-glass windows **3:***607*
Stalin, Joseph **3:**656
Stalingrad, Battle of (1942)
4:1107
Stångebro, Battle of (1598)
5:1308
stanza, Spenserian **5:**1290
Stanza della Segnatura
(Vatican) **5:**1181,
1186–1187
Stanza dell'Incendio di Borgo
(Rome) **5:**1187
Stanza di Eliodoro (Vatican)
5:1187
Star Chamber, Court of
5:1328
Starry Messenger, The (Galileo)
2:464, **5:**1253

Starry Messenger, The (Lilly)
1:*72*
stars **1:**68, 266, 271
celestial chart **1:***67, 69*
state and church *see* church-
state relations; established
churches
Stationers' Company **5:**1170
steam engine **3:**775, 785, 786,
812, **5:**1259
Stefaneschi, Cardinal **2:**487,
491
Stefaneschi altarpiece (Giotto)
2:490, 491
Steinau **5:**1337
stem family **2:**561
Sten Sture (the Elder), regent
of Sweden **5:**1304
Sten Sture (the Younger),
regent of Sweden
5:1304–1305
Stephen, Saint **5:***1284*
Stephen Báthory, king of
Poland **4:**1112
Stereometrics of Wine Casks
(Kepler) **3:**828, 831
Stevin, Simon **1:**275, **3:**831,
5:1250
Stewart, Walter **5:**1296
Stiatessi, Pierre Antonio
2:469, 471
Stiatessi, Prudentia **2:**471, 474
*Stigmatization of Saint Francis,
The* (Giotto) **2:**490
Stimmer, Tobias **2:***367,*
4:*1075*
Stirling Castle (Scotland)
5:*1263,* 1264
Stjerneborg observatory
5:1251
Stockholm **1:**228, **5:**1304,
1307, 1309
Descartes **2:**301
Stoffels, Hendrickje **5:**1212,
1215, 1217
Stolbova, Peace of (1617)
4:940, **5:**1309, 1334
Stonehenge **3:**665
Stone of Scone **5:***1301*
Stoning of Saint Stephen
(Rembrandt) **5:**1212

storage dam **1**:280

Stoss, Veit **4**:1112

Stow, J. **5**:*1161*

Strafford, earl of *see* Wentworth, Thomas

Stralsund **2**:503, **5**:1164, 1334

Strasbourg **1**:77, 179, 188, **2**:475, 482, 507, 558, **5**:1169

Strasbourg, University of **5**:1377

Stratford-upon-Avon **5**:1268, 1269, 1271, 1274–1275, 1322

Strigel, Bernhard **2**:550

Striggio, Alessandro **4**:919

Stroganovs, the **4**:936

Strozzi, Clarissa **1**:197

Strozzi, Filippo **2**:420

Strozzi, Tito and Ercole **1**:125

Struggle between Carnival and Lent, The (Bruegel the Elder) **4**:*1119*

Stuart, Mary *see* Mary, Queen of Scots

Stuarts, the **1**:189, **5**:*1296–1303,* 1426
  architecture **1**:40, 47, 48
  Church of England **1**:239–240
  England **5**:1262
  English civil wars **1**:109, **2**:347–355, **4**:906, **5**:1303, 1325
  iconoclasm **3**:609
  Jones's architecture **3**:663, 664–665, 666–667, 668
  monarchy **2**:342–346
  Puritans **1**:188
  Restoration **1**:240
  Scotland **5**:1260–1267
  theater **5**:1322
  Thirty Years War **5**:1336

Stubbes, Philip **4**:1118

studia humanitatis **3**:588, 592, 594

studium generale **5**:1366, 1368, 1371, 1372

Study of a Bather (Michelangelo) **4**:873

Sture *see* Sten Sture; Svante Sture

Styria **2**:557

Styrian Hapsburgs **2**:508, 509

Sudbury, Simon **4**:1043, 1046

Sufi, al- **1**:*271*

Sufism **3**:612, 614–615, 620, 621, 622, 625

sugar plantations **4**:1141

sugar trade **5**:1344, 1346, 1348, 1393

Süleyman I (the Magnificent), Ottoman sultan **1**:210, **2**:512, 555, **3**:623, 625, 681

Sulpicians **5**:*1361*

sultanate **3**:625–626, 628

Sumatra **4**:1142

Sumerians **1**:173

Summa theologiae (Thomas Aquinas) **1**:52

"Summoner's Tale, The" (Chaucer) **5**:1202

sumptuary laws **4**:979, 1041

sun **2**:464, 465, 467

sun-centered universe *see* heliocentric universe

Sunni Islam **3**:610, 611, 620, 621, 623, 626

supernova **1**:50, **2**:463

Surgant, Johann Ulrich **3**:698

surgeons **3**:840, 841, 843
  dissection **2**:302

Surprise de Meaux see Meaux, conspiracy of

surrealism **1**:131, 132

Surrender of Breda, The (Velázquez) **5**:1385, 1388

Surrey, earl of *see* Howard, Henry

Susanna and the elders **5**:1355

Susannah and the Elders (Gentileschi) **2**:470, 471, 473, 474

Susato, Tielman **4**:950

Svante Sture **5**:1304

Swabian League **2**:480, 550

Swammerdam, Jan **5**:1258

Swanenburg, Jacob Isaaczoon van **5**:1210

Swan Theatre (London) **5**:1326

sweating sickness **3**:841

Sweden **5**:**1304–1311**
  banking **1**:90
  Christina **1**:227–231
  Descartes **2**:301
  established church **2**:370, 372
  guilds **2**:493
  Hanseatic League **2**:503, 505, 506
  Hapsburgs **2**:480
  literacy **2**:323
  Lutheranism **2**:370
  Maximilian I **3**:839
  monarchy **4**:909, 911
  Muscovy **4**:933, 934, 937, 939, 940, 941
  Poland **4**:1111, 1112–1113, 1114
  Reformation **5**:1191
  Russia **3**:653
  Thirty Years War **1**:228, **2**:371, 372, **5**:1330, 1332–1338, 1415
  trade **5**:1341
  university **5**:1367

Swedish Africa Company **5**:*1349*

Swedish Polish War **5**:1309, 1334–1335

Sweelinck, Jan Pieterszoon **4**:954, 960

Swinburne, Algernon Charles **3**:823

Swiss Brethren **5**:1314

Swiss Guards **5**:1314

Switzerland **2**:509, **3**:742, **5**:**1312–1316**
  Black Death **2**:305
  Burgundy **1**:163
  Calvinism **1**:178, 188
  dams **1**:279, 280
  education **2**:322, 324
  humanism **2**:312, **3**:585
  iconoclasm **3**:606–607, 609
  infantry **3**:651
  Italian wars **3**:645, 646
  markets **3**:819
  national history **4**:964

Reformation **1**:178, 179, 181, 188, **5**:1193, 1195, 1196, 1198

Reformation music **4**:952
  warfare **5**:1313, 1315, 1411, 1413
  witch hunts **5**:1425
  see also Geneva

Swynford, Catherine **1**:214

syllogism **1**:50, 81

Sylvester I, Pope **3**:594, 686

Symbolic Logic (Venn) **4**:1068

symbolism, Dürer images **2**:313, 314

Symphoniae sacrae (Schütz) **5**:1246

Symposium (Plato) **4**:1092, 1095, 1102

synagogues **3**:669, 672, *675, 678,* 679, 681

Syndics of the Clothmakers' Guild, The (Rembrandt) **5**:*1216,* 1217

Syntagma musicum (Praetorius) **4**:958

syphilis **1**:255, **2**:308–309, 310, **3**:840, 841, 843–844

Syria **1**:260, **2**:429, **3**:623
  Islam **3**:612, 617, 623

Syriac language **3**:695

Systema naturae (Linnaeus) **5**:1258

szlachta (Polish nobility) **4**:1108, 1111, 1113

T

Table Talk (Luther) **1**:102

Taccola, Mariano **1**:280, **5**:*1407*

Tacitus **3**:588, 590, **4**:923

Tagus River **1**:280, **4**:1141

Taikosama *see* Hideyoshi Toyotomi

Tainos (people) **1**:250–251, 252–253

Talbot, Elizabeth **5**:*1264*

Talbot, George, earl of Shrewsbury **5**:1420

Talbot, Grace **5**:1420

Talbot, John, earl of Shrewsbury **2**:*404*

Talbot Shrewsbury Book of
Romances **3:**601
Tale of a Tub (Jonson) **3:**663
Tallinn (Reval) **2:**503, **5:**1307
Tallis, Thomas **4:**953
Talmud **3:**669, 672, 674
Tamburlaine the Great
(Marlowe) **3:**822, 824
Tamerlane *see* Timur Lenk
Tametsi decree (1563) **5:**1362
Taming of the Shrew, The
(Shakespeare) **5:**1271, 1274
tangents **3:**833
Tannenberg, Battle of (1410)
1:223, **4:**1106, 1107
Tannenberg, Battle of (1914)
4:1107
tapestries **1:**163, *242,* **5:**1237
Tapia, Gonzalo de **4:**890
Tartaglia, Niccolò **3:**829
Tartuffe (Molière) **4:**899,
900–901
Tasman, Abel **2:**385
Tassi, Agostino **2:**469–474
Tasso, Torquato **1:**223, **3:**721,
4:922
Tatars **3:**653, 654, **4:**933, 934,
936, 938, **5:**1337
Taula (Barcelona bank) **1:**89
Tauler, Johannes **1:**185, **3:**760,
4:1065
Taverner, John **1:**280
Tavola Strozzi **4:**1130
taxation **4:**1135
church-state tensions **1:**180
English civil wars **2:**347, 352
feudal levies **2:**407, 408, 409
Florence **2:**421
France **2:**456
households **2:**568–569
Maximilian I **2:**550
Ottoman **3:**617, 626
peasants' revolts **1:**216,
4:1042–1043, 1047
Sweden **1:**228
Tebaldeo, Antonio **1:**125
technology **5:**1248–1259
agriculture **1:**21, 24, 25,
26–27, 28, 29, **4:**1134
Brunelleschi's inventions
1:156

dams and drainage
1:273–281
Leonardo da Vinci's
inventions **3:**709, 710
machines **3:**774–786, 819
manufacturing **3:**804–812
seafaring **5:**1343, 1347
warfare **5:**1309, 1407–1415
see also printing
telescope **1:**60, **2:**539, **3:**699,
775, 783, **4:**1069, **5:**1250,
1251, 1252, 1253, 1258
Descartes **2:**297
Galileo **1:**271, **2:**460, 463,
464, **3:**774
Tell, William **5:**1312
Temperance (Pollaiuolo) **1:**134
Tempe Restored (Jones masque)
3:663
Tempest, The (Giorgione)
4:989
Tempest, The (Shakespeare)
5:1271, 1275
Tempietto (Rome) **1:**32, 37,
38, 139, 140, 141, **5:**1231
*Temptation of Saint Anthony,
The* (Bosch) **1:**128, 129
Ten, Council of (Venice)
5:1397, 1400
Ten Articles (1536) **2:**525
Ten Books on Architecture
(Vitruvius) **1:**33, 34, 35,
37, **3:**668, **4:**1001
Ten Commandments **5:**1158,
1170
tenebrism **4:**994, 997, **5:**1386
Tenochtitlán **2:**307
"Tenure of Kings and
Magistrates, The" (Milton)
4:884
Terbrugghen, Hendrik **4:**997
Terence **3:**683, 687, 729, 732,
733, **5:**1320
Teresa of Ávila **1:**100, **5:**1207,
1427
Terpsichore (Praetorius) **4:**950
Terra Australis myth
2:384–385
Tertiary Order of Saint Francis
1:206
terza rima **1:**113

Teseida (Boccaccio) **1:**113, 217
Tetrabiblos (Ptolemy) **1:**69
Tetzel, Johann **3:**757, **5:**1189,
1190, 1191
Teutonic Knights, Order of the
1:222, 223, **2:**506
Hanseatic League **5:**1304,
1306
Poland **4:**1104, 1106, 1107
textiles **3:**786, 808
Flanders **1:**157
German towns **2:**476, 477
Italian city-states **3:**630, 631,
633
manufacturing **3:**740, 741,
750, *753,* 805
milling **1:**279, **3:**806, *807,*
808
trade **5:**1341, 1344, 1350,
1393
Venice **5:**1394
see also wool trade
Textus Receptus **1:**109
Tezio, Paulo **1:**98
Thames River **3:**749, *750,*
751, *754, 755,* 820,
4:1047, **5:**1324, 1326,
1328
theater **3:**726–733, 735, 737,
748, 772, **5:**1317–1329
court masques **3:**663, 665,
666
England **2:**335–336
festivals **4:**1118, 1119, *1222,*
5:1317
London **3:**732, 733, 751,
754, 755
Marlowe **3:**822–826
Molière **4:**897–902
opera **4:**916, 920
Portural **4:**1145
Shakespeare **5:**1268–1276,
1322
tournaments **1:**225
Theater of Marcellus (Rome)
5:1430
Theatines **5:**1204
Theatre (London theater)
3:732, **5:**1326, 1327
*Theatre of the Empire of Great
Britain* (Speed) **5:**1297

*Theatre Wherein Be
Represented As Well the
Miseries and Calamities
That Follow the Voluptuous
Worldlings* (van der Noot)
5:1286
Themistius (Greek
rhetorician) **1:**56
Theobalds (Hertfordshire)
5:1289
theocracy **1:**186–187
theodicy **2:**360
Theodora, Byzantine empress
1:258
Theodosius II, Byzantine
emperor **1:**256, 257
Theodosius I (the Great),
emperor of Rome **1:**168,
2:531, **3:**696
Theologia Platonica (Ficino)
4:1100
Theological-Political Treatise
(Spinoza) **5:**1292, 1293,
1294, 1295
Theotokópoulos, Doménikos
see Greco, El
thermometer **3:**775
Thessaloníki (Thessalonica)
1:258, 262, **3:**680
Thevet, André **5:**1169
Thionville, Battle of (1638)
5:1338
Third Crusade **2:**505
third estate (France) **2:**439
third orders (lay orders)
5:1209
Thirty-nine Articles (1563,
England) **1:**104, 188,
2:341, 368, **3:**608–609,
5:1374
Thirty Years War **1:**46, 183,
3:767, **4:**911, 914, 1040,
1057, **5:**1191, 1225, 1246,
1330–1339, 1415
Augsburg, Peace of **1:**77, 78
Bohemia **1:**121–122
dams and drainage **1:**279
established churches
2:371–372
German towns **2:**476, 477,
478, 480, 514, *540,* 541

Thirty Years War *(cont.)*
  Holy Roman Empire **2:**476,
    480, 481, 483, 514, 558,
    560
  James I **2:**343
  Maximilian I **3:**835–839
  Poland **1:**228, **4:**1113
  printed propaganda **5:**1174
  Stuarts **5:**1301, 1302, 1336
  Sweden **1:**227, 228, **5:**1307,
    1310, 1330, 1333–1338
  Swiss neutrality **5:**1315
  see also Westphalia, Peace of
Thomas, Lord Camoys **1:**18
Thomas à Kempis **1:**99, 185,
  3:606, 760, **4:**1079
Thomas Aquinas **2:***398*, 461,
  3:696, 760, **4:**1075, **5:**1249
  Aristotelianism **1:**52, 56, 59,
    3:604
  astrology **1:**73
  blood-sports critique **1:**96
  divine right **4:**906
  Erasmus vs. **2:**357, 358–359
  Greek translation **1:**261
  iconoclasm **3:**604, 606
  idealism **1:**182
  magic **3:**797
  philosophy **4:**1062, 1064
Thomas of Reading (Deloney)
  3:738
Thomas Palaeologus **1:**169
Thomas Posthumous Hoby
  5:1422
Thomas the Apostle **2:**380
Thorne, Robert **2:**383
Thou, Jacques-Auguste de
  4:1033
Thrace **1:**165
three estates **2:**406, *407,* 439
Three Graces, The (Raphael)
  5:1181, 1183
Three Henrys, War of the
  2:454, 458
Thucydides **2:**542, **3:**588
Thunberg, Carl Peter **5:**1259
Tiber River **1:**38, 40, 41, 100,
  140, **4:**1025, **5:**1227, 1228,
  1230, 1231
Tibi Dam (Alicante Dam)
  1:280

Ticino River **3:**647, 688
tidal mills **3:**808
Tierra del Fuego **3:**791
Tiers Livre (Rabelais) **5:**1178
Tilbury **2:**331
Tilly, count of *see* Tserclaes,
  Johann
timekeeping **3:**775, 779–780,
  790
Time of Troubles (Russia)
  3:656, **4:**938, 940, 1113,
  5:1308
Timofeevich, Yermak **3:**656
Timon of Athens (Shakespeare
  and Middleton) **5:**1329
Timur Lenk **1:***71*, **3:**617, 621
tin **5:**1341
Tinctoris, Johannes **4:**944
Tintoretto **1:***259,* **5:**1236,
  1387, 1388, 1399
Tirsi e Clori (Monteverdi)
  4:916
Titian **2:***364,* **3:***701,* **4:**981,
  986, 988, 989, 994, *1012,*
  1056, **5:***1197,* 1222, 1236,
  1237, *1352, 1353, 1360,*
  1386, 1387, 1388, 1389,
  1399
  as Rembrandt influence
    5:1213, 1214
Titus Andronicus (Shakespeare)
  2:335
Titus at His Desk (Rembrandt)
  5:1217
Tlaxcalans **4:**891
tobacco **1:**28, **5:**1342, 1346,
  1348
Tobit, book of **5:**1355
toccata **4:**960
Tokugawa shogunate **4:**1142,
  1143
Toledo **3:**693, **5:**1207
Toledo, Antonio de **1:**204
Tomasso da Messina **4:**1055
Tomassoni, Ranuccio **1:**191
tomatoes **1:**28–29, **5:**1346
Tomeo, Niccolò Leonico **1:**56
tools *see* technology
Topkapi Palace **3:***625*
"To Posterity" (Petrarch)
  4:1052

Torah **3:**669, *679*
Tordesillas **5:**1280, 1281
Tordesillas, Treaty of (1494)
  2:381, 382, **3:**788, **4:**889,
  4:1142
Tordinona opera house (Rome)
  1:228, 230
Torgau, League of **2:**555
Toro, Battle of (1476) **5:**1277
Torquemada, Tomás de **2:**533,
  5:1278
Torre de la Parada (Madrid)
  5:1241
Torre delle Tilzie (Rome) **1:**39
Torricelli, Evangelista **3:**775
Torriti, Jacopo **2:**488
Tortosa Disputation
  (1413–1414) **3:**676
torture **2:**532, 534, **4:**1139,
  5:1278
  Inquisition **2:**396
  Viscontis **5:**1405
Torun **1:**265, 266
Totenfresser (Protestant
  pamphlet) **5:**1192
*To the Councilors of All German
  Cities That They Establish
  and Maintain Christian
  Schools* (Luther) **2:**321–322
"To the Lord General
  Cromwell" (Milton) **4:**885
*To the Younger Generation on
  Making Good Use of Greek
  Literature* (Basil of Caesarea)
  3:665
Tottel, Richard **3:**723
Tottel's Miscellany **3:**723–724
Toulon **3:**624
Toulouse **2:**455
Toulouse, University of
  5:1371
Touraine **2:**294, **5:**1176,
  1177
tourism **4:**1026
tournaments **1:**162, 221, *222,*
  224, 225, 226, **3:**598
Tours **2:**451
Tours, Truce of (1444) **3:**602
Tovey, Nathaniel **4:**880
Tower of Belém (Lisbon)
  4:1141, *1145*

Tower of London **1:**218,
  2:330, 332, **3:**597, 749,
  751, **4:**931–932, 1046,
  1047
towers, Italian *grandi* **3:**634
towns *see* cities and towns
Toynbee, Arnold **1:**166
*Trabaios de Persiles y
  Sigismunda, Los (The Trials
  of Persiles and Sigismunda)*
  (Cervantes) **1:**203, 206
Tractaet van Dyckague
  (Vierlingh) **1:**281
trade **4:**914, **5:1340–1351**
  agriculture **1:**22, 26
  Americas **3:**719
  ancient Greece **1:**166–167
  banking **1:**84–91
  Bardi family **2:**567
  Black Death **2:**306
  cannon use **3:**775
  Columbus **1:**247
  companies **2:**498–501
  Constantinople **1:**260–261,
    263
  disease **2:**302–303,
    304–305, 306
  England **3:**751, 752
  exploration **2:**373, 379,
    4:1139, 1140–1141
  fairs **3:**813–821
  Florence **2:**414–415
  German towns **2:**480, 481
  guilds **2:**494–496, 497, 498
  Hanseatic League
    2:475–476, 502–506,
    5:1306
  humanism **3:**588
  Hundred Years War **3:**596
  Islam **3:**613
  Italian city-states **2:**414–415,
    3:630–632, 633,
    634–635, 636, 640, 642,
    5:1401
  Judaism **3:**671
  Lombardy **3:**740, 741
  London guilds **3:**750, 753
  Lutheranism **2:**553
  machines **3:**774, 776
  manufacturing **3:**804, 806,
    811, **4:**1135–1136

markets **3:**813–821
Medicis **3:**849
missionaries **4:**892, 895
noble status **4:**977–978
Ottoman Empire **3:**624
pilgrimage **4:**1082, 1085
Portugal **4:**1142, 1143, 1145
ship design **3:**777–778
Silk Road **3:**805
Sweden **5:**1304–1306, 1311
towns **3:**809
Venice **5:**1340, 1341, 1344,
    1392–1394, 1395, 1398
see also ships and shipping
tradition **5:**1354, 1355
tragedy
    Aristotelian **4:**920
    Greek **5:**1321, 1322
    Shakespearean **5:**1271, 1272,
      1274
Training in Oratory
    (Quintilian) **3:**583
Trajan, emperor of Rome
    4:1040
transatlantic trade *see* Atlantic
    Ocean
Transfiguration (Raphael)
    1:242, **5:**1187
transportation
    canals **5:**1402
    disease **2:**302
    waterways **1:**277, **3:**741, 749
    see also ships and shipping
transubstantiation **1:**52,
    2:536, **3:**608, 764, **5:**1194,
    1268
    Calvin **1:**184
    Elizabeth I **2:**341
    Reformation **1:**178
    Trent, Council of **5:**1197,
      1358
    Zwingli **5:**1315
Transylvania **2:**555, **5:**1335,
    1337
    Gregorian calendar **1:**176
Trastevere (Rome) **1:**40,
    5:1230, 1231
Trato de Argel, El (Cervantes)
    1:204
Trattato dell'architettura
    (Cornaro) **4:**1001

travel **2:**311, 312, **3:**611 *see*
    also exploration; pilgrimage
Travels (Ibn Battutah) **3:**611
Treatise of the Virtues and
    Properties of Waters . . .
    (Sitoni) **1:**280
Treatise on Man (Descartes)
    5:1251
Treatise on the Abacus (Piero
    della Francesca) **3:**827
Treatise on the Astrolabe, A
    (Chaucer) **1:**213
Treatise on the Emendation of
    the Intellect (Spinoza)
    5:1292
tremolo **4:**922
trenches **5:**1407
Trent (Trento) **1:**279, **5:***1352,*
    1357
Trent, Cathedral of **5:**1353
    calendar reform **1:**175, *176*
    universities **5:**1375
Trent, Council of **1:**44, 75,
    175, *186,* **2:**430, 467, 540,
    3:593, 698, 747, **5:**1226,
    1234, **1352–1364**
    Bernini sculpture **1:**97, 99
    bibles **1:**104
    catechism **5:**1174
    Decree of Reunion **2:**431
    ecumenical or general status
      5:1364
    Eucharist **5:**1197
    holiness doctrine **1:**186
    missal **1:**175, **5:**1363
    music **4:**943, 954, 955
    painting **4:**992
    Paul III **4:**1016, 1017–1018
    Paul V **4:**1036
    Pius IV **4:**1020, 1024
    Sarpi critique **4:**1038
    Vulgate **3:**684, 689
Trevi fountain (Rome) **1:**37
Treviso **3:**647, **5:**1394
Trew Laws of Free Monarchies,
    The (James VI) **5:**1299
Triana, Rodrigo de **1:**248
Tridentine Mass **5:**1363
Triennial Act of 1641
    (England) **2:**349
Trier **2:**548

trigonometry **3:**728, 828, 829,
    831, 834
trinitarianism **3:**610–611, 669,
    757
    Decree of Reunion **2:**430
Trinitarian order **1:**204, 206
Trinity (ship) **5:**1350
Trinity College (Cambridge)
    1:262, **5:**1432
    library **5:***1375*
Trinity Guild of Lynn **4:**1081
Trinity Manuscript (Milton)
    4:881
Trionfi (Petrarch) **4:***1053*
Trismegistus (Hermes) **4:**1065
Trissino, Gian Giorgio **1:**43,
    125, **4:**1000, 1001, 1002
Triumph of Death, The
    (Bruegel) **1:**145, **4:***1125*
Triumph of Galatea (Raphael)
    1:41
Triumph of Saint Thomas
    Aquinas (Benozzo di Lesse
    Gazzoli) **1:***52*
trivium **2:**357, **5:**1366, 1372
Trivulzio, Giangiacomo **3:**651,
    743
Troilus and Criseyde (Chaucer)
    1:112, 113, 213, 217–218,
    220
trompe l'oeil **1:**139
troubadours and trouvères
    1:214
Troyes, Treaty of (1420) **1:**17,
    160, **3:**601, **4:**1030
Tsaritsyn *see* Volgograd
Tschudi, Aegidius **5:**1312
Tserclaes, Johann, count of
    Tilly **3:**835, 836, 837, 838,
    839, **5:**1333, 1334, 1335,
    1337, 1415
Tübingen, University of **2:**324,
    5:1371, *1372*
Tudor, Elizabeth *see* Elizabeth
    I, queen of England
Tudor, Margaret *see* Margaret
    Tudor, queen consort of
    Scotland
Tudor, Mary *see* Mary I
Tudors, the **1:**233, 236, **2:**410,
    521, **4:**912

Elizabeth I **2:**326–333
    male heir **1:**233
    printing **5:**1175
    Reformation **5:**1325
    Scotland **5:**1261, 1297,
      1298
    Shakespeare **5:**1271
    see also Edward VI; Elizabeth
      I; Henry VII; Henry VIII;
      Mary I
Tuileries **4:**1031
tulips **1:**26
Tull, Jethro **1:**27
Tunis **1:**202, 209, 211, **3:**624,
    5:1347
Tunstall, Cuthbert **1:**106
Turin, University of **2:**357,
    5:1367
Turkey, Republic of **1:**172 *see*
    also Ottoman Empire
Turriano, Juanelo **1:**280
Tuscan order **1:**30, *142*
Tuscany **3:***635,* **4:**1091
    Galileo **2:**464
    government **3:**637, 642
    Italian wars **3:**642, 649
    Petrarch **4:**1049
    see also Florence
Tusi, Nasir ad-Din al- **1:**271
Twelfth Night (Shakespeare)
    3:727, **5:**1271
Twelve Apostles **1:***154*
Twelver Shiism **3:**621
Twenty-third Psalm **1:**183
Two New Sciences (Galileo)
    2:468, **3:**690
Tyler, Wat **4:**1044, 1046,
    1048
Tyndale, William **1:**232, 234,
    240, **2:**524, **3:***697,* 698,
    4:931
    bibles **1:**103, 105, 106, 107,
      110
typhus **2:**307
Tyrol **1:**88, **2:**508, 509, 511
Tyrrhenian Sea **1:**277

U

Uccello, Paolo **4:**985
Uffizi Gallery (Florence)
    2:489, **3:**708

Ukraine **4:**1109, 1113–1114, **5:**1337

Ulászló II, king of Hungary **1:**120, **2:**510

ulema **3:**614

Ulm **2:**295, 475, *476*, 482

Ulozheniye (law code) **4:**940, *941*

Ulster **2:**350

Ulster, countess of **1:**212–213

Uluch Ali **3:**718

Umberto I, king of Italy **2:**466

Underweysung der Messung mit dem Zirckel und Richscheyt (Dürer) **2:**312

Unfortunate Traveller; or, The Life of Jacke Wilson (Nash) **3:**738

"Unigenitus" (Clement VI) **3:**757

United Provinces *see* Netherlands

United States
  architecture **1:**140
  disestablishment **2:**367, 372
  see also Americas; *specific states*

universe **2:**463, 464, 465, 467, 539

universitas vs. *conlegium* **5:**1376

universities **2:**317, 318, *322, 323*–325, **5:1365–1377,** *1406*
  Arabic studies **3:**618
  Aristotelianism **1:**51, 56–58
  Constantinople **1:**257, 258, 261
  degree holders **4:**973
  dramatic productions **5:**1328
  England **2:**336
  Greek studies **1:**264, **3:**685
  humanism **2:**319, 324, 336, **3:**582, 584, 585, 588–589, 590, 592, 593, 594, 683, **5:**1218–1219, 1220, 1224, 1282
  Jewish students **3:**679
  London law studies **3:**752

Luther at Wittenberg **3:**672, 758–759

Marlowe at Cambridge **3:**822–823

medicine **3:**840, 841, 844, 845, 846–847, 848, **5:**1367

Ottoman **3:**627

Platonism **1:**261

Portugal **4:**1144

Prague **1:**118, 119, 212

public **2:**323–325

Reformation **2:**321, 324, *325*

religious founders **4:**891

Roman Catholicism **2:***322,* 324

Scholasticism **1:**54, 57, 58–59, 261, **2:**294, 357

science **5:**1255

Scotland **5:**1263

Sweden **5:**1308

theater **3:**732

University Wits **3:**732, 824

unleavened bread **1:**259

Unmoving Mover **1:**52

Unterwalden **5:**1312

"Upon the Famous Voyage" (Jonson) **3:**755

Uppsala, University of **5:**1308, 1367

Ural Mountains **3:**656

Urania (Wroth) **3:***725*, 737

Uraniborg observatory **5:**1251

Urban V, Pope **1:**112, 115, **4:**1052

Urban VI, Pope **4:**1010, **5:**1424

Urban VIII, Pope **1:**73–74, **2:**466, **5:**1380
  Bernini works **1:**97, 98, 99, 100
  religious orders **5:**1208
  Rome **5:**1234
  Thirty Years War **5:**1332, 1333, 1336

urbanization *see* cities and towns

Urbina, Juan de **1:**205

Urbino **1:**139, 140, **2:**444, **3:**701, **5:1378–1383**
  Raphael **5:**1180, 1181, 1183

Urbino, duke of **3:**701

Uri **5:**1312

Ursulines **5:**1353

Ussher, James **1:**110

usury **1:**85, **3:**633, **5:**1316

Utopia (More) **3:**585, **4:**927–928, 1103, **5:**1173

utopias **4:**1048, 1103, **5:**1251

Uylenburgh, Hendrick van **5:**1212

Uylenburgh, Saskia van **5:**1212, 1214

Uzzanos, the **2:**417, **3:**850

V

vacuum pump **3:**775

Vaenius, Otto *see* Veen, Otto van

Val-de-Grâce, Church of (France) **1:**48

Valdor, Johannes **5:***1253*

Valencia **1:**205, **2:**396, 397, **4:**965, **5:**1277

Valentes, University of **5:**1371

Valla, Lorenzo **4:**1023
  Donation of Constantine forgery **3:**584, 594
  Erasmus **2:**358, 359, **3:**591
  Latin scholarship **3:**586, 591, 686–687, 688
  manuscript analysis **3:**587
  overview of **3:**586

Valladolid **1:**205, 206, 248, 255, **2:**396, **4:**1056, 1058, **5:**1280

Valladolid, Cathedral of **1:**47

Valois dynasty **2:**555, **4:**966
  Burgundy **1:**157–164
  Catherine de Médicis **1:**197–201
  France **2:**433, 436, 438, 451
  Francis I **2:**445–450
  Henry IV **2:**516–520
  Italian wars **2:**421

Valtellina **5:**1337

Valturio, Roberto **5:***1408*

Van de molens (Stevin) **1:**275

van de Velde *see* Velde

Van Dyck, Anthony **2:***347,* **3:***608,* **4:**993, **5:**1211, 1241, 1243, *1257, 1302*

van Eyck, Jan *see* Eyck, Jan van

van Somer, Paul **1:***81*

Vanson, Adrian **5:**1265

Varano, Giulia **5:**1380

Varcollier, Atala **5:***1179*

Vargas Manrique, Luis de **1:**204

Variata of 1540 **1:**76

Varmia **1:**265, 266

Varna, Battle of (1444) **3:**618

Varro, Marcus **1:**277

Vasa dynasty **5:***1304,* 1305–1310
  Christina **1:**227–231

Vasari, Giorgio **1:**34, 42, 148, **2:**485, **3:***649,* 714
  on Brunelleschi's dome **1:**150, 156
  Michelangelo **5:***1225*
  on Palladio **4:**1005
  on Raphael **5:**1183, 1185, 1187

Vasily I, grand prince of Muscovy **4:**934

Vasily II (the Blind), grand prince of Muscovy **4:**934

Vasily III, grand prince of Muscovy **3:**652, **4:**935, 936

Vasily Shuysky **4:**939

Vasnezov, Viktor Michailovitch **3:***653*

Vasquez, Daniel **1:***248*

vassal *see* feudalism

Vatican *see* papacy

Vatican archives **4:**1036, 1037

Vatican Council I **5:**1363, 1364

Vatican Council II **2:**430, **5:**1363, 1364

Vatican Library **1:**230, **4:**1022, *1023,* **5:**1230
  Paul III **5:**1353

Vatican Museum **3:**708

Vatican Palaces **4:**1025, **5:**1228, 1229–1232
  Cortile de Belvedere **1:**142, **4:**1040
  Villa del Belvedere **1:**140, 142, **3:**703, **5:**1231

Vecchi, Giovanni da **4:***1025*

Vecchietta, Lorenzo **4:**1090
Veen, Otto van **5:**1236
Vega, Garcilaso de la **3:**726
Vega, Lope de **1:**204, **3:**727, 728, **5:**1284, 1322–1323
on *Don Quixote* **1:**205
Vega Carpio, Lope Felix de **3:**726
Velázquez, Diego Rodríguez de Silva **4:**993, 994, **5:**1237, 1242, **1384–1391**
Velázquez, Juan **5:**1199
Velde, J. van de **5:***1168*
Velde, Willem van de, II **5:***1347*
Veli, Benedetto **5:***1201*
Veneto **3:**668
Venezuela **1:**249
Venice **2:**414, **3:**630, 853, **5:**1336, **1392–1400**
architecture **1:**32, 33, 42–43, **3:***640,* 641, 642, 666, 667, 668
banking **1:**87, 91, **2:**416
Black Death **2:**305, 306
Charles V **1:**210
Constantinople **1:**168, 260–261
dams and drainage **1:**276–277
France **2:**447
government **3:**637, 638–639, 642, 651, 668
Greek texts **1:**261, **2:**320, 430, **3:**688
Italian wars **1:**242, 244, **3:**545, 643, 647, 648
Jewish ghetto **3:**672, 679
Lepanto, Battle of **3:**715, 716, 718, *719*
Lombardy **3:**744, 745
Milan **5:**1404
Monteverdi **4:**9, 922
music **4:**951–952, 958–959, **5:**1244–1245, 1246
nationalism **4:**966–967, 969
nobility **4:**974, 977
opera **3:**734
Ottoman Empire **3:**616, 618–619, 626, 715, 716, 718

painting **2:**312, 313, **4:**981, 986, 988, 989, **5:**1236
Palladio **3:**664, 668, **4:**1000, 1006–1007, **5:**1399
papacy **4:**1012, 1020–1021, 1037, 1038–1039
Petrarch **4:**1051
printing **3:**819
silk manufacture **3:**805
telescope **5:**1252
territorial battles **2:**419
theater **3:**734
trade **2:**475, **3:**740, 741, **5:**1340, 1341, 1344, 1392–1394, 1395, 1398, 1401
Urbino **5:**1380, 1381
Velázquez **5:**1388, 1389
Venn, John **4:**1068
Venus (goddess) **1:**135, **2:***424,* 425
Venus (planet) **2:**464
Venus and Adonis (Shakespeare) **5:**1268
Venus and Cupid (Gentileschi) **2:**472
Venus and Mars (Botticelli) **1:**135
Venus at Her Toilette (Velázquez) *see Rokeby Venus*
Venus of Urbino (Titian) **5:**1389
Vera Cruz, College of (Valladolid) **5:**1280
Vere, Edward de **5:**1276
Vergerio, Piero Paolo **3:**584, **5:**1220
background of **2:**318
Verhaecht, Tobias **5:**1236
Vermeer, Jan **4:**997, 998, *999*
Vermuyden, Cornelius **1:**276
vernaculars *see* languages, vernacular
vernal equinox **1:**174, 176
Vernet, Emile-Jean-Horace **5:***1231*
Verona **5:**1394
Veronese **1:***203,* **4:**992, **5:**1388
Verrazano, Giovanni da **2:**382, **4:**914

Verrocchio, Andrea del **3:**706, 707, 708, 709, **4:**985
Verrocchio, Giuliano del **3:**707
Versailles **1:**45, 48, **2:**450, **4:**1007
gardens **1:**26
Vert, Cape **5:**1345
Vervins, Peace of (1598) **2:**458, **4:**1058, 1060
Vesalius, Andreas **2:**302, 303, **3:**840, 845, 846, 848, **5:**1250, 1254
Vespers (Monteverdi) *see Vespro della Beata Vergine*
Vespignano **2:**487
Vespro della Beata Vergine (Monteverdi) **3:**745, **4:**921, 943
Vespucci, Amerigo **1:***254,* 255, **2:***374,* 382
Vettori, Francesco **1:**245
Via della Lungara (Rome) **5:**1231
Via Giulia (Rome) **1:**40, 141, **5:**1231
Viaje del Parnaso (Cervantes) **1:**203
Vicente, Gil **4:**1145
Vicentino, Nicola **4:**943
Vicenza
Palladio **1:**42–43, **2:**563, **3:**664, 666, *668,* **4:**1000, 1002, 1004, 1005, 1006–1007
Venice **4:**996, **5:**1394
Vicenza, University of **5:**1371
Victoria, Tomás Luis de **4:**956–957
Victory (Michelangelo) **4:**874
Victory (ship) **1:**63
Vida del Buscón, La (Quevedo y Villegas) **3:**738–779
Vida es sueño, La (Calderón) **3:**728, **5:***1323*
Vie de Gargantua et de Pantagruel, La (Rabelais) **3:**436, **5:**1176, 1177, 1178
Vienna **2:**556, 557
Black Death **2:**305
Jewish purges **3:**672

Ottoman sieges (1529, 1683) **1:**209, **2:**555, **3:**612, 624, **4:**1114
Vienna, Concordat of (1448) **4:**970
Vienna, Council of (1312) **1:**85
Vier Bücher von Menschlicher Proportion (Dürer) **2:**312, 316
Vierlingh, Andries **1:**274–275, 276, 281
Viète, François **3:**828, 830
View of Delft (Vermeer) **4:***999*
View of the Present State of Ireland, A (Spenser) **5:**1287, 1289
Vignola, Giacomo da **1:**34, 38, 40, 44, 45, **3:**667
Vijd, Joos **2:**387
villa **2:**563
Villa Badoer (Vicenza) **4:**1005
Villa Barbaro (Vicenza) **1:**43
Villa Borghese (Rome) **4:***1037*
Villa Chiericati (Vicenza) **3:**666
Villa Coronaro (Vicenza) **1:**43, **4:**1005
Villa del Belvedere (Vatican) **1:**140, 142, **3:**703, **5:**1231
courtyard **1:**142, **4:**1040
Villa Emo (Vicenza) **4:**1005
Villa Farnesina (Rome) **1:***41*
Villa Foscari (Vicenza) **4:**1001, 1005
Villa Franca, Ana de **1:**204
Village Fair (Brueghel the Younger) **5:***1319*
Villa Godi (Vicenza) **4:**1005
Villa Madama (Rome) **1:**39
Villa Medici (Rome) **5:**1389
Villani Chronicle (Pucci) **2:**484
Villa Pisani (Vicenza) **1:**43, **4:**1005
Villa Poiani (Vicenza) **4:**1005
Villa Polano (Vicenza) **1:**43
Villa Rotunda (Vicenza) **1:***42,* 43, **4:**1005
Villa Thiene (Vicenza) **1:**43, **3:***668,* **4:**1001, 1004, 1005

Villiers, George, duke of Buckingham **2**:342–343, 347, **5**:1300, 1301, 1336
Vimercati, Francesco **1**:56
Vincent de Paul **5**:1208
Vincent Ferrer **3**:*676,* **5**:1160, 1161
Vincentians **5**:1208
Vincenzo II Gonzaga, duke of Mantua and Montferrat **5**:1336
viol **4**:958
violin **4**:942, 958
Virgil **1**:112, **3**:*594,* 737, **4**:1144, **5**:1219, 1289
  classical languages **3**:682, 683, 687
  English humanism **2**:336
  Petrarch **4**:1052–1053
Virgin and Child (Michelangelo) **4**:874, 876
Virgin by a Fountain (Eyck) **2**:390
Virginia **3**:609, **4**:892, 894, **5**:1342
Virginia Company **2**:375
Virgin Kykkotissa **2**:380
Virgin Mary **1**:137, *145,* 178, **2**:425, **3**:689, 709, **4**:890, *1062,* **5**:1222
  Assumption **1**:193, **4**:1081, **5**:1317, 1318
  Dürer paintings **5**:*1220*
  iconoclasm **3**:604, *606*
  Immaculate Conception **4**:1036
  prayer to **5**:1160
  Raphael paintings **5**:1180, 1182, 1184, *1221*
  shrines **4**:1081, 1083
  see also Madonna and Child
viruses **2**:302, 310
Vischer, Georg **1**:*178*
Visconti, Azzone **5**:1403, 1405
Visconti, Bernabò **1**:216, **3**:741, **5**:1404, 1405
Visconti, Bianca Maria **3**:742, **5**:1403, *1404*
Visconti, Filippo Maria **3**:742, **5**:1403, 1404, 1405

Visconti, Galeazzo I **5**:1403, 1404, 1405
Visconti, Galeazzo II **5**:1402, 1403, 1404, 1405–1406
Visconti, Gian Galeazzo **3**:741, **5**:1402, 1403, 1404, 1405
Visconti, Giovanni Maria **3**:742, **5**:1403
Visconti, Lucchino **5**:1403, 1404
Visconti, Matto I **3**:741, **5**:1405
Visconti, Ottone **3**:741, **5**:1403, 1404–1405
Visconti, Valentina **3**:645, 742
Viscontis, the **1**:213, **3**:638, 645, 740, 741–742, 744, 745, **5**:1394, **1401–1406**
Visigoths **1**:258
Vision of Delight (Jonson) **3**:663
Visscher, Jan Claesz **5**:*1271, 1328*
Vistula River **4**:*1105*
Vita nuova, La (Dante) **1**:217
Vitruvius **1**:*32,* 33–34, 35, 48, 141, **3**:668, 709, **4**:1001, **5**:1321
Vitruvian Man (Leonardo da Vinci) **3**:709
Vitry, Jacques de **3**:779
Vittoria, Alessandro **4**:1000
Vittoria d'Amore, La (Monteverdi) **4**:919
Vives, Juan Luis **5**:1282–1283, 1416, 1417
Viviani, Vincenzo **2**:460
Vladislav the Jagiellonian *see* Ulászló II, king of Hungary
vocal music **4**:950, 952
Volga River **3**:653, **4**:933
Volgograd **4**:933
Volterra, Daniele da **4**:992
Voorburg **5**:1292, 1293
Vorarlberg **2**:509
vows, chivalric **1**:226
Vroom, Hendrik **1**:*66*
Vulcan's Forge (Velázquez) **5**:1387
Vulgari eloquentia, De (Dante) **1**:217

Vulgate **1**:104, 107, 108, 109, **2**:337, **3**:591, *682,* 684, 696, **4**:1024
  Gutenberg Bible **3**:697
  translation errors **3**:688–689
  Trent, Council of **5**:1357

W

Wadham College (Oxford) **5**:1429, 1431
Waghenaer, Lucas Janszoon **2**:*376*
Wakefield play cycle **5**:1318
Waldensians **2**:530, 531, **3**:766
Waldo, Peter **2**:531
Waldseemüller, Martin **1**:*254,* 255, **2**:382
Walens, Mayses **5**:*1327*
Wales **1**:17, **3**:596, **4**:904, **5**:1416
Wales, prince of **3**:598, **4**:903
Walker, Anna **5**:1427
Wallace, William **4**:905
Wallachia **3**:616
Wallenstein, Albrecht von **3**:838–839, **5**:1332, 1333, 1334, 1335, 1337
  overview of **5**:1415
Waller, Edmund **3**:690
Walsingham, Francis **2**:330, 331
Walsingham, Thomas **3**:825
Walter, Johann **4**:943, 952, 954
Walworth, William **4**:1046
Wanderjahre **2**:311, 312
Warbeck, Perkin **1**:233
Ward, Mary **5**:1208
warfare **5**:**1407–1415**
  Agincourt battle **1**:16–20
  armada, Spanish **1**:62–66
  chivalric laws **1**:221, 222, 224, 226
  chivalric orders **1**:223
  dams and drainage **1**:279
  English archers **3**:596, *597,* 600
  feudalism **2**:402–403, 408–412
  France **2**:433, 449, 451, 458, 520

Gustavus II Adolphus **5**:1309, 1332
Henry VIII **2**:521, 522, 527
Holy Roman Empire **2**:554, 555
Islam **3**:612, 616, 617, 618, 628–629
Italian soldiers **3**:651
Japan **4**:1142
Joan of Arc **3**:658, 659, 660–661
Leonardo sketches **3**:710, *711,* **5**:1249
Lepanto, Battle of **3**:715–719
Machiavelli **3**:770, 772, 773
mercantilism **5**:1351
mercenaries **5**:1395, 1403, 1411
monarchy **4**:908–909, 912
Muscovy **4**:936–937, 938, 939, 940, 941
nationalism **4**:967–968, 970
naval **3**:650, 715–719, 778, **5**:1347, 1412
Ottoman **3**:617, 622, 623, 624, 626, 628, 629
papacy **4**:1090
Poland-Lithuania **4**:1104, 1106, 1107, 1109, 1112–1114
political philosophy **4**:1066
population effects **4**:1136
religious controversy **1**:183
Renaissance changes **5**:1335
ship design **3**:778, 786
Spain **4**:1145
Switzerland **5**:1313, 1315
technology **3**:774, 775, 782, 786
tournaments **1**:225
Venice **5**:1395
Viscontis **5**:1403, 1404, 1406
  see also English civil wars; French civil wars; Hundred Years War; Italian wars; Thirty Years War; weaponry; other *specific battles and wars*
Warham, William **1**:106, 235, 240

Warner, William **3**:753
Warrant Design (Wren) **5**:1432
Warsaw **4**:*1105,* 1112
Warsaw, Compact of (1573) **4**:1110
Wars in Italy *see* Italian wars
wars of religion *see* French civil wars; Thirty Years War
Wars of the Roses *see* Roses, Wars of the
Wartburg **3**:765
Warwick, earl of *see* Neville, Richard
Warwickshire **2**:351
Washington College **1**:189
waterpower **1**:24, **3**:741, 776–777, 805, 806, *807,* 808, 809, 812
water supply **1**:273–281, **4**:1133
waterways *see* canals; rivers
waterwheels **1**:*278,* **3**:776–777, 809, 812
waterworks *see* dams and drainage
Watson, Thomas **3**:822, 824
Watzenrode, Lucas **1**:265
Wavrin, Jean de **3**:*599,* **4**:*1127, 1137*
Wawel Castle (Kraków) **4**:1109, 1112
Wawel Cathedral (Kraków) **4**:1112
Way of Perfection, The (Teresa of Ávila) **5**:1207
Way of Reconciliation (Ponet) **5**:1419
wealth
  Bardi family **2**:567
  Calvinism **1**:190
  established churches **2**:365, 368
  exploration **2**:380, 381, 382, **3**:693
  Florence **2**:414–415, 416, 417
  households **2**:561–562, 563, 564, 565
  Italian city-states **3**:630, 632, 633, 637, 638, 640, 641

London **3**:751, 752, 754
market system **3**:821
Medicis **3**:849, 854
Milan **2**:414–415
Protestant ethic **1**:190
trade **5**:1342, 1350
Viscontis **5**:1401, 1402
women's household role **5**:1421
weaponry **3**:774, 775, 782, 793
  Agincourt **1**:*16,* 18, 19
  archers **3**:596, *597,* 600
  Hundred Years War **2**:435, **3**:596, *597*
  Italy **3**:632, 651
  knighthood **1**:221, 225
  Leonardo innovations **3**:710, *711,* **5**:1249
  naval gunnery **1**:63, 65, 66
  Ottoman **3**:618, 623, 717, 719
  pikes **5**:1309, 1313–1314, 1335, 1412, 1413
  Portugal **4**:1142
  Russia **3**:653, 654
  Safavids **3**:628 629
  Sweden **5**:1309
  Switzerland **5**:1313 1314
  Thirty Years War **5**:1335
  trade **5**:1341
  see also firearms; gunpowder
weather forecasts **1**:68
weather gauge **1**:66
weather lore **1**:177
Webb, John **1**:48, **3**:*667,* 668, **4**:1007
Weber, Max **1**:190, **4**:1123
Webster, John **5**:1325, 1329
Weerdt, Abraham van **5**:*1172*
Weissenfels **5**:1247
Welfs, the **2**:505
Well of Moses (Sluter) **4**:981
Wells, H. G. **4**:929
Welsers, the **5**:1344
Wenceslas, Saint **1**:117, *118*
Wenceslas III, king of Bohemia **1**:116, 117
Wenceslas IV, king of Bohemia *see* Wenceslas, Holy Roman emperor

Wenceslas, Holy Roman emperor **1**:118, 119, **3**:741, **5**:1403, 1404, 1405
Wendel, Lupold von **3**:749
Wendish towns **2**:506
Wentworth, Thomas **2**:350
Werewolf, The (Cranach the Elder) **4**:*1115*
werewolves **4**:*1115*
Werner, count of Hapsburg **2**:507
Weser River **2**:506, **5**:1335
Western Isles **5**:1296
Western Schism 1378–1417 **2**:366, 421, 429, 430, **4**:913, 1010–1011, 1052, **5**:1227, 1406 *see also* Avignon papacy
Westfall, James **2**:459
West Indies *see* Caribbean region
Westminster Abbey **1**:30, **5**:*1301*
  Chaucer's tomb **1**:218, *220*
  Newton's tomb **5**:1257
  Poets' Corner **1**:218, *220*
  Spenser's tomb **5**:1290
Westminster Confession **1**:104
Westphalia **5**:1236, 1237
Westphalia, Peace of (1648) **1**:46, **2**:511, *540,* 541, **3**:836, 839, **4**:914, **5**:1191, 1200, 1234, 1246, 1330, 1333, 1338
  Christina **1**:228
  German towns **2**:478, 480, 483
  religious toleration **5**:1339
  Sweden **5**:1307, 1310, 1311, 1330
Weyden, Rogier van der **1**:129, *161,* 163, *221,* **2**:316, **4**:982, *1129,* **5**:*1357*
Whaddon folio **4**:*1043*
What a Tailor Can Do! (Goya) **4**:*1123*
"What Can Be Called into Doubt" (Descartes) **2**:297
wheel lock **3**:782
Wheldon, James **2**:547

Whetstone of Witte, The (Recorde) **3**:829
Whichcote, Benjamin **4**:1070
Whistler, James McNeill **5**:1391
Whitehall (London) **2**:355, **3**:*666,* 668, 749, 751
Whitehead, Alfred North **4**:1092
White Mountain, Battle of (1620) **1**:122, **3**:836, 838, **4**:1040, **5**:1192, 1334, *1335, 1336*
White Sea **4**:933
Whitgift, John **1**:79
Whitney, Isabella **3**:726
Whittingham, William **1**:107
whooping cough **2**:307, 308
Whore of Babylon, The (Dekker) **5**:*1327*
Widow and Her Son (Moro) **5**:*1422*
widows **5**:1421, 1422
Wife of Bath (illustration) **4**:*1081*
Wight, Isle of **2**:353
Wignancourt, Alof de **1**:194
Wildeck, Magdalena **5**:1246
Wilhelm Tell (Schiller) **5**:1312
Willaert, Adriaan **4**:947, 951–952
William I (the Conqueror), king of England **2**:403, **3**:749, 751
William III (William of Orange), king of England *see* William and Mary
William I (William of Orange), stadtholder of the Netherlands **2**:331, 453, **4**:1057
William of Norwich (blood libel) **3**:673
William of Ockham *see* Ockham, William of
William of Orange *see* William I; William and Mary
William and Mary, king and queen of England **1**:24, 262, **2**:346, 499, **4**:906, **5**:1302

William and Mary, College of **4:**892
Willoughby, Francis **5:**1422
Willoughby, Hugh **2:**384
Wilton House (Wiltshire) **1:***47,* 48, **3:***667, 668*
windows **1:**31, 36, 40, *46*
wind power **1:**24, 275, 277, 278, **3:***777–778, 804, 807–808*
wine **4:**1139, **5:**1341, 1344, 1350
Wine Merchants' Guild **3:**633
Winter's Tale, The (Shakespeare) **3:**732, **5:**1271, 1275, 1321
Wisdom, book of *see* Wisdom of Solomon
Wisdom of Solomon **1:**103, **5:**1355
Wishart, George **1:**189
Wismar **5:**1334
witchcraft
  Inquisition **2:**534–535, **3:**801, **4:**1019
  Joan of Arc **3:**661
  magic **3:**795–796, 801–803
  Scotland **5:**1267
  witch hunts **2:**535, **5:**1425
Witt, Johannes de **5:***1326*
Wittelsbach family **2:**549, 550
Wittenberg
  altarpiece **5:***1163*
  bibles **1:**105
  church door **1:**178, **5:***1189,* 1191
  indulgences **5:**1190
  Luther **3:***756,* 758–759, 762, 765, **4:**929, **5:**1190
Wittenberg, University of **2:**482, **3:**585, 593, 606, 704, 705, **5:**1189
  Luther **4:**1013, **5:**1352, *1376*
  Melanchthon **2:**324
Witzel, George **3:**768
Wladyslaw I, king of Poland **4:**1112
Wladyslaw II, king of Poland **4:**911, 1104–1107
Wladyslaw III, king of Poland **4:**1105

Wladyslaw IV Vasa, king of Poland **4:**1113, 1114, **5:**1308
woad (blue dye) **5:**1350, 1402
Wolfgang of Zweibrücken **2:**453
Wolgemut, Michael **2:**311
Wolmar, Melchior **1:**179
Wolsey, Thomas **2:**521, 522, 523, **4:**930, **5:***1273,* 1373
  Hampton Court Palace **2:**334
  Henry VIII **1:**234, **2:**338
wolves **4:**1115
women **5:1416–1428**
  Borgia, Lucrezia **1:**123–126
  chivalry **1:**221, *222,* 226
  Christina **1:**227–231
  cities **4:**1132
  colonialism **5:**1285
  court society **5:**1383, 1427
  education **2:**319, 322
  Florentine artists' portrayal **2:***424,* 425
  Gentileschi **2:**469–474
  household roles **2:**562–563, 564–565, 566
  humanist education **3:**584, 588
  inheritance rights **2:**404–405, 413
  Joan of Arc **3:**657–662
  Judaism **3:**681
  literacy **5:**1172
  London advantages **3:**753
  marital age **4:**1129, **5:**1419
  Medicis **1:**197–202, 232, 246, **3:**857
  Middleton depictions **5:**1329
  midwives **3:**842
  in monarchical succession **3:**595, **4:**911
  as monarchs **1:**227–231, **2:**326–333, 393–400, 523, 528, **4:**1104, **5:**1221, 1225, 1267, 1277–1279, 1425–1427
  nude paintings **5:**1183, 1238
  pilgrimage **4:**1081
  popular culture **4:**1116, 1117, *1120*

as preaching audience **5:**1161, 1162
religious orders **5:**1201, 1202, 1207, 1208
Renaissance status **5:**1225
scientific pursuits **5:**1257
witchcraft charges **2:**534, **3:**796, 802, 803, **5:**1425
as writers **3:**724, 725, 726, 735–736, 737, **5:**1427
"Women's War against the Pope for Stealing Ten Days from the Calendar, The" (poem) **1:**177
Wonderful Magician, The (Calderón) 728
wood **3:**811
woodcuts **2:**310, 311, **5:**1170, *1171*
  Dürer **2:**311, 312, 313, 314
Woodroffe, Benjamin **1:**262
Woodward, William Harrison **5:**1219
wool trade **5:**1341, 1344, 1350
  Ciompi **2:**415, 419
  cloth **3:**740, 806, *807,* 849, 853
  Italian city-states **3:**630, 636
  Scotland **5:**1260
Worcester College (Oxford) **3:**668
Wordes unto Adam, His Owne Scriveyn (Chaucer) **1:***213*
Work for Armourers (Dekker) **1:**93
World, The (Descartes) **2:**296, 297
World Turned Upside Down, The (pamphlet) **5:***1175*
World War I **2:**512, **3:**629, **4:**1107
World War II **4:**1107, 1112, **5:**1312
Worms **2:**557
Worms, Diet of (1521) **1:**210–211, **2:**514, 553, **3:**762, 765, 768
Worms, Edict of (1521) **1:**104, **2:**555, **5:**193, 1192, 1200
Wotton, Henry **5:**1223

Wren, Christopher **1:**32, 33, 47, 48–49, 140, **3:**667, 668, 748, *755,* **4:**1007, **5:**1256, *1374, 1375,* **1429–1433**
Wright, Joseph **4:***1072*
writing system **3:**774, 776 *see also* literacy
Wroth, Mary **3:**725, 737
Wuchters, Abraham **5:***1311*
Wurst, Wider Hans **5:**1191
Würzburg, bishop of **1:**77
Wyatt, Thomas (the Elder) **3:**722–723, 724, 726
Wyatt, Thomas (the Younger) **2:**326–327
Wycliffe, John **1:**102, 103, 110, 232, **2:**536–537, **3:**761

X

Xanten, Treaty of (1614) **5:**1334
Xavier, Francis **4:**894, 1015, **5:**1205–1206
Xenophon **1:**261

Y

Yale College **1:**189
Yam Zapolsky, Truce of (1582) **3:**656, **4:**1112
Yarranton, Andrew **1:***276*
yellow fever **2:**307
Yermak Timofeyevich **4:**936
Yiddish language **3:**670
Yonge, Nicholas **4:**943
York, archbishop of **2:**346
York play cycle **5:**1318
Yorks, the **1:**233, **2:**408, **4:**903, 912, **5:**1273
Yorkshire **1:**235, **2:**351
Young, John **5:**1287
Young, Peter **5:**1264
Young, Thomas **4:**879, 880
Young Man Playing the Lute (Lievens) **5:***1211*
Young Woman with a Water Jug (Vermeer) **4:**998
Youthful Adventures of the Cid, The (Castro y Bellvís) **3:**728

Yucatán *see* Mexico
Yung-lo *see* Chu Ti
Yuriria dam **1:**280
Yuste **1:**209, 211

Z

Zabarella, Jacopo **1:**57
Zahir-ud-Din, Muhammad *see*
    Babur
Zayandeh River **1:***280*
Zeeman, Reinier **4:***1031*
Zeno **4:**1097
Zeno's paradoxes **4:**1097
Zuccari, Federico **2:***366,*
    3:*648,* **5:**1236, 1237
Zuccari, Taddeo **5:***1362*
Zuider Zee **1:**274
Zurbarán, Francisco de **4:**994,
    5:1386
Zurich
    Black Death **2:**304, 305
    public education **2:**322
    Reformation **1:**188, **5:**1193,
        1267, 1312, 1314, 1315,
        1316
    Renaissance map **5:***1316*
Zwingli, Huldrych **1:**178,
    181, 184, **2:**483, 539,
    3:761, 762, **4:**952, **5:**1193,
    1312, 1314, 1315, 1316
Zwinglians **1:**76